D1284484

RICK-PAULOS@UIOWA.EDU

Mastering
Turbo Pascal®
5.5

R E L A T E D   T I T L E S

Mastering Turbo Pascal® Files
Tom Swan

Pascal Programs for Games & Graphics
Tom Swan

Pascal Programs in Science and Engineering
Jules H. Gilder and J. Scott Barrus

Pascal with Excellence
Henry F. Ledgard with John Tauer

Turbo Pascal® 4.0 Application Developer's Library
Edward R. Rought and Thomas D. Hoops

Turbo C® Developer's Library
Edward R. Rought with Thomas D. Hoops

C: Step-by-Step
Mitchell Waite and Stephen Prata

The Waite Group's Advanced C Primer ++
Stephen Prata

The Waite Group's C++ Programming *(Version 2.0)*
Edited by The Waite Group

The Waite Group's C Primer Plus, Revised Edition
Mitchell Waite, Stephen Prata, and Donald Martin

The Waite Group's Microsoft® C Bible
Naba Barkakti

The Waite Group's Microsoft® C Programming for the PC, Revised Edition
Robert Lafore

The Waite Group's Turbo C® Bible
Naba Barkakati

The Waite Group's Turbo C® Programming for the PC, Revised Edition
Robert Lafore

Programming in C, Revised Edition
Stephen G. Kochan

Programming in ANSI C
Stephen G. Kochan

For the retailer nearest you, or to order directly from the publisher, call 800-428-SAMS. In Indiana, Alaska, and Hawaii call 317-298-5699.

Mastering
Turbo Pascal®
5.5

Third Edition

Tom Swan

HAYDEN BOOKS

A Division of Howard W. Sams & Company
4300 West 62nd Street
Indianapolis, Indiana 46268 USA

©1989 by Tom Swan

THIRD EDITION
FIRST PRINTING—1989

All rights reserved. No part of this book shall be reproduced, stored in a retrieval system, or transmitted by any means, electronic, mechanical, photocopying, recording, or otherwise, without written permission from the publisher. No patent liability is assumed with respect to the use of the information contained herein. While every precaution has been taken in the preparation of this book, the publisher and author assume no responsibility for errors or omissions. Neither is any liability assumed for damages resulting from the use of the information contained herein.

International Standard Book Number: 0-672-48450-1
Library of Congress Catalog Card Number: 89-62987

Acquisitions Editor: *Richard Swadley*
Development Editor: *C. Herbert Feltner*
Manuscript Editor: *Sara Bernhardt Black*
Production Coordinator: *Marjorie Jo Hopper*
Illustrator: *Don Clemons*
Cover Illustrator: *Keni Hill, Meridian Design Studio Inc.*
Indexer: *Ted Laux*
Technical Reviewer: *Kim Kokkonen, Turbo Power Software*
Compositor: *Shepard Poorman Communications Corp.*

Printed in the United States of America

Trademark Acknowledgments

All terms mentioned in this book that are known to be trademarks or service marks are listed below. In addition, terms suspected of being trademarks or service marks have been appropriately capitalized. Howard W. Sams & Company cannot attest to the accuracy of this information. Use of a term in this book should not be regarded as affecting the validity of any trademark or service mark.

Apple and Macintosh are registered trademarks of Apple Computer, Inc.
CP/M is a registered trademark of Digital Research, Inc.
IBM is a registered trademark of International Business Machines, Inc.
MS is a trademark of Microsoft Corporation.
Turbo Pascal is a registered trademark of Borland International, Inc.
UCSD-Pascal is a trademark of the Regents of the University of California, San Diego.
WordStar is a registered trademark of Micropro International Corporation.

Overview

Contents

5. Adding Structure to Data

13.   *Advanced Techniques*   **399**

15. *Object-Oriented Programming* 517

List of Tables

Preface
to the Third Edition

When I recently met Anders Heilsberg, the author of Turbo Pascal, I asked him what new features he was cooking up for future versions of Borland International's most famous computer language. Anders nodded at my question, took me aside, and whispered one word excitedly, "Objects."

I knew immediately what he meant. And I knew that the addition of Object-Oriented Programming (OOP) concepts to Turbo Pascal meant that I'd soon be revising *Mastering Turbo Pascal* to explore this intriguing facet of Pascal programming. The result is a new Chapter 15 that introduces the brave new world of OOP techniques and terminology.

But OOP is not all that's new in the Third Edition. I also combed out burrs and snags here and there, recompiled all programs, and made over 150 changes and additions—some short, others many pages long. The introduction now explains how to use Turbo Pascal's built-in debugger. I rewrote portions of chapters 10 and 13, adding details about Turbo Pascal 5.0 and 5.5 overlays and concentrating on the newest version's "probation-reprieve" memory manager, which can add speed to overlayed code. Chapter 16's Encyclopedia (formerly Chapter 15) lists all Turbo Pascal standard procedures and functions in a reference that will serve you long after you master the tutorial.

As in previous editions, the main feature in *Mastering Turbo Pascal 5.5* is source code—lots of source code. Over 400 examples show you every nook and cranny of Pascal programming in action. All programs are compatible with Turbo Pascal version 5.5, but many will work with versions 4.0 and 5.0 as well. To learn a new computer language, there's just no substitute for typing in *complete* programs and making them run on your own computer. If anything, this book is short on theory and long on practical advice. (See the order form inside the back cover for details on how you can order an optional disk of the book's programs or how you can upgrade your disk if you purchased an earlier version. You don't have to purchase the disk. All the programs are printed in the text.)

If you're new to Pascal, you'll find a complete tutorial in this book that, I hope you'll agree, doesn't waste time talking around subjects but gets to the meat in a hurry with real examples that explain key concepts—such as data structures, procedures, functions, units, BGI graphics, and pointers. If you've read a previous edition, I hope you'll enjoy learning about the new additions to Turbo Pascal as much as I have—especially the OOP extensions.

To the many thousands of readers who have supported this book's previous two editions, allow me to add a personal note of thanks. It's been a pleasure to hear from many of you and to have the opportunity to share Turbo Pascal experiences. Here's to another four great years!

Tom Swan
Compuserve ID: 73627,3241

Acknowledgments

I could never have completed this book without the help of the following: Jim Hill, Richard Swadley, Herb Feltner, Sara Black, Marj Hopper, Wendy Ford, Betty Kish, Ted Laux, Fred Amich, Glenn Santner, and all the employees of Howard W. Sams and Borland International.

Special thanks to my wife and assistant Anne Swan and to Kim Kokkonen for many fine suggestions.

Introduction

This book describes how to write computer programs in Turbo Pascal. In here you'll find:

- A complete introduction to Pascal programming specifically tailored for Turbo Pascal and assuming no prior programming knowledge.
- Chapters devoted to advanced techniques, pointers, separate compilation with units, and color graphics, as well as using a math coprocessor and mixing assembly language with Pascal.
- Full railroad (syntax) diagrams describing Turbo Pascal syntax, originally introduced in the first edition and now fully updated.
- An encyclopedia describing and listing complete example programs for every Turbo Pascal procedure and function.
- Hundreds of tested examples with line numbers for easy reference from the text.

About the Examples

By typing in and observing the actions of over 400 examples, some only a few lines, some longer, you'll learn how to write your own Turbo Pascal programs. If you don't have the time or patience to type the examples, you can order the programs on disk. You'll find instructions and an order form on the last page inside the back cover.

How to Use This Book

Many tutorials describe how to program with a generic form of Pascal that few professional programmers would actually use to write software. Some textbooks go so far as to use languages that don't even exist on real computers. While these approaches have some merit for generalizing the subject of programming, it's also true that you can't learn how to swim without getting wet! Therefore, I decided to write this book based on a *specific* language, Turbo Pascal, for a *specific* computer, the IBM PC and compatible systems.

The best way to use this book is to read the text, type the associated examples, and observe how the programs run. Make changes to the programs to test various theories. Experiment. If something doesn't interest you, or if some of the early material is old hat, jump ahead. Look up procedures and functions in Chapter 16 for more details and consult the index for other references. In general, chapters follow a natural progression from simple to complex subjects, avoiding items not yet introduced. You'll find very few places that discuss material "to be explained later." Even so, this book isn't a novel—you won't ruin the ending by reading the chapters out of order!

The following sections list the materials and equipment you will need and describe what the chapters do and do not cover.

Required Materials

To begin your study of Turbo Pascal, you need to have the following items:

1. Turbo Pascal version 4.0, 5.0, or 5.5.
2. The Turbo Pascal Reference Manual.
3. Several blank disks or a hard drive for storing examples.
4. Printer (optional).
5. Any IBM PC or compatible computer.

What This Book Contains

Following are brief descriptions of chapter contents. Each chapter begins with a list of key words and identifiers covered in the chapter and ends with a summary and suggested exercises to test your knowledge. You'll find answers to many exercises at the end of the book.

- Chapter 1, *Programming by Example*, introduces Turbo Pascal, explaining the fundamentals of simple programs and variables. You'll learn how to use railroad diagrams as quick references to the language.

- Chapter 2, *Data—What a Program Knows*, explains constants and numbers, introduces strings and comments, and shows how to deal with common programming errors.

- Chapter 3, *Action—What a Program Does*, adds the concept of a statement to your Pascal knowledge. You'll meet all Turbo Pascal's repetitive and conditional statements here.

- Chapter 4, *Divide and Conquer*, begins to show Turbo Pascal in full force, with procedures and functions that divide large programs into manageable chunks. The chapter details the tenets of top-down programming, an organizational method that many professional programmers use.

- Chapter 5, *Adding Structure to Data*, expands your knowledge about Pascal's data types, covering subranges and scalar types, arrays, records, and sets.

- Chapter 6, *Files*, melts the mysteries of working with disk files as well as accessing devices like printers and modems. You'll learn about text and structured files here.

- Chapter 7, *Pointers, Lists, and Trees*, dispels another mysterious subject of Pascal programming—a subject that even some experts avoid. Pointers are not difficult to understand, as this chapter explains.

- Chapter 8, *Strings*, completes your study of strings, string procedures, and functions, adding to your knowledge of string handling introduced in Chapter 2.

- Chapter 9, *Introducing the Unit*, explains how to use Turbo Pascal's method for compiling programs in separate pieces. The chapter contains descriptions of each of Turbo Pascal's standard units.

- Chapter 10, *Custom Units and Overlays,* shows how to write your own units, letting you develop custom programming libraries and overlays.

- Chapter 11, *The Borland Graphics Interface*, one of the largest chapters in this book, completely describes every procedure and function in Turbo Pascal's massive graphics unit for writing color graphics programs on CGA, EGA, and VGA systems.

- Chapter 12, *More About Numbers*, fully explains Turbo Pascal's integer and real numeric data types, concentrating on specific problems with programming numeric expressions. The chapter also explains how to make good use of Turbo Pascal's math coprocessor data types.

- Chapter 13, *Advanced Techniques*, details many of Turbo Pascal's special features for accessing memory, using typecasting and conditional compilation, writing large programs with the Exec function, and declaring structured variable constants. You'll also learn how to design custom exit routines and efficient overlays.

- Chapter 14, *Pascal Meets Assembly Language*, takes you down the dark alley of adding machine language to Pascal—not really so dangerous once you understand the fundamentals.

- Chapter 15, *Object-Oriented Programming*, introduces Turbo Pascal 5.5's new OOP extensions. Object-oriented programming is gaining new acceptance among programmers, and this chapter will help you to enter this brave new world. Many program examples, diagrams, and a glossary explain OOP concepts and terms.

- Chapter 16, *Turbo Pascal Encyclopedia*, praised in the first edition, is a completely updated reference to all Turbo Pascal's procedures and functions. You'll find this expanded reference valuable long after mastering Turbo Pascal.

What This Book Does Not Contain

Instructions for starting your computer, formatting blank diskettes, making disk copies, and using operating system commands are not covered. Consult your computer manuals or ask teachers and friends if you need help with these subjects.

The first edition of this book explained how to use Turbo Pascal on Z-80-based CP/M computers. Turbo Pascal 4.0 and later versions no longer run under CP/M; therefore, this material has been snipped.

Compiler syntax error numbers, runtime errors, installation instructions, information about how to use the editor, descriptions of the integrated and command-line compiler settings, and other details listed in the Turbo Pascal Reference Manual are not repeated here. Borland's Reference Manual describes Turbo Pascal, the program. This book teaches how to use Turbo Pascal, the language. You need both books to master Turbo Pascal.

For those who are having trouble getting started, though, the next section explains one way to type in example programs. There may be other, even better ways, for typing and running programs, methods you will best learn by reading your reference manual instructions on using the integrated and command-line compilers.

How to Enter Programs

Turbo Pascal comes in two varieties: integrated and command-line. The integrated compiler contains a text editor and can run programs in memory or compile to disk EXE code files. You can use either compiler to run the examples in this book.

Using the Integrated Compiler

1. Prepare your compiler diskette or hard drive subdirectory according to the Turbo Pascal Reference Manual. Type TURBO from the DOS command line to start Turbo Pascal.

2. Press < Alt > -FN to start a new work file. Turbo Pascal asks if you want to save a previous work file in case you forget.

3. Type the example.

4. Press F2 to save your work file, supplying a file name the first time. If you don't know what names to use, type the first eight letters of the name following the key word **PROGRAM** at the top of all programs. Turbo Pascal automatically attaches the PAS file name extension, identifying the text file as a Pascal program.

5. Press < Alt > -R to compile and run the program, then press Enter to return to the Turbo Pascal editor.

6. When the instructions in this book tell you to compile a program to disk, instead of step 5, press < Alt > -CD, changing the *Destination* from *Memory* to

Disk. Press C to compile the program to a disk EXE code file. Press D again to switch back to *Memory*. After compiling, temporarily quit Turbo Pascal by pressing <Alt>-FO. Then type the program name from the DOS command line, just as you run any other stand-alone program. Type EXIT and press Enter to return to Turbo Pascal.

7. From any menu, press <Esc> to return to editing your program text.

8. To quit Turbo Pascal, press <Alt>-X.

Using the Command-Line Compiler

1. Using your favorite ASCII text editor, type the program example and save as <name>.PAS, replacing <name> with the first eight letters of the program name following **PROGRAM** or **UNIT**. Don't use a word processor to type programs. Most word processors add invisible control characters to mark underlines and bold face and to specify printing features that Turbo Pascal doesn't understand. You might be able to use a word processor, though, if it allows you to edit and save plain ASCII text.

2. From the DOS command line, type TPC <name> to compile your program to <name>.EXE. This requires the command-line compiler, TPC.EXE, on disk.

3. Type <name> to run the program.

Using the Built-in Debugger

The integrated versions of Turbo Pascal 5.0 and 5.5 come with a built-in debugger that can help you find errors in programs and can also help you learn more about programming in Pascal. The debugger can run programs one command at a time, monitor values of variables, and stop a running program at planned locations.

The following notes describe the built-in debugger's commands. Professional versions of Turbo Pascal come with a more capable stand-alone Turbo Debugger that has many more features and can debug Pascal, C, and assembly language code. (My forthcoming book, *Mastering Turbo Debugger,* describes how to use this product.)

If you are new to Pascal, some of the terms in the following notes will be unfamiliar. But don't let that stop you from using the debugger. As you enter and run the example listings in this book, press F7 to execute statements one at a time. Press <Alt>-F5 to view the output display and then press any key to return to Turbo Pascal. This lets you examine the results of your program in slow motion—a very useful tool for learning about Pascal.

Some function keys in the integrated compiler apply only to the debugger; others have more general uses. For reference, the next section lists all function keys, some of which were introduced previously.

Function Keys

F1—On-line help. To get help with specific Turbo Pascal commands, position the cursor on any menu item and press F1. Then, follow the onscreen messages to see other help screens.

F2—Save the current text file. If you never saved the program text before, you'll be asked to supply a file name.

F3—Load a new file. If you made changes to the current file, you'll be asked if you want to save your changes before loading the new file.

F4—Run the program up to the current cursor position. This key is useful to execute just a few statements and see their effects. Place the cursor *after* the last statement to execute. Then press F4.

F5—Zoom current window to full screen or zoom a full-screen window back to its original size.

F6—Switch windows. Active windows have double-line borders. Inactive windows have single-line borders. The editor window must be active before you can enter program text.

F7—Trace the current statement. Use this key to single-step your program, executing one statement at a time. If that statement calls another procedure or function, the cursor will jump to the first statement in that section of the program. You can then continue pressing F7 to execute the procedure or function code one statement at a time. If pressing F7 "reverts" to a previously loaded program, try pressing F9 or < Alt > -F9 to compile the new code before pressing F7 the first time.

F8—Steps over the current statement. This key works exactly the same as F7 but for one difference: If the current statement calls a procedure or function, the cursor will not jump to the first statement in that section of the program. Instead, the statement is executed as an indivisible command. Use this key to step over a call to a procedure or function that you don't want to execute one statement at a time.

F9—Compiles (makes) the program text. Depending on the *Destination* setting in the *Compile menu,* "making" a program stores the executable code in memory or in a disk .EXE file. If the program uses any units (separate modules), pressing F9 compiles all modules that are out of date.

F9 is most useful for advanced work. You might want to set the *Compile* menu's *Primary* file: setting to your main program's name. Then, after modifying various modules, set *Destination* to *Disk* and press F9 to recompile only the minimum number of modules needed to bring the entire program up to date.

Debugger Menu Commands

There are two main menu commands related to debugging. Press <Alt>-D to open the *Debug* menu. Press <Alt>-B for the *Break* menu. Each menu has its own set of subcommands, described next.

After using a command, press <Esc> to return to editing. Some commands may require you to press <Esc> more than once.

Debug Menu (<Alt>-D)

Evaluate (<Ctrl>-F4) lets you enter expressions and evaluate their results. There are three parts to this command: Evaluate, Result, and New Value. Enter an expression such as 2 *3 in the Evaluate box. The value of the expression appears in the Result box. Use the Tab key to move to other boxes. Enter new values for variables in the bottom box.

You can call functions and use Turbo Pascal's built-in standard functions such as **Abs** and **Lo** in expressions. While debugging, type in the name of a variable to see its current value. Type in the name of a procedure or function to see where that code is stored in memory.

If some *Evaluate* expressions don't seem to work, press F7 to execute at least one program statement. The program must be "active" for *Evaluate* to be able to find the program's symbols.

Call stack shows the series of currently active procedure and function calls. Use this command to examine the path of events that led to this place in the code. Place the cursor on any identifier in the *Call stack* window and press <Enter> to jump to that place in the program text.

> Note: In simple programs without any procedures and functions, such as most example programs in this book, the *Call stack* command has no useful purpose.

Find procedure works like the search command in a word processor. Type the name of any procedure or function and press <Enter> to jump to that place in the program. This command is most useful in large programs with many procedures and functions.

Integrated debugging should be set to *On* for most programs. If this setting is *Off,* the built-in debugger commands are disabled.

Standalone debugging should be set to *Off* unless you are compiling to a disk .EXE file, which you plan to run under control of the stand-alone Turbo Debugger (available separately from Borland or in the Turbo Pascal Professional package).If you change this setting to *On,* you'll probably want to set *Integrated debugging* to *Off.*

Display swapping can be *Smart* (automatically switches to the display screen when something new appears there), *None* (never switches displays), or *Always* (switches to the display screen after every statement).

Unless the program prompts for input from the keyboard or is performing a lengthy operation, the screen may switch back to Turbo Pascal before you have a chance to read the text. When this happens, press <Alt>-F5 to view the output screen. Then press any key to return to Turbo Pascal.

Refresh display redraws Turbo Pascal's display screen. Use this command in case a runaway program overwrites the display. In severe cases where you can't read anything on the screen, you should be able to give this command with <Esc> <Alt>-DR. (This problem should be rare and is unlikely to occur for any of the programs in this book.)

Break Menu (<Alt>-B)

Add watch (<Ctrl>-F7) adds a new variable name to the Watch Window at the bottom of the display. The Watch Window lists the values of variables that you want to monitor while a program runs. For example, a graphics program might use two variables X and Y to position shapes on the display. You can view the values of X and Y by entering their names into the Watch Window. As the program changes the values of the variables, Turbo Pascal automatically updates the values in the Watch Window.

Instead of entering names by hand, you can also position the cursor on any letter of the variable name you want to monitor and press <Ctrl>-F7. Press <Enter> to add the variable to the Watch Window.

Because variables inside procedures and functions are "visible" to the program only when those procedures and functions are executing, listing those variables in the Watch Window may give "Unknown identifier" error messages. When the program runs those procedures and functions, the variables "come alive," showing their correct values. For this same reason, Turbo Pascal can't check that the variable names you enter actually exist. This is not a bug in the debugger.

Delete watch deletes one variable by name from the Watch Window.

Edit watch lets you edit the name of a variable in the Watch Window.

Remove all watches deletes the list of variables in the Watch Window.

Toggle breakpoint (<Ctrl>-F8) adds a breakpoint at the current cursor position. A breakpoint is like a bookmark that marks a certain page. The program stops just before executing a marked statement, shown in red (or dark gray probably if you have a black and white display).By entering a series of breakpoints in a program, you can run the code up to various stopping places. Then, you can use the Watch Window and *Evaluate* commands to examine the values of variables at those spots in the code.

After the program stops at a breakpoint, press F7 to single-step additional statements or press <Ctrl>-F9 to resume execution.

Breakpoints are not saved on disk. You have to set them again each time you load a program's text file.

Clear all breakpoints erases all breakpoint positions from the program.

View next breakpoint shows you where the program will stop next if you press <Ctrl>-F9 to run.

1

Programming by Example

1

Key Words and Identifiers

BEGIN, END, PROGRAM, Readln, String, VAR, Write, Writeln

The best way to master a programming language is to enter programs and make them run on a computer. Books might inspire, but they can never replace your own experience. To help you gain that experience, this book is filled with example Pascal programs of many kinds. Enter them all and do the exercises at the end of each chapter, and you'll be well on your way to mastering Turbo Pascal. With no further delay, then, let's turn to our first example of a complete Pascal program.

Program 1-1

```
1:  PROGRAM Welcome;
2:  BEGIN
3:    Writeln( 'Welcome to Pascal Programming!' )
4:  END.
```

There are four numbered lines in Program 1-1. When you enter the program, exclude the line numbers and colons along the left border. They have been added for reference to most example programs in this book.

The first line of Program 1-1 is the *program declaration*, which has three parts: the key word **PROGRAM**; a name, or *identifier*, that you make up; and a semicolon. All Pascal programs begin with a similar declaration.

Key Words and Identifiers

Pascal reserves *key words* for special purposes. *Key ide   rs*, on the other hand, are built-in commands and symbols in the Pascal langu   . Other identifiers are words that you create. You can reuse key identifiers, but\   risk redefining their original meanings. You can never reuse key words for yo\   wn purposes.

For example, **Welcome**, an identifier from Program \   describes what the program does. You could just as well name the program **X29**\   it that's no help to others who have to read what you write. **PROGRAM** is a k   ord with special meaning to the Pascal compiler. **Writeln** is a key identifier, a b   in language element.

In this book, key words are in all uppercase, while other   ntifiers are in upper- and lowercase. In the text, **boldface** words refer to thes   id other program elements. When entering programs, you may type in upper-\   owercase as you prefer. **BEGIN**, **begin**, and **BeGIn** are all the same to Pascal.\

When inventing your own identifiers, avoid duplicating key w\   , or you'll receive an error message from the compiler. Also, try not to use bui\   identifiers, or you might redefine their meanings. To help you avoid thes   oblems, chapters begin with a list of those key words and identifiers covered i   chap- ter. Some identifiers appear in more than one list.

The Program Body

Key words **BEGIN** and **END** mark the body of Program 1-1. Inside the prog   n body are the main actions that occur when you run the program. Notice the pe after **END**. A period is the last symbol in all Pascal programs. Turbo Pascal igno any characters after the **END** and its period.

Writeln (pronounced "write line") is a procedure—a Pascal command—tha writes lines of text and other things to the display. (In later chapters, you'll learn how to use **Writeln** to write to a printer or diskette file, too.) Inside **Writeln**'s parentheses is a *string*, marked with beginning and ending single quote marks. Together, the **Writeln**, parentheses, and string in line 3 form a *statement*—a de- scription of an action you want Pascal to perform. When you compile and run Program 1-1, you see the following message on your display.

```
Welcome to Pascal Programming!
```

Error Messages

Unfortunately for programmers, computers demand perfection. The tiniest typ- ing error brings the Turbo Pascal compiler to a halt. When that happens, read the error message on your display, then press the Esc key to see what the compiler did not understand.

Because you probably will make many errors while typing the examples in this book—a perfectly normal, if at times exasperating, experience—it helps to make a few errors on purpose now so you know how to deal with them later. Let's see what happens when you introduce a few common mistakes into Program 1-1.

Program 1-2 (with errors)

```
1:   PROGRAM Welcome:
2:   BEGIN
3:     Writelm( 'Welcome to Pascal Programming' )
4:   END
```

Program 1-2 is the same as Program 1-1, but it has three errors. First, a colon incorrectly replaces the semicolon at the end of line 1. Second, the **Writeln** statement is misspelled. And third, the period following **END** is missing. When you try to compile the program, you receive this error message:

```
Error 85: ; expected
```

Assuming you are using the integrated version of Turbo Pascal, you should see the cursor positioned on the faulty colon. Change the colon to a semicolon, and try again to compile the program. Instead of success, you see another error message:

```
Error 3: Unknown identifier
```

The cursor is now under the **W** of the misspelled **Writelm**. Pascal doesn't understand what a **Writelm** is and, therefore, gives the "unknown identifier" error. Correct the error by changing **Writelm** to **Writeln**, and compile. Once again, you receive an error message.

```
Error 10: Unexpected end of file
```

That simply means the program text, or *source code*, ended before the compiler found the program's final **END** and period. As you can see, Turbo Pascal insists on a complete program at all times. You can certainly add new things to a program, and your work may at times be unfinished, but the program must be officially, or *syntactically*, complete before it will compile. This helpful feature of Pascal lets you compile and test your programs at every stage of development, making sure before going on to the next stage that each new addition operates as you expect.

After adding the missing period to the **END** in line 4, compile Program 1-2 again. This time, you should receive no errors.

The process of programming, compiling, fixing errors, and recompiling, over and over, is normal, although in time you'll learn to avoid the more common mistakes. Don't think, however, that because you receive a lot of errors you're doing something wrong. Even top professional programmers make plenty of mistakes and spend a good bit, if not the major portion, of their time getting the bugs out of their programs. Knowing this, perhaps you should change Program 1-2 to display the string, 'Welcome to the club!'

Introducing Strings

Strings are sequences of characters that you want a program to treat as one object. Usually, the characters in a string are visible, constructed from all the letters, digits, punctuation marks, and other symbols available on your keyboard. Less frequently, strings contain invisible *control characters* that perform actions rather than display visible symbols. One example of a control character is Ctrl-I, produced by pressing the Tab key. The tab character is a character just like A or B, but it has no visible symbol. Control characters like Ctrl-I are often abbreviated with a caret as in ^I.

To create a string, place single quote marks, called *delimiters*, at the beginning and end of the characters you want to group. The entire string must fit on a single line. Although the maximum string length is 255 characters, Turbo Pascal can compile lines containing no more than 127 characters. Even so, the Turbo Pascal editor lets you type up to 248 characters per line. Other editors may impose different maximum line lengths. (Details like these can drive you nuts. Don't worry too much about them.) As you'll learn later on, there are ways to avoid these limitations by breaking long strings into pieces.

You already saw one example of a string in Program 1-1. Here's another:

```
'This is a Pascal string.'
```

Try inserting this string in place of the one in the **Writeln** statement of Program 1-1. Compile and run the program, then remove one or both of the quote marks, and recompile. Did you receive an error message?

You might wonder, if single quote marks delimit the beginning and end of a string, how do you display a quote mark itself? To do that, simply repeat the quote mark. This tells the compiler to display the quote, not to mark the end of the string. Here, for example, is a string with a contraction.

```
'Don''t give up the ship!'
```

There are no spaces between the single quotes in **Don''t**. Be careful to type *two* single quotes and not the double quote character("). Insert this new string into the **Writeln** statement of Program 1-1. When you run the program, you see:

```
Don't give up the ship!
```

Reading Railroad Diagrams

As you learn about the Pascal language, you'll encounter many definitions of various features. For clarity and future reference, there is a precise method for defining these features and explaining Pascal *syntax*, the rules for combining language elements into statements and programs. Language designers use these same methods to create new programming languages and to write compilers like Turbo Pascal.

Pictures, as the saying goes—at least among programmers— are worth a kiloword. And Pascal syntax is often best described in picturelike graphs called *railroad diagrams*.

Figure 1-1 is an example of a railroad diagram, also called a *syntax graph*. To read a railroad diagram, trace the heavy-line tracks with your finger. The diagram is a guide to Pascal symbols, showing their forms and relationships. Each diagram has one entry point (usually at the left) and one exit (usually at the right). For clarity, some of the diagrams here and in other chapters are modified versions of the full Turbo Pascal syntax diagrams in Appendix A.

program declaration

Figure 1-1 Railroad diagram describing the syntax of a program declaration, the first line of all Pascal programs.

Compare the diagram in Figure 1-1 with the first line of Program 1-1 while reading the following descriptions of the three essential railroad diagram components.

Each encircled part of a railroad diagram contains a symbol, word, or punctuation mark. A single encircled character tells you to type that character at this position. Capitalized, encircled words are language key words. Enter them exactly as spelled. As you learned earlier, the key word **PROGRAM** is the first word of a Pascal program, a fact the railroad diagram in Figure 1-1 confirms.

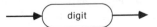

A lowercase encircled word stands for another symbol or group of symbols with an obvious meaning. For example, the lowercase *digit* tells you that one of the digits 0 through 9 is allowed at this place in a program.

Boxed-in words represent the contents of another diagram. This rule lets simple diagrams serve as building blocks in other more complex graphs while avoiding duplication and clutter. Looking at Figure 1-1, you would expect to find a separate diagram for the boxed *identifier* (see Figure 1-2). You could replace the boxed *identifier* in Figure 1-1 with the entire diagram in Figure 1-2 and still correctly show program declaration syntax.

There are many possible paths through the diagram in Figure 1-2. Notice that some of the arrows point to the left, indicating repetition. The diagram tells you

identifier

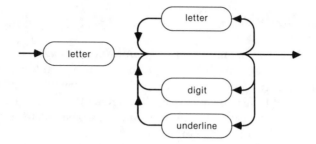

Figure 1-2 An identifier begins with a letter, followed by any number of digits, letters, and underlines.

that an identifier begins with a letter, followed by any combination of other letters, digits, and underlines.

By the way, underlines can make long identifiers more readable as in **speed _of_light**. When using underlines this way, be aware that Turbo Pascal considers **speed_of_light** and **SpeedOfLight** to be *different* identifiers. (Many other Pascal compilers ignore the underlines.) For this reason, the programs in this book do not use underlines in identifiers.

Compare the identifier railroad diagram in Figure 1-2 with the identifiers in Table 1-1. Listed on the left are correct identifiers; on the right, illegal or badly formed identifiers. Prove to yourself that each word conforms to the rules for well-formed identifiers.

Table 1-1 Identifier rights and wrongs

Right	Wrong
GoodSym	Bad sym
Fahrenheit_451	32_Degrees
ABCDEFG	9876.543
MoneyBags	$Moneybags$
OverWeight	Under-weight

Now that you know the basics of reading railroad diagrams, you should be able to draw a diagram for defining Pascal strings. Try a few designs before looking at the answer in Figure 1-3. How will you diagram the method described earlier for inserting single quote marks into strings?

string

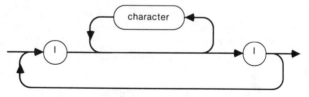

Figure 1-3 Railroad diagram showing how to delimit strings with single quote marks.

Declaring Variables

In Pascal, as in most other programming languages, *variables* hold data on which a program operates. In the program text, the variable's name represents the value of data stored somewhere in computer memory when the program runs. This value does not have to be numeric, although it often is. You can name variables for numbers, zip codes, and account balances, as well as for strings, names, addresses—even the colors of the rainbow.

Variables are like boxes that hold values, as Figure 1-4 illustrates. Pascal requires you to decide in advance on the type of values that fit in the box. For example, if you declare a variable as an *integer*, meaning a whole number, then that variable cannot hold a string or a floating point value.

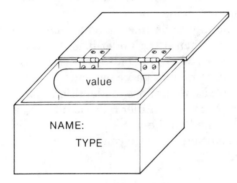

Figure 1-4 A variable is similar to a box with a name and type. The type defines what kind of value goes in the box; the program refers to the value by its name.

Likewise, a string variable may not hold a number. A variable, then, has an associated *data type*, indicating the kind of value it contains. Program 1-3 shows how to declare a string variable, **YourName**.

Program 1-3

```
1:   PROGRAM WhoAreYou;
2:   VAR
3:      YourName : String[40];
4:   BEGIN
5:      Write( 'What is your name? ' );
6:      Readln( YourName );
7:      Writeln( 'Hi there ', YourName, '!' )
8:   END.
```

There are several new elements in Program 1-3. Lines 2 and 3 make up the *variable declaration*, starting with the key word **VAR** and declaring a variable

YourName. The type of the variable is a **String** with a maximum character length of 40 in brackets. You can declare string variables with lengths from 1 to 255 characters. When the program runs, the string variable can hold from zero to its declared maximum number of characters.

If you don't specify a maximum string length in brackets, Turbo Pascal automatically assigns a 255-character limit. For example, these two strings, **String-Thing1** and **StringThing2,** can each hold up to 255 characters:

```
VAR
   StringThing1 : String[255];
   StringThing2 : String;
```

All variable declarations start with **VAR**. After that comes a series of identifiers, each followed by a colon and data type, ending with a semicolon. (See Figure 1-5.) To declare multiple variables of the same type, separate their identifiers with commas. For example, the following variable declaration creates three ten-character strings **A**, **B**, and **C**.

```
VAR
   A, B, C : String[10];
```

variable declaration

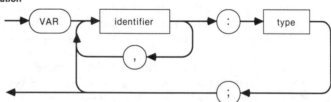

Figure 1-5 The variable declaration part of a program follows the
program declaration (see Figure 1-1).

Besides the variable declaration, there's another new feature of Program 1-3 in the three lines between **BEGIN** and **END**. The two previous examples had only single statements in the program bodies. This program has multiple statements separated from each other by semicolons. Together, lines 4–8 form a *compound statement*.

To show their relationships, each statement is indented on a separate line. You could put all statements on the same line with or without indentations. Turbo Pascal requires only that semicolons separate multiple statements. A statement's physical position and indentations are conveniences for your sake—and for others who have to read your programs.

Program 1-3 also shows how to use a **Write** statement (line 5). Except for one difference, **Write** is the same as **Writeln**. **Writeln** issues a carriage return, moving the cursor to the start of the next line down. **Write** does not end a line with a carriage return. After **Write**, the cursor stays on the same line just after the last character written.

Pascal Input—Reading Strings

Line 6 of Program 1-3 contains a new Pascal identifier, **Readln**. A **Readln** statement reads information into a variable, in this case, **YourName**. As used here, **Readln** takes its input from the keyboard. When the program gets to line 6, it waits for you to enter something. **Readln** restricts your typing to a maximum 127 characters even if the string variable can hold more. Of course, you may use shorter strings as in the example. In this case, you can still type up to 127 characters, but Pascal ignores characters beyond the declared string length.

    Readln lets you edit your typing. You can backspace over mistakes and type corrections before pressing Enter and sending to the program what you type. See Table 1-2 for a list of other editing keys you can use.

Table 1-2 Readln editing keys

Key	Operation
BS	The backspace key moves the cursor left, erasing mistakes.
←	The left arrow key works the same as the backspace key.
Esc	The escape key prints a backslash (\) and carriage return, cancelling any characters typed so far and letting you reenter the line.
Enter	Ends input, placing typed characters in **Readln**'s variable.
^C	Type Ctrl-C (the caret is shorthand for Ctrl) to end the program.

When you press Enter, the **Readln** statement deposits your typing into **YourName**, which the program then displays in a **Writeln** statement (line 7). Look closely at this line. There are two literal strings plus the variable **YourName** separated by commas inside parentheses. **Writeln** writes these individual elements as though they formed one string. Therefore, when you run the program, "Hi there" is followed by whatever you type into **YourName**, which is in turn followed by an exclamation point. The ability to combine various elements in a single **Write** or **Writeln** statement is powerful, and you'll see this feature again and again in future examples.

Summary

Studying, entering, and running program examples is the best way to master Turbo Pascal. This book has many examples. You should enter, compile, and run them all, and observe how they operate.

    Key words are reserved words in Pascal. Key identifiers are built-in language elements. Other identifiers are words that you invent. Statements are descriptions of actions to perform. Railroad diagrams describe the relationships between key words, identifiers, and other symbols and show how to write Pascal statements.

Strings are sequences of symbols, surrounded by single quotes. You can store strings, as well as other data types, in declared variables, giving descriptive names to values the program uses. Use two quote marks to display a single quote.

To display strings, use **Write** or **Writeln**. To read strings, letting people enter data into a program, use **Readln**. To display multiple items in **Write** and **Writeln** statements, separate the items with commas.

Exercises

1-1. Write a program to display the following message on your screen.

```
Pack my box with five dozen liquor jugs.
```

1-2. Write a program to display the following two lines. Use multiple **Writeln** statements. Watch out for the punctuation!

```
"It's eleven o'clock," she said,
"why aren't you in bed?"
```

1-3. Assume that the only parts of English speech are articles, adjectives, nouns, and verbs. Draw a syntax diagram (or diagrams) describing how to compose simple, but grammatically correct, sentences. Show how to punctuate multiple adjectives with commas as in "The quick, brown fox jumped over the lazy dog."

1-4. Add a definition for compound sentences to your diagram from exercise 1-3. Identify the key words.

1-5. Using a string variable and a combination of **Readln** and **Writeln** statements, write a program to prompt for a string, and then duplicate that string three times. For example, if you type "Apple," the program should write "AppleAppleApple." One solution uses five statements. Can you do it using three?

2

Data—What a Program Knows

- The Constant Declaration
- Numeric Constants
- Scientific Notation
- Formatting Numbers
- String and Character Constants
- Boolean Constants
- Variables
- The Assignment Operator
- Comparison Operators
- Declaring Variables
- Common Programming Errors
- Subrange Types
- Range Checking
- Expressions
- Operator Precedence
- Mixing Reals and Integers
- Inserting Comments in Programs
- Compiler Directives
- Variable Constants
- Constant Expressions

2

Key Words and Identifiers

Boolean, Byte, Char, CONST, Integer, LongInt, Real, ShortInt, String, Word

Data are facts that a computer program knows. A program might know your name, your weight, the time of day, the date, the amount of money you have in your savings, and the amount you owe to the telephone company. In Pascal, data that can change are stored in *variables*. *Constants*, on the other hand, hold data that do not change. This chapter explains how to get data in and out of programs using variables and constants.

The Constant Declaration

Figure 2-1 shows the railroad diagram for a constant declaration, which comes between the program declaration and body but before any variable declaration. Each constant has an identifier and an associated constant value. In a program, you might have constants named **Size** or **Height**. After declaring these and other constants, you can use their descriptive names in place of their values.

constant declaration

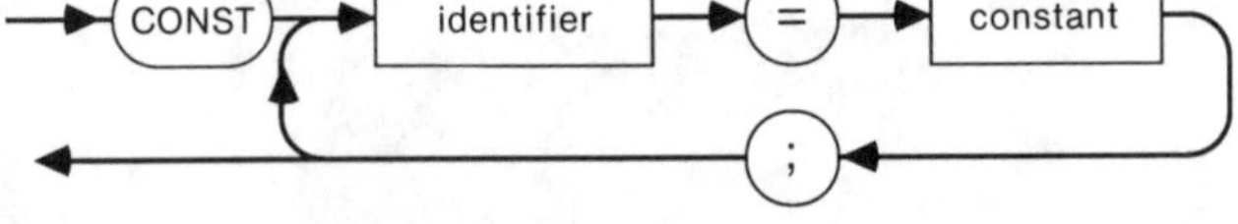

Figure 2-1 Railroad diagram describing the constant declaration part of a Pascal program.

The constant declaration part of Program 2-1 begins with the key word **CONST**, followed by a list of constants separated by semicolons (lines 2–5). Each constant declaration has an identifier, an equal sign, a value, and a semicolon. The value determines the data type of the constant. For example, line 3 declares a string constant, **Name**, while lines 4 and 5 declare two integer, or whole number, constants, **Weight** and **Savings**.

Program 2-1

```
 1:   PROGRAM Constants;
 2:   CONST
 3:      Name = 'Anne';
 4:      Weight = 118;
 5:      Savings = 375;
 6:   BEGIN
 7:      Writeln( 'Name   : ', Name );
 8:      Writeln( 'Weight: ', Weight, ' pounds' );
 9:      Writeln( Name, ' has $', Savings, ' in savings' )
10:   END.
```

As demonstrated in Program 2-1, there are two main advantages to using constants in Pascal. Well-chosen constant identifiers make a program more readable and, therefore, easier to understand. Calling 118 **Weight** and 375 **Savings** makes the meanings of the two values harder to confuse.

A second advantage is the concentration of constant values at the top of a program. Although a constant name may appear in many different statements, you can easily change the declared value in the constant declaration. When you recompile the program, all statements automatically recognize the new constant.

As an example, Program 2-1 uses the constant **Name** in two **Writeln** statements. If you change 'Anne' to your own name in line 3, the program displays your name in lines 7 and 9. With constants, you avoid hunting through a program for values that need changing. In a typical commercial program with thousands of lines, that advantage is a necessity.

In the special case of string constants, Turbo Pascal stores only one copy of a string in memory, even though you might use the string constant identifier many times throughout the program.

Numeric Constants

Whole number, or **Integer**, constants range from $-32,768$ to $+32,767$. Although commas appear in these numbers to make them more readable in this text, never use commas in a program's numbers. Figure 2-2 shows a few typical integer constants as they might appear in a program's constant declaration.

```
CONST
    MonthsInYear = 12;
    DaysInWeek   = 7;
    HoursInDay   = 24;
    Altitude     = 15000;
```

Figure 2-2 Examples of **Integer**, or whole number, constants.

Along with plain integers, Turbo Pascal has four other whole number types. **Byte** values range from 0 to 255. **ShortInt** values range from −128 to +127. **Word** values range from 0 to 65,535. And **LongInt** values range from a whopping −2,147,483,648 to +2,147,483,647.

Besides their upper and lower limits, the only difference between these four extra numeric types and **Integer** values is the amount of memory they occupy. **Byte** and **ShortInt** values each take one byte of memory. **Integer** and **Word** values each take two bytes. **LongInt** values take four bytes.

When declaring whole number constants, you never have to specify which type to use. As this example demonstrates, Turbo Pascal automatically selects the most efficient type—the one that takes the least memory—for you:

```
CONST
    c1 = 200;      { Byte }
    c2 = -2;       { ShortInt }
    c3 = 1024;     { Integer }
    c4 = 55678;    { Word }
    c5 = 2000000;  { LongInt }
```

Real number constants hold larger numbers or values with fractional parts. In mathematics, real numbers include the set of all rational and irrational values. In Pascal, a real number is simply any number with a decimal point. You might declare dollar values or the distance from the earth to the moon as real-number constants. Figure 2-3 lists a few other examples. Notice that values less than one must have a leading zero to the left of the decimal point as in 0.123, and that values with no fractional part must end in a period as in 999. or a period and 0 as in 999.0 to be **Real** numbers instead of **Integer**.

```
CONST
    MinimumWage   = 3.65;
    MilesToMoon   = 238857.0;
    InterestRate  = 0.123;
    MetersPerMile = 1609.344;
```

Figure 2-3 Examples of **Real** number constants.

Scientific Notation

To see the effect of using real-number constants instead of integers, change the value of **Savings** in Program 2-1 from 375 to 375.50. When you run the program, it now displays the following line:

```
Anne has $ 3.7550000000E+02 in savings
```

As you can see from that example, real numbers normally display in *scientific notation*, a convenient shorthand for expressing large and small values. Dropping trailing zeros for clarity, the value 3.755E + 02 is equivalent to the more common mathematical notation, 3.755×10^2. To read the shorthand value, move the decimal point the number of places indicated by the exponent E. Move the decimal point right for positive exponents. Move it left for negative exponents. Thus, 5.123E + 03 is equivalent to 5,123.00. 6.5E – 03 is the same as 0.0065. Moving the decimal place two digits to the right in the previous example, you can see that Anne has 375.50 in savings.

The range of real numbers is much larger than the range of integers. For most purposes, you can assume that real numbers have no limit, although in Turbo Pascal the actual range is approximately plus or minus 2.9E – 39 to 1.7E + 38. You can extend this range by using a numeric data processor (NDP)—either an 8087, 80287, or 80387—or by switching on Turbo Pascal's NDP emulation routines. See Chapter 12 for details.

Formatting Numbers

Of course, unless you're fussy about fractions of pennies, two decimal places are sufficient to display dollar amounts. To properly display the real number **Savings** constant in Program 2-1, rewrite line 9 to read:

```
Writeln( Name, ' has $', Savings:8:2, ' in savings' )
```

The notation **:8:2** is a formatting command, which tells **Writeln** to display the value of **Savings** in eight columns *including* a maximum of two decimal places. Specifying decimal places is optional. Try **Savings:8** or **Savings:20:4**. (The same formatting rules apply to **Write** and **Writeln** statements.) Also experiment with different values for **Savings** in the program's constant declaration. What happens when you use the values 50.459 or 123.456789?

A useful notation is **:0:n**, where **n** is the number of decimal places to display. Even though the zero appears to specify no columns for the value's whole number part, Turbo Pascal always displays the correct value in cases where numbers require more columns than you specify. Therefore, **:0:2** displays any real number with two decimal places but with no leading spaces. To see how this works, change **Savings** to **Savings:0:2** in line 9 of Program 2-1.

Another trick is to use **:0:0**, which displays the integer part of a **Real** value rounded to the nearest whole number. Change **Savings** to **Savings:0:0** and experiment with different constant values. For example, 375.49 displays as 375 while 375.50 is rounded up to 376. (Note: Some earlier Turbo Pascal versions rounded 375.50 down to 375 and 375.51 up to 376.)

Using a similar notation, you can also format integer values in **Write** and **Writeln** statements. Because integers have no fractional parts, specify only the number of columns. To format the integer constant **Weight** in a ten-character-wide column, replace line 8 in Program 2-1 with this line:

```
Writeln( 'You weigh ', Weight:10, ' pounds' );
```

In addition to letting you create your own constants, Turbo Pascal has two predeclared numeric constants, listed in Table 2-1. You can use **Maxint** and **MaxLongInt** without first defining their values.

Table 2-1 Predefined numeric constants

Constant	Value	Type
Maxint	32,767	Integer
MaxLongInt	2,147,483,647	LongInt

String and Character Constants

Figure 2-4 lists a few examples of string and character constants. Single-character constants are type **Char**. Multiple-character constants are type **String**. You can associate any string of characters with a constant identifier, which you may then use throughout a program in place of the actual, or *literal*, string.

```
CONST
    LastName      = 'Reagan';
    FirstName     = 'Ronald';
    MiddleInitial = 'W';
    Address       = '(No longer) The White House';
    CityStateZip  = 'Washington, DC 10000';
    PhoneNumber   = '201-555-1212';
```

Figure 2-4 Examples of string and character constants.

Because single characters are type **Char**, it apparently is not possible to declare single-character string constants. What type, for example, is **MiddleInitial** in Figure 2-4? Is it a single character or a single-character string? What's the difference?

To solve this ambiguity, Turbo Pascal's designers rightly chose to allow single characters like A or X in most places where strings are called for. This allowance may seem vague and unimportant to you now, but it is more understandable when you know that a string is stored in memory along with an invisible value that indicates its length. There is no such value stored with single characters, but there would be with single-character strings. Thus, in your program, the *character* Q appears identical to the *string* Q, but it is stored differently in memory, a difference that Turbo Pascal conveniently ignores.

Boolean Constants

Type **Boolean**, named after the nineteenth-century English mathematician George Boole (1815–1864), has two possible values, **True** and **False**. The Boolean data type is a critical feature of Pascal, and, because of its use in logical expressions, it's a fair assumption that the self-educated Boole would have approved of this use of his family name. Although Boole's formal education ended after elementary school, he went on to father modern Boolean algebra, without which today's digital computers—and programming languages like Pascal—could not have been designed.

Boolean constants, and Boolean variables, contribute to the readability of Pascal programs while making complex sequences seem logical and appropriate. For example, if you declare a Boolean constant **Debugging**, your program can test if **Debugging** is **True** or **False** and take appropriate action, perhaps displaying various things that only you, but not your clients, need to see. Used in this way, a Boolean constant is a kind of logical switch, the conceptual equivalent of a test switch that might be found inside a TV or a computer.

Another use for Boolean constants is to keep track of true or false facts. In Program 2-2, the five Boolean constants in lines 3–8 describe facts about a fictitious computer system. The **Writeln** statements in lines 12–17 display these values in a table. (The lone **Writeln** in line 18 writes a blank line on the display.) Let's say you're looking for a system that has graphics, is portable, and comes with a printer. Line 19 indicates whether the various settings conform to your specifications. The phrase **Graphics AND Portable AND Printer** is a Boolean expression that, when the program runs, evaluates to a single true or false result.

Program 2-2

```
 1:   PROGRAM LookAlike;
 2:   CONST
 3:      Graphics   = False;
 4:      Compatible = True;
 5:      Dvorak     = False;
 6:      Portable   = True;
 7:      Printer    = True;
 8:      HardDisk   = False;
 9:   BEGIN
10:      Writeln( '** Look-alike specifications **'    );
```

Program 2-2 *cont.*

```
11:       Writeln( '-------------------------------'    );
12:       Writeln( '   Graphics .......... ', Graphics   );
13:       Writeln( '   IBM compatible .... ', Compatible );
14:       Writeln( '   Dvorak keyboard ... ', Dvorak     );
15:       Writeln( '   Portable .......... ', Portable   );
16:       Writeln( '   Printer ........... ', Printer    );
17:       Writeln( '   Hard disk ......... ', HardDisk   );
18:       Writeln;
19:       Writeln( 'Good choice = ', Graphics AND Portable AND Printer )
20: END.
```

A Boolean expression may have any combination of Boolean constants or variables plus the key word operators **AND**, **OR**, **NOT**, and **XOR**. For example, you could replace line 19 with one of the following two **Writeln** statements:

```
Writeln( 'Good choice = ',
   Compatible AND Printer OR HardDisk );
Writeln( 'Good choice = ',
   NOT Portable AND Graphics AND Printer );
```

Pascal evaluates each Boolean expression into one final true or false value. Each of the Boolean operators has a different effect. **NOT** changes a Boolean value from true to false or from false to true. **AND** combines two Boolean values for a true result only if both operands are true. **OR** combines two Boolean values with a true result if one or both operands are true. **XOR** (exclusive or) combines two Boolean values with a true result if only one value, but not both, is true. This relationship is easier to see in a truth table, as shown in Table 2-2, which lists the results of **AND**ing, **OR**ing, and **XOR**ing two operands A and B for all possible true and false combinations.

Variables

Unlike constants, variables may change their values many times while a program runs. Earlier you learned how to declare a single string variable, **YourName**, in Program 1-3. The value of **YourName** changes to whatever you enter in response to the program's **Readln** statement. Most programs have many such variables, all of a variety of types: real numbers, integers, strings, and other Pascal data types.

The Assignment Operator

To assign literal values to variables, use Pascal's *assignment operator*, a double-character symbol composed of a colon and equal sign. For example, the following statement assigns 125 to an integer variable **Height**:

```
Height := 125;
```

The variable on the left takes on the value of the expression or literal value on the right of the assignment symbol. While reading a Pascal program, pronounce := as "becomes equal to" or just "becomes." Don't confuse a simple equal sign with Pascal's assignment symbol. The equal sign states a fact, such as the fact that **Height** = 125. This is not the same as assigning the value 125 to a variable named **Height**.

Comparison Operators

The equal sign is called a *comparison operator* because it compares its two operands—the values on either side—with each other. Table 2-3 lists other Turbo Pascal comparison operators.

Table 2-2 Boolean truth tables

A	AND	B	=	C
False		False		False
False		True		False
True		False		False
True		True		True

A	OR	B	=	C
False		False		False
False		True		True
True		False		True
True		True		True

A	XOR	B	=	C
False		False		False
False		True		True
True		False		True
True		True		False

Table 2-3 Comparison operators

Operator	Meaning	Example
=	Equal	(a = b)
<	Less than	(a < b)
>	Greater than	(a > b)
< =	Less than or equal	(a < = b)
> =	Greater than or equal	(a > = b)
< >	Not equal	(a < > b)

Having made an assignment to **Height**, it may then be true that **Height** = 125. This is intuitive, but many programming languages make no similar distinction between statements of fact and assignments of values to variables. In fact, many languages use the equal sign for both purposes, making programs difficult to understand. In Pascal, you can always distinguish assignments from statements of fact, an important quality of a professional computer language.

Declaring Variables

You already know how to declare a single variable. (See the **VAR** railroad diagram in Figure 1-5.) Declaring more than one is equally simple, as Program 2-3 demonstrates. The identifiers in lines 3–5 have the same names as the constants in Program 2-1. This time, though, the program assigns new values to the variables. Unlike constants, variables do not have predefined values. The first thing to do, then, is to initialize a program's variables with assignments.

Lines 7–9 do this by assigning initial values to **Name**, **Weight**, and **Savings**. After that, lines 10–12 display the assigned values. The same process then repeats in lines 16–21, but this time with new values assigned to the same variables. You now have a simple database program recording various facts about people. Try duplicating lines 16–21 yet again, adding another set of facts to the program.

Program 2-3

```
 1:  PROGRAM Vary;
 2:  VAR
 3:      Name    : String[20];
 4:      Weight  : Integer;
 5:      Savings : Real;
 6:  BEGIN
 7:      Name := 'Anne';
 8:      Weight := 118;
 9:      Savings := 375.75;
10:      Writeln( 'Name    : ', Name );
11:      Writeln( 'Weight  : ', Weight );
12:      Writeln( 'Savings : ', Savings:4:2 );
13:
14:      Writeln;
15:
16:      Name := 'Tom';
17:      Weight := 155;
18:      Savings := 0.25;
19:      Writeln( 'Name    : ', Name );
20:      Writeln( 'Weight  : ', Weight );
```

Program 2-3 *cont.*

```
21:    Writeln( 'Savings : ', Savings:4:2 )
22: END.
```

As lines 3–5 in Program 2-3 show, you must declare every variable as a specific data type. This example has **String**, **Integer**, and **Real** number variables.
You could also declare variables of the other types we've seen such as **Char**, **Boolean**, and **Byte**. Program 2-4 demonstrates this with six variables of various common data types.

When you assign a value to a variable, Pascal checks that the value matches
the variable's declared type. This characteristic, known as *strong type checking*,
helps prevent one of the most common programming errors—assigning the wrong
value to a variable, for example, confusing your age with your golf score. In another language, the variable **Married** from Program 2-4 might be a simple number, with 0 standing for true and 1 for false. In that case, there is nothing to prevent
you from accidentally assigning the value 125 to **Married**, clearly an error, but not
something the computer is able to catch. In Pascal, such an assignment would
never make it through the compiler. Program 2-4 declares **Married** as a **Boolean**
data type, which cannot hold a numeric value. **Married** can be only true or false.

Program 2-4

```
 1: PROGRAM ManyTypes;
 2: VAR
 3:    Weight  : Integer;
 4:    Age     : Byte;
 5:    Savings : Real;
 6:    Married : Boolean;
 7:    Sex     : Char;
 8:    Name    : String[20];
 9: BEGIN
10:    Name := 'Marvin';
11:    Age := 42;
12:    Sex := 'M';
13:    Married := true;
14:    Weight := 160;
15:    Savings := 12931.32;
16:
17:    Writeln( 'Name    : ', Name );
18:    Writeln( 'Age     : ', Age );
19:    Writeln( 'Sex     : ', Sex );
20:    Writeln( 'Married : ', Married );
21:    Writeln( 'Weight  : ', Weight );
22:    Writeln( 'Savings : ', Savings:6:2 )
23: END.
```

Common Programming Errors

To see what happens when you assign the wrong kind of value to a variable, breaking Pascal's strong type checking rule, change line 13 in Program 2-4 to read:

```
Married := 500;
```

When you compile the program, you receive:

```
Error 26: Type mismatch
```

The Boolean data type, remember, has only two values, **True** or **False**—numbers are not allowed.

Errors like these are called *syntax errors* because they break one of the syntactical rules of Pascal programming. When you receive a syntax error, check the appropriate railroad diagram in Appendix A. You'll often find your mistake this way.

Syntax errors cause the compiler to stop. A *runtime error*, on the other hand, occurs while the program is running. Syntax and runtime errors are two of the three most common kinds of programming errors. As you learn more about Pascal programming, you'll undoubtedly become old friends—or enemies—with all three.

The third kind of error, a *logical error*, occurs when you assign a value like 2000 to a variable such as **Weight** in Program 2-4. Logical errors are the most difficult to fix. The program has no way of knowing that a person can't weigh 2000 pounds—that's your responsibility.

Subrange Types

To help prevent logical errors, you can declare subranges of numeric variables, telling the compiler to limit the low and high values that variables can hold. Specify a subrange as two whole numbers separated with a double period, called an ellipsis. (In typesetting, an ellipsis has three periods. In Pascal, it has two—the economy model.)

Change the 160 in line 14 of Program 2-4 to 2000 and run the program. Although the weight is now incorrect, the compiler doesn't mind. To fix the error, change line 3 to read:

```
Weight : 7 .. 250;
```

You can now compile the program only if the assignment to **Weight** is within the range of 7 to 250, a reasonable human weight range. The subrange lets the compiler verify assignments to variables. You still could assign the wrong weight value, of course, but at least you get some protection against outlandish catastrophes.

Range Checking

One problem with subrange values is that the compiler can check only for literal assignments to variables. If you assign 5000 pounds to poor Marvin, the compiler can stop with an error message. But, if you assign a *variable* to a subrange data type, the compiler can't know the variable's value until the program runs. To see the problem, change line 14 to:

```
Write( 'Weight? ' );
Readln( Weight );
```

This prompts for the weight value, letting you type the answer. Run the program and type 2000. Are you surprised by the result? The reason you do not receive an error is that checking subranges takes time—and time is something that Turbo Pascal is rightfully stingy about wasting. When you want to check subranges automatically during program runs, you must turn on an option called *range checking*. To do this, surround the **Readln** or any other statement with compiler directives:

```
{$R+} Readln( Weight ); {$R-}
```

The {$R+} and {$R-} are commands to the compiler. They tell Pascal to create automatic range checks for statements in between. {$R+} turns on range checking. {$R-} turns it off. Some people place a single {$R+} at the beginning of their programs to turn on range checking for the entire program. This way, after debugging, it's easy to remove the directive and, therefore, remove the time-consuming code that has to perform the limit checks at every assignment to subrange variables.

For another example of a runtime error, add the following two lines between lines 15 and 16 in Program 2-4:

```
Write( 'How old are you? ' );
{$R+} Readln( age ); {$R-}
```

Compile and run the modified program. Type your age when the program asks, "How old are you?" Now rerun the program. This time, lie. Here's what happened when I said I was 500.

```
How old are you? 500
Runtime error 201 at 0000:00C0.
```

The **0000:00C0** is the address in memory where the error occurred. The number you see will probably be different. After pressing Enter to go back to the Turbo Pascal editor, the cursor jumps to the **Readln** statement and near the top of the screen is the message:

```
Error 201: Range check error
```

Error 201 stopped the program because 500 is outside the legal range of a **Byte** variable, which can hold values only from 0 to 255.

Run the modified program again. This time, if you type A for your age, you receive a different runtime error:

```
Error 106: Invalid numeric format
```

The letter A is not a number. Pascal doesn't let you type letters into the **Byte** variable, **Age**.

As you can see from these examples, data types have legal forms and limits, which Pascal can help enforce. Pascal's strong type-checking abilities encourage you to write correct programs by guarding against common errors that all programmers make.

Expressions

An expression combines constants, variables, and literal values into a single result. If A = 5 and B = 3, then the expression (A + B) equals 8. The result of an expression is the same type as its components. Integer expressions have integer results; Boolean expressions, Boolean results. The Boolean expression (A < B), for example, is **False**, because 5 is not less than 3.

Numeric expressions use the common mathematics programming operators plus (+), minus (–), and multiply (*). Division has two forms. To divide two **Byte**, **ShortInt**, **Word**, **Integer**, or **LongInt** values, use the key word **DIV** this way:

```
IntegerAverage := Sum DIV Count;
```

To divide two real numbers, use a slash (/). This always produces a real-number result. For example, even if **Sum** and **Count** are integer variables, the division result in this statement is a real number:

```
RealAverage := Sum / Count;
```

As an example of using numeric expressions, Program 2-5 converts degrees Fahrenheit to Celsius, named for the Swedish astronomer Anders Celsius (1701–1744), who invented the temperature scale with 0° at the freezing and 100° at the boiling points of water. There are two real-number variables in the program, **Fdegrees** and **Cdegrees**. Lines 1–8 should be familiar. Line 9 shows how to program the conversion formula for Fahrenheit to Celsius as an expression, with the result assigned to **Cdegrees**. When the program asks for a temperature, type a number such as 100 or 32.5. The program then displays the equivalent temperature in degrees Celsius.

Program 2-5

```
 1:  PROGRAM Celsius;
 2:  VAR
 3:     Fdegrees, Cdegrees : Real;
 4:  BEGIN
 5:     Writeln( 'Fahrenheit to Celsius conversion' );
 6:     Writeln;
 7:     Write( 'Degrees Fahrenheit ? ' );
 8:     Readln( Fdegrees );
 9:     Cdegrees := ( ( Fdegrees - 32.0 ) * 5.0 ) / 9.0;
10:     Writeln( 'Degrees Celsius = ', Cdegrees:8:2 )
11:  END.
```

Note: When running Program 2-5 and others in Turbo Pascal's integrated environment, the display returns to the editor before you have a chance to see the results. When this happens, press Alt-F5 to view the output screen, or insert a temporary **Readln** statement just before the program's **END.** This lets you view the output and then press Enter to return to the editor.

Operator Precedence

Notice the use of parentheses in line 9 of Program 2-5. Pascal first evaluates the parts of an expression inside the most deeply nested parentheses before it evaluates the rest of the expression. In the absence of parentheses, the order of operations in an expression follows a predefined *precedence*. (See Appendix E.) Expressions having operators with higher precedence are evaluated before expressions having lower precedence. Some of the operators and data types in Appendix E will be introduced in later chapters.

Program 2-6 demonstrates how operator precedence affects expression results. Although the three expressions in lines 6–8 are similar, the results are 610, 610, and 900. Because the multiply operator (*) has a higher precedence than plus (+), lines 6 and 7 evaluate to the same value. The extra parentheses in line 7 do not affect the result. In other words, the following statement is true:

$$(A + B * C) = (A + (B * C))$$

To add variables **A** and **B** before multiplying by **C** requires parentheses to force Pascal to evaluate the expression with the lower precedence first. Therefore, the following statement is also true, at least for the assigned values in Program 2-6. The symbol < > means "not equal."

$$(A + B * C) <> ((A + B) * C)$$

Even when not strictly required, extra parentheses often clarify complex expressions, as in Program 2-5. Additional parentheses have no effect on the size or speed of a program, and many programmers lavishly use them to avoid any chance of an ambiguity. The intention of $(A + (B*C))$ is perfectly clear, even though the expression $(A + B*C)$ gives the same result.

Program 2-6

```
1:   PROGRAM Precedence;
2:   VAR
3:      A, B, C : Integer;
4:   BEGIN
5:      A := 10; B := 20; C := 30;
6:      Writeln( A + B * C );
7:      Writeln( A + ( B * C ) );
8:      Writeln( ( A + B ) * C )
9:   END.
```

Mixing Reals and Integers

Although the two data types **Real** and **Integer** are different, you may freely mix values of both types in expressions. While this bends Pascal's strict type checking rule, it would be awkward if expressions such as $(2*3.141)$ were not allowed. The same rule applies for types **Byte**, **ShortInt**, **Word**, and **LongInt**. In general, you can mix all these types in numeric expressions. However, when you mix real numbers in any expression, the result is always real, not integer. Also, when assigning the result of integer expressions, you must be careful to choose variables that can safely hold the expression value.

For an example of mixing reals and integers, try changing the real-number variable **Fdegrees** in Program 2-5 to type **Integer**. Does the program still run? What happens if you change both **Fdegrees** and **Cdegrees** to type **Integer**? Try to predict the result before compiling and running the program.

Inserting Comments in Programs

Pascal programs tend to be very readable and understandable on their own. Even so, a clarifying comment or two helps explain complicated sections. It's appropriate to introduce comments in this chapter because they are a kind of private data—for your eyes only.

Add comments by surrounding text with braces { and } or with the alternate double-character symbols (* and *). The compiler ignores the text inside either pair of comment brackets. Comments, therefore, have no effect on the size or speed of the compiled program. Use whichever pair of symbols you prefer.

Program 2-7 converts miles to kilometers while demonstrating how to put comments into a program. The comments in lines 3–5 identify the program's purpose and author and refer to the source of the conversion factor for kilometers per mile. Other comments attached to lines 8 and 11 further clarify the constant and variable declarations. In lines 17 and 22, the alternate comment brackets (* and *) enclose descriptions about what is happening at various places in the program.

Program 2-7

```
1:  PROGRAM Kilometers;
2:
3:  { Purpose : Convert miles to kilometers }
4:  { Source  : World Almanac 1984 Units of Measurement pg 763 }
5:  { Author  : Tom Swan }
6:
7:  CONST
8:     KmPerMile = 1.609344;     { Number of kilometers in one mile }
9:
10: VAR
11:    Miles : Real;             { Number of miles to convert }
12:
13: BEGIN
14:    Writeln( 'Convert miles to kilometers' );
15:    Writeln;
16:
17: (* Prompt operator for number of miles *)
18:
19:    Write( 'How many miles? ' );
20:    Readln( Miles );
21:
22: (* Print answer *)
23:
24:    Writeln( 'Kilometers = ', Miles * KmPerMile : 8 : 2 )
25: END.
```

Be careful when using comments not to fall into the habit of automatically commenting every line. If the purpose of something is already clear, there's no need to add a comment. Commented lines like these are unnecessarily wordy:

```
PersonHeight : Integer;   { Height of person }
B := B + 10;              { Add 10 to B }
```

By the same reasoning, Program 2-7 probably needs no comments—it's perfectly understandable on its own. Because Pascal programs tend to be readable, almost storylike, the programs in this book use comments only where meanings might otherwise be unclear. Most examples have no comments at all. Try to write programs that are understandable without comments. But, if you think a note or two is needed to clarify program statements, don't hesitate to add as many comments as you need.

Debugging with Comments

Comments can also help you debug a program. Often, an interesting test is to see what happens after removing one or more program statements. Compiling and running a program without some of its vital parts and observing the results often isolate a tricky problem. What happens, for example, to Program 2-7 if you remove the **Readln** statement in line 20? To perform that test, instead of actually erasing the line, surround it with comment brackets like this:

```
(* Readln( Miles ); *)
```

Recompile and run the program, which now has a serious bug—it doesn't request the number of miles to convert. Remove the comment brackets and try again. Now the program works correctly again. When used this way, comment brackets are important programming tools.

Nesting Comments

Turbo Pascal lets you insert a comment inside another comment. Although it may seem strange to want to do that, there's a good reason for being able to nest two comments together. An example explains why. Go back to Program 2-5, **Celsius**, and add a comment to line 8, changing that line to read as follows:

```
Readln( Fdegrees );    { Get degrees in Fahrenheit }
```

Next, insert the opening comment bracket (* between lines 7 and 8, and the closing comment bracket *) between lines 9 and 10. The lines should now appear like this:

```
(*
Readln( Fdegrees );    { Get degrees in Fahrenheit }
Cdegrees := ( ( Fdegrees - 32.0 ) * 5.0 ) / 9.0;
*)
```

The effect of all this is to "comment out" lines 8 and 9, effectively removing them from the program. Notice that the comment you added to the original line 8 nests inside the larger commented-out portion that now occupies four lines. If Pascal did not allow nested comments, it would be impossible to comment out portions of programs that contain other comments.

A nested comment must always use the other kind of brackets. In other words, you can have the nested comments (* {*comment*} *) or {(* *comment* *)}. But, the nested comments {(*comment}*) and (*{comment*)} are incorrect—you must use the same kind of bracket at a comment's beginning and end, and you cannot overlap the two different kinds.

I usually reserve the braces { and } for permanent comments and save the alternates (* and *) for temporarily removing sections of programming. That way, I never accidentally nest two pairs of the same comment brackets together.

Compiler Directives

Earlier, you learned how to turn on range checking with the compiler directive, {$R + }. A compiler directive is a special kind of comment that gives a command to the compiler, changing the way Turbo Pascal compiles your program.

A compiler directive starts with an opening comment symbol and a dollar sign, for example, {$I – } and (*$R + *). {I – } is a plain comment. The directive's letter, in upper- or lowercase, selects one of several available options. Directive letters might be followed by values, {$M 8192,8192,655360}, or a plus or minus switch to turn features on {$R + } or off {$N – }, or a string {$L MYCODE.OBJ}.

You can mix compiler directives together by separating them with commas. The following compiler directive issues three commands and uses the alternate comment brackets instead of braces:

```
(*$I-,R+,N+*)
```

Appendix C lists Turbo Pascal's compiler directives. You'll meet them all in action as you proceed.

Variable Constants

Although *variable constant* seems contradictory—an oxymoron like *sweet sorrow*— it's a powerful feature in Turbo Pascal. A variable constant, called a *static variable* in some other languages, resembles a regular constant but has a colon and data type inserted between its identifier and declared value.

The Turbo Pascal Reference Manual calls variable constants *typed constants*. Because all constants have associated data types, the term variable constant more correctly describes this Pascal feature and is used throughout this book.

Variable constants are preinitialized variables. Programs can use them wherever regular variables might appear. Constants, as you know, represent predeclared, unchanging values. Variables, on the other hand, have no predeclared values but can change. Variable constants mix these ideas—they have predeclared values like constants but can also change like variables.

Program 2-8 demonstrates one way to use variable constants to save memory. Line 3 is different from previous declarations. The constant identifier (**MiscString**) has a data type like a variable (**:String[35]**) plus a value like a constant ('Welcome...'). Together, these elements create a variable constant.

The program uses **MiscString** like any other variable. Line 11 displays the string, welcoming you to the program. Line 13 uses the *same* string as a variable for storing your name, which the program then displays in lines 18 and 25.

Reusing a string variable constant this way saves memory. If the program declared the welcome message as a plain string constant, the message's characters would remain in memory as long as the program runs. But there's no need to keep the message around after displaying it in line 11. By using a variable constant to hold the message, and then reusing that same variable constant for other purposes, the program puts the memory occupied by **MiscString** to double use.

Even so, don't be tempted to declare all data as variable constants just to avoid initializing variables. There are several reasons why that's a bad idea. For one, all Pascal compilers do not recognize variable constants. Also, variable constants permanently take up memory space. It is possible, as you'll learn later on, to declare Pascal variables that are *dynamic*, existing only in the parts of a program where needed. The same is not true of variable constants, which have a voracious appetite for valuable computer memory. Use them sparingly.

Program 2-8

```
1:   PROGRAM Planets;
2:   CONST
3:      MiscString : String[35] = 'Welcome to Your Weight and Fortune!';
4:      Sun     = 27.9;
5:      Mercury = 0.37;
6:      Moon    = 0.17;
7:      Jupiter = 2.64;
8:   VAR
9:      Weight : Real;
10:  BEGIN
11:     Writeln( MiscString );  { Display welcome message }
12:     Write( 'What is your name? ' );
13:     Readln( MiscString );
14:     Write( 'How much do you weigh in pounds? ' );
15:     Readln( Weight );
16:
17:     Writeln;
18:     Writeln( MiscString, '''s weight:' );
19:     Writeln( ' On the Sun  = ', Sun * Weight:0:0, ' lbs' );
20:     Writeln( ' On Mercury  = ', Mercury * Weight:0:0, ' lbs' );
21:     Writeln( ' On the Moon = ', Moon * Weight:0:0, ' lbs' );
22:     Writeln( ' On Jupiter  = ', Jupiter * Weight:0:0, ' lbs' );
23:
24:     Writeln;
25:     Writeln( MiscString, '''s fortune:' );
26:     Writeln( ' You are fortunate not to be living on Jupiter!' );
27:  END.
```

Constant Expressions

Beginning with Turbo Pascal 5.0, you can write expressions in **CONST** declarations. This lets you create constants such as:

```
Minimum = 1;
Range = 100;
Maximum = Minimum + ( Range - 1 );
```

The first two constants are no different from others you've seen earlier. **Minimum** equals 1. **Range** equals 100. The third constant uses an expression involving the other two constants to calculate **Maximum.** Because of this, changing **Minimum** or **Range** automatically affects the value of **Maximum.** Previous versions of Turbo Pascal required updating all three constants manually, increasing the possibility of errors caused by miscalculations.

All items in a constant expression must be literal values such as 3.14159 or other constant identifiers declared earlier in the program. You may use parentheses along with any of the usual math operators. Variables are never allowed.

Constant expressions are useful for calculating the initial values of variable constants. For example, the declaration

```
StartValue : Integer = ( Minimum - 1 );
```

assigns to variable-constant **StartValue** the integer value of **Minimum** minus 1. You can't use variable constants such as this in other constant expressions. This declaration will not compile:

```
EndValue = StartValue + Maximum;    { ??? }
```

That doesn't work because variable constants can change like variables; therefore, their use in constant expressions is ambiguous and is not allowed.

Be sure to understand that constant expressions are calculated when the program is compiled, not later when the program runs. Constant expressions cost you nothing in runtime speed.

Summary

Constants, variables, and variable constants hold and specify data, the facts that a computer program knows. Pascal requires you to declare the data types of variables and checks that values assigned to variables match their declared types. Constants automatically assume the types of their values. With its strong type checking, Pascal helps guard against common programming errors, often not prevented in other languages.

The Pascal data types examined in this chapter are **Byte**, **ShortInt**, **Word**, **Integer**, **LongInt**, **Real**, **Char**, **Boolean**, and **String**. You can declare variables, constants, and variable constants of any of these types.

Subranges of integers limit the high and low values that variables can hold. The compiler can check for range errors only for literal constant values assigned to subrange variables. To check subranges when programs run, you must turn on range checking with the compiler directive, {$R+}.

Expressions combine variables, constants, and other values into a single result. The result of an expression is the same type as its elements. Real-number expressions produce real-number results. Boolean expressions evaluate to true or false. Operator precedence and parentheses determine the evaluation order of an expression's parts. Expressions with a mix of **Real** and **Integer** values are always type **Real**.

Descriptive names for variables and constants make programs more readable, while two kinds of comments let you further clarify a program. One special kind of comment, called a directive, gives the compiler an instruction, selecting among various options.

Variable constants, otherwise known as typed constants, are variables with preassigned values. They can represent fixed values like constants, but they can also change like variables.

Constant expressions let you declare constants that depend on the values of other constants. Only literal values, other constants, and the usual math operators may be used in constant expressions. Variables are prohibited.

Exercises

2-1. Given that water weighs 8.33 pounds per gallon, write a program to prompt for the number of gallons, and compute the weight of that much water. Use a constant to describe the relationship of gallons to weight. The program should accept fractions of gallons (e.g., 5.75 or 10.2) and display the result to two decimal places.

2-2. To convert Celsius to Fahrenheit temperatures, multiply by 9, divide the result by 5, and add 32. Using Program 2-5 as a guide, write this formula into a Pascal program.

2-3. For every 550 feet above sea level, water boils at about 1° less than 212° Fahrenheit. Write a Pascal program to calculate the boiling point of water at any altitude. Document the program with appropriate comments.

2-4. Modify your answer to exercise 2-1 to let someone decide how many decimal places should appear in the result. (Hint: Use an integer variable in the formatting command.) What would be the advantage of using a variable constant instead?

3

Action—What a Program Does

- Compound Statements
- Repetitive Statements
- Conditional Statements

3

Key Words and Identifiers

CASE-ELSE, FOR-TO-DO, FOR-DOWNTO-DO, GOTO, IF-THEN-ELSE, LABEL, MOD, Pred, REPEAT-UNTIL, Succ, WHILE-DO

As the examples in Chapters 1 and 2 demonstrate, a program's many statements normally execute in sequential order, one statement after the other. This chapter introduces two new kinds of statements that change the order in which statements execute. *Repetitive* statements make loops in a program, repeating operations. *Conditional* statements make decisions, selecting one statement over others and changing the program flow.

Compound Statements

A compound statement is a group of individual statements, each separated from the next with a semicolon. As shown in the railroad diagram of Figure 3-1, the key words **BEGIN** and **END** collect the compounded statements into one unit. You can use compound statements at any place in a program where Pascal allows ordinary statements. Railroad diagrams identify those places with the boxed-in word, *statement*.

Because you can use single and compound statements interchangeably, from now on, *statement* means either a single *or* compound statement.

Looking at Figure 3-1, you can see that the last statement before the key word **END** does not require a semicolon. Semicolons separate statements from each other—they do not terminate statements. In other words, you don't have to end

compound statement

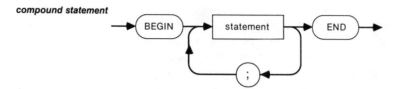

Figure 3-1 Railroad diagram defining a compound statement.

each statement with a semicolon. You do have to separate multiple statements with semicolons. Pascal relaxes its own rule, however, and lets you add an extra semicolon as demonstrated in Program 3-1, line 5.

Because there is no actual statement following the semicolon in line 5, you have to imagine an empty or *null* statement, shown as a comment in Program 3-1. This null statement doesn't do anything except satisfy the syntax of Figure 3-1, which says that a statement, not a semicolon, always precedes **END**. The existence of the null statement is a minor Pascal oddity—don't let it concern you. The extra semicolon before **END** has no effect on the compiled result. Add or delete it as you please.

Program 3-1

```
1:   PROGRAM Semicolon;
2:   BEGIN
3:      Writeln( 'Statement #1' );
4:      Writeln( 'Statement #2' );
5:      Writeln( 'Statement #3' );  { null statement }
6:   END.
```

Repetitive Statements

Repetitive statements cause one or more statements to repeat. In Pascal, there are three repetitive statement types: **WHILE**, **REPEAT**, and **FOR**.

WHILE Loops

Pascal's **WHILE-DO** or, more simply, **WHILE** statement executes another statement while some condition is true. Figure 3-2 shows the railroad diagram for a **WHILE** statement, also called a **WHILE** *loop* because of the way it causes program actions to cycle in a kind of logical loop.

while statement

Figure 3-2 Railroad diagram defining Pascal's repetitive **WHILE** statement.

The condition can be any Boolean expression that evaluates to true or false. It could also be a simple Boolean variable. While *expression* is true, the *statement* executes. When *expression* becomes false, the loop ends, and the program proceeds to whatever follows *statement*. Because *expression* may be false to begin with, the statements inside a **WHILE** loop might never execute.

Program 3-2 is a simple example of a **WHILE** loop in action. The program counts to ten and stops. Variable **Counter** is called a *control variable* because of the way it controls how many times the **WHILE** statement in lines 7–11 executes. First, line 6 initializes the control variable to a starting value, in this case, setting **Counter** to one. The compound statement in lines 8–11 then executes while the value of **Counter** is less than or equal to ten.

Program 3-2

```
 1:  PROGRAM WhileCount;
 2:  VAR
 3:     Counter : Integer;
 4:  BEGIN
 5:     Writeln( 'While count' );
 6:     Counter := 1;
 7:     WHILE Counter <= 10 DO
 8:     BEGIN
 9:        Writeln( Counter );
10:        Counter := Counter + 1
11:     END
12:  END.
```

Line 9 displays **Counter**'s value. Line 10 adds one to **Counter** each time through the loop. Eventually, **Counter** grows larger than ten, making the expression (**Counter** < = 10) false, ending the **WHILE** statement and, subsequently, the program.

What is the value of **Counter** after the loop ends? To find out, add the following statement between lines 11 and 12:

```
Writeln( 'Value of Counter = ', Counter )
```

You also have to add a semicolon to the end of line 11, separating the compound statement from the new addition.

Does the final value of **Counter** make sense? What value would you expect if you change the expression in line 7 to **Counter** < 10? Sometimes, when trying to answer questions like these, it helps to "play computer," writing down values of variables for statements as you execute the program by hand. What happens, for example, if you use the expression **Counter** = 10 in line 7? Before running the program, try to predict the results. Will the **WHILE** loop execute? If not, why not?

A control variable can also be a character, as demonstrated in Program 3-3, which prints the alphabet. The program is similar to Program 3-2, but, because of

Pascal's strict type-checking rule, it can't add one to the character variable **Ch** as the previous program did to the integer variable **Counter**. Instead, line 10 uses the standard function, **Succ**, to return the successor to the value of **Ch**. You'll learn more about functions in Chapter 4, but, for now, think of a function as a Pascal command that returns a value, in this case, the value that succeeds **Ch**. The successor of a character is the next character in sequence. For example, the successor of B is C. A similar function, **Pred**, returns the predecessor, or preceding, value. **Pred**('Z') is Y.

Program 3-3

```
1:    PROGRAM WhileAlphabet;
2:    VAR
3:        Ch : Char;
4:    BEGIN
5:        Writeln( 'While alphabet' );
6:        Ch := 'A';
7:        WHILE Ch <= 'Z' DO
8:        BEGIN
9:            Write( Ch );
10:           Ch := Succ( Ch )
11:       END;
12:       Writeln;
13:   END.
```

As in Program 3-2, you can check the value of the character variable **Ch** when the **WHILE** loop ends. To do this, add a statement between lines 12 and 13 of Program 3-3 to write **Ch** to the display. What do you think **Ch** will be? If you don't know, look up the ASCII character set in Appendix D. (ASCII stands for the American Standard Code for Information Interchange.) What character is next in sequence following Z?

Another way to write a **WHILE** loop is to use a Boolean variable for the conditional expression, as Program 3-4 demonstrates.

Program 3-4

```
1:    PROGRAM WhileBoolean;
2:    VAR
3:        Counter : Integer;
4:        Done : Boolean;
5:    BEGIN
6:        Writeln( 'While Boolean' );
7:        Counter := 1;
8:        Done := False;
9:        WHILE NOT Done DO
```

Program 3-4 *cont.*

```
10:    BEGIN
11:      Writeln( Counter );
12:      Counter := Succ( Counter );
13:      Done := ( Counter > 10 )
14:    END
15:  END.
```

With a well-chosen name, a Boolean variable improves the program's readability as shown in Program 3-4, which operates similarly to Program 3-2, counting to ten and stopping. This time the program uses a **Boolean** variable, **Done**, as the **WHILE** statement control variable. Line 8 initializes **Done** to false before starting the **WHILE** loop in lines 9–14. You could also write line 9 as follows:

```
WHILE ( Done = False ) DO
```

As shown in Program 3-4, though, the phrase **WHILE NOT Done DO** has the same effect and is more readable. Similar uses of Boolean variables often lead to Englishlike programs in Pascal that read more like stories than computer programs. For example, you might have two or more Boolean variables in **WHILE** loops:

```
WHILE Testing AND NOT InError
   DO <statement>;
```

Even out of context, you at least get the flavor of what happens at this place in the program. When looking at thousands of statements, you'll appreciate the ability to pick out a lone statement and understand its purpose. Of course, it's up to you to choose names that make sense! The purpose of **WHILE (A AND (NOT B OR C)) DO** is no clearer in Pascal than it is in any other language.

Despite its readability, line 13 of Program 3-4 may appear strange. This assignment is more understandable when you consider that Pascal evaluates the Boolean expression (**Counter** > 10) to a true or false result, which the program assigns to control variable **Done**, causing the loop to end when **Done** becomes true.

What happens if you move line 13 (plus a semicolon at the end of the line) to between lines 11 and 12? Predict the result before trying this on your computer. Was your assumption correct?

REPEAT Loops

Another kind of repetitive statement is the **REPEAT-UNTIL** or **REPEAT** loop, diagrammed in Figure 3-3. Notice that a compound statement is automatically allowed in this case, without using **BEGIN** and **END**. The key words **REPEAT** and **UNTIL** already mark the repeating group of statements—surrounding the same group with **BEGIN** and **END** is legal but unnecessary. Multiple statements may appear inside the **REPEAT** and **UNTIL** key words. The *statements* execute repeatedly until the *expression* is true.

repeat statement

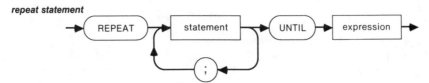

Figure 3-3 Railroad diagram from Pascal's **REPEAT** statement.

Counting to ten with **REPEAT-UNTIL** is only a little different from doing the same job in a **WHILE** loop. Once again, Program 3-5 uses an integer control variable, **Counter**, initialized to one in line 6. The program writes successive values of **Counter** to the screen (line 8), increasing **Counter** by one in line 9 for every pass through the loop. The loop ends in line 10 when **Counter** becomes greater than ten.

Program 3-5

```
 1:   PROGRAM RepeatCount;
 2:   VAR
 3:      Counter : Integer;
 4:   BEGIN
 5:      Writeln( 'Repeat count' );
 6:      Counter := 1;
 7:      REPEAT
 8:         Writeln( Counter );
 9:         Counter := Counter + 1
10:      UNTIL Counter > 10
11:   END.
```

A **REPEAT** loop, unlike a **WHILE** loop, always executes at least one time. If the conditional expression in the **WHILE** loop starts out false (see Figure 3-2 and Program 3-2), its statements never execute. This happens because Pascal evaluates the expression at the top of a **WHILE** loop. But a **REPEAT** loop evaluates its expression at the bottom (see Figure 3-3 and Program 3-5), and that doesn't happen until the statements inside the loop execute at least once.

Program 3-6 is the **REPEAT** loop equivalent of Program 3-3, which prints the alphabet. Again, the **Succ** function in line 9 advances the character control variable **Ch** after initializing **Ch** to A in line 6. When **Ch** becomes alphabetically greater than Z, the **REPEAT** loop, and therefore the program, ends.

Program 3-6

```
 1:   PROGRAM RepeatAlphabet;
 2:   VAR
 3:      Ch : Char;
 4:   BEGIN
```

Program 3-6 *cont.*

```
 5:     Writeln( 'Repeat alphabet' );
 6:     Ch := 'A';
 7:     REPEAT
 8:        Write( Ch );
 9:        Ch := Succ( Ch )
10:     UNTIL Ch > 'Z';
11:     Writeln
12:  END.
```

A **REPEAT** statement's ending expression might also be a Boolean control variable. In Program 3-7, line 11 sets Boolean variable **Done** to true or false, depending on the result of the expression (**Counter** > 10). The **REPEAT** loop executes until **Done** is true. When you read this program, the compound statement in lines 8–12, **REPEAT...UNTIL Done** seems natural and understandable.

Program 3-7

```
 1:  PROGRAM RepeatBoolean;
 2:  VAR
 3:     Counter : Integer;
 4:     Done : Boolean;
 5:  BEGIN
 6:     Writeln( 'Repeat Boolean' );
 7:     Counter := 1;
 8:     REPEAT
 9:        Writeln( Counter );
10:        Counter := Succ( Counter );
11:        Done := ( Counter > 10 )
12:     UNTIL Done
13:  END.
```

What does **Counter** equal after the end of the **REPEAT** loop in Programs 3-5 and 3-7? What does **Ch** equal after the loop in Program 3-6? Use **Writeln** statements to prove your guesses.

FOR Loops

The third and final repetitive statement in Pascal is the **FOR** loop, diagrammed in Figure 3-4. Although a **FOR** loop appears more complex than **WHILE** or **RE-PEAT** loops, in practice it often produces more concise programming. To see why, let's look at the same counting program, this time written with a **FOR** loop.

Program 3-8 counts to ten and stops, but it does it in fewer lines than Programs 3-2 and 3-5, which are similar. Although all three programs do the same thing, using a **FOR** loop in this case is the easiest and most efficient method.

for statement

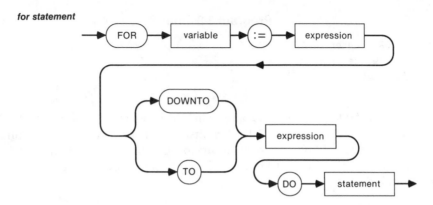

Figure 3-4 Railroad diagram for Pascal's **FOR** statement.

Program 3-8

```
1:   PROGRAM ForCount;
2:   VAR
3:      Counter : Integer;
4:   BEGIN
5:      Writeln( 'For count' );
6:      FOR Counter := 1 TO 10 DO
7:          Writeln( Counter )
8:   END.
```

Like other loops, the **FOR** loop needs a control variable, here the integer variable **Counter**. In English, line 6 tells you that **Counter** starts at one, goes up **TO** ten, and, for each successive **Counter** value, the loop should **DO** a statement, in this case, the **Writeln** in line 7. Line 6 handles the initialization of **Counter**, the increment by one each time through the loop, and the test for done when **Counter** is greater than ten—all of the "housekeeping" chores expressly added to the similar **WHILE** and **REPEAT** loops.

FOR loops can also count backwards, as shown in Program 3-9 which counts from ten down to one. Compare line 6 with its counterpart in Program 3-8. Notice that **DOWNTO** replaces the key word **TO**. When a **FOR** loop counts up, use **TO**. When it counts down, use **DOWNTO**.

Program 3-9

```
1:   PROGRAM ForCountdown;
2:   VAR
3:      Counter : Integer;
4:   BEGIN
5:      Writeln( 'For count down' );
```

Program 3-9 *cont.*

```
6:      FOR Counter := 10 DOWNTO 1 DO
7:          Writeln( Counter )
8:   END.
```

A **FOR** loop's control variable can be a character, as it was in the **WHILE** and **REPEAT** loops. Program 3-10 demonstrates this by printing the alphabet. The program uses a **FOR** loop to cycle variable **Ch** through the characters A to Z. Can you rewrite Program 3-10 to print the alphabet in reverse order, in other words, from Z *down to* A?

Program 3-10

```
1:   PROGRAM ForAlphabet;
2:   VAR
3:      Ch : Char;
4:   BEGIN
5:      Writeln( 'For alphabet' );
6:      FOR Ch := 'A' TO 'Z' DO
7:          Write( Ch );
8:      Writeln
9:   END.
```

From these examples, you might be thinking that **FOR** loops are more attractive than **WHILE** or **REPEAT** loops. There are many reasons, though, why you often cannot use **FOR**. The major restriction is that a **FOR** loop always counts by one value at a time. It cannot count up or down by two or three—only by one. Second, **FOR** loops must use simple control variables like integers and characters. They can't use Boolean expressions, as in Programs 3-4 and 3-7, to control the action of their loops.

And if these restrictions weren't enough, there is another important limitation to **FOR** loops: *The statements inside the loop must never alter the control variable in any way.* Never write a **FOR** loop like this:

```
FOR Counter := 1 TO 10 DO
BEGIN
   Writeln( Counter );
   Counter := Counter + 1
END;
```

At first glance, you might think this is a clever way to force the computer to count by twos with a **FOR** loop. Although the compiler accepts such programming, the results can be surprising. To live dangerously, replace lines 6 and 7 in

Program 3-8 with this five-line **FOR** loop, and run the program. In one experiment on an IBM PC, the program counted by twos up to 19 and then stopped.[1]

Similarly, you cannot trust the value of **Counter** in Program 3-8 or the value of **Ch** in Program 3-10, after the **FOR** loop ends. Earlier, in the **WHILE** and **REPEAT** examples, you inserted **Writeln** statements to test the ending values of the loop control variables. Although you can do the same thing in Programs 3-8 and 3-10, the results are unpredictable and could be different on other computers. Never write programs that rely on the uninitialized value of the control variable following a **FOR** loop.

Despite these restrictions, **FOR** loops are valuable to Pascal programming, as are **WHILE** and **REPEAT** loops. Of the three types of repetitive statements, a **FOR** loop, where appropriate, is usually the most efficient and fastest choice. The real problem is knowing how to choose among the three loops.

To help you decide, a few rules of thumb for choosing a **WHILE**, **REPEAT**, or **FOR** loop follow. Many times, the best choice is not clear, and you'll have to experiment with the following advice in mind.

When to Use WHILE

Ask yourself, "Is there at least one condition when the statements in the loop should not execute, not even once?" If the answer is yes, then a **WHILE** loop probably is the best choice. Because the **WHILE** (see Figure 3-2) evaluates its controlling expression at the top of the loop, if that expression is false, the statements in the loop do not execute.

When to Use REPEAT

If the answer to the question in the preceding paragraph is no, then use a **REPEAT** loop instead. As Figure 3-3 shows, the statements in a **REPEAT** loop execute before evaluating the controlling expression. Even if the expression is false the first time through the loop, the statements in the loop execute at least one time.

When to Use FOR

If you know, or the program can calculate in advance, the exact number of loops required, and if a simple control variable is available, then a **FOR** loop is often the best choice. As with a **WHILE** loop, the statements in a **FOR** loop might never

---

[1] Because of changes in Turbo Pascal, the **FOR** loop now correctly counts by twos, stopping with nine. Even so, I decided to let the example stand from the first edition—it's bad form to change a **FOR** loop's control variable inside the loop or to assume that the variable will have a specific value when the loop ends. The reason for this restriction is that the Pascal compiler might load the control value into an internal processor register or a memory location rather than use the memory reserved for the variable. This makes the **FOR** loop run more quickly, but it also makes the variable as stored in memory untrustworthy. Apparently, Turbo Pascal doesn't do this, but, more importantly, a future version *might* and still be consistent with the rules of Pascal. This means that you must not change a **FOR** loop's control variable even when doing so appears to produce no errors! The fact that this example used to fail and now works is fair warning of the consequences of disobeying this important rule.

execute. If you replace line 6 in Program 3-8 with the following, it writes nothing to the screen:

```
FOR Counter := 1 TO 0 DO
```

Obviously, because zero is less than one and because variable **Counter** starts with a value of one, the condition to end the **FOR** loop—namely that **Counter** is greater than or equal to zero—is true before the loop begins. Therefore, the **FOR** loop never runs, and the program continues with the next statement. In this example, the program simply ends. On the other hand, the following **FOR** loop executes exactly one time:

```
FOR i := 1 TO 1 DO
```

Repetitive statements add power to all computer languages, and Pascal's menu of three statements—**WHILE**, **REPEAT**, and **FOR**—gives you a choice of ways to construct loops. The ability to control the number of times a statement executes is vital to programming in Pascal. Next, you'll learn how a Pascal program selects one statement over another, and makes decisions affecting a program's flow.

Conditional Statements

Deciding which statement to execute based on one condition or another is a common feature among all programming languages. In Pascal, there are three ways to force a program to alter its operational flow. Figure 3-5 diagrams the first of these, the **IF-THEN-ELSE** conditional statement or, more simply, the **IF** statement.

if statement

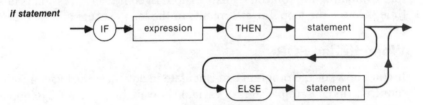

Figure 3-5 Railroad diagram defining Pascal's **IF-THEN-ELSE** conditional statement.

The IF Statement

The **IF** statement in Pascal is simple to use and operates just the way it sounds. If *expression* evaluates to true, then the *statement* following key word **THEN** executes; otherwise, the *statement* following **ELSE** executes. Notice that the **ELSE** *statement* is completely optional. As it is in repetitive statements, *expression* may be any expression that evaluates to true or false, or it may be a Boolean variable. The **THEN** and **ELSE** statements may be single or compound.

Program 3-11 demonstrates **IF** in lines 10 and 11. The example limits a response to a specific range of numbers, in this case, from one to ten. If you enter any other value, the program prints an error message and repeats the prompt. Controlling this action is the Boolean variable **Okay**, which the program sets equal to true or false in line 9. The **IF** statement in line 10 tests this variable and, if it's false, displays an error message.

Program 3-11

```
 1:   PROGRAM Choice;
 2:   VAR
 3:       Number : Integer;
 4:       Okay : Boolean;
 5:   BEGIN
 6:       Writeln( 'Enter a number between 1 and 10' );
 7:       REPEAT
 8:          Readln( Number );
 9:          Okay := ( 1 <= Number ) AND ( Number <= 10 );
10:          IF NOT Okay
11:              THEN Writeln( 'Incorrect. Try again.' )
12:       UNTIL Okay;
13:       Writeln( 'Okay' )
14:   END.
```

Line 9 of this example gives a lot of people trouble on first glance. It's simple to understand, though, if you carefully examine how Pascal evaluates this Boolean expression to a single true or false result:

```
( 1 <= Number ) AND ( Number <= 10 )
```

Only if **Number** is inclusively between one and ten is the entire expression true. The program assigns the result of this expression to the Boolean variable, **Okay**. You could rewrite this with the help of an **IF** statement as follows:

```
IF ( 1 <= Number ) AND ( Number <= 10 )
   THEN Okay := True
   ELSE Okay := False;
```

As demonstrated in Program 3-11, there's no reason to go to all this trouble. Instead, you can directly assign the result of any Boolean expression to a Boolean variable—they are, after all, of the same type.

Nested IF Statements

IF-THEN-ELSE statements can nest inside one another to make complex conditional decisions. To demonstrate nesting, Program 3-12 has three **IF** statements.

One statement, starting at line 11 and ending at line 19, tests the value of variable **Year**. *If* **Year** is greater than zero, *then* the compound statement in lines 12–19 executes; otherwise, the program goes directly to the **UNTIL** in line 20. Notice how indenting lines 13–18 helps make this action clear.

Program 3-12

```
1:   PROGRAM Leap;
2:   VAR
3:      LeapYear : Boolean;
4:      Year : Integer;
5:   BEGIN
6:      Writeln( 'Leap year' );
7:      REPEAT
8:         Writeln;
9:         Write( 'Year? (0 to quit) ' );
10:        Readln( Year );
11:        IF Year > 0 THEN
12:        BEGIN
13:           IF Year MOD 100 = 0
14:              THEN LeapYear := ( Year MOD 400 ) = 0
15:              ELSE LeapYear := ( Year MOD   4 ) = 0;
16:           IF LeapYear
17:              THEN Writeln( Year, ' is a leap year' )
18:              ELSE Writeln( Year, ' is not a leap year' )
19:        END { if }
20:     UNTIL Year = 0
21:  END.
```

Nested inside the compound statement in Program 3-12 are two more **IF** statements, the first starting in line 13 and the second in line 16. These statements test for leap years, which are evenly divisible by four, except for new centuries like 1900 and 2000, which are leap years only if divisible by 400. Therefore, 1900 was not a leap year, but 2000 will be.

The **IF** statement in lines 13–15 uses this formula. The **MOD** (modulus) operator returns the remainder of an integer division. 15 **MOD** 10 equals 5 (10 goes once into 15 with 5 remaining), 8 **MOD** 15 equals 8 (15 goes into 8 zero times with 8 remaining), 20 **MOD** 20 equals 0, and so on. If the year in question is evenly divisible by 100 (line 13), then it's a new century,[2] causing the Boolean **LeapYear** variable to become true in line 14 if the year is also evenly divisible by 400. Otherwise,

---

[2] Technically, new centuries begin with the first year after those evenly divisible by 100. In other words, 1901 was the start of the twentieth century, and 2001, not 2000, will be the first year of the twenty-first century. There was no year 0000—the first year was 0001; therefore, the one-hundredth year is always *last* in its century. I suspect you'll have trouble, though, convincing Times Square revellers that December 31, 1999 is not the end of the twentieth century!

LeapYear becomes true in line 15 if the year is divisible by 4. Keep in mind that expressions like **(Year MOD 4)** = **0** evaluate to a single true or false result, assigned here to Boolean variable **LeapYear**.

Another **IF** statement, starting at line 16, tests the Boolean **LeapYear** variable and writes a message on the screen to tell you if this is a leap year. Notice also that all these actions occur inside a **REPEAT** statement (lines 7– 20). This lets you enter more than one year without rerunning the program, which stops when you enter zero. The **REPEAT** statement is the correct choice here to make the statements in lines 8–19 execute at least one time.

Look at the position of the semicolon in line 15 of Program 3-12. Remember, the semicolon in Pascal separates one statement from another. The **IF-THEN-ELSE** in lines 13–15 is a *single* statement and, therefore, the semicolon at its end correctly separates it from the next **IF** statement. Try adding a semicolon to the end of line 14 and then recompile the program. Do you understand why you receive an error?

To avoid confusion, it helps to use one of the three popular styles in Figure 3-6 for writing **IF** statements. You can have an entire **IF-THEN-ELSE** on a single line, as shown at the top of Figure 3-6, or separate the **THEN** and **ELSE** statements to add clarity to the program. Most programmers prefer to line up an **ELSE** with its corresponding **THEN**. When nesting multiple **IF** statements, it may not be obvious which **ELSE** goes with which **THEN**. Lining them up improves the program's clarity. Of course, the Pascal compiler doesn't care how the program looks. A good-looking style is for your benefit, not the computer's.

```
IF <expression> THEN <statement> ELSE <statement>;

IF <expression>
   THEN <statement>
   ELSE <statement>;

IF <expression>
   THEN
      <statement>
   ELSE
      <statement>;
```

Figure 3-6 Three popular **IF** statement styles.

Style alone, however, does not guard against the most common **IF** statement error, demonstrated in Program 3-13. The example prompts for a value between one and ten, displaying an error message for any other value.

Although the **ELSE** in line 11 physically lines up with the **THEN** in line 8, it logically attaches to the **THEN** in line 10. The rule is that an **ELSE** statement goes with the closest preceding **THEN**, regardless of the indentations. When you run the program, entering a legal value between one and ten produces the faulty error message, "value < 1."

Program 3-13 (with errors)

```
1:   PROGRAM BadIf;
2:   VAR
3:      Counter : Integer;
4:   BEGIN
5:      Write( 'Value (1..10)? ' );
6:      Readln( Counter );
7:      IF Counter >= 1
8:        THEN
9:          IF Counter > 10
10:             THEN Writeln( 'Error: value > 10' )
11:        ELSE
12:            Writeln( 'Error: value < 1' )
13:   END.
```

You can easily fix the bug in Program 3-13 by isolating the inner **IF** statement with key words **BEGIN** and **END**, as shown in Program 3-14. This forms a compound statement in lines 9–12, forcing the **ELSE** clause to go with the **THEN** in line 8 as originally intended. Running the program now correctly gives the error message for values outside of the range one through ten.

Program 3-14

```
1:   PROGRAM GoodIf;
2:   VAR
3:      Counter : Integer;
4:   BEGIN
5:      Write( 'Value (1..10)? ' );
6:      Readln( Counter );
7:      IF Counter >= 1
8:        THEN
9:          BEGIN
10:            IF Counter > 10
11:                THEN Writeln( 'Error: value > 10' )
12:          END
13:        ELSE
14:            Writeln( 'Error: value < 1' )
15:   END.
```

Short-Circuit Boolean Expressions

Turbo Pascal evaluates Boolean expressions in a special way that helps make conditional statements run more quickly. Consider this:

```
IF ( <e1> AND <e2> AND <e3> )
   THEN <statement>;
```

The symbols <e1> ... <e3> represent any Boolean expressions or variables. Only if the three values are true does the entire expression evaluate to true, executing *statement*.

Now, think about what happens if <e1> is false. Because all three values in the expression must be true for the entire expression to be true, if <e1> is false, there is no need to examine <e2> and <e3>—their values are unimportant.

Turbo Pascal knows this and, whenever it can, stops evaluating the parts of an expression *as soon as the result is certain*. The expression *short circuits*, skipping the parts that have no bearing on the final outcome. The three-part Boolean expression could be written:

```
IF <e1> THEN IF <e2> THEN IF <e3>
   THEN <statement>;
```

In fact, this is the only way to achieve short-circuit expression evaluation in Pascals that don't have this ability. There's nothing wrong with this approach, but Turbo Pascal's expression evaluator makes the second two **IF** statements unnecessary.

You can turn off Turbo Pascal's ability to perform short-circuit expression evaluation by changing the *Options-Compiler-Boolean evaluation* setting in the integrated environment, or by inserting the compiler directive {$B+} at the start of the program. You can also use the /$B+ command with the command-line compiler. For example, to compile a program named MYPROG.PAS, use the DOS command:

```
tpc /$B+ myprog
```

Usually, the only reason to switch off short-circuit expression evaluation this way is to run programs written for other Pascals (or in previous Turbo Pascal versions) where entire expressions are expected to be evaluated regardless of the outcome. When you learn about functions in Chapter 4, you'll see that it is possible to cause the evaluation of expressions to perform actions, as well as to generate values. In this case, you may have to defeat short-circuit evaluation to ensure that all actions are performed—even if the result of the expression in which those actions participate is known beforehand. This is a shaky rock on which to stand, and you will do yourself a big favor if you never write expressions that require all parts to be evaluated. Use Turbo Pascal's short-circuit Boolean expressions—they make programs run faster and can reduce the complexity of multiple, nested **IF** statements.

The CASE Statement

Multiple **IF** statements often lead to a situation demonstrated in Program 3-15, which prints the complementary colors of a standard color wheel you might find in an interior decorating book. (Complementary colors look good together, and the program can pick color pairs for painting a room.) Lines 9–10 prompt for a choice of colors and read your single character answer. The program then tests this character, held in variable **Choice**, in seven subsequent **IF** statements. On matching one of the known colors, it writes the color complement. If you enter an unknown character, line 25 displays an error message. Notice that lines 23 and 24 set the Boolean variable **UserQuits** to true when you type Q to quit the program, ending the **REPEAT** statement in lines 8–26.

Program 3-15

```
1:  PROGRAM Color1;
2:  VAR
3:      Choice : Char;
4:      UserQuits : Boolean;
5:  BEGIN
6:      Writeln( 'Complementary Colors #1' );
7:      UserQuits := False;
8:      REPEAT
9:          Write( 'B.lue, G.reen, O.range, P.urple, R.ed, Y.ellow, Q.uit? ' );
10:         Readln( Choice );
11:         IF ( Choice = 'B' ) OR ( Choice = 'b' )
12:             THEN Writeln( 'Orange' ) ELSE
13:         IF ( Choice = 'G' ) OR ( Choice = 'g' )
14:             THEN Writeln( 'Red' ) ELSE
15:         IF ( Choice = 'O' ) OR ( Choice = 'o' )
16:             THEN Writeln( 'Blue' ) ELSE
17:         IF ( Choice = 'P' ) OR ( Choice = 'p' )
18:             THEN Writeln( 'Yellow' ) ELSE
19:         IF ( Choice = 'R' ) OR ( Choice = 'r' )
20:             THEN Writeln( 'Green' ) ELSE
21:         IF ( Choice = 'Y' ) OR ( Choice = 'y' )
22:             THEN Writeln( 'Purple' ) ELSE
23:         IF ( Choice = 'Q' ) OR ( Choice = 'q' )
24:             THEN UserQuits := True
25:             ELSE Writeln( 'Error: Try again.' )
26:     UNTIL UserQuits
27: END.
```

Although there is nothing technically wrong with successive **IF** statements as programmed in the example, the excessive clutter is hard to read. Luckily, there is a better way to write the same program.

Pascal's **CASE** statement (see Figure 3-7) offers an alternative to the multiple **IF** statements in Program 3-15. It can replace a series of **IF-THEN-ELSE** statements. An example helps clarify how **CASE** works. (It's not as difficult to understand as the figure may seem.) Program 3-16 does the same job of picking complementary colors but, with the help of a **CASE** statement, is much easier to read.

Except for lines 11–20, Program 3-16 is identical to Program 3-15. The **CASE** statement evaluates an *expression* (see Figure 3-7) and then applies the resulting value to a list of constants or *selectors*. Here the selectors are upper- and lowercase characters in lines 12–18.

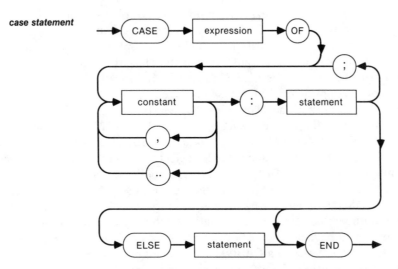

Figure 3-7 Railroad diagram for Pascal's **CASE** statement.

Program 3-16

```
1:  PROGRAM Color2;
2:  VAR
3:      Choice : Char;
4:      UserQuits : Boolean;
5:  BEGIN
6:      Writeln( 'Complementary Colors #2' );
7:      UserQuits := False;
8:      REPEAT
9:          Write( 'B.lue, G.reen, O.range, P.urple, R.ed, Y.ellow, Q.uit? ' );
10:         Readln( Choice );
11:         CASE Choice OF
12:             'B', 'b' : Writeln( 'Orange' );
13:             'G', 'g' : Writeln( 'Red'    );
14:             'O', 'o' : Writeln( 'Blue'   );
15:             'P', 'p' : Writeln( 'Yellow' );
16:             'R', 'r' : Writeln( 'Green'  );
17:             'Y', 'y' : Writeln( 'Purple' );
18:             'Q', 'q' : UserQuits := True;
```

Program 3-16 *cont.*

```
19:              ELSE Writeln( 'Error: Try again.' )
20:          END
21:      UNTIL UserQuits
22:  END.
```

If the result of the expression (in this example the character held in variable **Choice**) matches one of the selectors, then the associated statement following the colon executes. If no possibility matches, the optional **ELSE** clause executes instead. If there is no **ELSE** clause, and no matches, then the program simply continues after the end of the **CASE** statement. Remove line 19 to see what happens without the optional **ELSE** clause in place.

When Turbo Pascal compiles a **CASE** statement, it creates the finished code no differently than a multilevel equivalent **IF-THEN-ELSE** construction. Some Pascal compilers create fast *jump tables* for **CASE** statements, a method programs can use to skip directly to one **CASE** selector rather than test each value sequentially. Unfortunately, Turbo Pascal doesn't operate that way, and, in terms of the finished result, it doesn't matter whether you use **CASE** or **IF-THEN-ELSE**.

CASE statements work only with simple constants—you can't use strings or real numbers as selectors. In situations where you must compare a number of strings, you have no choice but to use a series of **IF-THEN-ELSE** statements.

The *expression* in a **CASE** statement (Figure 3-7) must reduce to an integer, character, or other *scalar* type. A type is scalar if it has regular, whole-number steps. Integers are scalar. Real numbers are not. **CASE** statements are especially handy, therefore, when writing "menu-driven" programs like Program 3-16 where you make a selection from a menu of choices.

Turbo Pascal allows ranges of selectors in a **CASE** statement. A range of values looks like this:

```
'A' .. 'D'
```

The double periods form an ellipsis—just as in the integer subranges in Chapter 2—indicating that what you really mean is:

```
'A', 'B', 'C', 'D'
```

This lets you write **CASE** statements to select actions for a range of selectors. For example, this selects **ActionA** for uppercase letters, **ActionB** for lowercase, and **ActionC** for digits:

```
CASE Choice OF
    'A' .. 'Z' : ActionA;
    'a' .. 'z' : ActionB;
    '0' .. '9' : ActionC
END;
```

To do the same thing in many other Pascal compilers, you have to type each individual character constant, separated by commas. The Turbo Pascal shorthand is a trick worth remembering.

The statement after each **CASE** selector may be single, compound, or any other kind. You can use **WHILE**, **REPEAT**, and **FOR** loops, insert **IF-THEN-ELSE** decision points, and even use additional **CASE** statements. Here's an example with no particular purpose but to demonstrate the various kinds of statements you can use inside **CASE**. Assume **i** is an integer variable:

```
CASE i OF
   1 : Writeln( 'i=', i );
   2 : BEGIN
         Write( 'What''s your name? ' );
         Readln( yourName )
       END;
   3 : REPEAT
         Writeln( j );
         j := j + 1
       UNTIL j >= 100;
   4 : IF ( j <> 100 ) AND ( j <> 200 )
         THEN j := 0 ELSE j := 100;
   5 : BEGIN
         ch := 'A';
         WHILE ch <= 'Z' DO
         BEGIN
            write( ch );
            ch := Succ( ch )
         END
       END
END; { case }
```

The GOTO Statement

Besides **IF** and **CASE** statements, there is a third way to alter statement flow in a program, a method that has achieved widespread notoriety. The infamous **GOTO** statement has a nasty reputation because of its ability to jump around at will to nearly any place in a program. This lack of control, according to some, invites programmers to pitch caution away, jumping from here to there, with little regard for the consequences.

Using a lot of **GOTO**s can produce what many call *spaghetti code*. If you could draw a line from every **GOTO** to its destination, a **GOTO**-infested program would look like that classic refrigerator art work—an explosion in a spaghetti factory.

In practice, with the rich and powerful **WHILE**, **REPEAT**, **FOR**, **IF**, and **CASE** statements, there are few situations that require a **GOTO**. Used indiscriminately, **GOTO**s can lead to chaos—but then, so can other Pascal features. There are a few rare situations when **GOTO**s come in handy, though, and should be used—with care.

The **GOTO** requires a **LABEL** declaration (Figure 3-8) coming before any program **CONST** or **VAR** declarations. Labels can be unsigned (positive) integers or unique identifiers. (In many Pascal systems, they must be integers.) Use commas to separate multiple labels, ending the list of all labels with a semicolon.

After defining your labels, you may then use them with a colon in front of any statement to mark that position in a program (Figure 3-9). To transfer control to a labeled statement, use the command **GOTO** *label*, where *label* is one of your predefined labels. Each label can mark only one position in a program (Figure 3-10).

label declaration

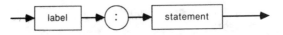

Figure 3-8 Each label to be used in a later **GOTO** statement must be declared in a label declaration.

labeled statement

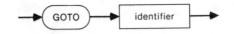

Figure 3-9 To mark a statement, precede it with a predefined label and a colon.

goto statement

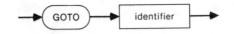

Figure 3-10 Railroad diagram for a **GOTO** statement, which transfers control to the statement marked by a label identifier.
(See also Figures 3-8 and 3-9.)

Program 3-17 demonstrates how to use **GOTO**s in Pascal in a situation where another kind of solution would be less elegant. In the example, certain statements repeat for some keypresses, others for other keypresses, and portions of both sequences for still other selections.

Program 3-17

```
1:   PROGRAM MultipleChoice;
2:   LABEL
3:      1, 2, 3, 4, 5;
```

Program 3-17 *cont.*

```
4:   VAR
5:      Choice : Char;
6:   BEGIN
7:      Write( 'Enter A, B, or C: ' ); Readln( Choice );
8:      CASE Choice OF
9:         'A', 'a' : GOTO 1;    { do statements 1, 3, 4 }
10:        'B', 'b' : GOTO 2;    { do statements 2, 4 }
11:        'C', 'c' : GOTO 3     { do statements 3, 4 }
12:               ELSE GOTO 5    { do no statements }
13:      END;
14:   1: Writeln( 'statement #1' ); GOTO 3;
15:   2: Writeln( 'statement #2' ); GOTO 4;
16:   3: Writeln( 'statement #3' );
17:   4: Writeln( 'statement #4' );
18:   5: Writeln( 'Done' )
19:   END.
```

There appear to be three approaches to solving this kind of problem. One approach repeats each group of statements for each appropriate selection. Another uses Boolean expressions and **IF** statements to select which statements to execute. The third uses **GOTO**s. Without **GOTO**s, Program 3-17 requires either the duplication of one or more statements or multiple, time-wasting, Boolean expressions.

That observation leads to a good rule to follow. If a **GOTO** avoids repeating the same statement at different places in a program, or if a **GOTO** saves extra programming steps, then use it. Duplication of effort is something to fight courageously in programming, and, on occasion, the **GOTO** is a useful weapon in the battle. As with all weapons, however, aim your **GOTO**s only at things you're sure you want to hit!

One important rule is never to jump into the middle of a **REPEAT**, **WHILE**, or **FOR** loop. Ignore this rule at your own peril. Jumping into the middle of a loop may skip an important initialization of the control variable or cause other problems and hard-to-find bugs.

Summary

Compound statements are individual statements, separated by semicolons and surrounded by **BEGIN** and **END**. Pascal allows compound statements anywhere a boxed-in *statement* appears in a railroad diagram.

Repeating a single or compound statement is a common programming operation. Pascal has three repetitive statements to choose from: **WHILE**, **REPEAT**, and **FOR**. A **WHILE** loop evaluates its condition at the top and may never execute. A **REPEAT** loop evaluates its condition at the bottom and always executes at least once. A **FOR** loop is often shorter and more efficient than the other two loops but requires a simple control variable and always goes up or down by single steps.

Conditional statements, **IF-THEN-ELSE** and **CASE**, allow programs to make decisions, changing the program's flow. **IF** statements choose one of two possible statements. **CASE** statements choose one of many possibilities. The notorious **GOTO** jumps to a specific place in a program, but its power is dangerous if used carelessly.

Exercises

3-1. Modify Program 3-2 or 3-5 to count down from ten to one. Add a prompt for a starting value to begin counting.

3-2. Program 2-5 calculates the Celsius temperature for degrees Fahrenheit, but you have to rerun it for every new temperature. Add a loop to the program making it repeat until you want to stop.

3-3. The following colors are complementary: yellow-green and red-purple; blue-green and red-orange; blue-purple and yellow-orange. Add these six new colors to Program 3-16. (Hint: Modify the **CASE** statement to select colors by number; for example, 1 = yellow, 2 = yellow-green, etc.)

3-4. A factorial, written *n!*, of a nonnegative integer is defined by the equation (using an asterisk for multiplication):

$$n! = 1 * 2 * \ldots * n$$

In other words, *n!* equals all the integer values from one up to and including *n* multiplied together. Write a program to calculate *n!* for any positive value of *n*. (Note: The factorial of zero is one, not zero. Your program should handle this special condition.)

3-5. Think of a number between one and 100. Now, if I try to guess your number, say 50, you tell me if I'm high or low, then I'll make another guess. I bet I can guess your number in seven tries or less. Write a program to play this game with you. What repetitive and conditional statements will you use?

3-6. Modify Program 3-17 to operate without using any **GOTO**s.

4

Divide and Conquer

- Top-Down Programming
- Procedures
- Functions
- Passing Parameters
- Nesting Procedures and Functions
- Scope Consequences
- Forward Declarations and Recursion
- Predeclared Procedures and Functions
- Function Side Effects
- Escape Artists: Halt and Exit
- Functions and Evaluation Order
- Procedures That Increment and Decrement

4

Key Words and Identifiers

Dec, Exit, FUNCTION, FOR, FORWARD, GOTO, Halt, Inc, Odd, PROCEDURE, Upcase, VAR

One approach to designing Pascal programs might be called the "brute-force method." That is, you state a goal, for example, converting temperatures from Fahrenheit to Celsius, then sit down and write the code. This may be adequate for small programs, but the same approach fails miserably for larger projects, database managers, spreadsheets, and sophisticated games. Such endeavors require too many complex steps to comprehend, much less program, all at once.

Instead of a brute-force, do-it-all approach, most professional programmers follow an organizational method called *top-down programming*. As you'll learn in this chapter, top-down programming and Pascal fit together like a glove on your hand.

Top-Down Programming

Experienced programmers divide large projects into pieces, then conquer each of the more manageable parts one by one. This way, the entire program falls into place while you concentrate on a few simple lines at a time.

This divide-and-conquer method is at the heart of top-down programming. You start at the top, with the main goal, and progress from overall concepts down to finer and finer details. Programmers, of course, are not the only people to use top-down methods in their work. A builder starts with a blueprint and lays the foundation before framing in the walls. A musician begins with a theme or melody before adding the trills. This book started with an idea, then progressed to an outline, and from there grew into chapters, paragraphs, and sentences. The top-down method is a natural, enjoyable way to tackle seemingly overwhelming problems. Pascal encourages top-down design, but you must consciously apply the method for it to work.

Procedures

One way to divide a large program into smaller parts is to use *procedures*. A procedure is a named group of statements, variables, constants, and other declarations, all with a particular purpose. Anywhere you write the procedure's name, its internal statements run as though you had copied those statements to this place in the program.

For example, you might design a procedure named **Calculate**. To use that procedure, you write **Calculate** any place in your program. Wherever **Calculate** appears, the statements in the procedure execute. In this way, procedures extend the Pascal language, letting you invent and name new commands. Procedures also reduce duplication by collecting operations that many other parts of a program require.

You can insert procedures anywhere between the last variable declaration of a program and the **BEGIN** of the main program body. After declaring a procedure, its identifier can be used anywhere in a program to call the procedure into action. Figure 4-1 shows the railroad diagram for a simple procedure declaration. An identifier (naming the procedure) and a semicolon follow the key word **PROCEDURE**. After that comes a *block* containing the statements and declarations that apply to this procedure. (Appendix A shows the complete procedure and block diagrams.) An example helps clarify procedure declarations while demonstrating top-down programming methods.

simple procedure

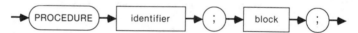

Figure 4-1 Railroad diagram describing a simple procedure.

Program 4-1 is going to be a U.S. Customary to International Metric measurements converter. The program is not finished. Five of the six options listed in lines 20–25 are missing. The only completed option is the first, "Inches to centimeters." This is a typical situation in top-down programming. Parts of the program are finished while others await your attention. After testing the finished parts, you add the rest of the programming, testing each new option before adding the others.

You should have no trouble understanding most of Program 4-1. The plan is to enter a value (line 19), select an option (line 27), then do the conversion (lines 29–32). The procedure **InchesToCentimeters** in lines 7–13 has an obvious purpose—converting inches to equivalent centimeters. Because the procedure name identifies what the procedure does, there's no need to add a comment here.

Program 4-1

```
1:   PROGRAM Metrics;
2:   { Metric conversion program }
3:   VAR
4:      Value : Real;
5:      Selection : Integer;
6:
7:   PROCEDURE InchesToCentimeters;
8:   CONST
9:      CentPerInch = 2.54;
10:  BEGIN
11:     Writeln( Value:1:2, ' inches = ',
12:             Value * CentPerInch:1:2, ' centimeters' )
13:  END; { InchesToCentimeters }
14:
15:  BEGIN
16:     Writeln( 'Metrics' );
17:     Writeln;
18:     Write( 'Value to convert? ' );
19:     Readln( Value );
20:     Writeln( '1 - Inches to centimeters' );
21:     Writeln( '2 - Centimeters to inches' );
22:     Writeln( '3 - Feet to meters' );
23:     Writeln( '4 - Meters to feet' );
24:     Writeln( '5 - Miles to kilometers' );
25:     Writeln( '6 - Kilometers to miles' );
26:     Writeln;
27:     Write( 'Selection? ' ); Readln( Selection );
28:     Writeln;
29:     CASE Selection OF
30:        1 : InchesToCentimeters;
31:        ELSE Writeln( 'Selection error' )
32:     END { case }
33:  END.
```

Notice how the procedure resembles a complete program. It has its own constant declaration and its own **BEGIN** and **END** with a semicolon at the end. In fact, anything that can go in a program can go in a procedure declaration. The only difference is that a procedure's final **END** has a semicolon, not a period. (Because of the multitude of **END**s in a large program, some programmers add clarifying comments as in lines 13 and 32 to show exactly what is ending.)

Line 30 activates the procedure as a selection in the **CASE** statement, which now has only one selector. The procedure name, **InchesToCentimeters**, could also go wherever else Pascal allows statements with one restriction: You cannot use a procedure before declaring it. (Later in this chapter you'll learn how to break even this rule.)

Scope of a Procedure

The procedure in Program 4-1 has a *scope*, a limited range of view, of the procedure's variable, constant, and other declarations. Declarations inside the procedure are *local*—they do not exist outside of the procedure's block. To prove this, try adding the following statement between lines 16 and 17, then rerun the program:

```
Writeln( CentPerInch );
```

If you had declared **CentPerInch** as a constant in the main program, you would not receive an error. But as now written, the procedure declares **CentPer-Inch** as a local constant in lines 8–9. Statements belonging to the procedure block can use the constant. Statements outside of the procedure's scope can't. When you refer to **CentPerInch** outside of the procedure, you receive:

```
Error 3: Unknown identifier
```

On the other hand, the two variables **Value** and **Selection** in lines 4–5 have a *global* scope. Declared in the main program block, which extends from line 2 to line 33, the variables are visible from everywhere in the program—including the procedure statements in lines 11–12 where the global **Value** helps compute inches to centimeters. Global declarations are visible from all places in a program; local declarations are limited to the scope of their declaring procedure.

Continuing with the top-down approach, finish Program 4-1, adding the next option to convert centimeters to inches. First, insert a new **CASE** selector between lines 30 and 31:

```
2 : CentimetersToInches;
```

Next, add the following procedure between lines 14 and 15:

```
PROCEDURE CentimetersToInches;
CONST
   InchPerCent = 0.3937;
BEGIN
   Writeln( Value:1:2, ' centimeters = ',
      Value * InchPerCent:1:2, ' inches' )
END; { CentimetersToInches }
```

When you're finished, the program has two procedures and two options. Test the program before continuing.

Now add the remaining options until the program is complete. You should be able to write the procedures on your own, using the previous examples as guides.

There are 0.3048 meters in 1 foot, 3.28084 feet in 1 meter, 1.609 kilometers in 1 mile, and 0.621 miles in 1 kilometer. In top-down fashion, add and test each formula before going on to the next.

Functions

A function is identical to a procedure but for one difference: A function returns a value where its name appears. You may use functions in expressions anywhere you normally could use a constant. Constants, as you already know, have predeclared values. Functions, on the other hand, calculate the values they return. Also, like constants and variables, functions have associated data types. Functions may return Boolean, real, integer, character, or string data types. They may also return other values such as pointers, a subject for Chapter 7.

As the railroad diagram in Figure 4-2 shows, a function declaration starts with the key word **FUNCTION** and a naming identifier. A colon, a data type, a semicolon, and a block follow. As in a procedure, the block contains the local declarations and program statements belonging to the function, starting with **BEGIN** and ending with **END** and a semicolon.

simple function

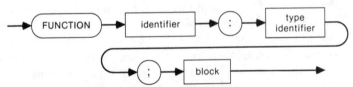

Figure 4-2 Railroad diagram describing a simple function, similar to that in Figure 4-1 but adding a colon and a data type.

Program 4-2 shows a function in action. Before looking at the function, examine the **REPEAT** loop in lines 18–21. The loop repeats until **UserQuits** is true, adding one to variable **i** and displaying **i**'s value for each repetition—just to give the example something to do.

Program 4-2

```
1:   PROGRAM QuitExample;
2:   VAR
3:     i : integer;
4:
5:   FUNCTION UserQuits : Boolean;
6:   { Return TRUE if user wants to end program. }
7:   VAR
8:     answer : Char;
```

Program 4-2 *cont.*

```
 9:  BEGIN
10:     Write( 'Another value? (y/n) ' );
11:     Readln( answer );
12:     UserQuits := ( Upcase( answer ) <> 'Y' )
13:  END; { UserQuits }
14:
15:  BEGIN
16:     Writeln( 'Quit example' );
17:     i := 0;
18:     REPEAT
19:        i := i + 1;
20:        Writeln( 'i=', i )
21:     UNTIL UserQuits
22:  END.
```

UserQuits is a Boolean function (lines 5–13) that returns true or false. The function's statements display a prompt (line 10) and request your answer (line 11). Closely examine line 12. If you type Y to the prompt, the program assigns a false result to the function name, **UserQuits**. If you type any other character, the program assigns a true result. When you run the program, you see a display something like this:

```
i=1
Another value? (y/n) Y
i=2
Another value? (y/n) Y
i=3
Another value? (y/n) N
```

Typing Y and pressing Enter causes **UserQuits** to report a false value back to the **REPEAT** loop at line 21. Therefore, the loop repeats. Pressing any other key, signaling you do not want to see another value, reports a false result, ending the loop.

There are two important rules to learn from this simple example. First, line 21 uses the function name, **UserQuits**, in the same way the program might use a Boolean constant. Second, line 12 *inside the function block* assigns a result to the function name, as though it were a Boolean variable. This passes the value back to the place where the function identifier appears in the program.

Line 12 of Program 4-2 uses another function, **Upcase**, built into Turbo Pascal. The function returns the uppercase equivalent of a character inside parentheses after the function name. For example, this statement displays a capital A:

```
Writeln( Upcase( 'a' ) );
```

Usually, you'll pass a variable to **Upcase** to convert letters to uppercase in statements such as:

```
VAR ch : Char;

REPEAT
    Readln( ch )
UNTIL Upcase( ch ) = 'Q';
```

The **REPEAT** loop reads characters from the keyboard until you press the Q key. Because of **Upcase**, it doesn't matter if you type a lower- or uppercase Q. Without the **Upcase** function, you would have to write the loop this way:

```
REPEAT
    Readln( ch )
UNTIL ( ch = 'q' ) OR ( ch = 'Q' );
```

Common Errors in Functions

Forgetting to assign a value to a function identifier is a common error. Assuming **Value** and **Factor** are global variables the function multiplies, as the following example demonstrates, there is no telling what value a function with such a serious bug returns:

```
FUNCTION Multiply : Real;
VAR
    Temp : real;
BEGIN
    Temp := Value * Factor
END;
```

Although the function calculates local variable **Temp**, the programmer forgot to assign that result to the function identifier, **Multiply**. Being a local variable, **Temp** has no meaning outside the function's scope. Therefore, when the function ends, the value of **Temp** is lost. To repair the problem, change the assignment to the following, assigning the result to the function identifier:

```
Multiply := Value * Factor;
```

Or, you can add a new line, assigning the temporary variable **Temp** to the function identifier:

```
Multiply := Temp;
```

Either way, you ensure that **Multiply** returns the calculated result. Such errors are all too common in programming and are a leading cause of erratic, hard-to-find bugs. To avoid problems, always assign a value to the function identifier for all possible conditions.

Passing Parameters

Parameters pass values to functions and procedures for processing. With parameters, you can write statements like:

```
Writeln( TenTimes(v):8:2 );
```

Earlier, you passed a character parameter to the built-in **Upcase** function. The parameter—a value the procedure or function needs or processes—appears in parentheses after the procedure or function name. In this example, the parameter value (**v**) passes to the function (**TenTimes**), which uses that value in its calculation, returning the result as the function value. Continuing this example, **TenTimes** declares the parameters it expects to receive, adding them in parentheses to the function declaration:

```
FUNCTION TenTimes( r : Real ) : Real;
BEGIN
   TenTimes := r * 10.0
END; { TenTimes }
```

Let's say that the program has a real number value **v** equal to 50.0. These statements then display that value times 10:

```
v := 50.0;
Writeln( TenTimes(v):8:1 );
```

The function receives the value of **v** in its local parameter, **r**. The value passed to a function must be the same type as the parameter declared in the function, but may have a different name. In this example, **v** equals 50.0. Therefore, when the program passes **v** to **TenTimes**, **r**—the function parameter—becomes equal to **v**'s value. **TenTimes** then multiplies **r** by 10.0 and passes the result back to the **Writeln** statement, which displays the finished value—500.0 here.

Figures 4-3, 4-4, 4-5, and 4-6 show new procedure and function railroad diagrams complete with parameter lists. Except for the addition of the boxed-in *parameters* in the first two of these figures, the procedure and function definitions are identical to the simple versions presented earlier.

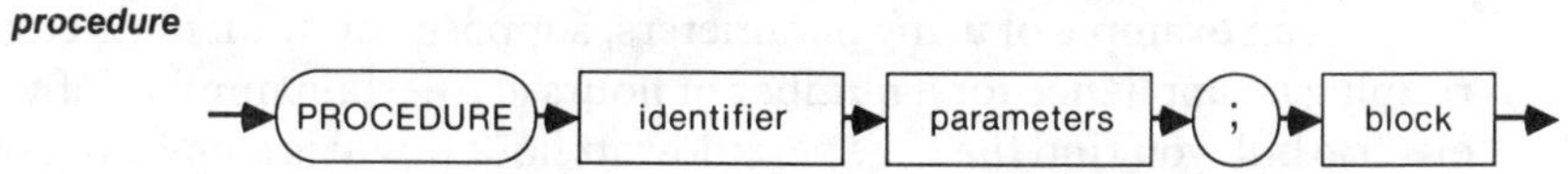

procedure

Figure 4-3 The complete railroad diagram for a procedure contains a
list of formal parameters.

For both procedures and functions, parameters are listed inside parentheses (Figure 4-5). Parameters are always optional. If your procedures and functions don't need any parameters, just omit them and the parentheses.

function

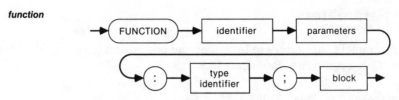

Figure 4-4 The complete railroad diagram for a function contains a list of formal parameters coming before the colon and type identifier.

parameters

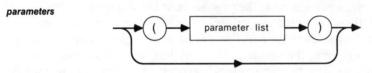

Figure 4-5 Formal parameters may be empty or may contain a parameter list in parentheses.

parameter list

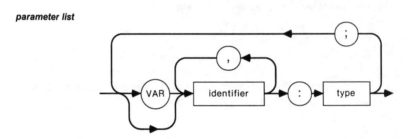

Figure 4-6 A parameter list contains typed identifiers, separated by semicolons, and is optionally preceded by **VAR**.

Figure 4-6 diagrams a parameter list, which is the same for procedures and functions. Notice the similarity of a parameter list and a **VAR** declaration. This is no accident. Parameters are named variables inside procedures and functions, just like any other variables. The only difference is that parameters *receive* values from the place in the program that calls the procedure or function. As you can see in Figure 4-6, each parameter has an identifier, followed by a colon and data type. You can separate multiple identifiers of the same type with commas. An optional **VAR** precedes the first such identifier. For the moment, let's postpone what the **VAR** does.

As an example of using parameters, suppose you want to calculate the cost of running an appliance for a number of hours at a certain number of watts. On your electric bill, you find the *Cost* per kilowatt hour (kwh) is something like 0.0687. At a certain kwh *Rate*, number of hours or *Time*, and number of watts or *Power*, the formula to calculate electric cost in dollars is:

$$Cost = Rate * (Power * 0.001 * Time)$$

You can write this same formula as a Pascal function, with the formal parameters **Time**, **Power**, and **Rate**:

```
FUNCTION Cost( Time, Power, Rate : Real ) : Real;
BEGIN
   Cost := Rate * ( Power * 0.001 * Time )
END;
```

To use the function, insert the function name **Cost** in your program along with actual values in parentheses. To set real number variable **Value** to the cost of running a 100-watt appliance for 10 hours, for example, you could use this statement:

```
Value := Cost( 10, 100, 0.0687 );
```

You must pass as many actual values as there are formal parameters in the function declaration. The following uses of **Cost** produce compiler errors:

```
Value := Cost( 10, 100 );   {Too few params.}
Value := Cost( 10, 100, 0.0687, 99 );   {Too many params.}
```

The first has too few parameters; the second, too many.

You can also pass variables as actual values. Your program might declare real number variables **Watts**, **Hours**, and **CostPerKwh**. After prompting for those values, display the cost using the statement:

```
Writeln( 'Cost = ',
   Cost( Hours, Watts, CostPerKwh ):8:2 );
```

The **Cost** function returns a real number and, as shown in the previous **Writeln** statement, you can format it (:8:2) just as you can any other real number. Being able to pass different actual values to the formal parameters of a procedure or function is a powerful Pascal feature. By changing values passed to functions, you can write a program to print a table listing the electric costs for various power ratings over time.

Program 4-3 uses the **Cost** function (lines 23–27), two procedures, and a Boolean function to print such a table for any number of watts over any length of time. It includes many Pascal features covered in this and earlier chapters. When trying to understand a larger Pascal program like this one, it helps to start not at the beginning, but at the main program body near the end. When you run the program, supply a starting number of hours, an hourly increment, the starting number of watts, an increment for the watts, and the cost per kilowatt hour. When typing the kilowatt-hour value, use a leading zero as in 0.0625.

Program 4-3

```
1:  PROGRAM Electricity;
2:  CONST
3:     MaxRow = 12;        { Number rows in table }
```

Program 4-3 *cont.*

```
 4:       MaxCol = 8;          { Number columns in table }
 5:   VAR
 6:       StartHours,
 7:       HourlyIncrement,
 8:       StartWatts,
 9:       WattsIncrement,
10:       CostPerKwh     : Real;
11:
12:   PROCEDURE Initialize;
13:   BEGIN
14:       Writeln( 'Cost of electricity' );
15:       Writeln;
16:       Write( 'Starting number of hours .. ? ' ); Readln( StartHours );
17:       Write( 'Hourly increment .......... ? ' ); Readln( HourlyIncrement );
18:       Write( 'Starting number of Watts .. ? ' ); Readln( StartWatts );
19:       Write( 'Watts increment ........... ? ' ); Readln( WattsIncrement );
20:       Write( 'Cost per kilowatt hour (KWH)? ' ); Readln( CostPerKwh )
21:   END; { Initialize }
22:
23:   FUNCTION Cost( Time, Power, Rate : Real ) : Real;
24:   { Return cost of running at "Power" watts for "Time" hours }
25:   BEGIN
26:       Cost := Rate * ( Power * 0.001 * Time )
27:   END; { Cost }
28:
29:   PROCEDURE PrintTable;
30:   VAR
31:       Row, Col : Integer;
32:       Hours, Watts : Real;
33:   BEGIN
34:       Writeln;
35:       Write( 'Hrs/Watts' );
36:       Watts := StartWatts;
37:       FOR Col := 1 TO MaxCol DO
38:       BEGIN
39:          Write( Watts:8:0 );
40:          Watts := Watts + WattsIncrement
41:       END; { for }
42:       Writeln;
43:
44:       Hours := StartHours;
45:       FOR Row := 1 TO MaxRow DO
46:       BEGIN
47:          Writeln;
48:          Write( Hours:6:1, ' - ' );
```

Program 4-3 *cont.*

```
49:        Watts := StartWatts;
50:        FOR Col := 1 TO MaxCol DO
51:        BEGIN
52:           Write( Cost( Hours, Watts, CostPerKwh ):8:2 );
53:           Watts := Watts + WattsIncrement
54:        END; { for }
55:        Hours := Hours + HourlyIncrement
56:     END; { for }
57:     Writeln;
58:     Writeln;
59:     Writeln( 'Cost of Electricity @ ', CostPerKwh:0:4, ' per KWH' )
60:  END; { PrintTable }
61:
62:  FUNCTION Finished : Boolean;
63:  VAR
64:     answer : Char;
65:  BEGIN
66:     Writeln;
67:     Write( 'Another table (y/n) ? ' );
68:     Readln( answer );
69:     Finished := Upcase( answer ) <> 'Y'
70:  END; { Finished }
71:
72:  BEGIN
73:     REPEAT
74:        Initialize;
75:        PrintTable
76:     UNTIL Finished
77:  END.
```

Notice that the entire main body of Program 4-3 occupies only six lines, 72–77. Typically, large Pascal programs have tiny main bodies, serving only to call various procedures and functions in some logical order. Figure 4-7 shows an example of the program's output.

When designing programs with the top-down method, you might start with a short main body and insert *dummy* procedures as place holders. For example, when I first wrote Program 4-3, I used a dummy **PrintTable** procedure to hold a place where the actual procedure would eventually go:

```
PROCEDURE PrintTable;
BEGIN
END;
```

With its collection of dummy procedures, the program compiles and runs but doesn't do anything. Temporarily, you might also insert **Writeln** statements in

```
Cost of electricity

Hrs/Watts    100    110    120    130    140    150    160    170
     4.0 -   0.03   0.03   0.03   0.04   0.04   0.04   0.04   0.05
     6.0 -   0.04   0.05   0.05   0.05   0.06   0.06   0.07   0.07
     8.0 -   0.05   0.06   0.07   0.07   0.08   0.08   0.09   0.09
    10.0 -   0.07   0.08   0.08   0.09   0.10   0.10   0.11   0.12
    12.0 -   0.08   0.09   0.10   0.11   0.12   0.12   0.13   0.14
    14.0 -   0.10   0.11   0.12   0.13   0.13   0.14   0.15   0.16
    16.0 -   0.11   0.12   0.13   0.14   0.15   0.16   0.18   0.19
    18.0 -   0.12   0.14   0.15   0.16   0.17   0.19   0.20   0.21
    20.0 -   0.14   0.15   0.16   0.18   0.19   0.21   0.22   0.23
    22.0 -   0.15   0.17   0.18   0.20   0.21   0.23   0.24   0.26
    24.0 -   0.16   0.18   0.20   0.21   0.23   0.25   0.26   0.28
    26.0 -   0.18   0.20   0.21   0.23   0.25   0.27   0.29   0.30


Cost of Electricity @ 0.0687 per KWH
```

Figure 4-7 Nested **FOR** loops and the **Cost** function in Program 4-3 printed this row and column table.

dummy procedures and functions. If you weren't ready to fill in function **Cost**, you could insert the following dummy function:

```
FUNCTION Cost( Time, Power, Rate : Real ) : Real;
VAR
    Temp : Real;
BEGIN
    Writeln;
    Write( 'DUMMY COST. Value? ' );
    Readln( Temp );
    Cost := Temp
END;
```

Eventually, you'll insert the proper formula to complete the function. Meanwhile, the program prompts you for the value that **Cost** should return. This lets you debug the program, testing what happens when **Cost** returns various values. After filling in the real programming, you can be confident in the operation of the other tested program statements.

There are a few other highlights you might want to examine more closely in Program 4-3. Procedure **PrintTable** shows how to use nested **FOR** loops to print row and column tables, a common computer problem you will encounter over and over again. Function **Finished** at lines 62–70 is similar to **UserQuits** in Program 4-2.

Value and Variable Parameters

Value parameters take their values from the caller of a function or procedure. For example, line 52 of Program 4-3 passes the value of **Hours**, **Watts**, and **CostPerKwh**, to function **Cost** at line 23. When the statements inside **Cost** execute, the formal parameter **Time** has the value of **Hours**; **Power** has the same value as **Watts**; and **Rate** equals **CostPerKwh**. This is called *passing parameters by value*. Even if **Cost** were to change the value of **Time**, the actual variable **Hours** would not also change. The two variables are distinct even though they have the same value.

The next example will help you to better understand value parameters. Program 4-4 has a single procedure, **PrintValues**, with three formal integer parameters, **X**, **Y**, and **Z**. The procedure multiplies these three values by two and then displays the results in line 9. In line 14, the program assigns initial values 10, 20, and 30 to three global integer variables, **A**, **B**, and **C**. Line 17 passes these parameters by value to **PrintValues**' formal parameters X, Y, and Z. The program tests the effect of the procedure on the global variables **A**, **B**, and **C**, printing their values (lines 16 and 19) before and after passing them to **PrintValues**. Running the program produces these results:

```
Before.... A=10, B=20, C=30
During.... X=20, Y=40, Z=60
After..... A=10, B=20, C=30
```

As you can see, **A**, **B**, and **C** do not change. Although **PrintValues** multiplies **X**, **Y**, and **Z** by two in line 7, the global variables **A**, **B**, and **C** keep their original values before and after the procedure executes, proving that the variables are distinct. **PrintValues**' formal parameters receive copies of the actual variables passed by value in line 17—the original variables (**A**, **B**, and **C**) are not disturbed.

Program 4-4

```
1:    PROGRAM ValueParameters;
2:    VAR
3:       A, B, C : Integer;
4:
5:    PROCEDURE PrintValues( X, Y, Z : Integer );
6:    BEGIN
7:       X := X * 2; Y := Y * 2; Z := Z * 2;
8:       Writeln;
9:       Writeln( 'During.... X=', X, ' Y=', Y, ' Z=', Z )
10:   END; { PrintValues }
11:
12:   BEGIN
13:      Writeln( 'Value parameters' );
14:      A := 10; B := 20; C := 30;
15:      Writeln;
```

Program 4-4 cont.

```
16:     Writeln( 'Before.... A=', A, ' B=', B, ' C=', C );
17:     PrintValues( A, B, C );
18:     Writeln;
19:     Writeln( 'After..... A=', A, ' B=', B, ' C=', C )
20:  END.
```

Program 4-5 is identical to Program 4-4 except for a new element in the parameter list in line 5. By declaring the formal parameters with the preceding key word **VAR**, the program has a different effect, producing these results:

```
Before.... A=10, B=20, C=30
During.... X=20, Y=40, Z=60
After..... A=20, B=40, C=60
```

Now, when procedure **PrintValues** multiplies **X**, **Y**, and **Z**, the original variables **A**, **B**, and **C** also change to the new values. When declared with the key word **VAR**, the formal parameters **X**, **Y**, and **Z** are called *variable parameters*. If changed inside the procedure, as in the example, the actual variables passed to the procedure also vary.

Program 4-5

```
1:   PROGRAM VariableParameters;
2:   VAR
3:      A, B, C : Integer;
4:
5:   PROCEDURE PrintValues( VAR X, Y, Z : Integer );
6:   BEGIN
7:      X := X * 2; Y := Y * 2; Z := Z * 2;
8:      Writeln;
9:      Writeln( 'During.... X=', X, ' Y=', Y, ' Z=', Z )
10:  END; { PrintValues }
11:
12:  BEGIN
13:     Writeln( 'Variable parameters' );
14:     A := 10; B := 20; C := 30;
15:     Writeln;
16:     Writeln( 'Before.... A=', A, ' B=', B, ' C=', C );
17:     PrintValues( A, B, C );
18:     Writeln;
19:     Writeln( 'After..... A=', A, ' B=', B, ' C=', C )
20:  END.
```

Passing values to variable parameters this way is called *passing parameters by reference*. The formal parameters (**X**, **Y**, and **Z** in the example) *refer* or point to the actual variables **A**, **B**, and **C**. Changing the value of the formal parameter also changes the value of the actual variable to which it refers.

While you can pass either variable or literal values to value parameters, you can pass only variables to variable parameters. For example, try changing line 17 in Program 4-4 to:

```
PrintValues( 100, 200, 300 );
```

The value parameters in line 5 accept these literal constants. Try changing the same line in Program 4-5, however, and the compiler displays:

```
Error 20: Variable identifier expected
```

The reason for this error is that variable parameters (line 5) cannot accept literal, constant values. You can pass only variables to variable parameters.

Parameter Names

Parameters in procedures and functions are similar to local variables. Like local variables, parameters are visible only within the routines in which you declare them. You can't refer to parameter names outside the procedure—the parameters exist only when the procedure is running.

Because they are local variables, parameter identifiers never conflict with identifiers declared outside the routine's scope. In other words, you could change line 5 in Program 4-5 to:

```
PROCEDURE PrintValues( VAR A, B, C : Integer );
```

even though the same names **A**, **B**, and **C** are used as global variables at line 3. Inside **PrintValues**, **A**, **B**, and **C** are distinct variables from the ones with the same names outside the routine.

Usually, though, it's a good idea to choose unique names for identifiers inside procedures and functions. This way, the program is perfectly clear. But if you want to repeat identifier names for global variables, parameters, and local variables inside procedures and functions, you may certainly do so.

Where Are My Parameters?

Turbo Pascal creates all value parameters and local variables on the stack, the memory area that stores return addresses to callers of procedures and functions among other items. This happens when the routine that declares the variables begins running. For example, in Program 4-5, **X**, **Y**, and **Z** exist only while **PrintValues** runs.

Local variables and value parameters, then, are *dynamic*, existing only while needed. Turbo Pascal dynamically reserves space for local variables and value parameters on demand, efficiently using memory. In a program with thousands of procedures, only the absolute minimum amount of variable space exists as needed at any one time.

Global variables always exist in memory, even when you don't need them. For this reason, it's a good idea to use global variables only when you must preserve their values between calls to various routines.

Try to use global variables sparingly, declaring most variables locally inside procedures and functions, and passing parameters for processing. This lets Turbo Pascal dynamically create space for your variables as needed—space that many other routines can share. If you follow this rule, you'll probably find that your programs take less memory.

Mixing Variable and Value Parameters

You can freely mix variable and value parameters in a parameter list, but when writing procedures with several formal parameters, you may want to use a style like the one shown at the bottom of Figure 4-8.

As with other stylistic concerns in Pascal, the compiler doesn't care about parameter cosmetics. To the compiler, the two styles for procedure **Test** in Figure 4-8 are equally beautiful. But a carefully written program is easier to read and understand, especially years later when your original intentions may be unclear. With hundreds or thousands of procedures and functions, many having multiple parameters, the beauty of a good programming style is more than just skin deep— to a programmer, that is.

```
PROCEDURE test( param1, param2 : Integer; VAR param3 :
   Real; param4 : Char );


PROCEDURE test(      param1,
                param2 : Integer;
            VAR param3 : Real;
                param4 : Char     );
```

Figure 4-8 These two procedure declarations are the same, but the one on top is more difficult to read. The bottom style has each formal parameter declared on a separate line.

Turbo Pascal allows two other kinds of parameters. *Untyped parameters* have no data types. *Procedural parameters* are the names of procedures and functions, passed as values to other procedures and functions. Chapter 13 discusses these advanced techniques.

Nesting Procedures and Functions

Procedures and functions can nest inside other procedures and functions. You can have one procedure with other subprocedures and subfunctions, which in turn can have sub-subprocedures, and so on.

A nested procedure or function is local to its surrounding parent. Statements outside the parent cannot call the locally nested procedure, just as they cannot use any locally declared variables or constants.

Program 4-6 demonstrates nested procedures. The program calculates the volume of a sphere from its radius. Designed using the top-down method, the main program in lines 31–36 is simple, writing the program title (line 32) and repeatedly calculating volumes until **Done**. **FindVolume** is a procedure (lines 5–29) that prompts for the radius (line 25) and writes the result (line 28). The procedure returns a Boolean variable parameter **Quitting** (line 5) equal to true if you enter zero, ending the program when the actual variable **Done** is false in line 35.

Program 4-6

```
1:   PROGRAM Sphere;
2:   VAR
3:      Done : Boolean;
4:
5:   PROCEDURE FindVolume( VAR Quitting : Boolean );
6:   { Compute volume, returning Quitting=true if user is done }
7:   VAR
8:      Radius : Real;
9:
10:     FUNCTION VolOfSphere( r : Real ) : Real;
11:     { Return volume of sphere with radius r }
12:
13:        FUNCTION Cube( n : Real ) : Real;
14:        { Return n*n*n }
15:        BEGIN
16:           Cube := n * n * n
17:        END; { Cube }
18:
19:     BEGIN
20:        VolOfSphere := ( 4.0 * Pi * Cube(r) ) / 3.0
21:     END; { VolOfSphere }
22:
23:   BEGIN
24:      Writeln;
25:      Write( 'Radius? (0 to quit) ' ); Readln( Radius );
26:      Quitting := ( Radius = 0.0 );
27:      IF NOT Quitting
28:         THEN Writeln( 'Volume = ', VolOfSphere( Radius ):1:3 )
29:   END; { FindVolume }
30:
31:   BEGIN
32:      Writeln( 'Volume of a sphere' );
33:      REPEAT
```

Program 4-6 *cont.*

```
34:        FindVolume( Done )
35:     UNTIL Done
36:  END.
```

There are two nested functions in the example. Function **VolOfSphere** in lines 10–21 calculates the volume according to this formula from solid geometry:

$$V_{sphere} = \frac{4\pi r^3}{3}$$

This formula appears as the expression in line 20. Another nested function returns the cube of a value. Function **Cube** at lines 13–17 lets line 20 write **Cube(r)** instead of **r∗r∗r**. Notice how the purely stylistic indentation (lines 10, 13, and 19) indicates the level of nesting.

Each nested function in Program 4-6 has a limited scope. For example, function **Cube** can be seen only from inside its parent function, **VolOfSphere**. You could not use **Cube** in the body of the program (lines 31–36) or in procedure **FindVolume** (lines 23–29). To prove this claim, try adding the following statement between lines 26 and 27 to print the cube of the radius:

```
Writeln( 'Radius cubed = ', Cube( Radius ) );
```

The compiler displays:

```
Error 3: Unknown identifier
```

because the **Cube** function is local to **VolOfSphere** and does not exist outside that function's limited scope. To fix the problem, you could move function **Cube** from its current position at lines 13–17 to between lines 9 and 10. Doing this declares the function local to **FindVolume** and, therefore, within the scope of everything inside that procedure. Although the modified program now runs, you still cannot access **VolOfSphere** or **Cube** from the main body of the program. Those functions are still local to **FindVolume**.

Limitations of Nesting

Technically, there is no limit to the number of subprocedures that can nest inside procedures on higher levels. You could have procedures inside procedures inside functions inside still other procedures until your program looks like a pyramid toppled onto one side.

In practice, though, nesting is rarely useful to a depth much greater than that shown in Program 4-6. If each nesting level is numbered with the main program at level zero, then procedure **FindVolume** is at level one, **VolOfSphere** is at level two, and **Cube** is at level three. As a general rule, most programs require nesting levels no deeper than three or four.

Another limitation of nested routines concerns the ability to access variables declared locally to other routines. In Program 4-6, variable **Radius** is local to **FindVolume**. Both **VolOfSphere** and **Cube** can use this variable because these two functions are within **FindVolume**'s scope.

Remember that value parameters and local variables are identical. The only difference is that parameters receive initial values from callers to procedures and functions. Parameter **r** in line 10 is a local variable inside **VolOfSphere**. Because of this, **FindVolume** cannot refer to **r**. But **Cube** could use **r** because **Cube** is within the **VolOfSphere**'s scope. Similarly, parameter **n** in line 13 is a local variable in **Cube**. Because **Cube** is the most deeply nested routine, only its own statements can use **n**.

If all this seems confusing, just remember that you can refer to items declared only in the same or in outer levels. You can never refer to items declared within inner levels.

It may help to picture this concept as a set of rooms constructed out of one-way glass facing out. Each room, representing a procedure or function, nests inside a larger room. The outermost room is the main program. While standing in any one room, you can see all the way to the outside, but you can't see into any other rooms nested inside the one you're in. You can see the furniture (variables) in outer rooms and in your own, but you can't look into inner rooms to see what they contain. If you fix this image firmly in mind, you'll avoid mixups when working with nested procedures and functions.

Scope Consequences

In Chapter 3, you learned about **GOTO** and **FOR** statements. When using these statements in procedures and functions, you need to be aware of two restrictions.

A **GOTO** inside a procedure or function can jump to labeled statements only within the same block. For example, if you define a global label between lines 1 and 2 of Program 4-4 and label the statement at line 18, you still can't jump to line 18 from inside the **PrintValues** procedure. This limitation forces you to use **GOTO** statements only for short hops within the block defining the **GOTO** label.

Another restriction concerns the scope of procedure and function blocks that contain **FOR** loops. The control variable for all **FOR** loops must be a global variable, a local variable, or a value parameter. You may never use a variable parameter (preceded by **VAR** in the parameter list) for a **FOR** loop control. If you try to do this, you receive:

```
Error 97: Invalid FOR control variable
```

These minor restrictions are rarely problems; you just have to memorize them. Don't be too concerned with the details, though. Turbo Pascal will tell you if you make a mistake—one of the reasons for using a language compiler in the first place.

Forward Declarations and Recursion

Earlier, you learned that you must declare procedures and functions before using them. Sometimes, you'll discover situations where you must break this rule, using a procedure before declaring it. To handle the problem, Turbo Pascal provides a special key word, **FORWARD**, which Program 4-7 demonstrates.

The example reads like an Abbott and Costello comedy routine. The program has two procedures **A** and **B**. The action begins (line 17) by calling **A**, which at line 7 calls **B** if **Ch** is less than Z. **B** in turn calls **A** at line 13 passing the successor of **Ch** by value back to **A**, after which **A** again calls **B**, which then calls **A**. Who's calling who?! Although the example may seem silly, it demonstrates a real programming situation that often occurs in Pascal.

Program 4-7

```
1:   PROGRAM WhosOnFirst;
2:
3:   PROCEDURE B( ch : Char ); FORWARD;
4:
5:   PROCEDURE A( ch : Char );
6:   BEGIN
7:      IF ch < 'Z' THEN B( ch );
8:      Write( ch )
9:   END;
10:
11:  PROCEDURE B( ch : Char );
12:  BEGIN
13:     A( Succ( ch ) )
14:  END;
15:
16:  BEGIN
17:     A('A');
18:     Writeln
19:  END.
```

Program 4-7 is an example of *mutual recursion*. Recursion is what happens when a procedure or function calls itself. Mutual recursion is what happens when procedure (or function) **A** calls *another* routine **B**, which again calls **A**—exactly what happens in Program 4-7. The recursion continues in layer upon layer until the procedures stop calling each other, usually when a variable reaches a certain value or when a condition becomes true or false.

Obviously, even though two mutually recursive procedures call each other, you cannot declare them ahead of each other. Either **B** must follow **A** or the other way around. To solve this problem, Pascal allows you to declare procedures and functions *forward* letting both **A** and **B** call each other, as shown in Program 4-7, line 3.

The forward-declared **B** has a normal procedure declaration with an optional parameter list but ends with the key word **FORWARD** in place of the usual block. Now, **A** may call **B**, while **B** may still call **A**. To understand how the program works, try to execute its statements by hand. The results may surprise you!

When you write the actual programming for a forward routine (see lines 11–14), you must repeat the procedure or function declaration exactly as it appears earlier with the **FORWARD** key word. If you declare different numbers of parameters in either case, you'll receive:

```
Error 131: Header does not match previous definition
```

(By "header," Turbo Pascal means the procedure or function declaration.)

Alternatively, you may declare the procedure with its parameters and the **FORWARD** key word and then later delete the parameters altogether. In other words, it's perfectly okay to change line 11 to:

```
PROCEDURE B;
```

The reason for this odd rule is that in most other Pascals—and in previous Turbo Pascal versions—you are not allowed to repeat the parameter lists from forward declarations. Therefore, for compatibility, Turbo Pascal lets you declare forward routines with parameters and then write the actual routines without redeclaring those same parameters. If you declare parameters in both places, though, the compiler insists that they match. Use whichever style you prefer.

More About Recursion

Program 4-7 demonstrates mutual recursion. Plain recursion occurs when a procedure or function calls itself. When this happens, several actions occur:

- The procedure or function starts running from its first statement for each time it calls itself.

- New and distinct copies of value parameters and local variables are created.

- The location that calls the procedure or function is put on hold, in effect pausing while the recursively generated level starts running.

An example helps explain these effects. Program 4-8 contains a recursive procedure, **Count**, which calls itself from line 5 if the value of **n** is less than ten. The main program calls **Count**, passing an initial value of one as a value parameter.

Program 4-8

```
1:   PROGRAM RecursiveCount;
2:
3:   PROCEDURE Count( n : integer );
```

Program 4-8 *cont.*

```
 4:  BEGIN
 5:     IF n < 10 THEN Count( n + 1 );
 6:     Writeln( n )
 7:  END; { Count }
 8:
 9:  BEGIN
10:     Count( 1 )
11:  END.
```

When Count starts running, **n** equals one. Because this is less than ten, the **IF** statement calls **Count** a second time, in this case passing **n + 1**, or two. This causes **Count** to start over from the top with a distinct value for **n**. Remember that all value parameters and local variables are distinct for each new level of recursion. Every call to a procedure or function, as you learned earlier, dynamically creates space for local variables and for value parameters. This is true also when routines call themselves recursively, and, therefore, each successive call to **Count** creates a new and distinct memory space on the stack to hold the value of parameter **n**.

Eventually, as these actions repeat, **n** increases to ten, causing the **IF** statement to fail. What happens next is the exciting part: The **Writeln** statement in line 6 executes for the first time.

After the **Writeln**, **Count** ends. Because the program calls **Count** a total of ten times, each successive level of the recursion also ends, unwinding each of the recursive calls until reaching the first. When you run the program, the effect is to count backward from ten!

If you have trouble understanding how this works, imagine that the procedure is like a mirror, with the light striking the glass representing the value passed to the procedure. As you probably have seen, aiming two mirrors at each other causes their light to reflect seemingly forever back and forth between them. Because each mirror "sees" the other as a smaller image, the reflections shrink as they infinitely repeat.

Recursion works like that. And, unless the recursive procedure stops itself at some point down the line, the process continues until the computer runs out of stack space to keep track of the recursive calls and local variables. To prove this, replace **Count** in Program 4-8 with the following:

```
PROCEDURE Count( n : integer );
BEGIN
   Count( n + 1 )
END;
```

When you run the modified program, **Count** calls itself repeatedly, adding one to **n** for each new call. The recursion never ends—just as the light bouncing between two mirrors presumably never stops alternating back and forth. Actually, though, because computers have limited memory space, when you run the modified program, you quickly receive a "Stack overflow" error. This makes sense because Turbo Pascal stores the successive values of **n** in memory, stacking each new value along with other items. As you can see, it doesn't take long for memory to fill to capacity, ending the program with an error.

Predeclared Procedures and Functions

Turbo Pascal contains a number of procedures and functions that extend standard Pascal commands as originally designed. You learned about one built-in function, **Upcase**, in Program 4-2. Chapter 16 lists all of Turbo Pascal's built-in routines. You'll meet every one in other chapters as well.

Use built-in procedures and functions the same as those you declare in your own programs. For example, the built-in **Odd** function returns true if an integer value passed to the function is an odd number. Program 4-9 demonstrates how to use **Odd**.

Program 4-9

```
 1:  PROGRAM AtOdds;
 2:  VAR
 3:     n : integer;
 4:  BEGIN
 5:     Write( 'Type any number: ' );
 6:     Readln( n );
 7:     IF odd( n )
 8:        THEN Writeln( n, ' is very odd' )
 9:        ELSE Writeln( n, ' evens the score' )
10:  END.
```

Function Side Effects

Be careful when using functions and procedures not to cause *side effects*, usually as the result of changing a global variable. Program 4-10 demonstrates this danger.

Program 4-10 (with errors)

```
 1:  PROGRAM SideEffect;
 2:  VAR
 3:     i : Integer;
 4:
 5:  FUNCTION Even : Boolean;
 6:  BEGIN
 7:     i := i + 1;
 8:     Even := Odd( i )
 9:  END; { Even }
```

Program 4-10 (with errors) *cont.*

```
10:
11:   BEGIN
12:     i := 1;
13:     WHILE i < 20 DO
14:     BEGIN
15:       Write( i:2 );
16:       IF Even THEN Write( ' : is even' );
17:       Writeln;
18:       i := i + 1
19:     END
20:   END.
```

Program 4-10 has a bug. The purpose of the program is to write a list of numbers, identifying the even values. Faced with this problem, you might decide to write a function based on the idea that **N** is even if **N + 1** is odd, a reasonable approach, if not the best one. This function is programmed in lines 5–9. Variable **i** increases by one, making function **Even** true or false depending on the result of the built-in Boolean function, **Odd**.

The problem is that the main loop of the program also uses **i** as a control variable inside the **WHILE** loop in lines 13–19. Because the program increases **i** in line 18 and, unknown to the main program, also in line 7, it lists no even numbers. The side effect of function **Even** changing the value of the global variable **i** causes the bug.

Because of the potential for causing side effects, statements inside procedures and functions should rarely, if ever, make assignments to global variables. In a large program, it's easy to forget which procedures affect which global variables. Using those variables elsewhere, as Program 4-10 demonstrates, can lead to difficult problems. To prevent side effects, pass parameters to your procedures. For example, you might rewrite Program 4-10 with the following lines in place of lines 5 and 16:

```
 5:   FUNCTION Even( i : Integer ) : Boolean;
16:   IF Even( i ) THEN Write( ' : is even' );
```

By declaring a formal parameter **i** in function **Even** and passing **i** by value, adding one in line 7 affects only the local parameter, not the global variable of the same name. The side effect is gone, and the program now runs correctly.

Escape Artists: Halt and Exit

Two special built-in procedures let you immediately end a program (**Halt**) and stop a procedure or function (**Exit**) at any place you want. **Halt** is useful when you want to display an error message and end a program:

```
PROCEDURE Error;
BEGIN
   Writeln( 'Error!  Halting program...' );
   Halt
END;
```

Exit lets you stop a procedure, rather than let it continue to the end. This is sometimes useful when, deep in the execution of a procedure, you want to escape quickly out of a loop and go on with the rest of the program.

Program 4-11

```
1:   PROGRAM FastExit;
2:
3:   PROCEDURE Error( ch : Char );
4:   BEGIN
5:      Writeln( 'Error! You did not type ', ch );
6:      Halt
7:   END;
8:
9:   PROCEDURE A;
10:  VAR ch : Char;
11:  BEGIN
12:     Write( 'Type X to quit procedure A: ' );
13:     Readln( ch );
14:     IF Upcase( ch ) <> 'X'
15:        THEN Error( 'X' )
16:  END;
17:
18:  PROCEDURE B;
19:  VAR ch : Char;
20:  BEGIN
21:     Write( 'Type Y to quit procedure B: ' );
22:     Readln( ch );
23:     IF Upcase( ch ) = 'Y'
24:        THEN Exit;
25:     Error( 'Y' )
26:  END;
27:
28:  BEGIN
29:     A; B
30:  END.
```

Program 4-11 demonstrates these Pascal escape artists. Procedure **A** asks you to type X. Procedure **B** asks you to type Y. If you type a different character, each procedure calls **Error** at line 3, halting the program. If you type the requested character, procedure **A** ends rather than calling **Error.** Procedure **B** ends a different way: by calling **Exit** at line 24, thus skipping the call to **Error** at line 25.

Exit in a program's outer block ends a program and, in this case, is identical to **Halt.** Either of the following two replacements for line 29 in Program 4-11 ends the program before calling procedure **B:**

```
29: A; Exit; B
29: A; Halt; B
```

Halt has two forms. You can use it with no parameters as in line 6, or you can pass an integer value in parentheses like this:

```
Halt( 5 );
```

The value passed to **Halt** goes back to DOS (or to another program that may have run your program). DOS or the other program can use the value for any purpose, but, usually, halt values represent error codes with zero meaning no error. **Halt** with no parameters is equivalent to **Halt(0).**

To demonstrate how to use a **Halt** parameter in DOS, type Program 4-12, save as TESTHALT.PAS, and compile to disk, creating TESTHALT.EXE. Next, type the following five lines and save as RUNHALT.BAT:

```
ECHO OFF
:LOOP
TESTHALT
IF ERRORLEVEL 1 GOTO LOOP
ECHO ON
```

With RUNHALT.BAT and TESTHALT.EXE on disk, quit Turbo Pascal and type RUNHALT to run this small batch file program. The batch file calls TEST-HALT, which asks you to type a number. Type 1, 2, 3, or any other whole number. The value you enter passes back to DOS through the **Halt(n)** statement in line 8. Back in the batch file, DOS tests this value by checking ERRORLEVEL. If the value is greater than or equal to one, the batch file goes back to :LOOP, again running TESTHALT. To stop the repetition, type 0.

Program 4-12

```
1:  PROGRAM TestHalt;
2:  VAR n : Integer;
3:  BEGIN
4:     Writeln;
5:     Writeln( 'Welcome to TEST HALT.' );
6:     Write( 'Enter 0 to stop repeating: ' );
7:     Readln( n );
8:     Halt( n )
9:  END.
```

Functions and Evaluation Order

A subtle side effect can occur when mixing functions in complex expressions. Program 4-13 demonstrates how this situation sometimes clashes with Turbo Pascal's short-circuited Boolean expression evaluator.

The program declares three functions at lines 6, 15, and 21. A **WHILE** statement at line 28 calls the functions to increment the test variable **i**, to check whether **i** is less or equal to a certain maximum, and to ask, "Another value?" Run the program, answering Y and pressing Enter to each prompt. As this demonstrates, even when **i** equals the maximum 10, the program still asks for another value. Obviously, this is a bug—the program should end when **i** equals **Maximum.**

Change line 1 to {**$B –** }, switching on short-circuit evaluation (the default setting), then run the program again. This time, the **WHILE** loop ends when **i** equals 10, skipping the call to function **Done.**

There are two observations to make about these different results. First, with short-circuit evaluation in effect, all functions in a complex expression such as the one in line 28 may or may not be called, possibly skipping a vital operation on which other parts of the program depend. Second, it's dangerous to rely on a specific evaluation order among all expression parts. For example, with short-circuiting switched on ({**$B –** }), functions **NextValue** and **Maximum** are called *before* **Done.** With short-circuiting off ({**$B +** }), **Done** is called first. If **Done** changes other values on which the program depends, these actions may affect the results in unexpected ways.

Be aware of these subtle details of expression evaluation. In expressions that call many functions, the results of a complex expression are often difficult to predict. The best solution in these cases is to assign function results in the correct order to temporary variables, and then use the variables instead of calling the functions directly in expressions.

Program 4-13 (with errors)

```
1:  {$B+}      { Turn off short-circuit evaluation }
2:  PROGRAM FnExpress;
3:  VAR
4:     i : Integer;
5:
6:  FUNCTION Done : Boolean;
7:  VAR
8:     answer : Char;
9:  BEGIN
10:    Write( 'Another value? ' );
11:    Readln( answer );
12:    Done := Upcase( answer ) <> 'Y'
13: END; { Done }
14:
```

Program 4-13 (with errors) *cont.*

```
15:  FUNCTION NextValue( VAR n : Integer ) : Integer;
16:  BEGIN
17:     Inc( n );
18:     NextValue := n
19:  END; { NextValue }
20:
21:  FUNCTION Maximum : Integer;
22:  BEGIN
23:     Maximum := 10
24:  END; { Maximum }
25:
26:  BEGIN
27:     i := 0;
28:     WHILE ( NextValue( i ) <= Maximum ) AND ( NOT Done ) DO
29:        Writeln( 'Value of i = ', i )
30:  END.
```

Procedures That Increment and Decrement

Program 4-13 demonstrates how to use a versatile procedure, **Inc.** Use **Inc** to add 1 to any **Byte, ShortInt, Integer, Word,** and **LongInt** variable. For example, if **n** is a **LongInt** variable, then these statements are equivalent:

```
n := n + 1;
Inc( n );
```

Because of the way Turbo Pascal evaluates expressions, **Inc** is faster than adding 1 to a value and assigning the result back to the same variable. Similarly, you can use **Dec** to decrement (subtract 1) from a value. These two statements have the same effects:

```
n := n - 1;
Dec( n );
```

Summary

Procedures and functions encourage top-down programming by dividing large programs into small, manageable parts.

Procedures operate as Pascal statements. To activate the statements inside the procedure, simply write the procedure's name.

Functions are the same as procedures except they return values. Use functions anywhere a constant value could go. Unlike constants, functions calculate their values.

Procedures and functions can declare formal parameters. Value parameters (passed by value) copy their initial values from the actual passed parameters. Variable parameters (passed by reference) refer directly to the actual variables passed. **FOR** statements may never use variable parameters as control variables.

Procedures and functions have limited scopes. The constants, variables, statements, and other declarations inside procedure and function blocks exist only within the routines. **GOTO** statements may jump only to labels defined in the same block.

Recursion is what happens when a procedure or function calls itself. Mutual recursion occurs when one procedure calls another, which again calls the original.

Turbo Pascal has many built-in procedures and functions such as **Odd**, **Exit**, and **Halt** that you can use exactly the same way as those you create yourself.

Beware of side effects, usually caused by procedures and functions making assignments to global variables. To avoid side effects, pass parameters to procedures and functions.

Exercises

4-1. The area of a square, of course, is the product of its length times its width. Other formulas for surface area S are: $S_{pyramid} = (n*b*h)/2$, where n is the number of faces, b is the length of the base, and h is the height; $S_{cube} = 6a^2$, where a is the length of one side; and $S_{cylinder} = (2*\pi*r)*h$, where r is the radius and h is the height. Using the top-down method, write a program to find the area for those objects. Use procedures and functions to calculate individual formulas and let people select one of several formulas.

4-2. Fuses and circuit breakers are rated by how many amperes it takes to break the connection. Ohm's law says that current measured in amperes equals voltage divided by resistance. Write a program that uses a function **Amperes** to compute the amount of current for a given voltage and resistance.

4-3. If E equals voltage, I equals current in amperes, and R equals resistance in ohms, then the three variations of Ohm's law are $R = E/I$, $E = I*R$, and $I = E/R$. Expand your program in exercise 4-2 to calculate all three of these formulas. Use functions, passing the appropriate parameters needed to complete each equation. How can you use the top-down method to make writing this program easier?

4-4. Program 4-3 uses a function **Finished** as the condition for ending its **REPEAT** loop. Write a new and more general function. For example, your prompt might simply ask "More? (y/n)."

4-5. What is a formal parameter? What is an actual parameter? Describe the difference between value (passed by value) and variable (passed by reference) parameters.

4-6. Modify Program 4-7 to print the alphabet in normal order.

4-7. Develop a procedure PETC, standing for "Press Enter to Continue." The procedure should display that message and then pause until you press the Enter key. Write a test program for your new procedure.

5

Adding Structure to Data

- The TYPE Declaration
- Subranges of Integers
- Scalar Types
- Arrays
- Records
- Sets

5

Key Words and Identifiers

ARRAY, CASE, Char, Chr, IN, Length, MaxInt, NOT, Ord, PACKED, Random, RECORD, SET, TYPE, WITH

Programs in previous chapters declared variables as common Pascal data types, **Boolean**, **Real**, **Integer**, and **Char**. Many programs, however, require more sophisticated kinds of data. In this chapter, you'll learn how to define custom data types and then declare variables of those new types. You'll also learn how to add structure to variables, organizing data into arrays, records, and sets.

The ability to create complex data structures is a prime feature of Pascal. With the many different ways to represent data at your fingertips, you can store and manipulate data in ways limited only by your imagination.

The TYPE Declaration

A Pascal **TYPE** declaration tells the compiler about new data types you want it to recognize. After creating a data type, you create variables of the new type for use in expressions or as parameters to procedures and functions.

A type declaration in Pascal (Figure 5-1) begins with the key word **TYPE**, followed by a naming identifier, an equal sign, and type definition. The type definition can take a variety of forms. One of those forms, the subrange, limits the minimum and maximum range of integer variables. You learned how to create subrange variables in Chapter 2. In the next section, you'll discover that subrange data types are even more useful.

type declaration

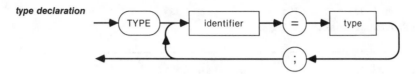

Figure 5-1 Railroad diagram for Pascal's **TYPE** declaration.

Subranges of Integers

Lines 3–4 in Program 5-1 declare a new data type **Index** as a subrange of the integers one through ten. The corresponding railroad diagram is in Figure 5-2. The two periods (called an ellipsis, remember) indicate a range of numbers between two literal constants, one and ten in this example. You must use plain constants to define the minimum and maximum ranges; variable constants are not allowed.

subrange type

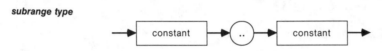

Figure 5-2 Railroad diagram for a subrange scalar data type.

After defining the new type, the program declares a variable, **i** (line 6) of type **Index**, limited to the range of values from one to ten. Turbo Pascal then checks that values assigned to **i** are within this limited range. Assigning a value outside the defined limits causes a runtime "range error."

Instead of declaring a new data type, you could declare **i** as a subrange type as explained in Chapter 2. There is no difference between line 6 in Program 5-1 and this:

```
i : 1 .. 10;
```

The new **Index** data type, though, is available to other parts of the program. You might declare dozens of local variables of type **Index**. Later, if you need to adjust the range—perhaps from ten to 20—all you have to do is modify the type declaration and recompile. All the variables of type **Index** then assume the new subrange limits. If you directly declare variables as subranges, you have to modify each one to change the range. With custom data types, you don't have to work so hard.

Another reason for declaring data type identifiers is to pass parameters of those types to procedures and functions. Parameter types must be simple identifiers, not constructions with multiple pieces like subranges. In other words, you cannot write:

```
PROCEDURE Work( i : 1 .. 15 );  { Incorrect!! }
```

Instead, you must declare a data type and then use the type identifier along with the parameter:

```
TYPE Index = 1 .. 15;
PROCEDURE Work( i : Index );
```

Program 5-1

```
 1:   {$R+}
 2:   PROGRAM Limits;
 3:   TYPE
 4:       Index = 1 .. 10;
 5:   VAR
 6:       i : Index;
 7:   BEGIN
 8:       i := 1;
 9:       WHILE i < 10 DO
10:       BEGIN
11:          Write( i : 5 );
12:          i := i + 1
13:       END;
14:       Writeln
15:   END.
```

To tell the Turbo Pascal compiler you want it to check for range errors, use the compiler option {$R+} as shown in line 1 of Program 5-1. You could also use the alternate style (*$R+*) to do the same thing, or you can turn on range checking by toggling the *Options-Compiler-Range checking* setting in the integrated environment. To see the effect of range checking, change line 9 to:

```
WHILE i <= 10 DO
```

When you run the program, you receive a runtime error 201, and the program stops. (Press Enter to see where the error occurred.) Why did the program fail? When **i** equals ten, adding one to **i** (line 12) makes 11, which is outside of the limited range declared in line 4. With range checking on, Pascal checks that values assigned to variables are within the allowed range.

Turbo Pascal checks for range errors during all assignments to variables, including **FOR** loops, **Readln** statements, and other places when values are assigned to variables of subrange data types.

Scalar Types

A *scalar* type is a data type containing a finite number of elements. Two examples of scalar data types are integers and characters. Simple integers like 1, 2, and 3 are scalar as are the simple characters A, B, and C. Real numbers are not scalar. Between 1.0 and 2.0 there is a third number, 1.5, and between 1.5 and 2.0 there is

1.75, and so on. Because the steps between real numbers are infinite, real numbers are not scalar.

As you can see in Figure 5-3, you can declare new scalar types as a list of identifiers in parentheses, called an *enumerated data type*. Turbo Pascal allows up to 65,536 scalar elements in an enumerated type, although most such types have only a few elements.

enumerated type

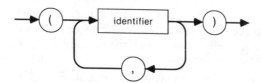

Figure 5-3 An enumerated data type is simply a list of identifiers inside parentheses.

An example of how to declare a new scalar type is shown in line 3 of Program 5-2. In this example, a new enumerated data type, **Colors**, has the seven scalar values, **Red**, **Orange**, **Yellow**, **Green**, **Blue**, **Indigo**, and **Violet**. Commas inside parentheses separate the scalar elements.

Using Enumerated Data Types

When the compiler reads Program 5-2, it translates scalar elements into sequential numbers, starting with zero. **Red** becomes 0 in the compiled program; **Orange** becomes 1, and so forth. This is why scalar types like **Color** are called enumerated data types. The advantage is that instead of your having to know that the value 3 represents Green, the compiler lets you ignore this technical detail and use the more descriptive identifiers instead. It also ensures that you assign individual colors to color variables. For example, assigning 4 to variable color in Program 5-2 is not allowed. Instead, you must write:

```
Color := Blue;
```

Program 5-2

```
1:  PROGRAM RainBow;
2:  TYPE
3:     Colors = ( Red, Orange, Yellow, Green, Blue, Indigo, Violet );
4:  VAR
5:     Color : Colors;
6:  BEGIN
7:     Color := Yellow;
8:     Color := Violet;
9:     IF Color = Violet
```

Program 5-2 *cont.*

```
10:        THEN Writeln( 'Color is Violet' )
11:  END.
```

Using Scalar Variables

You can use scalar variables in loops, expressions, parameter lists, and even as parts of other new data types. Earlier, you learned how to use the built-in functions **Succ** and **Pred** to return the successor and predecessor of integers and characters. Actually, those functions operate with all scalar data types.

Using the Colors types from Program 5-2, then, **Succ(Red)** is **Orange**, **Pred (Indigo)** is **Blue**, **Succ(Orange)** equals **Pred(Green)**, and **Pred(Pred(Yellow))** is **Red**. You can also directly compare scalar elements: **(Blue < Indigo)** and **(Violet > = Orange)** are true Boolean expressions.

Boolean variables are also scalar having the two indivisible scalar elements, **True** and **False**. If the Boolean data type were not predefined in Pascal, you could create it with the following **TYPE** declaration:

```
TYPE
   Boolean = ( False, True );
```

When, declaring scalar types with from one to 256 scalar elements, a variable of that type occupies one eight-bit memory byte. A scalar variable with 257 or more elements takes two eight-bit bytes. You can associate over 65,000 scalar elements with one enumerated data type, although you'll probably never declare more than a few dozen elements at a time. These details are rarely important, but worth keeping in mind.

Scalar and Ordinal Values

The built-in function, **Ord**, returns the underlying ordinal value of a scalar element—in other words, the element's numerical ordering. This is easier to explain with an example. Program 5-3 declares the same scalar type **Colors** from Program 5-2 and a variable **Color** of that type.

As shown here, enumerated scalars can be control variables in a **FOR** loop. The built-in **Ord** function writes the ordinal number of the successive values for colors **Red** through **Violet**. As you can see when you run the program, these values are the integers 0 through 6, the values that the compiler assigns to the seven scalar identifiers.

When using enumerated data types, it's useful to remember that the computer never actually knows anything about real colors. Identifiers like **Red**, **Blue**, **Indigo**, and **Violet** are for *your* benefit, not the computer's. Pascal digests these descriptive names, converting them to numbers, which are, of course, more suited to the tastes of a computer. In the compiled result, therefore, the scalar identifiers no longer exist and do not take up any space. One question I often hear is, "But how does Pascal know what orange is?" The answer is, "It doesn't." The scalar identifier **Orange** is just a convenience to avoid using numbers in programs that *you* would otherwise have to remember really mean something else.

Program 5-3

```
1:   PROGRAM ScalarValues;
2:   TYPE
3:      Colors = ( Red, Orange, Yellow, Green, Blue, Indigo, Violet );
4:   VAR
5:      Color : Colors;
6:   BEGIN
7:      FOR Color := Red TO Violet DO
8:         Writeln( Ord( Color ) )
9:   END.
```

Ordinals to Enumerated Types

In the same way that **Ord** lets you determine the ordinal value of a scalar element, a special Turbo Pascal feature called *typecasting* lets you do the reverse. That is, you can convert or cast an ordinal value, a number, into an enumerated scalar element.

Assuming you have a variable **Col** of the enumerated type **Colors**, you can assign the ordinal value 3 to **Col** like this:

```
Col := Colors(3);
```

The number in parentheses after an enumerated type identifier represents the scalar element with that ordinal value. In other words, **Colors(3)** is equivalent to **Green**. (Remember, the first element always has the value zero. **Green** is the fourth scalar element in type **Colors** and, therefore, has the ordinal value, 3.)

If you try to assign a value outside the declared range of scalar identifiers, the compiler squawks with:

```
Error 76 : Constant out of range
```

For example, this statement does not compile:

```
Col := Colors(30);
```

A similar technique converts ASCII values to characters. ASCII values (see Appendix D) range from 0 to 255. To convert a value to a character variable **Ch**, use the assignment:

```
Ch := Chr(67);
```

This sets **Ch** equal to the character with the ASCII ordinal value 67—in other words, a C. In Turbo Pascal you can do the same thing using the built-in enumerated type identifier, **Char**:

```
Ch := Char(67);
```

Even though the two methods appear to do the same thing, there is a difference. **Chr** is a built-in Pascal *function*. **Char** is an enumerated data type. The value in parentheses recasts the value as a different type, a technique we'll see again in Chapter 13.

Arrays

Arrays are collections of values, all of the same type. When you have many variables to keep track of, rather than store them individually, you can put them into a more manageable array.

Figure 5-4 shows the syntax for declaring arrays. The boxed-in *simple type* can be any subrange or enumerated scalar type enclosed in square brackets [and]. In place of brackets, you can also use the alternate double-character symbols (. and .)—a relic from the past that used to be important on keyboards lacking bracket keys. Today, there's little reason not to use square brackets.

index range

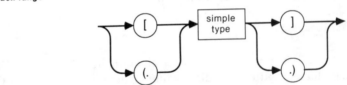

array

Figure 5-4 Railroad diagrams for Pascal arrays.

In Chapter 1, you learned that a variable is similar to a box that can hold one particular kind of thing. An array is like a stack of such boxes (Figure 5-5). Each box has a label, or index, so that a program can locate single elements at random. Because it takes no more time to locate element number fifty than it does element number one, an array is known as a *random access data structure*.

You can declare arrays as new data types. For example, the following **TYPE** declaration defines an array of ten integers:

```
TYPE
    IntegerArray = ARRAY[ 1 .. 10 ] OF Integer;
```

Or you can directly declare arrays as variables. A program might declare an array of 80 characters like this:

```
VAR
    CharArray : ARRAY[ 0 .. 79 ] OF Char;
```

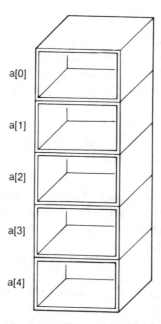

a[0]

a[1]

a[2]

a[3]

a[4]

Figure 5-5 An array is like a stack of boxes. To locate one array element, place the element index number inside square brackets.

Notice that one example uses an index range of [1 . . 10] while the other uses [0 . . 79]. The beginning and ending values are up to you. You could have arrays indexed [100 . . 200] if that makes sense in your program. In this case, Pascal is smart enough to not store extra positions [1 . . 99] wasted in many other languages that require a starting index of zero or one. You can also use negative index values. For example, this is perfectly legal:

```
VAR Score : ARRAY[ -10 .. +10 ] OF integer;
```

To locate one element of an array, use the array name followed by square brackets around the index of the element you want. To write the fifth element of the integer array declared earlier, you could use the statement:

```
Write( IntegerArray[5] );
```

Because this is an array of integers, **IntegerArray[n]**, with **n** equal to any array index, can go wherever Pascal normally allows integer variables. The identifier **IntegerArray** stands for the *entire* array. **IntegerArray[5]**, however, stands for a single array element at index five.

Assign values to array variables in the same way you assign values to simple variables. The following statement sets position two in the integer array to the value 1024:

```
IntegerArray[2] := 1024;
```

Be careful when using arrays with indexes beginning with zero. Failing to remember that the zero element is the first item in the array and, therefore, the element at index 5 is the sixth, not the fifth, is a frequent cause of programming bugs. These two arrays illustrate the problem:

```
VAR
    a1 : ARRAY[ 0 .. 9 ] OF integer;
    a2 : ARRAY[ 1 .. 10 ] OF integer;
```

Both arrays **a1** and **a2** contain spaces for ten integer values. The fifth value in array **a1** is at index 4, referenced in a program by writing **a1[4]**. The fifth value in array **a2** is at position 5, referenced by writing **a2[5]**, because the first index of the array begins at one.

There is no technical reason to use one method over the other, and you can begin your array indexes at zero or at one (or at any other value). If you want to use the method most programmers prefer, though, start your arrays at zero—even though you may think it easier to begin with one. The reason for this is that some languages—C for example—require arrays to begin with zero indexes. If you define most of your own arrays the same way, your programs will be easier to convert to C. Despite this suggestion, though, you should choose array indexes that make the most sense for the job you need to do. If it makes good sense to use array indexes from 12 to 99, then those are the values to use.

Strings and Arrays

A string in Turbo Pascal is a specialized array of characters, which you can also index with square brackets. A program might define a string variable and then use indexing to do something with individual characters in the string.

Program 5-4 demonstrates how to index a string as an array of characters. The program contains a handy procedure **StringUp** that converts from lower- to uppercase all characters in variable parameter **s**. The **FOR** loop at line 12 accomplishes this feat by incrementing control variable **Index** from one to the length of the string. (**Length**, a built-in function, returns the length of a string equal to the number of characters the string contains.) Line 13 converts each character in string **s** to uppercase through the built-in Turbo Pascal function, **Upcase**.

Program 5-4

```
1:  PROGRAM Capitals;
2:  TYPE
3:     String80 = String[80];
4:  VAR
5:     s : String80;
6:
7:  PROCEDURE StringUp( VAR s : String80 );
8:  { Convert characters in string to all uppercase }
9:  VAR
10:    Index : Integer;
11: BEGIN
12:    FOR Index := 1 TO Length( s ) DO
13:       s[ Index ] := Upcase( s[ Index ] )
14: END; { StringUp }
15:
16: BEGIN
17:    Writeln( 'Capitals' );
18:    REPEAT
19:       Writeln;
20:       Writeln( 'Enter any string (<ret> to quit).' );
21:       Readln( s );
22:       StringUp( s );
23:       Writeln( s )
24:    UNTIL Length(s) = 0
25: END.
```

Turbo Pascal hides the length of a string at index zero. In other words:

```
Length( s ) = ORD( s[0] );
```

In English, this tells you the ordinal value of the character at index zero—the first byte of the string variable—is equal to the number of characters in the string. Because Turbo Pascal automatically maintains the length of a string, you rarely need to use the length byte directly as shown here. It's nice to know where it is, though, in case you need it. For example, an advanced trick is to change the length of a string artificially by assigning a new value to the length byte. If **longString** has 25 characters, this statement effectively chops off the last five characters:

```
longString[0] := Chr(20);
```

This works by reducing the string length byte to 20. You must use the built-in **Chr** function to tell the compiler to assign a character—assigning plain integer 20 is not allowed. (Even though the length byte is not really a character, the compiler thinks it is.)

Use these tricks with care. If you fiddle with the length byte—changing it to 200 or something for a string originally declared to be 80 characters long, you can cause all sorts of strange problems.

Array Range Checking

If you use the compiler directive {$R+}, Turbo Pascal checks that array indexes are within declared boundaries. Normally, range checking is off, just as though you used the directive {$R–}. With this setting, Turbo Pascal does not check array boundaries.

As an example, assume you have an array of ten bytes declared this way:

```
VAR
    TenBytes : ARRAY[ 1 .. 10 ] OF Byte;
```

The compiler then checks constant indexes against the declared range. Regardless of whether you turn on range checking, the following statement does not compile:

```
TenBytes[ 11 ] := 128;
```

Index 11 is outside the declared range. Because 11 is a constant value, the compiler is able to catch the error. The compiler accepts the next statements, though:

```
VAR : Integer;

i := 11;
TenBytes[ i ] := 128;
```

Although those two statements compile correctly, with range checking on, you receive:

```
Runtime error 201: Range check error
```

Pascal checks that the value of **i** is in the declared array range. But, with range checking off, Pascal allows the bad assignment, possibly overwriting another variable in memory, causing a serious, hard-to-find program bug. A good rule is to turn on range checking with {$R+} until you are positive your program operates correctly. Because this generates code to check variable ranges while a program runs, though, most programmers turn off range checking for their finished and tested production versions, gaining every possible bit of speed.

Sorting Arrays

A useful demonstration of arrays is a program to sort a list of things into ascending order. The next example sorts an array of numbers, but you can use the same method to sort strings or other values.

Entire books are devoted to sorting algorithms, and there isn't room to compare all methods here. Of them all, though, the method in Program 5-5 offers a reliable compromise between speed and size—as long as the number of things to sort is not too large, no more than about 500 elements. The method is the *binary insertion sort*.

Program 5-5 declares an array in line 6 as a new type **ElementArray**. The square brackets following the key word **ARRAY** surround a scalar subrange indicating the maximum number of things that the array can hold. Line 5 declares single **Element**s as integers. You could also write line 6 this way:

```
ElementArray = ARRAY[ 1 .. 100 ] OF Integer;
```

Rather than directly using the constant 100 in the array declaration, the constant **MaxElements** lets other places in the program know what the array limits are. (See lines 38 and 40.) This also makes it easy to change the maximum number of elements in the array—just modify the constant in line 3. For a test, try setting **MaxElements** to 200. Because such changes are easy to make, it's usually a good idea to let constants rather than literal values define array limits.

Program 5-5

```
1:   PROGRAM BinarySort;
2:   CONST
3:      MaxElements = 100;   { Maximum array size }
4:   TYPE
5:      Element = Integer;
6:      ElementArray = ARRAY[ 1 .. MaxElements ] OF Element;
7:   VAR
8:      a : ElementArray;
9:      i, n : Integer;
10:
11:  PROCEDURE Sort( VAR a : ElementArray; n : Integer );
12:  { n = actual number elements in array a }
13:  { Algorithm = Binary Insertion }
14:  VAR
15:     i, j, Bottom, Top, Middle : Integer;
16:     Temp : Element;
17:  BEGIN
18:     FOR i := 2 TO n DO
19:     BEGIN
20:        Temp := a[ i ]; Bottom := 1; Top := i - 1;
21:        WHILE Bottom <= Top DO
22:        BEGIN
23:           Middle := ( Bottom + Top ) DIV 2;
24:           IF Temp < a[ Middle ]
25:              THEN Top := Middle - 1
26:              ELSE Bottom := Middle + 1
```

Program 5-5 *cont.*

```
27:        END; { while }
28:        FOR j := i - 1 DOWNTO Bottom DO
29:           a[ j + 1 ] := a[ j ];
30:        a[ Bottom ] := Temp
31:     END { for }
32:  END; { Sort }
33:
34:  BEGIN
35:     Writeln( 'Binary Insertion Sort' );
36:     Writeln;
37:     REPEAT
38:        Write( 'How many? (2 to ', MaxElements, ')? ' );
39:        Readln( n )
40:     UNTIL n <= MaxElements;
41:     FOR i := 1 TO n DO
42:     BEGIN
43:        a[ i ] := Random( Maxint );
44:        Write( a[ i ]:8 )
45:     END; { for }
46:     Writeln; Writeln;
47:     Sort( a, n );
48:     FOR i := 1 TO n DO
49:        Write( a[ i ]:8 );
50:     Writeln
51:  END.
```

Using the Sorting Program

Program 5-5 starts in line 35 by prompting for the number of elements to sort, setting **n** to this value. A **FOR** loop at line 41 inserts random values into the array from position 1 to **n**. In Turbo Pascal, the built-in function **Random** returns randomly sequenced numbers. (See line 43.) **Maxint** is a predeclared constant equal to the maximum integer value 32,767. The effect of **Random(Maxint)** is to select integers at random from the range of 0 to 32,766, one less than the parameter in parentheses. You could use other parameter values, too. For example, **Random(100)** returns values at random from 0 to 99. (Chapter 12 discusses **Random** in more detail.)

Notice how in line 43, variable **i** indexes the array **a**. Line 44 writes the value of **a[i]**, displaying the raw data before sorting. In a similar way, after sorting, another **FOR** loop at line 48 writes the now-ordered values in the array.

How the Binary Insertion Sort Works

Exercise 3-5 asks you to invent a number-guessing game. The solution is childishly simple—just keep dividing successive guesses in half, asking if each guess is high or low, until you get the answer. Surprisingly, this simple idea is the very basis for the binary insertion sort. It's a *binary* method because of the way it keeps dividing the array of elements in two, bisecting the remaining values, looking for the correct position where each value belongs.

The method operates by starting from the second element (it wouldn't make sense to sort only one number), and proceeding with a **FOR** loop at line 18, up to the number of elements (**n**) in the array. The program sets variable **Temp** equal to each element in turn (line 20) while two other variables **Bottom** and **Top** specify the range of indexes between **i** and **i − 1**, the portion of the array currently being sorted. This action repeats for successive values of **i** until the entire array is in order.

The **WHILE** loop (lines 21–27) uses the guessing-game strategy to find where between **Top** and **Bottom** the value of **Temp** belongs. Examine line 23 to see how the program locates the middle of **a[Bottom]** to **a[Top]**. After finding where **Temp** goes, the **FOR** loop at line 28 shuffles elements greater than **Temp** upward, dropping **Temp** into the correct place with an assignment statement in line 30.

If this description seems hard to understand, take eight playing cards ranking from two to nine, shuffle and lay them out as though they were the elements of the array, then play computer, manually following the binary insertion method to put your cards in order. Write down the values of program variables as you go along. A little experimenting—with Program 5-5 as a guide—shows you the inner workings of the binary insertion sort better than any possible narration of this fascinating algorithm.

Arrays with Multiple Dimensions

An array can have multiple dimensions. Such an array has another array at every indexed position. There are two ways to declare multiple-dimension arrays in Pascal. For example, the following declares two equivalent arrays, **A** and **B**:

```
VAR
    A : ARRAY[ 1 .. 4 ] OF ARRAY[ 1 .. 4 ] OF Char;
    B : ARRAY[ 1 .. 4, 1 .. 4 ] OF Char;
```

Both **A** and **B** are arrays of four four-character arrays. One way to visualize multiple-dimension arrays is to imagine their having rows and columns, as illustrated in Figure 5-6. Every array position has a unique row and column number. Writing **B[3,2]** locates the element at row 3, column 2. The computer screen you probably have nearby is a multidimensional array of characters that a program could represent like this:

```
VAR
    Screen : ARRAY[ 1 .. 25, 1 .. 80 ] OF Char;
```

```
                              COLUMNS
                    1         2         3         4
        R    1 | [1,1] | [1,2] | [1,3] | [1,4]
        O    2 | [2,1] | [2,2] | [2,3] | [2,4]
        W    3 | [3,1] | [3,2] | [3,3] | [3,4]
        S    4 | [4,1] | [4,2] | [4,3] | [4,4]
```

Figure 5-6 Two-dimensional arrays form a row and column matrix.

For better compatibility among different computers, though, you'd be wise to declare the maximum screen dimensions as constants and use those constants in the array declaration. That way, you can easily change your program to new display formats:

```
CONST
    RowMax = 25;    { Number rows on IBM PC }
    ColMax = 80;    { Monochrome display }
TYPE
    Rows = 1 .. RowMax;
    Cols = 1 .. ColMax;
VAR
    Screen : ARRAY[ Rows, Cols ] OF Char;
```

The new declaration uses constants and subranges of integers, building on those simple elements to finally declare the array variable, **Screen**. Notice how clear it is that **Screen** is an array of rows and columns. Because **Rows** and **Cols** already define subranges of integers, there is no need to use ellipses in the **ARRAY** declaration. Such clarity makes it easy to modify the program, changing the number of columns by revising one constant, **ColMax**, in this example. Redesigning an entire program to operate with a 40-column display also requires a single change—just replace constant 80 with 40. By following a similar approach for all array declarations, you'll make future modifications that much easier—especially in programs with hundreds or thousands of lines.

Beyond the Fourth Dimension

Be careful when declaring multidimensional arrays not to get carried away. While you can have up to 255 multiple dimensions in Turbo Pascal, there are few cases where more than three do much good. The following declares an array of three dimensions, each having ten elements:

```
VAR
    Cube : ARRAY[ 1 .. 10,1 .. 10,1 .. 10 ] OF Char;
```

In the same way that a two-dimensional array has rows and columns, a three-dimensional array resembles a cube, with depth as well as width and height. The cube declared here, though, occupies 1000 bytes ($10 \times 10 \times 10$) of computer memory! Adding a fourth dimension of ten elements increases that to 10,000 bytes, and adding a fifth, at 100,000 bytes, makes the array too large for Turbo Pascal to handle as a simple variable. (The maximum size for any variable is about 65,000 bytes. It's possible to create variables larger than that, but this is a technique for a later chapter.)

Scalar Indexes

Arrays may contain variables of any Pascal type, but array indexes must be scalar data types, such as integers, characters, or your own enumerated data types. For example, you can declare an array of strings, indexed by the scalar **Colors** type defined earlier:

```
VAR
    ColorNames : ARRAY[ Colors ] OF String[20];
```

This declares an array of four strings, each 20 characters long. Scalar elements like **Blue** and **Green** are the array indexes. The following seven lines assign strings to all array positions:

```
ColorNames[ Red    ] := 'Red';
ColorNames[ Orange ] := 'Orange';
ColorNames[ Yellow ] := 'Yellow';
ColorNames[ Green  ] := 'Green';
ColorNames[ Blue   ] := 'Blue';
ColorNames[ Indigo ] := 'Indigo';
ColorNames[ Violet ] := 'Violet';
```

The statements assign character strings to each array position, associating one string per scalar element. Remember, scalar elements like **Red**, **Orange**, and **Yellow** are just numbers as far as Turbo Pascal is concerned. The scalar identifiers exist only in the program text. The same identifiers do not exist in the compiled code. If you have a variable **Color** of type **Colors**, this means you cannot display the *name* of the color with the statements:

```
Color := Red;
Writeln( Color ); {Incorrect!!}
```

If you try this, the compiler complains with:

```
Error 64: Cannot Read or Write variables of this type
```

A variable of type **Colors**, or of any other enumerated data type, is not something that **Writeln** can directly display. Instead, you must use the string array of color names. This fixes the problem:

```
Color := Red;
Writeln( ColorNames[ Color ] );
```

ColorNames is an array of strings, which **Writeln** certainly can display. For an even better example, add the previous seven assignments along with the **ColorNames** array declaration to Program 5-3. Then change the **FOR** loop to read:

```
FOR Color := Red TO Violet DO
   Writeln( ColorNames[ Color ] )
```

When you run the program, you see the names of the colors instead of their scalar values as in the unmodified version. If all of this seems like a lot of trouble just to display seven strings, look back through the examples we've covered and notice how readable they are. The **FOR** loop is perfectly clear and, interestingly, is almost entirely composed of English words—anyway, at least Englishlike words.

As these examples illustrate, carefully chosen enumerated types help you to write clear and understandable programs that are easy to modify. Of course, it's up to you to put these features to work!

The Lack of Packing

Many Pascal compilers allow packing of arrays and other variables. Packing squeezes as many variables of a data type into as small a space as possible, usually at the expense of speed. Turbo Pascal, though, has no facilities for packing. If it did, you could declare an array like this:

```
VAR
   Switches : PACKED ARRAY[ 0 .. 7 ] OF Boolean;
```

In Turbo Pascal, the **Switches** array occupies eight bytes of memory. With some other Pascal compilers, the same declaration occupies one byte of memory with each bit of the byte taking one array position. This is possible because **Boolean** values **True** and **False** require only one bit to represent, with 0 equal to **False**, and 1 equal to **True**. Therefore, compilers that allow packing can squeeze eight Boolean variables into one eight-bit byte.

Although Turbo Pascal recognizes the word **PACKED**, it completely ignores it. Because of this, you may encounter published programs that do not operate correctly if they rely on packing.

Records

While arrays collect identically typed elements, another kind of collector, the Pascal record, assembles dissimilar elements under one roof. A record can contain any number of any kind of Pascal variables you can devise. To say the least, that's a powerful versatility.

A record declaration (Figure 5-7) begins with the key word **RECORD** and ends with **END**. In between is a *field list* of identifiers and types, which looks similar to a variable declaration. The similarity is no accident. Individual fields in records are just variables that the record contains. Having the fields in one record definition lets a program treat the collection of variables as a unit for some operations, or as individual variables for others.

record

field list

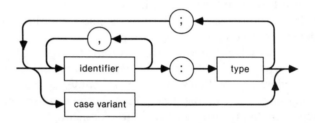

Figure 5-7 Pascal records contain lists of fields; individual fields are
variables that the record holds together.

Compare the field list railroad diagram in Figure 5-7 with the diagram for variable declarations (Figure 1-5). Like variables, record fields have identifiers and types separated by semicolons. To save typing, you can declare multiple variables of the same type together, separating their identifiers with commas. For now, ignore the part of the diagram in Figure 5-7 labeled *case variant*. We'll cover that in a moment.

Program 5-6 declares a new type **DateRec** as a record containing two subrange variables, **Month** and **Day**, plus an integer variable, **Year**. In lines 13–15, the program assigns values to the fields of the **Date** record variable declared in line 10 as type **DateRec**.

Program 5-6

```
1:   PROGRAM DateTest;
2:   TYPE
3:      DateRec =
4:         RECORD
```

Program 5-6 *cont.*

```
 5:          Month : 0 .. 12;   { 0 = no date }
 6:          Day   : 1 .. 31;
 7:          Year  : Integer
 8:       END;
 9:  VAR
10:     Date : DateRec;
11:  BEGIN
12:     Writeln( 'Date Test' );
13:     Date.Day := 16;
14:     Date.Month := 5;
15:     Date.Year := 72;
16:     Writeln( Date.Month, '/', Date.Day, '/', Date.Year )
17:  END.
```

To use a field of a record, precede it with a period. The statement **Write(Date.Day)**, for example, writes the **Day** field of a **Date**. After assigning values to all fields of the **Date** record, line 16 of Program 5-6 writes the assigned date in common mm/dd/yy format.

A shorthand method avoids typing the record name **Date** over and over as you did in line 16 of Program 5-6. Key word **WITH** (Figure 5-8) tells Pascal to associate identifiers with a specific record name, saving keystrokes while making the program more readable. Using **WITH**, you can use multiple field names without repeating the record name in front. For example, replace lines 13–16 of Program 5-6 with the following compound statement:

```
WITH Date DO
BEGIN
   Day := 16;
   Month := 5;
   Year := 72;
   Writeln( Month, '/', Day, '/', Year )
END;
```

Because of the **WITH**, the compiler knows that **Month**, **Day**, and **Year** are fields in record **Date**.

with

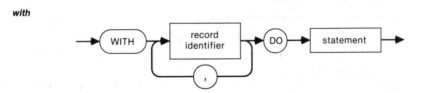

Figure 5-8 **WITH** statement railroad diagram.

Keeping Records

One of the most common uses for computers is to store and retrieve information about people and things. Let's say you are elected president of a neighborhood club and you want to computerize data on club members. You might start by inventing a Pascal record for each person's name.

NameRec in Program 5-7 defines a Pascal record containing four fields. The program lets you enter information into each of these fields (lines 15–18). Notice how the **WITH** statement (line 13) avoids having to type **Name.LastName** or **Name.FirstName**. Line 20 displays the fields in correct order.

By storing each part of a person's name in separate fields, you can write names in a variety of ways. For example, a directory listing of all club members would probably look best with names ordered last name first. To do that, replace line 20 of Program 5-7 with this statement:

```
Writeln( LastName, ', ', FirstName, ' ', Initial )
```

At other times, you might want to abbreviate a member's first name for printing on mailing labels. This is easily done by indexing the first character of the field, **FirstName**. (Remember, strings are just specialized arrays of characters.)

```
IF Length( FirstName ) > 0
    THEN Write( FirstName[1], ' ' );
Writeln( LastName )
```

Why use the **IF** statement? If the length of the string **FirstName** is zero, then indexing the first character of the string causes a runtime range error to occur (if range checking is turned on with the compiler option, {$R + }). Although most people have first names, and you may think a blank first name field is a situation that will never occur, it's a good idea to write programs that work for all cases, especially the unlikely ones.

Program 5-7

```
 1:  PROGRAM NameTest;
 2:  TYPE
 3:     NameRec =
 4:        RECORD
 5:           LastName  : String[20];
 6:           FirstName : String[20];
 7:           Initial   : Char;
 8:           Preface   : String[8]
 9:        END;
10:  VAR
11:     Name : NameRec;
```

Program 5-7 *cont.*

```
12:  BEGIN
13:     WITH Name DO
14:     BEGIN
15:        Write( 'Last name  ? ' ); Readln( LastName );
16:        Write( 'First name ? ' ); Readln( FirstName );
17:        Write( 'Initial    ? ' ); Readln( Initial );
18:        Write( 'Mr, Mrs, Ms? ' ); Readln( Preface );
19:        Writeln;
20:        Writeln( 'Name = ',
21:                  Preface, '. ', FirstName, ' ',
22:                  Initial, '. ', LastName            )
23:     END
24:  END.
```

Records As Building Blocks

Record fields can themselves be records containing still other fields. Such complex structures are easy to construct in Turbo Pascal. Starting with **NameRec** from Program 5-7, a program could define a new record like this:

```
VAR
    Couple :
      RECORD
          Husband, Wife : NameRec
      END;
```

Couple is a record variable containing two **NameRec** records. To write the husband's name, you could use this statement:

```
Writeln( Couple.Husband.LastName );
```

Husband is a field in the **Couple** record. **LastName** is a field in the **Husband** record. The periods and record variable identifiers define a sort of *path* down to the individual field you want, here **LastName**. Similarly, a program could read the wife's first name in a **Readln** statement:

```
Readln( Couple.Wife.FirstName );
```

From these examples, you can see the value of the **WITH** statement. Instead of repeating **Couple.Wife** over and over, to write the husband's name, you could use this simple statement:

```
WITH Couple.Husband DO
    Writeln( LastName, ', ', FirstName, ' ', Initial )
```

Nested WITH Statements

When using multiple **WITH** statements, you have a choice of two styles to choose from. Assume you have the following **RECORD** variable:

```
Student :
   RECORD
      Name : NameRec;
      Age : integer
   END;
```

To write fields **LastName** and **Age** in record **Student**, you could use the following statement:

```
WITH Student DO WITH Name DO
   Write( LastName, ' is ', Age, ' years old' );          .
```

The double **WITH**s tell the compiler first how to find fields **Age** and **Name** in **Student** and then how to find field **LastName** in **Name**. You can also use the following statement to do the same thing:

```
WITH Student, Name DO
   Write( LastName, ' is ', Age, ' years old' );
```

Separating multiple-level record fields with commas is the same as using multiple **WITH**s. In general, the form:

```
WITH r1 DO WITH r2 DO WITH r3 DO
```

reduces to the simpler:

```
WITH r1,r2,r3 DO
```

Mixing Data Structures

Pascal allows mixing complex data structures. A program can have arrays of records, records of arrays, and other combinations. For example, with an array of name records, you have the beginnings of a database system for keeping track of club members. Let's say there is a maximum of five members. (Yours is a very exclusive club.) Here's how the first part of the program looks:

```
CONST
   MaxMembers = 5;
TYPE
   {NameRec declaration from Program 5-7}
```

```
VAR
   Members : ARRAY[ 1 .. MaxMembers ] OF NameRec;
   Membership : 0 .. MaxMembers;
```

Members is an array of five **NameRec** records. **Membership** holds the number of members currently in the array. To complete the program, you need only a few simple procedures to enter and display individual records in the array. Program 5-8 contains some of these items.

Program 5-8

```
 1:   PROGRAM ClubDataBase;
 2:   CONST
 3:      MaxMembers = 5;
 4:   TYPE
 5:      Member =
 6:         RECORD
 7:            Name      : String[30];
 8:            Phone     : String[12];
 9:            Charges   : Real;
10:            Payments  : Real
11:         END; { Member }
12:   VAR
13:      Members : ARRAY[ 1 .. MaxMembers ] OF Member;
14:      Membership : 0 .. MaxMembers;
15:      Choice : Char;
16:
17:   PROCEDURE AddRecords;
18:   BEGIN
19:      IF Membership = MaxMembers
20:         THEN Writeln( 'Membership is full' ) ELSE
21:         BEGIN
22:            Writeln( 'Add new records' );
23:            Membership := Membership + 1;
24:            WITH Members[ Membership ] DO
25:            BEGIN
26:               Write( 'Name      : ' ); Readln( Name );
27:               Write( 'Phone     : ' ); Readln( Phone );
28:               Write( 'Charges   : ' ); Readln( Charges );
29:               Write( 'Payments  : ' ); Readln( Payments )
30:            END { with }
31:         END { else }
32:   END; { AddRecords }
33:
34:   PROCEDURE ListRecords;
35:   VAR
```

Program 5-8 *cont.*

```
36:     number : Integer;
37:  BEGIN
38:     FOR number := 1 TO Membership DO
39:        WITH Members[ number ] DO
40:           Writeln( number, ' : ', name,
41:                      ' ', Phone, Charges-Payments:8:2 );
42:  END; { ListRecords }
43:
44:  BEGIN
45:     Writeln( 'Club Database' );
46:     Membership := 0;
47:     REPEAT
48:        Writeln;
49:        Writeln( 'Number of members = ', Membership );
50:        Write( 'A.dd, E.dit, L.ist, Q.uit ? ' );
51:        Readln( choice ); choice := Upcase( choice );
52:        CASE choice OF
53:           'A' : AddRecords;
54:           'E' : Writeln( 'Sorry, no editing yet' );
55:           'L' : ListRecords
56:        END { case }
57:     UNTIL choice = 'Q'
58:  END.
```

In Program 5-8, procedures **AddRecords** and **ListRecords** enter and display names and phone numbers in the club membership database. The program evolved from a top-down design, starting at the main body in lines 44–58.

Line 46 initializes **Membership** to zero members. The **REPEAT** loop in lines 47–57 prompts for choices from a menu displayed by a **Write** statement (line 50). To simplify the **CASE** statement selectors, the built-in function, **Upcase**, converts character variable **Choice** to uppercase. The **CASE** statement in lines 52–56 tests **Choice**, calling procedure **AddRecords** if you type A or **ListRecords** if you type L. Because of pressure from the club business manager to market the program, this early release has an unfinished editing operation. If you type E, the program displays the message, "Sorry, no editing yet."

AddRecords at lines 17–32 adds one new record. First, an **IF** statement (line 19) tests if the number of members is already at the maximum. If so, it prints an error message; otherwise, the **ELSE** clause executes in lines 21–31. There, the number of members increases (line 23), and you're prompted for the new name, phone number, charges, and payments. For variety, the **Member** record definition (lines 5–11) includes two real-number fields, **Charges** and **Payments**.

Notice in line 24 how **WITH** indicates which record to use from the **Members** array. Without the **WITH** statement, you'd have to index the array directly in each of the four **Readln** statements in lines 26–29, something like this:

```
Readln( Members[ Membership ].Name );
```

Besides cluttering up the program and making the poor programmer work harder than necessary, repeating an array index also leads to slower running times. When you index an array, as in this **Readln** statement, the compiler generates programming to calculate the memory address of an array element. It repeats this time-consuming calculation for every array indexing operation. Using **WITH**, however, lets the compiler do the address calculation a single time, locating **Members[Membership]** and then using the same address repeatedly in lines 26–29. Appropriate **WITH** statements are not purely cosmetic, then. They often contribute to faster-running programs, too.

Procedure **ListRecords** displays the club database in a **FOR** loop at lines 38–41. Again, **WITH** easily—and efficiently—refers to individual member records in the **Members** array. The **Writeln** statement (lines 40–41) displays one name and phone number along with the club member's account balance, calculated by subtracting **Payments** from **Charges**.

Variant Records

The syntax diagram in Figure 5-7 indicates that a field list may have something called a *case variant* in addition to regular field identifiers and types. A case variant allows records to have different structures dependent on one condition or another.

case variant

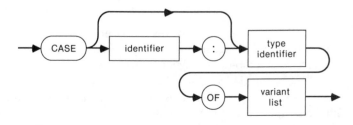

variant list

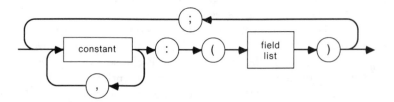

Figure 5-9 Records may contain a case variant part, overlaying different fields at the same physical position in the record.

Looking at the syntax for a case variant (top Figure 5-9), you see it begins with the key word **CASE** followed by an optional identifier and colon. After that comes a type identifier, the key word **OF** and then a variant list. Together, the identifier, colon, and type make up a *tag field*. For example, a case variant might begin:

```
CASE Married : Boolean OF
```

This prepares two cases: one if the Boolean tag **Married** is true; another if it's false. Tag fields can also be any scalar type such as **Char** or **Integer**. For example:

```
CASE Number : Integer OF
```

The integer **Number** tag field prepares two, three, a dozen or more case variants, with an individual record field list for each variation. You might complete the record definition this way:

```
RECORD
   CASE Number : Integer OF
      1 : ( i : Integer );
      2 : ( r : Real );
      3 : ( s : String[10] )
   END;
```

You now have three variations: one with an integer field **i**, another with field **r**, and a third with field **s**. Only one variation exists at a time. You can use field **i** or **s**, but not both. There is one **END**, not two, at the end of the record and case variant as correctly shown here.

In these examples, tag fields **Married** and **Number** are fields in the record definition, just like any other fields. However, the fields that follow them are based on the tag field values. A good example of how to use case variant records is the common database practice of storing certain parameters in the first record, with the real information beginning at record number two. To do this requires a record structure that varies according to what goes in the record. The program starts by defining a scalar type listing the different kinds of records in the database:

```
TYPE
   RecordType = ( Active, Deleted, System );
```

A record marked **Active** contains actual data, **Deleted** records contain old information, and **System** records indicate a special use. The record has a tag field of type **RecordType** with each scalar element selecting one variation of what goes in the record. Figure 5-10 shows the complete declaration.

```
OneRecord =
  RECORD
    CASE Kind : RecordType OF
      Active : ( Data : String[30] );
      Deleted : ( Link : Integer );
      System : ( NumRecs : Integer )
  END;
```

Figure 5-10 This record type has three variations, selected by the scalar elements, **Active**, **Deleted**, and **System**.

Kind is the tag field. If **Kind** is **Active**, then Pascal selects the **Active** variation field list in parentheses, allowing a string of **Data** in the record. If **Kind** is **Deleted**, then the record contains a **Link**, an integer variable intended to link together all deleted records. (How that is accomplished is not important here.) The final variation occurs when **Kind** is **System**, indicating a record that contains a special value, here the number of active records (**NumRecs**) currently in the database.

It is important to understand that each variation in a variant record physically overlays the others (Figure 5-11). **NumRecs**, **Link**, and **Data** all occupy the *same* memory space, and, therefore, only one variation exists inside the record at a time.

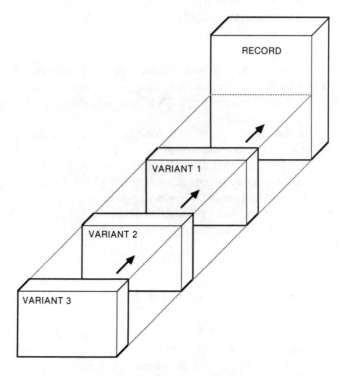

Figure 5-11 Variant parts of a record overlay each other at the same physical location in the record.

Records with a tag field case variant structure are called *discriminated unions*. All variations are united in one record definition, discriminated by the values of the tag field.

To allow for all variations, the total size of the record is equal to the size of the largest variant. In Figure 5-10, the largest variant is the **Data** string. Regardless of the actual tag field value, the record is always large enough to hold a 30-character string. Smaller variations, such as the two-byte integer fields **Deleted** and **System**, waste the extra space required by **Data** fields.

Another example shows how to mix regular fields with a case variant, which must always come last in the record declaration. Suppose you decide to add a case variant to the member club records in Figure 5-12. You want to indicate whether a member is married and, if so, you want to keep the name of that member's spouse along with a wedding date. For unmarried members, you instead plan to record the name and phone number of a friend. Combining these exclusive cases—a person can only be married or not—saves space in the record because the variations physically overlay each other in memory. Figure 5-12 shows the new record definition.

```
Member =
RECORD
    Name        : String[30];
    Phone       : String[12];
    Charges     : Real;
    Payments    : Real;
    CASE married : Boolean OF

      True : ( SpouseName : String[30];
               DateMarried : DateRec    );

      False : ( FriendName : String[30];
                FriendPhone : String[12] )

END; { Member }
```

Figure 5-12 The club **Member** record type redefined with a case variant indicating whether a member is married.

Tag field **Married** indicates if this member is married. If so, the **True** variation stores two fields, **SpouseName** and **DateMarried** in the record. If **Married** is false, then the false variant takes over, storing a friend's name and phone number. The **True** and **False** variations—both contained in parentheses—occupy the same space in the record. A program can test a member record tag field and take appropriate action:

```
WITH Members[3] DO
    IF NOT Married
        THEN InviteToBachelorParty
```

There is nothing to prevent you, however, from using the wrong variation. This faulty statement causes a bug in the club database program:

```
WITH Members[3] DO
   Writeln( 'Phone = ', FriendPhone );
```

The variant field **FriendPhone** exists only if **Married** is false, a fact the foregoing statement ignores. If **Married** is true, then **FriendPhone** does not exist, and the program must not use that field. It is up to you to write programs that access only existing fields. The compiler does not check this error for you.

In this example, **DateMarried** and **FriendPhone** overlay each other at the same physical location in the record (see Figure 5-11), but it's your responsibility to know which variation is active. From this observation, you can see that case variants let you overlay two fields of different types and simultaneously use them both. This ability also lets you easily translate a variable of one type to another. In this case, you don't even need a tag field, leading to one of Pascal's most infamous constructions, the *free union*.

Free Unions

A free union is a case variant record without a tag field. The **CASE** part of the record declares an unidentified type, a nameless entity that occupies no space. Most typical is the Boolean free union:

```
Trick :
   RECORD
      CASE Boolean OF
         True  : ( Ch : Char );
         False : ( n  : Byte )
   END;
```

A **Trick** record declared as above has two variations, a character variable **Ch** and a byte **n**. Because there is no tag field identifier, both variations occupy the same total space taken up by the record. This lets a program trick Pascal into translating characters into bytes. For example, you can write:

```
Trick.Ch := 'A';
```

This assigns 'A' to the character variant of the **Trick** record. To write this same data as a byte value, use the other variant:

```
Writeln( 'Value = ', Trick.n );
```

Or you can do the reverse, assigning a value to the byte variant and fooling Pascal into treating that value as a character:

```
Trick.n := 65;
Writeln( 'Character = s', Trick.ch );
```

Because 65 is the ASCII value for character A and because the freely united fields **n** and **Ch** occupy the same space, the foregoing **Writeln** displays an A. As you can see, this effectively subverts Pascal's normal type checking that ordinarily prevents mixing numbers and characters.

Nesting Case Variants

One case variant may contain another variant, which may contain yet another variant part, and so on. The only restriction is that case variants, however many there are, must be last in the record definition.

With variations on top of variations, you can design complex record structures in Pascal. As an example, imagine you are designing a computer operating system with a disk directory listing the files on a floppy disk. In the file directory, the software needs to distinguish between active and deleted files. It also needs to categorize the active entries further. All this is easily done in a single multivariant record definition (Figure 5-13).

```
FileEntry : RECORD
    CASE TypeOfDir : DirKind OF
       Deleted :
          (OldName : FileName;
           DeleteDate : DateRec);
       Active :
          (Fname : FileName; UpDated : DateRec;
           CASE TypeOfFile : FileKind OF
              TextFile :
                 ( CharsInFile : Integer;
                   Markers :
                    ARRAY[1..8] OF
                      RECORD
                        Label : String[8];
                        Offset : Integer
                      END );
              CodeFile :
                 ( Processor : (P6502,P8080,PZ80,P8088,P8086);
                   StartAddress : Integer );
              DataFile :
                 ( BytesPerRec : Integer )
END; { FileEntry record }
```

Figure 5-13 File name entry record from an imaginary disk operating system showing that multiple case variants allow complex, dynamic record structures in Pascal.

The example record makes use of two enumerated data types, **DirKind** and **FileKind**, defined as:

```
DirKind = (Deleted, Active);
FileKind = (TextFile, CodeFile, DataFile);
```

In a real system, those definitions probably would contain still other scalar elements. Each **FileEntry** record distinguishes its directory type with a case variant tag field, **TypeOfDir**.

Deleted variants store only **OldName** and **DeleteDate** fields while **Active** variants store a file name and date, plus a second, nested case variant with tag field **TypeOfFile**. **TextFile** variants store information possibly needed by a text editor or word processor. **CodeFile** variants store information about the computer processor. **DataFile** variants store the file size. With all variations under one tag field stored in the same space, the record compacts its information as much as possible, even if its definition looks long and complicated. Used this way, case variants lead to efficient record sizes.

Although imaginary, Figure 5-13 realistically illustrates how to use case variants. In fact, one operating system, the UCSD P-system, popular in the early 1980s, uses a similar record structure for its disk directories.

Sets

Sets define collections of zero or more elements of a certain scalar or subrange base type. The railroad diagram in Figure 5-14 shows that a set starts with the key words **SET OF** followed by a *simple type*, which might be a scalar or subrange of integer. For example, you could have a base type of months defined as an enumerated data type:

```
Months = (Jan,Feb,Mar,Apr,
          May,Jun,Jul,Aug,
          Sep,Oct,Nov,Dec );
```

set type

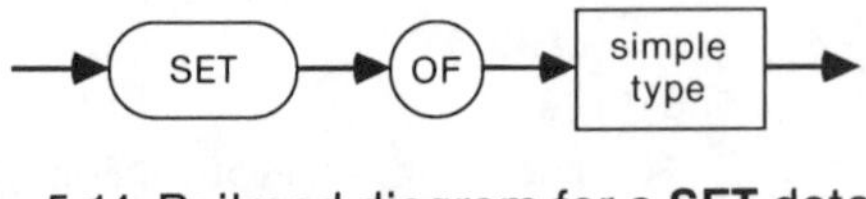

Figure 5-14 Railroad diagram for a **SET** data type.

Your program can then define set types and variables of the **Month** ranges, **Jan . . Dec**:

```
TYPE
    MonthSetType = SET OF Months;
```

```
VAR
   MonthSet : MonthSetType;
   Thirties : SET OF Months;
```

MonthSet and **Thirties** are set variables of the scalar base type, **Months**. To such variables, you can assign subsets of base type elements. One way to do this is to enclose a subrange of scalar elements in brackets:

```
MonthSet := [ Jan .. Dec ];
```

With this assignment, **MonthSet** defines the set of all 12 months. As it does in an array or integer subrange declaration, the ellipsis indicates a range between two scalar values. The first value must have an ordinal number less than or equal to the second. That's only logical. It would make no sense to write **[Dec . . Jan]**.

Another way to define sets is to bracket individual elements separated by commas. To assign to **Thirties** the set of months having 30 days, you could write:

```
Thirties := [ Sep, Apr, Jun, Nov ];
```

Thirties now defines a 4-month subset of its base type—the months with 30 days each. Notice that, unlike a subrange, the order of the individual elements is unimportant.

Sets may also be empty. To assign the empty or *null* set to **MonthSet**, use empty brackets. There aren't any months in this set:

```
MonthSet := [];
```

After assigning a set of elements to a set variable, Pascal's **IN** operator tests for the presence of a specific base type element. The following tests if April has 30 days:

```
IF ( Apr IN Thirties )
   THEN Writeln( 'Has 30 days!' );
```

The Boolean expression **(Apr IN Thirties)** evaluates to true or false. Program 5-9 uses a similar expression along with the **IN** operator to list which months have 30 days.

Program 5-9

```
1:  PROGRAM ThirtyDays;
2:  TYPE
3:     Months = (Jan, Feb, Mar, Apr, May, Jun,
4:               Jul, Aug, Sep, Oct, Nov, Dec );
5:  VAR
6:     Thirties : SET OF Months;
7:     MonthNames : ARRAY[ Months ] OF String[3];
```

Program 5-9 *cont.*

```
 8:     OneMonth : Months;
 9:  BEGIN
10:     Writeln( 'Thirty Days' );
11:     Writeln;
12:
13:     MonthNames[ Jan ] := 'Jan';     MonthNames[ Feb ] := 'Feb';
14:     MonthNames[ Mar ] := 'Mar';     MonthNames[ Apr ] := 'Apr';
15:     MonthNames[ May ] := 'May';     MonthNames[ Jun ] := 'Jun';
16:     MonthNames[ Jul ] := 'Jul';     MonthNames[ Aug ] := 'Aug';
17:     MonthNames[ Sep ] := 'Sep';     MonthNames[ Oct ] := 'Oct';
18:     MonthNames[ Nov ] := 'Nov';     MonthNames[ Dec ] := 'Dec';
19:
20:     Thirties := [ Sep, Apr, Jun, Nov ];
21:     FOR OneMonth := Jan TO Dec DO
22:     BEGIN
23:       Write( MonthNames[ OneMonth ] );
24:       IF OneMonth IN Thirties
25:           THEN Writeln( ' has 30 days' )
26:           ELSE Writeln( ' does not have 30 days' )
27:     END
28:  END.
```

Assignments to the string array **MonthNames** take up most of Program 5-9. We need the array because compiled programs numerically represent elements of scalar types like **Months**, similar to the **ColorNames** example explained earlier. In other words, when the program runs, **Jan** = 0, **Feb** = 1, **Mar** = 2, and so on. To write the month *names*, therefore, you have to associate visible strings with each scalar value. This is accomplished with Program 5-9's **MonthNames** array, indexed by the scalar elements of type **Months**.

Line 20 assigns the 30-day months to set variable **Thirties**. Then the **IN** operator (line 24) tests each month for presence in the set, displaying an appropriate message.

Relational Set Operators

Relational operators = (equal) and < > (not equal) compare two sets. Both of the following expressions are true:

```
[ Jun,Jul,Aug ] <> [ Apr,May,Jun ]
[ Jan,Feb,Mar ] =  [ Mar,Feb,Jan ]
```

Inclusion operators < = and > = test if one set is a subset of another. Pronounce < = "is a subset of" and > = "has the subset." If you use this trick to read the following three statements, you immediately see all three are true:

```
[Apr,May,Jun] <= [Jan .. Dec]
         [ ] <= [Jan .. Dec]
[Jan .. Dec ] >= [Jan,Dec]
```

Notice that the null set [] is a subset of [Jan .. Dec]. In fact, by definition, the null set is a subset of *any* set.

Logical Set Operators

Three other set operators combine two or more sets according to the logical rules of *union* (+), *intersection* (∗), and *set difference* (−). The example expressions in Figure 5-15 make these operations clear.

Union
```
[Jan,Feb,Mar] + [Feb,Mar,Apr] = [Jan,Feb,Mar,Apr]
```

Intersection
```
[Jan,Feb,Mar] * [Feb,Mar,Apr] = [Feb,Mar]
```

Difference
```
[Jan,Feb,Mar] - [Feb,Mar,Apr] = [Jan]
```

Figure 5-15 Examples of the three set operators: Union (+), Intersection (∗), and Difference (−).

The *union* of two sets is the combined set of elements from set A and set B. The *intersection* of two sets is the set of common elements found in set A and set B. The *difference* of two sets is the set of elements found in set A that are not also found in set B.

Program 5-10 demonstrates these concepts. (Lines 29–34 are the same as lines 13–18 in Program 5-9. To save time, you can copy those lines rather than re-typing.)

Program 5-10

```
1:  PROGRAM SetOperators;
2:  TYPE
3:      Months = (Jan, Feb, Mar, Apr, May, Jun,
4:              Jul, Aug, Sep, Oct, Nov, Dec );
5:      MonthSet = SET OF Months;
6:  VAR
7:      MonthNames : ARRAY[ Months ] OF String[3];
8:      seta, setb : MonthSet;
9:
```

Program 5-10 *cont.*

```
10:   PROCEDURE ShowSet( S : MonthSet );
11:   VAR
12:       Separator : String[2];
13:       OneMonth : Months;
14:   BEGIN
15:     Write( '  [' );
16:     Separator := ' ';
17:     FOR OneMonth := Jan TO Dec DO
18:       IF OneMonth IN S THEN
19:         BEGIN
20:           Write( Separator, MonthNames[ OneMonth ] );
21:           Separator := ', '
22:         END; { for / if }
23:     Writeln( ' ]' );
24:     Writeln
25:   END; { ShowSet }
26:
27:   BEGIN
28:
29:       MonthNames[ Jan ] := 'Jan';      MonthNames[ Feb ] := 'Feb';
30:       MonthNames[ Mar ] := 'Mar';      MonthNames[ Apr ] := 'Apr';
31:       MonthNames[ May ] := 'May';      MonthNames[ Jun ] := 'Jun';
32:       MonthNames[ Jul ] := 'Jul';      MonthNames[ Aug ] := 'Aug';
33:       MonthNames[ Sep ] := 'Sep';      MonthNames[ Oct ] := 'Oct';
34:       MonthNames[ Nov ] := 'Nov';      MonthNames[ Dec ] := 'Dec';
35:
36:       seta := [Jan,Feb,Mar];
37:       setb := [Feb,Mar,Apr];
38:
39:       Writeln;
40:       Writeln( 'Set operators' );
41:       Writeln;
42:       Write( 'SETA = ' ); ShowSet( seta );
43:       Write( 'SETB = ' ); ShowSet( setb );
44:       Writeln;
45:
46:       Writeln( 'Union SETA + SETB' );
47:       ShowSet( seta + setb );
48:       Writeln( 'Intersection SETA * SETB' );
49:       ShowSet( seta * setb );
50:       Writeln( 'Difference SETA - SETB' );
51:       ShowSet( seta - setb )
52:   END.
```

Lines 47, 49, and 51 apply the three set operators to **seta** and **setb**. For different results, change the assigned set elements in lines 36–37 and rerun the program.

Practical Use of Sets

Besides sets of scalar types, you can also have sets of integers and characters. Turbo Pascal, however, limits sets to a maximum of 256 elements with ordinal values 0 to 255. The following variable declaration, therefore, defines the largest possible integer set:

```
NumberSet : SET OF 0 .. 255;
```

Because Turbo Pascal limits set types to subsets of the positive integers, this also limits the size of set variables. In memory, each element of a set occupies a single bit, indicating the presence (1) or absence (0) of individual elements; therefore, a set of 256 elements takes 256 bits of memory. At eight bits per memory byte, this maximum-size set takes 32 (256/8) bytes. Sets with fewer defined elements take less room. A set of zero to 127, for example, takes 16 bytes (128/8) of memory.

Character Sets

One of the more useful kinds of sets is a set of characters. Characters are scalar by nature and, as defined in Turbo Pascal, fall in the ordinal range 0 . . 255. To define a set of characters, use this declaration in your program:

```
TYPE
    CharSet = SET OF Char;
VAR
    UpperCase, LowerCase, Digits : CharSet;
```

With these declarations, you can assign appropriate character ranges to set variables **UpperCase**, **LowerCase**, and **Digits**:

```
UpperCase := [ 'A' .. 'Z' ];
LowerCase := [ 'a' .. 'z' ];
Digits    := [ '0' .. '9' ];
```

Because these are character sets, set elements are literal characters surrounded by quote marks. The set of digit characters ['0' . . '9'] is not the same as the subset of integers [0 . . 9]! The first is a set of characters; the second is a set of positive numbers.

A common programming problem is to prompt for one character from a specific set. The program rejects anything else, perhaps allowing only digits when it asks you to type a number. With character sets, the solution is simple, as demonstrated in Program 5-11.

Program 5-11

```
 1:   PROGRAM CharacterSets;
 2:   TYPE
 3:       CharSet = SET OF Char;
 4:       String40 = String[40];
 5:   VAR
 6:       UpperCase, LowerCase, Digits : CharSet;
 7:       ch : Char;
 8:
 9:   PROCEDURE GetCommand(       Prompt      : String40;
10:                              LegalChars : CharSet;
11:                          VAR Command    : Char        );
12:   { Prompt for a command character }
13:   { Return Command char only if IN LegalChars set }
14:   BEGIN
15:       REPEAT
16:          Write( prompt );
17:          Readln( Command );
18:          Writeln;
19:          IF NOT ( Command IN LegalChars )
20:             THEN Writeln( chr(7), '*** Entry error!  Try again.' )
21:       UNTIL Command IN LegalChars;
22:       Writeln( 'Character entered is: ', Command )
23:   END; { GetCommand }
24:
25:   BEGIN
26:       Writeln( 'Character Sets' );
27:       Writeln;
28:       UpperCase := [ 'A' .. 'Z' ];
29:       LowerCase := [ 'a' .. 'z' ];
30:       Digits := [ '0' .. '9' ];
31:       GetCommand( 'Enter uppercase letter: ', UpperCase, ch );
32:       GetCommand( 'Enter lowercase letter: ', LowerCase, ch );
33:       GetCommand( 'Enter a digit 0 to 9: ', Digits, ch )
34:   END.
```

Procedure **GetCommand** (lines 9–23) takes a character set parameter **LegalChars**. The routine prompts you to press a key, returning variable **Command** only if you enter one of the characters from the legal subset. This general procedure works for any subset of characters, digits, punctuation, or letters and avoids writing complicated logic tests like:

```
IF ( ch <> 'A' ) AND ( ch <> 'D' ) AND ( ch <> 'F' ) AND ( ch <> 'Q' )
   THEN Writeln( 'Error' )
```

Character sets allow a more concise statement that accomplishes the same job:

```
IF NOT (ch IN ['A','D','F','Q'])
   THEN Writeln( 'Error' );
```

Or, with the **GetCommand** procedure in Program 5-11, use this single statement, limiting variable **ch** to a specific set of responses:

```
GetCommand( '? ', ['A','D','F','Q'], ch );
```

A common mistake when using character sets is to attempt a line such as:

```
IF ch NOT IN ['A'..'Z'] THEN...
```

This will not compile because the **NOT** is in the wrong place. The correct form is:

```
IF NOT (ch IN ['A'..'Z']) THEN ...
```

The parentheses force evaluation of the Boolean expression **(ch IN ['A' .. 'Z'])**. You need to use parentheses because **NOT** has a higher precedence than **IN** (see Appendix E). Without parentheses, **NOT** incorrectly applies to **ch**, and, of course, you cannot negate characters, only numbers or Booleans.

This observation leads to dangerous grounds in Boolean set expressions. If **B** is a Boolean set, and **V** a Boolean variable, then:

```
NOT V IN B
```

does not have the expected meaning:

```
NOT (V IN B)
```

Because **NOT** has a higher precedence than **IN**, the expression **NOT V IN B** evaluates as though it were **(NOT V) IN B**. You must use parentheses as shown above if that is not your intention.

Another more serious danger occurs with numeric sets. Turbo Pascal permits negating integer values, a permission other Pascal compilers do not often grant. If **K** is an integer, then **NOT K** negates all bits in **K**. In other words, bits take their opposite values: ones turning to zeros, and zeros to ones. The result is called the *one's complement* of **K**. Be especially wary of set expressions such as these:

```
IF NOT K IN [ 1 .. 50 ] THEN...
IF NOT (K IN [ 1 .. 50 ]) THEN...
```

Those two statements may produce different results and, because of the way **NOT** applies to integers in Turbo Pascal, might cause bugs especially when you are converting programs from one Pascal compiler to another.

The answer to these problems is to *always* use parentheses to resolve even the slightest potential ambiguity. Extra parentheses come at no extra cost; the compiler merely uses them to determine the evaluation order of expressions. The parentheses themselves do not end up in the compiled program. A good rule is to use as many parentheses as needed to force the order you want. Especially when programming with sets, this is a rule to follow religiously.

Summary

In this chapter you learned how to declare new data types and add structure to Pascal variables. Subranges limit scalar variables to specific minimum and maximum values. Enumerated types use descriptive names to create new scalar data types.

Arrays collect identically typed elements together, whereas records assemble variables of mixed data types. Case variant records allow different fields to coexist in the same record space. Set variables specify subsets of scalar elements.

Pascal lets you mix these and other data structures, making arrays of arrays, arrays of records, even records of arrays or sets.

Set logical operators let you combine and compare sets in a variety of ways.

Exercises

5-1. How can you prevent illegal date assignments in Program 5-6? Test your solution with illegal dates like March 42, – 1999.

5-2. Write a program to print out the ordinal values of the Boolean scalar elements, True and False. What are the ordinal values of the expressions (NOT True), (NOT False), and (NOT(NOT True AND NOT False))?

5-3. Write a program to prompt for a string and then display individual characters vertically on the screen. Modify your program to write the characters in a diagonal line. Recall that a string is similar to an array of characters.

5-4. Modify Program 5-5 to sort strings instead of numbers. Let the user enter a variety of strings to sort. (Hint: Convert all strings to uppercase before sorting. See Program 5-4. Why?)

5-5. The mileage chart in Table 5-1 is similar to those found in many roadmaps. Write a program to initialize a multiple-dimension array with these mileages, then let the operator enter the names of two cities, printing out the distance between them.

5-6. (Advanced) Finish Program 5-8, adding a procedure to edit the records in the database.

Table 5-1 City mileage chart

	Atlanta	Baltimore	Boston	Chicago	Dallas	Los Angeles	New York
Atlanta	0	654	1108	708	822	2191	854
Baltimore	654	0	427	717	1357	2647	199
Boston	1108	427	0	1004	1753	3017	208
Chicago	708	717	1004	0	921	2048	809
Dallas	822	1357	1753	921	0	1399	1559
Los Angeles	2191	2647	3017	2048	1399	0	2794
New York	854	199	208	809	1559	2794	0

5-7. Add an address field to Program 5-8.

5-8. (Advanced) Add a feature to Program 5-8 to sort the database by last name before listing the records.

5-9. (Advanced) Incorporate the new **Member** record type (Figure 5-12) into Program 5-8. Modify procedures **AddRecords** and **ListRecords** to handle the case variant part of the new record structure.

5-10. Starting with the scalar data type:

```
DaysOfWeek = ( Sun, Mon, Tue, Wed, Thu, Fri, Sat )
```

write a program to assign work days to employee records, as might be done in a company scheduling office. Use sets to record data for each employee. A chart listing all employees and the next week's schedule is posted on the company bulletin board. Your program should create this chart.

6

Files

- Text Files
- End of File—Eof
- Closing Files
- Input and Output
- Processing Text Files
- A Utility in Disguise
- Text File Filters
- Adding Line Numbers
- One Char at a Time
- End of Line—Eoln
- Structured Files
- Files of Records
- Sequential Processing
- Chicken and Egg Files
- Testing IoResult
- Random Access Processing
- Seeking and Writing
- Appending Records
- Appending Text Files
- Processing Text Files at Random
- Advanced File Handling
- Special Functions
- Untyped Files
- Passing Files As Parameters

6

Key Words and Identifiers

Append, Assign, BlockRead, BlockWrite, Close, Eof, Eoln, Erase, FILE, FILE-OF, FilePos, FileSize, Flush, Input, IoResult, Output, Read, Readln, Rename, Reset, Rewrite, Seek, Sizeof, Text, Truncate, Write, Writeln

Computers talk to a variety of devices such as modems, printers, and disk drives. Although most devices have different characteristics, programs need standard ways to communicate with them. Files are the solution.

A file is a kind of magic door (Figure 6-1) through which programs communicate with the outside world. To establish communications, a program *opens* a file to a device. After that, it sends data to the device and, if it makes sense to do so, receives information back. When completed, the program *closes* the file, telling the computer it has finished communicating.

It is important to distinguish Pascal files from disk files, a distinction that confuses a lot of people. You are probably saving this book's example programs in files on a floppy disk. In this sense, a file is simply a named location, or group of locations, on disk. But in Pascal the meaning of a file is much broader. A Pascal file is a special kind of variable that sets up communication with *any* device. This may include not only named disk files but also printers, modems, and plotters, to name a few examples.

To avoid confusion from now on, *disk file* specifically means a data file stored by name on disk. *File* alone, however, refers to any Pascal file, including disk files but also files to communicate with printers, keyboards, and other devices. Figure 6-2 shows the railroad diagram for declaring file types.

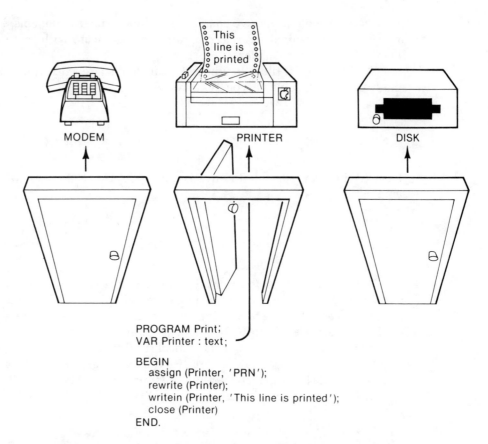

```
PROGRAM Print;
VAR Printer : text;

BEGIN
    assign (Printer, 'PRN');
    rewrite (Printer);
    writein (Printer, 'This line is printed');
    close (Printer)
END.
```

Figure 6-1 A Pascal file is like a magic door through which programs communicate with devices. This figure shows a file named **Printer** open to the computer's listing device, PRN. The program writes a line of text on paper.

file type

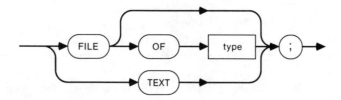

Figure 6-2 Railroad diagram for declaring Pascal file variables.

Text Files

Devices that send and receive characters include printers, modems, keyboards, and computer terminals. Pascal programs communicate with these and other character devices through *text files*.

Text is a special file data type in Pascal. To declare a text file in a program, simply create a variable of type **Text**:

```
VAR
   Printer : Text;
```

Declared this way, variable **Printer** is a text file. Here's another way to do the same thing:

```
VAR
   Printer : FILE OF Char;
```

To Pascal programs, **Printer** is just a file of characters—a place to send text. Both **FILE OF Char** and **Text** are similar, but not identical, in Turbo Pascal. In general, to read and write text in lines, use **Text**. To read and write text as individual characters, use either form. In other Pascals and Turbo Pascal versions 3.0 and earlier, these two declarations had identical results.

In a similar way, you can declare disk files of integers, strings, real numbers, or any other data type. In fact, the only data type you can't have in a file is another file. In other words, Pascal does not allow a **FILE OF FILE**.

Table 6-1 Text device file names

FileName	Description	Input	Output
'AUX'	Auxiliary device (COM1)	Yes	Yes
'CON'	Console and keyboard	Yes	Yes
'PRN'	Printer (LPT1)	No	Yes
'COM1'	Communications port 1	Yes	Yes
'COM2'	Communications port 2	Yes	Yes
'LPT1'	Line printer 1	No	Yes
'LPT2'	Line printer 2	No	Yes
'LPT3'	Line printer 3	No	Yes
'NUL'	Bit bucket	Yes	Yes
''	Standard input and output	Yes	Yes

Before you use a declared file variable, the first step is to name the device or disk file you want to access. All devices in Turbo Pascal have short three-character names (Table 6-1) that programs assign to file variables with the built-in procedure, **Assign**. For example, to prepare a file for printing, write:

```
Assign( Printer, 'PRN' );
```

This links the program text file variable **Printer** with the physical device or, more accurately, the interface circuit and cable that somewhere, you trust, attach to the actual printer. Other device names are explained in Table 6-1. After assigning a name to a text file variable, open the file for output with a **Rewrite** statement this way:

```
VAR
   printer, console : TEXT;

Assign( printer, 'PRN' );
Rewrite( printer );
Writeln( printer, 'This is printed' );
Writeln( 'This is not printed' );
```

Assigning a name to **printer** and then rewriting the file variable opens the file for later use. Here, a **Writeln** statement prints a line of text. The second **Writeln**, which does not have the opened file variable as its first parameter, operates normally, displaying a string on the screen. Including the opened file variable in **Writeln** (or **Write**) redirects the text to where you want it to go.

Why "rewrite"? In olden days of computing, which were not so long ago, a tape drive was the common file device, and **Rewrite** wound the tape to the beginning and prepared the drive for writing characters to tape—overwriting whatever was there before. Of course it makes no sense to rewind printers and modems. You just have to remember that **Rewrite** in its modern meaning opens files for output.

When used with a disk file, **Rewrite** creates a new file on disk ready to receive data. It also erases an old disk file of the same name.

Program 6-1 creates a new disk file named MYTEXT.TXT containing four lines of text. Line 5 assigns a name to the text file variable **FileVar**. Because this name is not a device name from Table 6-1, the file is created on disk. Line 6 creates the new file, and line 11 closes it, locking the new file name in the disk directory and writing any information held in memory buffers to disk. Lines 7–10 do the actual writing, using this form of the familiar **Writeln** and **Write** statements:

```
Write( [f,] v1, v2, ..., v3 );
Writeln( [f,] v1, v2, ..., v3 );
```

Write or **Writeln** may include a file variable *f*--which must be of type **Text**—followed by a comma and the things you want to write. The square brackets indicate that *f* is optional. If you don't specify a file, output normally goes to the display. Similarly, **Readln** reads lines of text from a file:

```
Read( [f,] v1, v2, ..., v3 );
Readln( [f,] v1, v2, ..., v3 );
```

Using **Readln** with a file variable reads the lines of text from MYTEXT.TXT, which you created with Program 6-1. But with a simple change, the reading program becomes a useful utility, as shown in Program 6-2.

Program 6-1

```
 1:   PROGRAM MakeText;
 2:   VAR
 3:      FileVar : Text;
 4:   BEGIN
 5:      Assign( FileVar, 'MYTEXT.TXT' );
 6:      Rewrite( FileVar );
 7:      Writeln( FileVar, 'MYTEXT -- A sample text file.' );
 8:      Writeln( FileVar, ' This program demonstrates how' );
 9:      Writeln( FileVar, ' to create and write to a disk' );
10:      Writeln( FileVar, ' text file.' );
11:      Close( FileVar )
12:   END.
```

Instead of using the literal file name 'MYTEXT.TXT', Program 6-2 lets you enter the name of any file into string variable **FileName**. Line 10 assigns **FileName** to the text file variable. Because we don't want to create a new disk file this time, line 11 uses **Reset** to open the file. **Reset** opens an existing disk file for reading and writing but does not disturb data already there. (Contrary to **Rewrite**, which works with all files, **Reset** works only with disk files and with devices that can send information to the program.)

Program 6-2

```
 1:   PROGRAM ReadText;
 2:   VAR
 3:      FileName : String[14];
 4:      FileVar  : Text;
 5:      OneLine  : String[80];
 6:   BEGIN
 7:      Writeln( 'Read text' );
 8:      Write( 'File name? ' );
 9:      Readln( FileName );
10:      Assign( FileVar, FileName );
11:      Reset( FileVar );
12:      WHILE NOT Eof( FileVar ) DO
13:      BEGIN
14:         Readln( FileVar, OneLine );
15:         Writeln( OneLine )
16:      END;
```

Program 6-2 *cont.*

```
17:     Close( FileVar )
18: END.
```

End of File—Eof

Line 12 of Program 6-2 demonstrates the built-in Boolean function, **Eof**, for "end of file." **Eof** is true after the program reads the last line from a text file. In most cases, a Ctrl-Z character (ASCII 26) marks the end of text files. **Eof** automatically becomes true when Pascal reads that character. For other kinds of files, **Eof** is true after reading the last unit of data. The **WHILE** loop at lines 12–16 tests **Eof**, ending the loop after exhausting all text in the file.

Closing Files

To avoid losing information, be sure to close your files as shown in line 11 of Program 6-1. This releases any data temporarily held by DOS in memory, a process called buffering because of the way memory, acting as a buffer zone, sits between the program and disk. Accessing disk drives takes time, and buffering data in memory speeds up disk operations by reading and writing many bytes at a time.

Closing also tells the operating system to clean up its internal file variables or *handles*, not normally accessible to your programs. If you forget to close your files, the operating system may eventually run out of handles. If this happens, you'll no longer be able to **Reset** and **Rewrite** new files.

To force the operating system to write buffered data to disk without closing the file, use **Flush**:

```
Flush( FileVar );
```

There are two main uses for **Flush**. When the computer stands idle for a time—for example, while displaying a selection menu—it's a good idea to flush buffered data to disk. Experience teaches that people sometimes turn down the brightness knob on displays. If somebody turns the computer off at that time without checking to see if a program is running, any buffered data would be irretrievably lost. For safety, the menu program could simply **Flush** all file variables. This method also avoids the time-consuming process of closing and then reopening all program files for each new menu selection.

The second place where **Flush** comes in handy is in multiuser or networked systems. Local microcomputers in the network—called *nodes*—may hold buffers of data in memory, making that data unavailable to other users. Multiuser software **Flushes** a local node's memory, making the buffered information available to all users again. Usually, there are **Lock** and **Unlock** commands for making sure that only one node receives a block of information at a time, but these are operating system commands, not part of Pascal.

Input and Output

Without a file variable, **Write** and **Writeln** default to the standard file **Output**, whereas **Read** and **Readln** default to **Input**. In other words, the following statements are equivalent:

```
Readln( s )   =  Readln( Input, s )
Writeln( s )  =  Writeln( Output, s )
```

Input and **Output** are default text files, automatically supplied for you in the absence of explicit text file variables. They are there if you want to use them, but usually they are not required.

Processing Text Files

A useful program *template*, or shell, to have around is a standard program for reading and writing text files. The program reads lines of text from a file, does something with that text, and then writes the new text somewhere else. With minor modifications, the program converts text to uppercase, counts words, searches for data, and writes output to another file, the console, or maybe the printer.

Program 6-3

```
 1:  PROGRAM CopyText;
 2:  CONST
 3:     Title = 'Copy Text';
 4:  TYPE
 5:     String132 = String[132];
 6:  VAR
 7:     InFile, OutFile : Text;
 8:
 9:  PROCEDURE OpenFiles;
10:  VAR
11:     FileName : String[14];
12:  BEGIN
13:     Write( 'Input file? ' ); Readln( FileName );
14:     Assign( InFile, FileName );
15:     Reset( InFile );
16:     Write( 'Output file? ' ); Readln( FileName );
17:     Assign( OutFile, FileName );
```

Program 6-3 *cont.*

```
18:       Rewrite( OutFile )
19:   END; { OpenFiles }
20:
21:   PROCEDURE ProcessString( VAR s : String132 );
22:   BEGIN
23:   END; { ProcessString }
24:
25:   PROCEDURE ProcessFiles;
26:   VAR
27:       s : String132;
28:   BEGIN
29:       WHILE NOT Eof( InFile ) DO
30:       BEGIN
31:          Readln( InFile, s );
32:          ProcessString( s );
33:          Writeln( OutFile, s )
34:       END { while }
35:   END; { ProcessFiles }
36:
37:   BEGIN
38:      Writeln( Title );
39:      Writeln;
40:      OpenFiles;
41:      ProcessFiles;
42:      Close( Outfile );
43:      Close( Infile )
44:   END.
```

In its basic form, Program 6-3 simply copies a text file from one place to another. When you run the program, you're asked for input and output file names which may be device names or the names of disk files. The program contains the dummy procedure **ProcessString** (lines 21–23), which you can fill in to do whatever you want to each line of text from the input file.

Procedure **OpenFiles** (lines 9–19) prompts for input and output file names. It then resets the input file and rewrites the output file. Notice that the same string variable **FileName** holds both input and output names. After assigning **FileName** to **InFile** (line 14), **FileName** is reused in line 16.

Now that the files are open, procedure **ProcessFiles** reads lines of text from the input file (line 31), calls the dummy procedure **ProcessString** (line 32), and then writes the string to the output file (line 33). These three steps repeat until reaching the end of the input file, setting **Eof** to true in line 29.

The **WHILE** loop (lines 29–34) is the correct repetitive statement to use. Why is the following procedure *not* correct?

```
REPEAT                      {Incorrect!!}
   Readln( InFile, s );
   ProcessString( s );
   Writeln( OutFile, s )
UNTIL Eof( InFile );
```

The reason this **REPEAT** loop fails is obvious if you consider what happens when reading empty files. In that case, **Eof** is true when the program opens the file. The end of an empty file, in other words, is at its beginning. The **REPEAT** loop, which always executes at least one time, tries to read a line of text from the empty file, causing an error to occur. The **WHILE** loop in Program 6-3, however, never executes if the file is empty. For bug-free results, it's always a good idea to test your programs against unusual cases such as what happens when processing empty files.

A Utility in Disguise

Program 6-3 has other uses that may not be obvious. In fact, the program is a useful utility in disguise. Of course, it copies disk text files to other disk text files, but it also displays text files on your screen. To do that, enter the name of a disk text file as the input—remember to type in the whole name, for example, MYTEXT.TXT—and then enter CON as the output file. The program reads the disk text file and writes each line to the console.

You can do the reverse, too. Enter CON as the input file and a new disk file name as the output. Don't enter the name of an existing disk file, or the **Rewrite** statement in line 18 erases it! Whatever you then type, the program writes to disk, with Program 6-3 functioning as a primitive text editor. To end typing, enter ^Z (Ctrl-Z), the character DOS recognizes as the end of file marker.

It may surprise you to learn that Program 6-3 not only copies and creates text but also serves as an electronic typewriter. Enter CON for the input file and PRN for output, and the program prints every line you type giving you the chance to edit mistakes before pressing Enter to print.

It's certainly impressive that a single program serves in so many capacities—displaying text files, creating new files, making copies of disk files, and running the printer—all by simply changing the input and output files. But let's not stop there. Filling in procedure **ProcessString** makes the program do even more.

Text File Filters

By modifying Program 6-3 in various ways, you build a collection of text file *filters* to do a number of things. A filter is a program that reads a file, modifies what it reads, and then writes the result to a new file.

As an example of writing text filters, you can easily make Program 6-3 convert text files to all uppercase. Insert a new **ProcessString** procedure (Figure 6-3) in place of lines 21–23. At the same time, change the title in line 3 to read:

```
Title  = 'Uppercase Converter';
```

```
PROCEDURE ProcessString( VAR s : String132 );
VAR
   i : Integer;
BEGIN
   FOR i := 1 TO Length( s ) DO
      s[i] := UpCase( s[i] )
END; { ProcessString }
```

Figure 6-3 To convert text files to all uppercase, insert this procedure
into Program 6-3, replacing lines 21–23.

You can also make the program display what it's doing—a visual feedback or
confirmation of the program's operation—by adding this **Writeln** statement between lines 32 and 33:

```
Writeln( s );
```

Adding Line Numbers

With an integer variable **Line** between lines 7 and 8, a statement to initialize **Line**
to zero, and a different **ProcessString** procedure (Figure 6-4), Program 6-3 adds
line numbers to text files. I used a similar program to print the listings in this book.

Add this line between lines 7 and 8

```
Line : Integer;
```

Replace lines 21–23 with this procedure

```
PROCEDURE ProcessString( VAR s : String132 );
BEGIN
   Line := Line + 1;
   Write( OutFile, Line:5, ': ' )
END; { ProcessString }
```

Add this line between lines 37 and 38

```
Line := 0;
```

Figure 6-4 Modifications to Program 6-3 to add reference line numbers
to text files.

One Char at a Time

Because of the maximum string length of 255 characters, reading text files a line at a time limits you to files with lines that are no longer. Some word-processing programs, however, use carriage returns to separate paragraphs, not lines. In this case, you have no choice but to process text one character at a time.

To demonstrate how to do this, Program 6-4 converts WordStar text files to standard ASCII format. WordStar, a popular word-processing program, stores characters in a special way that makes text unreadable by editors like Turbo Pascal's.

To avoid the line-length problem, Program 6-4 reads single characters with a **Read** statement in line 20. It then forces the character to the ordinal range 0–127 with the expression in line 21, converting eight-bit nonstandard characters to standard ASCII seven-bit format. The **Mod** operator returns the remainder of an integer division, here with the ordinal value of the original character.

Lines 22–23 convert plain carriage-return characters to carriage returns and line feeds—the output of the **Writeln** in line 23. Lines 24–25 write only characters in the visible ASCII range, skipping control characters whose values are lower than a blank.

Finally in lines 27–28, the program closes both input and output files. Notice that all program output initially goes to file TEMP.@@@ (see lines 4 and 16–17). The two lines at 29–30 erase the original input file and then rename TEMP.@@@ to whatever file name you enter to the prompt at line 36. This has the effect of preserving the original file until all processing is complete.

Program 6-4

```
 1:   PROGRAM WS2ASCII;
 2:   { Convert WordStar to ASCII text file }
 3:   CONST
 4:       TempName  = 'TEMP.@@@';
 5:   VAR
 6:       FileName : String[64];
 7:
 8:   PROCEDURE ProcessFile;
 9:   VAR
10:       i : Integer;
11:       InFile, OutFile  : Text;
12:       Ch : Char;
13:   BEGIN
14:       Assign( InFile, FileName );
15:       Reset( InFile );
16:       Assign( OutFile, TempName );
17:       Rewrite( OutFile );
18:       WHILE NOT Eof( InFile ) DO
19:       BEGIN
```

Program 6-4 *cont.*

```
20:        Read( InFile, Ch );
21:        Ch := Chr( Ord( Ch ) MOD 128 );
22:        IF Ch = Chr( 13 )
23:           THEN Writeln( OutFile ) ELSE
24:        IF Ch >= ' '
25:           THEN Write( OutFile, Ch )
26:      END; { while }
27:      Close( InFile );
28:      Close( OutFile );
29:      Erase( InFile );
30:      Rename( OutFile, FileName )
31:    END; { ProcessFile }
32:
33:    BEGIN
34:      Writeln( 'WordStar to ASCII Converter' );
35:      Writeln;
36:      Write( 'Convert what file? ' );
37:      Readln( FileName );
38:      IF Length( FileName ) > 0
39:         THEN ProcessFile
40:    END.
```

End of Line—Eoln

Processing text files a character at a time requires a special function to know when you've reached the ends of lines. **Eoln** (end of line) returns true when, during the course of sequentially reading characters, Turbo Pascal detects the end of a line, marked by a carriage return character, ASCII 13. To process a text file a character at a time with **Eoln**, use a **WHILE** loop such as this:

```
VAR inFile : Text; ch : Char;

WHILE NOT Eof( inFile ) DO
BEGIN
   IF Eoln( inFile )
      THEN Writeln;
   Read( inFile, ch );
   ProcessChar( ch )
END;
```

While this works, I prefer to check explicitly for carriage return and other control characters such as line feeds as in line 22 of Program 6-4. Most word processors do not adhere to the convention of ending lines with plain carriage returns and, therefore, **Eoln** is unable to recognize line endings except for standard ASCII text.

Structured Files

Text files are only one of the many varieties of disk files that programs can process. Regardless of how programs interpret file contents, disk files all contain the same thing—binary data bytes. Programs may freely interpret those bytes as they please. One program might interpret them as characters, another as integers, real numbers, Boolean true and false values, name and address records, and other structures. The interpretation of data in disk files is up to you and your program. There is nothing in a file (unless you put it there) to indicate the nature of its contents.

To declare a file of bytes, create a file variable like this:

```
VAR
   ByteFile : FILE OF Byte;
```

Byte is a predeclared data type with values ranging from 0 to 255, the range of values that fit in one eight-bit byte. With this declaration, a program can open any file as a sequence of bytes, and then copy it unchanged to another file. Because the program doesn't change or process the data in the file, it doesn't matter if the data represent other structures, characters, integers, or records.

Program 6-5 is similar to Program 6-3, except that it copies any disk file, not only ones containing text. Procedure **OpenFiles** is unchanged; no matter what kind of files you declare, you open them the same way. Line 3 declares **InFile** and **OutFile** as files of **Byte**. **ProcessFiles** reads and writes single bytes at a time (lines 25–26) while the **LongInt** variable **Size** keeps track of the number of bytes processed. (An integer **Size** could count no higher than 32,767 bytes, smaller than many common disk files. The **LongInt** variable lets the program handle files with over 2 *billion* bytes—larger than the total capacity of most personal computer disk drives.)

Program 6-5

```
1:   PROGRAM CopyBytes;
2:   VAR
3:      InFile, OutFile : FILE OF Byte;
4:
5:   PROCEDURE OpenFiles;
6:   VAR
7:      FileName : String[14];
8:   BEGIN
9:      Write( 'Input file? ' ); Readln( FileName );
```

Program 6-5 *cont.*

```
10:    Assign( InFile, FileName );
11:    Reset( InFile );
12:    Write( 'Output file? ' ); Readln( FileName );
13:    Assign( OutFile, FileName );
14:    Rewrite( OutFile )
15: END; { OpenFiles }
16:
17: PROCEDURE ProcessFiles;
18: VAR
19:    OneByte : Byte;
20:    Size : LongInt;
21: BEGIN
22:    Size := 0;
23:    WHILE NOT Eof( InFile ) DO
24:    BEGIN
25:       Read( InFile, OneByte );
26:       Write( OutFile, OneByte );
27:       Size := Size + 1
28:    END; { while }
29:    Writeln( Size, ' bytes copied' )
30: END; { ProcessFiles }
31:
32: BEGIN
33:    Writeln( 'Copy any file' );
34:    Writeln;
35:    OpenFiles;
36:    ProcessFiles;
37:    Close( OutFile );
38:    Close( InFile )
39: END.
```

Notice that the program uses **Read** and **Write**, not **Readln** and **Writeln** in lines 25–26. It can't use **Readln** because a file of bytes is just a stream of values with no defined structure. You can only use **Readln** with lines of text that end in carriage returns.

Files of Records

Disk files can hold any Pascal data structure. In Chapter 5, you developed a database for storing information about the members of a fictitious club. A better version saves its data on disk, then reads it back the next time you run the program.

Program 6-6

```
 1:   PROGRAM ClubDataBase2;
 2:   CONST
 3:      MaxMembers = 5;
 4:      FileName = 'CLUB.DAT';
 5:   TYPE
 6:      FileType = (SystemRec,ActiveRec);
 7:      Member =
 8:         RECORD
 9:            CASE RecKind : FileType OF
10:                SystemRec : ( NumMembers : Integer );
11:                ActiveRec : ( Name      : String[30];
12:                              Phone     : String[12];
13:                              Charges   : Real;
14:                              Payments  : Real      )
15:         END; { Member }
16:   VAR
17:      Members : ARRAY[ 0 .. MaxMembers] OF Member;
18:      Membership : 0 .. MaxMembers;
19:      Choice : Char;
20:
21:   PROCEDURE WriteMembers;
22:   VAR
23:      MemberFile : FILE OF Member;
24:      i : Integer;
25:   BEGIN
26:      WITH Members[0] DO
27:      BEGIN
28:         RecKind := SystemRec;
29:         NumMembers := Membership
30:      END;
31:      Assign( MemberFile, FileName );
32:      Rewrite( MemberFile );
33:      Writeln( 'Writing ', Membership, ' records.' );
34:      FOR i := 0 TO Membership DO
35:         Write( MemberFile, Members[i] );
36:      Close( MemberFile )
37:   END; { WriteMembers }
38:
39:   PROCEDURE ReadMembers;
40:   VAR
41:      MemberFile : FILE OF Member;
42:      i : Integer;
43:   BEGIN
44:      Assign( MemberFile, FileName );
```

Program 6-6 *cont.*

```
45:  {$i-}
46:     Reset( MemberFile );
47:  {$i+}
48:     IF IoResult <> 0 THEN
49:     BEGIN
50:        Writeln( 'New file' );
51:        Membership := 0
52:     END ELSE
53:     BEGIN
54:        Read( MemberFile, Members[0] );
55:        Membership := Members[0].NumMembers;
56:        Writeln( 'Reading ', Membership, ' records.' );
57:        FOR i := 1 TO Membership DO
58:           Read( MemberFile, Members[i] );
59:        Close( MemberFile )
60:     END { else }
61:  END; { ReadMembers }
62:
63:  PROCEDURE AddRecords;
64:  BEGIN
65:     IF Membership = MaxMembers
66:        THEN Writeln( 'Membership is full' ) ELSE
67:        BEGIN
68:           Writeln( 'Add new records' );
69:           Membership := Membership + 1;
70:           WITH Members[ Membership ] DO
71:           BEGIN
72:              Write( 'Name     : ' ); Readln( Name );
73:              Write( 'Phone    : ' ); Readln( Phone );
74:              Write( 'Charges  : ' ); Readln( Charges );
75:              Write( 'Payments : ' ); Readln( Payments )
76:           END { with }
77:        END { else }
78:  END; { AddRecords }
79:
80:  PROCEDURE ListRecords;
81:  VAR
82:     Number : Integer;
83:  BEGIN
84:     FOR Number := 1 TO Membership DO
85:        WITH Members[ Number ] DO
86:           Writeln( Number, ' : ', name,
87:                    ' ', Phone, Charges-Payments:8:2 );
88:  END; { ListRecords }
89:
```

Program 6-6 *cont.*

```
90:   BEGIN
91:      Writeln;
92:      Writeln( 'Club Data Base' );
93:      ReadMembers;
94:      REPEAT
95:         Writeln;
96:         Writeln( 'Number of members = ', Membership );
97:         Write( 'A.dd, E.dit, L.ist, Q.uit ? ' );
98:         Readln( input, choice );
99:         choice := Upcase( choice );
100:        Writeln( choice );
101:        CASE choice OF
102:           'A' : AddRecords;
103:           'E' : Writeln( 'Sorry, no editing yet' );
104:           'L' : ListRecords
105:        END { case }
106:     UNTIL choice = 'Q';
107:     WriteMembers
108:  END.
```

Program 6-6 adds two procedures **WriteMembers** and **ReadMembers** to the club database in Program 5-8. Procedures **AddRecords** and **ListRecords** are copied from Program 5-8.

One improvement in this new version is a **FileName** constant at line 4. There's also a new case variant in the **Member** record type. Its two variations, **System** and **Active**, define the record contents. A **System** record holds the current number of members in the data file while **Active** records hold actual data. Other fields in **Member** are the same.

Another important difference is the array of **Members** (line 17), which now begins at index zero instead of one as it did before. The new program stores a special system record at **Members[0]**, keeping track of how many member records are in the array.

This is done in the **WriteMembers** procedure (lines 21–37). File variable **MemberFile**, declared in line 23, is a file of type **Member**. In other words, the disk file contains records with the structure declared earlier in lines 7–15. The **WITH** statement (lines 26–30) sets tag field **RecKind** to **System** and stores the number of members in the **NumMembers** field. Later, when reading data back from disk, this technique lets the program know how many records are in the disk file.

Sequential Processing

A simple **FOR** loop (lines 34–35 in Program 6-6) writes member records to disk, one after the other, demonstrating one way to process disk files sequentially.

Even so, it is not correct to label the file a "sequential data file." (Later in this chapter is an equally misused term, "random access file.") Disk files are neither sequential nor random. Programs, however, may *process* files in sequential or random order—a subtle though important distinction to keep in mind.

As shown in procedure **ReadMembers** (lines 39–61), reading a disk file in sequence is simply the reverse process of writing. Again, **MemberFile** is a file of type **Member** (line 41). Line 44 is also familiar, assigning the file name to the **MemberFile** variable. Line 46 uses **Reset** to open the existing club disk file. But observant readers might spot a problem with this approach, as described in the next section.

Chicken and Egg Files

Program 6-6 solves a typical problem which might be called the "chicken and egg disk file syndrome." Looking near the end of the program in line 93, you see that the first thing the program does is to read the old data file. But, the first time the program runs, there is no old file, and resetting the file variable in line 46 causes an error.

To prevent halting the program when this happens, the compiler directives in lines 45 and 47 temporarily switch off input and output (I/O) error checking {$i–}, and then switch it back on {$i+} after the **Reset** command executes.

Normally, Turbo Pascal automatically checks I/O errors during read and write operations on files. If an error occurs, the program stops with an error message. Switching off I/O error checking lets the program test the result, called the **IoResult**, of file operations and take appropriate actions instead of screeching to a halt.

Testing IoResult

Line 48 in Program 6-6 checks the built-in **IoResult** integer function for **Reset** errors from line 46. If **IoResult** is zero, then no error occurred, and the program continues to read the file from disk. But if **IoResult** is not zero, something went wrong. In this example, the program assumes any error means that the old file doesn't exist, setting **Membership** to zero (line 51) and ending the procedure. A more complete program would test the **IoResult** code, checking the error type according to the list of "I/O Errors" in your Turbo Pascal Reference Guide. These error codes are identical to those reported by DOS; therefore, you can find descriptions of all codes returned by **IoResult**—too numerous to list here—in a DOS technical reference.

With I/O error checking off, you must follow every file operation—even simple **Readln** and **Writeln** statements—with **IoResult** checks. This is not optional—you must do it. See Figure 6-5 for a list of file operations that require **IoResult** checking.

Note: Chapter 13 explains how to use the directory procedures **ChDir**, **GetDir, MkDir,** and **RmDir** listed in Figure 6-5. Chapter 16 lists examples for the special text-file seek functions **SeekEof** and **SeekEoln.**

```
Append, BlockRead, BlockWrite, ChDir, Close, Erase, Flush,
GetDir, MkDir, Read, Readln, Rename, Reset, Rewrite, RmDir, Seek,
SeekEof, SeekEoln, Truncate, Write, Writeln
```

Figure 6-5 When you turn off I/O checking with the compiler directive {$I – }, you must check function **IoResult** following these file operations.

IoResult Side Effect

Chapter 4 investigates side effects caused by procedures and functions that change global variables. **IoResult** is an example of a function with the intended side effect of resetting a global, internally stored error code. You can't reference this code directly—it's private to Pascal. Using **IoResult** returns the current error setting while also resetting the internal value to zero. In other words, the **IoResult** value is valid only on its *first* use following an I/O operation.

Program 6-7 shows the wrong way to use **IoResult**. After prompting for a disk file name, the program tries to reset the file, checking **IoResult** in line 12 to see if any errors occurred. If so, line 14 writes the error code before ending. This doesn't work because checking **IoResult** in line 12 resets the internal error code to zero. Therefore, even if the program detects an error, it always reports "Error #0." Run the program and type existing and nonexisting file names to see the problem.

Program 6-7 (with errors)

```
 1:  PROGRAM BadCheck;
 2:  VAR
 3:     FileVar : Text;
 4:     FileName : String[14];
 5:  BEGIN
 6:     Write( 'Reset what file? ' );
 7:     Readln( FileName );
 8:     Assign( FileVar, FileName );
 9:  {$i-}
10:     Reset( FileVar );
11:  {$i+}
12:     IF IoResult <> 0
13:       THEN
14:         Writeln( 'Error #', IoResult )
```

Program 6-7 (with errors) *cont.*

```
15:    ELSE
16:      BEGIN
17:        Writeln( 'File opened' );
18:        Close( FileVar )
19:      END { else }
20:  END.
```

Program 6-8 fixes the bug in Program 6-7 by saving **IoResult** in an integer variable, **ErrorCode** (line 12). The program then tests **ErrorCode** (line 14) and, if the value is not zero, correctly displays the error message. Storing **IoResult** in a variable eliminates the side effect.

Program 6-8

```
1:  PROGRAM GoodCheck;
2:  VAR
3:    FileVar : Text;
4:    FileName : String[14];
5:    ErrorCode : Integer;
6:  BEGIN
7:    Write( 'Reset what file? ' );
8:    Readln( FileName );
9:    Assign( FileVar, FileName );
10: {$i-}
11:    Reset( FileVar );
12:    ErrorCode := IoResult;
13: {$i+}
14:    IF ErrorCode <> 0
15:      THEN
16:        Writeln( 'Error #', ErrorCode )
17:      ELSE
18:        BEGIN
19:          Writeln( 'File opened' );
20:          Close( FileVar )
21:        END { else }
22:  END.
```

Random Access Processing

Processing disk files at random resembles array indexing. The difference is that on disk a file might be much larger than the largest array you could hold in memory. For example, a hard disk drive can store many millions of bytes, while variables in memory are limited to about 65,000 bytes. Future microcomputer devices will store billions of bytes on disk. These *megabyte* and *gigabyte* devices expand the computer's memory but operate more slowly than fast memory circuits. For this reason, programs need special methods for reading and writing large disk files.

To randomly locate one record requires knowing the item's *record number*. A record number is similar to an array index. It uniquely identifies one record in a disk file. To access a particular record by its number, use Turbo Pascal's **Seek** command:

```
Assign( FileVar, 'CLUB.DAT' );
Reset( FileVar );
Seek( FileVar, 2 );
Read( FileVar, OneMember );
```

These four statements assign and open a file variable to the club database disk file. The third line seeks, or positions, an internal *file pointer* to the third record stored in the file. (The first record has record number *zero*. Therefore, seeking the second record number positions the file pointer to the *third* record, not the second.) Finally, the **Read** statement transfers a single record from disk to variable **OneMember**.

Program 6-9 uses this method to prompt for a record number, then print out the member's phone number and name in the club database. When you enter a record number (lines 27–28), the program seeks that record (line 31), reads it (line 32), and prints the phone number (lines 33–34).

Notice that the program no longer has to read all records into an array. Instead, it reads the specific record you request, leaving the others on disk.

Program 6-9

```
 1:   PROGRAM ClubPhone;
 2:   CONST
 3:      FileName = 'CLUB.DAT';
 4:   TYPE
 5:      FileType = (SystemRec,ActiveRec);
 6:      Member =
 7:        RECORD
 8:          CASE RecKind : FileType OF
 9:             SystemRec : ( NumMembers : Integer );
10:             ActiveRec : ( Name      : String[30];
11:                           Phone     : String[12];
12:                           Charges   : Real;
13:                           Payments  : Real      )
14:        END; { Member }
15:   VAR
16:      OneMember : Member;
17:      MemberFile : FILE OF Member;
18:      RecordNumber : Integer;
```

Program 6-9 *cont.*

```
19:
20:   BEGIN
21:      Assign( MemberFile, FileName );
22:      Reset( MemberFile );
23:      Writeln;
24:      Writeln( 'Club Member Phone Numbers' );
25:      REPEAT
26:         Writeln;
27:         Write( 'Member number? (0 to quit) ' );
28:         Readln( RecordNumber );
29:         IF RecordNumber > 0 THEN
30:         BEGIN
31:            Seek( MemberFile, RecordNumber );
32:            Read( MemberFile, OneMember );
33:            WITH OneMember DO
34:               Writeln( Phone, ' ....... ', Name )
35:         END { if }
36:      UNTIL RecordNumber = 0;
37:      Close( MemberFile )
38:   END.
```

Seeking and Writing

With **Seek**, you can modify individual records without disturbing the others. You might, for example, add the programming in Figure 6-6 to Program 6-9. Now, after reading a record and displaying its phone number, the program lets you correct the number if it's wrong.

Notice in Figure 6-6 that another **Seek** repositions the file pointer before writing the modified record back to disk. Reading the record (Program 6-9, line 32) advances Pascal's internal file pointer to the *next* record. A **Write** also advances the file pointer one record. To avoid reading or writing the wrong records, when processing files at random, always precede each **Read** or **Write** statement with a **Seek**.

Appending Records

In a typical large database, an interrelated collection of many data files, operators often enter new data into separate disk files. Then a simple program appends the new data onto a main disk file, ready for sorting and further processing.

Although there are several ways to append records to disk files, the first step is to locate the end of the file. One approach does this by reading records until **Eof** becomes true:

Add this line between lines 18 and 19

```
ch : Char;
```

Replace lines 33–34 with the following

```
WITH OneMember DO
BEGIN
   Writeln( Phone, ' ....... ', Name );
   Write( 'Change it? ' );
   Readln( ch );
   IF Upcase(ch) = 'Y' THEN
   BEGIN
      Write( 'New number? ' );
      Readln( Phone );
      Seek( MemberFile, RecordNumber );
      Write( MemberFile, OneMember )
   END { if }
END { with }
```

Figure 6-6 Modifications to Program 6-9 to change individual member phone numbers.

```
WHILE NOT Eof( MemberFile ) DO
   Read( MemberFile, OneMember );
```

Because the file might be empty, **WHILE** is the correct repetitive statement to use. After the loop, a simple **Write** statement adds a new record at the file's end:

```
Write( MemberFile, OneMember );
```

Another approach takes advantage of the way Program 6-6 stores the number of records in the club database, keeping that value in a system record (record number zero). When you know where to find the last record, seeking the end of the file is easy:

```
Seek( MemberFile, 0 );
Read( MemberFile, OneMember );
Seek( MemberFile, OneMember.NumMembers + 1 );
```

The first **Seek** and **Read** load record zero, containing the case variant with the number of records stored in the file (see Program 6-6, lines 10 and 26–30). Having discovered how many records there are, the third statement seeks past the last record. As with the **WHILE** loop approach, a simple **Write** can then add a new record.

After appending new records, regardless of the method you choose, the system record (number zero) no longer correctly shows the number of records in the file. To update this record, modify it like this:

```
Seek( MemberFile, 0 );
Read( MemberFile, OneMember );
WITH OneMember DO
   NumMembers := NumMembers + NumAppends;
Seek( MemberFile, 0 );
Write( MemberFile );
```

Of course, this assumes you kept track of the number of appended records in a variable, **NumAppends**.

Appending Text Files

To append new text to the end of existing text files, use the **Append** procedure in place of **Reset**. **Append** opens a text file just like **Reset**, but positions the file to its end, ready to accept more text.

To use **Append**, first give a text file a name. Then pass **Append** the file variable. After that, use **Write** and **Writeln** statements to write text to the end of the file. Finally, **Close** the file, preserving your changes. For example, this adds two lines to a file named TEST.TXT:

```
VAR
   tf : TEXT;

Assign( tf, 'TEST.TXT' );
Append( tf );
Writeln( tf, 'This is the first appended line' );
Writeln( tf, 'This is the second appended line' );
Close( tf );
```

Processing Text Files at Random

Unlike the club database, where all records have identical structures and are therefore the same size, common text files have many lines all of different lengths. There is no easy way to seek a single line of text at random without reading all preceding lines.

Program 6-10 demonstrates one way to access disk text file strings at random. After opening the file in lines 11–12, the program prompts for a line number (lines 15–16). A **FOR** loop in lines 20–21 advances to that line, which is then displayed in line 22. Try entering the name of an example Pascal program, stored in a disk file, and then ask for one of the line numbers as printed in this book. As you can see in the **FOR** loop, Program 6-10 simulates random access by skipping over preceding strings until it finds the one you want.

The program also demonstrates how to use **Reset** to reposition the file pointer to the top of the file, similar to rewinding a video tape to its beginning. Every time you enter a new line number (line 16), the program resets the file (line 19). Earlier, you learned that **Reset** opens existing disk files. When used this way, **Reset** repositions an already open file to its beginning.

Program 6-10

```
 1:  PROGRAM SeekStrings;
 2:  VAR
 3:      TextFile : Text;
 4:      FileName : String[14];
 5:      LineNumber, i : Integer;
 6:      OneLine : String[80];
 7:  BEGIN
 8:      Writeln;
 9:      Write( 'Seek strings in what file? ' );
10:      Readln( FileName );
11:      Assign( TextFile, FileName );
12:      Reset( TextFile );
13:      REPEAT
14:         Writeln;
15:         Write( 'Line number? (0 to quit) ' );
16:         Readln( LineNumber );
17:         IF LineNumber > 0 THEN
18:         BEGIN
19:            Reset( TextFile );
20:            FOR i := 1 TO LineNumber DO
21:               Readln( TextFile, OneLine );
22:            Writeln( LineNumber, ': ', OneLine )
23:         END { if }
24:      UNTIL LineNumber = 0;
25:      Close( TextFile )
26:  END.
```

Advanced File Handling

Turbo Pascal has a few special disk file-handling procedures. You can erase a file from disk with the **Erase** procedure:

```
Assign( MemberFile, 'OLDDATA.DAT' );
Erase( MemberFile );
```

When erasing files, do not open them first. Erasing an open file is like closing a door with your foot in the doorway (see Figure 6-1). You could do some serious damage!

Another thing you can do is change the name of a disk file. The following statements rename the club database file to keep a backup copy on disk:

```
Assign( MemberFile, 'CLUB.DAT' );
Rename( MemberFile, 'CLUB.BAK' );
```

As with **Erase**, do not open the file before renaming. You could add similar statements to Program 6-6 to create a backup disk file before writing the new records array. Many word-processing programs use a similar method. For example, Turbo Pascal's text editor keeps backup copies of files in case of disk problems, or to allow going back to a previous revision if by mistake you delete something.

To create backup disk files properly, use programming similar to Figure 6-7. First, erase the old backup (if it exists), then rename the current disk file, making it the new backup. Finally, write the new data to disk. This avoids accidentally having the same name appear twice in a directory, a situation DOS does not allow. **Rename** does not check whether a new file name already exists. That's your responsibility.

Add this new constant between lines 4 and 5

```
BackName = 'CLUB.BAK';
```

Add the following statements between lines 30 and 31

```
{$i-}
   Assign( MemberFile, BackName );
   Erase( MemberFile );
   IF Ioresult <> 0
      THEN {ignore it};
   Assign( MemberFile, FileName );
   Rename( MemberFile, BackName );
   IF Ioresult <> 0
      THEN {ignore it};
{$i+}
```

Figure 6-7 Modifications to Program 6-6 to create a backup CLUB.BAK file before writing new records to disk.

Special Functions

FilePos returns the current position of the internal file pointer, equal to the current record number. The function value is type **LongInt**. Because programs can seek any record number, even outside of the range of records stored on disk, **File-**

Pos can't detect attempts to seek beyond the end of the file. To catch this error, check **IoResult** after a disk-read operation, not after **Seek.** If you run the following sample, you'll see that, regardless of whether **IoResult** reports an error, **File-Pos** returns the value last given to **Seek:**

```
Seek( MemberFile, RecordNumber );
{$i-} Read( MemberFile, OneMember ); {$i+}
IF IoResult <> 0
   THEN Writeln( '**Error reading file' );
Writeln( 'File position = ', FilePos( MemberFile ) );
```

Another special function, **FileSize**, returns the number of records in a file and is also a **LongInt** value. You can use it to write a handy function that checks for empty files:

```
FUNCTION FileEmpty( VAR f : FileType ) : Boolean;
BEGIN
   FileEmpty := FileSize( f ) <= 0
END;
```

Notice the check for a file size less than or equal to zero. Presumably, if the size of the file is negative, something is seriously wrong. But even so, it would be a mistake to return **FileEmpty** equal to true in that unusual case! Although it might seem adequate to write **FileSize(f) = 0**, it takes no more time or effort to check **FileSize(f) < = 0**, which returns a correct value for even the most remote possibility. Covering all possibilities, no matter how unlikely, is a sound programming practice.

Untyped Files

Pascal treats untyped files as sequences of blocks, normally 128 bytes long. To declare an untyped file, use key word **FILE** alone. (See Figure 6-2.) The following declares an untyped file, **F:**

```
VAR
   F : FILE;
```

Using BlockRead and BlockWrite

Two special procedures read and write untyped files. **BlockRead** reads and **BlockWrite** writes one or more blocks at a time. Each has two different formats.

```
{Format A}
   BlockRead( F, Buffer, N );
   BlockWrite( F, Buffer, N );
```

```
{Format B}
   BlockRead( F, Buffer, N, Result );
   BlockWrite( F, Buffer, N, Result );
```

File **F** is an untyped file variable; **Buffer** is any variable, usually an array; **N** is the number of blocks you want to read or write. In Format B, **Result** equals the number of blocks actually read or written after calling **BlockRead** or **Block-Write**. If **Result** does not equal **N**, then something prevented the procedure from completing the request to read or write this many blocks.

These procedures are extremely fast, transferring blocks of disk data to and from memory with no regard for data structure. The procedures might be used in high-speed database systems or in disk backup or copy programs.

Because **BlockRead** and **BlockWrite** operate on files in chunks, the file size must be a multiple of the chunk size to avoid an error when reading the last block in a file. In other words, if you are reading 256-byte chunks, then the file size must be evenly divisible by 256 or you'll receive an I/O error when trying to read the last partial block.

In truth, on disk, all files are stored in multiples of some chunk size—most likely, 512 bytes per sector. Therefore, you might think that reading files 512 bytes at a time will almost always work. Unfortunately, that's not the case. Even though DOS physically stores data in 512-byte sectors, it keeps track in the disk directory of the actual number of bytes the file uses. This value, representing the usable file size, probably will not be a multiple of 512.

There are two ways around the dilemma, which, by the way, was not a problem in Turbo Pascal 3.0 and earlier versions. First, you can create files with sizes evenly divisible by a certain chunk size with **BlockWrite** and then read the file with **BlockRead**. This always works. For example, to create a file with ten, 256-byte blocks, you could write:

```
VAR
   f : FILE;
   buffer : ARRAY[ 0 .. 255 ] OF Byte;
   i : Integer;

Assign( f, 'TEST.DAT' );
Rewrite( f, 256 );
FOR i := 1 TO 10 DO
BEGIN
   { Insert data in buffer }
   BlockWrite( f, buffer, 1 )
END;
Close( f );
```

File **f** is untyped. The **buffer** is large enough to hold 256 bytes. After naming the file with **Assign**, **Rewrite** creates a new file on disk. The second parameter to **Rewrite** specifies the block (chunk) size for subsequent **BlockWrite**s, in this case, 256. Then, a **FOR** loop calls **BlockWrite** ten times, each time writing one buffer of data to disk. (The example doesn't check for errors, which a real program would, of course, have to do.) How the data gets in the buffer is up to you.

To read this same file a chunk at a time, simply reverse the process, using **Reset** instead of **Rewrite** and **BlockRead** instead of **BlockWrite**. Here's the code, using the same variables:

```
Assign( f, 'TEST.DAT' );
Reset( f, 256 );
WHILE NOT Eof(f) DO
BEGIN
   BlockRead( f, buffer, 1 );
   { Process buffer }
END;
Close( f )
```

After assigning the file name, **Reset** opens the file, specifying 256 bytes per block for subsequent **BlockRead** statements. Then, a **WHILE** loop cycles, reading buffers full of data one by one until reaching the end of the file.

These methods of reading and writing files in blocks are extremely useful for rapidly getting data into and out of a program. You might stuff all sorts of things into buffers and transfer them to disk, then reload that same information later in a flash.

Single Byte Chunks

To read and write existing disk files using **BlockRead** and **BlockWrite**, open your file variables with a chunk size of one byte. This trick neatly guarantees that file sizes are multiples of the chunk size because every possible file size is, of course, a multiple of one!

Along with the **Sizeof** function, which returns the number of bytes occupied by a variable or data type, these ideas make it easy to write a fast file copy program. Program 6-11 shows the result. First, the program creates a 10,000-byte buffer (lines 2–5). You can make this byte array any size you want, within Turbo Pascal's usual limits. **Original** and **Copy** are untyped file variables. **BytesRead** and **BytesWritten** control the copying action.

After typing file names for the original and copy (lines 9–19), a **REPEAT** loop cycles until the copying is finished or until an error occurs. Carefully examine this loop. It demonstrates the correct way to use **BlockRead** and **BlockWrite** to process files of any size.

Line 24 calls **BlockRead** with four parameters: an untyped file variable, a buffer to hold the incoming data, the size of the buffer in bytes, and a variable, **BytesRead**. The third parameter tells **BlockRead** to load 10,000 bytes (or however big you make the buffer), using **Sizeof** to return the size of **Buffer**. Of course, the file might not have exactly 10,000 bytes, and, in that case, **BlockRead** reads what it can, setting **BytesRead** equal to this number.

If **BytesRead** is not zero (line 25), then **BlockWrite** writes this same number of bytes from the buffer to the copy file (line 27). If the number of bytes requested to write (the third parameter to **BlockWrite**) does not equal the number of bytes actually written, **BytesWritten**, then a disk error must have occurred.

Program 6-11

```
 1:  PROGRAM CopyFile;
 2:  CONST
 3:      MaxBuff = 10000;  { Bytes transferred at one time }
 4:  VAR
 5:      Buffer : ARRAY[ 1 .. MaxBuff ] OF Byte;
 6:      Original, Copy : FILE;
 7:      BytesRead, BytesWritten : Integer;
 8:
 9:  PROCEDURE OpenFiles;
10:  VAR
11:      FileName : String;
12:  BEGIN
13:      Write( 'Original file name? ' ); Readln( FileName );
14:      Assign( Original, FileName );
15:      Reset( Original, 1 );
16:      Write( 'Copy to file name? ' ); Readln( FileName );
17:      Assign( Copy, FileName );
18:      Rewrite( Copy, 1 )
19:  END; { OpenFiles }
20:
21:  BEGIN
22:      OpenFiles;
23:      REPEAT
24:         BlockRead( Original, Buffer, Sizeof(Buffer), BytesRead );
25:         IF BytesRead > 0 THEN
26:         BEGIN
27:            BlockWrite( Copy, Buffer, BytesRead, BytesWritten );
28:            IF BytesRead <> BytesWritten THEN
29:            BEGIN
30:               Writeln( 'Disk write error' );
31:               {$i-} Close( Copy );
32:               Erase( Copy ); {$i+}
33:               Close( Original );
34:               Halt( 1 )
35:            END { if }
36:         END { if }
37:      UNTIL BytesRead = 0;
38:      Close( Copy );
39:      Close( Original )
40:  END.
```

Passing Files As Parameters

Files are variables and, as such, you can pass them by reference as parameters to procedures and functions. This lets you write procedures that redirect their input and output.

Program 6-12 demonstrates how to do this with a simple program to write a line of text to three output files. The program passes each file to variable parameter **f** in procedure **WriteText**. Because Pascal does not allow passing files by value, you must use the **VAR** key word as shown here.

Program 6-12

```
 1:  PROGRAM FileParams;
 2:  VAR
 3:     printer, console : Text;
 4:     n : Integer;
 5:
 6:  PROCEDURE WriteText( VAR f : Text );
 7:  BEGIN
 8:     Writeln( f, 'Test string number', n );
 9:     n := n + 1
10:  END;
11:
12:  BEGIN
13:     n := 1;
14:     Assign( printer, 'PRN' );
15:     Assign( console, 'CON' );
16:     Rewrite( printer );
17:     Rewrite( console );
18:
19:     WriteText( output );
20:     WriteText( printer );
21:     WriteText( console )
22:  END.
```

Although the example uses the predeclared file **Text**, you can pass other kinds of files too. However, because of the requirement that parameter types must be simple identifiers, you must first define a new file data type. Let's say you want to design a procedure to operate on integer data files. You might put the following declaration into your program:

```
TYPE
   DataFile : FILE OF Integer;
```

You can then write your procedure header with a formal file parameter **DF** of type **DataFile**:

```
PROCEDURE Operate( VAR DF : DataFile );
```

With another special procedure, you can chop off the end of a file with **Truncate**. Let's say you want to limit a file to 100 records. These statements do it:

```
Seek( FileVar, 100 );
Truncate( FileVar );
Close( FileVar );
```

Records numbered 0 through 99 remain in the file. Any records above that are now gone.

Summary

Files are like magic doors through which computers communicate with the outside world. Programs can have files for talking to devices such as printers, keyboards, and modems. They can also store and retrieve data in disk files.

Turbo Pascal has a variety of procedures for creating, reading, writing, and appending disk files. Programs read and write disk files sequentially or at random, plucking out only the records they want. Because all files exist as binary data on disk, programs are free to interpret data as characters, records, single bytes, sectors, or blocks.

BlockRead and **BlockWrite** read and write data in chunks in sizes from 1 to 512 or more bytes. These procedures are useful for rapidly reading and writing disk files. Another useful procedure is **Truncate**, which lops off the ends of files from any position.

You can pass file variables as parameters to procedures and functions, but only by reference. Turbo Pascal requires file parameters to be declared with the **VAR** key word.

Exercises

6-1. Write a program to read a text file and display all its lines backwards.

6-2. Write a program to concatenate (join) two text files into a single, long file.

6-3. Write the reverse program—in other words, a program to split a large text file into two smaller parts. Some text editors have a file size limit, and the program might be used to reduce long files to manageable size.

6-4. How might you increase the speed of Program 6-10? (Hint: Do you always have to reset the file for each new line, or is there another possibility?)

6-5. (Advanced) Write a program to read files as collections of blocks or sectors. Encrypt the file data with a user-entered "key." The same key should also recover the original text of a previously encrypted file. Because of the potential for destroying data, test your program thoroughly on copies of files, before trusting it on valuable data.

6-6. (Advanced) Write a program to read lines of text, sort them into ascending order, and then write the sorted lines to a new file. (Use the sorting method described in Chapter 5.)

6-7. Start your own database system. Design a program to read and write disk files of fixed length, eight-character strings. Write procedures to search, edit, delete, sort, and print reports.

7

Pointers, Lists, and Trees

- Creating Pointers
- Using Pointer Variables
- Comparing Pointers
- Pointers to Nowhere
- Notes on Drawings
- Why Use Pointers?
- One-Way Lists
- Memory Management
- Circular Lists
- Trees
- Dynamic Arrays
- Explicit Addressing
- Absolute Variables
- Absolute Pointers
- Overlaying Absolute Variables

7

Key Words and Identifiers

@, Absolute, Addr, Dispose, FreeMem, GetMem, Mark, MaxAvail, MemAvail, New, Nil, Ptr, Release, Sizeof

Memory bytes have addresses, unique values that identify where bytes are located. Ignoring electronic technicalities, when a computer reads a byte's value, it sends the byte's address to memory circuits, which return the value of the addressed byte. To store a new value in memory, the computer again sends the address, followed by the value to store at that location.

In Pascal, a *pointer* variable holds a memory address. That's all a pointer is—a memory address. By specifying an address, a pointer *points* to a unique location in memory. Stored at that location is the actual value the pointer addresses. There is a difference, therefore, between the value of a pointer and the value stored at the location where the pointer points—an important difference to keep in mind.

Pointers can point to simple byte values, integers, real numbers, records, strings—any Pascal data type. The actual value is stored in memory. The pointer locates the first byte of that value.

Creating Pointers

To create a pointer, type a caret, which resembles the point of an arrow, in front of any data type identifier. For example, the following creates a pointer named **ValuePointer**:

```
VAR
   ValuePointer : ^Integer;
```

ValuePointer is a pointer to an integer stored somewhere in memory. You can declare pointers to other Pascal types, too. Here are a few more examples:

```
TYPE
   ArrayType = ARRAY[1..10] OF Byte;
VAR
   RealPointer  : ^Real;
   ArrayPointer : ^ArrayType;
   RecPointer   : ^Member;
```

These statements create pointers to a real number (**RealPointer**), to an array of ten bytes (**ArrayPointer**), and to a **Member** record (**RecPointer**) borrowed from Chapters 5 and 6. Each pointer is associated with, or *bound to*, a specific type of value. Notice that in the case of the array, you first have to declare an **ArrayType** identifier and then create a pointer to it. The same is true for records, sets, and other structured types.

Using Pointer Variables

Before a program uses a pointer, it first requests memory space for the type of data the pointer addresses. In other words, a program must initialize its pointers—simply declaring them is not enough. To initialize a pointer, use the **New** command with any pointer variable:

```
New( ValuePointer );
```

New does two things. First, it reserves space for a value of the type **ValuePointer** addresses, in this case, an integer, taking two memory bytes. Second, **New** assigns the address of the reserved memory to **ValuePointer**. After executing **New**, **ValuePointer** points to a two-byte integer stored in memory.

You rarely have to examine or use the actual address of a pointer. In fact, a main reason for using pointers is to eliminate explicit addressing from programs while giving you the advantages only pointers can give. To store a value in memory at the location addressed by **ValuePointer**, use a caret after the pointer name:

```
ValuePointer^ := 100;
```

This stores 100 at the location addressed by **ValuePointer**. The caret signifies not the pointer itself, but the intent to access the thing pointed to—an action called *dereferencing the pointer*. When you do want to use the pointer directly, omit the caret. By doing this, you can transfer an address of one pointer variable to another. Let's say you have these two pointers to type integer:

```
VAR
   PointerA, PointerB : ^Integer;
```

A program can then reserve memory for **PointerA** and assign the same *address* to **PointerB** with the two statements:

```
New( PointerA );
PointerB := PointerA;
```

PointerB now addresses the same location in memory as **PointerA** (see Figure 7-1). The program hasn't assigned a value to this place in memory and, therefore, the value is unknown (shown by a question mark in the drawing). On the other hand, suppose the program reserves two different locations in memory. To transfer the *value* addressed by **PointerA** to the location addressed by **PointerB**, use carets to signify the things to which the pointers point (see Figure 7-2):

```
New( PointerA );
New( PointerB );
PointerA^ := 100;
PointerB^ := PointerA^ + 1;
```

In these four statements, **New** assigns to each pointer the address of newly reserved memory space. The third statement then assigns 100 to the location addressed by **PointerA**. It can do this because the value addressed by the pointer is type integer; therefore, the program can store integers at this place in memory. Finally, as Figure 7-2 illustrates, the fourth and final statement assigns one plus the value at the location addressed by **PointerA** to the location addressed by **PointerB**.

Comparing Pointers

Because pointers ignore the specifics of memory addressing, you can compare them only for equality in expressions. As these **IF** statements show, Pascal allows equality and inequality comparisons on pointers:

```
IF ( PointerA = PointerB )
   THEN <statement>;
IF ( PointerA <> PointerB )
   THEN <statement>;
```

You cannot compare the ordering of pointers with the relative operators $<$, $>$, $< =$, and $> =$. Because Pascal guarantees nothing about the actual locations of pointer-addressable items in memory, it makes no sense to test if a pointer to one item is less or greater than another. If such comparisons were allowed, they would likely produce different results on computers with different memory organizations.

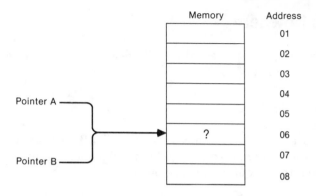

Figure 7-1 After the assignment **PointerB: = PointerA**, the two pointers have the same address and, therefore, point to the same memory location.

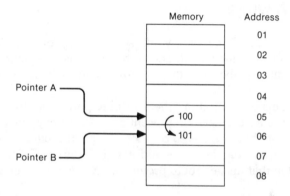

Figure 7-2 The result of the assignment **PointerB^: = PointerA^ + 1**. After using **New** to reserve memory for the two pointers, the value stored at the location addressed by one pointer is assigned to the location addressed by the other.

Despite this limitation, you can compare values addressed by pointers, provided such comparisons would normally be allowed on variables of the same data type. For instance, if **PointerA** and **PointerB** point to two integers, then Pascal allows this statement:

```
IF PointerA^ <= PointerB^
   THEN <statement>;
```

With carets attached to the two pointer identifiers, Pascal compares the values addressed by the pointers, not the pointers themselves.

Pointers to Nowhere

Pascal defines a special value, **Nil**, meaning no specific address. You can assign **Nil** to a pointer of any type:

```
PointerA := Nil;
```

Setting **PointerA** to **Nil** signifies that the pointer does not address a valid memory location. If you assign **Nil** to all pointers, programs can test the pointers to see if they require initialization:

```
IF PointerA = Nil
   THEN New( PointerA );
```

Notes on Drawings

Throughout this chapter, you'll see drawings of data structures, some that have **Nil** pointer values. Look ahead, for example, to Figure 7-3. There, an electrical grounding symbol—the three horizontal lines to the right of the figure—represents the value, **Nil**.

This drawing and others display pointer-addressable values conceptually and do not necessarily represent actual memory bytes. One of the best ways to understand pointers is to develop a mental model of the relationships between pointers and the data they address. The purpose of the diagrams is to help you develop that image, not to provide an X-ray picture of actual memory circuits.

Why Use Pointers?

If a pointer simply addresses a value—a variable like any other—what's the difference? Why go to the trouble of creating a pointer to a variable? Why not just use a simple Pascal variable instead?

The answer is that pointer-addressable variables occupy memory taken from a pool called the *heap*. Programs declare pointers and let the system figure out where in the heap to store the actual values. With hundreds or thousands of pointers—a common situation when using pointers to construct lists and trees as explained later in this chapter—it's easier to let the computer calculate where to store new values than to do the address calculations yourself.

The second reason pointers are valuable is their ability to use memory efficiently. As a contrast, consider arrays. Programs have to specify the maximum number of items in an array. If the array is half full, the unused positions are wasted. Pointers eliminate such waste by creating data structures that dynamically expand, taking only as much or as little memory as required. Such programs run on small systems while automatically taking advantage of a larger computer's extra memory. A spreadsheet program that has more "cells" on a larger computer than on a smaller one is a good example of this dynamic approach to memory management.

One-Way Lists

By creating pointers to values in memory and then using other pointers to link the values, programs create lists. Lists do not have fixed sizes. They might be empty, or they might contain thousands of items. To get to individual values, you search through the items in a list as though you were thumbing through the pages of a book.

Lists are easier to understand if you draw them out as in Figure 7-3. Paper and pencil, it turns out, are one of the best tools for learning about lists!

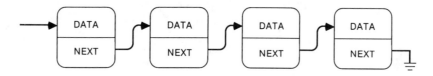

Figure 7-3 Links in values point to other values, creating a list.

If you could see a list in memory, it would appear as shown in Figure 7-3. Each item in the list points to the next item. Items in the list are Pascal records declared as follows:

```
TYPE
   ItemPointer = ^Item;
   Item = RECORD
          Data : String[20];
          Next : ItemPointer
        END;
```

These type declarations define **ItemPointer** as a pointer to type **Item**, a record with two fields. Notice that the pointer type declaration comes *before* **Item**, the thing to which an **ItemPointer** points—the one time in Pascal where you may use identifiers before defining them. This bending of the rules lets you define a pointer field of the same type inside the record. As shown here, **Item**'s second field, **Next**, is such a pointer. It points to another **Item** record of the same structure. This would be impossible if Pascal didn't allow pointer types to be declared in advance of the values they address.

Earlier, you learned about recursive procedures and functions—routines that call themselves into action. In similar fashion, a record type like **Item** is an example of a *recursive data structure*. It recursively points to a value of its own type.

List Insertion

To insert a value into a list is a simple matter of requesting memory space for the new value and then adjusting two pointers. If **newItem** is a variable of type **ItemPointer**, and **oldItem** addresses the value in front of where you want to insert this new record (Figure 7-4), then the following statements insert the new record into the list of Figure 7-3.

```
New( newItem );
newItem^.Next := oldItem^.Next;
oldItem^.Next := newItem;
```

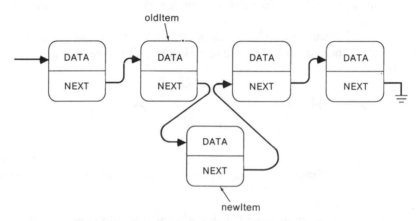

Figure 7-4 Inserting variables into linked lists is a matter of adjusting two pointers.

Take that a step at a time, and it's easy to understand. First, **New** creates space on the heap for one **Item** record, assigning the address to **newItem**. Then, two assignment statements adjust **Next** pointers to link the new **Item** record into the list. Notice how the carets access **Next** fields in the records addressed by the **newItem** and **oldItem** pointers. Remember that these two variables are *pointers*, but with carets attached, **newItem**^ and **oldItem**^ refer to **Item** records, the values to which the pointers point.

List Deletion

Deleting a value from a list is even easier. Again, given pointers **newItem** and **oldItem** as in Figure 7-4, this statement deletes the item addressed by **newItem**:

```
oldItem^.Next := newItem^.Next;
```

After the assignment, the list again resembles Figure 7-3. Assigning the **Next** pointer field of **newItem**^ to **oldItem**^.**Next** effectively *unlinks* the item addressed by **newItem**. But you don't even need the **newItem** pointer at all. This does the same thing:

```
oldItem^.Next := oldItem^.Next^.Next;
```

That may look confusing, but it's not hard to follow if you remember **Next** is just a pointer to another **Item**, which also has a **Next** pointer field. A few more examples further explain this idea. Given the list in Figure 7-5, then:

```
A^.Next             --    addresses B
A^.Next^.Next       --    addresses C
A^.Next^.Next^.Next --    addresses D
```

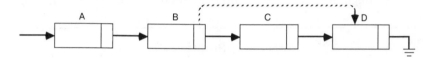

Figure 7-5 Linked lists are joined by pointers inside the
variables in the list.

Having pointer **A**, to delete item **C**, you can write:

```
A^.Next^.Next := A^.Next^.Next^.Next
```

In English, this statement assigns the **Next** field of **C** to the **Next** field of **B**, thus skipping **C**. After the assignment, **B**'s **Next** field directly addresses **D**, shown by the dotted line in Figure 7-5.

But, you might wonder, where does the deleted variable go? In Figure 7-5, what happens to deleted **C**? Ideally, its memory space is automatically reclaimed for use by other pointers and variables later in the program. Unfortunately, Pascal does not realize this ideal and, in practice, leaves deleted variables floating *out there*, scattered wastelands in memory, unreachable by your program. To reuse that space, programs have to manage computer memory carefully as the next section explains.

Memory Management

As you just learned, procedure **New** allocates memory space for a pointer-addressable variable. This memory is taken from an available-memory pool called the *heap*, an area of memory independent of the stack, where Pascal stores local variables among other things. Manipulating the heap does not affect any other program variables, only those addressed by pointers. To put that another way, values on the heap are always global—they exist outside of the scope of any procedures and functions.

In Program 7-1, variable **newItem** is a pointer to an **Item** record. The program demonstrates that using **New** to create variables in memory decreases the amount of total memory available for other values. To test available memory, lines

15 and 23 use a built-in **LongInt** function **MemAvail** in **Writeln** statements similar to this:

```
Writeln( 'Memory = ', MemAvail );
```

MemAvail returns the number of bytes available on the heap. Usually, this equals the total amount of memory in your computer minus the memory occupied by DOS, your program, and a few other miscellaneous items.

Program 7-1 calls **New** ten times in a **FOR** loop (lines 17–21). On each pass through the loop, **MemAvail** displays the amount of free memory left (line 20).

Program 7-1

```
1:   PROGRAM HeapDemo;
2:   TYPE
3:      ItemPointer = ^Item;
4:      Item = RECORD
5:                 Data : String[20];
6:                 Next : ItemPointer
7:             END;
8:   VAR
9:      newItem : ItemPointer;
10:     i : Integer;
11:  BEGIN
12:     Writeln;
13:     Writeln( 'Heap Demonstration' );
14:     Writeln;
15:     Writeln( 'Starting memory = ', MemAvail );
16:     Writeln;
17:     FOR i := 1 TO 10 DO
18:     BEGIN
19:        New( newItem );
20:        Writeln( i:3, ': After new, memory = ', MemAvail:5 )
21:     END; { for }
22:     Writeln;
23:     Writeln( 'Ending memory = ', MemAvail )
24:  END.
```

As you can see when you run the program, using **New** reduces the amount of memory available on the heap by adjusting an internal heap pointer that Pascal keeps hidden from view. Figure 7-6 illustrates the heap before and after running Program 7-1. Allocating space for new variables increases the heap pointer, raising the top of the heap and reducing the amount of free memory available for other values. (Higher memory addresses are at the top of Figure 7-6.)

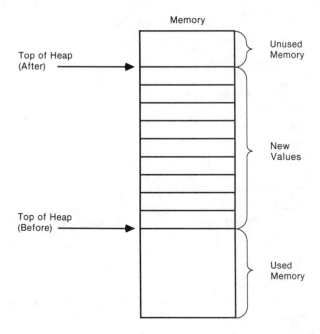

Figure 7-6 New allocates space for variables in a memory area called the heap.

Recording the value of the heap pointer before using **New** and then restoring that value later reclaims the memory space occupied by pointer-addressable variables. The reclaimed memory is then available for new variables. Two built-in procedures, **Mark** and **Release**, manage the usually invisible heap pointer to make this possible.

Except for lines 11, 13, and 25, Program 7-2 is similar to Program 7-1. Line 11 declares **Heap** of type **Pointer**, a generic type that is compatible with any other Pascal pointer. In this example, we are interested in the pointer values themselves—not in the variables that pointers address. Generic **Pointer** variables don't address specific values—they just hold address values.

Mark in line 13 sets **Heap** equal to the current value of the internal heap pointer. After the **FOR** loop executes (lines 19–23), **Release** restores the internal heap pointer to its original value (line 25). When you run the program, the amount of available memory before and after the **FOR** loop is the same, proving that the used space has been reclaimed.

Program 7-2

```
1:   PROGRAM HeapDemo2;
2:   TYPE
3:      ItemPointer = ^Item;
4:      Item = RECORD
5:              Data : String[20];
```

Program 7-2 *cont.*

```
 6:                 Next : ItemPointer
 7:              END;
 8:  VAR
 9:     newItem : ItemPointer;
10:     i : Integer;
11:     Heap : Pointer;
12:  BEGIN
13:     Mark( Heap );
14:     Writeln;
15:     Writeln( 'Heap Demonstration' );
16:     Writeln;
17:     Writeln( 'Starting memory = ', MemAvail );
18:     Writeln;
19:     FOR i := 1 TO 10 DO
20:     BEGIN
21:        New( newItem );
22:        Writeln( i:3, ': After new, memory = ', MemAvail:5 )
23:     END; { for }
24:     Writeln;
25:     Release( Heap );
26:     Writeln( 'Ending memory = ', MemAvail )
27:  END.
```

Using **Mark** and **Release** to record and reset the internal heap pointer can be dangerous. After resetting the heap pointer to its original value, variables previously created remain in the unused portion of memory, as shown by "Old Data" in Figure 7-7. Old pointers still may address portions of this memory. There's nothing to prevent you from using them, which is likely to cause serious problems if you subsequently create new variables *in the same space*, overwriting any values stored at the old pointer locations.

The rule to remember is: After releasing the heap, never use pointers allocated by **New** since you last marked the top of the heap. As another example, these statements create two variables on the heap:

```
New( Item1 );
Mark( Heap );
New( Item2 );
Release( Heap );
```

Item1 is in protected memory. **Item2** is in the unused portion of the heap after **Release**. **Heap** is a plain **Pointer**. Figure 7-8 shows the heap after those four statements execute. When you release the heap pointer, **Item2** is in unprotected memory.

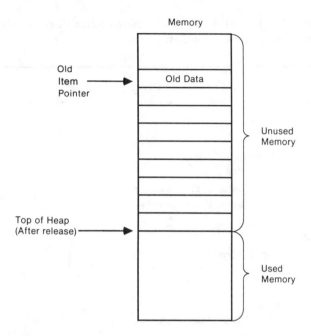

Figure 7-7 One way to reclaim heap space is to **Mark** the top of the heap and then execute **Release** to reset the heap pointer to the marked location.

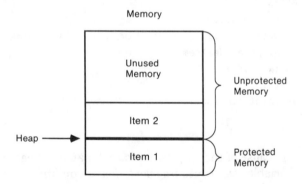

Figure 7-8 A danger of releasing the heap is that old pointers may address unprotected memory.

Disposing Variables

In addition to **Mark** and **Release**, Turbo Pascal offers a more sophisticated way to manage heap memory. In this new approach, programs *dispose* individual variables to return their space to the available memory pool. Pascal automatically keeps track of all such disposed items.

As Program 7-3 demonstrates, **Dispose** reclaims the memory occupied by variables (line 21) allocated by **New**. After disposal, the same memory space is available for new variables.

Program 7-3

```
 1:   PROGRAM HeapDemo3;
 2:   TYPE
 3:       ItemPointer = ^Item;
 4:       Item = RECORD
 5:                   Data : String[20];
 6:                   Next : ItemPointer
 7:              END;
 8:   VAR
 9:       newItem : ItemPointer;
10:       i : Integer;
11:   BEGIN
12:       Writeln;
13:       Writeln( 'Heap Demonstration' );
14:       Writeln;
15:       Writeln( 'Starting memory = ', MemAvail );
16:       Writeln;
17:       FOR i := 1 TO 10 DO
18:       BEGIN
19:          New( newItem );
20:          Writeln( i:3, ': After new, memory = ', MemAvail:5 );
21:          Dispose( newItem )
22:       END; { for }
23:       Writeln;
24:       Writeln( 'Ending memory = ', MemAvail )
25:   END.
```

Because of the way Turbo Pascal manages heap memory, disposing numerous variables can cause *fragmentation*, a condition that shatters the heap into islands of occupied and unoccupied territory. If it weren't for this disadvantage, disposing pointer-addressable variables would attain the earlier-mentioned ideal of automatically reclaiming used memory space. An example illustrates the problem. If a program has four pointers and then executes the following statements, the heap appears as shown in Figure 7-9.

```
New( Item1 );
New( Item2 );
New( Item3 );
New( Item4 );
Dispose( Item2 );
```

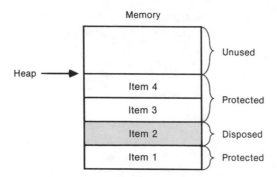

Figure 7-9 Disposing an individual item in the heap reclaims the item's space but can also fragment the heap.

As the shaded portion of Figure 7-9 shows, **Item2**'s disposed space is available for new items. Even so, that space is only large enough for items no bigger than **Item2**. In seriously fragmented memory, with hundreds or more unconnected, disposed variables, there might be plenty of total memory available but no single space large enough to hold new variables. Although Turbo Pascal can join adjacent items—for example, combining **Item3** and **Item4** in Figure 7-9 if these records were disposed—memory spaces are not shuffled to maximize the amount of free space available, a process called *garbage collection*, found in some other languages, most famously in Lisp.

Usually, you can minimize fragmentation by applying a few simple rules. First, avoid designing programs that create many small values of different sizes. Larger variables tend to produce less fragmentation; smaller variables, more. You might also add dummy fields to records to make them the same size as others. This way, new records fit neatly into disposed spaces. In fact, if *all* records are identical sizes, the danger of fragmentation is *completely eliminated*. Of course, this drastic solution may not be practical in all cases. Creating variables of sizes in bytes that are multiples of other record sizes (16, 32, 64, and so on) can also help reduce fragmentation.

Turbo Pascal keeps track of disposed variables in a private list that resembles Figure 7-3. The list is stored high in the heap, away from other variables created by **New. Release** empties this list, effectively resetting the heap to its condition before the first use of **Dispose**. In past Turbo Pascal versions, you could not use the **Mark** and **Release** methods for heap management along with **Dispose**. In newer versions starting with 4.0, you may combine the two

Measuring Disposed Memory

Function **MaxAvail** returns a value equal to the largest available disposed memory space. This lets you test whether there is enough space for new variables. **MemAvail** returns the *total* space available, which may be greater than **MaxAvail** after disposing other values on the heap. To use **MaxAvail** properly, you also need the help of function **Sizeof**, which returns the number of bytes occupied by a variable or data type. Assuming **p** is a pointer to type **RecType**, this **IF** statement tests whether there is adequate memory for a **RecType** variable:

```
IF MaxAvail >= Sizeof( RecType )
   THEN New( p )
   ELSE Writeln( 'Out of memory' );
```

Remember that **MaxAvail** returns the value of the largest unbroken space. **MemAvail** returns the *total* amount of available memory, including all disposed spaces. In seriously fragmented memory, **MemAvail** might indicate plenty of room even though no single area of memory is large enough for new variables.

The Avail Stack

A third memory-management technique, one that works under all versions of Turbo Pascal as well as with other Pascal compilers, links disposed variables into a list of available memory space. Although there is no active data in these values, the method uses existing pointer fields to link deleted items.

The list is handled as a stack, a data structure that resembles a stack of dishes in a spring-loaded bin. The first dish placed on the stack is the last taken off. The data structure, a list, operates in the same fashion. The first item inserted, or *pushed*, into the list is the last one to be taken, or *popped*, off.

To use the avail stack method, first declare a pointer **Avail** as an **Item-Pointer**, addressing a list of disposed variables (Figure 7-10). Initialize **Avail** to **Nil**. To remove an item from the **Avail** list, use the following **IF** statement:

```
IF Avail = Nil THEN New( newItem ) ELSE
BEGIN
   newItem := Avail;
   Avail := Avail^.Next
END;
```

Figure 7-10 Another method for managing memory is to link disposed items into an **Avail** stack.

The effect of the **IF** statement (Figure 7-11) is to pop one disposed item from the **Avail** list. If the list is empty (**Avail = Nil**), **New** creates a new variable on the heap. Therefore, additional heap space is taken up only if there are no disposed spaces available.

To push an item onto the **Avail** stack, do this:

```
newItem^.Next := Avail;
Avail := newItem;
```

Those two statements link the disposed item (addressed by pointer

newItem) into the list and set **Avail** to the item's address, changing Figure 7-11 back into Figure 7-10.

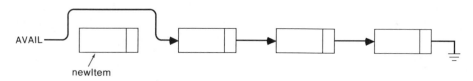

Figure 7-11 Popping the **Avail** stack removes the first item
from the linked list.

To demonstrate these concepts, Program 7-4 declares two lists, **Avail** and **ItemList**, both pointers to **Item** records. Lines 63–64 initialize these pointers to **Nil**, emptying both lists at the start.

When you press key A, **AddItem** (lines 49–54) adds a new item to **ItemList**. When you press D, **DeleteItem** (lines 56–60) deletes an item from the list, inserting the item into the **Avail** list. If you delete more items than you add, the program pushes empty uninitialized items onto the **Avail** stack. After each addition and deletion, the program displays both lists along with the total amount of free memory (lines 28–47).

The critical procedures in this program are **Push** (lines 13–17) and **Pop** (lines 19–26). **Push** inserts an item into a list. **Pop** removes one item. Notice that **Pop** creates a new variable if the list is empty. When writing programs to manipulate lists, it's especially important to handle empty lists correctly. Forgetting to deal with this situation is a common cause of bugs.

When you run the program, you'll see memory decreasing for each newly added item. After making a few deletions and inserting deleted items into the **Avail** list, you'll see that new items use disposed memory space before taking up new memory from the heap.

Adding a new variable (lines 49–54) is a matter of popping space from the **Avail** stack and assigning values to the item. To demonstrate this, the example assigns a random integer (line 52) before pushing the item into the **ItemList**. Of course, in your own programs, you'd assign whatever data you want to insert in the list.

Reversing the process deletes variables. As lines 56–60 show, the program does this by popping the **ItemList** and then pushing the popped item onto the **Avail** stack.

Program 7-4

```
1:   PROGRAM AvailStack;
2:   USES Crt;
3:   TYPE
4:      ItemPointer = ^Item;
5:      Item = RECORD
```

Program 7-4 *cont.*

```
 6:              Data : Integer;
 7:              Next : ItemPointer
 8:          END;
 9: VAR
10:     Avail, NewItem, ItemList : ItemPointer;
11:     ch : Char;
12:
13: PROCEDURE Push( VAR NewItem, List : ItemPointer );
14: BEGIN
15:     NewItem^.next := List;
16:     List := NewItem
17: END; { Push }
18:
19: PROCEDURE Pop( VAR NewItem, List : ItemPointer );
20: BEGIN
21:     IF List = Nil THEN New( NewItem ) ELSE
22:     BEGIN
23:         NewItem := List;
24:         List := List^.Next
25:     END
26: END; { Pop }
27:
28: PROCEDURE ShowList( p : ItemPointer );
29: BEGIN
30:     WHILE p <> Nil DO
31:     BEGIN
32:         writeln( p^.Data:8 );
33:         p := p^.Next
34:     END;
35:     Writeln
36: END; { ShowList }
37:
38: PROCEDURE Display;
39: BEGIN
40:     ClrScr;
41:     Writeln( 'MEMORY = ', MemAvail );
42:     Writeln;
43:     Writeln( ' AVAIL list' );
44:     ShowList( AVAIL );
45:     Writeln( ' ITEM list' );
46:     ShowList( ItemList )
47: END; { Display }
48:
49: PROCEDURE AddItem;
50: BEGIN
```

Program 7-4 *cont.*

```
51:     Pop( NewItem, AVAIL );
52:     NewItem^.Data := Random( Maxint );
53:     Push( NewItem, ItemList )
54: END; { AddItem }
55:
56: PROCEDURE DeleteItem;
57: BEGIN
58:     Pop( NewItem, ItemList );
59:     Push( NewItem, AVAIL )
60: END; { DeleteItem }
61:
62: BEGIN
63:     AVAIL := Nil;
64:     ItemList := Nil;
65:     REPEAT
66:        Display;
67:        Writeln; Writeln( '-----------' );
68:        Write( 'A.dd, D.elete, Q.uit ? ' );
69:        ch := Readkey;
70:        CASE Upcase( ch ) OF
71:           'A' : AddItem;
72:           'D' : DeleteItem
73:        END { case }
74:     UNTIL Upcase( ch ) = 'Q'
75: END.
```

Circular Lists

Stacks are only one of the many kinds of dynamic structures that are easy to create with Pascal pointers. So far, we've created lists organized in only one direction. For example, all the pointers in the one-way list illustrated in Figure 7-10 point the same way.

Adding a second pointer to variables creates bidirectionally linked lists—a structure that's easier to visualize by imagining linear lists of items with pointers to the right and left (Figure 7-12). There are several advantages to using such *doubly linked* lists.

One advantage is the ability to search for items either backward or forward. You must search one-way lists (Figure 7-10) in a forward direction. When a program points to the third item in a one-way list, it has no way to go back to the previous item. But from any place in a two-way list (Figure 7-12), a search can go to the right or left—all items are readily available from any starting place.

Besides being doubly linked, the list in Figure 7-12 is circular. Follow either the right (thin-line) or left (heavy-line) pointers, and you'll discover no beginning or end to this list. (Doubly linked lists do not have to be circular, although they

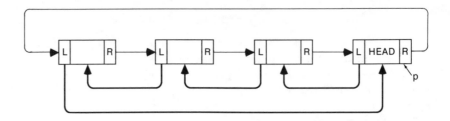

Figure 7-12 Items in doubly linked circular lists have both
left and right pointers.

often are. The leftmost L and rightmost R pointers in Figure 7-12 could be **Nil**, still
linking the list in two ways, but giving it a beginning and end.)

Because a circle has no beginning or end, and therefore no explicit beginning
of a circular list for a program to address, managing circular lists is easier with a
dummy item, called the *list head*, as one of the variables in the list. As explained
earlier, empty lists require careful handling. Unfortunately, with circular lists, the
programming tends to be complicated unless the dummy circular list head is
never deleted from the list. That way, a circular list is never empty—avoiding, if
not solving, the problem. The dummy list head also makes insertions and deletions simple to program.

To create a circular list, first declare a pointer to a record type with **Left** and
Right pointer fields as follows:

```
ItemPointer = ^Item;
Item = RECORD
         Data : String[20];
         Left, Right : ItemPointer
       END;
```

Initialize the list by allocating a new variable in memory, setting the item's **Left**
and **Right** fields to point to their own record:

```
New( p );
p^.Left := p;
p^.Right := p;
```

Pointer **p** is a variable of type **ItemPointer**. The statements create the list
illustrated in Figure 7-13.

If you compare Figures 7-12 and 7-13, you can see that the list is empty when
either the **Left** or **Right** field of the list head points to its own record. Knowing this
leads to a simple **Boolean** function test for an empty list:

```
FUNCTION empty : Boolean;
BEGIN
   empty := ( p^.Left = p )
END;
```

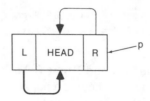

Figure 7-13 A list head, which is never deleted, makes doubly linked
circular lists easier to handle. The list head shown here is initialized
to point to itself.

However, when $p^\wedge.\text{Left} = p^\wedge.\text{Right}$, the list is not necessarily empty, even
though it may appear so from Figure 7-13. Look at Figure 7-14 for an example—the
list head left and right pointers are equal (because they address the same item), but
the list is not empty.

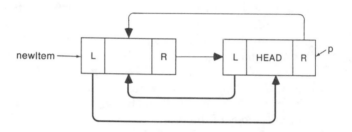

Figure 7-14 Adding a new item to the list head in Figure 7-13 produces
this new, two-variable list.

The next four statements insert new items into a circular list. Pointer **p** addresses the list head. Another pointer **newItem** addresses the new item to insert.
First execute **New(newItem)** and then:

```
newItem^.Left := p;
newItem^.Right := p^.Right;
p^.Right^.Left := newItem;
p^.Right := newItem
```

These statements applied to Figure 7-13 create the two-element list shown in Figure 7-14. For a better understanding of how this works, execute the four statements by hand.

You can also insert new items anywhere in the list, not only at the list head.
To do this, replace **p** with a pointer to any list variable and execute the same four
statements. One of the primary advantages to using doubly linked circular lists is
the ability to insert new items given only a single pointer to any list element.

Similarly, it's easy to delete doubly linked items. For example, these statements delete **newItem**$^\wedge$ in Figure 7-14:

```
newItem^.Left^.Right := newItem^.Right;
newItem^.Right^.Left := newItem^.Left;
```

This reassigns the **Left** and **Right** fields of the items surrounding the one to delete. Again, try the statements on paper, applying them to Figure 7-14. You should end up with the list in Figure 7-13. Also, try deleting items from the longer list in Figure 7-12. What happens if by accident you delete the dummy list head?

After unlinking **newItem**^ this way, you would normally **Dispose** it or link it into an **Avail** stack using one of the methods described earlier.

Trees

A tree is a special kind of linked list. Trees are difficult to describe—there are many variations and many disagreements among computer scientists about how to define them. For our purposes, though, a computer tree is more like a family tree than a tree in nature.

Family trees come in two varieties: pedigree trees listing an individual's ancestors and lineal trees showing the descendants of parents. Computer trees more closely resemble the lineal type. The *nodes* in a family tree are people. When drawn out, these nodes, linked with branching lines, have a treelike structure.

You probably have seen lineal trees like the one in Figure 7-15, which represents the genealogy of the rulers of Tenochtitlan, the nation centered in the land that is now Mexico City. In Pascal trees, pointer variables replace the lines. Records replace the people. By the way, I chose this particular example to illustrate trees because the Aztec names in the figure remind me of the unreadable identifiers Pascal programmers sometimes create.

The analogy between family trees and trees in computer memory is imperfect. Genealogies like the one in Figure 7-15 have several complications normally disallowed in computer trees. For example, the same name often appears more than once, or there might be unusual links as in the case of the prolific Huitziliahuitl (top right of Figure 7-15).

Roots

One similarity between family trees and the computer kind is that both have roots. Your great-great-grandparents might be at the root of your family tree. Opochtzin and Atotoztli are the root parents of the genealogy in Figure 7-15.

In Pascal, the root is simply a pointer to the starting place in the tree. In fact, some authorities recursively define a tree as any structure with a root that is empty or points to the root of another tree. In other words, a tree is a structure composed of subtrees, linked to a common root. Cut off the root, and what's left is a forest of subtrees. Join two subtrees, and you have a single tree with a common root.

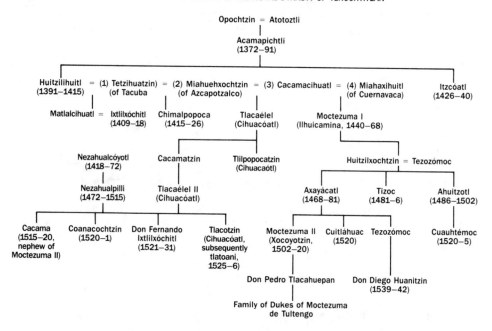

TENTATIVE GENEALOGY OF THE ROYAL DYNASTY OF TENOCHTITLAN

Figure 7-15 Computer trees resemble family trees, similar to this genealogy of the leaders of Tenochtitlan. (Davies, N. *The Aztecs*. London: Macmillan, 1973. Reprinted with permission of the publisher.)

Binary Trees

A special kind of tree is the binary tree. Binary trees have roots and nodes each with a maximum of two branches, one to the left and one to the right. Every node in a binary tree, including the root, either points nowhere or points to a subtree. When both branches point nowhere, the node is called a *leaf.*

Figure 7-16 shows a binary tree of fruit names. The root of this fruit tree is MANGO, which has two subtrees, {BANANA,APPLE,CHERRY} and {PEACH, PEAR}. Removing the root MANGO makes a forest of two subtrees with roots BANANA and PEACH.

The leaves of the fruit tree are APPLE, CHERRY, and PEAR. There are no branches growing from these nodes. PEACH is the root of a lopsided subtree with no branches to the left.

Programs can represent binary tree nodes as Pascal records defined like this:

```
ItemPointer : ^Item;
RECORD
   Item : String[20];
   Left, Right : ItemPointer
END;
```

Surprisingly, this definition is identical to the **Item** records used earlier in doubly linked, circular lists. This is an important observation. A structure's organization makes it a tree—not the composition of nodes or the data in them.

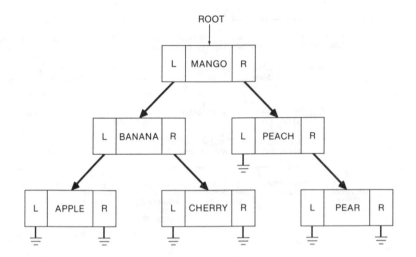

Figure 7-16 A "fruit tree" as it might appear in a computer's memory.

Tree Traversal

Programs traverse binary trees in three ways. Traversing means going from node to node and doing something with the data in each node. The three methods are *pre-order*, *in-order*, and *post-order*.

Clearly, at any single node, a program has three choices. It can move to the node on the left, move to the right, or process the data in the node. The exact nature of what it means to "process the data in the node" is unimportant for now. You might print out a string variable, increment a counter, or assign a value to a node variable. Important here is the concept of *when* a process activates, not *what* the process does.

Table 7-1 lists the three ways of traversing binary trees. It's easy to remember the three methods by observing when node processing occurs. Pre-order traversal processes nodes *before* going left and right. In-order processes nodes *in between* going left and right, and post-order processes nodes *after* going left and right.

Table 7-1 Binary tree traversal methods

Pre-order	In-order	Post-order
Process node	Go left	Go left
Go left	Process node	Go right
Go right	Go right	Process node

Each of the three traversal methods is recursive. The instruction "Go left" means to follow the left pointer to the next node and then start that traversal method over *from the top*. If a pointer has the value **Nil**, then simply go on to the next step.

If "process node" means to write out data stored in that node, then pre-order traversal of the fruit tree in Figure 7-16 produces (MANGO, BANANA, APPLE, CHERRY, PEACH, PEAR). In-order traversal produces (APPLE, BANANA, CHERRY, MANGO, PEACH, PEAR). Post-order makes (APPLE, CHERRY, BANANA, PEAR, PEACH, MANGO). Each traversal order produces a differently ordered list of data from the same tree.

Notice that in-order traversal of the tree in Figure 7-16 alphabetizes the fruit names. This happens because, in this particular tree, nodes branching left are alphabetically less and nodes branching right are alphabetically greater than their parent nodes. In-order traversal respects this ordering, and the list comes out in alphabetic order.

Trees and Recursion

The definition of a tree is recursive because it states that a tree is any root node that points to another tree. Because trees are naturally recursive, it is equally natural to write recursive procedures to manipulate them. This leads to simple procedures for traversing binary trees according to the three traversal methods described in Table 7-1.

Program 7-5 implements the three traversal methods in three recursive procedures: **PreOrder**, **InOrder**, and **PostOrder**. **InOrder** (lines 18–26) first tests if the passed node is **Nil** (line 20). If not, lines 22–24 execute the in-order method, that is, following all left branches, processing the node, then following the right branches. The **IF** test satisfies the requirement that the recursion end, as it must if the tree has a finite number of leaves with **Nil** branches. The other two procedures (lines 28–36 and 38–46) operate similarly but process the node at different times.

Notice how the procedures in Program 7-5 mirror the descriptions of the three traversal methods in Table 7-1. The algorithm becomes the program—supporting evidence for Pascal's reputation as an *algorithmic* language.

Without recursion, these same procedures are much more difficult to write. There isn't room here to examine the alternative, but it can be done. Recursion is never a requirement, only a convenience. All recursive programs have equivalent, nonrecursive solutions.

Program 7-5 creates a tree by adding new data that you type in—fruit names for example—with calls to procedure **Search** in lines 48–66. **Search** also calls itself recursively (lines 62–63).

The procedure does two things. First, in lines 52–59, if **Root** is **Nil**, the program creates a new root node (line 54). It also adds new data to this node and sets both left and right pointers to **Nil** (line 57). The actual **Root** value might represent any root of any subtree, not necessarily the main root.

The second job for procedure **Search** is to find the correct place in the tree to add new data. This happens in lines 62–64, which execute only if the current **Root** is not **Nil**. In two **IF** statements, **Search** recursively calls itself, tracing the left branches if **NewData < Data** or right branches if **NewData > Data**. If the new data is neither greater nor less, then it is already stored in a node, and the program prints the error message in line 64. **Right** and **Left** are pointers, remember, and **Search** takes a variable parameter in line 48. Passing these pointers as the roots of subtrees eventually finds the **Nil** pointer to which the new data should attach.

It is remarkable that the entire search and insert procedure is so concisely written while taking only a single pointer as its input. Once again, for a better understanding of the process, execute **Search** by hand, inserting new nodes into a paper tree.

Program 7-5

```
1:   PROGRAM Tree;
2:   TYPE
3:       String20 = String[20];
4:       ItemPointer = ^Item;
5:       Item = RECORD
6:                   Data : String20;
7:                   Left, Right : ItemPointer
8:               END;
9:   VAR
10:      NewData : String20;
11:      Root : ItemPointer;
12:
13:  PROCEDURE Process( Node : ItemPointer );
14:  BEGIN
15:      Write( Node^.Data, ' ' )
16:  END;
17:
18:  PROCEDURE InOrder( Node : ItemPointer );
19:  BEGIN
20:      IF Node <> Nil THEN
21:      BEGIN
22:         InOrder( Node^.Left );
23:         Process( Node );
24:         InOrder( Node^.Right )
25:      END
26:  END;
27:
28:  PROCEDURE PreOrder( Node : ItemPointer );
29:  BEGIN
30:      IF Node <> Nil THEN
31:      BEGIN
32:         Process( Node );
33:         PreOrder( Node^.Left );
34:         PreOrder( Node^.Right )
```

Program 7-5 *cont.*

```
35:     END
36:   END;
37:
38:   PROCEDURE PostOrder( Node : ItemPointer );
39:   BEGIN
40:     IF Node <> Nil THEN
41:     BEGIN
42:       PostOrder( Node^.Left );
43:       PostOrder( Node^.Right );
44:       Process( Node )
45:     END
46:   END;
47:
48:   PROCEDURE Search( VAR Root : ItemPointer );
49:   { Search for global NewData string in tree. }
50:   { If not found, insert it, else give error. }
51:   BEGIN
52:     IF Root = Nil THEN
53:     BEGIN
54:       New( Root );
55:       WITH Root^ DO
56:       BEGIN
57:         Data := NewData; Left := nil; Right := nil
58:       END
59:     END ELSE
60:     WITH Root^ DO
61:     BEGIN
62:       IF NewData < Data THEN Search( Left ) ELSE
63:       IF NewData > Data THEN Search( Right )
64:         ELSE Writeln( 'Error: Duplicate data!' )
65:     END
66:   END;
67:
68:   BEGIN
69:     Writeln( 'Tree test' );
70:     Root := Nil;
71:     REPEAT
72:       Write( 'Data (RET to quit)? ' );
73:       Readln( NewData );
74:       IF Length( NewData ) > 0
75:         THEN Search( Root )
76:     UNTIL Length( NewData ) = 0;
77:     Writeln;
78:     Writeln( 'PREORDER:' );
79:     PreOrder( Root );
```

Program 7-5 *cont.*

```
80:    Writeln; Writeln;
81:    Writeln( 'INORDER:' );
82:    InOrder( Root );
83:    Writeln; Writeln;
84:    Writeln( 'POSTORDER:' );
85:    PostOrder( Root );
86:    Writeln
87:  END.
```

Balanced Trees

When you run Program 7-5, enter the fruit names in this order: MANGO, BANANA, APPLE, CHERRY, PEACH, PEAR. What happens if you enter the names in a different order?

If you enter data in alphabetic order, the tree becomes unbalanced (Figure 7-17). An unbalanced tree has all or most of its branches going in one direction. You could balance the tree in Figure 7-17 by making BANANA the root and setting its LEFT pointer to address APPLE, the current root node. A good explanation of balanced trees in Pascal is in Niklaus Wirth's *Algorithms + Data Structures = Programs* (see Bibliography).

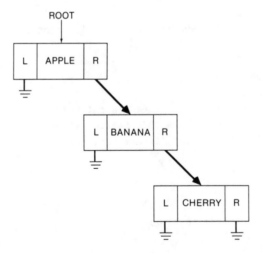

Figure 7-17 This binary tree is unbalanced. All its branches
go in one direction.

Dynamic Arrays

One common complaint about Pascal is the inability of a program to change the size of an array at run time. In some languages, you can declare array boundaries as variables, changing the size of arrays as needed when programs run. In Pascal, array index ranges must be constants, and, therefore, array sizes are fixed when you compile the program. If you have this array declaration:

```
VAR
    BigArray : ARRAY[ 1 .. 100 ] OF String[80];
```

then, to change the size of the array, you have to manually change the 100 to something else and recompile.

Some programmers get around the problem by declaring arrays like this:

```
VAR
    BigArray : ARRAY[ 1 .. 1 ] OF String[80];
```

Because Turbo Pascal normally has range checking off, as though you included the compiler directive {$R–} at the top of all programs, it allows statements such as the following even though **BigArray** has only one, and not 20, declared elements:

```
BigArray[ 20 ] := 'String Twenty';
Writeln( BigArray[20] );
```

Unfortunately, the element at **BigArray[20]** might be at the same position as other variables or program code in memory! Assignments like the one above can easily destroy data or wreck your program.

Allocating Heap Space

One way to have dynamic arrays and protect memory at the same time is to use two special Turbo procedures, **GetMem** and **FreeMem**, to allocate and dispose heap space in a way that is different from other pointer methods.

Use **GetMem** to allocate a specific number of bytes on the heap and assign the address of the first byte to a pointer variable. To dynamically create an array of 20 strings, use the statement:

```
GetMem( p, NumElements * Sizeof( OneElement ) );
```

Function **Sizeof** returns the number of bytes occupied by a data type or variable, here **OneElement**. **GetMem** reserves enough bytes on the heap for **NumElements** elements and assigns the address of the first element to **p**. Assuming **p** points to an array data type, the following statement assigns a string to element number twenty, and displays it:

```
p^[20] := 'String Twenty';
Writeln( p^[20] );
```

To deallocate space on the heap, use **FreeMem** with the same arguments to **GetMem**:

```
FreeMem( p, NumElements * Sizeof( OneElement ) );
```

FreeMem is equivalent to **Dispose** except that it gives you full control over the number of bytes to free. After freeing heap space, do not use pointer **p**. The memory that **p** addresses is no longer reserved for your use!

Program 7-6 demonstrates how to use this idea to create dynamically expanding arrays. Line 12 calls **GetMem** to allocate space for **NumElements** array items, which two **FOR** loops then fill and display (lines 13–16).

The declaration in line 4 may seem odd. (In fact, I frequently receive letters from readers claiming array declarations like this are typographical errors.) Declaring the array boundaries as [0 . . 0] is not a mistake. Although this appears to specify an array with only one index entry [0], with range checking off as it normally is, Turbo Pascal allows programs to ignore the declared boundaries and use indexes like [100] or [50]. Of course, it's up to you to make sure there is a variable at those locations, as done here in line 12.

The program declares **Item** as type **Integer** in line 3, using **Item** in the array declaration (line 4) and again later when allocating memory for the array (line 12). This makes it easy to change the array element type. For example, you can change **Integer** to **LongInt** in line 3, and the program still runs correctly.

Program 7-6

```
 1:  PROGRAM DynamicArray; {$R-}
 2:  TYPE
 3:     Item = Integer;
 4:     StringArray = ARRAY[ 0 .. 0 ] OF Item;
 5:  VAR
 6:     Dynarray    : ^StringArray;
 7:     NumElements, i : Integer;
 8:  BEGIN
 9:     Write( 'How many array elements? ' );
10:     Readln( NumElements );
11:     Writeln( 'Memory before = ', MemAvail );
12:     GetMem( Dynarray, NumElements * Sizeof( Item ) );
13:     FOR i := 0 TO NumElements - 1 DO
14:        Dynarray^[i] := i;
15:     FOR i := 0 TO NumElements - 1 DO
16:        Write( Dynarray^[i] : 8 );
17:     Writeln; Writeln;
18:     Writeln( 'Memory after = ', Memavail )
19:  END.
```

Explicit Addressing

Usually, you don't have to worry about where in memory Turbo Pascal stores variables. In fact, that's one reason for using a high-level language like Pascal in the first place—to avoid using explicit addresses as you must do in assembly language programming.

Sometimes, though, you will need to know where a certain variable is. Or, you might need to assign specific addresses to pointers. Turbo Pascal contains several features for handling these situations.

To find the address of any variable, procedure, or function, precede the identifier with an @ (at) sign. For example, suppose you have these declarations:

```
VAR
    q : Real;
    p : ^Real;
```

Variable **q**, a **Real** number, exists somewhere in memory. Variable **p** is a pointer to type **Real**. To make **p** point to **q**, you can write:

```
p := @q;
```

This assigns the *address* of **q** to pointer **p**. Because **p** now points to **q**, the following statements both assign **pi** to the *same* variable in memory:

```
q := pi;    { Assign pi to q }
p^ := pi;   { Same as above! }
```

There's no practical reason for making such assignments to simple variables—you may as well just use the variable identifier. But there is an advantage to using a similar idea to assign values to array elements, as the next two programs demonstrate. (You can use @ to find the addresses of procedures and functions, too.)

Programs 7-7 and 7-8 assign **pi** to item number 52 of an array of **Real** numbers. The two **FOR** loops in both programs repeat this step five million times. (Change the 500 to 50 or lower for PC or XT computers. The program takes about 30 seconds to finish on an 80386, 16-MHz system. It will take longer on slower systems.)

Program 7-7 uses typical array indexing, assigning **pi** to **a[k]** in line 11, with **k** equal to 52. On my system, five million such assignments takes about 28 seconds.

Program 7-7

```
1:  PROGRAM ArrayIndexA;
2:  VAR
3:      a : ARRAY[ 1 .. 100 ] OF Real;
4:      i, j, k : Integer;
5:  BEGIN
6:      k := 52;
7:      Write( 'Press Enter to start...' );
8:      Readln;
```

Program 7-7 *cont.*

```
9:      FOR j := 1 TO 500 DO      { 50 on PC, XT and clones }
10:     FOR i := 1 TO 10000 DO
11:        a[k] := pi;
12:     Write( chr(7) )    { Beep! }
13:  END.
```

Program 7-8 uses the pointer method to assign **pi** to the same array element as in Program 7-7. Line 7 of the new program sets pointer **p** to the address of **a[52]**. Then, inside the two **FOR** loops, line 12 assigns **pi** to the address to which **p** points. Because the program no longer has to calculate this same address, as it does in Program 7-7, the results are better—about 26 seconds.

Program 7-8

```
1:  PROGRAM ArrayIndexB;
2:  VAR
3:     a : ARRAY[ 1 .. 100 ] OF Real;
4:     i, j : Integer;
5:     p : ^Real;
6:  BEGIN
7:     p := @a[52];
8:     Write( 'Press Enter to start...' );
9:     Readln;
10:    FOR j := 1 TO 500 DO      { 50 on PC, XT and clones }
11:    FOR i := 1 TO 10000 DO
12:       p^ := pi;
13:    Write( chr(7) )    { Beep! }
14: END.
```

Even this small, 7% improvement could be important in a critical program. Remember that you can always take the address of any variable (@v), assign the address to a pointer to the same data type (p: = @v), and then use the pointer with a caret (p^) in place of the variable identifier (v).

Turbo Pascal has a function, **Addr**, that you can use in place of @. Both of the following statements assign the address of **q** to **p**:

```
p := @q;        { Assign address of q to p }
p := Addr(q);   { Same as above }
```

The only reason to use **Addr** instead of @ is if you plan to transfer your programs to other Pascal compilers, which might not recognize the @ symbol. In this case, you could write your own **Addr** function to return the address of variables and save time modifying your program.

Absolute Variables

Absolute variables exist at specific memory addresses. They can be any data type and exist anywhere in memory. You can declare variables at known locations or declare absolute variables on top of other Pascal variables and let the compiler figure out the addresses. An absolute variable is a sort of antipointer. Instead of using pointers to avoid explicit addressing, you can use absolute variables to force Pascal to use specific memory locations.

The form of an absolute variable is the same as any other variable declaration but includes the key identifier **Absolute** plus a memory address with both segment and offset values. For example, this declares a variable at the location of the print-screen status byte:

```
VAR
    status : Byte Absolute 0000:$0500;
```

Variable **status** is *not* a pointer to 0000:$0500. It's a variable at a specific location that you specify in the **Absolute** declaration. Use **status** like any other variable. For example, this sets the print-screen status byte to 1:

```
status := 1;
```

Doing this disables the print-screen key by fooling the computer into thinking a print-screen operation is in progress. Change the 1 to 0 to enable the key again.

Absolute Pointers

Another way to fix variables at specific locations is to assign a known address to a pointer variable. With a single pointer, all computer memory is available to your program. Such control is powerful but dangerous. You can easily overwrite portions of your program in memory, the operating system, or both.

Be sure you understand the difference between using an absolute variable and a pointer to a fixed address. To create a pointer variable to the address of the status byte and disable the print-screen key, you would have to write:

```
VAR
    statPtr : ^Byte;
BEGIN
    statPtr := Ptr( 0000, $0500 );
    statPtr^ := 1
END.
```

The **Ptr** function takes a segment and offset value, which together specify one location in memory. **Ptr** returns memory pointer, assigned here to **statPtr**, a pointer to type **Byte**. Storing 1 at this location disables the print-screen key. Storing 0 enables the key again. Although this has the same effect as using the absolute variable, one extra step is required to assign the address to the pointer variable. Also, four bytes of memory are required to hold the **statPtr** pointer. Absolute variables occupy no memory—they merely tell the compiler at which address to store and retrieve values.

Overlaying Absolute Variables

Specifying the identifier of a declared variable in place of a literal address overlays the variable at the same address. When you assign a value to one variable, the value of the other changes, too.

Program 7-9 shows how this works. Line 3 declares a byte variable, **ASCII**. Line 4 declares a character variable, **ch**. The program prints the alphabet by using **ASCII** in a **FOR** loop but writing **ch**. Although the program assigns nothing to **ch**, it cycles through letters A to Z! It does this because at line 4, the program declares **ch** to coexist in memory at the absolute address of **ASCII**.

Program 7-9

```
1:   PROGRAM DoubleUp;
2:   VAR
3:      ASCII : Byte;
4:         ch : Char Absolute ASCII;
5:   BEGIN
6:      FOR ASCII := 65 TO 90 DO
7:         Write( ch : 2 );
8:      Writeln
9:   END.
```

Summary

An understanding of pointers is vital to mastering Turbo Pascal. In this chapter, you learned that pointers are memory addresses that point to variables in memory. Programs manage the heap, where Pascal stores pointer-addressable variables, and use the **Mark** and **Release**, **Dispose**, or **Avail** stack methods to reclaim space occupied by old data.

Linked lists and trees are two important data structures, easily managed with the help of Pascal pointers. Using pointers, programs create lists, insert and delete objects, and manage stacks and doubly linked, circular list structures. Trees, recursive by nature, are easily managed with recursive procedures to create, search, and traverse nodes containing data.

By using **GetMem**, you can allocate memory on the heap, a method that lets you create dynamic arrays. **FreeMem** disposes the allocated memory.

Explicit addressing techniques let you assign addresses of variables, procedures, and functions to pointers. You can also declare absolute variables at specific locations in memory. Such abilities are powerful but dangerous if used improperly.

Exercises

7-1. Write a program to read a disk file of strings and insert the strings into a one-way list. Include a procedure to display the strings after reading.

7-2. Revise your answer in 7-1 to use a circular, two-way list. Add a procedure to search the list for specific values, printing the previous and next string.

7-3. (Advanced) Develop a procedure to exchange two objects in a circular list. It should take as parameters pointers to the two objects to exchange. Use your procedure in a program to sort a list *without* moving data, only adjusting pointers. Why is this better than the array-sorting method in Chapter 5?

7-4. Revise Program 7-5 to take its input from a disk text file.

7-5. Describe the three methods of memory management and explain the advantages and disadvantages of each.

7-6. Rewrite Program 7-4 *without* using any pointers.

7-7. (Advanced) Write a family-tree program. It should print out nodes in a tree-like graph similar to Figure 7-15. Develop a set of general procedures for saving tree nodes on disk. What special problems does this present?

8

Strings

- String Length
- Directly Setting String Length
- String Operations
- String Procedures
- String Functions
- Strings As Parameters
- Writing Your Own String Functions
- Special Characters
- Numbers to Characters
- Character Constants in Strings

8

Key Words and Identifiers

Chr, Concat, Copy, Delete, Insert, Length, PACKED, Pos, String

In early versions of Pascal, strings were simple arrays of characters, and the only string operation was assignment. Today, most Pascal compilers, including Turbo Pascal, come equipped with built-in string procedures and a string data type. Previously, you would declare a 20-character string variable like this:

```
VAR
   Name : PACKED ARRAY[ 1 .. 20 ] OF Char;
```

The key word **PACKED** tells the compiler to place each character in as little space as possible—usually a single byte. Assignments to **Name** require exactly 20 characters, including extra blanks:

```
Name := 'Susan
```

Turbo Pascal's string data type simplifies character strings by allowing *dynamic* string variables that expand or contract according to the number of significant characters in the string. You can still declare strings as arrays of characters, but there is seldom a good reason for doing so. (Turbo Pascal ignores the **PACKED** key word, automatically putting characters into single bytes in character arrays.) To declare a 20-character string variable, type a length value in brackets after the key identifier, **String**:

```
VAR
   Name : String[20];
```

Declared this way, the length of **Name** depends on its contents. The size of the variable in memory—the total amount of space it occupies—doesn't change but can hold anywhere from zero to 20 characters. You now can assign both short and long strings to **Name** without worrying about trailing blanks.

```
Name := 'Susan';                  { 5 characters }
Name := 'abcdefghijklmnopqrst';   { 20 characters }
```

Figure 8-1 shows the railroad diagram for Turbo Pascal's string data type. Inside the brackets, or the alternate symbols (. and .), you can specify lengths from one to 255 characters. The declared length represents the maximum number of characters that the string may hold. The actual length of the string varies according to how many significant characters the string contains. If you don't specify a string length in brackets, Turbo Pascal creates a 255-character, maximum-length string. In other words, these declarations have identical results:

```
VAR
   MyString : String[255];
   YourString : String;
```

Program 8-1 demonstrates function **Length**, which returns the number of characters in a string. Although you can also use **Length** with character arrays, the value the function returns always equals the number of bytes in the array, rather than the number of significant characters. Therefore, you should normally use **Length** only with string variables.

string type

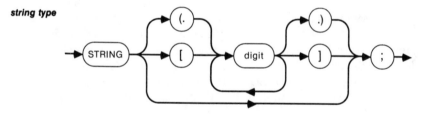

Figure 8-1 Railroad diagram for declaring string data types.

Program 8-1

```
1:   PROGRAM StringLength;
2:   VAR
3:      s : String[80];
4:   BEGIN
5:      REPEAT
```

Program 8-1 *cont.*

```
 6:        Writeln;
 7:        Write( 'Enter a string: ' );
 8:        Readln( s );
 9:        Writeln( 'Length = ', Length(s) )
10:     UNTIL Length(s) = 0
11:  END.
```

String Length

To record a string's actual length, Pascal stores a normally invisible single byte in front of all string variables. For example, the eight-character string in Figure 8-2 has five significant characters (HELLO) and three wasted positions. Because of the added length byte, string variables occupy one byte more than their declared lengths.

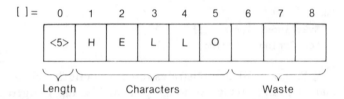

Figure 8-2 In memory, a string variable begins with a length byte followed by an array of characters.

As you can see from Figure 8-2, a string is simply an array of characters with the addition of a length byte. As with other arrays, you can index strings a character at a time. But, you cannot do the same with string constants—you can index only variables or variable constants. To demonstrate in-memory string representation, Program 8-2 is similar to Program 8-1 but shows the indexed characters of whatever string you enter. Enter HELLO, and you'll see a display that resembles Figure 8-2.

Program 8-2

```
1:  PROGRAM StringIndexing;
2:  CONST
3:     Blank = ' ';   { Single blank }
4:  VAR
5:     s : String[14];
6:     i : Integer;
7:  BEGIN
8:     REPEAT
```

Program 8-2 *cont.*

```
 9:        Writeln;
10:        Write( 'Enter a string: ' );
11:        Readln( s );
12:        FOR i := 0 TO Length(s) DO
13:            Write( '[',i:2,']', Blank );
14:        Writeln;
15:        Write( Ord( s[0] ):3, Blank:2 );
16:        FOR i := 1 TO Length(s) DO
17:            Write( s[i]:3, Blank:2 );
18:        Writeln
19:    UNTIL Length(s) = 0
20: END.
```

Line 15 of Program 8-2 shows a different way to find the length of a string. We know that the first byte of any string holds the length; therefore, the following statement is true:

```
Length(s) = Ord( s[0] );
```

In other words, the ordinal (integer) value of the byte at string index zero equals the length of the string. Because the **Length** function returns this value, there are few good reasons for directly accessing the length byte as shown here. At times, however, it's helpful to be able to preset the length of a string to some value before actually assigning any characters:

```
s[0] := Chr( 5 );
```

This sets the length of string **s** to five. The first five characters, left over from previous operations, are again made significant. Because all positions in the string are characters, to avoid a "Type mismatch" error, you must use the **Chr** function to assign the length value.

The result of this assignment is simply to store a 5 in the length byte of the string. The method works even if you turn range checking on with the compiler option {$R+}. Unlike other arrays, Turbo Pascal always allows you to index **s[0]**, although many other compilers consider zero to be outside the normal string range of **s[1]** . . . **s[n]**, where **n** is the declared string length.

Directly Setting String Length

As a practical example of setting the string length byte, procedure **DeTrail** (Program 8-3, lines 9-20) removes trailing blanks from string parameter **s**. The procedure searches for the first nonblank character starting from the end of the string and proceeding in a **WHILE** loop to the front. It correctly handles empty strings as well as those with all blanks.

Program 8-3

```
 1:   PROGRAM Trailers;
 2:   CONST
 3:      MaxLen = 80;
 4:   TYPE
 5:      String80 = String[80];
 6:   VAR
 7:      s : String80;
 8:
 9:   PROCEDURE DeTrail( VAR s : String80 );
10:   VAR
11:      i : Integer;
12:      Looking : Boolean;
13:   BEGIN
14:      i := Length(s); Looking := true;
15:      WHILE ( i > 0 ) AND Looking DO
16:        IF s[i] = ' '
17:           THEN i := i - 1
18:           ELSE Looking := false;
19:      s[0] := Chr( i )
20:   END; { DeTrail }
21:
22:   BEGIN
23:      Writeln( 'Remove trailing blanks' );
24:      REPEAT
25:         Writeln;
26:         Write( 'Enter a string: ' );
27:         Readln( s );
28:         Writeln( 'Length before ..... ', Length(s) );
29:         DeTrail( s );
30:         Writeln( 'Length after ...... ', Length(s) )
31:      UNTIL Length(s) = 0
32:   END.
```

DeTrail indexes the string with variable **i**, while looking for blank characters (line 16). If the procedure finds a blank, it sets **i** to **i − 1** and continues searching. Otherwise, it sets Boolean variable **Looking** to false, ending the **WHILE** loop at lines 15–18. The **WHILE** loop also ends if **i** becomes equal to zero.

String Operations

As with numbers, you can check if two strings are equal or if one is less than the other. The usual mathematics operators (= , < > , < , > , < = , and > =) apply to strings as well as to numeric values. The results, however, depend on the alphabetic order of characters in the string.

In addition to comparing two strings, you can combine them with **Concat**, short for "concatenate." **Concat** combines two or more strings into a single string variable. Program 8-4 demonstrates how **Concat** works. In line 8, the program adds to **Result** each new string you enter. You could replace line 8 with the following statement, which does the same thing:

```
Result := Result + Entry;
```

When concatenating strings, be careful to keep the result within the maximum declared string length. No harm is done if you exceed the maximum, but Turbo Pascal ignores any extra characters.

Program 8-4

```
 1:   PROGRAM Concatenation;
 2:   VAR
 3:      Entry, Result : String[80];
 4:   BEGIN
 5:      Result := '';
 6:      REPEAT
 7:         Write( 'Entry? ' ); Readln( Entry );
 8:         Result := Concat( Result, Entry );
 9:         Writeln( 'Result = ', Result )
10:      UNTIL Length( Entry ) = 0
11:   END.
```

You can combine several strings with one operation. Let's say you have three string variables, **Last** = 'Smith', **First** = 'John', and **Middle** = 'Q'. A mailing label program might concatenate the three strings this way:

```
Name := First + ' ' + Middle + '.' + ' ' + Last;
```

This sets **Name** to the string, 'John Q. Smith', inserting the proper spacing and punctuation.

Because the plus sign has a higher precedence than the relational operators (see Appendix E), you can safely compare concatenated strings in expressions like these:

```
IF s = 'IBM' + 'XT'
   THEN <statement1> ELSE
IF s = 'IBM' + 'AT'
   THEN <statement2>
```

Turbo Pascal concatenates the literal strings 'IBM' and 'XT' or 'AT' before comparing with **s**.

String Procedures

There are several procedures and functions available to manipulate strings. Procedure **Delete** removes a specified number of characters from anywhere inside a string. **Insert** does the opposite, inserting characters into a string at any position.

Insert requires three parameters: the string or character to insert, the string into which the insertion goes, and the indexed position where the insertion begins. Program 8-5 demonstrates how this works, inserting successive characters from A to K into string **s** at index six, in other words, at **s[6]**. When you run the program, you see characters already in the string move to the right to make room for new insertions.

Program 8-5 also demonstrates **Delete**, which takes three parameters: a string, the starting position of the deletion, and the number of characters to remove. Line 16 deletes one character from **s** at indexed position six (**s[6]**). Doing this eleven times removes the previous insertions.

Program 8-5

```
 1:   PROGRAM InsDelDemo;
 2:   VAR
 3:      s : String[80];
 4:      ch : Char;
 5:      i : Integer;
 6:   BEGIN
 7:      s := 'abcdefghijk';
 8:      Writeln( s );
 9:      FOR ch := 'A' TO 'K' DO
10:      BEGIN
11:         Insert( ch, s, 6 );
12:         Writeln( s )
13:      END;
14:      FOR i := 1 TO 11 DO
15:      BEGIN
16:         Delete( s, 6, 1 );
17:         Writeln( s )
18:      END
19:   END.
```

String Functions

Two functions copy strings and search for substrings inside string variables. Function **Copy** takes the same parameters as **Delete**, but, instead of removing characters, **Copy** simply transfers them to another variable. If string **Name** equals 'WASHINGTON', then the following sets **Name** to 'SHING':

```
Name := Copy( Name, 3, 5 );
```

The first **Copy** parameter is a string variable, the second is the starting indexed position in the string, and the third is the count of characters to copy. This writes the first character of any string:

```
Write( Copy( s, 1, 1 ) );
```

If you ask for more characters than available, **Copy** returns only as many characters as it can, up to the end of the string. If you use an index beyond the actual string length, **Copy** returns the null string (")—a string with zero length.

Function **Pos** returns the indexed position of one string in another. **Pos** returns zero if it fails to find the substring. Using **Pos**, you can easily write a program to search for embedded strings in a text file.

Program 8-6, which demonstrates **Pos**, prompts for the name of a text file in which to search for strings. (Enter the full file name, for example, PROG1.PAS or TEST.TXT.) The program prints all lines containing your search string. As a programmer's utility, the program finds statements that use a certain variable name. For example, try searching for all uses of **ch** and **FOR** in Program 8-5 (assuming, of course, you saved the program on disk.) What happens when you search for single-character variables such as **i** or **N**?

The program holds your search string in variable **SubString** (line 29). Procedure **UpperCase** converts all characters in the string to uppercase. Failing to do this would require the exact upper- and lowercase spelling of search strings. (Remove lines 32 and 39 to see the effect of not converting to uppercase.)

Variables **OneLine** and **Temporary** hold lines of text. After converting **Temporary** to uppercase (line 39), function **Pos** searches for **SubString** (line 40). **Pos** takes two parameters: the string to search for and the string in which to search. It returns the indexed position where it finds the first character of **SubString**, or zero if the string is absent. If **SubString** = 'SHING' and **Temporary** = 'WASHINGTON', then:

```
Pos( SubString, Temporary )
```

returns three, indicating the index where SHING starts in WASHINGTON.

Program 8-6

```
1:  PROGRAM Search;
2:  TYPE
3:     BigString  = String[132];
4:  VAR
5:     FileName   : String[14];
6:     FileVar    : Text;
7:     LineNumber : Integer;
8:     OneLine,
```

Program 8-6 *cont.*

```
 9:      Temporary,
10:      SubString  : BigString;
11:
12:  PROCEDURE UpperCase( VAR s : BigString );
13:  { Convert all chars in s to uppercase }
14:  VAR
15:     i : Integer;
16:  BEGIN
17:     FOR i := 1 TO length(s) DO
18:        s[i] := Upcase( s[i] )
19:  END; { UpperCase }
20:
21:  BEGIN
22:     Write( 'Search what text file? ' );
23:     Readln( FileName );
24:     Assign( FileVar, FileName );
25:     REPEAT
26:        Writeln;
27:        Reset( FileVar );
28:        Write( 'Search for? (RET to quit) ' );
29:        Readln( SubString );
30:        IF Length( SubString ) > 0 THEN
31:        BEGIN
32:           UpperCase( Substring );
33:           LineNumber := 0;
34:           WHILE NOT Eof( FileVar ) DO
35:           BEGIN
36:              Readln( FileVar, OneLine );
37:              LineNumber := LineNumber + 1;
38:              Temporary := OneLine;
39:              UpperCase( Temporary );
40:              IF Pos( SubString, Temporary ) > 0
41:                 THEN Writeln( LineNumber:3, ': ', OneLine )
42:           END { while }
43:        END { if }
44:     UNTIL Length( SubString ) = 0
45:  END.
```

Strings As Parameters

When designing your own procedures and functions with string parameters, Turbo Pascal normally insists that the declared lengths of actual parameters match the lengths of formal parameters. In other words, if you design a procedure with a variable parameter **ParamString** of type **String[40]**, you can pass only string variables of that same size to the procedure.

While this automatic check prevents a dangerous error, it also imposes an often annoying restriction. The danger looms when you pass to a procedure or function by reference a string smaller than the type of the formal parameter. In this situation, a concatenation or other operation in the procedure might cause the formal parameter to grow larger than the maximum length of the actual variable, thus overwriting other items in memory. On the negative side, restricting formal parameters to the same size actual variables, while preventing this error, also makes it hard to design procedures to operate on all strings, regardless of length.

Luckily, it's easy to turn string length checking off, as Program 8-7 demonstrates with a procedure **DownCase** that converts strings from upper- to lowercase. Line 11 adds 32 to the ordinal (ASCII) value of each string character found in line 10 to be in the set **['A' . . 'Z']**.

The procedure's formal parameter **s** is of type **String**, with a maximum length of 255 characters. Because the **FOR** loop restricts index **i** to the actual string length, you cannot accidentally index past the end of a shorter string. The main program at line 17 passes **LittleString**, with a maximum of 40 characters, to procedure **DownCase**. The compiler directives {$V –} and {$V +} temporarily turn off string length checking, allowing the procedure to accept the short parameter.

To see the difference string length checking makes, remove the directives in line 17 and recompile. You receive:

```
Error 26: Type mismatch
```

because the actual string parameter type is shorter than the declared length of **s**.

You can turn off string parameter length checks by inserting a {$v –} compiler directive at the beginning of a program or by changing the Options:Compiler: Var-string-checking setting from Strict to Relaxed. Usually, though, it's best to turn off string length checks temporarily as in Program 8-7. This way, you aren't likely to run programs with the wrong setting in effect.

Program 8-7

```
1:   PROGRAM MixedLengths;
2:   VAR
3:      LittleString : String[40];
4:
5:   PROCEDURE DownCase( VAR s : String );
6:   VAR
7:      i : Integer;
8:   BEGIN
9:      FOR i := 1 TO Length( s ) DO
10:        IF s[i] IN [ 'A' .. 'Z' ]
11:           THEN s[i] := Chr( Ord( s[i] ) + 32 )
```

Program 8-7 *cont.*

```
12:  END; { DownCase }
13:
14:  BEGIN
15:    REPEAT
16:      Write( '? ' ); Readln( LittleString );
17:      {$V-} DownCase( LittleString ); {$V+}
18:      Writeln( LittleString )
19:    UNTIL Length( LittleString ) = 0
20:  END.
```

Writing Your Own String Functions

Many Pascal compilers restrict function results to scalar and real-number data types. But in the special case of a string type, Turbo Pascal breaks the common mold, letting you write functions that return strings. For example, here's a simple function that removes blank characters from a string:

```
FUNCTION NoBlanks( s : String ) : String;
VAR j : Integer;
BEGIN
   j := 1;
   WHILE ( j <= Length(s) ) DO
     IF s[ j ] = ' '
        THEN Delete( s, j, 1 )
        ELSE Inc( j );
   NoBlanks := s
END; { NoBlanks }
```

NoBlanks operates on a single value parameter **s**. After using **Delete** to remove blanks from **s**, the final statement in **NoBlanks** assigns **s** to the function name, thus passing the edited string back to the caller. To use the function, create a string variable, say **MyName**. Then, to remove blanks from **MyName**, write an expression such as:

```
MyName := NoBlanks( MyName );
```

Technically, **NoBlanks** returns an address, even though it appears to return a **String** data type. The address points to the actual string variable stored somewhere in memory. At most times, you can ignore this detail and use string functions as though they were actual strings. This doesn't always hold true. For instance, you can't index a string function:

```
writeln( NoBlanks(s)[4] );      { Incorrect! }
```

Although that appears to index the fourth character in the string result of **NoBlanks**, Turbo Pascal rejects the statement. If you remember the earlier-stated rule that string and other function results may be used where *constants* can normally appear, you'll avoid backing yourself into such corners. (You can't index string constants, either.)

You may be wondering how it is possible for Turbo Pascal to return strings as function results, which are usually restricted to real numbers, integers, and other scalar values. Because string functions actually return addresses that point to string variables in memory, and because functions can, of course, return pointers, string functions obey Pascal's rules by returning a kind of secret string pointer that doesn't require you to use the pointer techniques described in Chapter 7.

Related to this is the fact that all arrays, of which strings are merely special subsets, are passed by address to procedure and function parameters. Even if you don't use the **VAR** key word to declare string and array parameters, the variables are passed by address. Most times, you can ignore this technical detail, which helps keep compiled code running fast. String and array parameters operate like parameters of other types, but you should be aware that Turbo Pascal always passes these items around by address.

When designing your own string functions, you may first have to declare a new string data type. This is necessary because you cannot write function declarations like this:

```
FUNCTION Name : String[40];    {Incorrect!}
```

Instead, you first have to declare a new string data type. Then you can write the function declaration to return the new type:

```
TYPE
    String40 = String[40];


FUNCTION Name : String40;
```

To demonstrate how to design string functions, Program 8-8 writes the color names for enumerated type **Colors** (line 4). Function **ColorName** takes a parameter **Col** of that type and, with the help of a **CASE** statement, returns an appropriate string as the function value. The **Writeln** statement in line 19 activates the function to write the names of the three colors, Red, White, and Blue.

Program 8-8

```
1:  PROGRAM StringFunctions;
2:  TYPE
3:      String8 = String[8];
4:      Colors = ( Red, White, Blue );
5:  VAR
6:      C : Colors;
```

Program 8-8 *cont.*

```
 7:
 8:   FUNCTION ColorName( Col : Colors ) : String8;
 9:   BEGIN
10:      CASE Col OF
11:         Red   : ColorName := 'Red';
12:         White : ColorName := 'White';
13:         Blue  : ColorName := 'Blue'
14:      END
15:   END; { ColorName }
16:
17:   BEGIN
18:      FOR C := Red TO Blue DO
19:         Writeln( ColorName( C ) )
20:   END.
```

Special Characters

There are two special ways to assign values to character and string variables, methods not usually found in Pascal compilers.

In the ASCII character set, characters with ordinal values 0 to 31 are called *control characters* because, when written to the display or printer, they typically cause actions to occur rather than visible symbols to appear. For example, this statement:

```
Write( Chr(7) );
```

rings the bell or beeps the beeper on terminals and computers that recognize ASCII code 7 as the bell control character. Another control character, ASCII 12, advances most printers to the top of a new page. As originally designed, Pascal has a procedure **Page** that does the same thing. Although Turbo Pascal lacks a built-in **Page**, it's easy to write your own procedure:

```
PROCEDURE Page( VAR f : Text );
BEGIN
   Write( f, Chr( 12 ) )
END;
```

To use the new procedure, **Rewrite** a text file **f** to 'PRN' and execute **Page(f)** to advance the printer to the top of a new page. Some terminals, but not all, clear the screen if you use **Page(Output)**. This doesn't always work because not all terminals recognize ASCII 12 as a screen control character. On the IBM PC, for example, paging the standard **Output** file displays the astronomy symbol for Venus ♀ (or, depending on your specialty, the biology symbol for a female organism). This may come as a surprise, but it's a good example of why you should not expect all ASCII terminals to understand the same control characters.

In Turbo Pascal, you can also write control characters with a preceding caret. The following statement rings the bell.

```
Write( ^G );
```

Pascal translates the symbol ^G (control G) into the equivalent of Chr(7). All other control characters have associated letters starting with ^A = Chr(1), ^B = Chr(2), and so on. The letters correspond to the values generated by pressing the Ctrl key and that same letter on the keyboard. (Although letters are capitalized, you don't have to press the shift key.) For instance, to check if an operator enters Ctrl-E, a program could use these statements:

```
Read( ch );
IF ch = ^E
   THEN DoSomething;
```

Numbers to Characters

You can also assign ASCII values to character variables. Precede a value with a number sign (#), and the compiler considers that value to be an ASCII character, not an integer. This is most useful in constant declarations:

```
CONST
   BellChar = #7;
   CtrlE    = #5;
```

To do the same thing with most other Pascal compilers, you'd have to declare a **BellChar** variable and then assign to it the ASCII value you want. Using such special features may be convenient, but it can also make transporting programs to other compilers more difficult.

Character Constants in Strings

Because values like #7 and ^H are character constants, you can use them in strings as long as you insert the characters with no intervening symbols *outside* the string's quote delimiters. For example, to beep the terminal and display a string at the same time, use the **Writeln** statement:

```
Writeln( #7'Beep!' );
```

One useful application of this idea is in error messages. Because errors might occur at any time during a program run, it's usually wise to first execute a carriage return and then display the message. This way, all messages line up along the left screen border where they are easy to see. Program 8-9 demonstrates the idea and shows how to mix character constants and control characters in literal strings (line 5). Notice that although line 6 executes a **Write** statement, the error message starts on a new display line because of the carriage return (#13) and line feed (#10) character constants assigned to **s** in line 5.

Program 8-9

```
1:   PROGRAM CharConstants;
2:   VAR
3:      s : String[80];
4:   BEGIN
5:      s := #13#10'***'^G'Error!';
6:      Write( 'I detect an...' );
7:      Writeln( s )
8:   END.
```

Summary

Along with Turbo Pascal's built-in string data type, there are a number of procedures and functions for combining, checking length, copying, searching substring positions, and doing other string operations. Early versions of Pascal used character arrays for strings. While you can do the same in Turbo Pascal, dynamic strings are more versatile.

String variables may hold from zero to 255 characters. Physically, string variables are arrays of characters with a length byte at index zero (s[0]). The declared string length limits the maximum characters the string can hold. The actual length of the string changes depending on how many characters are in the string. You can index string variables similar to the way you index other arrays. You cannot index string constants.

Length returns the actual length of a string. **Concat** joins two or more strings. You can use a plus sign (+) in place of **Concat**. Other string routines, **Copy**, **Insert**, and **Delete**, let you manipulate strings. **Pos** finds a substring, if it exists, in another string.

Turbo Pascal checks that string parameters to procedures and functions have the same declared lengths. You can turn off this feature with the {$V – } compiler directive at the risk of introducing a bug in your program if you increase a string's actual length beyond the declared maximum.

Even though Turbo Pascal normally limits function results to scalars and real numbers, it breaks the rules for strings, letting you write string functions. Actually, string functions return pointers to string variables, thus obeying Pascal's rules for function data types. Related to this is the fact that Turbo Pascal passes all string and array procedure and function parameters by address, regardless of whether the parameters are declared with **VAR**.

Exercises

8-1. Design a mailing list program (or several programs) to store names and addresses in a disk file. Let the operator select one of three printout formats: labels, directory, and envelopes. The directory should come out last name first, while labels and envelopes should show names in normal order. Use string procedures and functions in your program.

8-2. Write a utility program to hunt for all key words in a Pascal text and convert them to uppercase.

8-3. Write a search and replace program to hunt for any string in a text file and change it to something else.

8-4. Design a procedure for editing strings. Use control characters to delete characters, move forward and back, and insert blanks. After testing, add your procedure to your program in exercise 8-1.

9

Introducing the Unit

- The USES Declaration
- Unit Disk Files
- Using Units in Programs
- The System Unit
- The Crt Unit
- The Dos Unit
- The Printer Unit
- The Turbo3 Unit
- The Graph3 Unit

9

Key Words and Identifiers

AssignCrt, ClrEol, ClrScr, Delay, DelLine, DiskFree, DiskSize, DosVersion, EnvCount, EnvStr, FExpand, FindFirst, FindNext, FSearch, FSplit, GetCBreak, GetDate, GetEnv, GetFAttr, GetFTime, GetTime, GetVerify, GotoXY, HighVideo, InsLine, Intr, Keypressed, LowVideo, MsDos, NormVideo, NoSound, PackTime, ReadKey, SetCBreak, SetDate, SetFAttr, SetFTime, SetTime, SetVerify, Sound, TextBackground, TextColor, TextMode, UnPackTime, USES, WhereX, WhereY, Window

A unit is a precompiled collection of Pascal goodies, ready for other programs to share. A kind of programmer's warehouse, a unit stocks raw materials—constants, types, variables, procedures, and functions—in a form that Turbo Pascal can quickly attach to programs.

Although a unit can store anything that you might find in a normal Pascal program, a unit is not itself a complete program. You can't run a unit on its own. Instead, you have to write a *host program* that uses the unit's features, just as though you declared those same features directly in the program.

This chapter explains how to use Turbo Pascal's standard units as well as other precompiled units that you might purchase from software companies. Chapter 10 explains how to write your own units and how to convert units to *overlays*, which can share memory to reduce a large program's RAM consumption.

The USES Declaration

To attach a unit to a program, insert the unit's name in a **USES** declaration, which appears immediately after the **PROGRAM** line but before any **LABEL**, **CONST**, **TYPE**, **VAR**, **PROCEDURE**, or **FUNCTION** declarations. For example, to use unit **Crt**, you could start your program like this:

```
PROGRAM UsesOneUnit;
USES Crt;
```

A semicolon must come at the end of the **USES** declaration. To use more than one unit, separate the unit names with commas:

```
PROGRAM UsesManyUnits;
USES Crt, Dos, Graph;
```

This program uses three units: **Crt**, **Dos**, and **Graph**. For each unit a program uses, Turbo Pascal reads from the unit disk file a special section called the *unit interface*. Inside the interface are the declarations describing the unit's contents. The compiler needs this information to know what's in a unit.

Of course, you also need to know what's in a unit before you can put the unit's features to work. To find this information, you can't read a unit disk file, which is stored in precompiled form for the compiler's use only. Instead, you have to read the unit interface in its original text form. For example, Turbo Pascal's standard units come with .DOC text files that describe the unit's contents. These files are purely for reference—you can't modify and compile them to change how units operate. If you purchase units from other companies, you'll probably receive similar files or printed interface documentation.

Table 9-1 lists Turbo Pascal's standard units. The TURBO.TPL (Turbo Pascal Library) file stores multiple units in a single file. The .TPU (Turbo Pascal Unit) files store individual compiled units. Each unit has an associated .DOC file. Depending on your installation, these files may be stored in different subdirectories. We'll cover the Crt, Dos, Graph3, Printer, System, and Turbo3 units in this chapter. Chapter 10 describes how to use the Overlay unit. Chapter 11 is devoted to the Graph unit.

Table 9-1 Turbo Pascal standard units

Name	Disk file	Description
Crt	TURBO.TPL	Fast direct-video display routines
Dos	TURBO.TPL	DOS functions
Graph	GRAPH.TPU	Graphics kernel
Graph3	GRAPH3.TPU	Version 3.0 graphics
Overlay	TURBO.TPL	Overlay manager
Printer	TURBO.TPL	Printer output
System	TURBO.TPL	Standard run-time library
Turbo3	TURBO3.TPU	Version 3.0 miscellaneous

Unit Disk Files

Individual units are compiled to files ending in .TPU, which you may transfer to TURBO.TPL for faster loading when using the integrated environment. Turbo Pascal reads all TURBO.TPL into memory, making the library's precompiled units instantly available to host programs. Use the TPUMOVER program (described in Chapter 10) to transfer compiled units in and out of TURBO.TPL. To gain extra memory during compilation, you can remove the **Turbo3** and **Graph3** units, needed only to compile version 3.0 programs. Table 9-1 lists the units that you'll probably want to keep in TURBO.TPL.

If a unit listed in a **USES** declaration is not in TURBO.TPL, the compiler searches for a file *unitname*.TPU in the current directory. If it still can't find the compiled unit, it searches all the paths specified in *Options-Directories-Unit directories*. This lets you store compiled units in various subdirectories, but still allows the compiler to find them. For example, to make the compiler search for compiled units in GRAPH, TURBO3, and MYUNITS subdirectories of C:\TP, you could change your *Unit directories* entry to:

```
C:\TP\GRAPH;C:\TP\TURBO3;C:\TP\MYUNITS
```

Using Units in Programs

A simple example demonstrates how to compile programs that use units. Program 9-1 uses the **Crt** unit (line 2). The program displays a message (line 4) and executes a **REPEAT** loop (lines 5–7) until function **ReadKey** returns ASCII character 13, the value generated by pressing the Enter key. When you press Enter, line 8 clears the display by calling **ClrScr**.

Function **ReadKey** and procedure **ClrScr** are not part of the Pascal language. They are precompiled routines stored inside the **Crt** unit. (For more information on these routines, look them up in Chapter 16, which lists all Turbo Pascal procedures and functions in alphabetic order.) Because of the **USES Crt** declaration, the routines are available—just as though they were Pascal natives. To prove this, remove line 2 and recompile. Instead of success, when the compiler reaches **ReadKey**, it displays the error message:

```
Error 3: Unknown identifier
```

Because **ReadKey** is defined in **Crt**, you must use the unit for the compiler to know what **ReadKey** means. You would receive the same error at line 8 if the compiler got that far. **ClrScr** is a routine in **Crt**. You have to specify **USES Crt** for the compiler to know what **ClrScr** is. As you can see, using units adds new commands to Pascal, customizing the language to understand how to accomplish new tasks.

Program 9-1

```
1:  PROGRAM Clear;
2:  USES Crt;
3:  BEGIN
4:     Write( 'Press Enter to clear the screen' );
5:     REPEAT
6:        { wait }
7:     UNTIL ReadKey = Chr(13);
8:     ClrScr
9:  END.
```

The System Unit

The **System** unit is a phantom, always around even if you don't insert it in your program's **USES** declaration. Inside **System** are most of Turbo Pascal's standard procedures and functions, such as the string routines described in Chapter 8. You never have to tell the compiler to use **System**—it will anyway.

Think of the **System** unit as a kind of shell enveloping every program you write. Chapter 16 lists all of **System**'s many routines, too numerous to discuss individually here.

SYSTEM.DOC details the **System** unit's interface, which does not list standard procedures and functions such as **Writeln** and **Read**, even though these and other native routines are actually stored in **System**, sometimes also called the *runtime library*. **System** includes several variable (typed) constants that define Turbo Pascal's internal values, for example, the location of the heap and the size of the stack. You'll meet many of these values again in Chapter 13. Also in the **System** unit are the standard **Input** and **Output** text file variables plus a series of pointers in which Turbo Pascal saves interrupt vectors when programs start running. Interrupt vectors are pointers to routines stored in your computer's ROM and in DOS. Because Turbo Pascal hooks into some of these routines, it saves the original pointers for restoring when the program ends.

It's probably best to be aware that the **System** unit exists—and then forget about it. Because you never have to tell the compiler to use **System**, you may as well consider this unit's features to be native Turbo Pascal residents.

The Crt Unit

The **Crt** unit contains constants, variables, and routines to control the display and keyboard. (Crt stands for *Cathode Ray Tube* but, in computer jargon, generally refers to the display and keyboard together.)

Adding the **Crt** unit to programs does more than simply give you a few neat procedures and functions to use. Using **Crt** also replaces the **Write** and **Writeln** standard text output routines with super-fast, direct-video code. Using **Crt**, then, has three important side effects:

1. Writing text to the display goes as fast as possible by transferring characters directly to video display memory buffers rather than calling slower BIOS (Basic Input Output System) ROM routines.

2. Program output from **Write** and **Writeln** statements can no longer be redirected or piped with the DOS <, >, and | command characters. As you'll learn in a moment, there is a way to provide this ability by using a text file along with **Crt**.

3. Programs might not run correctly under control of some multitasking software, which shares computer time among several programs stored together in memory.

The Crt Unit Variables

This section describes **Crt**'s several variables, which you can examine and change. The unit also declares a number of constants described in the sections that follow:

CheckBreak : Boolean;

Normally true, **CheckBreak** controls whether programs halt on the *next* **Write** or **Writeln** statement to execute after you press Ctrl-Break. Set **CheckBreak** to false to disable Ctrl-Break checking:

```
CheckBreak := FALSE;  { Disable Ctrl-Break checking }
```

CheckEof : Boolean;

Use **CheckEof** to control the effect of pressing Ctrl-Z during **Read** and **Readln** statements. Normally, **CheckEof** is false, ignoring Ctrl-Z. When true, pressing Ctrl-Z during input sets **Eof** to true. A few examples clarify the importance of this action:

```
VAR s : String; i, j, k : Integer;

CheckEof := TRUE;   { Enable Ctrl-Z checking }
Readln( s );
Reset( input );
Read( i, j, k );
```

With **CheckEof** true, the **Readln** statement ends as soon as you press Ctrl-Z, setting **Eof** true for the standard input file. If **CheckEof** were false, then pressing Ctrl-Z in **Readln** would have no effect—you'd have to press Enter to continue as you normally do in **Readln** statements.

The **Reset** statement is necessary after **Readln** because **Eof**, once set to true, remains true until resetting the file. If you did not reset the standard input file and if you typed Ctrl-Z to **Readln**, the next **Read** statement would not execute.

The **Read** statement lets you type three numbers separated with spaces. When **CheckEof** is true, pressing Ctrl-Z immediately ends input—even before you supply values for all variables. Pressing 5 and then Ctrl-Z sets **i** to 5, and **j**, **k** to 0. When **CheckEof** is false, pressing Ctrl-Z has no effect; you must supply values for all variables before the **Read** statement ends.

DirectVideo : Boolean;

Set **DirectVideo** to false (it's normally true) to disable writing characters directly to video display memory. Because this slows text output by calling inefficient BIOS ROM routines, do this only if you have problems with text I/O when using **Crt**. If you have this problem, set the variable to false:

```
DirectVideo := FALSE;   { Disable direct video output }
```

Setting **DirectVideo** to false does not reenable the ability to redirect program output with the <, >, and | DOS command-line characters. To use **Crt** and be able to redirect program output, **Rewrite** a text file with a null file name. Program 9-2 demonstrates how this works, attaching a text file to standard output, bypassing **Crt**'s direct video effects on **Write** and **Writeln**. Compile the program to disk as TEST.EXE (or any other name) and type:

```
TEST >TEST.TXT
```

This redirects the line "This text is redirectable" to file TEST.TXT. You could also type >PRN to redirect output to the printer. The **Writeln** statement in line 8, though, is not redirectable—the text always appears on screen because of **Crt**'s direct video routines. Setting **DirectVideo** to false would still not allow line 8 to be redirected.

Program 9-2

```
 1:  PROGRAM CrtRedirection;
 2:  USES Crt;
 3:  VAR f : TEXT;
 4:  BEGIN
 5:     Assign( f, '' );
 6:     Rewrite( f );
 7:     Writeln( f , 'This text is redirectable');
 8:     Writeln( 'This text is not redirectable');
 9:     Close( f )
10:  END.
```

CheckSnow : Boolean;

If you see "snow storms" on some older CGA video systems, especially during scrolling and when clearing the display, set **CheckSnow** to true. Monochrome and newer EGA and VGA displays do not have this problem.

You might want to include a command in your program's setup procedure to ask people if they see snow on their screens. If so, set **CheckSnow** to true to cure the problem. Unfortunately, this also slows output so don't take this step unless absolutely necessary.

LastMode : Word;

When calling **TextMode** to switch video text modes, **Crt** stores the mode number in **LastMode**. (This variable probably would be better named *CurrentMode*.) To switch to a different mode, use programming such as:

```
VAR mode : Word;

mode := LastMode;     { Save current text mode value }
TextMode( CO40 );     { Switch to color 40-column mode }
:
{ commands in Color 40-column mode }
:
TextMode( mode );     { Restore previous text mode }
```

TextAttr : Byte;

Normally, use procedures **TextColor** and **TextBackground** to change foreground and background colors or attributes such as underlining and bold characters on monochrome systems. When speed is important, though, you can accomplish the same job by storing values directly in the **TextAttr** byte.

Figure 9-1 shows this byte's format. Bit 7 controls whether characters are solid or blinking. Bits 4–6 specify the background color, 0 to 7. Bits 0–3 set the foreground color from 0 to 15. Use **Crt**'s 16 color constants to set the blink attribute, foreground, and background colors in one assignment statement. Here are a few examples:

```
{ White on blue, no blink }
TextAttr := White + Blue * 16;

{ Blinking "red alert" warning }
TextAttr := Red + LightGray * 16 + Blink;

{ Normal white on black, no blink }
TextAttr := White + Black * 16;
```

WindMin : Word; and WindMax : Word;

These two variables hold the minimum and maximum display coordinates. The low byte of each word equals the horizontal (x) coordinate. The high byte equals

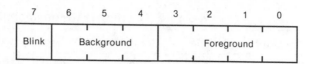

Figure 9-1 The **TextAttr** byte in unit **Crt** packs background and foregound color values plus a single blink bit into one eight-bit variable.

the vertical (y) coordinate. To set four variables to the top-left (x1,y1) and bottom-right (x2,y2) window corners, write:

```
x1 := Lo( WindMin ) + 1;
y1 := Hi( WindMin ) + 1;
x2 := Lo( WindMax ) + 1;
y2 := Hi( WindMax ) + 1;
```

Notice that you must add one to each value for the correct coordinate values. While **WindMin** and **WindMax** range from 0 to the maximum coordinate less one, **Crt**'s **GotoXY** cursor positioning procedure requires coordinate values from 1 to the maximum.

Controlling the Cursor

One procedure (**GotoXY**) and two functions (**WhereX** and **WhereY**) change and examine the cursor position. Use **GotoXY** (some people call it "go-toxy", others say "go-to-x-y") to position the cursor anywhere on screen. **GotoXY**(1,1) sends the cursor to the upper-left corner of the current window. Use functions **WhereX** and **WhereY** to locate the current cursor position. For example:

```
VAR x, y : Integer; yourName : String;

GotoXY( 10, 21 );  { Position cursor at x=10, y=21 }
Write( 'Enter your name: ' );   { Display prompt }
Readln( yourName );   { Get answer }

x := WhereX;       { Assign cursor location }
y := WhereY;       {  to x and y. }
```

Controlling the Display

Crt has a number of routines to help you design good-looking displays. You can clear portions of the screen, turn on special video modes, and select foreground and background colors.

To switch video modes, use **TextMode** along with one of the constant values from Table 9-2. Each time you do this, **Crt** saves the mode value in variable **LastMode** as explained earlier. Remember that this variable always specifies the text mode *now* in effect—not the mode last in effect as its name implies.

Table 9-2 Crt unit TextMode constants

Constant	Value	Columns	Lines	Display mode
BW40	0	40	25	Black and white
CO40	1	40	25	Color
C40	1	40	25	Color
BW80	2	80	25	Black and white
CO80	3	80	25	Color
C80	3	80	25	Color
Mono	7	80	25	Monochrome
Font8x8	256	80	43	EGA compressed text
Font8x8	256	80	50	VGA compressed text

Notes. BW40, CO40, C40, BW80, CO80, and C80 require a color video system such as CGA, EGA, or VGA. Mono requires a monochrome adapter (MDA), Hercules, or equivalent. Font8x8 must be added to CO80 to select either 43- or 50-line compressed text displays.

Compressed 43- and 50-Line Text

Add the **Font8x8** constant to **CO80** to select EGA 43-line or VGA 50-line displays:

```
TextMode( CO80 + Font8x8 );
```

Use **LastMode** to leave the video mode unchanged but select between normal and compressed EGA 43-line or VGA 50-line displays. Assuming the display is compressed, this switches to normal 25-line text:

```
TextMode( Lo( LastMode ) );
```

To switch back to 43- or 50-line text, add back the **Font8 × 8** constant like this, leaving the video mode unchanged while returning to compressed text:

```
TextMode( Lo( LastMode ) + Font8x8 );
```

Clearing, Inserting, and Deleting Text

Call **ClrScr** to clear the entire screen or window. **ClrEol** clears from the cursor to the end of the line. To clear the entire line and leave the cursor position unchanged, insert this procedure into your program:

```
PROCEDURE ClrLine;
VAR x, y : Integer;
BEGIN
   x := WhereX; y := WhereY;
   GotoXY( 1, y );
   ClrEol;
   GotoXY( x, y )
END;
```

ClrLine simulates the clear-line operation found on many video terminals. To clear from the cursor position to the end of the screen requires a bit more work:

```
PROCEDURE ClrEosc;
VAR xx, yy, y : Integer;
BEGIN
   ClrEol;
   yy := WhereY; xx := WhereX;
   FOR y := yy + 1 TO Hi(WindMax)+1 DO
   BEGIN
      GotoXY( 1, y ); ClrEol
   END;
   GotoXY( xx, yy )
END;
```

By carefully using **ClrEol**, **WhereY**, **WhereX**, **GotoXY**, and **WindMax**, **ClrEosc** works correctly for all video modes, inside restricted windows (described in the next section) and in 43- and 50-line compressed displays.

To insert a blank line at the current cursor position, call **InsLine**. All lines from the cursor below move down one line within the current window. The last line in the window is permanently lost. To delete a line at the current cursor position, call **DelLine**. The deleted line is permanently lost, all lines below the cursor move up one line, and a blank line replaces the last line in the window.

Text Windows

Windows have become such a popular subject in modern software design that any language or product that doesn't have them may have serious trouble competing in the market. Turbo Pascal offers a limited form of windows demonstrated in Program 9-3. The **Window** procedure changes the relative display borders. It has the form:

```
PROCEDURE Window( x1, y1, x2, y2 : Byte );
```

Technically, this is the correct definition as found in **Crt**'s interface. But you might find it easier to work with **Window** if you pretend it to be declared like this:

```
PROCEDURE Window( Left, Top, Right, Bottom : Byte );
```

The four byte parameters represent the screen coordinates of the new corners. Normally, **Left** and **Right** range from 1 to 80, and **Top** and **Bottom,** from 1 to 25.

After setting a new window's parameters, the top-left corner has the coordinate (1,1). In other words, executing **GotoXY(1,1)** always sends the cursor to the top-left window corner, regardless of where that is on the entire screen. Other procedures such as **ClrScr** and **ClrEol** also respect the new window borders.

Program 9-3 demonstrates these ideas. A record type, **WindRec**, keeps track of the borders of two display windows, **Wind1** and **Wind2**. Procedure

OpenWind (lines 16–24) uses the **Window** procedure to set the new borders and put the cursor in the lower-left corner (lines 20–21). Procedure **TextBox** (line 64) draws a simple box around the window, using an extended character, ASCII 176.

After initializing two windows (lines 97–98), the program lets you enter a file name (see function **OpenFile**, line 26). The function returns true only if it can open the file you request.

With the file open, procedure **DisplayFile** at line 50 reads and displays the file's contents in the larger window. Because line 54 switches to **Wind2**, the contents of the smaller entry window are not disturbed while lines of text scroll off the screen.

By separating the input and output windows, you can view text but still see the command you gave to open the file. In a way, the program runs as though there were separate computer screens, each with a different purpose. The windows help you form a mental image of what the program is supposed to do, even if they don't actually do much to help the computer complete its task.

Program 9-3

```
 1:   PROGRAM Windows;
 2:   USES Crt;
 3:
 4:   TYPE
 5:      WindRec = RECORD
 6:                    WindTop,
 7:                    WindBottom,
 8:                    WindLeft,
 9:                    WindRight : Integer
10:                END;
11:   VAR
12:      Done : Boolean;
13:      Wind1, Wind2 : WindRec;
14:      TextFile : Text;
15:
16:   PROCEDURE OpenWind( Wind : WindRec );
17:   BEGIN
18:      WITH Wind DO
19:      BEGIN
20:         Window( WindLeft, WindTop, WindRight, WindBottom );
21:         Gotoxy( 1, 1 + WindBottom - WindTop );
22:         Writeln
23:      END
24:   END; { OpenWind }
25:
26:   FUNCTION OpenFile : Boolean;
27:   { True if file open; False if user quits }
28:   VAR
```

Program 9-3 *cont.*

```
29:     ErrCode : Integer;
30:     FileName : String;
31: BEGIN
32:    OpenWind( Wind1 );
33:    REPEAT
34:       Writeln( 'Enter a file name' );
35:       Write( ']' );
36:       Readln( FileName );
37:       IF Length( FileName ) = 0 THEN
38:       BEGIN
39:          OpenFile := False; Exit
40:       END;
41:       Assign( TextFile, FileName );
42:       {$i-} Reset( TextFile ); {$i+}
43:       ErrCode := IoResult;
44:       IF ErrCode <> 0
45:          THEN Writeln( 'Error #', ErrCode, #7#13#10 )
46:    UNTIL ErrCode = 0;
47:    OpenFile := True
48: END; { OpenFile }
49:
50: PROCEDURE DisplayFile;
51: VAR
52:    s : String[132];
53: BEGIN;
54:    OpenWind( Wind2 );
55:    Writeln;
56:    WHILE NOT Eof( TextFile ) DO
57:    BEGIN
58:       Readln( TextFile, s );
59:       Writeln( s )
60:    END;
61:    Close( TextFile )
62: END; { DisplayFile }
63:
64: PROCEDURE TextBox( Top, Bottom, Left, Right : Integer );
65: VAR
66:    x, y : Integer;
67:
68:    PROCEDURE TwoChar( x1, y1, x2, y2 : Integer );
69:    BEGIN
70:       Gotoxy( x1, y1 ); Write( chr(176) );
71:       Gotoxy( x2, y2 ); Write( chr(176) )
72:    END;
73:
```

Program 9-3 *cont.*

```
74:  BEGIN
75:     FOR x := Left TO Right DO
76:        TwoChar( x, Top, x, Bottom );
77:     FOR y := Top TO Bottom DO
78:        TwoChar( Left, y, Right, y )
79:  END; { TextBox }
80:
81:  PROCEDURE InitWind( VAR Wind : WindRec;
82:                          Top, Bottom, Left, Right : Integer );
83:  BEGIN
84:     TextBox( Top, Bottom, Left, Right );
85:     WITH Wind DO
86:     BEGIN
87:        WindTop    := Top+1;
88:        WindBottom := Bottom-1;
89:        WindLeft   := Left+1;
90:        WindRight  := Right-1
91:     END
92:  END; { InitWind }
93:
94:  PROCEDURE Initialize;
95:  BEGIN
96:     ClrScr;
97:     InitWind( Wind1, 1, 12, 1, 21 );
98:     InitWind( Wind2, 5, 22, 26, 80 )
99:  END; { Initialize }
100:
101: BEGIN
102:    Initialize;
103:    REPEAT
104:       Done := NOT OpenFile;
105:       IF NOT Done
106:          THEN DisplayFile
107:    UNTIL Done;
108:    Window( 1, 1, 80, 25 );
109:    ClrScr
110: END.
```

Controlling the Keyboard

The **Keypressed** Boolean function returns true if it senses a key was pressed sometime earlier. This lets you write **REPEAT** loops such as:

```
REPEAT {wait} UNTIL Keypressed;
```

The loop waits until you press a key. The comment {*wait*} is not necessary—it merely makes the purpose of the statement clear. Actually, there is a null statement (which isn't really there, of course) between the **REPEAT** and **UNTIL**. You may be amused by this bit of sorcery, but null statements are no joke. If Pascal did not allow them, you could never write a "do-nothing" loop like this one—you'd have to use a real statement. And then, the do-nothing loop would no longer do nothing!

Reading Characters in Silence

For some odd reason, reading a single character from the keyboard without displaying the character is one of those tricky subjects that most computer languages never seem to get right. Even older Turbo Pascal versions made the job unnecessarily difficult. Luckily, the **Crt ReadKey** character function threatens an end to this controversy once and for all. To read a single character, use the following statement:

```
ch := ReadKey;
```

(Variable ch is of type Char.)

The statement pauses for you to press a key, depositing the ASCII result in variable **ch**. **ReadKey** has absolutely no effect on any text now on display, and there is no way to make it have any such effect. If you want to display the character—so people can see what they type—do this:

```
ch := ReadKey;
Write( ch );
```

There are other neat tricks you can teach your program with **ReadKey**. For example, this waits for you to press the Escape key:

```
REPEAT
   {wait}
UNTIL ReadKey = Chr(27);
```

There's that null statement again inside the **REPEAT** loop, which waits until **ReadKey** returns ASCII 27, the code for the Esc control character. Notice that loops like this do not require a program variable.

ReadKey always pauses for input. Often, that's not convenient. Suppose your program is printing a long text file and you want to check periodically if someone has pressed Esc to stop printing. You could write:

```
IF Keypressed THEN
   IF ReadKey = Chr(27)
      THEN Halt;
```

By checking **Keypressed** *before* **ReadKey**, the program reads the keyboard only *after* you type something. If you don't type anything, the program continues normally.

Reading Function Keys

All PC keyboards have ten or 12 function keys plus several other special keys, arrows, Insert, Home, and so on. Unlike regular alphanumeric, punctuation, and control keys, these special function keys generate two ASCII codes, not just one. For this reason, it takes extra care to recognize them properly. Again, **ReadKey** makes the job easier than in earlier Turbo Pascal versions.

If the first character returned by **ReadKey** equals ASCII 0, then the *next* key specifies a key from Table 9-3. Special keys like Home and the up arrow always generate one character following ASCII 0. Function keys F1–F10 produce one of four possible characters depending on whether you press the key alone or hold down the Alt, Ctrl, or Shift keys. For example, to check for Alt-F4, you could write:

```
IF Keypressed
   THEN IF ReadKey = Chr(0)
      THEN IF ReadKey = 'k'
         THEN DoAltF4;
```

Program 9-4 tests these and other key combinations. Run the program and press any key, try out various function keys, and experiment with control and Alt keys. The program displays the visible character that a key produces (except for a few that do not display visible symbols) and lists the ASCII code in parentheses. Press Esc to end the program.

Program 9-4

```
 1:  PROGRAM KeyTest;
 2:  USES Crt;
 3:  VAR
 4:     ch : Char;
 5:     done : Boolean;
 6:
 7:  FUNCTION ASCII( ch : Char ) : Char;
 8:  BEGIN
 9:     Write( ch, ' (', Ord(ch), ') ' );
10:     ASCII := Chr(0)
11:  END; { Ascii }
12:
13:  BEGIN
14:     Writeln( 'Key test. Press Esc to quit.' );
15:     done := False;
16:     REPEAT
17:        IF Keypressed THEN
18:        BEGIN
19:           ch := ReadKey;
20:           IF ch = Chr( 0 )
```

Program 9-4 *cont.*

```
21:            THEN Writeln( ASCII(Chr(0)), ASCII(ReadKey) )
22:            ELSE Writeln( ASCII(ch) );
23:         done := ( ch = Chr(27) )
24:      END { if }
25:   UNTIL done
26: END.
```

Table 9-3 Special function keys

Key label	Normal	Alt	Ctrl	Shift
F1	; (59)	h (104)	^ (94)	T (84)
F2	< (60)	i (105)	_ (95)	U (85)
F3	= (61)	j (106)	' (96)	V (86)
F4	> (62)	k (107)	a (97)	W (87)
F5	? (63)	l (108)	b (98)	X (88)
F6	@ (64)	m (109)	c (99)	Y (89)
F7	A (65)	n (110)	d (100)	Z (90)
F8	B (66)	o (111)	e (101)	[(91)
F9	C (67)	p (112)	f (102)	\ (92)
F10	D (68)	q (113)	g (103)	] (93)
Home	G (71)			
Up arrow	H (72)			
PgUp	I (73)			
Left arrow	K (75)			
Right arrow	M (77)			
End	O (79)			
Down arrow	P (80)			
PgDn	Q (81)			
Ins	R (82)			
Del	S (83)			

Note. Some keyboards label keys Page Up, Page Down, Insert, and Delete instead of PgUp, PgDn, Ins, and Del.

Text Attributes

Table 9-4 lists the **Crt** unit text color constants, which you can use with **TextColor** and **TextBackground** to select foreground and background colors. Use the first eight constants for both foregrounds and backgrounds. Use the second eight constants only for foregrounds. This prepares to display yellow text on a blue background:

```
TextColor( Yellow );
TextBackground( Blue );
```

Table 9-4 Crt unit color constants

Constant	Value	Fg	Bg
Black	0	x	x
Blue	1	x	x
Green	2	x	x
Cyan	3	x	x
Red	4	x	x
Magenta	5	x	x
Brown	6	x	x
LightGray	7	x	x
DarkGray	8	x	
LightBlue	9	x	
LightGreen	10	x	
LightCyan	11	x	
LightRed	12	x	
LightMagenta	13	x	
Yellow	14	x	
White	15	x	

To make characters blink on and off, add another **Crt** constant, **Blink**, equal to 128, to any foreground color. (You can't blink the background.) You might use this to display warnings:

```
TextColor( Red + Blink );
TextBackground( LightGray );
Write( 'You are about to erase your disk!' );
```

On monochrome monitors, various color combinations select underlined, dim, bold, and blinking text. **Blue** and **LightBlue** constants select underlined text. Other colors from **Green** to **Brown** select dim text. **LightGreen** to **White** select bold text. Blinking works as it does on color displays—just add the **Blink** constant to any foreground color. Here are a few examples:

```
TextColor( Blue );
Writeln( 'This is underlined' );
TextColor( LightGray );
Writeln( 'This is not underlined' );
Writeln;
TextColor( LightBlue );
Writeln( 'This is underlined' );
TextColor( White );
Writeln( 'This is not underlined' );
```

Another way to change text attributes is to use the **LowVideo**, **HighVideo**, and **NormVideo** procedures. **LowVideo** turns off the high intensity bit in the character attribute byte, bit number 3 in Figure 9-1. **HighVideo** turns the bit on. As you can see from Figure 9-1, **LowVideo** and **HighVideo** do not add additional colors or attributes over what you can achieve with color constants. They simply convert between the first and second eight foreground color constant values in Table 9-4. In other words, if the foreground color is **Green**, executing **HighVideo** has the identical effect as setting **TextColor** to **LightGreen**.

Use **HighVideo** and **LowVideo** to intensify and dim letters after selecting the colors you want, as in this example, which intensifies the word NOT in mid sentence:

```
LowVideo;
TextColor( Green );
TextBackground( Red );
Write( 'Press N if you do ' );
HighVideo;
Write( 'NOT ' );
LowVideo;
Writeln( 'want to continue' );
```

Unfortunately, **HighVideo** selects several light colors (color numbers 9–13) while **LowVideo** selects more brilliant hues (1–5)—exactly opposite of what the procedure names suggest. If the color is now green and you execute **HighVideo**, the color changes to light green. But if the color is light gray, **HighVideo** changes to bright white—a confusing contradiction we just have to endure.

A final way to change text attributes is to call **NormVideo**, which resets the **TextAttr** byte to the value it had when the program started. To restore text to original colors, call this procedure just before your program ends:

```
NormVideo;    { Restore original text attributes }
```

Waiting Around

Usually, programmers spend much of their time making programs faster. Occasionally, though, it's helpful to be able to slow things down—perhaps to let people read text as though it were coming from a ticker tape. To do this, call **Delay** with a value representing the number of milliseconds you want to pause at this point:

```
Delay( 1000 );    { Wait a sec. }
```

Don't put too much faith in the amount of delay—it's accurate only to plus or minus about ¼ second. Turbo Pascal uses a timing loop to set the amount of delay when programs begin, so this feature works whether or not the computer has a built-in clock. One use for **Delay** is to pause between important text displays—for example, sign-on copyright notices and error messages. Because different computer models run at different speeds, unless you insert **Delays**, your program's messages may zip by too fast to read on super fast computers.

Sounding Off

Crt's **Sound** procedure starts a tone at approximately the frequency specified in parentheses:

```
Sound( 440 );   { 'A' }
```

Sound continues until you call **NoSound**—even after the program ends! Therefore, in any program that uses **Sound**, it's a good idea to end with a call to **NoSound**:

```
NoSound;   { Turn off tone generator }
```

Crt Reassignments

Sometimes, it's nice to give people the choice of printing text or displaying it on screen. A database program, for example, might have a command to preview a report on screen before printing a copy on paper. One way to accomplish this is to design a procedure with a text file parameter, something like this:

```
PROCEDURE Report( VAR f : TEXT );
VAR i : Integer;
BEGIN
   Writeln( f, 'Report header' );
   FOR i := 1 TO NumLines DO
      Writeln( f, lines[i] )
END;
```

This is just a simple example and a real report generator would be much more complex, but the idea is to pass text file **f** to **Writeln**, optionally redirecting the report to one device or another. For example, this displays the report on screen by specifying the standard output text file, normally the display:

```
Report( output );
```

And this opens a file to the printer, printing a paper copy of the report by writing to a file named PRN:

```
VAR printer : TEXT;

Assign( printer, 'PRN' );
Rewrite( printer );
Report( printer );
Close( printer );
```

These methods work but introduce a nasty problem that may not be obvious. One of the reasons for using the **Crt** unit is to display text as fast as possible, storing characters directly in video display memory. Redirecting text to the standard output file as just described defeats this feature, displaying text through the slower BIOS ROM routines.

To have your direct-video text and print it too, use the **AssignCrt** procedure to attach a text file to the **Crt** unit. Doing this tells **Crt** that you plan to use the text file in **Write** and **Writeln** statements but that you still want the unit to use its direct-video routines for displaying text on screen. Continuing the earlier report example, instead of specifying the standard output file, you could write:

```
VAR console : TEXT;

AssignCrt( console );
Rewrite( console );
Report( console );
Close( console );
```

Except for the **AssignCrt** statement, this is identical to the earlier method for printing text. By assigning the unnamed text file to **Crt**, subsequent **Write** and **Writeln** statements that use the file go through **Crt**'s direct-video routines. You can now pass to procedures a 'PRN' file to print text but pass the **console** file to display text as fast as possible.

The Dos Unit

The **Dos** unit contains constants, type declarations, one variable, and several routines to call DOS functions. The following covers most of the **Dos** unit routines except for a few advanced subjects postponed until Chapter 13.

> Note: To avoid confusion, *Dos* refers to the **Dos** unit. *DOS* in all capital letters refers to the Disk Operating System software.

Dos Variables

The **Dos** unit has a single variable, **DosError**, of type **Integer**. Table 9-5 lists **DosError**'s possible values. After calling **Dos** routines, check this variable to see if an error occurred.

Calling BIOS Interrupts

In all PCs, there are many low-level routines available for controlling various computer features. These routines are called "low level" because they directly access computer hardware to control the display, communications ports, timers, disk drives, and other devices. Together, the routines form the ROM BIOS, or *Basic Input Output System*.

Table 9-5 DosError codes

DosError Value	Meaning
0	No error
2	File not found
3	Path not found
5	Access denied
6	Invalid handle
8	Not enough memory
10	Invalid environment
11	Invalid format
18	No more files

Each BIOS routine has a unique *interrupt number*. An interrupt is a process that stops the computer at whatever it is doing and makes it do something else. When that something else finishes, the original operation resumes where it left off. Except for the time this takes, the interrupted process is normally unaware of the interruption.

There are two kinds of interrupts: hardware and software. *Hardware interrupts* come directly from devices like the keyboard. Every time you press a key, circuits inside the keyboard generate an interrupt signal, which causes a BIOS routine to read your keystroke and store its value in memory where programs can find it. Contrasting that action, *software interrupts* are more like Pascal procedures. You call them by issuing a *software interrupt number*.

To generate software interrupts in Turbo Pascal, use the **Dos** unit **Intr** procedure as demonstrated in Program 9-5, line 33. **Intr** takes two parameters: an interrupt number and a simulated register record, which contains fields that represent the processor registers AX, BX, CX, and others. Figure 9-2 lists the **Registers** data type.

```
Registers =
   RECORD
      CASE Integer OF
         0: (AX,BX,CX,DX,BP,SI,DI,DS,ES,Flags: Word);
         1: (AL,AH,BL,BH,CL,CH,DL,DH: Byte);
   END;
```

Figure 9-2 The **Dos** unit **Registers** record contains fields
to simulate processor registers.

Program 9-5 changes the cursor shape by calling interrupt $10 with register ah equal to 1 (line 32). This selects interrupt $10's cursor style routine, changing the cursor size by specifying its start line in register ch and its end line in cl. Although the cursor looks like a solid block, it's composed of horizontal lines numbered from the top 0 to 7 for color and 0 to 13 for monochrome displays. The two variable constant arrays in lines 9–10 specify start and end line numbers for each of three settings, normal, half, and full, which, when passed to interrupt $10, change the cursor.

After running the program, the cursor may or may not keep its new shape, depending on other software installed in your computer.

Program 9-5

```
1:  PROGRAM Cursor;
2:  USES Crt, Dos;
3:
4:  TYPE
5:      Settings = ARRAY[ 0 .. 5 ] OF Byte;
6:
7:  CONST                        {  0      1      2    }
8:                               { ch  cl  ch  cl  ch  cl }
9:      Monochrome : Settings = ( 11, 12, 07, 12, 00, 12 );
10:     Color      : Settings = ( 06, 07, 04, 07, 00, 07 );
11:
12: VAR
13:     Choice : Integer;
14:
15: PROCEDURE SetCursor( n : Integer );
16: { n = 0, 1, or 2 to select Monochrome or Color settings }
17: VAR
18:     Reg : Registers;
19: BEGIN
20:     n := n * 2;
21:     WITH Reg DO
22:     BEGIN
23:        IF LastMode = Mono THEN
24:        BEGIN
25:           ch := Monochrome[n];
26:           cl := Monochrome[n+1];
27:        END ELSE
28:        BEGIN
29:           ch := Color[n];
30:           cl := Color[n+1]
31:        END; { else }
32:        ah := 1;
33:        Intr( $10, Reg )
34:     END { with }
35: END; { SetCursor }
36:
37: BEGIN
38:     Writeln( 'Change cursor style:' );
```

Program 9-5 *cont.*

```
39:        Write( '-1=No change; 0=Normal; 1=Half block; 2=Full block ? ' );
40:        Readln( Choice );
41:        IF ( 0 <= Choice ) AND ( Choice <= 2 )
42:           THEN SetCursor( Choice );
43:        Writeln( 'Press Enter to end program.' );
44:        Write( 'New cursor style: ' );
45:        Readln
46:    END.
```

Calling DOS Functions

Of course, one of the main purposes for the **Dos** unit is to call routines in the MS-DOS or PC-DOS operating system. These operating system calls are readily available to assembly language programmers and, with the help of the **Dos** unit, to Turbo Pascal programmers, too. In assembly language, the conventional way to call a DOS routine is to place a function number in register ah, initialize other registers the function needs, and then execute interrupt $21. For example, this fragment displays the character A by calling the DOS character output routine, number 2:

```
DISPLAY:   mov   ah,2
           mov   dl,'A'
           int   21H
```

That, obviously, is not Pascal. The **mov ah,2** instruction is assembly language for "move the value 2 into register ah." But in Turbo Pascal, you cannot move values into computer registers, which are physically located on the processor chip inside your system. Instead, you have to use the simulated **Registers** record of Figure 9-2 and then call the **Dos** unit **MsDos** routine, which loads the real registers and calls DOS for you.

There are two ways to call DOS routines: You can call **MsDos** with simulated register values as just described, or you can call several predeclared **Dos** unit procedures and functions that simplify common DOS operations. The **MsDos** method takes a single variable parameter of type **Registers**:

```
PROCEDURE MsDos( VAR reg : Registers );
```

For each DOS call you make, be sure to assign appropriate values to the simulated register fields in record **reg**. The slightest mistake can cause serious problems and can even erase disk files unexpectedly. Use **MsDos** carefully. It bites.

In all cases, assign to register ah the number of the DOS routine you want to call. Also assign values to other registers that this routine requires. You don't have to initialize unused register fields. Finally, pass **reg** to **MsDos**. Afterwards, if the DOS routine returns any register values, you'll find them in the same **reg** record.

A simple example shows how to use **MsDos**. Program 9-6 displays the DOS version number—similar to typing VER at the command line prompt. Line 6 assigns the DOS version routine number, $30, to register field ah. Then, line 7 calls **MsDos**, which passes the version number back in registers al and ah. Line 8 displays this number.

Consult a DOS technical reference for other interrupt and DOS function numbers and their requirements.

Program 9-6

```
1:   PROGRAM Version;
2:   USES Dos;
3:   VAR
4:       reg : Registers;
5:   BEGIN
6:       reg.ah := $30;
7:       MsDos( reg );
8:       Writeln( 'DOS Version = ', reg.al, '.', reg.ah )
9:   END.
```

Starting with Turbo Pascal 5.0, you can call the **Dos** unit's **DosVersion** function to perform the same action that Program 9-6 demonstrates. **DosVersion** returns a **Word** value representing the DOS version. Use the **Lo** function to extract the major version number from this value. Use **Hi** to extract the minor revision number. To try **DosVersion**, replace lines 3–9 in Program 9-6 with:

```
VAR
   v : Word;
BEGIN
   v := DosVersion;
   Writeln( 'DOS Version = ', Lo( v ), '.', Hi( v ) )
END.
```

The first statement assigns **DosVersion**'s result to **v**. This saves time by not calling **DosVersion** twice in the **Writeln** statement—a good programming technique to remember. Limiting the number of times a program calls functions and procedures keeps the code running fast.

The System Date

Two routines inspect and change the computer's system date. **GetDate** reads the current date. **SetDate** changes the date to anything you want. The procedures are defined as:

```
PROCEDURE GetDate( VAR year, month, day, dayOfWeek : Word );
PROCEDURE SetDate( year, month, day : Word );
```

GetDate returns the year, month, day, and day of week. Years are full values like 1988 and 2001. Months range from 1 for January to 12 for December. Days are the day of month. And the day of week equals 0 for Sunday, 1 for Monday, 2 for Tuesday, and so forth.

SetDate takes one less parameter than **GetDate**. There's no need to specify the day of week when setting the date. Program 9-7 demonstrates these procedures by calculating the day number for dates after January 1, 1980. (DOS stores years relative to 1980, so the program doesn't work with earlier dates.) Line 13 preserves the current date for restoring later in line 20. Lines 17–18 change the date by calling **SetDate** and then immediately calling **GetDate**, which returns the day of week.

Program 9-7

```
1:  PROGRAM Days;
2:  USES Dos;
3:
4:  CONST
5:     dayName : ARRAY[ 0 .. 6 ] OF String[3] =
6:        ( 'Sun', 'Mon', 'Tue', 'Wed', 'Thu', 'Fri', 'Sat' );
7:
8:  VAR
9:     oldYear, oldMonth, oldDay,
10:    year, month, day, dayOfWeek : Word;
11:
12: BEGIN
13:    GetDate( oldYear, oldMonth, oldDay, dayOfWeek );
14:    Write( 'Year? ' ); Readln( year );
15:    Write( 'Month? ' ); Readln( month );
16:    Write( 'Day? ' ); Readln( day );
17:    SetDate( year, month, day );
18:    GetDate( year, month, day, dayOfWeek );
19:    Writeln( 'Day = ', dayName[ dayOfWeek ] );
20:    SetDate( oldYear, oldMonth, oldDay )
21: END.
```

Two similar routines, **GetTime** and **SetTime**, inspect and change the system time:

```
PROCEDURE GetTime( VAR hour, minute, second, sec100 : Word );
PROCEDURE SetTime( hour, minute, second, sec100 : Word );
```

GetTime reads the current hour, minute, second, and hundredths of seconds. **SetTime** changes the system time to any values you want. The hundredths parameter **sec100** is not very accurate. In general, you should not expect accuracy of most PC system times to be any greater than about ¼ second.

If your computer has a hardware clock, the **Dos** unit date and time routines do not change the clock's internal settings. They change only the date and time that DOS maintains—whether or not the computer has a hardware clock. Therefore, after changing the date and time, you don't have to change it back if you have a hardware clock. You can simply reboot or use the DOS DATE and TIME commands.

File and Disk Routines

A number of **Dos** unit routines perform special operations on disks and disk files—operations that Turbo Pascal file-handling routines cannot do on their own. Two of the simplest in this set are:

```
FUNCTION DiskFree( drive : Byte ) : LongInt;
FUNCTION DiskSize( drive : Byte ) : LongInt;
```

DiskFree returns the number of bytes available on any drive. **DiskSize** returns the total of all bytes used and unused on any drive. Specify the drive as a number with 0 for the current drive, 1 for drive A:, 2 for B:, and so on. These **LongInt** functions make it easy to display a report of disk usage with only three **Writeln** statements:

```
Writeln( 'Disk size  = ', DiskSize( 0 ) );
Writeln( 'Bytes free = ', DiskFree( 0 ) );
Writeln( 'Bytes used = ',
   DiskSize( 0 ) - DiskFree( 0 ) );
```

File Attributes

Procedures **GetFAttr** (Get File Attribute) and **SetFAttr** (Set File Attribute) examine and change the single-bit attributes stored with every entry in disk directories. See Figure 9-3 for a description of each attribute bit. Table 9-6 lists corresponding **Dos** unit constants that you can use to examine and change these bits.

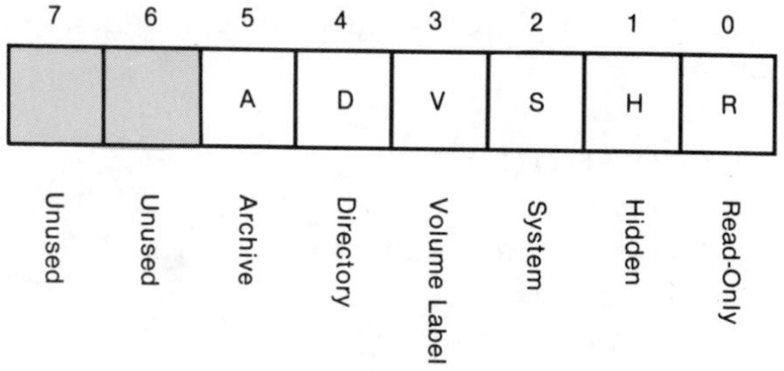

Figure 9-3 The directory attribute byte.

Table 9-6 Dos file attribute constants

Constant	Hex value	Bit number
ReadOnly	$01	0
Hidden	$02	1
SysFile	$04	2
VolumeID	$08	3
Directory	$10	4
Archive	$20	5
AnyFile	$3F	0–5

To examine a file's attribute, assign the file name to a file variable, which can be any type, and call **GetFAttr**, passing the unopened file and a **Word** variable:

```
VAR f : FILE; attr : Word;

Assign( f, 'TEST.DAT' );
GetFAttr( f, attr );
IF DosError <> 0
   THEN Writeln( 'Error locating file' )
   ELSE Writeln( 'Attribute = ', attr );
```

Checking **DosError** detects errors, most likely a bad file name. To check for specific attributes, use the sum of the first six constants from Table 9-6 logically ANDed with the attribute byte. For example, this tells you if the archive bit is set, indicating a recent change to the file:

```
GetFAttr( f, attr );
IF ( attr AND Archive ) = 0
   THEN Writeln( 'File is backed up' )
   ELSE Writeln( 'File has been changed' );
```

You can also change a file's attribute. Again, assign a name to any file and pass the unopened file variable plus the sum of the attributes you want to set. **SetFAttr** does not preserve the current attribute settings. To do that, precede **SetFAttr** with **GetFAttr** as in this example, which sets the file's hidden and read-only bits:

```
Assign( f, 'TEST.TXT' );
GetFAttr( f, attr );
attr := attr + ReadOnly + Hidden;
SetFAttr( f, attr );
```

Setting the hidden bit this way hides the program name in directories. To undo this change, turn off all attribute bits with:

```
Assign( f, 'TEST.TXT' );
SetFAttr( f, 0 );
```

File Dates and Times

As you no doubt know, DOS stores the date and time when a file was most recently changed. The **Dos** unit lets you examine and change this information—but not as easily as it lets you work with the system clock. To save disk space, DOS encodes the date and time in two 16-bit values, which the **Dos** unit further packs together into one 32-bit **LongInt** value. Table 9-7 lists the components of this value while Figure 9-4 shows the **Dos** unit **DateTime** record, which makes it easy to work with encoded dates and times.

Table 9-7 Date and time packing format

Field	Range	Bits
Sec	0–59	0–5
Min	0–59	6–11
Hour	0–23	12–16
Day	1–31	17–21
Month	1–12	22–25
Year	0–99	26–31

Note. For the correct year, add 1980.

```
DateTime =
  RECORD
     Year, Month, Day, Hour, Min, Sec : Word;
  END;
```

Figure 9-4 The **Dos** unit **DateTime** record.

Call **PackTime** to convert a **DateTime** record into a packed, 32-bit **LongInt** variable. Call **UnPackTime** to do the reverse, unpacking a **LongInt** value into a **DateTime** record. These procedures are defined as:

```
PROCEDURE PackTime( VAR t : DateTime; VAR p : LongInt );
PROCEDURE UnPackTime( p : LongInt; VAR t : DateTime );
```

To read the date and time of any file, assign its name to a file variable and pass the unopened file along with a **LongInt** variable to **GetFTime**:

```
VAR unpacked : DateTime; packed : LongInt; f : FILE;

Assign( f, 'TEST.DAT' );
GetFTime( f, packed );
UnpackTime( packed, unpacked );
```

Unpacking the encoded value into a **DateTime** record makes the date values more accessible. To change a file's date and time, pass the unopened file variable plus a packed **LongInt** value to **SetFTime**:

```
WITH unpacked DO
BEGIN
   { fill in year, date, month, ..., fields }
END;
PackTime( unpacked, packed );
Assign( f, 'TEST.DAT' );
SetFTime( f, packed );
```

Directory Routines

FindFirst and **FindNext** make listing directories far simpler than in previous Turbo Pascal versions. Both of these handy routines use the record type listed in Figure 9-5. DOS uses Field **Fill** for its own purposes. For each file entry located in a directory, **Attr** equals its attribute (see Figure 9-3), **Time** equals the packed date and time (see Table 9-7 and Figure 9-4), **Size** equals the file size in bytes, and string **Name** is the file's name.

```
SearchRec =
   RECORD
      Fill: ARRAY[ 1 .. 21 ] OF Byte;
      Attr: Byte;
      Time: Longint;
      Size: Longint;
      Name: String[12];
   END;
```

Figure 9-5 The **Dos** unit **SearchRec** record.

To read file name entries from a directory, first call **FindFirst** with three parameters:

```
PROCEDURE FindFirst( path : String; attr : Word;
   VAR f : SearchRec );
```

The **path** can be any string you would normally type to the DOS DIR command, for example, *.* or C:\PROG*.EXE. The **attr** word equals the attributes you want to find. Use the constant **AnyFile** (see Table 9-6) to locate all files including those normally hidden from view, subdirectories, plus regular files. The last **FindFirst** parameter is a **SearchRec** variable. After **FindFirst**, any file entries matching the parameters are in this record.

The next step is to call **FindNext**, this time with the same **SearchRec** variable filled in by **FindFirst**. **FindNext** is defined as:

```
PROCEDURE FindNext( VAR f : SearchRec );
```

Never call this procedure without first calling **FindFirst** and never modify the **Fill** field in the **SearchRec** record. DOS needs the information in this field to continue searching for file name entries after finding the first one.

Program 9-8 shows how to put these ideas together to list a disk directory, displaying file names and sizes in parentheses, and adding the total space occupied by all listed files. Line 13 tests **DosError** after **FindFirst**, looping until either this procedure or **FindNext** in line 17 fail to execute, indicating there are no more matching files to be found. Compile this program to a disk file DR.EXE (or any other name). Then type DR *.*, or DR C:\UTIL*.PAS for a directory.

Program 9-8

```
1:   PROGRAM Directory;
2:   USES Dos;
3:   VAR
4:      arg : String;
5:      total : LongInt;
6:      fileStuff : SearchRec;
7:   BEGIN
8:      IF ParamCount = 0
9:         THEN arg := '*.*'
10:        ELSE arg := ParamStr(1);
11:     total := 0;
12:     FindFirst( arg, AnyFile, fileStuff );
13:     WHILE DosError = 0 DO WITH FileStuff DO
14:     BEGIN
15:        Writeln( name, ' (', size, ')' );
16:        total := total + size;
17:        FindNext( fileStuff )
18:     END; { while / with }
19:     Writeln;
20:     Writeln( 'Total size = ', total, ' bytes' )
21:   END.
```

Taking a Break

As explained earlier, you can disable Ctrl-Break checking for **Write** and **Writeln** statements by setting the **Crt** unit **CheckBreak** switch to **False**. DOS maintains a similar variable, called the *Break switch*. When this switch is off, DOS checks for Ctrl-C key presses during console input and output, printer operations, and serial communications. When the switch is on, DOS checks for Ctrl-C at *every* system call.

To read the current setting of DOS's Break switch, call the **Dos** unit procedure **GetCBreak** procedure as in Program 9-9, line 6, passing the name of a **Boolean** variable. The procedure sets the variable equal to the current Break-switch value. To change the Break-switch setting, pass **True** or **False** (or a **Boolean** variable) to **SetCBreak** as in lines 8 and 15.

Program 9-9 counts from 1 to 10, pausing for about 1 second between displaying each number. Run the program and press Ctrl-C to stop execution before reaching 10. This works even though **CheckBreak** is set to **False** because line 8 turns on the DOS Break switch, causing DOS to check for Ctrl-C during all system calls. In this example, the program halts during the call to **DosVersion** at line 13. Now, change **True** to **False** in line 8 and run the program again. This time, because no DOS I/O is performed, you can no longer break out of the code by pressing Ctrl-C.

> Note: The **Crt** unit **CheckBreak** switch is not the same as the DOS Break switch, which affects only calls to DOS routines. The **Crt** unit's fast direct-video routines ignore the setting of the DOS switch.

Program 9-9

```
 1:  PROGRAM BreakOut;
 2:  USES Crt, Dos;
 3:  VAR i, j : Integer;
 4:      oldBreak : Boolean;
 5:  BEGIN
 6:     GetCBreak( oldBreak );
 7:     CheckBreak := False;
 8:     SetCBreak( True );
 9:     FOR i := 1 to 10 DO
10:     BEGIN
11:        Write( i, ' ' );
12:        Delay( 1000 );
13:        j := DosVersion
14:     END; { for }
15:     SetCBreak( oldBreak )
16:  END.
```

Trust but Verify

Programmers are trusting soles. They (or, I should say, we) are prone to believing that writing data to disk safely stores the data away, ready for reading later. But that's not always what happens. Despite built-in safeguards in disk controller circuits, it's possible to write data to disk only to discover that same data was somehow changed in the process, usually due to a flaw on the disk surface.

One way to increase the security of saved data is to read the same disk sectors immediately after writing them. If this operation fails, the program can take corrective action. Or, at the very least, it can display an error message. Better to know now than months later that a save instruction didn't work!

DOS has the ability to read back every disk sector following a disk write operation. To switch on this ability, give the DOS command VERIFY ON. To switch it off, type VERIFY OFF. To see the current setting, just type VERIFY. Most of the time, you'll want to leave the switch off—disk writes go at half speed when verification is in effect.

In Turbo Pascal programs, call **GetVerify** to read the state of the DOS *read-after-write-verify* switch. Call **SetVerify** to change the state of this switch. Program 9-10 demonstrates how to use these procedures (see lines 50, 51, 54, and 55). The program writes four hundred, 512-byte blocks to a test file named TEST.$$$. (Be sure to have at least 204,800 bytes of free space before running the test.) Doing this with verification on and then off demonstrates the effect of different switch settings. The program also serves as a useful benchmark of disk performance—you might want to run it to compare drive speeds on different systems.

Program 9-10

```
1:   PROGRAM DiskBenchmark;
2:   USES Crt, Dos;
3:   CONST
4:      FileName = 'TEST.$$$';  { Test file name }
5:      Blocks = 400;     { Warning: requires 204800 bytes disk space }
6:   TYPE
7:      ArrayType = ARRAY[ 0 .. 511 ] of Byte;
8:   VAR
9:      f : FILE OF ArrayType;
10:     verify : Boolean;
11:     hour1, minute1, second1, hundredths1 : Word;
12:     hour2, minute2, second2, hundredths2 : Word;
13:     v : ArrayType;
14:
15:  FUNCTION Seconds( hour, minute, second, hundredths : Word ) : Real;
16:  BEGIN
17:     Seconds := ( hour * 3600 ) + ( minute * 60 ) + second
18:         + ( hundredths / 100 )
19:  END; { Seconds }
20:
21:  PROCEDURE ShowTime;
22:  VAR
23:     time1, time2 : Real;
24:  BEGIN
25:     time1 := Seconds( hour1, minute1, second1, hundredths1 );
26:     time2 := Seconds( hour2, minute2, second2, hundredths2 );
27:     Writeln( 'Time1 ........ ', time1:8:2, ' second(s)' );
28:     Writeln( 'Time2 ........ ', time2:8:2, ' second(s)' );
```

Program 9-10 *cont.*

```
29:        Writeln( 'Elapsed time = ', time2 - time1:8:2, ' second(s)' )
30:  END; { ShowTime }
31:
32:  PROCEDURE Test;
33:  VAR
34:     i : Integer;
35:  BEGIN
36:     Writeln( 'Start: Writing ', Blocks, ' blocks' );
37:     GetTime( hour1, minute1, second1, hundredths1 );
38:     Assign( f, FileName );
39:     Rewrite( f );
40:     FOR i := 1 TO Blocks DO
41:        Write( f, v );
42:     Close( f );
43:     GetTime( hour2, minute2, second2, hundredths2 );
44:     Erase( f );
45:     Writeln( 'End of test' );
46:     ShowTime
47:  END; { Test }
48:
49:  BEGIN
50:     SetVerify( True );
51:     GetVerify( verify );
52:     Writeln( '--- Testing with Verify = ', verify );
53:     Test;
54:     SetVerify( False );
55:     GetVerify( verify );
56:     Writeln( '--- Testing with Verify = ', verify );
57:     Test
58:  END.
```

Environmental Concerns

The DOS environment is a block of memory composed of ASCII character variables in the form *name = value*. Standard environment variables such as COM-SPEC, which specifies the directory path to COMMAND.COM, and PROMPT, which sets the DOS prompt characters, are stored along with others that you can create with the SET command. For example, to create an environment variable named TMP and assign to it the name of a RAM disk drive E:\, you'd give the command SET = E:\ either directly from the DOS command line or in a batch file.

In Turbo Pascal programs, the **Dos** unit **EnvCount** function tells you how many environment variables exist. A simple statement displays this number:

```
Writeln( EnvCount, ' variables' );
```

The **EnvStr** function returns a string equal to a specific variable. To display the value of the first variable, you can write:

```
Writeln( 'Variable #1:', EnvStr(1) );
```

Program 9-11 demonstrates how to use these two functions to display all environment variables. The program operates similarly to typing SET and pressing Enter at the DOS prompt.

Program 9-11

```
 1:   PROGRAM Environment;
 2:   USES Crt, Dos;
 3:   VAR
 4:      i : Integer;
 5:   BEGIN
 6:      Writeln;
 7:      Writeln( 'There are ', EnvCount, ' environment strings' );
 8:      Writeln;
 9:      FOR i := 1 TO EnvCount DO
10:         Writeln( i:2, ' : ', EnvStr(i) );
11:   END.
```

Another function, **GetEnv**, reads environment variables just as **EnvStr** does but lets you specify variables by name. For example, this sets a string **s** to the value of the PATH variable:

```
s := GetEnv( 'PATH' );
Writeln( 'Path is ', s );
```

If the PATH environment variable doesn't exist, that statement sets the length of string **s** to 0.

Using environment variables is a great way to pass information around in DOS. Programs can look for specific variables, using their values in place of various defaults. For example, you might design your program to place temporary files in the current directory, but give people the option to direct those files elsewhere, perhaps to a RAM disk for extra speed. The program uses an environment variable TMP for the directory name:

```
dirName := GetEnv( 'TMP' );
IF Length( dirName ) > 0
   THEN Writeln( 'Writing files to ', dirName );
```

Program 9-12 demonstrates **GetEnv** and also serves as a useful utility that enhances the DOS CD (CHDIR) command. To use the program, first set up an environment variable CDPATH with a command such as:

```
SET CDPATH=C:\;C:\APPL;C:\PROJ;C:\USR
```

This assumes that your main drive is C: and that you have several subdirectories named APPL, PROJ, and USR. Substitute your actual subdirectory names for these and add others separated by semicolons. You'll probably want to insert this line into your AUTOEXEC.BAT file to create CDPATH automatically when you boot.

Next, compile Program 9-12 and save (or rename) the result to XD.EXE. Copy this file to any file listed in your DOS PATH setting (another environment variable that tells DOS where to look for executable programs and batch files).

After completing these steps, type XD *name*, where *name* is the name of a subdirectory located in any of the directories listed in CDPATH. You may have to try this a few times to understand the value of this utility, but I think you'll be pleased with the results. Suppose, for example, you have two subdirectories named C:\APPL\WS4 and C:\APPL\WORK. To change to WORK, you'd normally type:

```
CD C:\APPL\WORK
```

But, with the XD program, as long as C: \APPL is one of the CDPATH directories, you can instead type the shorter:

```
XD WORK
```

This performs the same task as the CD command with a lot less typing. And it works no matter which directory happens to be current.

Program 9-12

```
 1:   {$i-}              { Switch off I/O error checking }
 2:   PROGRAM XDir;   { Compile to XD.EXE }
 3:   USES Crt, Dos;
 4:   VAR
 5:       tryPath, paths : String[80];
 6:       p : Integer;
 7:   BEGIN
 8:       ChDir( paramStr(1) );
 9:       IF IoResult <> 0 THEN
10:       BEGIN
11:         paths := GetEnv( 'CDPATH' ) + ';';
12:         WHILE Length( paths ) > 0 DO
13:         BEGIN
14:           p := Pos( ';', paths );
15:           tryPath := Copy( paths, 1, p - 1 );
16:           Delete( paths, 1, p );
17:           IF Length( tryPath ) > 0 THEN
```

Program 9-12 *cont.*

```
18:           BEGIN
19:               IF tryPath[ Length( tryPath ) ] <> '\'
20:                   THEN tryPath := tryPath + '\';
21:               ChDir( tryPath + paramStr(1) );
22:               IF IoResult = 0
23:                   THEN Halt(0)
24:             END { if }
25:         END; { while }
26:         Writeln( 'Can''t change to ', paramStr(1) )
27:     END { if }
28: END.
```

File and Path Names

Programs that read and write disk files usually store file names in string variables. As long as the files are in the current directory, keeping track of file names is simple. But the best programs are not so restrictive, letting people enter complex path names such as A:\MYWORK\ACCOUNTS.DAT to read and write files on floppy disks and in subdirectories. To make this easy, the **Dos** unit has three useful routines for working with path names.

The **FExpand** function expands a simple file name such as INIT.TXT to its full path, prefacing the name with a drive letter and subdirectories, thereby pinpointing the file's exact location on disk. **FExpand** returns a **PathStr** defined along with these other special strings in the **Dos** unit:

```
PathStr = String[79];
DirStr  = String[67];
NameStr = String[8];
ExtStr  = String[4];
```

To use **FExpand**, declare a **PathStr** variable, perhaps named **path**, and then prompt for new file names this way:

```
Write( 'File name? ' );
Readln( path );
path := FExpand( path );
```

The call to **FExpand** adds drive and subdirectory information to **path**, letting the program change the current directory with **ChDir** but still be able to open the file by specifying the complete path.

FSplit reverses what **FExpand** does, taking a full path name and splitting it into pieces. **FSplit**'s parameters are four string variables (see Program 9-13, lines 6–9 and 21). Also demonstrated here is function **FSearch**, which tries to locate a file in a series of subdirectories. For example, assuming **path** is a **PathStr** string variable, to search for INIT.DAT in the three directories, C:\, C:\DOS, and C:\WORK, you can use the statement:

```
path := FSearch( 'INIT.DAT', 'C:\;C:\DOS;C:\WORK' );
```

If INIT.DAT is found in any of the listed paths, **FSearch** returns the full path name. If INIT.DAT is not found, **FSearch** returns a zero-length string.

Usually, you'll call **FSearch** with the value of the PATH environment variable (or another), using a statement such as:

```
path := FSearch( 'PROG.EXE', GetEnv( 'PATH' ) );
```

To demonstrate these routines, run Program 9-13 and enter the name of a file to locate among the directories listed in **SearchPath** (line 4). Try entering GRAPH.DOC and TURBO.EXE. Lines 13, 19, and 21 show the **FSearch**, **FExpand**, and **FSplit** routines in action.

Program 9-13

```
 1:   PROGRAM FindFile;
 2:   USES Crt, Dos;
 3:   CONST
 4:      SearchPath = 'C:\;C:\TP;C:\TP\UNIT;C:\TP\BGI;C:\TP\DOC';
 5:   VAR
 6:      fname, path : PathStr;
 7:      name : NameStr;
 8:      dir : DirStr;
 9:      ext : ExtStr;
10:   BEGIN
11:      Write( 'Find what file? ' );
12:      Readln( fname );
13:      path := FSearch( fname, SearchPath );
14:      IF Length( path ) = 0
15:        THEN
16:          Writeln( 'Can''t find ', fname )
17:        ELSE
18:          BEGIN
19:             path := FExpand( path );
20:             Writeln( 'Path      = ', path );
21:             FSplit( path, dir, name, ext );
22:             Writeln( 'Dir       = ', dir );
23:             Writeln( 'Name      = ', name );
24:             Writeln( 'Extension = ', ext )
25:          END { else }
26:   END.
```

The Printer Unit

The **Printer** unit is the shortest in Turbo Pascal's standard library. It contains only one **TEXT** variable, **Lst**, which makes it easy to send text to the printer.

Use **Lst** in **Write** and **Writeln** statements. You don't have to initialize **Lst** or close it when your program ends. The **Printer** unit takes care of these details, attaching **Lst** to LPT1:, the logical device normally connected to printers. Program 9-14 uses **Lst** to read and print any text file. Line 12 writes a form feed control character (ASCII 12) to **Lst**, which advances the paper to the top of a new page. Line 24 shows how to print one line of text.

Program 9-14

```
 1:  PROGRAM Lister;
 2:  USES Crt, Printer;
 3:  VAR
 4:     inFile : TEXT;
 5:     fileName : String;
 6:     oneLine : String;
 7:     lines : LongInt;
 8:
 9:  PROCEDURE Page;
10:  { Start a new page }
11:  BEGIN
12:     Write( Lst, Chr(12) )   { Send form feed command to printer }
13:  END; { Page }
14:
15:  BEGIN
16:     Write( 'List what file? ' );
17:     Readln( fileName ); IF Length( fileName ) = 0 THEN Halt;
18:     Assign( inFile, fileName );
19:     Reset( inFile );
20:     lines := 0;
21:     WHILE NOT EOF( inFile ) DO
22:     BEGIN
23:        Readln( inFile, oneLine );
24:        Writeln( Lst, oneLine );
25:        lines := lines + 1;
26:        IF lines MOD 58 = 0
27:           THEN Page
28:     END; { while }
29:     IF lines MOD 58 <> 0
30:        THEN Page;
31:     Close( inFile )
32:  END.
```

The Turbo3 Unit

The **Turbo3** unit contains two variables and several routines that make it possible to compile most Turbo Pascal version 3.0 and earlier programs.

If you receive the source code to a 3.0 program, which you have trouble compiling, add a **USES** declaration after the program name:

```
USES Turbo3;
```

Often, this is all you need to do to compile an older program. If this doesn't work, though, refer to your Turbo Pascal Manual for hints on converting programs and on using the UPGRADE program on your disks.

The Graph3 Unit

The **Graph3** unit contains the programming from Turbo Pascal 3.0's GRAPH.BIN file. Use this unit to compile Turbo Pascal version 3.0 and earlier graphics programs.

For new graphics programs, use the **Graph** unit, described in Chapter 11. **Graph3** commands aren't up to the high quality in the new graphics unit, which works on any of the PC's various video displays. Graph3 works only on CGA (Color Graphics Adapter) systems. To convert 3.0 graphics programs, remove all references to GRAPH.BIN and GRAPH.P and add this **USES** declaration after the program name:

```
USES Graph3;
```

Summary

Units add new features to the basic Turbo Pascal language by attaching to programs precompiled libraries of procedures, functions, constants, types, and variables. Units are like warehouses, stocked with raw materials that all programs can share.

The **USES** declaration adds everything inside a unit to a program. You can specify one or more units in a **USES** declaration, which must come immediately after the **PROGRAM** header.

Units are stored in one of two kinds of disk files. TPU (Turbo Pascal Unit) files store individual units. TPL (Turbo Pascal Library) files store one or more units together. The Turbo Pascal compiler automatically loads a special library file, TURBO.TPL, making the units in this file instantly available to programs.

Turbo Pascal comes with several ready-to-use units: **Crt, Dos, Graph, Graph3, Overlay, Printer, System**, and **Turbo3**. You do not have to specify the

System unit in a **USES** declaration. When compiling programs, Turbo Pascal always includes **System**, which contains standard runtime procedures and functions. To use the features in other units, you must list the unit names after **USES**.

The **Crt** unit contains items for controlling the display and keyboard. **Crt** also improves the performance of **Write** and **Writeln** statements with fast direct-video code. The **Dos** unit makes it easy to call MS-DOS routines. The **Printer** unit helps you print text. **Turbo3** and **Graph3** contain declarations that help you to compile Turbo Pascal programs written for version 3.0 or earlier. The **Graph** unit, described in Chapter 11, contains a powerful set of graphics commands. The **Overlay** unit, described in Chapter 10, lets you convert other units to overlay modules.

Exercises

9-1. Write a program to display a menu and let people read and view any text file. Use the **Crt** unit **ClrScr**, **ClrEol**, and other features to create a good-looking display.

9-2. Add a procedure to your answer for exercise 9-1 to let people choose various colors and screen attributes for menus, text, and program messages.

9-3. Write a custom directory lister using the **Dos** unit to display file names in columns instead of one file name on a line as in Program 9-8.

9-4. (Advanced) Write a procedure to use in any program to select file names by moving a highlighted bar around in a directory. Your program should use the **Dos** and **Crt** units.

9-5. Pick any DOS function from a technical reference and use the **Dos** unit's **MsDos** procedure to call the function.

9-6. Write a utility to determine the space free and used for all disk drives installed on the computer.

9-7. Write a program to print and view a text file simultaneously. Use the **Printer** unit.

10

Custom Units and Overlays

- The Parts of a Unit
- Writing Your Own Units
- Declaring Procedures and Functions in Units
- Compiling Units
- Using Your Own Units
- The Unit Directory
- Using the XtraStuff Unit
- Units That Use Other Units
- Circular Unit References
- Multiple Units in Memory
- Unit Identifier Conflicts
- Units in Memory
- Near and Far
- Installing Units in Library Files
- Using TPUMOVER
- Large-Program Development with Units
- Overlays

10

Key Words and Identifiers

BEGIN, END, IMPLEMENTATION, INTERFACE, OvrGetBuf, OvrInit, OvrInitEMS, OvrResult, OvrSetBuf, UNIT, USES

By storing your favorite routines in units, you build programming libraries for other programs to share. You can also divide large programs into pieces, storing different parts in separate units, which you compile individually. Called *separate compilation*, this process reduces compilation time and helps you to better organize the many thousands of statements in a large program.

This chapter explains how to write and use your own units. You'll learn about the design of a unit, how to compile units to memory and to disk, and how to install compiled units in library files. You'll also learn how to convert units into *overlay modules*, a technique for constructing programs that are too large to fit entirely in memory.

The Parts of a Unit

All units have four parts, whether or not you write them yourself. The four parts are:

1. Unit declaration.
2. Unit interface.
3. Unit implementation.
4. Unit initialization.

The *unit declaration* is like a program declaration. It gives the unit a name and tells Turbo Pascal this is a unit and not a program. On disk, precompiled units store the unit's name along with the unit's contents. Programs that use the unit must specify this name in a **USES** declaration in order to use a unit's contents.

The *unit interface*, sometimes called the unit's *public* section, describes all the features inside a unit that host programs, and other units, can share. In text form, the interface contains labels, constants, types, and variables, plus procedure and function declarations. In compiled form, Turbo Pascal stores an encoded form of the unit interface section along with the unit's other items. When you later compile a program that uses the unit, the interface tells the compiler the syntax of the unit's features.

The *unit implementation* contains items that are *private* to the statements inside the unit. Contained in the implementation are the actual statements that *implement* the procedures and functions described in the interface. The implementation can also contain additional labels, constants, types, and variables—as well as private procedures and functions—that are strictly for the unit's own use.

The last part of a unit is the *initialization*, an optional block of statements that resembles the main body of a normal Pascal program. The statements in the initialization run before the statements in a program that uses the unit, giving the unit the ability to initialize its own variables and automatically perform other jobs immediately before the host program begins. Some units have no initialization section and, therefore, perform no startup actions.

Writing Your Own Units

Writing your own units is as easy as writing programs. Anything a program can do, a unit can do—if not better, at least as well.

To illustrate the basic design of all units, Program 10-1 lists a shell, a starting place for your own unit designs. Line 1 is the unit declaration, which gives the unit a name and tells the compiler this is a unit and not a program. In your own units, replace **Shell** with your unit's name.

Line 3 begins the unit interface, the public parts you want other programs (and other units) to know about. The comments in lines 5, 7, and 9 show where to insert various declarations such as **USES, CONST, TYPE, VAR, PROCEDURE,** and **FUNCTION**.

Line 12 begins the implementation containing the unit's private parts. In this section, you can insert a second **USES** declaration in place of the comment at line 14—an advanced technique that allows multiple units to refer to each other in circular fashion. Line 16 shows where you can insert **LABEL, CONST, TYPE,** and **VAR** declarations, all of which are for the unit's internal use—none of these declarations is visible to host programs that use the unit. Line 18 shows where to place procedure and function bodies. Every procedure and function declared in the interface (see line 9) must have a corresponding statement block in the implementation. You may also insert private procedures and functions here.

The final part of the unit shell in Program 10-1 is the initialization, lines 21–25. Insert the statements between **BEGIN** and **END** that you want to execute before a host program begins running. When a host program uses more than one unit, all initialization parts run in the order the units appear in the host's **USES** declaration. If you have no initialization statements to perform, you can write **BEGIN END** with nothing between, or take out **BEGIN** and end the unit with a lone **END**.

Program 10-1

```
 1:   UNIT Shell;
 2:
 3:   INTERFACE
 4:
 5:   { Place a USES declaration here }
 6:
 7:   { Place CONST, TYPE, and VAR declarations here }
 8:
 9:   { Place PROCEDURE and FUNCTION declarations here }
10:
11:
12:   IMPLEMENTATION
13:
14:   { Place a second USES declaration here }
15:
16:   { Place private LABEL, CONST, TYPE, and VAR declarations here }
17:
18:   { Place PROCEDURE and FUNCTION bodies here }
19:
20:
21:   BEGIN { optional }
22:
23:   { Insert initialization statements here }
24:
25:   END.
```

Declaring Procedures and Functions in Units

An example of a real unit will help you to understand the outline in the unit **Shell**. Program 10-2 is a collection of seven general-purpose procedures and functions plus one data type that I've been using for years. Precompiling these routines in a unit makes them readily available. To add my favorite library to any program, I simply type **USES XtraStuff** after the **PROGRAM** declaration.

Look carefully at Program 10-2's interface (lines 3–15). The seven procedure and function declarations appear without their usual **BEGIN** and **END** key words and do not have any statements. Remember that the interface merely describes what's in the unit—the actual programming comes later. The **TYPE** declaration (line 7) declares **CharSet** as a set of type **Char**. Because this declaration is in the interface section, any program using **XtraStuff** can declare variables of type **CharSet** as though this were a native Pascal data type.

The implementation section (lines 18–78) contains the programming for the routines declared in the interface. As you can see, the procedures and functions now have bodies and statements that make the routines do their stuff.

When writing your own units, be careful to duplicate all function and procedure declarations in both the interface and implementation parts. This dual format—declaring procedures and functions in the interface and then fleshing them out later in the implementation—resembles the **FORWARD** declarations you learned about in Chapter 4. To demonstrate what happens if you make a mistake, change the parameter type in line 20 from Char to Integer:

```
FUNCTION Dncase( ch : Integer ) : Char;
```

Because **Dncase**'s implementation no longer matches the interface declaration in line 9, compiling the modified unit produces:

```
Error 131: Header does not match previous definition
```

Turbo Pascal insists that procedures and functions are exactly the same in both the interface and implementation.

If you receive this error frequently, you can optionally remove the parameter lists in the implementation. Turbo Pascal relaxes its own rule and lets you specify procedure and functions with no parameters in the implementation. For an example of how this works, change line 20 to:

```
FUNCTION Dncase;
```

Even though this new declaration does not match the interface, Turbo Pascal compiles the unit with no errors. If you include parameters, though, the compiler checks that they match their counterparts in the interface. The choice is yours. Some programmers repeat the parameters in both places; others leave them out. In a long unit, it's nice to have the parameters in both places for reference, although you then have to remember to modify both the interface and the implementation to add or subtract new parameters. Try both approaches until you find the one that works best for you.

> Note: If you are following along, undo your changes to the **Dncase** function now.

Occasionally, you'll see units with their implementation parameter lists surrounded with comment brackets like this:

```
FUNCTION Dncase(* ( ch : Char ) : Char *);
```

Of course, this is effectively the same as not declaring the parameter and function type at all. I point this out only because you will see listings that use this style, the result of other compilers such as UCSD Pascal that do not allow parameter lists to repeat in the implementation. In these systems, the comments are merely references to avoid having to look up parameters in the interface.

Before moving on to the next example, notice that line 78 ends the unit without a **BEGIN**. There are no initializations to perform in this unit and, therefore, no need for an initialization section. This is the only time when an **END** in a statement block does not have to be preceded by **BEGIN**.

Program 10-2

```
 1:   UNIT XtraStuff;
 2:
 3:   INTERFACE
 4:
 5:   USES  Crt;
 6:
 7:   TYPE  CharSet = Set of Char;
 8:
 9:   FUNCTION Dncase( ch : Char ) : Char;
10:   PROCEDURE GetCommand( VAR command : Char; commandset : Charset );
11:   PROCEDURE BumpStrup( VAR s : String );
12:   FUNCTION InRange( n, min, max : Integer ) : Boolean;
13:   FUNCTION Verified( message : String ) : Boolean;
14:   PROCEDURE PromptAt( x, y : Integer; message : String );
15:   PROCEDURE Center( y : Integer; message : String );
16:
17:
18:   IMPLEMENTATION
19:
20:   FUNCTION Dncase( ch : Char ) : Char;
21:   { Convert ch from upper- to lowercase }
22:   BEGIN
23:     IF ( 'A' <= ch ) AND ( ch <= 'Z' )
24:         THEN Dncase := Chr( Ord(ch) + 32 )
25:         ELSE Dncase := ch
26:   END; { Dncase }
27:
28:   PROCEDURE GetCommand( VAR command : Char; commandset : Charset );
29:   { Return command from keyboard from chars in commandset }
30:   BEGIN
31:     REPEAT
32:         command := Upcase( Readkey )
33:     UNTIL command IN commandset
34:   END; { GetCommand }
```

Program 10-2 *cont.*

```
35:
36: PROCEDURE BumpStrup( VAR s : String );
37: { Convert (bump) string s to uppercase }
38: VAR i : Integer;
39: BEGIN
40:    FOR i := 1 TO Length(s) DO
41:       s[i] := Upcase( s[i] )
42: END; { Bumpstrup }
43:
44: FUNCTION InRange( n, min, max : Integer ) : Boolean;
45: { True if min <= n <= max }
46: BEGIN
47:    InRange := ( min <= n ) AND ( n <= max )
48: END; { Inrange }
49:
50: FUNCTION Verified( message : String ) : Boolean;
51: { True if you type Y or y to message }
52: VAR ch : Char;
53: BEGIN
54:    Write( message, ' ? (y/n) ' );
55:    ClrEol;
56:    GetCommand( ch, [ 'Y', 'N' ] );
57:    Writeln( ch );
58:    Verified := ( ch = 'Y' )
59: END; { Verified }
60:
61: PROCEDURE PromptAt( x, y : Integer; message : String );
62: { Display message at (x,y), clearing to end of line }
63: BEGIN
64:    GotoXY( x, y );
65:    Write( message );
66:    ClrEol
67: END; { PromptAt }
68:
69: PROCEDURE Center( y : Integer; message : String );
70: { Center message at row y, clearing line }
71: BEGIN
72:    GotoXY( 1, y );
73:    ClrEol;
74:    Write( message : 40 + ( Length(message) DIV 2 ) )
75: END; { Center }
76:
77:
78: END. { unit }
```

Compiling Units

As you can with programs, you can compile units either to disk or to memory. Most of the time, though, you'll compile units to disk files, which end in TPU (for Turbo Pascal Unit). Compiling units to memory is faster than compiling to disk, but it has a serious disadvantage: Host programs can use the units only as long as you remain in Turbo Pascal. If you compile your units to disk, then you don't have to recompile them for each new programming session.

To compile a unit to disk, first change the Compile:Destination command from Memory to Disk. (Pressing D when the Compile menu is visible toggles this setting, a handy shortcut to remember.) Then press C to compile. If the destination already is set to Disk, press < Alt >-F9 at any time to compile the unit.

Try this now with Program 10-2. Save the listing text as XTRASTUF.PAS and compile to disk, creating the unit code file XTRASTUF.TPU. You must use the same name for the .PAS file and the unit identifier in line 1. Use the first eight characters for the file name if the unit name is longer. (Previous Turbo Pascal versions recognized the {$U *unitname*} option to refer to units named differently than their disk files. Versions starting with 5.0 no longer permit this option.)

Using Your Own Units

Now that you've written your own unit and compiled it to memory or to disk, you're ready to write a host program that uses the unit's features. You should already have typed Program 10-2, saved as XTRASTUF.PAS and compiled to XTRASTUF.TPU on disk.

Next, type Program 10-3 and press < Alt >-R to run. This test program demonstrates several of **XtraStuff**'s features in a design that a larger program might use in a main menu. Press Esc to clear the screen; press A, B, or C to test the **GetCommand** procedure; press Q to quit.

Program 10-3

```
 1:   PROGRAM TestXtraStuff;
 2:   USES Crt, XtraStuff;
 3:   CONST
 4:       TheEndOfTime = False;   { As far as I know }
 5:   VAR
 6:       command : Char;
 7:   BEGIN
 8:       ClrScr;
 9:       Center( 8, 'A Great New Program' );
10:       Center( 10, 'from Ugly Duckling Software' );
11:       Center( 14, '(C) 2001. No rights reserved.' );
```

Program 10-3 *cont.*

```
12:     REPEAT
13:        PromptAt( 1, 1, 'Menu: A, B, C, Q-uit ' );
14:        GetCommand( command, ['A', 'B', 'C', 'Q', #27 ] );
15:        ClrScr;
16:        CASE command OF
17:           'A', 'B', 'C'
18:              : BEGIN
19:                    PromptAt( 1, 18, 'You typed ' );
20:                    Write( command )
21:                 END;
22:           'Q'
23:              : BEGIN
24:                    GotoXY( 1, 24 );
25:                    IF Verified( 'Do you want to quit' )
26:                       THEN Halt
27:                 END
28:        END { case }
29:     UNTIL TheEndOfTime
30: END.
```

A few quick experiments with Program 10-3 help explain several other features about writing your own units and host programs. Suppose you make a change to the host (or write a new host). You do not have to recompile the unit—you already did that. For example, add the following line to Program 10-3 between lines 11 and 12:

```
Center( 23, '(this is the bottom line)' );
```

You can compile and run the new host without recompiling the **XtraStuff** unit. The only time you have to recompile a unit is if you make changes to the items in the unit.

To handle situations involving many units, some which require recompilation and others that don't, two Turbo Pascal commands automate compiling out-of-date units. Again, a simple experiment helps explain how to use the commands. Reload XTRASTUF.PAS (Program 10-2) and modify line 78, adding an initialization section:

```
78: BEGIN
79:    ClrScr
80: END.
```

Because the new initialization section clears the screen, any host program that **USES XtraStuff** can now assume that the display is clear when the program begins running. If you permanently make this change, remove line 8 from Program 10-3. **XtraStuff**'s initialization statements automatically run before the host program's first statement; therefore, the display is already clear when the program starts.

Having made this and other changes to **XtraStuff**, there are three ways to recompile both the unit and the host program. These methods assume you either have the host program in the Turbo Pascal editor or you've set the *Compile-Primary file* setting to the name of the host text file. To bring both the unit and host program up to date, follow one of these three steps:

1. Use the *Compile-Make* command. This automatically checks the .PAS text files of all units the host program uses. Any unit text files with dates and times later than the unit's TPU file are recompiled, bringing all units up to date before compiling the main program.

2. Use the *Compile-Build* command, which is identical to *Make* except that Turbo Pascal compiles all unit .PAS files without checking if any are out of date.

3. Manually recompile each unit the program uses and then compile the program.

The first method—*Compile-Make*—is the best in most cases. You can change various units, modify your program, and use this single command to recompile only the necessary modules to bring the entire project up to date.

The second method—*Compile-Build*—is less helpful, but handy when you have the text files to a multiunit program but not the TPU code files. For example, you might download a multiunit program in text form from a bulletin board or time-sharing system. Use this command to recompile the entire program including all units.

Of course, you can always use the third method, recompiling each unit individually and then compiling (or running) the host program. But, why work so hard when you have easier methods at your disposal?

The Unit Directory

One alternative to storing compiled unit TPU files in the current directory is to change Turbo Pascal's unit directory setting. To do this, use the *Options-Directories* command and type the name of a directory in the space labeled *Unit directories*. After compiling a unit text file, copy your TPU disk files into this directory.

Some programmers prefer to store all their TPU files in one place, building a programming library of common routines for many host programs to share. If Turbo Pascal can't find a unit TPU file in the current directory, it looks in the library subdirectory. Only if it still doesn't find the file needed does the compiler display the message:

```
Error 15: File not found
```

Using the XtraStuff Unit

The **XtraStuff** unit (Program 10-2) contains many useful routines, described in this section. For reference, the procedure and function declarations are repeated.

FUNCTION Dncase(ch : Char) : Char;

Pass any character to **Dncase** to change uppercase letters to lowercase. Only characters A though Z are affected. Other characters are unchanged. **Dncase** is the reverse of Turbo Pascal's built-in function, **Upcase**.

PROCEDURE GetCommand(VAR command : Char; commandset : Charset);

Use **GetCommand** to read a single uppercase character from the keyboard, perhaps in a menu as in Program 10-3, line 14. Pass a character variable and a set of characters. **GetCommand** rejects any characters not in the set. For example, to prompt for a digit from 1 to 4, you could write:

```
VAR digit : Char;

Write( 'Type a digit from 1 to 4: ' );
GetCommand( digit, [ '1' .. '4' ] );
```

PROCEDURE BumpStrup(VAR s : String);

Pass any string to **BumpStrup** to convert characters in the string to all uppercase. Characters not in the set 'A' . . 'Z' are unaffected. To pass short strings to **BumpStrup**, use the {$V –} compiler directive as in this example which prompts for a file name, converting your answer to uppercase:

```
VAR filename : String[64];

Write( 'File name? ' );
Readln( filename );
{$V-} BumpStrup( filename ); {$V+}
```

FUNCTION InRange(n, min, max : Integer) : Boolean;

InRange returns true only if **n** is within the range **min . . max**. Use the function in place of **IF** statements as in this example, which prompts for a number from 1 to 100:

```
VAR n : Integer;

REPEAT
   Write( 'Enter a number from 1 to 100: ' );
   Readln( n )
UNTIL InRange( n, 1, 100 );
```

FUNCTION Verified(message : String) : Boolean;

Verified returns true if you type Y or y to the **message**, to which the function adds a question mark and the reminder, (y/n). This function is particularly handy in constructions like this one:

```
IF Verified( 'Do you want to print the report' )
   THEN PrintTheReport
```

On screen, the message appears as follows, waiting for you to respond yes or no:

```
Do you want to print the report? (y/n)
```

PROCEDURE PromptAt(x, y : Integer; message : String);

Use this procedure to display strings at any (x,y) location on screen. I find the routine particularly handy for constructing data entry screens where people type information into *fields*. For example, you could write:

```
PromptAt( 1, 10, 'Name           : ' );
   Readln( name );
PromptAt( 1, 11, 'Address        : ' );
   Readln( address );
PromptAt( 1, 12, 'City, State, Zip : ' );
   Readln( citystzip );
```

PROCEDURE Center(y : Integer; message : String);

Call **Center** to display **message** centered on row **y**. For a few examples, see lines 9–12 in Program 10-3.

Units That Use Other Units

Any unit can use any other unit by inserting a **USES** declaration after the **INTERFACE** key word. For example, if you write a new unit that needs some of the declarations in **XtraStuff**, start the new unit with:

```
UNIT MoreStuff;
INTERFACE
USES XtraStuff;
{ Okay to refer to XtraStuff items }
```

Or, hide **USES** inside the new unit's **IMPLEMENTATION**, in which case only the unit's implementation details, not items in the interface, can use **XtraStuff**'s stuff:

```
UNIT MoreStuff;
INTERFACE
{ Interface declarations }
{ Can't refer to XtraStuff items yet }
IMPLEMENTATION
USES XtraStuff;
{ Okay to refer to XtraStuff items }
```

Having told the compiler that the new unit uses **XtraStuff**, you can then declare variables of **XtraStuff**'s **CharSet** data type, and you can call any of the procedures and functions declared in **XtraStuff**'s interface. A host program can also use either or both units. In the previous examples, because **MoreStuff** uses **XtraStuff**, both units will be loaded into memory when the program runs. Even so, for the host program to be able to use the features in both units, it must also declare both unit names in a **USES** declaration:

```
PROGRAM Sample;
USES XtraStuff, MoreStuff;
```

The order of the unit names doesn't matter—you could put **MoreStuff** first. (Some other compilers such as UCSD Pascal require units to be declared in "nesting" order. In other words, units used by others must be named first.)

Circular Unit References

If UnitA uses UnitB, which uses UnitA—and if these units are listed between **INTERFACE** and **IMPLEMENTATION**—Turbo Pascal refuses to compile the units, instead displaying the error message:

```
Error 68: Circular unit reference
```

You might also see this error in cases where UnitA uses UnitB, which uses UnitC, which in turn uses UnitA. The situation is more common than you may suppose. For example, if you write a unit named **Math** that uses **XtraStuff**, you may decide later to revise **XtraStuff** to use one of the procedures declared in **Math**. But that won't work because it introduces a circular-unit reference, and you'll receive error 68 when you try to compile the units.

Turbo Pascal 5.0 solves this tricky problem by permitting circular-unit references in a private **USES** declaration inside the unit's implementation (see Program 10-1, line 14). As long as you insert your **USES** declarations into the implementation, multiple units may refer to each other in round-about order, and the final result will come out correctly. The restriction against circular-unit references applies only to units listed in interface sections.

Unfortunately, this also means that if UnitA uses UnitB, which uses UnitA, then UnitB may not declare new constants, types, and variables in UnitB's interface using declarations from UnitA's interface. In other words, two interface sections may never use each other. You can usually get around this restriction by copying all such circular declarations to another unit, perhaps named GLOBALS.PAS, compile that unit separately, and then insert **USES GLOBALS** in as many other units as you need.

Multiple Units in Memory

Multiple units do not nest inside each other in memory. If UnitA uses UnitC, and UnitB also uses UnitC, then only one copy of UnitC is loaded into memory. UnitC is not *inside* UnitA or UnitB. A unit is a distinct entity even though other units (and the main program) use it. In cases where many units use others—a common situation in a large program—only one copy of each unit exists in memory, no matter how many other units refer to that copy. If 15 units use **Crt**, Turbo Pascal knows the program doesn't need 15 copies of the same code in memory!

Unit Identifier Conflicts

One common multiunit problem arises when the same identifiers exist in two or more units. For example, suppose you purchase a precompiled unit, let's say it's called **Video**, that has a **ClrScr** procedure—the same name as the procedure in unit **Crt**. You may think that, because of the conflict, you can't use both units. Actually, you can. Here's an example. (Don't try to run this. There is no **Video** unit in Turbo Pascal.)

```
PROGRAM Test;
USES Video, Crt;
BEGIN
   ClrScr
END.
```

If both **Video** and **Crt** contain a **ClrScr** procedure, which procedure does this program call? The answer is: the procedure in the unit *last* declared in **USES**. The following program would call the **ClrScr** procedure in **Video**:

```
PROGRAM Test;
USES Crt, Video;
BEGIN
   ClrScr
END.
```

Switching the unit names in **USES** now calls **ClrScr** in **Video**, which follows

Crt. With many conflicting identifiers, though, this method won't always work. Instead, you can use a technique called *dot notation* to distinguish between duplicate identifiers.

Unit-identifier dot notation is similar to the dot notation in record and field identifiers. Turbo Pascal lets you precede any identifier by a period (the dot) and the name of the unit or host program that declares the identifier. For example, to call the **Video ClrScr** procedure, but declare the **Video** unit first in **USES**, you can write the program this way:

```
PROGRAM Test;
USES Video, Crt;
BEGIN
   Video.ClrScr
END.
```

The dot notation **Video.ClrScr** tells the compiler to call the **ClrScr** procedure in **Video** instead of **Crt**. If the host program declares a conflicting identifier, you can also use the program name to resolve the problem.

Program 10-4 demonstrates these ideas with an example of dot notation carried to the extreme. The program uses the **Crt** unit but also declares its own **ClrScr** procedure, causing an identifier conflict with the **Crt** procedure of the same name. To call **Crt's ClrScr**, the program uses this statement at line 26:

```
Crt.ClrScr;
```

The dot notation resolves the conflict, even though the program redefines **ClrScr**. To call the host program's procedure, use the program name and dot notation:

```
Lotsadots.ClrScr;
```

Other uses of dot notation in **Lotsadots** show how to refer to global variables when there are identical local variables as **i** and **j** in procedure **FillScreen** (lines 13–22). By writing:

```
FOR Lotsadots.i := 1 TO 25 DO
```

the program refers to the global variable. The local integers **i** and **j** at line 14 are not used.

Line 27 uses dot notation to call a **System** unit routine, **Readln**. Even though the program does not include **System** in the **USES** declaration (line 2), recall from Chapter 8 that Turbo Pascal always uses the **System** unit even if you do not specify **System** in **USES**. Of course, you would have to do this only if the program or another unit redefined **Readln** and you want to use the **System** routine instead.

Program 10-4

```
 1:  PROGRAM Lotsadots;
 2:  USES Crt;
 3:  VAR i, j : Integer;
 4:
 5:  PROCEDURE ClrScr;
 6:  VAR i : Integer;
 7:  BEGIN
 8:     Crt.GotoXY( 1, 25 );
 9:     FOR i := 1 TO 25 DO
10:        System.Writeln
11:  END; { Lotsadots.ClrScr }
12:
13:  PROCEDURE FillScreen;
14:  VAR i, j : Integer;    { Not used! }
15:  BEGIN
16:     FOR Lotsadots.i := 1 TO 25 DO
17:     BEGIN
18:        Writeln;
19:        FOR Lotsadots.j := 1 TO 79 DO
20:           System.Write( '*' )
21:     END { for }
22:  END; { Lotsadots.FillScreen }
23:
24:  BEGIN
25:     Lotsadots.FillScreen;
26:     Crt.ClrScr;
27:     System.Readln;
28:     Lotsadots.FillScreen;
29:     Lotsadots.ClrScr
30:  END.
```

Units in Memory

Simple programs that do not use any units have four main sections in memory. These sections are:

1. Code segment.

2. Data segment.

3. Stack segment.

4. Heap.

The *code segment* contains all of the program's procedures and functions plus the main program body. The *data segment* contains global variables and variable constants plus a few items for Turbo Pascal's private use. The *stack segment* contains return addresses for calls to procedures and functions plus most local variables declared inside those routines. The *heap* contains nothing until you reserve memory with **New** and store data in that memory via pointers as described in Chapter 7.

Figure 10-1 shows the relationship of these four sections. (Appendix B contains a detailed memory map, more complete than the simplified version here.) The code, data, and stack segments can each be up to 64K long while the heap takes up whatever remaining memory is available. As you can see from this diagram, discounting the variable-sized heap, the maximum simple program size is about 192K (64 × 3).

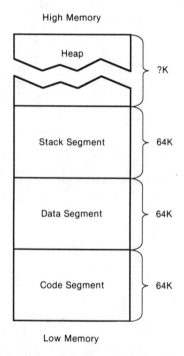

Figure 10-1 Simplified memory map of compiled Turbo Pascal programs.

Carefully dividing large programs into units can increase the program code-size limit. This works because the procedures and functions in a unit are stored in separate memory segments. Each unit segment, which can be as large as 64K, occupies only as much memory as needed. The unit code segments fit between the main code and data segments, as Figure 10-2 shows. The first units in a **USES** declaration are higher in memory. Figure 10-2 corresponds with this program declaration:

```
PROGRAM UnitsInMem;
USES UnitA, UnitB, UnitC;
```

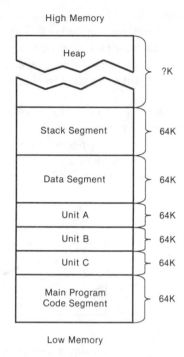

High Memory

Figure 10-2 In addition to the three main segments in Figure 10-1, each unit occupies its own memory segment, which can be as large as 64K. Segmenting programs into units, then, allows programs to grow as large as available memory.

Near and Far

All unit public procedures and functions—those declared in the interface section—are *far* routines. Calls to a far routine push onto the stack both the segment and offset addresses after the calling instruction. Because the complete return address is on the stack, far routines can be called from any place in memory, even from other code segments.

All private procedures and functions—those declared exclusively in the implementation section plus those in the host program—are *near* routines. Calls to near routines push only the offset address. Because the segment address is not saved on the stack, near routines can be called only from inside their own code segment.

Because of the additional address on the stack, far calls are slightly less efficient than near calls. Usually, the difference is minor and nothing to worry about. Be aware, though, that there is a small time penalty for calling far routines declared in unit interface sections.

Despite the fact that each unit's code segment is distinct, all global variables declared in the unit interface and implementation sections are lumped together in a single data segment. This means that the space occupied by all the program's own global variables plus all public and private global variables in all units the program uses cannot total more than 64K. To store more data than that, you must use pointers and reserve memory on the heap as Chapter 7 explains.

Installing Units in Library Files

The TPUMOVER program on your Turbo Pascal disks collects individual unit .TPU files into single library files, ending in .TPL (Turbo Pascal Library). You can also use the program to extract or delete individual units from library files.

Turbo Pascal automatically loads the special library file TURBO.TPL into memory when it starts, making all units in this library file available to programs without additional disk reads. Because this is faster than loading individual unit files from disk, you can store your most-used units in TURBO.TPL to reduce compilation time.

Using TPUMOVER

Turbo Pascal's TPUMOVER utility program adds and subtracts compiled units to and from TURBO.TPL. Run TPUMOVER interactively from DOS by typing "tpumover" and pressing Enter. You'll see a display window listing the current TURBO.TPL contents, showing the units used by others. A second window lists the contents of another library file or individual units on their way in and out of TURBO.TPL. Function keys are listed at the bottom of the screen. Press F1 for more help. Refer to Table 10-1 for a complete list of TPUMOVER function keys.

> Note: You must store units separately in .TPU files or in TURBO.TPL, even though TPUMOVER can create and edit library files of other names. Perhaps someday in the future you'll be able to load units from such libraries, using TPUMOVER to maintain a collection of unit tools. Alas, for now, this intriguing idea is nothing but "computer-science fiction."

Although you can run TPUMOVER as just described, an easier way is to give commands directly from DOS. This also lets you create batch files with multiple TPUMOVER commands. In this form, TPUMOVER's full syntax is:

```
TPUMOVER [libfile] /<option>unit[.TPU] [/<option>unit[.TPU]]...
```

The square brackets represent optional items. The *libfile* is normally TURBO.TPL. The *unit* must be the name of a unit (as named in a **UNIT** declaration), or the name of a compiled .TPU file name. The *<option>* may be one of these four characters:

+   Add Unitname to library
−   Delete Unitname from library
*   Extract Unitname to UNITNAME.TPU
?   Display TPUMOVER instructions

You may specify one or more *<option>unit* combinations for one *libfile*, inserting, deleting, and extracting many compiled units at once. For example, to delete the **Turbo3** and **Graph3** units from TURBO.TPL, enter the command:

```
TPUMOVER TURBO.TPL /-turbo3 /-graph3
```

Be careful with delete commands like that one, which permanently discards the named units. A safer approach is to extract the units with:

```
TPUMOVER TURBO.TPL /*turbo3 /*graph3
```

The safer command removes the two units from TURBO.TPL and stores the extracted unit code in TURBO3.TPU and GRAPH3.TPU. You can then save these files elsewhere, or later reload them into TURBO.TPL if necessary.

You may want to insert the **XtraStuff** unit (Program 10-2) into TURBO.TPL, especially if many of your programs use this unit. To do that, enter the command:

```
TPUMOVER TURBO.TPL /+xtrastuf.tpu
```

Notice that, in this case, you have to specify the .TPU file name extension (in upper- or lowercase as you wish).

Table 10-1 TPUMOVER command keys

Key	Operation
F1	Display help screen
F2	Save active window to disk
F3	Load a new .TPL or .TPU file
F4	Display additional information about marked unit
F6	Switch windows (active window has double border)
+	Mark or unmark unit at selection bar
Ins	Transfer marked units to opposite window
Del	Delete marked units
Esc	Quit program and return to DOS
Up arrow	Move selection bar up
Dn arrow	Move selection bar down

Large-Program Development with Units

Besides collecting program libraries of common routines, variables, and other items, units are also useful for writing large programs. Dividing a program into separate units can drastically reduce compile times.

Programs 10-5 through 10-8 show a typical multiunit, large-program setup. Of course this example is small and you could just as easily write the entire program in one text file. But the design is similar to what you could use in a program with thousands of statements.

To compile and run the complete example, type Program 10-5 and save as UCHOICEA.PAS. Type Program 10-6 and save as UCHOICEB.PAS. Finally, type Program 10-7 and save as UCHOICEC.PAS. You do not have to compile the units at this time.

Next, type Program 10-8 and save as MAIN.PAS. With **Main** in memory, to compile and run the entire program use the *Compile-Make* command. (You could also use *Compile-Build*.) When the program is running, press A, B, or C to run the **ChoiceA**, **ChoiceB**, and **ChoiceC** procedures in the three units. Type Q to quit.

Program 10-5

```
 1:   UNIT UChoiceA;
 2:
 3:   INTERFACE
 4:
 5:   PROCEDURE ChoiceA;
 6:
 7:   IMPLEMENTATION
 8:
 9:   PROCEDURE ChoiceA;
10:   BEGIN
11:      Write( 'Choice A....' );
12:      Readln
13:   END;
14:
15:   END.
```

Program 10-6

```
 1:   UNIT UChoiceB;
 2:
 3:   INTERFACE
 4:
 5:   PROCEDURE ChoiceB;
 6:
 7:   IMPLEMENTATION
```

Program 10-6 *cont.*

```
 8:
 9:    PROCEDURE ChoiceB;
10:    BEGIN
11:       Write( 'Choice B...' );
12:       Readln
13:    END;
14:
15:    END.
```

Program 10-7

```
 1:    UNIT UChoiceC;
 2:
 3:    INTERFACE
 4:
 5:    PROCEDURE ChoiceC;
 6:
 7:    IMPLEMENTATION
 8:
 9:    PROCEDURE ChoiceC;
10:    BEGIN
11:       Write( 'Choice C...' );
12:       Readln
13:    END;
14:
15:    END.
```

Program 10-8

```
 1:    PROGRAM Main;
 2:    USES Crt, UChoiceA, UChoiceB, UChoiceC;
 3:    VAR
 4:       ch : Char;
 5:    BEGIN
 6:       ClrScr;
 7:       REPEAT
 8:          GotoXY( 1, 1 );
 9:          Write( 'Choice-A, Choice-B, Choice-C, Q-uit ? ' );
10:          ch := UpCase( ReadKey );
11:          ClrScr;
12:          CASE ch OF
13:             'A' : ChoiceA;
14:             'B' : ChoiceB;
15:             'C' : ChoiceC
```

Program 10-8 *cont.*

```
16:        END { case }
17:     UNTIL ch = 'Q'
18:  END.
```

The importance of this multiunit design is the way each main program opera-
tion is in its own unit. This makes it easy to change individual operations without
having to recompile the entire program. To see how this works, add a few lines to
Program 10-5 (UCHOICEA.PAS). Before loading that file, though, use the *Compile-
Primary file* command to make MAIN.PAS the current work file. Then, load
UCHOICEA.PAS and replace procedure **ChoiceA** (lines 9–13) with these statements:

```
USES Crt;

PROCEDURE ChoiceA;
VAR ch : Char;
BEGIN
   Write( 'Ch? ' );
   ch := Readkey;
   Writeln( 'ASCII value = ', Ord(ch) );
   Write( 'Press <Enter>...' );
   Readln
END;
```

Insert the **USES Crt** declaration in place of line 4. Press F2 to save these
changes and then press <Alt>-R to recompile and run the whole shebang. Because you made MAIN.PAS the primary file, you don't have to reload the host
program before compiling.

When designing your own large programs, start by dividing the project into
sections, each in its own unit. For test purposes, you might also write separate
programs and then, after debugging, convert each program into a unit, ready for
attaching to the main host. Either way, units help you organize even the most mon-
strous of projects.

Clearing the Primary File

In the previous section, you used the *Compile-Primary file* command to make
MAIN.PAS the current work file. To clear the work file, select the same command,
type a Space, and press the Backspace and Enter keys. You must do this before
typing and compiling other programs.

Overlays

Most Turbo Pascal programs fit easily into memory. Even large programs composed of many separate units rarely require more than about 256K of RAM, and
most PCs today have at least that much.

But what do you do if your programs grow larger than available RAM? With Turbo Pascal 4.0, the answer wasn't encouraging. If your program didn't fit entirely in memory, you had little choice but to divide your code into separate .EXE files and run the pieces separately from a batch-file menu or under control of another program.

Turbo Pascal 5.0 solves this problem with an *overlay manager* unit, appropriately named **Overlay**. Version 5.5 adds additional enhancements that let you fine-tune overlay efficiency. (Chapter 13 discusses these enhancements in detail.)

What are overlays? They are units that remain on disk until needed and, when loaded into RAM, share the same memory addresses with other overlay units. Because there's no practical limit to the number of units that can overlay each other in the same memory, there's no longer any restriction on program size. If your program grows too large to fit entirely in RAM, just divide the code into overlays and let the **Overlay** unit manage the dirty details of loading the pieces into memory as needed.

Using Overlays

In most cases, writing overlay units is only a little more difficult than writing regular units. The primary rule to remember is: Only entire units may be converted to overlays. Turbo Pascal 3.0 allowed you to write overlay procedures and functions. Versions 5.0 and up restrict overlays to whole units.

Using overlays correctly takes careful planning. A common mistake is to misuse overlays, writing inefficient programs that spend too much time reloading portions of themselves from disk into RAM. One way to avoid this problem is to design your programs in top-down fashion. When following this idea, the main program typically calls various submodules as demonstrated in Program 10-8. Because of this natural organization, each submodule—**ChoiceA**, **ChoiceB**, and **ChoiceC** in this example—is an excellent candidate for converting to an overlay.

To demonstrate how to accomplish that goal, in this section, you'll convert Programs 10-5 through 10-8 into a main program and three overlays. First, add the directive {$O+} to each of the units. (That's a capital O, not the digit zero.) The directive tells the compiler that the units *might* be called as overlay modules. To make this change, add {$O+} to line 2 in Programs 10-5, 10-6, and 10-7. Save these units in files named UCHOICEA.PAS, UCHOICEB.PAS, and UCHOICEC.PAS.

Next, enter Program 10-9, a modified version of Program 10-8. Save this file as MAIN.PAS. Instructions for compiling and running the program follow the listing.

Program 10-9

```
1:  {$O+,F+}
2:  PROGRAM Main;
3:
4:  USES Overlay, Crt, UChoiceA, UChoiceB, UChoiceC;
```

Program 10-9 *cont.*

```
 5:
 6:    {$O UChoiceA}
 7:    {$O UChoiceB}
 8:    {$O UChoiceC}
 9:
10:    VAR
11:       ch : Char;
12:
13:    BEGIN
14:       OvrInit( 'MAIN.OVR' );
15:       IF OvrResult <> ovrOk THEN
16:       BEGIN
17:          Writeln( 'Overlay error' );
18:          Halt(1)
19:       END; { if }
20:       ClrScr;
21:       REPEAT
22:          GotoXY( 1, 1 );
23:          Write( 'Choice-A, Choice-B, Choice-C, Q-uit ? ' );
24:          ch := UpCase( ReadKey );
25:          ClrScr;
26:          CASE ch OF
27:             'A' : ChoiceA;
28:             'B' : ChoiceB;
29:             'C' : ChoiceC
30:          END { case }
31:       UNTIL ch = 'Q'
32:    END.
```

Compiling Overlays

Compiling overlay units and programs is different in only one aspect from compiling nonoverlay programs. You must compile all the program's parts to disk. The Turbo Pascal integrated environment can compile, but it can't run overlay programs.

If you are using the integrated environment, set *Compile-Destination* to *disk* and specify MAIN.PAS as the *Compile-Primary file:*. Then use the *Compile-Build* or *Compile-Make* commands to compile the entire program. Remember to recompile any units to which you added the {$O+} directive.

If you are using the command-line compiler, just compile as you normally do, using option switches to compile all (/B) or only modified (/M) units.

In either case, the result is two files, in this example, MAIN.EXE and MAIN.OVR. The .EXE file contains the code that stays permanently in memory. The .OVR file contains the overlay code that the **Overlay** manager loads from disk as needed.

Note: When running this example, you may not see the disk light come on when calling procedures in the overlay modules. This example is so small that overlays aren't needed, and the entire program may therefore be loaded into RAM.

Understanding Overlays

Line 1 of Program 10-9 declares two options. The overlay switch O + tells the compiler that this program uses overlays. The Far code switch F + forces all procedures and functions to use far call and return instructions. A far call pushes both the 16-bit segment and offset address values onto the stack. This way, the called code can return to the original location, even if that code is in a different memory segment. Normally, Turbo Pascal assumes that all procedures and functions are near and, therefore, require only the 8-bit offset address of the return location in the same code segment.

When writing overlay programs, if there is any chance no matter how remote that a procedure or function will result in an overlay being loaded from disk, then that procedure or function must have been compiled with the {$F + } directive in effect. Ignore this rule at your own peril. If a near {$F − } procedure or function calls another procedure or function in an overlay unit, the stack may become corrupted because of the way the **Overlay** manager unit intercepts the call. Every active procedure and function at the time the overlay is loaded *must* have been compiled with {$F + } in effect.

This rule is true even in cases where a near procedure calls a far procedure, which activates the overlay. Because the earlier near procedure hasn't yet ended, disaster may strike. For this reason, it's usually wise to add the {$F + } directive to every part of the program unless you are 100% positive that an overlay cannot be activated.

Lines 4–8, repeated here from Program 10-9, list the units that this host program uses:

```
USES Overlay, Crt, UChoiceA, UChoiceB, UChoiceC;

{$O UChoiceA}
{$O UChoiceB}
{$O UChoiceC}
```

List the **Overlay** unit in the host program's **USES** declaration along with other overlay and nonoverlay units. After that, list each overlay unit in separate {$O unitname} directives. (Again, that's a capital O, not the digit zero.) Together, the **USES** declaration and the directives tell the compiler which units to place in the .OVR file.

In addition to these setup chores, the main program must call an initialization procedure in the **Overlay** unit. As line 14 shows, pass the name of the overlay disk file to **OvrInit**:

```
OvrInit( 'MAIN.OVR' );
IF ovrResult <> OvrOk THEN
BEGIN
   Writeln( 'Overlay error' );
   Halt(1)
END; { if }
```

Normally, you'll want to check **ovrResult** this way, an **Integer** variable (typed) constant in the **Overlay** manager. If **ovrResult** is not equal to **OvrOk**, then an error occurred and the program must not be allowed to continue. Table 10-2 lists all possible **ovrResult** values.

Table 10-2 Overlay manager OvrResult values

Constant	Value	Meaning
OvrOk	0	No error
OvrError	−1	General error code
OvrNotFound	−2	Overlay file not found
OvrNoMemory	−3	Not enough memory for overlays
OvrIOError	−4	Disk I/O error loading overlay
OvrNoEMSDriver	−5	Expanded-memory driver missing
OvrNoEMSMemory	−6	Not enough EMS memory available

When you call an overlay unit (see lines 27–29 in Program 10-9), the **Overlay** manager automatically intercepts the call and loads the appropriate overlay code from disk. That code is stuffed into an internal buffer that occupies a portion of the heap. When another overlay is needed, the buffer is emptied, and the new code is brought into memory. Actually, the **Overlay** manager is smart enough to keep multiple overlays in the buffer simultaneously, but that's a subject to which we'll return in Chapter 13.

Most of the time, the preceding steps are all you need to write your own overlays. Here are a few hints and tips that will help you get started:

- Remember to add {$O + } to every overlay unit.

- Add {$O + ,F + } to the beginning of the main host program and to any unit that **USES** another overlay unit.

- With no exceptions, any procedure or function that eventually results in an overlay being loaded into memory must have been compiled with the {$F + } switch in effect.

- Specify the **Overlay** unit in your host program's **USES** declaration along with your own overlay units.

- List the overlay units in {$O unitname} directives after the host program's **USES** declaration.

- Call **OverInit** with the name of the overlay file, usually the same as the program name but ending in .OVR. Check **ovrResult** for any errors, halting the program if the overlay file isn't found.

Note: The standard **Dos** unit is compiled with an {$O+} switch. Use the directive {$O Dos} to add the **Dos** unit to the program's .OVR file to save memory in programs requiring only occasional access to **Dos** routines, for example, when prompting for file names at the beginning of a program. No other standard units may be loaded as overlays.

Finding the .OVR File

When you execute **OvrInit('MAIN.OVR');**, the **Overlay** manager tries to open the file MAIN.OVR in the current directory. If this doesn't work and you're running DOS 3.0 or a later version, **OvrInit** searches for the file in the same directory that contains the main program code file, in this example, MAIN.EXE. If it still can't find the overlay file, **OvrInit** searches all the directories listed in a PATH command. Only if this fails does the procedure give up, returning error **OvrNotFound** (see Table 10-2).

Loading Overlays into Expanded Memory

The **Overlay** unit can load overlay code into *expanded memory* (EMS), the kind of extra RAM that works on all PCs, XTs, and ATs. *Extended memory* works only on ATs and 80386 systems. If you have extended memory, your system probably came with a software driver to convert some or all of the extra RAM into simulated EMS. Installing the driver should allow overlays to use extended memory.

To enable the use of EMS RAM, call **OvrInitEMS** after successfully calling **OvrInit**. To do this with Program 10-9, change lines 14–19 to:

```
OvrInit( 'MAIN.OVR' );
IF OvrResult <> ovrOk THEN
BEGIN
   Writeln( 'Overlay error' );
   Halt(1)
END; { if }
OvrInitEMS;
```

You can also check **ovrResult** for errors after **OvrInitEMS**. If equal to **OvrNoEMSDriver** or **OvrNoEMSMemory**, then the **Overlay** manager either did not find any or enough EMS RAM. But, if there isn't enough EMS RAM to hold the overlays, the program simply uses main memory as it normally does.

If it finds enough EMS RAM, the **Overlay** manager loads *all* overlays from the .OVR file into memory. Then, instead of loading individual overlay units from disk, **Overlay** transfers the overlays as needed from EMS to main RAM. Because of this action, EMS RAM doesn't reduce a program's memory requirements—it just makes overlay programs run more quickly.

Changing the Overlay Buffer Size

The overlay buffer size is normally set to the size of the largest overlay unit. If enough memory is available, you can increase the buffer size to a value large enough to hold two or more overlays simultaneously. That way, if two overlay units are used frequently, the program runs faster because the overlays tend to stay in memory longer. The **Overlay** manager automatically detects this condition, loading overlays from disk only if they are not already in RAM.

Note: Chapter 13 explains how to use advanced features in Turbo Pascal 5.5's **Overlay** unit to help keep multiple overlays in memory for even longer times. The overlay buffer actions described in this section apply to both Turbo Pascal 5.0 and 5.5.

Call **OvrGetBuf** for the size of the current overlay buffer. For example, to display the buffer size, add this statement between lines 22 and 23 in Program 10-9:

```
Writeln( 'Overlay buffer size = ', OvrGetBuf, ' bytes' );
```

To change the buffer size to 6000 bytes (or any other size), call **OvrSetBuf**:

```
OvrSetBuf( 6000 );
```

Do this *after* calling **OvrInit** but *before* calling **New** or **GetMem** to allocate variables on the heap. The overlay buffer occupies the bottom portion of the heap; therefore, **OvrSetBuf** ignores a request to increase the buffer size if you've allocated any pointer-addressable variables. (See Appendix B for a memory map showing the overlay buffer location.)

Note: You may not want to increase the overlay buffer size if **OvrInitEMS** returns **ovrOk**. In that case, all overlays are stored in EMS RAM and a larger overlay buffer in main RAM offers little or no advantage.

Joining Overlays and Program Code

If you're using Turbo Pascal 5.5, you can combine your .EXE and .OVR files into one .EXE file. For this to work, you must compile all programs and units *without* debugging information for the stand-alone or built-in Turbo Debuggers. If you want to run your overlays under control of Turbo Debugger, you must store your programs in separate .EXE and .OVR files.

To join the MAIN.EXE and MAIN.OVR files from program 10-9, edit line 14 to:

```
OvrInit( 'MAIN.EXE' );
```

Or, because **ParamStr(0)** under DOS 3.0 or later returns the name of the program code file, you can use the statement:

```
OvrInit( ParamStr(0) );
```

After editing **OvrInit** to open the .EXE file, and after compiling your program, join the result with the DOS command:

```
COPY /B MAIN.EXE + MAIN.OVR
```

The /B option with DOS COPY stands for "binary copy." This attaches MAIN.OVR to the end of MAIN.EXE. You can then delete MAIN.OVR with:

```
DEL MAIN.OVR
```

Summary

Units collect procedures, functions, types, variables, constants, and other items in separate modules, which you compile apart from other program sections. Units are good for collecting libraries of common features for many host programs to share. They are also helpful for dividing large programs into manageable pieces. And, because a unit's code goes in its own memory segment, you can use units to write Pascal programs limited only by the amount of memory in your computer.

Units have four parts: the declaration, interface, implementation, and initialization. The initialization section resembles a program's main body and runs before the statements in a host program.

Use dot notation to resolve conflicts between duplicate identifiers in multiple units and in the main program text. Unit dot notation is similar to the notation used in record and field expressions.

To add a unit's features to a program (or to another unit), type the unit name in a **USES** declaration, which comes after the **PROGRAM** header or, in another unit, after the key word **INTERFACE**. No matter how many units a program and other units use, only one copy of the unit's code is loaded into memory.

Use the TPUMOVER program to install and remove compiled units in library TPL disk files. Installing units in the special TURBO.TPL file lets Turbo Pascal preload the units into memory, speeding compilation but also reducing memory space.

Units may use other units. But, when two or more units refer to each other in circular fashion, the **USES** declaration must appear in the unit's implementation section. Units listed in **USES** in the unit's interface may not refer to each other circularly.

To construct Turbo Pascal programs larger than available memory, you can selectively convert units to overlays. Overlay units share the same memory. The **Overlay** manager unit loads overlay units as needed into RAM. Programs can also load overlays into EMS memory.

Exercises

10-1. Create your own unit of favorite routines, culled from programs in your personal library. Or, extract several procedures and functions from other examples in this book and insert them in a unit.

10-2. Write a test program to put your custom unit in exercise 10-1 through the paces.

10-3. Install your custom unit from exercise 10-1 in TURBO.TPL. What effect does this have on memory and compilation speed?

10-4. Where does the unit's code exist in memory? Where are the global variables? Where are the variables declared in procedures and functions inside the unit?

10-5. Describe the difference between a *far* and a *near* procedure or function.

10-6. If UnitA uses UnitB, which uses UnitC, which uses UnitA, Turbo Pascal may not compile the program. Why not? How would you instruct a programmer to fix this problem?

11

The Borland Graphics Interface

- Choosing a Graphics Mode
- The Borland Graphics Interface
- Setting Up for Graphics
- Viewports and Coordinates
- Plotting Points
- Drawing Lines
- Relative Lines
- Stylish Lines
- Color Palettes
- Changing Display Colors
- In the Background
- Setting the Write Mode
- Shape Routines
- Arcs and Circles
- Drawing Ellipses
- A Slice of Pie
- Bit-Map Images
- Displaying Text on Graphics Screens
- Animation
- Loading Multiple Fonts and Drivers
- Creating a Graphics Application
- Advanced BGI Graphics

11

Arc, Bar, Bar3D, Circle, ClearDevice, ClearViewPort, CloseGraph, DetectGraph, DrawPoly, Ellipse, FillEllipse, FillPoly, FloodFill, GetArcCoords, GetAspectRatio, GetBkColor, GetColor, GetDefaultPalette, GetDriverName, GetFillPattern, GetFillSettings, GetGraphMode, GetImage, GetLineSettings, GetMaxColor, GetMaxMode, GetMaxX, GetMaxY, GetModeName, GetModeRange, GetPalette, GetPaletteSize, GetPixel, GetTextSettings, GetViewSettings, GetX, GetY, GraphDefaults, GraphErrorMsg, GraphResult, ImageSize, InitGraph, InstallUserDriver, InstallUserFont, Line, LineRel, LineTo, MoveRel, MoveTo, OutText, OutTextXY, PieSlice, PutImage, PutPixel, Rectangle, RegisterBGIdriver, RegisterBGIfont, RestoreCrtMode, Sector, SetActivePage, SetAllPalette, SetAspectRatio, SetBkColor, SetColor, SetFillPattern, SetFillStyle, SetGraphBufSize, SetGraphMode, SetLineStyle, SetPalette, SetRGBPalette, SetTextJustify, SetTextStyle, SetUserCharSize, SetViewPort, SetVisualPage, SetWriteMode, TextHeight, TextWidth

There are few areas in computer programming more satisfying than graphics. Programmers who spend their time designing graphics software live in a heaven of colors, shapes, animations, and three-dimensional objects limited only by their imaginations and their computer's video display circuits.

With Turbo Pascal's extensive graphics commands, anyone can become a computer graphics artist, whether you write business software, games, or simulations or just like to have fun. Even simple programs can produce remarkable patterns, giving your programs an extra touch that text-only software can never match.

Choosing a Graphics Mode

All PCs can display text—individual characters with fixed bit patterns stored in ROM or, sometimes, in RAM. Although several special characters have fixed line and angle segments giving a limited ability to construct lines and boxes on text displays, the real excitement in computer graphics comes from the ability to control each tiny display dot, called a *picture element*, or *pixel*.

Depending on the type of display and video card or circuits in your PC, you can have from 320 × 200 pixels to 1024 × 768 pixels in as few as two to as many as 256 colors on screen at one time. That's anywhere from 64,000 to 786,432 pixels at your control. Also called an All Points Addressable (APA) display, a PC graphics screen is the Etch-a-Sketch of many a programmer's dreams.

Perhaps the most difficult aspect of PC graphics is writing programs to choose among the number of display formats, some of which do not exist on various computer models. Turbo Pascal simplifies the process by automatically detecting and initializing the best possible graphics mode available. And, by following a few simple rules, you can write graphics software that runs correctly on all the graphics modes listed in Table 11-1.

Table 11-1 Turbo Pascal graphics modes

Mode	Description	Interface file
CGA	Color Graphics Adapter	CGA.BGI
MCGA	Multicolor Graphics Array	CGA.BGI
EGA	Enhanced Graphics Adapter	EGAVGA.BGI
VGA	Video Graphics Array	EGAVGA.BGI
Hercules	Hercules Monochrome Graphics	HERC.BGI
AT&T	AT&T 400 line graphics	ATT.BGI
PC3270	IBM PC 3270 Graphics	PC3270.BGI
IBM8514	IBM PC 8514 Graphics	IBM8514.BGI

Most of the programs in this chapter look best with EGA or VGA color graphics and an RGB (Red, Green, Blue) monitor. You can use CGA graphics or a less expensive color monitor but the results may not be as colorful or as clear. Hercules and other monochrome graphics systems will also work, although you'll see only shades of green or amber instead of different hues.

The Borland Graphics Interface

The right column in Table 11-1 lists the BGI (Borland Graphics Interface) disk files containing the machine language software for the graphics modes on the left. A BGI file is called a *driver* because it drives the video display. The graphics driver is also known as a *kernel*, an operating system term that refers to a core of low-level routines with some particular purpose.

To run graphics programs, you need at least one BGI driver file on disk. To compile programs, you need only the GRAPH.TPU file, which contains the **Graph** unit's interface and implementation (see Chapter 9). The information inside GRAPH.TPU tells the compiler how to make calls to the routines inside a BGI driver. When the program runs, Turbo Pascal automatically loads the correct driver, connecting your program with the necessary machine language programming for your graphics system. You do not need GRAPH.TPU on disk to run graphics programs.

If you have a floppy disk system, you can remove the BGI driver files from your compiler disk to save room. You might also remove all but the BGI driver needed by your graphics hardware. If you want to write programs that automatically run on any display, though, it's best to keep all the BGI drivers on disk. (It's also possible to link drivers directly into your compiled code, a subject for later in this chapter.)

Another important disk file type ends in CHR and contains information for drawing text characters. A CHR file is also called (somewhat incorrectly) a *font* file. In typesetting, a font is one type size and style. In Turbo Pascal graphics, a font is a text style, which you can scale up or down to many different sizes. I'll follow the modern trend here and use font to describe a text style in *all* its sizes.

Setting Up for Graphics

The easiest way to prepare your disks for compiling and running graphics programs is to store GRAPH.TPU and all your BGI and CHR files in the same directory as the Turbo Pascal compiler. Assuming this is your setup, Program 11-1 shows the correct way to initialize a graphics mode and draw a circle in the center of the screen.

Program 11-1

```
1:   PROGRAM InTheRound;
2:   USES Graph;
3:   VAR grDriver, grMode, grError : Integer;
4:       xCenter, yCenter : Integer; radius : Word;
5:   BEGIN
6:      grDriver := Detect;
7:      InitGraph( grDriver, grMode, '' );
8:      grError := GraphResult;
```

Program 11-1 *cont.*

```
 9:     IF grError <> GrOk
10:       THEN
11:         Writeln( 'Graphics error : ', GraphErrorMsg( grError ) )
12:       ELSE
13:         BEGIN
14:            xCenter := GetMaxX DIV 2;
15:            yCenter := GetMaxY DIV 2;
16:            radius := GetMaxY DIV 4;
17:            SetColor( Green );
18:            Circle( xCenter, yCenter, radius );
19:            Readln;
20:            CloseGraph
21:         END { else }
22:     END.
```

If you have EGA or VGA graphics, Program 11-1 should display a green circle in the center of the display. If you have a different graphics system and your circle is not green, don't worry—we'll get to colors and how to change them later. If you don't see a circle, or if you receive an error message, be sure you typed the program correctly and that you have the BGI, CHR, and GRAPH.TPU files on your compiler disk.

Note: If you don't see a circle and you're sure your system supports graphics, try changing **Green** to **White**, or remove line 17.

Program 11-1 contains many elements that you will use in all your graphics programs. Lines 6–8 automatically detect and initialize a graphics display mode. The first step is to set integer variable **grDriver** to **Detect**, a constant defined in the **Graph** unit. Passing **Detect** to **InitGraph** (line 7) automatically detects the best graphics mode for your computer. Therefore, the most common initialization sequence is:

```
grDriver := Detect;
InitGraph( grDriver, grMode, '' );
```

You can change the third **InitGraph** parameter to the path where you store the BGI driver and CHR character files. This lets you run graphics programs from other directories and disks. A null string indicates the current drive and directory. If you save your BGI and CHR files in a subdirectory named C:\TPAS\GRAPH, use these statements:

```
grDriver := Detect;
InitGraph( grDriver, grMode, 'C:\TPAS\GRAPH' );
```

InitGraph loads the proper graphics BGI driver file from disk, initializes various internal variables and default conditions, and erases the display. The procedure also returns a second integer variable **grMode** equal to the mode now in effect for the driver specified by **grDriver**.

Table 11-2 explains **grMode** and **grDriver** values. As you can see, most drivers can handle many different modes with various resolutions and pages. A single

Table 11-2 Graphics modes, resolutions, and pages

Driver	Mode	Resolution	Pages
CGA	CGAC0	320 × 200	1
	CGAC1	320 × 200	1
	CGAC2	320 × 200	1
	CGAC3	320 × 200	1
	CGAHI	640 × 200	1
MCGA	MCGAC0	320 × 200	1
	MCGAC1	320 × 200	1
	MCGAC2	320 × 200	1
	MCGAC3	320 × 200	1
	MCGAMed	640 × 200	1
	MCGAHi	640 × 480	1
EGA	EGALo	640 × 200	4
	EGAHi	640 × 350	2
EGA64	EGA64Lo	640 × 200	1
	EGA64Hi	640 × 350	1
EGAMono	EGAMonoHi	640 × 350	1–2*
VGA	VGALo	640 × 200	4
	VGAMed	640 × 350	2
	VGAHi	640 × 480	1
HecMono	HercMonoHi	720 × 348	2
ATT400	ATT400C0	320 × 200	1
	ATT400C1	320 × 200	1
	ATT400C2	320 × 200	1
	ATT400C3	320 × 200	1
	ATT400Med	640 × 200	1
	ATT400Hi	640 × 400	1
PC3270	PC3270Hi	720 × 350	1
IBM8514	IBM8514LO	640 × 480, 256 colors	n/a
	IBM8514HI	1,024 × 768, 256 colors	n/a

*64K on card = 1 page; 256K = 2 pages.

page equals the amount of memory needed to hold all the pixels from one display. Multipage modes let you draw offscreen while viewing graphics on other screens—an especially useful technique for animation and slide show programs.

Initializing Graphics the Hard Way

If you don't care for Turbo Pascal's automatic mode selection, you can choose a different mode by assigning a driver from Table 11-2 to **grDriver** and a mode to **grMode** before calling **InitGraph**. For example, to initialize EGA low resolution, 640 × 200, 16-color graphics, you can write:

```
grDriver := EGA; grMode := EGALo;
InitGraph( grDriver, grMode, '' );
```

When manually selecting graphics modes this way, it's up to you to determine what graphics hardware the computer has. Usually, it's best to let Turbo Pascal automatically select a graphics mode for you, but you might want to include an option in your programs to let people select specific modes, overriding auto-detection. Be careful when experimenting. Initializing display modes not available on your computer can cause the computer to hang, forcing you to reboot or, in some cases, to shut off power.

One way to avoid these problems is to call **DetectGraph** instead of passing the default **Detect** constant to **InitGraph**. **DetectGraph** checks the hardware and sets integer variables **grDriver** and **grMode** to the values Turbo Pascal considers ideal for this system. But, unlike **InitGraph**, **DetectGraph** does not initialize the display. The initialization sequence now becomes:

```
DetectGraph( grDriver, grMode );
InitGraph( grDriver, grMode );
```

This is identical to passing **Detect** to **InitGraph** as in the previous examples. But, because most graphics drivers can support more than one mode, **DetectGraph** gives you the option of initializing the display to a different mode. You might use this idea to detect CGA graphics, but initialize the display to 640 × 200 resolution instead of the default 320 × 200 mode. This does the job:

```
DetectGraph( grDriver, grMode );
IF grDriver = CGA THEN
BEGIN
   grMode := CGAHi;
   InitGraph( grDriver, grMode, '' );
   :
   { graphics statements }
   :
END;
```

Another possibility is to call function **GetMaxMode** after **InitGraph** to find the range of modes supported by the automatically selected driver. To select another display mode, you can then pass a value in the range 0 to **GetMaxMode** to **SetGraphMode**, which clears the display and selects a specified graphics mode. For example, to initialize graphics for the highest possible mode number, execute these statements:

```
DetectGraph( grDriver, grMode );
InitGraph( grDriver, grMode, '' );
IF GraphResult = GrOk THEN
BEGIN
   SetGraphMode( GetMaxMode );
   :
   { graphics statements }
   :
END;
```

Prior to Turbo Pascal 5.0, the only way to detect the maximum mode number was to call **GetModeRange**, which returns two values representing the low and high modes for a graphics driver. Unlike **GetMaxMode**, you may call **GetModeRange** before **InitGraph**, as in this fragment, which selects the lowest possible mode number for the default graphics driver:

```
DetectGraph( grDriver, grMode );
GetModeRange( grDriver, loMode, hiMode );
InitGraph( grDriver, loMode, '' );
```

loMode and **hiMode** are **Integer** variables. One drawback with this method is that it works only with standard BGI drivers. As you'll discover later in this chapter, starting with Turbo Pascal 5.0, it's possible to link in custom graphics drivers. **GetMaxMode** returns the maximum mode number for custom and BGI standard drivers. **GetModeRange** works only with the standards.

You can also pass the **Graph** unit constant **CurrentDriver** to **GetModeRange** instead of calling **DetectGraph**. This may be useful for obtaining the mode range values after calling **InitGraph**. The previous code then becomes:

```
grDriver := Detect;
InitGraph( grDriver, grMode, '' );
IF GraphResult = GrOk THEN
BEGIN
   GetModeRange( CurrentDriver, loMode, hiMode );
   SetGraphMode( loMode );
   :
   { graphics statements }
   :
END;
```

Note: If your computer has VGA graphics, depending on how much memory your hardware has, you may have some trouble running programs that use multiple display pages. If you see "garbage" on screen or a band of interference patterns, you may have to force Turbo Pascal to initialize graphics in EGA mode in order to run the program. Most programs in this chapter initialize the default mode by setting **grDriver** to **Detect**. For most VGA displays, this selects 640 × 480, 16-color graphics. To initialize a VGA card for EGA 640 × 350, 16-color graphics, change **Detect** to **EGA**. That should clear up any problems.

Detecting Graphics Errors

The final step in preparing a graphics mode is to check whether the initialization worked. **InitGraph**, as well as several other routines, stores an internal error code that describes the success or failure of an operation. You can examine this code through the integer function **GraphResult**. Be careful, though. **GraphResult** returns the current error code but also resets the code to zero. Therefore, you can check **GraphResult** only once after any operation. Checking it again always returns zero, the value meaning no error.

Lines 8–11 in Program 11-1 show the correct way to check **GraphResult** for errors. First, assign the function result to a temporary integer variable, here **grError**. All graphics errors are either zero or negative—you must use integer variables to store their values. Line 11 displays an appropriate message if an error occurs (**grError** is not equal to **GrOk**). Table 11-3 lists graphics error values and messages. You could decode the values and display your own messages, but it's easier just to call string function **GraphErrorMsg** as in line 11, displaying the messages shown in the table. **GraphErrorMsg** fills empty parentheses (error values – 3 and – 8, for example) with the offending file names for these errors.

Displaying Driver and Mode Names

After initializing graphics with **InitGraph**, you can ask the **Graph** unit for the names of the current driver and mode. To do this, call the string functions **GetDriverName** with no parameters and **GetModeName** with a single parameter equal to any valid mode number in the range 0 to **GetMaxMode**.

To see how these functions work, replace lines 6–21 of Program 11-1 with the following:

```
grDriver := Detect;
InitGraph( grDriver, grMode, '' );
IF GraphResult = GrOk THEN
BEGIN
   Writeln( 'Graphics driver: ', GetDriverName );
   Writeln( 'Graphics mode:   ', GetModeName( grMode ) );
```

```
    Readln;
    CloseGraph
END
```

For the **Writeln** statements to work in graphics modes, the program may *not* use the **Crt** unit. This doesn't work with Hercules displays.

Table 11-3 Graphics error numbers and messages

GraphResult	GraphErrorMsg
0	No error
−1	(BGI) graphics not installed
−2	Graphics hardware not detected
−3	Device driver file not found ()
−4	Invalid device driver file ()
−5	Not enough memory to load driver
−6	Out of memory in scan fill
−7	Out of memory in flood fill
−8	Font file not found ()
−9	Not enough memory to load font
−10	Invalid graphics mode for selected driver
−11	Graphics error
−12	Graphics I/O error
−13	Invalid font file ()
−14	Invalid font number
−18	Invalid version

Detecting Screen Resolution

Lines 13–21 in Program 11-1 execute if no errors occur when initializing a graphics mode. At this point, the screen is clear and ready for drawing. The first three statements, repeated here for reference, show how to prepare drawings for any of the many possible resolutions:

```
xCenter := GetMaxX DIV 2;
yCenter := GetMaxY DIV 2;
radius := GetMaxY DIV 4;
```

The integer functions, **GetMaxX** and **GetMaxY**, return the maximum horizontal (x) and vertical (y) coordinate values. By designing your programs around these values, instead of assuming you have so many pixels high or wide to work with, you write programs that work correctly in different modes. Here, **xCenter** and **yCenter** are set to the midpoint of the display x and y axes, while radius is set to one-quarter the height. Because the height is never greater than the width in PC graphics display modes, these three values ensure that the circle drawn in line 18 is centered and is *relatively* the same size no matter what graphics mode you are using.

Lines 17 and 18 draw the circle, using the command **SetColor** to choose a drawing color and **Circle** to draw the figure in that color. The three parameters to **Circle** specify the x and y center position and the radius.

Switching Between Text and Graphics

The final two statements in Program 11-1 wait for you to press a key (line 19) and perform an optional deinitialization step (line 20) before the program ends. To return to the display mode in effect before calling **InitGraph**, end your programs with **CloseGraph**. If you don't do this, you may confuse people by leaving the computer in an unfamiliar graphics display mode. This is harmless and you can always reboot or use the DOS MODE command to return to the normal text display. (See your DOS or computer manual for information on using MODE.)

CloseGraph also removes the BGI driver previously loaded by **InitGraph**. You might use **CloseGraph** in programs that display graphics and then switch to a text display. To perform this same action but keep the BGI driver in memory, use the method in Program 11-2 to go back and forth between graphics and text.

Program 11-2

```
 1:   PROGRAM MixedModes;
 2:
 3:   USES Crt,Graph;
 4:
 5:   CONST
 6:      Esc = #27;
 7:
 8:   VAR
 9:      graphDriver, graphMode : integer;
10:      xCenter, yCenter : integer;
11:
12:   BEGIN
13:      graphDriver := Detect;
14:      InitGraph( graphDriver, graphMode, '' );
15:      xCenter := GetMaxX DIV 2; yCenter := GetMaxY DIV 2;
16:
17:      SetColor( Cyan );
18:      Rectangle( xCenter-50, yCenter-50, xCenter+50, yCenter+50 );
19:      OutText( 'This is the graphics page. Press <Enter>...' );
20:      Readln;
21:
22:      RestoreCrtMode;
23:      Write( 'This is the text page. Press <Enter>...' );
24:      Readln;
25:
26:      SetGraphMode( graphMode );
```

Program 11-2 *cont.*

```
27:      Circle( xCenter, yCenter, yCenter DIV 2 );
28:      OutText( 'Back on the graphics page. Press <Enter>...' );
29:      Readln;
30:
31:      CloseGraph
32: END.
```

To save space, Program 11-2 and other programs in this chapter do not check for errors after **InitGraph** as in Program 11-1. Add these checks to all examples if you want. Lines 17–20 change the drawing color to cyan (blue-green) and display a box with procedure **Rectangle**, which takes the form:

```
Rectangle( x1, y1, x2, y2 );
```

Coordinate (x1,y1) specifies the upper-left corner and (x2,y2) the lower-right corner of the box. Line 19 displays a line of text in the current font. (You'll meet the **OutText** command in more detail later in this chapter.)

After you press Enter, line 22 calls **RestoreCrtMode** to return to the text display temporarily. After you press Enter once more, line 26 calls **Set-GraphMode**, passing the same **graphMode** value you originally fed to **Init-Graph** back at line 14. This restores the display to graphics for the **Circle** command in line 27. Press Enter a final time to end the program.

If you called **CloseGraph** instead of **RestoreCrtMode** in line 22, you'd have to call **InitGraph** again to reload a graphics driver before displaying more graphics. For this reason, **RestoreCrtMode** is faster, although the graphics driver takes up memory space that only **CloseGraph** can recover.

Unless you are using a monochrome or CGA graphics mode, you'll notice that the cyan color selected in line 17 changes when switching back to graphics in line 26. Also, the rectangle is gone. **SetGraphMode** erases the display and resets all graphics parameters to their default settings. There's no easy way to preserve screens when switching modes—except maybe storing a display on disk or in a memory buffer, and then reloading it when going back to graphics.

Graphics Defaults

After changing colors and selecting other graphics features, to return to the default conditions, call procedure **GraphDefaults**. Doing this does not erase the display.

If you need to know what graphics mode is now in effect, use integer function **GetGraphMode**. If you don't want to keep a global **graphMode** variable as in Program 11-2, you could write:

```
graphMode := GetGraphMode;
RestoreCrtMode;
  :
```

```
{Text display commands}
:
SetGraphMode( graphMode );
```

This records the current graphics mode in a variable before restoring the text display with **RestoreCrtMode**. Passing this value to **SetGraphMode** returns to the graphics screen, erases the display, and resets all default conditions.

Viewports and Coordinates

Every graphics display pixel has unique x and y coordinate values. The x axis is horizontal; the y is vertical. The pixel in the upper-left corner of the display has the coordinate (0,0). Positive x coordinates move to the right. Negative y coordinates move down. In the vertical direction, this is the reverse of common mathematics notation where positive values move up along the y axis.

All coordinate values in Turbo Pascal graphics are integers, which can be negative or positive. As the inner rectangle in Figure 11-1 shows, the visible portion of the graphics display is merely a restricted view of the entire *logical* surface, or plane, on which programs can draw. This area is called the *viewport*. Drawing outside the viewport is invisible. Only points within the viewport's boundaries are displayed.

At all times, Turbo Pascal stores an internal coordinate, called the *current point* (CP). The CP is the point at which many graphics operations begin. The CP might be the beginning of a line, or it might be the position where text appears. To find out where CP is, use the integer functions **GetX** and **GetY**. After initializing a graphics mode, CP equals (0,0). To find out the maximum x and y coordinates available within the viewport, use the integer functions **GetMaxX** and **GetMaxY**. Together, the four functions test whether points are inside the viewport regardless of the graphics mode in effect:

```
IF ( 0 <= GetX ) AND ( GetX <= GetMaxX ) AND
   ( 0 <= GetY ) AND ( GetY <= GetMaxY )
   THEN { CP is inside viewport }
   ELSE { CP is out of view }
```

The total number of horizontal coordinate values equals **GetMaxX** + 1. The total number of vertical coordinate values equals **GetMaxY** + 1. By using these functions instead of fixed limits, you can write programs that work correctly in any resolution.

Clearing the Viewport

To erase the viewport, call **ClearViewPort**, which paints the screen with the current background color. To erase the viewport and reset CP to (0,0), call **Clear-Device**. To clear the viewport, reset CP, and restore all default conditions, call

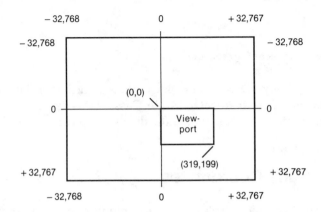

Figure 11-1 A viewport defines the visible area of the logical coordinate
surface, or plane.

ClearViewPort followed by **GraphDefaults**. Calling **ClearDevice** in this case
would be redundant.

Changing the Viewport

There are two reasons to change the viewport illustrated in Figure 11-1. You can
restrict drawing to a portion of the display, protecting graphics in other locations.
Or, you can shift the *origin*—the viewport's top-left corner—to make some kinds of
graphics operations easier to write.

Program 11-3 calls **SetViewPort** in line 12 to restrict drawing to the coordinates (0,0) to (100,75). The procedure takes the form:

```
SetViewPort( x1, y1, x2, y2 : Integer; clip : Boolean );
```

Coordinate (x1,y1) is the new upper-left corner while (x2,y2) is the new
lower-right corner of the viewport. The four values must be greater or equal to
zero, x1 must be less than x2, and y1 must be less than y2. Set **clip TRUE** to restrict drawing to within these new boundaries. Set **clip FALSE** to allow drawing
outside the viewport. Instead of **TRUE** and **FALSE**, you can use the more descriptive **Graph** constants **ClipOn** and **ClipOff**.

Program 11-3

```
1:  PROGRAM RestrictedViews;
2:
3:  USES
4:     Crt, Graph;
5:
6:  VAR
7:     graphDriver, graphMode : integer;
```

Program 11-3 *cont.*

```
 8:
 9: BEGIN
10:    graphDriver := Detect;
11:    InitGraph( graphDriver, graphMode, '' );
12:    SetViewPort( 0, 0, 100, 75, ClipOn );
13:    WHILE NOT Keypressed DO
14:    BEGIN
15:       SetColor( 1+Random(GetMaxColor) );
16:       Line( Random(GetMaxX), Random(GetMaxY),
17:             Random(GetMaxX), Random(GetMaxY) )
18:    END; { while }
19:    CloseGraph
20: END.
```

Experiment with different coordinate values in line 12 of Program 11-3. Change **ClipOn** to **ClipOff** and observe the difference clipping makes. Add a check to **GraphResult** to test for bad viewport settings. For example, you could change line 12 to:

```
SetViewPort( 0, 0, 100, 75, ClipOn );
IF GraphResult <> GrOk THEN
BEGIN
   CloseGraph;
   Writeln( 'Error in viewport settings' )
END;
```

After changing the viewport, the upper-left corner again has the coordinate (0,0). This seems confusing at first. Consider the statement:

```
SetViewPort( 100, 50, 200, 150, ClipOn );
```

Although this sets the viewport to the coordinates (100,50) and (200,150), plotting a point at the relative viewport location (0,0) appears at the absolute screen coordinate (100,50). You'll avoid confusion if you think of a viewport as having its own coordinate system—with (0,0) always in the upper-left corner no matter where the viewport appears on display. Coordinates inside the viewport are relative to the viewport boundaries.

To reset the viewport to the entire display, call **GraphDefaults** followed by **ClearViewPort** if you want to erase the screen as well. You can also write:

```
SetViewPort( 0, 0, GetMaxX, GetMaxY, ClipOn );
```

If you need to know the current viewport settings, call **GetViewSettings** passing a variable of type **ViewPortType**:

```
ViewPortType =
   RECORD
      x1, y1, x2, y2 : Integer;
      clip : Boolean
   END;
```

Another viewport setting you can check is the *aspect ratio*, defined as:

$$\frac{\text{Display width}}{\text{Display height}}$$

NTSC (National Television Standard Code) standard aspect ratio is 4:3, suggesting an ideal display with a multiple of four pixels wide by a multiple of three pixels tall, a ratio equal to 1.333. On Macintosh computers and some VGA modes, the aspect ratio is very nearly 1.000—pixels are just about square. In 640 by 350 EGA display mode on PCs, the aspect ratio is 0.7750—nowhere near the ideal.

Turbo Pascal uses the aspect ratio when drawing circles and arcs to make them round. If it didn't compensate for the display's aspect ratio, a round circle would look oval.

Note that the aspect ratio is *not* equal to the horizontal divided by the vertical *resolutions*. The display resolution has no relation to the aspect ratio. To find the correct aspect ratio for any display mode, call **GetAspectRatio** with two **Word** parameters:

```
GetAspectRatio( xaspect, yaspect );
```

Run Program 11-4 to display the aspect ratio for the automatically selected graphics mode on your computer.

Program 11-4

```
 1:  PROGRAM AspectRatio;
 2:  USES Crt, Graph;
 3:  VAR grDriver, grMode : Integer;
 4:      xaspect, yaspect : Word;
 5:  BEGIN
 6:      grDriver := Detect;
 7:      InitGraph( grDriver, grMode, '' );
 8:      RestoreCrtMode;
 9:      GetAspectRatio( xaspect, yaspect );
10:      Writeln( 'Graph driver = ', grDriver );
11:      Writeln( 'Graph mode   = ', grMode );
12:      Writeln( 'xaspect      = ', xaspect );
13:      Writeln( 'yaspect      = ', yaspect );
14:      Writeln( 'Aspect ratio = ',
15:          (xaspect*1.0) / (yaspect*1.0) :0:3 )
16:  END.
```

In EGA 640 × 350 mode, Program 11-4 displays the following information:

```
Graph driver = 3
Graph mode   = 1
xaspect      = 7750
yaspect      = 10000
Aspect ratio = 0.775
```

These values indicate that, for graphics driver 3 in mode 1, a one-unit-tall pixel is 0.775 unit wide. Assuming the aspect ratio is less than zero, multiplying the height of a line by the aspect ratio compensates for the disparity, letting you draw lines of equal display sizes even though the lines cover different numbers of pixels. Program 11-5 demonstrates how to do this.

Program 11-5

```
1:   PROGRAM EqualLines;
2:   USES Crt, Graph;
3:   VAR grDriver, grMode : Integer;
4:       xaspect, yaspect : Word;
5:       ratio : Real;
6:
7:   PROCEDURE DrawLines( x, y, len : Integer );
8:   BEGIN
9:      Line( x, y, x + len, y );  { Horizontal line }
10:     Line( x, y, x, y + Round(len*ratio) );  { Vertical line }
11:  END; { DrawLines }
12:
13:  BEGIN
14:     grDriver := Detect;
15:     InitGraph( grDriver, grMode, '' );
16:
17:     ratio := 1.0;   { No adjustment }
18:     DrawLines( 25, 25, 75 );
19:
20:     GetAspectRatio( xaspect, yaspect );
21:     ratio := (xaspect*1.0) / (yaspect*1.0);
22:     DrawLines( 110, 110, 75 );
23:
24:     REPEAT UNTIL Keypressed;
25:     CloseGraph
26:  END.
```

Program 11-5 draws two right angles. The first in the upper-left corner is not adjusted for the display's aspect ratio. As you can see, the vertical line is longer than the horizontal. This only makes sense. Pixels are taller than they are wide; therefore, lines of the same pixel length are similarly taller.

The second right angle to the lower-right adjusts the vertical line length by the aspect ratio, calculated in program line 21. This adjustment makes the horizontal and vertical lines equal lengths on display. If you measure these lines accurately, though, don't be too surprised if the results are imperfect. Minor differences in display monitors can also affect the aspect ratio.

If the default aspect ratio is not correct—in other words, if circles aren't perfectly round—call **SetAspectRatio** with two parameters representing the x (display width) and y (display height) axes. The actual values aren't too important. It's the *ratio* of x to y that matters. For instance, to change the display ratio to the NTSC standard 4:3, a ratio of 1.333, you can execute:

```
SetAspectRatio( 4, 3 );
```

Shifting the Origin

By turning off clipping and moving the viewport so that (0,0) is at dead center, you can write graphics that use both negative and positive coordinate values. Doing this divides the viewport into quadrants, simplifying some kinds of operations. Figure 11-2 shows the relationship of this new viewport to the entire coordinate plane.

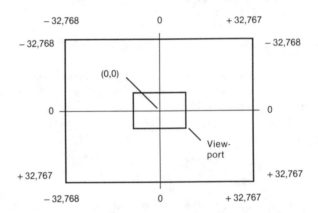

Figure 11-2 Changing the viewport so that (0,0) is at center screen makes some kinds of graphics programs easier to write.

To accomplish this requires a small trick: Set the viewport so that the absolute center of the screen becomes the new (0,0) coordinate and then turn off clipping:

```
xCenter := GetMaxX DIV 2;
yCenter := GetMaxY DIV 2;
SetViewPort( xCenter, yCenter, GetMaxX, GetMaxY, ClipOff );
```

Using **ClipOn** instead would restrict drawing to the lower-right quadrant of the display. With clipping off, the other three quadrants are visible. Even though the viewport is technically in the lower-right of the display, positive and negative coordinate values now locate points on the entire screen, with (0,0) in the center. Figure 11-3 shows this new arrangement. Four combinations locate points in the four quadrants according to the scheme:

- (−x, −y) Upper-left quadrant.
- (−x, +y) Lower-left quadrant.
- (+x, −y) Upper-right quadrant.
- (+x, +y) Lower-right quadrant.

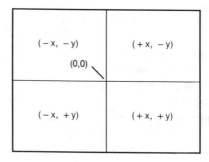

Figure 11-3 With (0,0) at the center, the display is divided into four quadrants.

Plotting Points

Two fundamental routines display and read individual pixels:

```
PutPixel( x, y : Integer; pixel : Word );
GetPixel( x, y : Integer ) : Word;
```

A pixel is the **Word** value equal to the displayed dot's color number. (Later in this chapter, you'll learn how to associate different display colors with color numbers. **GetPixel** always returns the color number—in other words, the logical color—not necessarily the color you see on screen.)

   PutPixel displays one dot at location (x,y) in the color number specified by parameter **pixel**. Program 11-6 demonstrates how to use **PutPixel** and **GetPixel**. The program displays dots at random locations (line 17) unless **GetPixel** discovers a dot already there. In this case, line 16 turns the pixel off by painting it black. The effect is to create a display full of pixels, evenly distributed like sand on the beach. Let the program run for several minutes. This is also a good test of the random number generator as well as a check on your monitor's ability to resolve individual pixels.

   Line 14 of the program shows how to use function **GetMaxColor** to determine the maximum color number available for any graphics mode.

Program 11-6

```
 1:   PROGRAM Twinkler;
 2:   USES Crt, Graph;
 3:   VAR grDriver, grMode, grError : Integer;
 4:       x, y, xMax, yMax, color : Integer;
 5:   BEGIN
 6:      grDriver := Detect;
 7:      InitGraph( grDriver, grMode, '' );
 8:      xMax := GetMaxX; yMax := GetMaxY;
 9:      Randomize;
10:      WHILE NOT Keypressed DO
11:      BEGIN
12:        x := Random( xMax );
13:        y := Random( yMax );
14:        color := Random( GetMaxColor );
15:        IF GetPixel( x, y ) <> Black
16:           THEN PutPixel( x, y, Black )
17:           ELSE PutPixel( x, y, color )
18:      END; { while }
19:      CloseGraph
20:   END.
```

Drawing Lines

Of course you could draw lines by plotting individual pixels along a path between two coordinates. Instead of doing this yourself, it's easier—and much faster—to call one of Turbo Pascal's three line generators: **Line**, **LineTo**, and **LineRel**.

Procedure **Line** connects two points, (x1,y1) and (x2,y2). The procedure has the form:

```
Line( x1, y1, x2, y2 );
```

The two points can be anywhere, even off screen, although you'll see lines only in the visible portion of the current viewport. Program 11-7 demonstrates how to use **Line** to draw a border around the graphics display. Notice how **GetMaxX** and **GetMaxY** (line 8) let this program work correctly for all display resolutions.

Program 11-7

```
 1:   PROGRAM GraphBorder;
 2:   USES Crt, Graph;
```

Program 11-7 *cont.*

```
 3:    VAR graphDriver, graphMode : Integer;
 4:        xMax, yMax : Integer;
 5:    BEGIN
 6:        graphDriver := Detect;
 7:        InitGraph( graphDriver, graphMode, '' );
 8:        xMax := GetMaxX; yMax := GetMaxY;
 9:
10:        Line( 0, 0, xMax, 0 );
11:        Line( xMax, 0, xMax, yMax );
12:        Line( xMax, yMax, 0, yMax );
13:        Line( 0, yMax, 0, 0 );
14:
15:        REPEAT UNTIL Keypressed;
16:        CloseGraph
17:    END.
```

Instead of specifying the first (x, y) coordinate, you can use **LineTo** to join the current CP to a new (x, y) location:

```
LineTo( x, y );
```

Drawing lines with **Line**, **LineTo**, or **LineRel** changes CP to the line's new end point. Calling **LineTo** then continues drawing with the previous end point as the start for the next line. Because **LineTo** has two fewer parameters than **Line**, it runs a tiny bit faster—enough to make a noticeable difference in speed when you have many lines to draw.

Another way to change CP before drawing lines is to use **MoveTo**. The statements:

```
MoveTo( x1, y1 );
LineTo( x2, y2 );
```

have the identical effect as:

```
Line( x1, y1, x2, y2 );
```

Program 11-8 duplicates Program 11-7, but uses **MoveTo** and **LineTo** to outline the display. The previous program (11-7) is obviously wasteful in lines 10–13 because the end point of each line is the starting point of the next. Therefore, **LineTo** is faster. The **MoveTo** statement at line 10 is not necessary in this example because **InitGraph** positions CP to (0,0). The statement would be necessary, though, if you had previously changed CP.

Program 11-8

```
 1:  PROGRAM BetterBorder;
 2:  USES Crt, Graph;
 3:  VAR graphDriver, graphMode : Integer;
 4:      xMax, yMax : Integer;
 5:  BEGIN
 6:      graphDriver := Detect;
 7:      InitGraph( graphDriver, graphMode, '' );
 8:      xMax := GetMaxX; yMax := GetMaxY;
 9:
10:      MoveTo( 0, 0 );
11:      LineTo( xMax, 0 );
12:      LineTo( xMax, yMax );
13:      LineTo( 0, yMax );
14:      LineTo( 0, 0 );
15:
16:      REPEAT UNTIL Keypressed;
17:      CloseGraph
18:  END.
```

Relative Lines

Two procedures, **MoveRel** and **LineRel**, move CP to a new coordinate relative to the present CP or draw a line with its starting point relative to CP. With these procedures, it's easy to design figures that display correctly at any screen position. The procedures are defined as:

```
MoveRel( dx, dy );
LineRel( dx, dy );
```

Parameters **dx** (delta x) and **dy** (delta y) are integer values representing the change in x and y. Positive values move down and to the right; negative values move up and to the left.

Program 11-9 shows how to use these routines in a procedure, **DrawFigure** at lines 6–17, that draws a design centered relative to a point (x,y). Because of the **MoveRel** and **LineRel** statements, the same figure is easy to draw at any screen location.

Program 11-9

```
 1:  PROGRAM Relativity;
 2:  USES Crt, Graph;
 3:  VAR graphDriver, graphMode : Integer;
```

Program 11-9 *cont.*

```
 4:        xMax, yMax : Integer;
 5:
 6:    PROCEDURE DrawFigure( x, y, size : Integer );
 7:    BEGIN
 8:        MoveTo( x, y );
 9:        MoveRel( x-size, y-size );
10:        LineRel( size, 0 );
11:        LineRel( 0, size );
12:        LineRel( -size, 0 );
13:        LineRel( 0, -size );
14:        LineRel( size, size );
15:        MoveRel( 0, -size );
16:        LineRel( -size, size )
17:    END; { DrawFigure }
18:
19:    BEGIN
20:        graphDriver := Detect;
21:        InitGraph( graphDriver, graphMode, '' );
22:        xMax := GetMaxX; yMax := GetMaxY;
23:        Randomize;
24:        WHILE NOT Keypressed DO
25:        BEGIN
26:            Delay( 100 );
27:            DrawFigure( Random(xMax), Random(yMax), 10+Random(40) )
28:        END; { while }
29:        CloseGraph
30:    END.
```

Stylish Lines

Two procedures, **GetLineSettings** and **SetLineStyle**, examine and change three line characteristics:

1. Style.
2. Pattern.
3. Thickness.

The line style can be one of the following constants:

```
SolidLn   = 0;
DottedLn  = 1;
CenterLn  = 2;
DashedLn  = 3;
```

The first four of these constants specify solid lines (**SolidLn**), dotted lines (**Dot-tedLn**), alternating dash-dot lines (**CenterLn**), and dashes (**DashedLn**). Two other constants change line width to normal or thick:

```
NormWidth  = 1;
ThickWidth = 3;
```

These are the only automatic thicknesses available. In other words, to draw two-pixel wide lines, you have to draw two lines of normal width.

Call **SetLineStyle** to change line styles and thickness. For example, to draw a fat center line, dividing the top and bottom of the display, you can write:

```
SetLineStyle( CenterLn, 0, ThickWidth );
Line( 0, GetMaxY DIV 2, GetMaxX, GetMaxY DIV 2 );
```

The second parameter to **SetLineStyle** is significant only when the first parameter equals another constant, **UserBitLn**. In this case, the second parameter is the **Word** bit pattern you want the line generator to use to draw lines. For example, to display a faint line of sparse dots in the center of the screen, write:

```
VAR pattern : Word;

pattern := $1010;
SetLineStyle( UserBitLn, pattern, NormWidth );
Line( 0, GetMaxY DIV 2, GetMaxX, GetMaxY DIV 2 );
```

The custom **pattern** equals hex $1010, or in binary, 0001 0000 0001 0000. Each 1 in the pattern becomes a dot on screen; each 0, an invisible point that is not plotted. Using the **UserBitLn** constant lets you draw lines with any repeating pattern of 16 ones and zeros.

To read the current line style settings, call **GetLineSettings** with a record variable defined as:

```
LineSettingsType =
   RECORD
      lineStyle : Word;
      pattern   : Word;
      thickness : Word
   END;
```

The three fields in this record correspond with the three parameters passed to **SetLineStyle**. Use **GetLineSettings** to preserve the current line style when you want to change styles temporarily to draw other lines. Here's an example:

```
VAR style : LineSettingsType;

GetLineSettings( style );
```

```
     :
{ change line style and draw lines }
     :
WITH style DO
   SetLineStyle( lineStyle, pattern, thickness );
```

This preserves the current line style in variable **style** and then, after changing styles and drawing other lines, restores the previous settings with a call to **SetLineStyle**, passing the three record fields, **lineStyle**, **pattern**, and **thickness**.

Color Palettes

Different graphics modes can display different numbers of colors on screen at once. CGA graphics shows up to four colors including the background. EGA and VGA graphics display up to 16 colors. And, by using the special driver VGA256.BGI, available from Borland, VGA graphics can display a full 256 colors. IBM 8514 graphics modes can also display 256 colors.

Because most people have CGA and EGA adapters, it's a good idea to limit your graphics programs to 16 colors—especially, of course, if you plan on distributing your program to others. The following discussion, therefore, assumes that you'll be using a maximum of 16 colors.

In each of these modes, and in other less popular graphics displays, a *palette* controls what actual colors (or shades of gray on monochrome systems) you see on screen. Changing palettes instantly changes the colors of points already on display. You can't draw a few objects in one set of colors and then change palettes to get more colors on screen. Changing palettes merely tells the computer what colors to use for all points, whether already displayed or to be displayed in the future.

In memory, a palette is an array of color values. The indexes to each arrayed value represent the *color numbers*—the values programs use to specify the colors of lines and points. When you draw in a certain color, say **Red**, a **Graph** unit constant equal to 4, the actual color you see on screen depends on the color value of palette[4]. If you change that color value to **Blue**, all the previously red points as well as future red points will be **Blue**. Turbo Pascal defines a palette this way:

```
CONST
   MaxColors = 15;
TYPE
   PaletteType =
      RECORD
         size : Byte;
         colors : ARRAY[ 0 .. MaxColors ] OF ShortInt
      END;
```

A **PaletteType** record starts with a **Byte** field **size**, which tells how many significant bytes follow. The actual number of bytes changes for different modes but is never greater than **MaxColors** + 1. To find out how many colors are available, use the function **GetMaxColor**. Assuming you have a **PaletteType** record **pt**, this always sets the **size** field correctly:

```
WITH pt DO
   size := GetMaxColor + 1;
```

Remember that a **PaletteType** variable only represents the actual palette stored somewhere in memory. To load a **PaletteType** variable with the contents of the in-memory palette, use **GetPalette** like this:

```
VAR pt : PaletteType;

GetPalette( pt );
```

GetPalette initializes the **size** field in **pt** and inserts color values into the **colors** array. You can then inspect or change the values to create different palettes and pass the result to **SetAllPalette**:

```
pt.colors[1] := Brown;
SetAllPalette( pt );
```

A value of − 1 in the **colors** array causes no change to a color. This lets you change some colors while leaving others alone. For example:

```
WITH pt DO
BEGIN
   size := GetMaxColor+1;
   FOR i := 1 TO size DO
     colors[i] := -1;
   colors[1] := Brown
END; { with }
SetAllPalette( pt );
```

An easier way to change a single color entry is to use **SetPalette**. This changes the first color to brown:

```
SetPalette( 1, Brown );
```

The first **SetPalette** parameter is a **Word** equal to the color number—the index into the color palette array. The second parameter is the color value, a **ShortInt** value, which can be any number from − 128 to + 127. After this statement, passing 1 to **SetColor** will draw in **Brown**—or in whatever actual color or gray shade this value produces in one or another graphics modes.

In most programs, **PaletteType** records are useful for preparing several different palettes and switching among them with **SetAllPalette**. To change individual palette entries, use the simpler **SetPalette**.

Another way to determine the maximum palette number is to call **GetPaletteSize**, newly added to Turbo Pascal 5.0. The **Integer** function returns the same value as the **size** field in a **PaletteType** record returned by **GetPalette**. Use **GetPaletteSize** to check that palette color numbers are within range. Because the maximum value equals **GetPaletteSize** − 1, the correct way to verify that a **Word** variable **color** is within limits is:

```
IF color >= GetPaletteSize
   THEN { error--color out of range }
   ELSE SetPalette( color, Red );
```

The Default Palette

The **Graph** unit maintains a copy of the original palette initialized by **InitGraph**. To read this palette, call **GetDefaultPalette** with a variable of type **PaletteType**. Unlike **GetPalette**, which returns the *current* palette, including any modifications you made to palette entries, **GetDefaultPalette** returns an unblemished copy of the original palette. Assuming **pt** is a **PaletteType** variable, to restore the original palette at any time takes only two statements:

```
GetDefaultPalette( pt );
SetAllPalette( pt );
```

Changing Display Colors

Because of the variety of different display modes, it's a good idea to call **GetMaxColor** early in your program. This tells you the maximum color number (palette index) that you can pass to **SetColor**, changing the color for subsequent drawing.

Color number 0 is the background color. Values from 1 to **GetMaxColor** equal the full range of color numbers that you can use. Program 11-10 demonstrates these ideas along with **GetMaxX** and **GetMaxY** to fill the screen with randomly positioned lines, in randomly selected colors, for any display mode.

Program 11-10

```
1:  PROGRAM RandomLines;
2:  USES Crt, Graph;
3:  VAR graphDriver, graphMode : Integer;
4:      xMax, yMax : Integer;
5:  BEGIN
6:     graphDriver := Detect;
7:     InitGraph( graphDriver, graphMode, '' );
8:     xMax := GetMaxX; yMax := GetMaxY;
9:     Randomize;
```

Program 11-10 *cont.*

```
10:    WHILE NOT Keypressed DO
11:    BEGIN
12:      Delay( 100 );
13:      SetColor( 1+Random(GetMaxColor) );   { 1 .. GetMaxColor }
14:      LineTo( Random(GetMaxX+1),           { 0 .. GetMaxX }
15:              Random(GetMaxY+1) );         { 0 .. GetMaxY }
16:    END; { while }
17:    CloseGraph
18: END.
```

Remove line 12 to increase the speed of this example, slowed for effect. Line 13 calls **SetColor** with the expression:

```
SetColor( 1+Random(GetMaxColor) );
```

to select a drawing color at random between 1 and **GetMaxColor** + 1. This skips the background color (which would draw invisible lines) and is usually the correct way to generate colors at random in the entire spectrum available for all graphics modes.

If you need to find out the current drawing color, use **GetColor**, assigning this function's result to any **Word** variable:

```
VAR theColor : Word;

theColor := GetColor;
```

In the Background

Two other color procedures examine and change the background color, which always has the color palette number 0 no matter what actual color you see. To change the background to cyan, write:

```
SetBkColor( Cyan );  { Change background color }
```

This is identical to changing the palette entry for color number 0:

```
SetPalette( 0, Cyan );   { Change background color }
```

Like other palette changes, the visual effect is immediate. You don't have to clear the screen or perform any other steps to see the new background color. Lines and other shapes are preserved and appear on top of the new background—as long as they aren't of the same color of course! To find out the current background color, call **Word** function **GetBkColor**:

```
VAR theBkColor : Word;


theBkColor := GetBkColor;
```

Setting the Write Mode

Changing the **Graph** unit's Write Mode affects the method used to poke new pixels into the display. Normally, routines such as **DrawPoly, Line, LineRec, LineTo,** and **Rectangle**—some of which you haven't yet seen in action—simply turn on the appropriate pixels to draw lines and other shapes. To set the Write Mode to XOR (exclusive OR), call **SetWriteMode** with the predefined constant **XORPut**:

```
SetWriteMode( XORPut );
```

To change the Write Mode back to normal, pass **CopyPut** to **SetWriteMode**:

```
SetWriteMode( CopyPut );
```

When setting the Write Mode to **XORPut**, redrawing a line in the same color erases the line. This is useful in graphics programs that display shapes on top of other shapes. After setting Write Mode to **XORPut**, you can remove a shape on top of another simply by redrawing the foreground image—without disturbing the shape below.

For a demonstration of how **XORPut** Write Mode works, make a copy of Program 11-10 and replace line 4 with this procedure:

```
PROCEDURE DoLines( n : Integer );
{ Recursive XORPut demonstration }
VAR
    color, x1, y1, x2, y2 : Integer;
BEGIN
    Delay( 50 );
    x1 := GetX; y1 := GetY;
    x2 := Random( GetMaxX + 1 );
    y2 := Random( GetMaxY + 1 );
    color := 1 + Random( GetMaxColor );
    SetColor( color );
    LineTo( x2, y2 );
    IF n < 30 THEN DoLines( n + 1 );
    Delay( 50 );
    SetColor( color );        { Must reset color! }
    Line( x1, y1, x2, y2 )  { Can't use CP! }
END; { DoLines }
```

Next, replace lines 8–16 with:

```
SetWriteMode( XORPut );
Randomize;
DoLines( 0 );
```

  When you run the modified program, you'll see random lines as in the original. This time, because **SetWriteMode** changes the Write Mode to **XORPut**, redrawing lines in the same colors erases the lines one by one, leaving the display clear. Change **XORPut** to the default **CopyPut** (or remove the **SetWriteMode** statement) to see the difference that exclusive-OR drawing makes.

Shape Routines

Turbo Pascal offers three basic shapes, all composed of lines: rectangles, bars, and polygons. You can also fill a shape's insides with various patterns and colors. And, in the case of bars, you can display a pseudo-three-dimensional box, popular for business graphs.

Rectangles

Rectangles are the easiest shapes to draw. Pass the coordinates of the upper-left and lower-right corners of the area to enclose. Then call **Rectangle**, which has the form:

```
Rectangle( x1, y1, x2, y2 : Integer );
```

  Line 9 of Program 11-11 calls **Rectangle** to outline the screen in the default drawing color, usually white. This is far simpler than our attempts to do the same job in Programs 11-7 and 11-8. Program 11-11 calls **Rectangle** again at lines 15–18, drawing boxes at random locations and colors until you press a key to stop the program. Notice how the **Random** statements carefully restrict the boxes to within the outline borders.

Program 11-11

```
1:  PROGRAM Rects;
2:  USES Crt, Graph;
3:  VAR graphDriver, graphMode : Integer;
4:      xMax, yMax : Integer;
5:  BEGIN
6:      graphDriver := Detect;
7:      InitGraph( graphDriver, graphMode, '' );
```

Program 11-11 *cont.*

```
 8:     xMax := GetMaxX; yMax := GetMaxY;
 9:     Rectangle( 0, 0, xMax, yMax );  { Outline screen }
10:     Randomize;
11:     WHILE NOT Keypressed DO
12:     BEGIN
13:        Delay( 100 );
14:        SetColor( 1+Random(GetMaxColor) );  { 1 .. GetMaxColor }
15:        Rectangle( 1+Random(GetMaxX-1),
16:                   1+Random(GetMaxY-1),
17:                   1+Random(GetMaxX-1),
18:                   1+Random(GetMaxY-1)  )
19:     END; { while }
20:     CloseGraph
21:  END.
```

Bars

A simple bar, helpful for drawing bar graphs, is just a rectangle painted with a color and a bit pattern. When drawing these and other filled shapes, it's helpful to think of the color as the *paint* and the bit pattern as the *brush*. Executing this command:

```
Bar( x1, y1, x2, y2 );
```

is the same as calling **Rectangle** with these same coordinates and then filling the inside of the box with the current paint (white unless you change it) and brush pattern (normally solid). To see an example, replace **Rectangle** in line 15 of Program 11-11 with **Bar** and rerun the demo.

If you're following along on your computer, you now see a problem—the color passed to **SetColor** does not affect the paint color for filled shapes. To fix the problem, replace line 14 in Program 11-11 with:

```
SetFillStyle( SolidFill, 1+Random(GetMaxColor) );
```

SetFillStyle takes two parameters, both **Word** types. The first parameter is the pattern, which can be any one of the identifiers listed in Table 11-4. The second pattern is the color of paint you want to use. To fill boxes with both random patterns and colors, replace line 14 with:

```
SetFillStyle( Random(12), 1+Random(GetMaxColor) );
```

If none of Turbo Pascal's standard brush patterns will do, you can create your own patterns with **SetFillPattern**. This procedure takes an array of type **FillPatternType**, defined as:

```
TYPE
  FillPatternType =
    ARRAY[ 1 .. 8 ] OF Byte;
```

Table 11-4 Pattern constants for SetFillStyle

Constant	Value	Fill effect
EmptyFill	0	Background color
SolidFill	1	Solid color
LineFill	2	Lines (---)
LtSlashFill	3	Thin slashes (////)
SlashFill	4	Thick slashes (////)
BkSlashFill	5	Thick backslashes (\\\\)
LtBkSlashFill	6	Thin backslashes (\\\\)
HatchFill	7	Light hatch marks
XHatchFill	8	Heavy hatch marks
InterleaveFill	9	Interleaved lines
WideDotFill	10	Sparse dots
CloseDotFill	11	Dense dots
UserFill	12	Previous SetFillPattern

A custom pattern is an 8 × 8 block, with each bit corresponding to a pixel on display. To fill shapes with tiny boxes, assign values to a **FillPatternType** array with the appropriate bits.

A simple experiment demonstrates how to design custom patterns. Starting with a copy of Program 11-11, change **Rectangle** in line 15 to **Bar** and add a variable between lines 4 and 5:

```
pattern : FillPatternType;
```

Next, add these assignments between lines 10 and 11 (after **Randomize**):

```
pattern[1]:=$00;    {00000000}
pattern[2]:=$3C;    {00111100}
pattern[3]:=$24;    {00100100}
pattern[4]:=$24;    {00100100}
pattern[5]:=$24;    {00100100}
pattern[6]:=$24;    {00100100}
pattern[7]:=$3C;    {00111100}
pattern[8]:=$00;    {00000000}
```

This creates the custom pattern array, assigning hex values to each of the eight array bytes. For reference, the equivalent binary values are shown in comments to the right of the assignments. Notice that the 1s form a box inside the 8 × 8 grid.

The final step is to pass this custom bit pattern to the graphics kernel. Replace line 14 with:

```
SetFillPattern( pattern, 1+Random(GetMaxColor) );
```

When you pass a custom pattern to **SetFillPattern** this way, Turbo Pascal makes a copy of the pattern in memory. Rather than call **SetFillPattern** a second time, to use the most recent custom pattern, write:

```
SetFillStyle( UserFill, 0 );
```

In this case, the color is the value you passed to **SetFillPattern**. The 0 in this example is ignored.

To preserve the current fill pattern, call **GetFillPattern** with a **FillPattern-Type** variable. You can then restore this pattern by calling **SetFillPattern**:

```
VAR pattern : FillPatternType;

GetFillPattern( pattern );
:
{ design and draw with custom patterns }
:
SetFillPattern( pattern, color );  {restore pattern}
```

To preserve both the current fill pattern and color, call **GetFillSettings**. This procedure takes a record defined as:

```
TYPE
   FillSettingsType =
   RECORD
      pattern : Word;
      color   : Word
   END;
```

After calling **GetFillSettings**, you can restore both the original pattern and color by passing the fields of this record to **SetFillStyle**. Here's an example:

```
VAR settings : FillSettingsType;

GetFillSettings( settings );
:
{ design and draw with other patterns }
:
WITH settings DO
   SetFillStyle( pattern, color );
```

Three-D Bars

A special bar procedure, **Bar3D**, draws a pseudo-three-dimensional box, with three visible sides. The box has no depth and is technically called an *orthographic* *projection*. Even so, this object is useful for breathing some realism into an otherwise boring two-dimensional bar chart.

Program 11-12 displays a series of three-dimensional bars. When you run the program, you'll see that the face of the bar is filled with a solid color (probably white), while the top and right sides are only outlines. To change the number of bars, adjust constant **NumBars** in line 5. To change the depth of the pseudo-three-dimensional effect, change **Depth** in line 4.

Change the face of the bars the same way you changed the brushes and paint colors in earlier examples. Use either **SetFillStyle** or **SetFillPattern**. For example, to fill the bars with red slashes, insert this statement between lines 14 and 15:

```
SetFillStyle( SlashFill, Red );
```

When you run this modified program, the bars fill with red slashes instead of solid white—a definite improvement. Notice that the bar outlines remain white, unaffected by **SetFillStyle**. To change outline color, call **SetColor**. Try this statement after the **SetFillStyle** you just inserted:

```
SetColor( Yellow );
```

You now should see red-faced, slash-filled bars, outlined in yellow. On older CGA graphics systems, you might see the reverse—yellow faces outlined in red. This just goes to show that you can't trust the names of color constants to hold true for all graphics modes!

Program 11-12

```
 1:  PROGRAM FancyBarChart;
 2:  USES Crt, Graph;
 3:  CONST
 4:      Depth = 14;
 5:      NumBars = 9;
 6:  VAR
 7:      graphDriver, graphMode : Integer;
 8:      width, height : Integer;
 9:      i, x1, y1, x2, y2, xMax, yMax : Integer;
10:  BEGIN
11:      graphDriver := Detect;
12:      InitGraph( graphDriver, graphMode, '' );
13:      xMax := GetMaxX; yMax := GetMaxY;
14:      Randomize;
15:      width := xMax DIV NumBars;
16:      height := yMax - ( yMax DIV 4 );
17:      FOR i := 1 TO numBars DO
18:      BEGIN
```

Program 11-12 *cont.*

```
19:        x1 := width * ( i - 1 );
20:        y1 := Depth + Random( height );
21:        x2 := x1 + ( width DIV 2 );
22:        y2 := yMax - ( yMax DIV 6 );
23:        Bar3D( x1, y1, x2, y2, Depth, TopOn )
24:     END; { for }
25:
26:     REPEAT UNTIL Keypressed;
27:     CloseGraph
28:
29: END.
```

Polygons

A polygon is any enclosed shape with sides made of straight lines. Triangles and boxes are polygons. Because there are easy ways to draw such simple shapes, though, a polygon is usually a more complex object with many sides.

One good analogy to the way Turbo Pascal draws polygons is a child's connect-the-dots game. Each dot is a coordinate on the screen. The graphics kernel is the child, connecting the dots to draw a picture.

In memory, a polygon is an array of x and y coordinates—two integers per coordinate point. The array can be any size within practical limits; the more points you have, the longer it takes to draw the figure. Unlike some other graphics data types, there is no predefined polygon structure. Probably, the best design is to use an array of **PointType** records:

```
VAR
    polygon : ARRAY[ 1 .. NumPoints ] OF PointType;
```

Each **PointType** record has two fields, x and y. To fix the starting point of the polygon to (0,0), you could write:

```
WITH polygon[1] DO
BEGIN
   x := 0; y := 0
END;
```

You could also use a two-dimensional array indexed by x and y values, but this method uses the more efficient **WITH** statement and a single index operation to get to the x and y components of each polygon point.

Another good possibility is to use a variable constant prefilled with coordinate values. Program 11-13 uses this idea to define a five-point star, the **polygon** constant at lines 4–10. Passing this array to **DrawPoly** at line 18 draws the star by connecting the points in the array.

The first parameter to **DrawPoly** tells how many coordinates follow—in this case, six. The second parameter is the array itself. Notice that this five-point object requires six array entries to close the shape. Replace line 18 with the following to see what happens if you forget this important rule:

```
DrawPoly( 5, polygon );
```

Program 11-13

```
 1:   PROGRAM StarStruck;
 2:   USES Crt, Graph;
 3:   CONST
 4:     polygon : ARRAY[ 1 .. 6 ] OF PointType =
 5:        ( ( x :  50; y :  0 ),
 6:          ( x :  90; y : 75 ),
 7:          ( x :   0; y : 25 ),
 8:          ( x : 100; y : 25 ),
 9:          ( x :  10; y : 75 ),
10:          ( x :  50; y :  0 ) );
11:   VAR
12:     graphDriver, graphMode : Integer;
13:   BEGIN
14:     graphDriver := Detect;
15:     InitGraph( graphDriver, graphMode, '' );
16:
17:     SetColor( Cyan );
18:     DrawPoly( 6, polygon );
19:
20:     REPEAT UNTIL Keypressed;
21:     CloseGraph
22:   END.
```

Filling Polygons

You can fill polygons with patterns and colors the same way you fill two- and three-dimensional bars. Use **SetFillStyle** and **SetFillPattern** to select a brush and paint. Then call **FillPoly** instead of **DrawPoly**. For a test, replace line 18 in Program 11-13 with these two statements:

```
SetFillStyle( InterLeaveFill, LightBlue );
FillPoly( 5, polygon );
```

The 5 is not a mistake. **FillPoly** operates a bit differently than its sister procedure, **DrawPoly**. Because painting a polygon with an unconnected side would leak paint all over the screen, Turbo Pascal automatically closes the shape for you. Therefore, **FillPoly** always requires one less point than **DrawPoly**. (You can specify the last point with no harm, though, passing 6 instead of 5 to **FillPoly** with no bad effects.)

When you run this new program, you'll see the star tips filled with light blue, using an interleaved line pattern. Use **SetColor** to change the color of the lines outlining the polygon.

Flood Filling

So far, you've learned how to draw and fill regular shapes like boxes, bars, and polygons connected with straight sides. To fill other shapes, use **FloodFill**, defined as:

```
FloodFill( x, y : Integer; border : Word );
```

Coordinate (x,y) specifies a *seed*, which can be anywhere inside the shape. Parameter **border** is the color of the lines that make up the shape, which must be completely enclosed. If the shape has gaps in its outline, the paint will leak into the surrounding areas, possibly filling the screen and ruining your drawing. Change the paint color and brush with **SetFillStyle** and **SetFillPattern** as you did in previous examples. To complete the program, replace line 18 with the next statements. (The earlier modifications are repeated here for reference.)

```
SetColor( White );
SetFillStyle( InterLeaveFill, LightBlue );
FillPoly( 6, polygon );
FloodFill( 50, 50, White );
```

Arcs and Circles

Three useful procedures round out Turbo Pascal's set of basic graphics commands: **Arc**, **Circle**, and **Ellipse**. A variant of these routines, **PieSlice**, makes it easy to design pie charts or to draw wedges for other purposes.

To draw an arc, specify a starting (x,y) coordinate, equal to the center of the circle containing the arc. Also specify the starting and ending angles, as though spokes from the center reached to the arc end points. Finally, specify the circle radius. The complete definition for procedure **Arc** is:

```
Arc( x, y, : Integer; stAngle, endAngle, radius : Word );
```

Figure 11-4 shows how these parameters cooperate to draw arcs. On screen, only the heavy line is visible. The center point is at (x,y). The starting angle is at A in the figure. The ending angle is at B. The radius is the dotted line r. Angles and the radius must be positive integers or zero. An angle of zero is at 3 o'clock, with greater angles rotating counterclockwise.

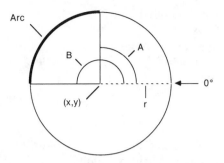

Figure 11-4 Of the many parameters that specify arcs, only the arc itself
(the heavy line here) is visible.

Program 11-14 draws a rainbow—not true to nature's colors—by cycling
through all colors available on your system, and calling **Arc** at line 18. To draw full
circles instead of arcs, replace that line with:

```
Arc( x, y, 0, 360, radius );
```

You must specify a starting angle of 0 and an ending angle of 360 to enclose a
circle completely.

Program 11-14

```
 1:   PROGRAM Rainbow;
 2:   USES Crt, Graph;
 3:   VAR
 4:      graphDriver, graphMode : Integer;
 5:      color, x, y : Integer;
 6:      radius : Word;
 7:   BEGIN
 8:      graphDriver := Detect;
 9:      InitGraph( graphDriver, graphMode, '' );
10:
11:      x := GetMaxX DIV 2;
12:      y := GetMaxY DIV 2;
13:      radius := y;
14:
15:      FOR color := 1 TO GetMaxColor DO
16:      BEGIN
17:         SetColor( color );
18:         Arc( x, y, 0, 180, radius );
19:         y := y + 10
20:      END; { for }
21:
22:      REPEAT UNTIL Keypressed;
```

Program 11-14 *cont.*

```
23:     CloseGraph
24:   END.
```

As Figure 11-4 shows, arcs have three important coordinates: the center point (x,y), the starting point of the first pixel in the arc (x1,y1), and the ending point of the last pixel (x2,y2). Call **GetArcCoords** after drawing an arc to get these points from the graphics kernel.

Program 11-15 demonstrates how to do this with a program that draws a figure similar to the illustration in Figure 11-4. A variable **arcCoords** in line 7 is declared of type **ArcCoordsType**, which has the definition:

```
TYPE
   ArcCoordsType =
   RECORD
      x, y : Integer;
      xStart, yStart : Integer;
      xEnd, yEnd : Integer
   END;
```

Six integer fields locate the center, starting, and ending points associated with the arc most recently drawn. Program 11-15 uses this information to draw a blue wedge inside a brown circle with a white arc. (In CGA displays, you'll probably see different colors.)

Program 11-15

```
1:   PROGRAM GetArc;
2:   USES Crt, Graph;
3:   VAR
4:     graphDriver, graphMode : Integer;
5:     xCenter, yCenter : Integer;
6:     stAngle, endAngle, radius : Word;
7:     arcCoords : ArcCoordsType;
8:   BEGIN
9:     graphDriver := Detect;
10:    InitGraph( graphDriver, graphMode, '' );
11:
12:    xCenter := GetMaxX DIV 2;
13:    yCenter := GetMaxY DIV 2;
14:    radius := GetMaxY DIV 3;
15:    stAngle := 0;
16:    endAngle := 59;
17:
18:    SetColor( Brown );
```

Program 11-15 *cont.*

```
19:     Circle( xCenter, yCenter, radius );
20:
21:     SetColor( White );
22:     Arc( xCenter, yCenter, stAngle, endAngle, radius );
23:
24:     GetArcCoords( arcCoords );
25:     WITH arcCoords DO
26:     BEGIN
27:       SetColor( Blue );
28:       Line( x, y, xStart, yStart );
29:       Line( x, y, xEnd, yEnd )
30:     END; { with }
31:
32:     REPEAT UNTIL Keypressed;
33:     CloseGraph
34:   END.
```

Program 11-15 also demonstrates the **Circle** procedure, which has three parameters:

```
Circle( x, y : Integer; radius : Word );
```

Circle draws a circle (what else) centered at (x,y) with a certain **radius**. Program 11-16 demonstrates one problem with the **radius** parameter, which Turbo Pascal adjusts according to your display's aspect ratio in order to draw round circles.

Program 11-16

```
1:  PROGRAM RadiusDemo;
2:  USES Crt, Graph;
3:  VAR
4:     graphDriver, graphMode : Integer;
5:     color, x, y : Integer;
6:     radius : Word;
7:  BEGIN
8:     graphDriver := Detect;
9:     InitGraph( graphDriver, graphMode, '' );
10:
11:    x := GetMaxX DIV 2;
12:    y := GetMaxY DIV 2;
13:    radius := y DIV 2;
14:
15:    SetColor( Yellow );
16:    Circle( x, y, radius );
```

Program 11-16 *cont.*

```
17:     SetColor( White );
18:     Line( x, y, x + radius, y );
19:     Line( x, y, x - radius, y );
20:     Line( x, y, x, y + radius );
21:     Line( x, y, x, y - radius );
22:
23:     REPEAT UNTIL Keypressed;
24:     CloseGraph
25: END.
```

When you run this program, you'll see a circle in the center of the display with a cross in the center. The horizontal lines exactly fit inside the circle. But on most displays, the vertical lines extend beyond the circumference. This happens even though program lines 18–21 use the same radius value. This shows that you cannot assume the radius of displayed circles to have a certain number of pixels along their diameters.

Drawing Ellipses

An ellipse in Turbo Pascal graphics is any oval shape, including perfectly round circles. You can also draw a portion of an oval, similar to what the **Arc** routine produces, but with finer control over the results. One procedure, **Ellipse**, draws all these shapes. It has this definition:

```
Ellipse( x, y : integer; stAngle, endAngle : Word;
   xRadius, yRadius : Word );
```

The (x,y) coordinate is at the center of the ellipse (or ellipse-like arc). Angles **stAngle** and **endAngle** correspond to A and B in Figure 11-4 and have the same purpose as the angle parameters to **Arc**. The last two parameters control the shape of the ellipse, altering its width (**xRadius**) and height (**yRadius**).

Unlike **Circle**, the ellipse is not adjusted for the display's aspect ratio. This usually means that, if **xRadius** equals **yRadius**, the ellipse will *not* be circular. In other words, to draw a circle with the **Ellipse** procedure, you must allow for the display's aspect ratio. The graphics kernel does not do this for you.

Program 11-17 demonstrates **Ellipse** while drawing an interesting shape. A **WHILE** loop (lines 16–22) varies the x and y radii to draw successive ovals from fat to skinny and short to tall.

Program 11-17

```
1: PROGRAM Ovaltine;
2: USES Crt, Graph;
```

Program 11-17 *cont.*

```
 3:  VAR
 4:     graphDriver, graphMode : Integer;
 5:     xMax, yMax, xRadius, yRadius : Integer;
 6:     xCenter, yCenter, maxColor : Integer;
 7:  BEGIN
 8:     graphDriver := Detect;
 9:     InitGraph( graphDriver, graphMode, '' );
10:     xMax := GetMaxX; yMax := GetMaxY;
11:     xCenter := xMax DIV 2; yCenter := yMax DIV 2;
12:     maxColor := GetMaxColor + 1;
13:
14:     yRadius := yCenter DIV 4;
15:     xRadius := xCenter DIV 2;
16:     WHILE xRadius > 40 DO
17:     BEGIN
18:        SetColor( 1 + ( xRadius MOD maxColor ) );
19:        Ellipse( xCenter, yCenter, 0, 360, xRadius, yRadius );
20:        xRadius := xRadius - 1;
21:        yRadius := yRadius + 1;
22:     END; { for }
23:
24:     REPEAT UNTIL Keypressed;
25:     CloseGraph
26:  END.
```

Filling Ellipses

Starting with Turbo Pascal 5.0, a new **Graph** unit procedure, **FillEllipse**, operates much like other fill procedures such as **FloodFill** and **FillPoly**. The new procedure takes four parameters:

```
PROCEDURE FillEllipse( x, y : Integer; xRadius, yRadius : Word );
```

Except for the missing **stAngle** and **endAngle** fields, the four parameters are identical to those in **Ellipse**. **FillEllipse** can't fill in partial ellipses; therefore, the two additional angle values that **Ellipse** requires aren't needed.

Use **SetFillStyle** as explained earlier to modify the ellipse fill pattern and color. To see how **FillEllipse** works, replace lines 14–22 in Program 11-17 with the following statements, which draw a tennis racket (or maybe it's a fly swatter).

```
yRadius := yCenter DIV 2;
xRadius := xCenter DIV 4;
SetColor( White );
SetFillStyle( HatchFill, LightRed );
FillEllipse( xCenter, yRadius, xRadius, yRadius );
```

```
SetFillStyle( SolidFill, White );
Bar( xCenter-8, yRadius*2, xCenter+8, GetMaxY );
```

Filling Partial Ellipses

Another new routine, with the somewhat unusual name **Sector**, has the identical parameters as **Ellipse**:

```
PROCEDURE Sector( x, y : Integer; stAngle, endAngle,
   xRadius, yRadius : Word );
```

Sector draws a full or partial ellipse filled with the current pattern and color initialized by **SetFillStyle**. Except for filling what it draws, **Sector** operates identically to **Ellipse**. Adjust the two angle parameters, **stAngle** and **endAngle**, as explained earlier to draw partial ellipses or filled ellipses.

To see what **Sector** does differently from **FillEllipse**, replace lines 14–22 in Program 11-17 with the following statements, which draw an umbrella (or maybe it's a mushroom).

```
yRadius := yCenter DIV 2;
xRadius := xCenter DIV 3;
SetColor( White );
SetFillStyle( HatchFill, LightGreen );
Sector( xCenter, yRadius*2, 0, 180, xRadius, yRadius );
SetFillStyle( SolidFill, White );
Bar( xCenter-8, yRadius*2, xCenter+8, GetMaxY );
```

A Slice of Pie

A special **Graph** unit routine, **PieSlice**, makes it easy to draw pie charts—one of the more common shapes needed in business graphics programming. **PieSlice** is defined as:

```
PieSlice( x, y : Integer; stAngle, endAngle, radius : Word );
```

Except for its name, **PieSlice** is identical to **Arc**. In fact, that's what a pie slice is—a filled arc, or wedge, with its end points joined at the center point (x,y) (see Figure 11-4). You could use other commands to draw arcs, join their ends, and fill their centers, but using **PieSlice** is easier.

Each slice of pie has an outline color, changed by **SetColor**, and a fill pattern and interior color, changed by **SetFillStyle** or **SetFillPattern** as described earlier for other filled shapes. If you don't want outlined pie wedges, use the same colors for the interior and outline.

Program 11-18 draws a pie chart from a data set, which you must enter into a separate file. You can specify from one to 50 wedges. For example, type the following lines into a file named PIE.DAT:

```
8
12.0
5.0
7.0
29.0
13.0
22.0
8.0
4.0
```

The first number tells how many values follow, in this case eight. Each value can be any number with or without a fractional part. Usually, the values following the first number should total 100.0 as they do here, but they don't have to.

After saving the data, type Program 11-18, compile, and run. When the program asks for a file name, type PIE.DAT and press Enter. For reference, the program first displays the data in tabular form. Press Enter a second time to see the pie chart.

Program 11-18

```
 1:   PROGRAM SweetyPie;
 2:   USES Crt, Graph;
 3:
 4:   CONST
 5:      MaxData = 50;    { Maximum number of wedges }
 6:
 7:   TYPE
 8:      WedgeRec =       { Holds precalculated wedge parameters }
 9:         RECORD
10:            stAngle, endAngle : Integer
11:         END;
12:
13:   VAR
14:      graphDriver, graphMode : Integer;
15:      xMax, yMax, radius : Integer;
16:      xCenter, yCenter, maxColor : Integer;
17:      total : Real;
18:      numWedges : 1 .. MaxData;
19:      percentage, data : ARRAY[ 1 .. MaxData ] OF Real;
20:      wedge : ARRAY[ 1 .. MaxData ] OF WedgeRec;
21:
22:   PROCEDURE ReadData;
23:   { Text file format: count, d1, d2, ..., dcount }
```

Program 11-18 *cont.*

```
24:   VAR tf : TEXT; fileName : String; i : Integer;
25:   BEGIN
26:     Write( 'Read data from what file? ' );
27:     Readln( fileName );
28:     Assign( tf, fileName );
29:     Reset( tf );
30:     Readln( tf, numWedges );
31:     FOR i := 1 TO numWedges DO
32:     BEGIN
33:       Readln( tf, data[i] );
34:       Writeln( i:2, ' : ', data[i]:12:3 )
35:     END; { for }
36:     Close( tf )
37:   END; { ReadData }
38:
39:   PROCEDURE Calculate;
40:   { Calculate wedge parameters from data }
41:   VAR
42:     i, startAngle, arcAngle : Integer;
43:   BEGIN
44:     total := 0.0;
45:     FOR i := 1 TO numWedges DO
46:       total := total + data[i];
47:     Writeln( '=================' );
48:     Writeln( 'Total =', total:10:3 );
49:     startAngle := 0;
50:     FOR i := 1 TO numWedges DO WITH wedge[i] DO
51:     BEGIN
52:       percentage[i] := data[i] / total;
53:       IF i = numWedges THEN arcAngle := 360 ELSE
54:         arcAngle := startAngle + round( percentage[i] * 360.0 );
55:       stAngle := startAngle;
56:       endAngle := arcAngle;
57:       startAngle := endAngle
58:     END { for }
59:   END; { Calculate }
60:
61:   PROCEDURE DisplayChart;
62:   { Display the pie chart }
63:   VAR i : Integer;
64:   BEGIN
65:     FOR i := 1 TO numWedges DO WITH wedge[i] DO
66:     BEGIN
67:       SetFillStyle( solidFill, i MOD maxColor );
68:       PieSlice( xCenter, yCenter, stAngle, endAngle, radius )
```

```
69:    END { for }
70:  END; { DisplayChart }
71:
72:  BEGIN
73:    ReadData;
74:    Calculate;
75:    Write( 'Press <Enter> for pie chart...' );
76:    Readln;
77:    graphDriver := Detect;
78:    InitGraph( graphDriver, graphMode, '' );
79:    xMax := GetMaxX; yMax := GetMaxY;
80:    xCenter := xMax DIV 2; yCenter := yMax DIV 2;
81:    maxColor := GetMaxColor + 1;
82:    radius := yMax DIV 3;
83:    DisplayChart;
84:    REPEAT UNTIL Keypressed;
85:    CloseGraph
86:  END.
```

Program 11-18 displays a pie chart by calculating the percentage of 360° for each data value (lines 50–58) along with the **PieSlice** angles, stored in an array of **WedgeRec** records (lines 8–11 and 20). After this step, procedure **DisplayChart** (lines 61–70) calls **SetFillStyle** and **PieSlice** to display each wedge.

On monochrome monitors, the wedge divisions might be difficult to see. To fix this problem, use different fill patterns. For example, you might change line 67 to:

```
SetFillStyle( 1+(i MOD 11), i MOD maxColor );
```

When you make this change, each wedge fills with both a different color and pattern, making the pie chart visible on all types of graphics displays.

Bit-Map Images

Three routines, **ImageSize**, **GetImage**, and **PutImage**, copy display pixels into variables and then display those pixels anywhere on screen. The **Graph** unit defines these routines as:

```
ImageSize( x1, y1, x2, y2 : Integer ) : Word;
GetImage( x1, y1, x2, y2 : Integer; VAR bitMap );
PutImage( x, y : Integer; VAR bitMap; copyMode : Word );
```

ImageSize calculates the number of bytes required to store a copy of pixel image within a rectangle with its upper-left corner at (x1,y1) and its lower-right corner at (x2,y2). **GetImage** copies pixels from the display inside a similar rectangle, depositing the image plus width and height information in the untyped variable, **bitMap**. It's your responsibility to ensure that a **bitMap** is large enough to store the image. If not, **GetImage** can overwrite other information or programs in memory, causing serious program bugs.

PutImage copies a **bitMap** image to the screen with the upper-left corner at (x,y). The **copyMode** parameter specifies one of the constants:

```
CopyPut     = 0;    { or NormalPut = 0 }
XORPut      = 1;
OrPut       = 2;
AndPut      = 3;
NotPut      = 4;
```

These values select the logical method used to combine the copied image with pixels already on display. **CopyPut** overwrites existing pixels. (**CopyPut** used to be called **NormalPut**, which still exists for compatibility and has the same effect.) The other four values perform the listed bit-by-bit logical operations—XOR (exclusive or), OR, AND, and NOT.

The final **PutImage** parameter is named **BitBlt** in GRAPH.DOC and in Borland's references. Apparently, **BitBlt** stands for "bit blitter," a hardware device used by some computers, but not PCs, for high-speed graphics. I've renamed **BitBlt** in this text to **copyMode** for clarity—a change that has no effect on how **PutImage** works.

Normally, you will use the three routines together following these steps to copy and display images:

1. Draw the image using various **Graph** unit commands.
2. Use **ImageSize** to create a variable large enough to hold a copy of the image.
3. Call **GetImage** to copy pixels from the screen into the variable created in step 2.
4. Call **PutImage** to display the image, possibly at a different location.

Program 11-19 demonstrates these steps, drawing a green house with **DrawPoly** (line 30), using the variable constant values initialized at lines 5–14. Line 32 shows how to create a variable to hold the bit image. Two data types are needed:

```
ByteArray = ARRAY[ 0 .. 0 ] OF Byte;
ByteArrayPtr = ^ByteArray;
```

A **ByteArray** is an array of bytes. Because the actual size of the variable will change, the array dimensions are unimportant. The range [0 . . 0] is typical, although any other legal range values would work equally well. The **ByteArrayPtr** type is a pointer to a **ByteArray**, which the program creates on the heap. Line 32 reserves memory for this purpose, calling **GetMem** with the statement:

```
GetMem( image, ImageSize(0,0,50,50) );
```

Variable **image** is a **ByteArrayPtr**. Using the **ImageSize** function as the **GetMem** size parameter allocates the correct number of bytes needed to hold the pixels within the rectangle at (0, 0) to (50, 50). If enough memory is not available, **GetMem** halts the program with a runtime error. To avoid this problem, see Chapter 16's discussion of **HeapFunc**, which causes **GetMem** to return a **nil** pointer if memory is tight. In that case, you'd follow the **GetMem** call by testing if **image** is **Nil**, in which case the program must not use the **image** pointer.

This step of reserving memory with **ImageSize** is vital to writing graphics programs that work correctly in all display resolutions. You could, of course, create a fixed-size variable to hold display pixels but then your program would be fixed to one display mode. Avoid this limitation whenever you can.

After reserving memory, line 35 uses this statement to copy the displayed green house to the location addressed by **image**:

```
GetImage( 0, 0, 50, 50, image^ );
```

The coordinate values must be the same as those used to create the image variable on the heap. **GetImage** copies the pixels from the display—actually, from the video memory buffer—transferring the data to the location addressed by pointer **image**. At the same time, the procedure copies the width and height of the image for later use by **PutPixel**.

Lines 36–37 replicate the copied image at randomly selected locations, calling **PutImage** to create a rapidly expanding development of little green houses. Try other display mode constants in place of **NormalPut**, the last parameter to **PutImage**.

Program 11-19

```
 1:  PROGRAM Developments;
 2:  USES Crt, Graph;
 3:
 4:  CONST
 5:     house : ARRAY[ 1 .. 9 ] OF PointType =
 6:        ( ( x :   0; y : 50 ),
 7:          ( x :   0; y : 25 ),
 8:          ( x :  25; y :  0 ),
 9:          ( x :  50; y : 25 ),
10:          ( x :   1; y : 25 ),
11:          ( x :  50; y : 50 ),
12:          ( x :  50; y : 26 ),
13:          ( x :   1; y : 50 ),
14:          ( x :  50; y : 50 ) );
15:
16:  TYPE
```

```
17:      ByteArray = ARRAY[O..0] OF Byte;
18:      ByteArrayPtr = ^ByteArray;
19:
20: VAR
21:      graphDriver, graphMode : Integer;
22:      xMax, yMax : Integer;
23:      image : ByteArrayPtr;
24:
25: BEGIN
26:      graphDriver := Detect;
27:      InitGraph( graphDriver, graphMode, '' );
28:      xMax := GetMaxX; yMax := GetMaxY;
29:      SetColor( Green );
30:      DrawPoly( 9, house );
31:
32:      GetMem( image, ImageSize( 0, 0, 50, 50 ) );  { Reserve memory }
33:      IF image <> NIL THEN
34:      BEGIN
35:        GetImage( 0, 0, 50, 50, image^ );  { Copy image from screen }
36:        WHILE NOT Keypressed DO
37:            PutImage( Random(xMax), Random(yMax), image^, NormalPut )
38:      END; { if }
39:
40:      CloseGraph
41: END.
```

Displaying Text on Graphics Screens

As long as you do not use the **Crt** unit, **Write** and **Writeln** work the same on graphics displays as they do normally. Using **Crt** switches to direct-video routines for **Write** and **Writeln**, which display characters more quickly on text screens, but which can't show characters on graphics displays.

Another and probably better way to display text with graphics is to use Turbo Pascal's built-in font routines. Fonts are stored in disk files ending in CHR and containing the information needed to display characters on graphics screens. Your Turbo Pascal disks come with several of these files and you'll probably find others on bulletin boards and advertised in magazines.

There are two kinds of graphics fonts: bit-mapped and vectored, or *stroked*. The default font is bit-mapped—its character shapes are stored as fixed bit patterns, similar to the PC's usual character images in ROM. All other fonts are stroked, formed out of line segments much like the polygon shapes you drew earlier in this chapter.

The advantage of using a stroked font becomes obvious when you enlarge characters. Because the patterns are formed of line segments, characters retain their relative shapes as they grow larger. A B's humps stay round no matter how large they grow. Also, the lines in a character have the same thicknesses in all font sizes. A straight line in an uppercase I, for example, may grow taller but it won't get fatter.

Bit-mapped fonts are different. As a bit-mapped character grows, jagged edges along diagonals become more pronounced. Each bit—normally a single pixel in the font's default size—grows in all directions, making lines grow fatter as well as taller. You've probably seen this effect on paper banners created by dot matrix printers.

Bit-mapped fonts do have one important advantage over stroked fonts, though—they are faster to display. Because a stroked character is composed of individually drawn lines, it takes longer to display than a bit-mapped image, which the graphics kernel can plop directly into video memory with fast memory move commands. Turbo Pascal handles both kinds of graphics text, letting you choose quality or speed, whichever is more important to you.

An example explains how to load character fonts from disk and display text. Because Program 11-20 does not use the **Crt** unit, it can display text with **Write** and **Writeln** (as in line 11) as well as with Turbo Pascal's two analogous routines, **OutText** and **OutTextXY**. When you run the program, you'll see two lines of text, the first displayed by a **Writeln** statement and the second by **OutText**.

Program 11-20

```
 1:  PROGRAM GraphText;
 2:  USES Graph;
 3:  VAR graphDriver, graphMode : integer;
 4:  BEGIN
 5:     graphDriver := Detect;
 6:     InitGraph( graphDriver, graphMode, '' );
 7:
 8:     SetColor( Blue );
 9:     SetTextStyle( DefaultFont, HorizDir, 2 );
10:
11:     Writeln( 'This text is displayed by Writeln' );
12:     MoveTo( 0, 25 );
13:     OutText( 'This text is displayed by OutText' );
14:
15:     Readln;
16:     CloseGraph
17:  END.
```

Line 9 loads a character font and specifies two characteristics: direction and size. **SetTextStyle** takes three **Word** parameters:

```
SetTextStyle( font, direction, charsize : Word );
```

Set **font** to one of the numbers in Table 11-5. The default bit-mapped font is number 0 and is always available to programs. Other fonts require a corresponding CHR file in the directory path previously passed to **InitGraph** (see line 6). For best results, store your BGI graphics drivers and CHR files in the same directory.

Table 11-5 Graphics text fonts

Constant	Value	Type	Disk file
DefaultFont	0	Bit map	none
TriplexFont	1	Stroked	TRIP.CHR
SmallFont	2	Stroked	LITT.CHR
SansSerifFont	3	Stroked	SANS.CHR
GothicFont	4	Stroked	GOTH.CHR

The **direction** parameter displays text horizontally or vertically. Use one of these two constant values:

```
HorizDir = 0;
VertDir  = 1;
```

The final parameter, **size**, controls the size of text on screen. You need only one font in memory for all sizes—Turbo Pascal scales the font patterns up and down as needed. Different fonts do not have the same relative sizes for the same **size** values. Unfortunately, text sizes have no direct relation to typesetting points, which measure character size in $1/72$-inch increments.

Experiment with Program 11-20, inserting different values in the **SetTextStyle** statement in line 9. If you don't see different font styles, check that your CHR files are on disk. You might also follow **SetTextStyle** with an error check after loading the font pattern from disk. To do this, add an integer variable **grError** and replace blank line 10 with:

```
grError := GraphResult;
IF grError <> GrOk THEN
BEGIN
   RestoreCrtMode;
   Writeln( 'Graphics error : ',
     GraphErrorMsg( grError ) );
   Halt
END; { if }
```

Of course, you might want to take a more friendly action than halting the program. Unlike more serious errors, such as a failure to initialize the graphics display with **InitGraph**, an error loading a font simply causes text to appear in a different style.

Notice the **MoveTo** statement in line 12 of Program 11-20. **MoveTo** changes

CP, where **OutText** displays the upper-left corner of the first character. To prove this, replace blank line 14 with:

```
PutPixel( 0, 25, White );
```

When you run the modified program, you'll see a small white dot at the upper-left corner of the cross in the T. (You might have trouble seeing this dot on CGA systems or on poor-quality monitors.)

Instead of using **MoveTo** to change CP for **OutText**, you can use the simpler **OutTextXY** to do both jobs at once. For example, replace lines 12 and 13 with:

```
OutTextXY( 0, 25, 'This text...' );
```

One important difference between **OutText** and **OutTextXY** is the effect on CP. After **OutText**, CP changes to the next position *after* the last character drawn. After **OutTextXY**, CP equals the (x,y) coordinate passed to the procedure. A little experiment helps make this clear. Replace line 13 in Program 11-20 with:

```
OutText( 'This is a test' );
SetColor( White );
LineTo( GetMaxX, GetMaxY );
```

You should see a line from just after the end of the text to the bottom-right display corner.

Now, change the **OutText** to **OutTextXY** with this statement:

```
OutTextXY( 0, 50, 'This is a test' );
```

This time, the line extends from the first character to the bottom-right corner, proving that **OutTextXY** changes CP to (0,50).

Text Justification

SetTextJustify changes where **OutText** displays text in relation to CP or to the coordinate passed to **OutTextXY**. The procedure takes two **Word** parameters:

```
SetTextJustify( horiz, vert : Word );
```

The **horiz** parameter determines whether text starts at CP and moves right, starts at the center, or starts at the right and moves left. The **vert** parameter determines whether text is above, below, or centered at CP. For the **horiz** parameter, use one of these constants:

```
LeftText   = 0;
CenterText = 1;
RightText  = 2;
```

For the **vert** parameter, use one of the constants:

```
BottomText = 0;
CenterText = 1;
TopText    = 2;
```

Combinations of these values change where text displays in relation to CP. Program 11-21 shows all possible combinations of these values and also explains how to display numeric values with **OutText** and **OutTextXY**, which can display only character strings. When you run the program, press Enter to redisplay a line of text at different locations relative to CP, represented as a small cross.

Program 11-21

```
1:   PROGRAM Justification;
2:   USES Crt,Graph;
3:   VAR
4:       graphDriver, graphMode : integer;
5:       xCenter, yCenter : word;
6:       horiz, vert : integer;
7:       hs, vs : String[5];
8:   BEGIN
9:       graphDriver := Detect;
10:      InitGraph( graphDriver, graphMode, '' );
11:      xCenter := GetMaxX DIV 2; yCenter := GetMaxY DIV 2;
12:      FOR vert := 0 TO 2 DO
13:         FOR horiz := 0 TO 2 DO
14:         BEGIN
15:            ClearViewPort;
16:            SetTextJustify( LeftText, TopText );
17:            SetColor( White );
18:            Str( horiz, hs ); Str( vert, vs );
19:            MoveTo( 0,  0 ); OutText( 'Horiz = ' ); OutText( hs );
20:            MoveTo( 0, 25 ); OutText( 'Vert  = ' ); OutText( vs );
21:            SetTextJustify( horiz, vert );
22:            SetColor( LightRed );
23:            OutTextXY( xCenter, yCenter, 'Justification Test' );
24:            SetColor( White );
25:            Line( xCenter, yCenter-2, xCenter, yCenter+2 );
26:            Line( xCenter-2, yCenter, xCenter+2, yCenter );
27:            IF Readkey=CHR(27) THEN Halt
28:         END; { for / for }
29:      CloseGraph
30:   END.
```

Lines 18–20 display the current **horiz** and **vert** justification values, calling

Str to convert integers to strings. It's necessary to use **MoveTo** and **OutText** here because **OutTextXY** would not leave CP in the correct position to display the string values, **hs** and **vs**.

Line 21 changes the justification for the **OutTextXY** statement in line 23. Lines 25–26 draw the cross.

Text Width and Height

To determine how many pixels a character occupies on screen in the current font and size, call the functions:

```
TextHeight( textString : String ) : Word;
TextWidth( textString : String ) : Word;
```

The two functions help you write programs with graphics that change relatively to the font size. Program 11-22, for example, displays underlined text by using **TextHeight** and **TextWidth** to draw a line under a string.

Program 11-22

```
 1:   PROGRAM GraphUnderline;
 2:   USES Graph;
 3:   CONST s = 'This text is underlined.';
 4:   VAR graphDriver, graphMode : integer;
 5:   BEGIN
 6:      graphDriver := Detect;
 7:      InitGraph( graphDriver, graphMode, '' );
 8:
 9:      SetColor( White );
10:      SetTextJustify( LeftText, BottomText );
11:      SetTextStyle( GothicFont, HorizDir, 4 );
12:      OutTextXY( 0, TextHeight(s), s );
13:      Line( 0, TextHeight(s), TextWidth(s), TextHeight(s) );
14:
15:      Readln;
16:      CloseGraph
17:   END.
```

Try changing the font and size in line 11. In every case, the underline automatically grows and shrinks as necessary. In your own programs, try to design text and graphics that work the same for other sizes and styles. This makes modifying your programs much easier.

Controlling Font Size

For finer control over character width and height, use **SetUserCharSize** with four **Byte** parameters:

```
SetUserCharSize( multX, divX, multY, divY : Byte );
```

The four parameters specify two ratios, which the graphics kernel uses to change the width and height of text in the current style and size set by **SetText-Style**. The horizontal ratio equals multX/divX. The vertical ratio equals multY/divY. A ratio of 1 causes no change. A ratio less than 1 reduces the horizontal or vertical size. A ratio greater than 1 increases the size. For example, to display text half as wide as normal, you could write:

```
SetUserCharSize( 1, 1, 1, 1 );
SetTextStyle( TriplexFont, HorizDir, UserCharSize );
OutTextXY( 0, 0, 'Normal width' );
SetUserCharSize( 1, 2, 1, 1 );
SetTextStyle( TriplexFont, HorizDir, UserCharSize );
OutTextXY( 0, 40, 'Half width' );
```

The first call to **SetUserCharSize** prepares to display text in its normal size—not necessarily the same as a size parameter of 1, but in the size of a font with no adjustment to the width and height. After **SetUserCharSize**, you must call **SetTextStyle** to choose a font and direction. Instead of the usual size parameter, specify **UserCharSize**, a **Graph** unit constant equal to 0. This tells the graphics kernel to use your ratios in place of the standards.

The second call to **SetUserCharSize** in this example prepares for displaying text half as wide as previously. In this case, multX equals 1 and divX equals 2, a ratio of 1:2 or 0.5. Notice that you must again call **SetTextStyle** after changing ratios. (Take this statement out to see the difference.) To display text twice as wide, use the statement:

```
SetUserCharSize( 2, 1, 1, 1 );
```

This specifies the ratio 2:1 or 2.0—twice as wide as 1:1. Here's another example:

```
SetUserCharSize( 2, 1, 4, 1 );
```

This displays text twice as wide (2:1) and four times as tall (4:1) as normal.

Reading Text Parameters

When you need to know the current text settings, call **GetTextSettings** with a record variable of this type:

```
TYPE
   TextSettingsType =
      RECORD
         font      : Word;
         direction : Word;
         charsize  : Word;
```

```
         horiz     : Word;
         vert      : Word
      END;
```

Turbo Pascal fills in the fields of this record with the current text parameters. You might use **GetTextSettings** to save the current settings, change to a new font and size, display some text, and then restore the original settings before proceeding. Here's how:

```
VAR settings : TextSettingsType;

GetTextSettings( settings );
:
{ change settings and display text }
:
WITH settings DO
BEGIN
   SetTextStyle( font, direction, charsize );
   SetTextJustify( horiz, vert )
END; { with }
```

First, save the current text settings by calling **GetTextSettings** with a variable of type **TextSettingsType**. Then, change to other fonts and display text in various sizes. To restore the original settings, pass the five fields in the **settings** record to **SetTextStyle** and **SetTextJustify** as shown here.

Animation

EGA, VGA, and Hercules video modes have enough memory to store more than one display page. With these systems, the graphics kernel lets you choose on which page to draw and which page to view. You can draw on offscreen pages and then switch rapidly to the finished drawing. Because of this action, people don't see your graphics in the process of forming—they see only the final result. Using this technique, you can also store more than one chart, picture, or graph and then switch among them like slides in a projector.

Another use for multipage graphics is in animation. Drawing offscreen while viewing a second page, and then rapidly alternating between the two screens, smoothly animates pictures by hiding the drawing details from your eyes. This process, called *ping ponging* or *page swapping*, is similar to the way cartoons appear to move by showing successive still frames fast enough to produce an illusion of motion.

To change the page you see, call **SetVisualPage**. To change the page on which drawing commands operate, call **SetActivePage**. Each of these procedures takes a single **Word** parameter, **page**.

It's up to you to make sure the pages you request exist in your system. The first page is number 0, the second number 1, and so on. Table 11-2 lists the number of pages for various modes. Never attempt to select nonexistent pages—you can cause serious bugs and, in some video systems, even cause the computer to hang.

To animate a sequence, follow these steps:

1. Initialize two word variables. Set **active** to 0 and **visual** to 1.

2. Execute these statements to draw on the active page and view the other:

```
SetActivePage( active );
SetVisualPage( visual );
```

3. Erase any drawing on the unseen page and draw your new figures.

4. Swap the **active** and **visual** variables and go back to step 2.

An example demonstrates how these steps smooth animations by hiding the drawing details. Program 11-23 draws a "Pac Person" figure, opening and shutting its hungry mouth by changing the starting and ending angles in a **PieSlice** statement (line 34).

Procedure **Initialize** first checks that you have an EGA, Hercules, or VGA video system (lines 11–16). If not, the program halts with an error. Otherwise, lines 17–21 prepare for the upcoming graphics. Line 21 initializes the page swapping variables described earlier.

Lines 41–42 set the active and visual page. Then, procedure **DoGraphics** draws a figure on the offscreen page while you view the other. After lines 44–46 swap **active** and **visual**, the **WHILE** loop repeats until you press a key to end the program.

A simple experiment proves that page swapping makes the animation work smoothly. Assign 0 to **visual** instead of 1 in line 21 and run the program again. This ruins the animation by displaying the details of drawing the Pac Person pie slice.

Program 11-23

```
 1:   PROGRAM PacPerson;
 2:   USES Crt,Graph;
 3:   VAR graphDriver, graphMode : Integer;
 4:       active, visual, temp : Word;
 5:       xCenter, yCenter, radius, stAngle, endAngle : Integer;
 6:
 7:   PROCEDURE Initialize;
 8:   BEGIN
 9:       graphDriver := Detect;
10:       InitGraph( graphDriver, graphMode, '' );
11:       IF NOT ( graphDriver IN [EGA, HercMono, VGA] ) THEN
12:       BEGIN
13:           RestoreCrtMode;
14:           Writeln( 'Error : Requires multi-page video graphics' );
```

Program 11-23 *cont.*

```
15:       Halt
16:     END; { if }
17:     SetColor( Red );
18:     SetFillStyle( SolidFill, Blue );
19:     xCenter := GetMaxX DIV 2; yCenter := GetMaxY DIV 2;
20:     stAngle := 0; radius := GetMaxY DIV 8;
21:     active := 0; visual := 1
22:   END; { Initialize }
23:
24:   PROCEDURE DoGraphics;
25:   BEGIN
26:     ClearViewPort;
27:     IF stAngle = 0 THEN
28:       BEGIN
29:         stAngle := 30; endAngle := 330
30:       END ELSE
31:       BEGIN
32:         stAngle := 0; endAngle := 360
33:       END; { else }
34:     PieSlice( xCenter, yCenter, stAngle, endAngle, radius )
35:   END; { DoGraphics }
36:
37:   BEGIN
38:     Initialize;
39:     WHILE NOT Keypressed DO
40:       BEGIN
41:         SetActivePage( active );
42:         SetVisualPage( visual );
43:         DoGraphics;
44:         temp := active;
45:         active := visual;
46:         visual := temp
47:       END; { while }
48:     CloseGraph
49:   END.
```

Loading Multiple Fonts and Drivers

By preloading fonts and drivers into memory, you speed up programs that need to switch modes and character styles. The only disadvantage to this method is the extra memory it takes. The main advantage is speed—sometimes, a lot of speed.

The idea is simple. Load each driver and font you need into a memory buffer exactly as big as required. Then, register the drivers and fonts with the graphics kernel. That's *register*, as in registering to vote. By registering your drivers and fonts, you tell the graphics kernel that they are already in memory. Knowing this, the kernel won't reload the files from disk every time you switch modes and text styles.

An example demonstrates how this idea dramatically improves performance. Program 11-24 displays five lines of text in as many fonts (lines 57–61) and then writes the alphabet, alternating fonts for each character (63–68). Procedures **LoadOneFont** and **LoadFonts** load Turbo Pascal's four standard disk-based fonts into memory. Pass the same path name to **LoadFonts** used later in **InitGraph** (see lines 50 and 52).

Notice how lines 24–25 calculate the font file size, which is different for different fonts, and then reserve that much memory with **GetMem**. You could use a different method or even store fonts in global variables, but storing fonts on the heap is easy and, in most cases, best. The **BlockRead** statement in line 26 loads the font into memory, storing bytes at the location addressed by pointer **fp**.

Never load fonts into local variables declared in procedures and functions. When the routines end, the variable space disappears, a fact the graphics kernel won't know.

The final step is to register the font by calling **RegisterBGIfont**, an integer function, passing the address of the first byte of the font image now in memory (line 28). If the function returns a value less than zero, then an error occurred— probably because the font file is not recognized. (Perhaps you tried to load a file that is not actually a graphics font.) In this case, check **GraphResult** for the error number (lines 31–32).

That's all you need to do to load multiple fonts into memory. When you later call **SetTextStyle** to switch fonts, the graphics kernel knows the font is already in memory and won't reload the .CHR file from disk.

Preloading multiple fonts takes extra care and programming, but the results are worth every bit of trouble. For proof, remove line 50 from Program 11-24 and run the program again. Now, because each new font number passed to **SetTextStyle** loads that font from disk into memory, the program runs sluggishly, especially when displaying the multifont alphabet.

You could use a similar method to load multiple graphics drivers into memory, too. In this case, just replace **RegisterBGIfont** with **RegisterBGIdriver**. Everything else is the same except, of course, you will load driver files like 'CGA.BGI' instead of fonts.

Usually, however, loading multiple drivers this way is not as advantageous as loading multiple fonts. It's the rare program that needs to switch rapidly between different graphics modes. The next section explains a superior approach to attaching multiple drivers to programs.

Program 11-24

```
1:   PROGRAM MultiFonts;
2:   USES Graph;
3:   CONST
4:      message = 'Turbo Pascal 5.5';
```

Program 11-24 *cont.*

```
 5:  VAR
 6:     graphDriver, graphMode, y : Integer;
 7:     ch : Char;
 8:
 9:  PROCEDURE ShowText( font : Word );
10:  BEGIN
11:     SetTextStyle( font, HorizDir, 4 );
12:     OutTextXY( 0, y, message );
13:     y := y + TextHeight( message ) + 4
14:  END; { ShowText }
15:
16:  PROCEDURE LoadOneFont( fileName : String );
17:  VAR
18:     f : FILE;        { Untyped file for reading disk file }
19:     fp : Pointer;    { Pointer to font in memory }
20:     bytes : LongInt; { Bytes required to hold font in memory }
21:  BEGIN
22:     Assign( f, fileName );
23:     Reset( f, 1 );              { Open with block size = 1 byte }
24:     bytes := FileSize( f );     { Get size of file }
25:     GetMem( fp, bytes );        { Reserve memory for font }
26:     BlockRead( f, fp^, bytes ); { Read font into memory }
27:     Close( f );
28:     IF RegisterBGIfont( fp ) < 0 THEN  { Resister font number }
29:     BEGIN
30:        Writeln( 'Error loading ', fileName );
31:        Writeln( 'Graphics Error : ',
32:           GraphErrorMsg( GraphResult ) );
33:        Halt
34:     END { if }
35:  END; { LoadOneFont }
36:
37:  PROCEDURE LoadFonts( path : String );
38:  BEGIN
39:     IF Length( path ) > 0 THEN
40:        IF path[ Length( path ) ] <> '\'
41:           THEN path := path + '\';
42:
43:     LoadOneFont( path + 'TRIP.CHR' );
44:     LoadOneFont( path + 'LITT.CHR' );
45:     LoadOneFont( path + 'SANS.CHR' );
46:     LoadOneFont( path + 'GOTH.CHR' );
47:  END; { LoadFonts }
48:
49:  BEGIN
```

Program 11-24 *cont.*

```
50:      LoadFonts( '' );
51:      graphDriver := Detect;
52:      InitGraph( graphDriver, graphMode, '' );
53:      y := TextHeight( message );
54:
55:      SetColor( Cyan );
56:
57:      ShowText( DefaultFont );
58:      ShowText( TriplexFont );
59:      ShowText( SmallFont );
60:      ShowText( SansSerifFont );
61:      ShowText( GothicFont );
62:
63:      MoveTo( 0, y + 16 );
64:      FOR ch := 'A' TO 'Z' DO
65:      BEGIN
66:        SetTextStyle( (Ord(ch)-Ord('A')) MOD 5, HorizDir, 2 );
67:        OutText( ch )
68:      END; { for }
69:
70:      Readln;
71:      CloseGraph
72:  END.
```

Creating a Graphics Application

For programs that you plan to sell or, perhaps, to distribute to the public domain on bulletin boards, it's inconvenient to require people to have Borland's BGI driver and CHR font files on disk. Besides, you certainly don't want to limit your market to only those people who own Turbo Pascal.

One way to proceed is to combine driver and font files directly into your disk EXE code file. Although this makes the disk file grow up to 50,000 or more bytes larger, it makes a convenient package of one file containing all the elements needed to run your graphics program.

The first step is to convert BGI and CHR files into a new form, called *object files*, that Turbo Pascal can link into a program. To do this, locate the program BIN-OBJ.EXE on your Turbo Pascal disks. Make sure you have in the same directory BINOBJ.EXE along with the four CHR files listed in Table 11-5 plus the first five BGI files listed in Table 11-1. Then from the DOS command line, type the following lines exactly as shown here:

```
binobj goth.chr goth GothicFontProc
binobj litt.chr litt SmallFontProc
binobj sans.chr sans SansSerifFontProc
```

```
binobj trip.chr trip TriplexFontProc

binobj cga.bgi cga CGADriverProc
binobj egavga.bgi egavga EGAVGADriverProc
binobj herc.bgi herc HercDriverProc
binobj pc3270.bgi pc3270 PC3270DriverProc
binobj att.bgi att ATTDriverProc
```

Alternatively, you could type these lines into a batch file named MAKEOBJ.BAT, and then just type MAKEOBJ to convert all files at once.

After executing these unseemly instructions, you should have the following object files on disk:

```
GOTH.OBJ
LITT.OBJ
SANS.OBJ
TRIP.OBJ
CGA.OBJ
EGAVGA.OBJ
HERC.OBJ
PC3270.OBJ
ATT.OBJ
```

Type DIR *.OBJ to make sure.

The *binobj* instructions you just typed to create these files converted the driver and font files from their binary form into object files that, to Turbo Pascal, look like code modules—in other words, procedures and functions even though that's not what they really are. The next step is to create two units containing these phony procedures. Type Program 11-25, save as GRDRIVER.PAS, and compile to disk as GRDRIVER.TPU. Type Program 11-26, save as GRFONTS.PAS, and compile to disk as GRFONTS.TPU.

After these steps, you no longer need the .OBJ files on disk to compile and run graphics programs. In fact, you don't even need the BGI or CHR files any longer. (Don't delete your only copies of these files, though!)

Programs 11-25

```
1:   UNIT GrDrivers;
2:
3:   { Graphics drivers }
4:
5:
6:   INTERFACE
7:
8:   USES Graph;
9:
```

Programs 11-25 *cont.*

```
10:
11:    IMPLEMENTATION
12:
13:    PROCEDURE ATTDriverProc; External;          {$L ATT.OBJ }
14:    PROCEDURE CGADriverProc; External;          {$L CGA.OBJ }
15:    PROCEDURE EGAVGADriverProc; External;       {$L EGAVGA.OBJ }
16:    PROCEDURE HercDriverProc; External;         {$L HERC.OBJ }
17:    PROCEDURE PC3270DriverProc; External;       {$L PC3270.OBJ }
18:
19:    PROCEDURE ReportError( s : String );
20:    BEGIN
21:       Writeln;
22:       Writeln( s, ' : ', GraphErrorMsg( GraphResult ) );
23:       Halt( 1 )
24:    END; { ReportError }
25:
26:    BEGIN
27:       IF RegisterBGIdriver( @ATTDriverProc    ) < 0
28:          THEN ReportError( 'AT&T' );
29:       IF RegisterBGIdriver( @CGADriverProc    ) < 0
30:          THEN ReportError( 'CGA' );
31:       IF RegisterBGIdriver( @EGAVGADriverProc ) < 0
32:          THEN ReportError( 'EGA-VGA' );
33:       IF RegisterBGIdriver( @HercDriverProc   ) < 0
34:          THEN ReportError( 'Hercules' );
35:       IF RegisterBGIdriver( @PC3270DriverProc ) < 0
36:          THEN ReportError( 'PC-3270' );
37:    END.
```

Program 11-26

```
1:    UNIT GrFonts;
2:
3:    { Graphics fonts }
4:
5:
6:    INTERFACE
7:
8:    USES Graph;
9:
10:
11:    IMPLEMENTATION
12:
13:    PROCEDURE GothicFontProc; External;        {$L GOTH.OBJ }
```

Program 11-26 *cont.*

```
14:  PROCEDURE SansSerifFontProc; External;      {$L SANS.OBJ }
15:  PROCEDURE SmallFontProc; External;          {$L LITT.OBJ }
16:  PROCEDURE TriplexFontProc; External;        {$L TRIP.OBJ }
17:
18:  PROCEDURE ReportError( s : String );
19:  BEGIN
20:     Writeln;
21:     Writeln( s, ' font : ', GraphErrorMsg( GraphResult ) );
22:     Halt( 1 )
23:  END; { ReportError }
24:
25:  BEGIN
26:     IF RegisterBGIfont( @GothicFontProc     ) < 0
27:        THEN ReportError( 'Gothic' );
28:     IF RegisterBGIfont( @SansSerifFontProc ) < 0
29:        THEN ReportError( 'SansSerif' );
30:     IF RegisterBGIfont( @SmallFontProc      ) < 0
31:        THEN ReportError( 'Small' );
32:     IF RegisterBGIfont( @TriplexFontProc    ) < 0
33:        THEN ReportError( 'Triplex' );
34:  END.
```

The two units in Programs 11-25 and 11-26 are similar. Except for the **USES** declaration at line 8, neither has any public items for programs to use. In Program 11-25, five private procedures are declared **External**, which tells the compiler that the code for these procedures is stored on disk in the files specified by the {$L} directives at the end of each line. Remember that these are only phony procedures—place holders for our font patterns and graphics drivers. You never directly call the phony procedures.

Compiling each unit combines the external object files to produce a single unit TPU disk file. When the program runs, the unit initialization parts execute (lines 26–37 in Program 11-25 and lines 25–34 in Program 11-26). The series of **IF** statements in these sections register the fonts and drivers with the graphics kernel, telling the system to use the in-memory copies of these items instead of loading them from disk.

To finish your graphics application, simply add Program 11-25 or 11-26 or both to your program's **USES** declaration along with unit **Graph**. When you compile your program to disk, the resulting EXE file is completely self-contained, runs correctly under any graphics mode, and does not require driver or font files on disk. To convert any of the previous examples to a stand-alone program, follow these steps. We'll use Program 11-18 here, although the same steps work for any graphics program.

1. Load or type Program 11-18 and save as SWEETY.PAS.

2. Change the **USES** declaration in line 2 to read:

```
USES Crt, Graph, GrDrivers;
```

3. Compile to disk, creating SWEETY.EXE. Exit to DOS and type SWEETY to run the program.

Simple, no? For an example of how to use both the **GrDrivers** and **GrFonts** units, follow these steps for converting Program 11-24.

1. Load or type Program 11-24 and save as MULTIFON.PAS.
2. Change the **USES** declaration in line 2 to read:

```
USES Graph, GrDrivers, GrFonts;
```

3. Delete lines 16–47 and 50. All fonts are stored in **GrFonts**—there's no need to load them from disk.
4. Compile this much shorter program to disk, creating MULTIFON.EXE. Exit to DOS and type MULTIFON to run the example. Notice that switching between multiple fonts is now as fast as it was when you manually loaded the font files.

Advanced BGI Graphics

If you have a VGA 256-color display, an IBM-8514 adapter, or custom hardware, you can write BGI programs to take full advantage of these high-quality display resolutions and colors.

Two functions, **InstallUserDriver** and **InstallUserFont**, provide a way to link low-level graphics driver software to **Graph** unit routines. You can also write your own low-level drivers, although this subject is too involved to cover in detail here. For more information, refer to Chapter 16's discussion of **InstallUserDriver** and **InstallUserFont**.

Another procedure, **SetRGBPalette**, lets you program IBM-8514 256-color displays:

```
PROCEDURE SetRGBPalette( colorNum,
    redValue, greenValue, blueValue : Integer );
```

On IBM-8514 displays, **colorNum** may range from 0 to 255. The three values **redValue, greenValue**, and **blueValue** specify the color levels to assign to the palette entry indexed by **colorNum**. The first 16 such palette entries on IBM-8514 displays default to the standard EGA and VGA colors. Even though the color values are type **Integer**, only 6 bits of the low bytes in each value are significant.

Summary

Borland's graphics kernel automatically detects the best possible display mode for any PC graphics card or circuitry. This eases the job of programming graphics for a variety of display types, traditionally one of the most difficult aspects of writing PC graphics software.

Graphics drivers contain the machine language to implement graphics routines and other items described in the **Graph** unit. Drivers are stored in BGI disk files. Character fonts, which can be bit-mapped or stroked, are stored in CHR files. Normally, these files must be on disk to run graphics programs. For finished applications, follow the instructions in this chapter to combine drivers, character fonts, and your program into a single disk file.

A viewport restricts the visible viewing area of the logical coordinate grid in which programs can draw. Various **Graph** routines draw lines, circles, ellipses, polygons, and arcs. A host of other commands help you write programs to run correctly in various screen resolutions and colors.

Exercises

11-1. Write a program to bounce a ball around on screen. Your program should run correctly on any PC graphics display.

11-2. Draw a line graph using a data set of values. Label the x and y axes.

11-3. (Advanced) Design procedures to save and restore graphics images in disk files.

11-4. Write a sketching program, using the arrow keys to move a cursor around the graphics display, drawing lines.

11-5. Add shapes to your program in exercise 11-4, drawing boxes, circles, and other patterns at the cursor.

11-6. Use page-swapping animation techniques to display a short cartoon of your own design. (Hint: It requires a multipage graphics display.)

11-7. (Advanced) Design a fade-in, fade-out procedure to transfer a graphics image in memory gradually to the display.

11-8. Convert any of your answers to preceding questions into a stand-alone application. Your program should run without graphics drivers and font files on disk.

11-9. Design your own circle procedure using only **PutPixel** commands.

11-10. Improve the bar chart example (Program 11-12) to display a z axis, showing several rows of bars.

11-11. Improve Program 11-18 to display one wedge pulled out of the pie chart.

11-12. Animate your answer to exercise 11-11.

12

More About Numbers

- Integer Numbers
- Real Numbers
- Coprocessors and Emulation Routines
- Coprocessor Emulation in Units
- Reading and Writing Numbers
- Word Alignment
- Numeric Expressions
- A Horse of a Different Radix
- Hex and Decimal Conversions
- Logical Operations on Integers
- Numeric Functions
- Transcendentals
- Advanced Constant Expressions
- Raising to a Power
- Round-Off Error
- Numbers in Business
- The Comp Data Type
- Math Coprocessor Blues
- Numbers at Random

12

Key Words and Identifiers

Abs, AND, ArcTan, Byte, Comp, Cos, DIV, Double, Exp, Extended, Frac, Hi, Int, Integer, Ln, Lo, LongInt, MaxInt, MaxLongInt, NOT, OR, Random, Randomize, RandSeed, Real, Round, Shl, ShortInt, Shr, Sin, Single, Sqr, Sqrt, Str, Trunc, Val, Word, XOR

Real numbers, as you learned in Chapter 2, range from about plus or minus 2.9E−39 to 1.7E+38 (in scientific notation). While integer values range from −32,767 to +32,768, real numbers can express much larger or smaller values and can have fractional parts as in 3.14159 and 0.0001.

Turbo Pascal offers several variations on these two fundamental numeric data types. It also has many built-in procedures and functions useful for working with numbers. This chapter explores more about numbers and shows how to make use of a math coprocessor chip if your computer has one. You'll also learn how to enable coprocessor emulation for writing extended real-number programs that run almost identically with and without a real coprocessor.

Integer Numbers

Table 12-1 lists Turbo Pascal's integer data types. To avoid confusion from now on, the capitalized and bold face **Integer** refers to the **Integer** data type while the uncapitalized integer refers to any of the types from Table 12-1. Values in this table have commas for clarity only—in programs, you can never type commas in numbers.

Table 12-1 Integer data types

Type	Minimum . . Maximum	Sign	Size
ShortInt	− 128 . . 127	Signed	1
Byte	0 . . 255	Unsigned	1
Integer	− 32,768 . . 32,767	Signed	2
Word	0 . . 65,535	Unsigned	2
LongInt	− 2,147,483,648 . . 2,147,483,647	Signed	4

Note. Values in programs cannot have commas. They have been added here for clarity.

Each type in Table 12-1 can express values ranging from a minimum to a maximum. Two types, **Byte** and **Word** are *unsigned*—they can represent only positive numbers. The other three types, **ShortInt**, **Integer**, and **LongInt**, are *signed*—they can represent positive and negative numbers. The table also lists the size in bytes that a variable of each type occupies in memory.

All integer types can represent zero, traditionally considered to be a positive number. Because of zero, the negative and positive values for signed types **ShortInt**, **Integer**, and **LongInt** are not mirror images. For example, the minimum **Integer** value is − 32,768 while the positive maximum is 32,767—*not* 32,768. *Including* zero, though, there are equal numbers of positive and negative values in a signed-number range. (There are 32,768 positive **Integer** values including zero and 32,768 negative values excluding zero.)

The built-in constant **MaxInt** equals the maximum **Integer** value. The built-in constant **MaxLongInt** equals the maximum **LongInt** value. The other types do not have similar constants. Be aware that − **MaxInt** and − **MaxLongInt** do not equal the minimum values for their data types for the reasons just explained.

Real Numbers

Table 12-2 lists Turbo Pascal's real-number data types. The table also lists the size in bytes that variables of each type occupy in memory plus the approximate maximum number of significant digits values can have.

Table 12-2 Real-number data types

Type	Minimum . . Maximum	Size	Significant digits
Single *	1.5E − 45 . . 3.4E38	4	7–8
Real	2.9E − 39 . . 1.7E38	6	11–12
Double *	5.0E − 324 . . 1.7E308	8	15–16
Extended *	1.9E − 4951 . . 1.1E4932	10	19–20
Comp *	− 2^{63} + 1 . . 2^{63} − 1	8	18–19

* Math coprocessor or emulation required.

Note: As with integers, the uncapitalized word, real, from now on stands for any of these types. The capitalized and bold **Real** refers only to the six-byte **Real** data type.

Coprocessors offer two main advantages: speed and accuracy. Numeric expression processing can run up to 200 times faster, while reducing round-off errors by increasing the range of values you can represent with standard **Real** numbers.

All programs can use the standard **Real** type. The other four types, **Single**, **Double**, **Extended**, and **Comp** require emulation routines or a coprocessor chip—an 8087, 80287, or 80387.

Coprocessors and Emulation Routines

Two settings in the integrated compiler's *Options-Compiler* menus control the use of data types in Table 12-2. *Numeric processing* (NP) tells the compiler whether to generate code for a math coprocessor. Set NP to "8087/80287" to use the types in Table 12-2 or to "Software" to restrict variables to type **Real**. ("8087/80287" was called "Hardware" in Turbo Pascal 4.0.) Another selection in this same menu, *Emulation*, selects coprocessor emulation routines. Set this switch "On" if you *don't* have a math coprocessor or to "Off" if you do. If NP equals "Software", the *Emulation* switch has no effect.

Instead of changing these settings, you can use the {$N+/−} and {$E+/−} compiler directives to select the same options. The *Emulation* setting and {$E+/−} directive do not exist in Turbo Pascal 4.0.

The following notes will help you to decide which settings and switch combinations to use in different situations.

- If you are using Turbo Pascal 4.0, change NP to "Hardware" to enable the types in Table 12-2, or use the {$N+} directive. There are no emulation routines in this version—you must have a math coprocessor to use the extended real-number types. The rest of these notes apply to Turbo Pascal 5.0 and 5.5.

- If you don't need the data types in Table 12-2, set NP to "Software" and *Emulation* to "Off," equivalent to the directives {$N−,E−}. Real-number variables are then restricted to type **Real**.

- If you are positive that a numeric coprocessor will be available, set NP to "8087/80287" and *Emulation* to "Off," or use the {$N+,E−} directives. If a coprocessor is not installed, a program compiled with these settings displays "Numeric co-processor required" and halts. You don't need a coprocessor to compile such programs; you need it only to run the compiled code.

- If you want your programs to use the data types in Table 12-2 but run on systems with and without math coprocessors, set NP to "8087/80287" and *Emulation* to "On," equivalent to the directives {$N+,E+}. When compiled with these options, the program automatically senses and uses a coprocessor if one is present. If not, the code calls the emulation routines. (Note: this option adds about 10K to the compiled .EXE file size.)

- Setting NP to "Software" and *Emulation* to "On"—or using the directives {$N – ,E + }—restricts the program to using **Real** data types. These settings have no practical value.

Coprocessor Emulation in Units

Emulation routines are never linked into compiled units; therefore, there's never any reason to use the {$E + / – } directive inside a unit. If a unit uses any of the data types from Table 12-2, insert the directive {$N + } above the **UNIT** key word (or change NP to "8087/80287") before compiling.

In the host program, insert the directives {$N + ,E – } to force the unit's code to use a numeric coprocessor. Or, to link in emulation routines, insert the directives {$N + ,E + }.

Reading and Writing Numbers

As many previous examples demonstrate, programs can directly assign the results of expressions to real or integer variables, or use **Read** and **Readln** to let operators enter values from their keyboards.

Program 12-1 demonstrates a problem that often occurs when directly reading real or integer values. When you run the program, type 3.14159 or any other number and press Enter. You should see the same value formatted in scientific notation. Run the program again, but this time press a letter key such as A and then press Enter. What happens? You receive:

```
Runtime error 106: Invalid numeric format
```

This error occurs because the **Readln** statement (line 8) expects a number. Typing a letter is the same as trying to assign a character or string to a number, which, of course, you cannot do.

Program 12-1

```
1:   PROGRAM InputNumbers;
2:   VAR
3:      r : Real;
4:   BEGIN
5:      Writeln( 'Input Numbers' );
6:      Writeln;
7:      Write( 'Value? ' );
8:      Readln( r );
```

Program 12-1 *cont.*

```
 9:    Writeln( 'r = ', r )
10:    END.
```

Error-Free Input

As Program 12-1 demonstrates, when reading integer or real-number variables in a **Read** or **Readln** statement, Pascal halts the program if you enter anything other than a valid number. Of course, software reviewers would hang your program from the yardarm if it halted at every typing error. To pass scrutiny, programs need error-free methods for reading numbers.

One way to avoid the problem is to read values as strings and then convert the digits from characters to numeric values with Turbo Pascal's built-in procedure, **Val**. Because you can type any characters into strings, this method lets people make typing mistakes without halting the program.

Val takes three parameters, a string, a real or integer variable, and an integer error code. In Program 12-2, **s** is the string, **r** is the real number variable, and **e** is the error code. In line 11, **Val** converts string **s** to value **r**, setting error code **e** to zero if it detects no errors.

When you run the program and enter an illegal character, the program itself detects errors and takes appropriate action—in this case, displaying the error code value or, if the error is zero, the converted number **r**. The same method works with integer values, too. Change the type of **r** from **Real** to **Integer**, and recompile. What happens if you now enter 3.14159?

Program 12-2

```
 1:    PROGRAM InputNumbers2;
 2:    VAR
 3:       e : Integer;
 4:       r : Real;
 5:       s : String[20];
 6:    BEGIN
 7:       Writeln( 'Input Numbers' );
 8:       Writeln;
 9:       Write( 'Value? ' );
10:       Readln( s );
11:       Val( s, r, e );
12:       IF e = 0
13:          THEN Writeln( 'r = ', r )
14:          ELSE Writeln( 'Error code = ', e )
15:    END.
```

The error code that **Val** returns (**e** in Program 12-2) represents the position of an illegal character in the string. You can use this information to write a general-purpose numeric input procedure, demonstrated in Program 12-3.

Procedure **GetReal** (lines 5–18) prompts for a real-number value. Line 12 reads your response into string variable **s**. When you enter an illegal character, the **IF** statement in lines 14–16 writes a caret pointing to your mistake. To find the column position of the error, **GetReal** adds the length of the prompt string to the error code returned by **Val** (line 13).

Program 12-3

```
 1:  PROGRAM InputNumbers3;
 2:  VAR
 3:      r : Real;
 4:
 5:  PROCEDURE GetReal( prompt : String; VAR r : Real );
 6:  VAR
 7:      Error : Integer;
 8:      s : String;
 9:  BEGIN
10:      REPEAT
11:         Write( prompt );
12:         Readln( s );
13:         Val( s, r, Error );
14:         IF Error <> 0
15:            THEN Writeln( '^' : length(prompt) + Error,
16:                          '-- Entry error!' )
17:      UNTIL Error = 0
18:  END; { GetReal }
19:
20:  BEGIN
21:      Writeln( 'Input Numbers' );
22:      Writeln;
23:      GetReal( 'Value? ', r );
24:      Writeln( 'r = ', r )
25:  END.
```

Type a few illegal entries such as 3.141A5 or 123@7.2 to see how Program 12-3 responds. You can also enter values in scientific notation. Try a few values such as 7.5025E4 and −45E−3.

Pressing Enter instead of a number is an error in this version of **GetReal**. To return zero in this case—a reasonable response to someone deciding not to type a number—add an **IF** statement between lines 12 and 13, calling **Val** only if the string length is greater than zero:

```
IF Length( s ) = 0 THEN
BEGIN
    r := 0.0; Error := 0
END ELSE
```

Val works equally well for any real or integer type. Try changing **Real** in lines 3 and 5 in Program 12-3 to any of the types in Tables 12-1 and 12-2. Some of the answers may surprise you. As you can see, different data types have subtle effects on the accuracy and representation of numbers as program variables. If you have a numeric coprocessor, insert the directive {$N + } above **PROGRAM**. If you don't have a numeric coprocessor and are using Turbo Pascal 5.0 or a later version, use the directives {$N + ,E + }.

Formatted Output

Procedure **Str** reverses what **Val** does, converting numbers to strings. A database program might use **Str** to store numeric values in disk files but convert them to strings for editing. **Val** could then reconvert edited numbers back into values.

Program 12-4 demonstrates **Str**. Enter a value followed by the number of digits and decimals that you want in the formatted result. Line 16 converts **Value** to string **s** with no formatting. Line 19 does the same thing but formats the result to the number of **Digits** and **Decimals** you specify.

The number of digits specifies the column width for the *entire* number, including the decimal point character plus all digits to the left and right. The number of decimals limits how many digits appear to the right of the decimal point, rounding values to the next highest value. The best way to understand these specifications is to run Program 12-4 and type 3.14159 (or any other value) with various numbers of decimals and digits.

Program 12-4

```
 1:  PROGRAM Num2String;
 2:  VAR
 3:     Value : Real;
 4:     Digits, Decimals : Integer;
 5:     s : String;
 6:  BEGIN
 7:     Writeln( 'Number to string converter' );
 8:     REPEAT
 9:        Writeln;
10:        Write( 'Value (0 to quit)? ' ); Readln( Value );
11:        IF Value <> 0.0 THEN
12:        BEGIN
13:           Write( 'Digits? ' ); Readln( Digits );
14:           Write( 'Decimals? ' ); Readln( Decimals );
15:
16:           Str( Value, s );
17:           Writeln( 'Unformatted result ===> ', s );
18:
19:           Str( Value : Digits : Decimals, s );
20:           Writeln( 'Formatted result =====> ', s );
```

Program 12-4 *cont.*

```
21:            Writeln( 'String length ========> ', length( s ) )
22:        END { if }
23:     UNTIL Value = 0.0
24:  END.
```

If the value to be formatted has fewer digits than the formatting values **Digits** and **Decimals**, **Str** right-justifies the result in the string. If the value has more digits, the result occupies as much space in the string as needed.

You can also convert integer values to strings with **Str**, but in that case you may specify only the number of digits, not the number of decimals, as **Str**'s parameter. To experiment, change **Real** in line 3 to **Integer** and revise line 19 to read:

```
Str( Value : Digits, s );
```

In addition to **Integer** and **Real**, **Str** can convert to strings any of the types in Tables 12-1 and 12-2. You might want to try some of these types before continuing.

Word Alignment

Turbo Pascal optimizes memory accesses by aligning all variables larger than 1 byte on even addresses. For example, if a 2-byte **Integer** variable would fall on an odd address, the compiler wastes a byte of memory to ensure that the variable's address is even.

Word alignment speeds program execution because the 16-bit 8086-family processors (but not the 8088) can load 2-byte variables faster if the first address is even. The speed increase is usually worth a little wasted memory—especially in programs that use many **Integer** and **Word** variables interspersed with other multibyte arrays, records, sets, and so forth. If you prefer to save as much memory as possible, include the directive {$A – } above the **PROGRAM** or **UNIT** headers to turn off word alignment. Be aware that this may slow your program.

With alignment on, as it normally is, multibyte records are also aligned on even address boundaries. But, individual fields in such records are *not* word aligned. If you want to align **Integer** and **Word** fields inside records, you must insert your own dummy variables to make sure that preceding fields occupy an even number of bytes. Or, just list all **Integer** and **Word** fields first in the record.

Numeric Expressions

As you learned in Chapter 2, you can mix real numbers and integers in expressions. The results of mixed expressions, however, are always **Real** numbers, which you cannot assign to **Integer** variables. Instead, you first have to convert real-number values to integers using one of two available methods.

Function **Round** converts a real number to a **LongInt** value, rounded up or down to the nearest whole number. Function **Trunc** also converts real numbers to **LongInt** values but truncates with no rounding all digits to the right of the decimal. Figure 12-1 lists a few example rounded and truncated values.

```
Round( 3.14159 ) = 3
Round( 100.5   ) = 101
Round( 1.99999 ) = 2

Trunc( 3.14159 ) = 3
Trunc( 100.5   ) = 100
Trunc( 1.99999 ) = 1
```

Figure 12-1 Functions **Round** and **Trunc** convert real numbers to integers.

When converting real numbers to integers, be careful to stay within the allowed integer range. This does not work:

```
{$R+}
r := 5.5E8;
i := Round( r );      {Incorrect!}
```

If range checking is on and if **i** is type **Integer**, assigning **Round**(r) to **i**, when **r** is not in the range $-32,767$ to $+32,768$, generates:

```
Runtime error 201: Range check error
```

There is no simple way to prevent Turbo Pascal from stopping your program if this error occurs. The only solution is never to allow the condition to arise. You could use the following sequence to avoid the problem:

```
{$R+}
IF (r >= -32767.0) AND
   (r <=  32768.0)
   THEN i := Round( r )
   ELSE i := 0;
```

Of course, it may not be adequate in all cases to set **i** to zero if **r** is out of range, but at least that approach avoids halting the program. Another possibility is to assign **Round** and **Trunc** to a **LongInt** variable. Except for very large real numbers, this will rarely generate runtime errors.

Converting integers to real numbers, on the other hand, is easier. Turbo Pascal automatically converts integer values to reals as needed. To convert an integer value, therefore, just assign it to a real-number variable. This sequence displays the value $1.234E+03$ (plus trailing zeros):

```
i := 1234;
r := i;
Writeln( r );
```

A Horse of a Different Radix

A number's radix is the *base* to which the number belongs. The standard radix in Turbo Pascal is base ten decimal, but you may also write numbers in base 16, more commonly called *hexadecimal*. Literally, hexadecimal means "ten and six." The word refers to the 16 symbols in the hexadecimal number system: the ten digits, 0 to 9, plus the six letters, A to F.

Hexadecimal and integer numbers are just different forms of the *same* values. Hexadecimal $FF represents the same number of things as decimal 255. Hex numbers are just horses of a different color—or radix.

You might wonder, if hex and decimal numbers represent the same values, why use one over the other? The answer is intimately related to the fact that all PCs (indeed, most computers in existence) operate on binary numbers, having the digits 0 and 1. Any number can be expressed in binary, decimal, hexadecimal—or in any other radix. For example, these values are equivalent:

```
1234               (decimal)
$04D2              (hexadecimal)
0100 1101 0010     (binary)
```

And each of the following statements sets integer variable **Num** to 255.

```
Num := 255;
Num := $FF;
Num := 240 + $0F;
Num := $F0 + $000F;
```

Because 16 is a power of two and because there are 16 symbols in the hexadecimal radix, there is a direct relationship between hexadecimals and binary, or radix-two, values. Because of this relationship, most programmers use hexadecimals to express specific binary values. For example, this assigns to an **Integer** variable the binary value, 01001101:

```
Number := $4D;    { Binary 0100 1101 }
```

Rather than memorize complicated conversion formulas to change between binary and hexadecimal values, refer to Table 12-3's list of binary equivalents for the 16 hexadecimal digits 0 through F. Because of the direct relationship between four-digit binary and single-digit hexadecimals, simple substitution converts hexadecimal values to binary. For instance, from Table 12-3, these expressions are equivalent:

```
$1234 = 0001 0010 0011 0100
$ABCD = 1010 1011 1100 1101
$8001 = 1000 0000 0000 0001
```

Each hexadecimal digit in the values on the left corresponds with a four-digit binary value on the right, taken from Table 12-3. From these examples, you can see why hexadecimal numbers are convenient for binary computer programmers. It's a lot easier to write and remember $ABCD than the equivalent binary value, 1010101111001101.

Table 12-3 Hexadecimal to binary converter

Hex	Binary	Hex	Binary
0	0000	8	1000
1	0001	9	1001
2	0010	A	1010
3	0011	B	1011
4	0100	C	1100
5	0101	D	1101
6	0110	E	1110
7	0111	F	1111

The custom in programming is to write hex values with a leading dollar sign ($) and to always write two- or four-digit groups. For example, you would normally write $0F or $000F, not $F, even though all three forms are technically correct. Similarly, the custom is to write binary values in groups of four digits. The number 111 (7 in decimal) is correct, although most people write 0111.

Turbo Pascal recognizes hexadecimal and decimal notations. It does not directly let you express numbers in binary. You can assign hexadecimal and decimal values to any of the integer types in Table 12-1.

Integers and Words in Hex

When assigning hexadecimal values to variables of Turbo Pascal's two 16-bit integer types, **Integer** and **Word**, the results may be different than you expect. As you probably know, the uppermost bit in positive **Integer** values is 0. An example makes this clear (with hexadecimal equivalents in parentheses):

```
32,767  =   0111 1111 1111 1111    ($7FFF)
```

The maximum positive **Integer** value 32,767 in binary has all 1 bits except for bit number 15. (Bits are numbered from right to left. The first bit is numbered 0.)

In negative 16-bit **Integer**s, the leftmost bit (number 15) is 1. For example, −1 in binary is:

```
-1      =    1111 1111 1111 1111     {$FFFF)
```

And, the lowest possible **Integer** value is:

```
-32,768 =    1000 0000 0000 0000     {$8000)
```

Considering that **Word** and **Integer** variables are both 16-bits long, the binary values are ambiguous. Hexadecimal $8000 equals the *signed* **Integer** value −32,768. But the same hex value also equals the *unsigned* **Word** value 32,768, implying (falsely) that −32,768 = +32,768! Because of this discrepancy, assignments such as the following do not compile:

```
i := $FFFF;        { ??? }
i := $8000;        { ??? }
```

Internally, Turbo Pascal stores those and other 16-bit hexadecimal values as 32-bit **LongInt** values. The statements fail to compile because they are really trying to do this:

```
i := $0000FFFF;    { 65,535 ??? }
i := $00008000;    { 32,768 ??? }
```

When viewed as full 32-bit values, it's easy to see why the assignments are incorrect. In both cases, the decimal equivalents (shown here as comments) are outside of the range allowed for signed **Integer**s.

To assign negative values to **Integer** variables, add an additional four F hex digits, specifying full 32-bit signed values. For example, to fix the above statements, you must write:

```
i := $FFFFFFFF;    { i = -1 }
i := $FFFF8000;    { i = -32,768 }
```

Remember that in negative values, the leftmost bit is 1. Because the 16-bit values −1 and −32,768 are stored internally as 32-bit values, bits 16 through 31 (the uppermost four hex digits) must *all* be 1 for Turbo Pascal to consider the values to be negative and in the proper range.

A similar problem occurs with **Word** values. These assignments do not compile:

```
w := $FFFFFFFF;    { ??? }
w := $FFFF8000;    { ??? }
```

The two hex values are negative 32-bit long integers—and you can't assign negative values to unsigned **Word**s. The correct assignments are:

```
w := $7FFF;        { w = 32,767 }
w := $FFFF;        { w = 65,535 }
```

Or, you can use the full 32-bit values:

```
w := $00007FFF;    { w = 32,767 }
w := $0000FFFF;    { w = 65,535 }
```

Hex and Decimal Conversions

Unfortunately, converting between hexadecimal and decimal is not as simple as converting between hexadecimal and binary—except for a Pascal program, that is.

There are many published methods for converting values from one radix to another. Rather than repeat these methods here, Program 12-5 solves the problem by taking advantage of the way Pascal stores integers in memory. It's not always a good idea to rely on such system dependencies, but neither should clever solutions be discounted just because they don't go strictly by the book. At the same time, the program demonstrates several new Turbo Pascal features.

Integers take two eight-bit bytes, with the low-order byte preceding the high. In other words, the two bytes are reversed from the order you might expect.

To convert a decimal value to hexadecimal, Program 12-5 separates an integer's two bytes and writes the appropriate hexadecimal digit for each four-bit part or *nybble*. The first nybble equals the byte divided by 16; the second nybble equals the byte modulo 16 (the remainder left after dividing by 16). Procedure **ConvertHex** uses this idea at lines 20–24, calling function **Digit** for each of the four nybbles in an integer.

To extract eight-bit bytes from **Integer** values, function **Hi** (lines 20–21) returns the upper eight bits while **Lo** (lines 23–24) returns the lower eight bits of parameter **Number**. Both **Hi** and **Lo** return values from 0 to 255 and ignore the sign of the original number.

Digit (lines 7–13) returns the appropriate character 0 through F for any value **n** from zero to 15. Values zero through nine return the *characters* 0 to 9 while values ten through 15 return characters A to F.

To convert to binary (see lines 28–40), the built-in operator **Shl** (line 37) shifts the bits in **Number** one bit to the left each time through the **FOR** loop starting at line 33. Notice that **Shl** is an *operator*, like plus ($+$) or minus ($-$). The number to the right indicates the number of shifts, which in this example is one. Not shown here is the alternate operator **Shr**, which shifts bits to the right.

The **Shl** in line 37 successively shifts each bit in **Number** to the leftmost position. The program passes the ordinal value of the Boolean expression (**Number** < 0) to function **Digit** (line 36). Negative integers have their leftmost bit set equal to one; therefore, if the value is less than zero, line 36 displays 1, otherwise, it displays 0.

As shown in line 50, converting to decimal couldn't be simpler in Turbo Pascal. To convert hexadecimal numbers you type into **Readln** statements, just precede your entry with a dollar sign. For example, try entering 255, $FF, -1, and $FFFF.

Program 12-5

```
1:   PROGRAM Radix;
2:   CONST
3:      Blank  = ' ';    { Single blank character }
4:   VAR
5:      Number : Integer;
6:
7:   FUNCTION Digit( n : Byte ) : Char;
8:   { For 0 <= n <= 15 }
9:   BEGIN
10:     IF n < 10
11:        THEN Digit := Chr( ord('0') + n )
12:        ELSE Digit := Chr( ord('A') + ( n - 10 ) )
13:   END; { Digit }
14:
15:  PROCEDURE ConvertHex( Number : Integer );
16:  BEGIN
17:
18:     Write( 'Base 16 =  ' );
19:
20:     Write( Digit( Hi( Number ) DIV 16 ),
21:            Digit( Hi( Number ) MOD 16 ) );
22:
23:     Writeln( Digit( Lo( Number ) DIV 16 ),
24:              Digit( Lo( Number ) MOD 16 ) )
25:
26:  END; { ConvertHex }
27:
28:  PROCEDURE ConvertBin( Number : Integer );
29:  VAR
30:     i : Integer;
31:  BEGIN
32:     Write( 'Base 02 = ' );
33:     FOR i := 0 TO 15 DO
34:     BEGIN
35:        IF i MOD 4 = 0 THEN Write( blank );
36:        Write( Digit( Ord( Number < 0 ) ) );
37:        Number := Number Shl 1
38:     END; { for }
39:     Writeln
40:  END; { ConvertBin }
41:
42:  BEGIN
43:     Writeln( 'Radix Conversion' );
44:     REPEAT
```

Program 12-5 *cont.*

```
45:        Writeln;
46:        Write( 'Value (0 to quit)?  ' );
47:        Readln( Number );
48:        ConvertHex( Number );
49:        ConvertBin( Number );
50:        Writeln( 'Base 10 =  ', Number )
51:    UNTIL Number = 0
52: END.
```

Logical Operations on Integers

In addition to the usual integer math operators, $*$, DIV, $+$, and $-$, Turbo Pascal understands six logical operators listed in Table 12-4. The table also shows an example expression and result in both hexadecimal and decimal.

Table 12-4 Logical operators

Operator	Description	Example	Results Hex	Decimal
Shl	Shift left	$55 Shl 1	$ 00AA	170
Shr	Shift right	$55 Shr 2	$ 0015	21
NOT	Negate	NOT $55	$ FFAA	−86
OR	Logical OR	$55 OR $80	$ 00D5	213
AND	Logical AND	$55 AND $0F	$ 0005	5
XOR	Logical XOR	$55 XOR $55	$ 0000	0

Shl and **Shr** shift integer values to the left or right. If **n** is an integer, then (**n Shr 4**) shifts the bits in **n** four bits to the right. **Shl** shifts in the opposite direction. Notice that the value to be shifted comes *before* the operator.

NOT negates an integer value, turning all 0 bits to 1 and all 1 bits to 0. Logical operators **OR**, **AND**, and **XOR** (exclusive or) combine two integer values bit for bit (see Table 12-5). Compare Table 12-5 with Table 2-2, which shows the true and false results of applying these same operators with Boolean operands. Don't confuse these operations. Integer expressions evaluate to integer results. Boolean expressions evaluate to Boolean true and false results.

The IBM PC Keyboard Flag

The PC keyboard BIOS routines change certain bits in memory when you press special keys like CapsLock or Alt. Program 12-6 tests some of these bits by declaring an absolute byte variable at the location of the keyboard flag byte (line 16). To end the program, press Ctrl-Break. The constants at lines 4–12 relate keys to individual bits in a byte. The program uses these constants along with a logical integer operator to determine whether bits are on (1) or off (0).

Table 12-5 Integer OR, AND, and XOR truth tables

A	OR	B	=	C
0		0		0
1		0		1
0		1		1
1		1		1

A	AND	B	=	C
0		0		0
1		0		0
0		1		0
1		1		1

A	XOR	B	=	C
0		0		0
1		0		1
0		1		1
1		1		0

To test for the presence of a bit, use a logical **AND**, as shown in lines 33–36 and 39–42. **AND**ing the keyboard flag byte with the appropriate constant isolates one bit, tested by procedure **Display**.

Program 12-6

```
 1:  PROGRAM KeyStat;
 2:  USES Crt;
 3:
 4:  CONST
 5:     InsState    = $80;
 6:     CapsState   = $40;
 7:     NumState    = $20;
 8:     ScrollState = $10;
 9:     AltShift    = $08;
10:     CtlShift    = $04;
11:     LeftShift   = $02;
12:     RightShift  = $01;
13:  TYPE
14:     String40 = String[40];
15:  VAR
16:     KbFlag  : Byte Absolute $0040:$0017;
17:     OldFlag : Byte;
```

Program 12-6 *cont.*

```
18:
19:  PROCEDURE Display( Message : String40; Value : Byte );
20:  BEGIN
21:     Write( Message );
22:     IF Value = 0
23:        THEN Writeln( 'Off' )
24:        ELSE Writeln( 'On ' )   { On + 1 blank }
25:  END;
26:
27:  BEGIN
28:     ClrScr;
29:     Writeln( 'Keyboard Status Byte--(Type Ctrl-Break to quit)' );
30:     REPEAT
31:        Gotoxy( 1, 4 );
32:        Writeln( 'State Bits (Press and release)' );
33:        Display( '  Insert ........ ', KbFlag AND InsState );
34:        Display( '  Caps Lock ..... ', KbFlag AND CapsState );
35:        Display( '  Num Lock ...... ', KbFlag AND NumState );
36:        Display( '  Scroll Lock ... ', KbFlag AND ScrollState );
37:        Writeln;
38:        Writeln( 'Shift Bits (Press, hold, and release)' );
39:        Display( '  Alt ........... ', KbFlag AND AltShift );
40:        Display( '  Ctrl .......... ', KbFlag AND CtlShift );
41:        Display( '  Left Shift .... ', KbFlag AND LeftShift );
42:        Display( '  Right Shift.... ', KbFlag AND RightShift );
43:        Gotoxy( 1, 23 );
44:        Write( 'Press above keys to change states...' );
45:        OldFlag := KbFlag;
46:        REPEAT { wait } UNTIL OldFlag <> KbFlag
47:     UNTIL False
48:  END.
```

Numeric Functions

Turbo Pascal has several general-purpose numeric functions for operating on real and integer numbers. Function **Abs** (*abs*olute value) returns the positive equivalent of negative or positive integers or real numbers. The result of **Abs** is the same type as its argument. In other words, the absolute value of an integer is an integer. The absolute value of a real number is real.

Function **Int** returns the integer portion of a real number in a form similar to the result of **Trunc**. But the type of **Int** is real, not integer. This seems contradictory until you examine the alternate function, **Frac**, which returns the fractional part of a real number. The two functions complement each other. **Int** returns all digits to the left of the decimal place while **Frac** returns the digits to the right of the decimal. For real-number r, then:

```
r = Int( r ) + Frac( r )
```

Figure 12-2 lists a few examples of applying **Abs**, **Int**, and **Frac** to different values.

```
Abs( -3.14159 ) = 3.14159      Int( 123.456  ) =  123.000
Abs( 10       ) = 10           Int( -3.14159 ) = -3.00000

            Frac( 123.456  ) = 4.5599999989E-01
            Frac( -3.14159 ) = -0.14159;

        Frac(-3.14159)+(Abs(Int(-3.14159))) = 2.85841
```

Figure 12-2 Examples of functions **Abs**, **Int**, and **Frac**.

Transcendentals

In mathematics, **transcendentals are quantities** for which no finite algebraic formulas exist. These include **exponential, logarithmic**, and trigonometric functions. Turbo Pascal has **all the usual transcendentals** found in most programming languages plus **Sqr and Sqrt** as listed in Table 12-6. You can find additional details on these functions in Chapter 16.

Table 12-6 Real-number functions

Function	Description
Abs(n)	Absolute value of n
ArcTan(n)	Arctangent of n
Cos(n)	Cosine of n
Exp(n)	Exponential equal to e^n (e = 2.7182818285)
Frac(n)	Fractional portion of n
Int(n)	Whole number portion of n
Ln(n)	Natural logarithm of n
Sin(n)	Sine of n
Sqr(n)	Product of n * n
Sqrt(n)	Square root of n

Derived functions are easy to program from Turbo Pascal's built-ins. For example, Figure 12-3 lists functions for **Tangent, Secant, CoSecant**, and **CoTangent**, which are not provided in Turbo Pascal. These functions, along with the built-in **ArcTan, Cos**, and **Sin**, operate and return angles expressed in *radians*.

```
FUNCTION Tangent( n : Real ) : Real;
BEGIN
   Tangent := Sin(n) / Cos(n)
END;

FUNCTION Secant( n : Real ) : Real;
BEGIN
   Secant := 1 / Cos(n)
END;

FUNCTION CoSecant( n : Real ) : Real;
BEGIN
   CoSecant := 1 / Sin(n)
END;

FUNCTION CoTangent( n : Real ) : Real;
BEGIN
   CoTangent := 1 / Tangent(n)
END;
```

Figure 12-3 Other trigonometric functions are easily derived from those provided in Turbo Pascal.

One radian is defined as any arc equal in length to the radius of a circle containing the arc. Joining the two end points of such an arc to the center of the circle creates an inner angle equal to about 57.296°. You don't have to memorize this formula, but you do have to be careful to express angles in the correct form. If your program uses integer angles from 0 to 360, you must convert values to radians.

Program 12-7 shows how to do the conversions. Function **Radians** (lines 6–9) converts angles to equivalent radians. Function **Degrees** (11–14) does the reverse, converting radians to angles. As a test, the program prints a table listing several angles converted both ways.

Program 12-7

```
1:  PROGRAM RadsToDegrees;
2:  VAR
3:     angle : Integer;
4:     ang, rad : Real;
5:
6:  FUNCTION Radians( angle : Real ) : Real;
7:  BEGIN
8:     Radians := Abs( angle ) * Pi / 180.0
9:  END; { Radians }
```

Program 12-7 *cont.*

```
10:
11:   FUNCTION Degrees( radians : Real ) : Real;
12:   BEGIN
13:      Degrees := ( 180.0 * radians ) / Pi
14:   END; { Degrees }
15:
16:   BEGIN
17:      angle := 0;
18:      Writeln( 'Angle    Radians    Degrees' );
19:      Writeln( '--------------------------' );
20:      WHILE angle <= 360 DO
21:      BEGIN
22:         rad := Radians( angle );
23:         ang := Degrees( rad );
24:         Writeln( angle:5, rad:10:3, ang:10:3 );
25:         angle := angle + 20
26:      END { while }
27:   END.
```

Using the functions from Program 12-7, the following statements are true:

```
Radians( 57.296 ) = 1.000;
Degrees( 1.000  ) = 57.296;
Radians( 180.0  ) = Pi;
```

Notice that the number of radians in 180° equals **Pi**.

Advanced Constant Expressions

Chapter 2 explains the concept of constant expressions, first introduced in Turbo Pascal 5.0. Compiling such expressions is sometimes called *constant folding* because the expressions are reduced (folded) to a single value. Constant expressions never generate code that runs; they simply give you a way to assign fixed values based on the values of other constants. For example, you can write **CONST** declarations such as:

```
min = 5;
max = 29;
size = 1 + ( max - min );
```

Now that you know more about numbers in Turbo Pascal, you'll be glad to learn that you can use *any* expression to the right of the equal sign. You can employ built-in operators such as **Shl** and **XOR**, and you can even call built-in functions

Abs and **Trunc**. This lets you create fancy expressions that appear similar to statements:

```
size2 = Abs( size );
size3 = size shl 4;
```

The only restriction is that all values must be literal or must refer to the identifiers of other constants. Typed constants and variables are not allowed. Also, you may "call" only built-in pseudo-functions such as **Abs** in the previous example. Real function calls—for example, to the built-in **Pi**—are not permitted. (**Pi** was a constant at one time in Turbo Pascal, but now, because extended NDP data types are available, **Pi** was changed to a function that automatically adjusts to an expression's numeric precision.)

Remember always that such constants do not execute at runtime. In all cases, the compiler reduces constant expressions to fixed values.

Raising to a Power

Many languages, but not Turbo Pascal, have an operator for raising a number to a power. While it's easy to write equivalent formulas for integer powers, raising a real number to a real power is not so simply done. For example, two to the fourth power (2^4) is simply $2*2*2*2$, or 16. But how do you calculate $3.14159^{2.321}$?

One solution is to write a function, **Raise**, that returns a number raised to any power. The standard method is to use the exponential function in an expression:

```
r := Exp( p * Ln( n ) )
```

This sets real number **r** equal to **n** raised to the power **p**. Unfortunately, there are complications with the method. For one, **Ln(0)** generates:

```
Runtime error 207: Invalid floating point operation
```

In some languages, **Ln(0)** simply returns zero, a value on which many published programs rely. Also, powers of negative numbers cause the formula to fail.

The **Raise** function in Program 12-8, however, works for all reasonable values. (Unreasonable values are those that raise numbers to values outside of the allowed real-number range.) The method used here operates similarly to the power operator found in many languages, handling two special cases according to these assumptions:

$$n^0 = 1.0$$
$$0.0^{n \ne 0} = 0.0$$

This follows the definition that any value (including zero) to the zero power equals 1.0, but zero to any nonzero power equals zero.

To deal with negative values, Program 12-8 includes another useful function, **Sign**, which returns −1 for negative values and +1 for positive values. The function considers zero to be positive. The **IF** statement (line 8) avoids a fatal divide by zero in line 10.

Function **Raise** uses **Sign** to raise negative numbers. This is done by passing the absolute value of **Number** to function **Ln** and multiplying the result of the power formula by the sign of the original number (line 20). Raising a negative number to any power, therefore, has a negative result.

Program 12-8

```
1:   PROGRAM TestRaise;
2:   VAR
3:      x, y : Real;
4:
5:   FUNCTION Sign( Number : Real ) : Real;
6:   { Return -1 if Number < 0, or +1 if Number >= 0 }
7:   BEGIN
8:      IF Number = 0.0
9:         THEN Sign := 1
10:        ELSE Sign := Abs( Number ) / Number
11:  END; { Sign }
12:
13:  FUNCTION Raise( Number, Power : Real ) : Real;
14:  { Raise Number to Power }
15:  BEGIN
16:     IF Number = 0.0
17:       THEN IF Power = 0.0
18:               THEN Raise := 1.0
19:               ELSE Raise := 0.0
20:       ELSE Raise := Sign( Number ) * exp( Power * ln( abs( Number ) ) )
21:  END; { Raise }
22:
23:  BEGIN
24:     REPEAT
25:       Write( 'X? ' ); Readln( x );
26:       Write( 'Y? ' ); Readln( y );
27:       Writeln( x:0:3, ' ^ ', y:0:3, ' = ', Raise( x, y ):0:3 )
28:     UNTIL x = 0.0
29:  END.
```

Round-Off Error

Real numbers expressed as fixed-size binary values can suffer from round-off error. Figure 12-2 illustrates this problem in the result of **Frac**(123.456). Although the correct answer should be 0.456, the fractional part of the value 123.456, the answer given is 4.5599999989E – 01. Close, but no cigar.

The problem occurs because of lost bits during certain operations on real numbers expressed in binary, leading to insignificant but annoying errors in the result.

Scientists have long been aware of round-off error. They effectively deal with the problem by agreeing on a system of significant digits where the result of any operation cannot have more digits than the smallest number of significant digits among all operands. In other words, (1/7) may read 0.1428571 on your calculator, but it is accurate to state only that the answer lies somewhere between 0.1 and 0.2. If, however, you divide 1.0000000 by 7.0000000, then you can safely trust the answer to eight significant digits.

In accounting programs, where lost pennies are unacceptable, programs often deal with the problem by formatting output in **Writeln** statements:

```
Writeln( Frac(123.456):3:3 );
```

By specifying three digits and three decimal places, the foregoing statement now gives the correct result. However, this approach works only with relatively small numbers. Because real numbers may have up to 11 or 12 significant digits in Turbo Pascal (more with a math coprocessor) results approaching or exceeding the maximum limits can suffer from round-off errors.

One solution is to install a numeric coprocessor and use the **Double** or **Extended** types instead of **Real**. Because more bits are used to represent numbers of these types, the values are more accurate—at least for values well within the ranges listed in Table 12-2. Also, the coprocessor does all calculations internally using the ten-byte **Extended** format, which improves the accuracy of all real-number calculations, not just those involving **Extended** variables.

If you do plan to use a numeric coprocessor, you should probably not use Turbo Pascal's six-byte **Real** data type. With a coprocessor, your program calls time-wasting routines to convert **Real** numbers to **Extended** and back again in expressions. It does not perform these conversions with the other types listed in Table 12-2. Therefore, using **Single**, **Double**, and **Extended** types usually makes programs run faster. (We'll get to the **Comp** type in a moment.)

Numbers in Business

A certain amount of error is acceptable, indeed expected, in scientific calculations. But it's a different story in business. I'll never forget the customer who, when I was a part-time clerk in a computer store, vehemently insisted that his computer language (an early BASIC) had a bug. An accounting program he had written refused to account accurately for every penny. Despite my best efforts, I was unable to convince him that real numbers represented by fixed numbers of binary digits cannot be perfectly accurate for all fractional values.

In truth, a degree of inaccuracy in real-number variables is not a bug. As any mathematician will tell you, there is a difference between measuring and counting. No measurement is perfectly accurate. For example, if you measure your backyard, the result is no more accurate than the smallest spacings on your tape measure. If the tape is marked in inches and you say your yard is 175 feet, 12½ inches long, you may be making a good guess, but it is still a guess. On the other hand, if you have six trees in your backyard, then you have *exactly* six trees—no more and no less.

In programming, integer values count things exactly. Real-number values represent measurements and, therefore, are accurate only to a certain number of significant digits—equivalent to the precision of a measuring tape. My poor customer's problem was that he was trying to use real-number measurements to count his pennies. You'd have no more luck balancing your checkbook with a slide rule. (Remember those?)

Dollars and Cents

In science, a mistake of a few inches in measuring the distance from the earth to the moon won't bother anyone. But in business, the loss of just one penny is enough to keep an army of grey suits sweating long past martini time. (Okay, maybe it would take two pennies.)

The problem for programmers is to choose an appropriate data type to represent dollars and cents. A common mistake is to use a **Real** number, assuming this is necessary to represent fractions of dollars such as $123.45. This invites all the round-off problems mentioned earlier and is generally unacceptable.

A better idea is to use an integer type and pretend there is a decimal point before the last two digits. The integer value 6578, then, equals $65.78; 256 equals $2.56 and so on. Because integers count things exactly, the program can't lose pennies due to round-off errors. The integer values represent cents, the smallest monetary division.

The **Integer** data type, though, is too limited for most dollar and cents values. You'll find a pretty small market for your accounting package if it can handle values no greater than $327.67!

The **LongInt** type is a much better choice, able to represent up to $21,474,836.47—big enough for my checkbook certainly but still miniscule in our world of trillion-dollar deficits and 300-billion-dollar defense budgets.

The Comp Data Type

For truly large counting jobs, use the **Comp** data type (see Table 12-2). **Comp** requires a math coprocessor (compile with {$N+}) or coprocessor emulation (compile with {$N+,E+}).

Comp is shorthand for *computational real*, a sort of cross-breed real and integer that's good for counting large quantities—but only up to a point. In memory, **Comp** variables are stored as 8-byte integers, twice the size of **LongInt** values.

But, in expressions, **Comp** values are treated as reals, so they can suffer from round-off errors when individual values are very large.

Comp 64-bit variables can represent values from exactly -2^{63} to $2^{63}-1$, approximately equal to the range $-9E18$ to $9E18$ with 18 significant digits. Assuming two decimal places, the largest **Comp** dollar and cents value you can represent is about 92 million, billion dollars, or exactly:

$92,233,720,368,547,758.09

Don't put too much faith in this extreme limit of the **Comp** data type, though. For practical use, limit your values to 18 significant digits. Internal calculations with values having 19 digits do not produce accurate results. In other words, anything under 10 million, billion dollars is okay.

When displaying **Comp** values, treat them as you do other real data types. Use the :0:0 formatting command in **Write** and **Writeln** statements to prevent values displaying in scientific notation. These two **Writeln** statements explain the difference, showing in braces what appears on screen:

```
c := MaxInt * MaxInt;
Writeln( c );           { 1.07367628900000E+0009 }
Writeln( c:0:0 );       { 1073676289 }
```

You can also specify the number of columns. **Writeln(c:9:0)** right justifies **Comp** numbers in nine columns, with no decimal places. In this example, the formatting command :9:2 displays 1073676289.00. Because **Comp** variables, like all integer types, cannot represent fractions less than one, the ability to display **Comp** values with decimal places is not that useful. You might do this, however, if your values represent whole dollar amounts but you want to display $9.00 instead of just $9.

Comp to String

As explained earlier in this chapter, **Str** and **Val** convert between values and strings, easing the job of getting numbers in and out of programs. You can use these procedures with all data types in Tables 12-1 and 12-2, including **Comp**.

Program 12-9 demonstrates one way to use **Str** and **Val** to help represent and display dollar and cents values in **Comp** variables. The program lets you type in dollar amounts, keeping a running total. Procedure **StrToComp** (lines 6–20) converts strings to **Comp** values. Procedure **CompToStr** (lines 22–28) converts **Comp** values into strings.

When running this program, type numbers as you would on a mechanical calculator. You do not have to type a decimal point. Typing 7654 is the same as typing 76.54. If you do type a decimal point, you must type two digits. Typing 15.5 equals 1.55, not 15.50 as you might expect. This happens because the procedures in Program 12-9 simply ignore the decimal point—a cheap but useful trick.

StrToComp removes any decimal points in the strings you enter at line 35. Line 17 calls **Val** to convert the string to a **Comp** value, returning 0 if you make any typing errors. **CompToStr** calls **Str** at line 24, converting raw values into strings. The **WHILE** loop (lines 25–26) adds leading zeros so that 3, for example, comes out as 0.03. Line 27 inserts the decimal point.

Program 12-9

```
1:   {$N+,E+}
2:   PROGRAM GoodCents;
3:   VAR
4:      total, amount : Comp;
5:      s : String;
6:
7:   PROCEDURE StrToComp( s : String; VAR c : Comp );
8:   VAR
9:      e : Integer;  { Val error code }
10:     p : Integer;  { Position of decimal point (if any) }
11:  BEGIN
12:     p := Pos( '.', s );
13:     WHILE p > 0 DO
14:     BEGIN
15:        Delete( s, p, 1 );   { Remove any decimal point }
16:        p := Pos( '.', s )
17:     END; { while }
18:     Val( s, c, e );
19:     IF e <> 0
20:        THEN c := 0   { Any errors return c = 0 }
21:  END; { StrToComp }
22:
23:  PROCEDURE CompToStr( c : Comp; VAR s : String );
24:  BEGIN
25:     Str( c:0:0, s );
26:     WHILE Length( s ) < 3 DO   { Add leading zeros if needed }
27:        Insert( '0', s, 1 );
28:     Insert( '.', s, Length(s) - 1 )  { Insert decimal point }
29:  END; { CompToStr }
30:
31:  BEGIN
32:     total := 0;
33:     Writeln( 'Count your pennies.  Press Enter to end.' );
34:     REPEAT
35:        Write( '$' );
36:        Readln( s );
37:        IF Length( s ) > 0 THEN
38:        BEGIN
39:           StrToComp( s, amount );
40:           total := total + amount;
```

Program 12-9 *cont.*

```
41:            CompToStr( total, s );
42:            Writeln( '$' + s : 20 )
43:        END
44:    UNTIL Length( s ) = 0
45: END.
```

Math Coprocessor Blues

Note: The following discussion about math-coprocessor function results and the NDP internal stack applies only to Turbo Pascal 4.0. Versions 5.0 and 5.5 no longer store intermediate function results on the coprocessor stack.

The 8087, 80287, and 80387 math coprocessor chips have eight, 80-bit, internal registers that operate as a stack. To save time when calling functions that return numeric coprocessor data types—or procedures and functions with numeric coprocessor value parameters—Turbo Pascal stores intermediate values in the math-chip stack. Because there are only eight registers available, functions and procedures that nest more than eight levels can cause a stack overflow:

```
Error 207: Invalid floating point operation
```

Program 12-10 demonstrates the problem, which is not difficult to fix. (You must have a math coprocessor for this example.) Function **Fact** (lines 7–12) returns the factorial of a positive integer n equal to the values in the sequence 1, 2, . . . , n multiplied together. The factorial of 2 is 2. The factorial of 4 is 24, and so on. The factorial of 0, a special case, is 1, not 0.

When you run Program 12-10, type any small integer value from 0 to about 100. As you will quickly learn, values above 7 generate the error mentioned previously. Line 10, which calls function **Fact** recursively, generates code to stack the temporary results of the expression **Fact(i – 1)** in math coprocessor registers *before* multiplying by **i**. Eight of these calls is all the coprocessor can handle before returning a fatal error.

Program 12-10

```
1: {$N+,E+}
2:
3: PROGRAM BlowYourStack;
4:
```

Program 12-10 *cont.*

```
 5:    VAR   n : Integer;
 6:
 7:    FUNCTION Fact( i : Integer ) : Extended;
 8:    BEGIN
 9:      IF i > 0
10:        THEN Fact := Fact( i - 1 ) * i
11:        ELSE Fact := 1.0
12:    END; { Fact }
13:
14:    BEGIN
15:      Write( 'Factorial of? ' );
16:      Readln( n );
17:      Writeln( 'Factorial = ', Fact( n ) )
18:    END.
```

There are two ways out of the mess in Program 12-10: Store temporary results in local variables or reorder expression evaluation to force Turbo Pascal to pop a value from the math coprocessor stack. The first solution adds a local variable to function **Fact**, assigns the recursive function result to the variable, and then multiplies by **i**:

```
FUNCTION Fact( i : Integer ) : Double;
VAR temp : Extended;
BEGIN
   IF i > 0
     THEN BEGIN
             temp := Fact( i - 1 );
             Fact := temp * i
          END
     ELSE Fact := 1.0
END; { Fact }
```

This cures the problem because procedures and functions create local variables on the main-memory stack, not the coprocessor's. An even better solution, but one that might not work in all situations, is to reorder the expression. For example, replace line 10 in the original Program 12-10 with this:

```
10: THEN Fact := i * Fact( i - 1 )
```

Simply placing **i** first causes Turbo Pascal to begin processing the expression *before* calling **Fact** recursively. The program now works because the compiled program stores intermediate expression results in memory, not on the math coprocessor stack. Obviously, you can't play this trick with every kind of expression, but if you can save an extra assignment, this is the best solution.

Numbers at Random

The expression "random number" is popular but imprecise. There is no such thing as a random number; there are only numbers taken from random sequences. The value 1024 is random only if it is statistically unpredictable from previous values in the sequence to which 1024 belongs. Obviously, 1024 is not at random if taken from the sequence:

$$1, 2, \ldots, 1023, 1024, 1025, \ldots, n$$

There are two methods for producing numbers at random in Turbo Pascal. Used with no parameters, function **Random** returns a real number in the range:

$$0.0 < = \text{Random} < 1.0$$

With an integer parameter, **Random** returns a positive integer in the range:

$$0 < = \text{Random(m)} < = m$$

In other words, **Random(m)** produces a random integer modulo **m**, equal to the remainder following a division by **m**, which must be an **Integer** value.

One property of a random sequence is a statistically even distribution. In other words, any value from a random sequence should be as likely to occur as any other. But how can you test that assumption? It is not adequate to simply count the occurrences of various randomly selected values. With that as the only test of randomness, the following sequence proves perfectly random:

$$1,1,1,2,2,2,3,3,3,4,4,4,5,5,5$$

Each value in this sequence occurs as often as any other, but the sequence is obviously not random! A better test simulates the action of a *known* series of random events and then uses statistical methods to verify the randomness of the **Random** function.

Rolling the Dice

Program 12-11 simulates dice rolls as a "benchmark" test of Turbo Pascal's random number generator. (A benchmark is a program that tests the performance of a computer or language.)

Line 67 calls **Randomize** to begin a new random sequence. **Randomize** seeds the random number generator, ensuring that new program runs use different random sequences. A seed is a starting value, or a value that produces a new starting value, also taken at random.

Assuming a pair of six-sided dice is on the up and up, it's easy to calculate the probability of all possible dice-roll combinations. For example, there are three ways to make four: $3 + 1$, $2 + 2$, and $1 + 3$. Because there are 36 ($6*6$) different pairings of two six-sided die, the probability of rolling four is 3/36, or 1/12.

Program 12-11 similarly calculates probabilities for dice-roll values 2 to 12, assigning the results to real-number array **p** (lines 61–66). Another array, **Count**, remembers the number of times the program rolls each value. The program compares these counts to the known probabilities. The random number generator is working if the results are more or less equal to expectations.

Line 19 simulates a dice roll. The statement **Succ(Random(6))** produces a number at random in the range one to six, simulating the roll of one die. The program adds the results of two such values to simulate the roll of a pair of dice. It would not be correct to simulate dice rolls with the expression **2 + Random(11)** although this also produces values from 2 to 12. Because a single value at random equalizes the probability of all rolls, this would destroy the test, to say nothing of the house percentage.

Program 12-11

```
 1:  PROGRAM Dice;
 2:  CONST
 3:      Min = 2;                { lowest category }
 4:      Max = 12;               { highest category }
 5:  TYPE
 6:      RealArray = ARRAY[ Min .. Max ] OF Real;
 7:  VAR
 8:      n       : LongInt;      { number of throws }
 9:      Count : RealArray;      { result counts }
10:      p       : RealArray;    { probabilities }
11:
12:  PROCEDURE ThrowDice( n : LongInt );
13:  VAR
14:      k : Min .. Max;         { holds value of one throw }
15:      i : LongInt;
16:  BEGIN
17:      FOR i := 1 TO n DO
18:      BEGIN
19:          k := Succ( Random(6) ) + Succ( Random(6) );
20:          Count[ k ] := Count[ k ] + 1.0;
21:      END { for }
22:  END; { ThrowDice }
23:
24:  FUNCTION ChiSquare( n : Real ) : Real;
25:  VAR
26:      v : Real;
27:      i : Integer;
28:  BEGIN
29:      v := 0;
```

Program 12-11 *cont.*

```
30:    FOR i := Min TO Max DO
31:       v := v + ( ( Sqr( Count[i] ) ) ) / p[i] );
32:    ChiSquare := ( ( 1.0 / n ) * v ) - n
33: END; { ChiSquare }
34:
35: PROCEDURE PrintResults( n : Real );
36: VAR
37:    i : Integer;
38: BEGIN
39:    Writeln;
40:    Writeln( 'Dice      Proba-   Expected   Actual ' );
41:    Writeln( 'Value     bility   Count      Count  ' );
42:    Writeln( '========================================' );
43:    FOR i := Min TO Max DO
44:       Writeln( i : 5,             ' ':4,        { dice value }
45:                 p[i] : 1 : 3,     ' ':5,        { probability }
46:                 p[i] * n : 8 : 0, ' ':4,        { expected count }
47:                 Count[i] : 8 : 0            );  { actual count }
48:    Writeln;
49:    Writeln( 'Chi Square result = ', ChiSquare( n ):0:3 )
50: END; { PrintResults }
51:
52: PROCEDURE initialize( VAR n : LongInt );
53: VAR
54:    i : Integer;
55: BEGIN
56:    Writeln( 'Dice - A random number benchmark' );
57:    Writeln;
58:    Write( 'How many throws? ' );
59:    Readln( n );
60:    FOR i := Min TO Max DO Count[i] := 0.0;
61:    p[ 2] := 1.0/36;   p[ 3] := 1.0/18;
62:    p[ 4] := 1.0/12;   p[ 5] := 1.0/9;
63:    p[ 6] := 5.0/36;   p[ 7] := 1.0/6;
64:    p[ 8] := 5.0/36;   p[ 9] := 1.0/9;
65:    p[10] := 1.0/12;   p[11] := 1.0/18;
66:    p[12] := 1.0/36;
67:    Randomize
68: END; { initialize }
69:
70: BEGIN
71:    initialize( n );
72:    IF n > 0.0 THEN
73:    BEGIN
74:       ThrowDice( n );
```

Program 12-11 *cont.*

```
75:        PrintResults( n )
76:     END { if }
77:  END.
```

The program prints a chart of the results of however many rolls you request. The more rolls the better, with 10,000 or more a minimum for accurate results. The chart shows the probability, expected count, and actual count received for each possible value, 2 to 12. Figure 12-4 lists an example chart for 50,000 rolls.

```
Dice - A random number benchmark

How many throws?  50000
```

Dice Value	Proba- bility	Expected Count	Actual Count
2	0.028	1389	1387
3	0.056	2778	2848
4	0.083	4167	4087
5	0.111	5556	5467
6	0.139	6944	6896
7	0.167	8333	8379
8	0.139	6944	7070
9	0.111	5556	5539
10	0.083	4167	4136
11	0.056	2778	2800
12	0.028	1389	1391

```
Chi Square result = 8.027
```

Figure 12-4 Example output of Program 12-11.

When you examine the chart in Figure 12-4 or from running Program 12-11, the distribution (*Actual Count*) should closely match the anticipated results (*Expected Count*). This, however, does not complete the test. To verify randomness, the program also compares the counts received against the expected probabilities using a statistical method called the Chi Square, written X^2. Function **ChiSquare** evaluates the formula:

$$V = \frac{1}{n} \sum_{1 \le i \le K} \left(\frac{o_i^2}{p_i} \right) - n$$

In the formula, o is the observed result, and p is the probability over the range 1 to n. Compare the result of the formula to a Chi Square distribution table, found in most elementary statistics books. (Table 12-7 shows a portion of a typical Chi Square table.) Table rows represent *degrees of freedom*, equal to one less than the number of categories in the original data. In the case of dice, there are 11 categories for the values 2 to 12. One less than that is 10, the row in which to look.

From Table 12-7, you expect the Chi Square result of Program 12-11 to fall in the range between 6.737 and 12.55 about 50% of the time. (See bottom of Figure 12-4.) A value greater than or equal to 23.21 should occur no more often than 1% of the time. To interpret the Chi Square result accurately, then, run Program 12-11 several times, at least three. A single bad result has a low statistical probability but does not necessarily indicate a faulty random number generator.

Table 12-7 Chi Square distribution (sample)

v	99%	95%	75%	50%	25%	05%	01%
9	2.088	3.325	5.899	8.343	11.39	16.92	21.67
10	2.558	3.940	6.737	9.342	12.55	18.31	23.21
11	3.053	4.575	7.584	10.34	13.70	19.68	24.73

Restarting Random Sequences

When you call **Randomize** to begin a new random sequence, Turbo Pascal scrambles a **LongInt** variable, **RandSeed**, in the **System** unit. This causes new random sequences to begin at random, generating different values for each program run.

To repeat the same random sequence, assign a starting value to **RandSeed**. For example, you might use these statements to display ten values at random:

```
RandSeed := 100;
FOR i := 1 TO 10 DO
   Writeln( Random(MaxInt) );
```

Because of the assignment to **RandSeed**, the **FOR** loop displays the same ten-number random sequence every time the program runs. Each different value you assign to **RandSeed** starts a different random sequence.

Repeating random sequences this way can be helpful during debugging. For example, a flight simulator is, of course, supposed to behave randomly. Controlled by random sequences, the simulated winds shift, causing changes in direction and altitude, and it wouldn't do to have the winds shift in exactly the same way during every flight!

But testing such randomly acting programs can be difficult. To repeat identical conditions, perhaps as a test of a hard-to-find bug, you could assign the same value to **RandSeed**—shifting the winds in a sort of instant replay fashion—and then later take out the assignment when you compile the final program.

Random numbers, and tests of randomness, are subjects that could fill books. It is time to move on before they fill this one!

Summary

Turbo Pascal has many built-in functions and procedures for converting and for manipulating numbers in various ways. Two functions, **Val** and **Str**, convert numbers and strings for error-free input. Other functions convert and process numbers in a variety of ways.

Real-number values measure things. Integer values count things.

Real-number calculations suffer from round-off errors, which can be minimized by careful programming. A math coprocessor gives several real number types that can help avoid round-off error by increasing the number of significant digits values can represent.

The 6-byte **Real** data type is always available, but offers only a limited range of values and suffers from round-off error in all but the simplest calculations. For better results, use the **Double, Extended**, and **Comp** types. To use these types with Turbo Pascal 5.0 and later versions, programs compiled with the directives {$N+,E-} require a math coprocessor. Use the directives {$N+,E+} to select a coprocessor automatically or to use emulation routines. Instead of using these directives, you can also enable a coprocessor or emulation by changing the integrated compiler's *Numeric processing* and *Emulation* settings in the *Options-Compiler* menu. Turbo Pascal 4.0 does not have math coprocessor emulation abilities.

For large dollar and cents values, use either the **LongInt** or **Comp** data types. **Comp** requires a math coprocessor.

Turbo Pascal produces random number sequences of real numbers or integers. With random sequences, simulations of real events, such as the rolling of dice, are easy to program.

Exercises

12-1. The formula to find the hypotenuse of a right triangle is:

$$\sqrt{a^2 + b^2}$$

Write the formula into a program. It should handle input errors in a friendly way.

12-2. Write a simple program to simulate a hand-held calculator. Add programmer's utilities to convert numbers to hexadecimal and binary and to do logical operations such as shifting left (**Shl**) and right (**Shr**).

12-3. Using random sequences, write a game to simulate a one-armed bandit slot machine. Keep track of the player's winnings.

12-4. As mentioned in the text, one of the many tests of randomness is to record the frequency of values in a range. Over many repetitions, all frequencies should be more or less the same. Write a program to test this assumption against the output of Turbo Pascal's **Random** function.

12-5. A popular radix in programming is *octal*, which has the eight digits 0 to 7. Write a program to convert hexadecimal, octal, and decimal values. (Hint: Each octal digit directly represents three binary digits. See the two left columns of Table 12-3.)

12-6. Write a procedure to set and reset specific bits in a **Word** variable. Use logical operators in your solution.

13

Advanced Techniques

- Conditional Compilation
- Typecasting
- Mem, MemW, and MemL
- Port and PortW
- Writing Large Programs
- Compiling Large Programs
- Untyped Parameters
- Filling Memory
- Memory Moves
- Text File Device Drivers
- Increasing Text-File Buffer Size
- Free Declaration Ordering
- Structured Variable Constants
- Special Directory Commands
- Custom Exit Procedures
- Procedure Types
- Dealing With Heap Errors
- Dealing With the Stack
- Other Memory Concerns
- Passing Command-Line Parameters
- Inside a File Variable
- Advanced Overlay Management

13

Key Words and Identifiers

Absolute, ChDir, DosExitCode, Exec, FillChar, Halt, Mem, MemL, MemW, MkDir, Move, OvrClearBuf, OvrFileMode, OvrGetRetry, OvrLoadCount, OvrReadBuf, OvrReadFunc, OvrSetRetry, OvrTrapCount, ParamCount, ParamStr, Port, PortW, PROCEDURE, FUNCTION, RmDir, SetTextBuf, SwapVectors

This chapter collects various tips, tricks, and tidbits that make Turbo Pascal special. In here you'll learn about conditional compilation, typecasting, special variables, text file device drivers, and designing custom exit procedures—plus several other juicy items.

Conditional Compilation

With a special set of compiler directives, you can write programs that compile differently based on one condition or another. This technique, called *conditional compilation*, is useful for debugging and for designing software that's easy to customize.

The process is simple. First you define various symbols, similar to other Pascal identifiers. (See Figure 1-2.) Then, you tell Turbo Pascal to compile either one section or another based on whether certain symbols are defined. Defining different symbols changes which sections of code are compiled.

The commands, in the form of compiler directives, form a kind of minilanguage inside Pascal. Always keep in mind, though, that conditional compilation commands are not Pascal statements. Like other compiler directives, these commands are merely instructions that change how the compiler operates. Table 13-1 lists the compiler directives of this minilanguage within a language.

Table 13-1 Conditional compilation directives

Directive	Description
{$DEFINE id}	Define symbol (id)
{$UNDEF id}	Undefine symbol (id)
{$IFDEF id}	Continue normally if (id) is defined
{$IFNDEF id}	Continue normally if (id) is not defined
{$IFOPT id}	Continue normally depending on switch (id)
{$ELSE}	Compile next section if preceding IF . . . fails
{$ENDIF}	Mark end of IF and optional ELSE section

In Table 13-1, *id* represents a conditional symbol. You can invent your own symbols or use one of several that are predefined. For example, this defines a symbol named Debugging:

```
{$DEFINE Debugging}
```

Having defined a symbol, you can use the directives IFDEF (if defined) and IFNDEF (if not defined) to test whether certain symbols exist. To compile two **Writeln** statements for a test of two program variables, you could write:

```
{$IFDEF Debugging}
    Writeln( 'Debugging' );
    Writeln( 'i=', i, ' j=', j );
{$ENDIF}
```

This is not the same as a Pascal **IF** statement. The two **Writeln** statements are compiled only if you have previously defined the Debugging symbol. If you have not used the {**$DEFINE Debugging**} command, the two **Writeln** statements *are completely ignored*. A typical program might contain hundreds of such debugging statements. After testing the program, change the DEFINE to UNDEF:

```
{$UNDEF Debugging}
```

Undefining the Debugging symbol is the same as never defining it in the first place. Now, the two **Writeln** statements, although still in the source code text, are not compiled. You could, of course, delete the debugging statements, but, then, you'd have to retype them if a later problem develops and you want to continue debugging. With conditional compilation, you simply define the Debugging symbol and recompile.

Be sure to understand that conditional compilation symbols like Debugging are not variables or constants. Symbols have no values. They are not true or false; they simply exist or don't exist. The conditional command {$IFDEF Debugging} does not test whether Debugging is true or false, but only whether you have previously defined the Debugging symbol.

In place of IFDEF, which tests if a symbol is defined, you can use IFNDEF, which tests if a symbol is not defined. You could use this idea to display a message identifying the program as the real McCoy or the debugging version:

```
{$IFNDEF Debugging}
    Writeln( 'Production version 1.00' );
{$ELSE}
    Writeln( 'Debugging version 1.00' );
{$ENDIF}
```

Notice that the {$ELSE} directive identifies an alternate **Writeln** statement. Only one **Writeln** is compiled depending on whether the program previously defines Debugging. The {$ENDIF} follows the optional {$ELSE} section.

Testing Options

As you know, Turbo Pascal has various options that you can select. For example, you can turn on numeric coprocessor data types with {$N+} or turn them off with {$N–}. Likewise, {$R+} and {$R–} turn range checking on and off.

Use the {$IFOPT id} conditional compilation directive to test the state of any option and, if the option has the value you specify, to compile the text that follows until reaching the next {$ELSE} or {$ENDIF}. For example, to compile a program with a variable **distance** of type **Real** on plain systems but of type **Extended** on systems with math coprocessors, you could write the **VAR** section like this:

```
VAR
    {$IFOPT N+}
        distance : Extended;
    {$ELSE}
        distance : Real;
    {$ENDIF}
```

With this declaration, changing {$N+} to {$N–}, or changing the Options:Compiler:Numeric-processing setting to Software, is all you have to do to compile the program on systems without coprocessors. The conditional compilation commands alter the source code for you automatically selecting the **Extended** or **Real** types.

Predefined Symbols

In addition to defining your own symbols, you can test whether certain built-in symbols exist. Table 13-2 lists Turbo Pascal's predefined conditional symbols.

Use the VERn symbol to design programs to compile under different Turbo

Pascal versions where *n* is 40 for version 4.0, 41 for version 4.1, 50 for version 5.0, and so on. Suppose that only version 3.9 (there is no such release number) supports a data type called **Quark**. Other versions require you to use **Real** instead. To design the program to compile correctly under both versions, you could write:

```
VAR
   {$IFDEF VER39}
      BlackHole : Quark;
   {$ELSE}
      BlackHole : Real;
   {ENDIF}
```

I suppose physicists will wince at my choice of terms, but you get the idea. The MSDOS and CPU86 predefined symbols in Table 13-2 may be valuable in the future if compatible Turbo Pascal versions become available on a variety of systems. Presumably, this is the reason for these symbols, which are of little use today.

The final symbol in Table 13-2, CPU87, is defined only if the computer has an '87-family math coprocessor chip. Remember that the conditional check for a coprocessor occurs at compile time—not when the program runs. Program 13-1 demonstrates how to use CPU87 along with IFOPT to write programs to use a coprocessor data type automatically if a math chip is available.

Table 13-2 Predefined conditional symbols

Symbol	Meaning if defined
VER40	Turbo Pascal version 4.0
VER50	Turbo Pascal version 5.0
VER55	Turbo Pascal version 5.5
VERn	Turbo Pascal version n
MSDOS	This computer supports MS-DOS or PC-DOS
CPU86	This computer has an '86-family processor
CPU87	This computer has a math coprocessor

The conditional directives in lines 1–5 test if the compiler is Turbo Pascal version 4.0, which does not have math-coprocessor emulation. If so, and if CPU87 tests positive in line 2, the directive {$N+} enables extended real-number data types; otherwise, {$N−} disables them. Lines 3–5 handle Turbo Pascal versions 5.0 and higher; in which cases, {$N+,E+} automatically detects and uses a coprocessor if present, or enables emulation routines if not. Notice that you can string directives together, as in line 2, or insert them separately, as in lines 1 and 3–5.

Lines 11–15 use IFOPT, ELSE, and ENDIF to define the variable constant **SpeedOfLight** as type **Double** if {$N +} is in effect, or **Real** if not (version 4.0 only). A similar technique in lines 23–27 defines two variables, **Miles** and

Seconds. Depending on the version and setting of the N +/− compiler option, lines 30–38 display one of the messages:

```
Coprocessor installed
Coprocessor not installed
Coprocessor or emulator installed
```

Remember that all these decisions are made at compile time, *not* at runtime. Conditional compilation directives generate no code—they merely tell the compiler which sections to compile and which sections to skip.

Program 13-1

```
 1:   {$IFDEF VER40}
 2:       {$IFDEF CPU87} {$N+} {$ELSE} {$N-} {$ENDIF}
 3:   {$ELSE}
 4:       {$N+,E+}
 5:   {$ENDIF}
 6:
 7:   PROGRAM Light;
 8:
 9:   CONST
10:
11:   {$IFOPT N+}
12:       SpeedOfLight : Double = 186282.3976; { Miles per second }
13:   {$ELSE}
14:       SpeedOfLight : Real = 186282.3976;
15:   {$ENDIF}
16:
17:       PromptChar = ']';
18:       ProgramName = 'S p e e d   O f   L i g h t';
19:       PromptString = 'Enter number of miles';
20:
21:   VAR
22:
23:   {$IFOPT N+}
24:       Miles, Seconds : Double;
25:   {$ELSE}
26:       Miles, Seconds : Real;
27:   {$ENDIF}
28:
29:   BEGIN
30:       Writeln( ProgramName );
31:       Write( 'Coprocessor ' );
32:   {$IFNDEF VER40}
33:       Write( 'or emulator ' );
```

Program 13-1 *cont.*

```
34:   {$ENDIF}
35:   {$IFOPT N-}
36:      Write( 'not ' );
37:   {$ENDIF}
38:      Writeln( 'installed' );
39:      Writeln;
40:      Writeln( PromptString );
41:      Writeln;
42:      Write( PromptChar );
43:      Readln( Miles );
44:      Seconds := Miles / SpeedOfLight;
45:      Writeln( 'Light travels ', Miles, ' miles in ' );
46:      Write( Seconds, ' seconds, or ' );
47:      Writeln( Seconds/60.0, ' minutes.' )
48:   END.
```

Typecasting

In assignment statements, Turbo Pascal normally requires values, expressions, and variables on opposite sides of the assignment operator := to be of the same types. *Typecasting* is a technique for breaking this rule, which you should do only when absolutely necessary. Subverting Turbo Pascal's strong type-checking abilities is potentially dangerous.

There are two different kinds of typecasting: value and variable. A value typecast transforms the *value* of an expression from one type to another. A variable typecast tells the compiler to consider a *variable* to be of a different type than originally declared. The following value typecast converts the value 66 into a character B in a **Writeln** statement:

```
Writeln( 'The letter is ', Char(66) );
```

The data type identifier **Char** encloses the value in parentheses you want the compiler to recast as a different type, here the character B. Variable typecasts look similar, but operate differently. This converts an array of four bytes into a string of three characters:

```
TYPE
   Str3 = String[3];
VAR
   a : ARRAY[ 0 .. 3 ] OF Byte;

a[0]:=3;
a[1]:=Byte('A'); a[2]:=Byte('B'); a[3]:=Byte('C');
Writeln( Str3(a) );
```

The array and **Str3** data types each occupies four bytes. The assignment to **a[0]** tells how many characters follow. Because this is an array of **Byte** and not **Char**, three value-typecasts assign characters as ASCII values to index positions 1, 2, and 3. Finally, the **Writeln** statement displays this oddly constructed array recast as type **Str3**, overcoming the compiler's natural reluctance to allow byte arrays in **Writeln** statements. (Try compiling **Writeln(a)** to see the error message you receive.) The variable typecast in the **Writeln** statement bypasses the compiler's check for proper data types, requiring you to ensure that the array in this example contains the correct values.

Sometimes the difference between value and variable typecasts is unclear. Casting a simple **Byte** variable to type **LongInt**, for example, is a value typecast because **Byte** variables represent values. The same is true for all scalar variables and pointers. Typecasting these types of objects is always a value, not a variable, cast.

Though obscure, the difference can be important. Turbo Pascal allows value typecasts between objects of different sizes. For example, you can write:

```
VAR
    Short : ShortInt;
    Long : LongInt;

Short := -123;
Long := LongInt( Short );
```

This is a *value* typecast, even though the second assignment uses the *variable* **Short**. (This particular example is for demonstration only—you could more simply assign the **Short** variable directly to **Long**.) The *value* of **Short** is converted to a **LongInt** data type. Also, the sign of **Short** is extended to **Long**. In other words, after the typecast, **Long** has the same value as **Short**.

Contrast this with the variable array typecast demonstrated earlier. In that case, the array was interpreted as a different data type—no conversion was performed. This is an important and subtle difference to understand. In general:

- A value typecast converts the value of an expression or scalar variable to a different data type. In an assignment, the two types do not have to be the same size. Values are sign-extended, meaning that negative values come out negative; positive values, positive.

- A variable typecast interprets the bytes in a variable as a different data type. In an assignment, the two types must be exactly the same size.

Typecasting Versus Free Unions

Chapter 5 explains how to use a free union record to trick the compiler into treating a variable as two or more different data types. Instead of a free union, you can accomplish the same task with a variable typecast. For example, suppose you need to access the high and low 16-bit words in a 32-bit **LongInt** variable. You can't use the **Lo** and **Hi** functions—they return the low and high *bytes* of 16-bit quantities. Instead, a variable typecast extracts the individual bytes and words in a **LongInt** variable.

Program 13-2 demonstrates how to do this. The program typecasts a **LongInt** variable into two record types, **Words** (lines 3–5) with two word fields and **Bytes** (lines 6–8) with two byte fields. The **Writeln** statement displays the original value (**Long**), the low and high words in this value, and the four bytes in these two words. (You don't have to type the comment in line 14, which just makes typing the previous two lines easier.)

Notice the qualifiers—the periods and field names after the closing parentheses in the typecast—in lines 18–23. Only variable typecasts may have such qualifiers. A value typecast cannot have qualifiers. As you can see from this example, typecasting with record types is one way to accomplish a variable typecast (transforming one type to another) when using values.

Program 13-2

```
 1:  PROGRAM LongBytes;
 2:  TYPE
 3:     Words = RECORD
 4:                 LoWord, HiWord : Word
 5:             END;
 6:     Bytes = RECORD
 7:                 LoByte, HiByte : Byte
 8:             END;
 9:  VAR
10:     Long : LongInt;
11:  BEGIN
12:     Writeln( '                              LoWord          HiWord'  );
13:     Writeln( '  Value LoWord HiWord LoByte HiByte LoByte HiByte' );
14:          (* 12345678123456781234567812345678123456781234567812345678 *)
15:
16:     FOR Long := -10 TO 10 DO
17:       Writeln( Long : 8,
18:                Words( Long ).LoWord : 8,
19:                Words( Long ).HiWord : 8,
20:                Bytes( Words( Long ).LoWord ).LoByte : 8,
21:                Bytes( Words( Long ).LoWord ).HiByte : 8,
22:                Bytes( Words( Long ).HiWord ).LoByte : 8,
23:                Bytes( Words( Long ).HiWord ).HiByte : 8 )
24:  END.
```

Typecasting Pointers

Another use for typecasting is to convert pointers of one kind of data type into another. Suppose you have a pointer to type **String** but you want the compiler to treat the variable as a byte instead, perhaps to get to the length byte in the front of all string types. You have these declarations:

```
TYPE
   sPtr = ^String;
   bPtr = ^Byte;
VAR
   sp : sPtr;
   bp : bPtr;
```

You then create a string variable on the heap with **New** and assign a string to the variable:

```
New( sp );
sp^ := 'String em up';
```

The **New** statement creates a string variable on the heap. The second statement assigns a 12-character string to the variable. Because of Turbo Pascal's strong type-checking ability, you can't write:

```
bp := sp;   { Incorrect! }
Writeln( 'Length of string = ', bp^ );
```

Turbo Pascal does not allow you to assign one pointer to another of a different type. To get around the problem, and address the first byte of the string, use a typecast:

```
Writeln( 'Length of string = ', bPtr(sp)^ );
```

This recasts the string pointer **sp** as a **bPtr** type, displaying 14, the length of the string. (You no longer need variable **bp**.) The importance of this technique is that it doesn't generate any code. The typecast **bPtr(sp)** is *not* a function call, although it appears to be. It is just an instruction to the compiler to pretend for the moment that **sp** addresses a variable of type **bPtr**.

Mem, MemW, and MemL

Three arrays, **Mem**, **MemW**, and **MemL**, open all computer memory to your program. These special variables are predeclared—all you have to do is use them.

To access a single byte of memory, use **Mem**. For two-byte memory words, use **MemW**. To read and write memory as four-byte long integers, use **MemL**. In each case, you specify a memory address as an array index with a segment and an offset value. You can read or assign values to and from memory. For example, this statement reads the current timer value into **TimerCount**, a **Word** variable:

```
TimerCount := MemW[ 0000:$046C ];
```

If you know BASIC, you'll recognize this as equivalent to a PEEK command. To assign a value to memory, move the array to the left of the assignment symbol (in BASIC, similar to a POKE). The next example toggles the IBM PC print-screen key on and off. After executing the statement once, the SHIFT-PrtSc keys no longer print the screen contents. Execute the same statement again to turn the print screen feature back on:

```
Mem[ $0050:0 ] := Mem[ $0050:0 ] XOR 1;
```

Program 13-3 uses this idea to assign the 16-bit value, located at address 0000:$0410, to variable **EquipFlag** (line 16). The program uses **MemW** because the value is a two-byte word, containing information about devices attached to the computer. The program uses logical **AND**s and shifts to decipher the information and display a configuration list.

Of course, a program of this kind assumes that the value at 0000:$0410 has the needed information. Because there is no guarantee that all computers store the same information at the same place, Program 13-3 is an example of a "system-dependent" program—one that might not run on other systems. (The program should run on most PCs and compatibles, though.)

Program 13-3

```
 1:  PROGRAM Devices;
 2:  VAR
 3:      EquipFlag : Integer;
 4:
 5:  PROCEDURE ShowVid( n : Integer );
 6:  BEGIN
 7:      CASE n OF
 8:          1 : Writeln( '40×25 (Color)' );
 9:          2 : Writeln( '80×25 (Color)' );
10:          3 : Writeln( '80×25 (Monochrome)' );
11:          ELSE Writeln( '<not used>' )
12:      END { case }
13:  END; { ShowVid }
14:
15:  BEGIN
16:      EquipFlag := MemW[ 0000:$0410 ];
17:      Writeln;
18:      Writeln( 'IBM PC Devices' );
19:      Writeln;
20:      Writeln( 'Number of printers ......... ',
21:          EquipFlag SHR 14 );
22:      Writeln( 'Game I/O attached .......... ',
23:          ( EquipFlag AND $1000 )=1 );
24:      Writeln( 'Number of serial ports ..... ',
```

Program 13-3 *cont.*

```
25:       ( EquipFlag SHR 9 ) AND $07 );
26:    Writeln( 'Number of diskette drives .. ',
27:       ( ( EquipFlag AND 1 ) * ( 1 + ( EquipFlag SHR 6 ) AND $03 ) ) );
28:    Write(  'Initial video mode ......... ' );
29:       ShowVid( ( EquipFlag SHR 4 ) AND $03 );
30:    Writeln
31: END.
```

Port and PortW

Two other built-in arrays, **Port** and **PortW**, access the computer's input and output ports. A port is a special channel attached to the computer processor. Accessing a device through a data port is the most direct way to communicate with hardware peripherals. You can, for example, directly read and write data stored in the controlling circuits and chips for various devices such as the video display or serial communications line.

Use **Port** to access eight-bit data ports. Use **PortW** to access 16-bit ports. To read a port, place the array identifier on the right side of an assignment statement. To write to a port, place the array on the left. The following duplicates an assembly language IN instruction and assumes you have the monochrome video display and printer adapter in your IBM PC (variable **PrintStatus** is type **Byte**):

```
PrintStatus := Port[ $03BD ];
```

Try using the foregoing statement in a short program, then run it with your printer on and then off. Provided you have the correct hardware in your system, you should see different values from port address $3BD. Programs could decipher this information to determine the printer's status.

To write a value to a port, reverse the process. The following commands set and clear the nonmaskable interrupt:

```
Port[ $A0 ] := $80;   { Set }
Port[ $A0 ] := 0;     { Clear }
```

Be especially careful when experimenting with data ports. Although I chose these examples for their relative safety, some ports activate events when you *read* them, not only when you write to them. You can easily turn on disk drive motors, affect your video display, destroy data in disk sectors, and experience other nasty surprises if you fiddle indiscriminately with ports.

For experimenting with ports, one relatively safe device is the PC's timer, which has special data registers at ports $40, $42, and $43. An associated chip, an 8255A Programmable Peripheral Interface (PPI) at port address $61, connects the timer with the computer's speaker to make sounds.

Program 13-4 assigns initializing values to timer registers through the **Port** array (lines 16–18). It then turns on PPI output bit numbers 0 and 1 (line 20), sending the output of the timer to the speaker and making it beep. Because the PPI has other purposes, it's important to preserve all bits other than the ones that control the output of the timer to the speaker. The program does this by saving the original port value (line 19) and then restoring that value at line 22. This also turns off the speaker.

You can find more information about ports and the meaning of various port values in an IBM PC Technical Reference Manual.

Program 13-4

```
 1:   PROGRAM Beeper;
 2:   USES Crt;
 3:   CONST
 4:       PortB        = $61;    { 8255 address }
 5:       Timer        = $40;
 6:       TimerOut     = $42;
 7:       TimerControl = $43;
 8:   VAR
 9:       ch : Char;
10:       Pitch, Duration : Integer;
11:
12:   PROCEDURE Beep( Frequency, Milliseconds : Integer );
13:   VAR
14:       SavePortB : Byte;
15:   BEGIN
16:       Port[ TimerControl ] := $B6;                { Select timer mode }
17:       Port[ TimerOut     ] := lo( Frequency );    { Set frequency divisor }
18:       Port[ TimerOut     ] := hi( Frequency );
19:       SavePortB := Port[ PortB ];                 { Save old PortB setting }
20:       Port[ PortB ] := SavePortB OR $03;          { Turn on speaker }
21:       Delay( Milliseconds );                      { Wait }
22:       Port[ PortB ] := SavePortB                  { Turn off speaker }
23:   END; { Beep }
24:
25:   BEGIN
26:       Writeln( 'Beeper' );
27:       Pitch := $255; Duration := 75;  { Default values }
28:       REPEAT
29:           Writeln;
30:           Write( 'Pitch? '    ); Readln( Pitch );
31:           Write( 'Duration? ' ); Readln( Duration );
32:           Writeln;
33:           Writeln( '  Pitch    = ', Pitch );
34:           Writeln( '  Duration = ', Duration );
35:           Writeln;
```

Program 13-4 *cont.*

```
36:        Write(    '   Press any key to stop...' );
37:        WHILE NOT Keypressed DO
38:        BEGIN
39:           Beep( Pitch, Duration );
40:           Delay( 100 )
41:        END; { while }
42:        Write( Readkey );
43:        Writeln; Writeln;
44:        Write( 'Again? ' );
45:        ch := Readkey;
46:        Writeln( ch )
47:     UNTIL Upcase( ch ) <> 'Y'
48:  END.
```

Writing Large Programs

Finished programs, like those you might find on a computer store shelf, are often the compiled results of thousands, maybe even tens of thousands, of programming lines, or *source code*. With its top limit of 60,000 or so characters, how can the Turbo Pascal editor handle such large programs? There are several answers.

Compiling Large Programs

Turbo Pascal can compile huge programs with thousands of symbols. But, if your system has limited free memory, it's possible for the compiler to run out of room. When this happens, follow these hints to gain more space:

- Reboot without installing memory-resident utilities, keyboard enhancers, function-key macros, and so on.

- Use the command-line TPC.EXE compiler instead of the integrated TURBO.EXE. All the memory that the Turbo Pascal editor and debugger use is then available for compiling.

- Change the integrated compiler's *Options-Linker-Link buffer* setting from "Memory" to "Disk," or use the /L option with the command-line compiler. This lengthens compilation time but frees up memory normally used by the compiler during linking—in other words, when references to various symbols are *resolved* into actual addresses.

- Use units to "hide" information in unit implementation sections. Organizing your program into units, and placing only the absolute minimum number of symbols in the unit interface sections, reduces the total number of symbols the compiler stores in memory.

- Run the TPUMOVER utility and remove one or more units from TURBO.TPL. Keep only the most frequently used units in TURBO.TPL.

The Turbo Pascal User's Guide lists a few other memory-saving tips, but the hints listed here give the best results.

Of course, you can also purchase more memory. Turbo Pascal automatically detects and uses 64K of expanded (EMS) memory for editing. If you have other programs that use EMS RAM, check if there's a way to reserve 64K for Turbo Pascal.

Include Files

One way to handle large programs is to divide them into editable pieces, storing program text in *include* files. An include file is just a separate disk text file that the compiler includes at some moment during compilation of another text. For example, the following line tells the compiler to include file LIBRARY.PAS, presumably a collection of procedures and functions that the program uses:

```
{$I LIBRARY.PAS}
```

Don't confuse this directive with {$I+} and {$I-}, which turn I/O error checking on and off. With a space after the **I**, the compiler expects to find a file name. You can also use the alternate comment brackets (* and *) like this:

```
(*$I LIBRARY.PAS*)
```

When the compiler comes to an include directive, it reads the include file as though the text is part of the original source code. Include files themselves may include other files, up to about eight levels deep, although simple tests indicate you can nest beyond this stated maximum. (Don't be too concerned with the actual limit—nesting include files more than a few levels deep is rarely necessary.) The only restriction is that an include directive may not appear between **BEGIN** and **END**. You can't include parts of procedures, for example.

When the compiler exhausts the included text, it continues where it left off in the source. Of course, the included file must be on disk when you compile the parent file. If not, you receive:

```
Error 15: File not found
```

If you don't use a file name extension, Turbo Pascal automatically adds .PAS to a file name. This directive also includes LIBRARY.PAS:

```
{$I LIBRARY}
```

Using the Dos Unit Exec Procedure

Another way to segment large programs is to divide them into modules—independently running subprograms—and then write a controller to call each module

---

413

in turn. The controller might be a main menu from which you select major program operations. Each operation is a separate module, which you design, compile, and test separately.

The **Dos** unit contains a procedure, **Exec**, that lets you run other programs or, to use the operating system term, *processes*. When a process ends, control returns to the calling program. **Exec** takes two string parameters:

```
Exec( path, cmdLine : String );
```

The **path** string is the name of the EXE or COM program you want to run. This can be a compiled Turbo Pascal program or any other program you normally run from the DOS command line. The **path** may include drive and subdirectory names as in C:\UTIL\FORMAT.

The **cmdLine** string holds any information you need to pass to a program. For example, if you have a program named SORT.EXE (not shown here) that takes input and output file names, then to sort NAMES.TXT to NAMES.SRT, you might use **Exec** like this:

```
Exec( 'SORT', 'NAMES.TXT NAMES.SRT' );
```

Programs 13-5, 13-6, and 13-7 show how to use **Exec** to design a multimodule program. To compile the complete program, save Program 13-5 as MENU.PAS and compile to MENU.EXE. Save Program 13-6 as SUB1.PAS and compile to SUB1.EXE. Finally, save Program 13-7 as SUB2.PAS and compile to SUB2.EXE. Quit Turbo Pascal and, with the three .EXE files on disk, type Menu to run the program. Press key 1 to select subprogram 1. Press key 2 to select subprogram 2. Press key 3 to quit.

Line 1 in each program uses a special compiler directive to restrict memory use. This directive takes the form:

```
{$M stacksize, heapmin, heapmax}
```

The *stacksize* is the number of bytes, ranging from a low of 1024 to a high of 65,520. Values *heapmin* and *heapmax* control the minimum and maximum heap (free memory) size available to variables created by **New** and **GetMem**. These two values must be in the range of 0 to 655,360.

You must restrict the stack and heap size when running programs that call **Exec** because Turbo Pascal and DOS normally reserve all available memory for programs. Therefore, unless you change your main program's memory requirements, there won't be any room left to run subprograms.

If your program does not use **New** or **GetMem**, set *heapmin* and *heapmax* to zero. Setting the *stacksize* limit correctly is tricky. Every program has different stack requirements, depending largely on how many procedures call others (in other words, the overall nesting level of all procedures and functions), plus the numbers and types of parameters passed to routines. In general, though, a stack size of about 8K should be adequate for most small to medium-sized programs. The default stack is 16K. A 32K stack is huge.

Lines 36–37 of Program 13-5 call **Exec**, passing the name of the subprogram to run. The first such call passes no parameters. The second passes two parameters. Notice that the two parameters are written as a *single* string (line 37).

Program 13-5

```
 1:  {$M 4000, 0, 0 }       { 4K stack, no heap minimum or maximum }
 2:
 3:  PROGRAM Menu;           { Compile to MENU.EXE }
 4:
 5:  USES Crt, Dos;
 6:
 7:  CONST
 8:      TheCowsComeHome = False;
 9:  VAR
10:      Choice : Char;
11:
12:  PROCEDURE Center( row : Integer; s : String );
13:  { Center string s at this display row }
14:  BEGIN
15:      GotoXY( 40 - ( Length(s) DIV 2 ), row );
16:      Write( s )
17:  END; { Center }
18:
19:  PROCEDURE DisplayMenu;
20:  BEGIN
21:      ClrScr;
22:      Center(  8, '    Main Menu' );
23:      Center(  9, '------------------' );
24:      Center( 10, '1 = Sub program 1' );
25:      Center( 11, '2 = Sub program 2' );
26:      Center( 12, '3 = Quit         ' );
27:      Center( 16, 'Which? ' );
28:  END; { DisplayMenu }
29:
30:  BEGIN
31:      DisplayMenu;
32:      REPEAT
33:          Choice := Readkey;
34:          Writeln( Choice );
35:          CASE Choice OF
36:              '1' : Exec( 'SUB1.EXE', '' );
37:              '2' : Exec( 'SUB2.EXE', 'Param1 Param2' );
38:              '3' : Halt
39:          END; { case }
40:          IF Choice IN [ '1', '2' ]
```

Program 13-5 *cont.*

```
41:           THEN DisplayMenu { on return from sub process }
42:    UNTIL TheCowsComeHome
43: END.
```

Program 13-6

```
1:  {$M 2000, 0, 0 }
2:
3:  PROGRAM Sub1;
4:  { Compile to SUB1.EXE }
5:
6:  USES Crt;
7:
8:  BEGIN
9:     ClrScr;
10:    Writeln( 'Here we are in SUB1.EXE!' );
11:    Writeln;
12:    Write( 'Press <Enter> to return to menu...' );
13:    Readln
14: END.
```

Program 13-7

```
1:  {$M 2000, 0, 0 }
2:
3:  PROGRAM Sub2;
4:  { Compile to SUB2.EXE }
5:
6:  USES Crt;
7:
8:  VAR i : Integer;
9:
10: BEGIN
11:    ClrScr;
12:    Writeln( 'Here we are in SUB2.EXE!' );
13:    Writeln;
14:    Writeln( 'Number of params = ', ParamCount );
15:    FOR i := 1 TO ParamCount DO
16:       Writeln( i:2, ' : ', ParamStr(i) );
17:    Writeln;
18:    Write( 'Press <Enter> to return to menu...' );
19:    Readln
20: END.
```

Exec Return Codes

Often, a subprogram needs to pass a return code back to its caller. Usually, the value indicates whether an error occurred. The usual way to do this is through the **Halt** procedure with an optional parameter. For example, instead of simply ending subprogram 1 (Program 13-6), insert this statement between lines 13 and 14:

```
Halt( 1 );
```

The main program can inspect the value passed to **Halt** by calling function **DosExitCode** in the **Dos** unit. The result of this function is a **Word** and, therefore, cannot be negative. Usually, zero means no error, although interpreting the code is up to you. To examine the return code, you might replace line 36 in Program 13-5 with:

```
'1' : BEGIN
        Exec( 'SUB1.EXE', '' );
        IF DosExitCode <> 0 THEN
        BEGIN
           GotoXY( 1, 24 ); Writeln;
           Writeln( 'Error # ', DosExitCode );
           Readln
        END
      END;
```

Unlike the **IoResult** function, you may use **DosExitCode** more than once to receive the value passed to **Halt** by a subprogram.

Executing DOS Commands

You can also use **Exec** to issue DOS commands like DIR, COPY, and FORMAT. To do this requires starting a temporary copy of COMMAND.COM, the program that displays the DOS prompt (C:>) and executes commands. The parameter string passed to **Exec** is the DOS command you want COMMAND.COM to execute. Because you don't want this second copy of COMMAND.COM to install itself in memory, you must also pass option /C, telling DOS that this is not the primary command processor.

To execute simple commands, make sure your program **USES Dos**; and includes a directive such as {$M 8192, 1024, 1024} before the **PROGRAM** header, setting the stack and heap memory sizes. Then, insert single **Exec** statements such as:

```
Exec( '\COMMAND.COM', '/C DIR' );
```

to start COMMAND.COM and execute a DIR command. When the command ends, the statement following **Exec** runs. If your program clears or writes to the display, you may want to follow **Exec** with a pause:

```
Writeln;
Write( 'Press Enter to continue...' );
Readln;
```

People often move COMMAND.COM to another location, usually to a RAM drive for extra speed. Deal with this by inspecting the COMSPEC environment variable for COMMAND.COM's current location. Assuming that variable **comspec** is a **String**, the previous command expands to:

```
comspec := GetEnv( 'COMSPEC' );
IF Length( comspec ) = 0
   THEN comspec := '\COMMAND.COM';
Exec( comspec, '/C DIR' );
```

Testing whether **GetEnv** returns a null string (indicating that COMSPEC is not defined) is probably unnecessary—COMSPEC is *always* defined. (See Chapter 9 for more information about **GetEnv** and environment variables.) If you are more trusting than I am, you can probably just write:

```
Exec( GetEnv( 'COMSPEC' ), '/C DIR' );
```

Vector Swapping

A subtle problem can develop when using **Exec**. Because Turbo Pascal installs several low-level routines to handle disk errors, to check for Ctrl-Break keypresses, and to handle other critical conditions, if such events happen when a subprogram is running, then the parent program's error handlers receive the calls.

If this is not what you want, you must restore the original error handlers before calling **Exec**. Then, after **Exec**, you must replace Turbo Pascal's handlers. To do this, call the **Dos** unit **SwapVectors** routine before and after **Exec**. This swaps Turbo Pascal's vectors (copied by the **System** unit when the program starts) with those stored in system memory at RAM addresses starting with 0000:0000.

Program 13-8 demonstrates how to use **SwapVectors** and **Exec** to return temporarily to DOS—similar to using the integrated environment's *File-OS shell* command. Lines 16–18 surround **Exec** with calls to **SwapVectors**, thus restoring and then resetting interrupt vectors. Line 19 tests **DosError** in case the attempt to run COMMAND.COM fails—usually due to a lack of memory. Notice that line 17 passes no parameters to COMMAND.COM. Because of this, you must type "EXIT" and press Enter to return to the program.

Program 13-8

```
1:  {$M 8096, 1024, 1024}
2:  PROGRAM ExitToDos;
3:  USES Crt, Dos;
4:  VAR
5:     choice : Integer;
```

Program 13-8 *cont.*

```
 6:
 7:    PROCEDURE RunDosCommands;
 8:    VAR comspec : String[80];
 9:    BEGIN
10:       Writeln;
11:       Writeln( 'Type EXIT to return to program' );
12:       Writeln;
13:       comspec := GetEnv( 'COMSPEC' );
14:       IF Length( comspec ) = 0
15:          THEN comspec := '\COMMAND.COM';
16:       SwapVectors;
17:       Exec( comspec, '' );
18:       SwapVectors;
19:       IF DosError <> 0 THEN
20:       BEGIN
21:          Writeln;
22:          Writeln( '*** Error: Can''t run COMMAND.COM' )
23:       END { if }
24:    END; { RunDosCommands }
25:
26:    PROCEDURE DoNothing;
27:    BEGIN
28:       Writeln;
29:       Writeln( 'Doing (almost) nothing' );
30:       Write( 'Press Enter...' );
31:       Readln
32:    END; { DoNothing }
33:
34:    BEGIN
35:       REPEAT
36:          ClrScr;
37:          Writeln( 'Test Menu' );
38:          Writeln( '---------' );
39:          Writeln( '1 - Do nothing' );
40:          Writeln( '2 - Run DOS commands' );
41:          Writeln( '3 - Quit' );
42:          Writeln;
43:          Write( 'Which? ' );
44:          Readln( choice );
45:          CASE choice OF
46:             1 : DoNothing;
47:             2 : RunDosCommands
48:          END { case }
49:       UNTIL choice = 3
50:    END.
```

Untyped Parameters

Procedures and functions may declare untyped variable parameters. Such parameters have identifiers but no colons and data types. For example, the following declares two untyped parameters, V1 and V2:

```
PROCEDURE Demo( VAR V1, V2 );
```

You can declare only variable untyped parameters. To say that another way, you must pass untyped parameters by reference, not by value. You can still mix typed and untyped parameters in the same declaration, though:

```
PROCEDURE Demo( VAR V1, V2; Count : Integer );
```

Declared this way, **Count** is an integer value parameter of the normal variety, but **V1** and **V2** can represent any kinds of variables. To these two untyped parameters, you can pass strings, arrays, records, or variables of any other data type. The procedure itself, though, must eventually define what **V1** and **V2** are. Let's say you want to treat **V1** and **V2** as arrays of characters. To do this, **Demo** makes the following declarations:

```
TYPE
    ChArray = Array[ 1 .. 1 ] OF Char;
VAR
    Ch1 : ChArray Absolute V1;
    Ch2 : ChArray Absolute V2;
```

After declaring data type **ChArray**, two local variables **Ch1** and **Ch2** are given the same address as the parameters **V1** and **V2**, using the **Absolute** identifier. Any variable passed to **Demo** appears inside the procedure as an array of characters, regardless of its original data type.

To demonstrate the usefulness of untyped parameters, Program 13-9 includes a procedure to erase a variable of any data type. You can use **ZeroVar** (line 8) to clear arrays, strings, real numbers, buffers—or any other type. (Using **ZeroVar** on files is allowed but not recommended.)

The test program asks for four values: a character, an integer, a real number, and a string. The procedure at lines 19–26 displays your entry values before and after passing each variable to **ZeroVar**. Notice how function **Sizeof** determines the correct number of bytes for **ZeroVar** to clear (lines 36–39).

Program 13-9

```
1:  PROGRAM UnTypedParameters;
2:  VAR
3:      ch : Char;
4:      s : String[80];
5:      i : Integer;
```

```
 6:        r : Real;
 7:
 8:    PROCEDURE ZeroVar( VAR V; Count : Integer );
 9:    TYPE
10:        Vtype = ARRAY[ 1 .. MaxInt ] OF Byte;
11:    VAR
12:        A : Vtype Absolute V;
13:        i : Integer;
14:    BEGIN
15:        FOR i := 1 TO Count DO
16:            A[i] := 0
17:    END;
18:
19:    PROCEDURE Display;
20:    BEGIN
21:        Writeln;
22:        Writeln( 'ch = ', ch, ' (ASCII ', Ord(ch), ')' );
23:        Writeln( ' i = ', i );
24:        Writeln( ' r = ', r );
25:        Writeln( ' s = ', s, ' (LENGTH ', Length(s), ')' )
26:    END;
27:
28:    BEGIN
29:        Write( 'Enter a character ..... ' ); Readln( ch );
30:        Write( 'Enter an integer ...... ' ); Readln( i );
31:        Write( 'Enter a real number ... ' ); Readln( r );
32:        Write( 'Enter a string ........ ' ); Readln( s );
33:        Writeln;
34:        Writeln( 'Before zeroing:' );
35:        Display;
36:        ZeroVar( ch, Sizeof(ch) );
37:        ZeroVar( i, Sizeof(i) );
38:        ZeroVar( r, Sizeof(r) );
39:        ZeroVar( s, Sizeof(s) );
40:        Writeln;
41:        Writeln( 'After zeroing:' );
42:        Display
43:    END.
```

Filling Memory

As written in Program 13-9, **ZeroVar** (lines 8–17) resembles another built-in procedure, **FillChar**. Use **FillChar** as in the following statement, which inserts zero bytes at every position in string **s** (including the length byte at **s[0]**):

```
FillChar( s, Sizeof(s), 0 );
```

FillChar takes three parameters: the variable to fill, the variable's size in bytes, and the value or character to insert into the variable. You can also index array variables, filling at a starting point anywhere in the array. For example, this inserts five bytes equal to character A starting at index ten in array **a**:

```
FillChar( a[10], 5, 'A' );
```

Memory Moves

Another built-in procedure moves bytes from one place to another, generally faster than doing the same operation in a loop. If you have two string variables of the same type, **S1** and **S2**, this sets **S1** equal to **S2**:

```
Move( S2, S1, Sizeof(S2) );
```

Move takes three parameters: the source, the destination, and the number of bytes to transfer. In this example, function **Sizeof** tells **Move** to move all bytes in **S2** to **S1**. Of course, you can do the same thing with the simple assignment:

```
S1 := S2;
```

Move shines when moving many bytes in large arrays. Assume you have this array variable:

```
VAR
   BigArray : ARRAY[ 1 .. 10000 ] OF char;
```

To transfer 1000 characters from **BigArray[1]** to **BigArray[100]**—in other words, to move 1000 characters down 100 array positions—you could use the FOR loop:

```
FOR i := 1000 DOWNTO 1 DO
   BigArray[i+100] := BigArray[i];
```

Notice that you have to start at the end of the block of characters you want to move. **Move** does the same thing in one easy step:

```
Move( BigArray[1], BigArray[100], 1000 );
```

Using **Move** also avoids a problem with the **FOR** loop approach that may at first not be obvious. Consider this **FOR** loop:

```
FOR i := 1 TO 1000 DO
   BigArray[i+100] := BigArray[i];
```

The problem here is that the indexes overlap, assigning characters to positions that the **FOR** loop control variable hasn't come to yet. **Move** avoids the problem by always moving data in the correct direction to prevent overlapping when the source and destination variables are the same. For example, to move the same 1000 bytes back to index one, simply reverse the indexes:

```
Move( BigArray[100], BigArray[1], 1000 );
```

To do the same in a **FOR** loop, you have to be careful to index in the correct direction:

```
FOR i := 1 TO 1000 DO
   BigArray[i] := BigArray[i+100];
```

Text File Device Drivers

The **Dos** unit defines record **TextRec**, which you can use to attach custom routines for controlling devices. Suppose, for example, you attach a graphics plotter or a speech synthesizer to a computer port. Because Turbo Pascal has no native commands to control such devices, you can write your own controlling routines and attach them to Turbo Pascal. Together, the custom routines make up a *device driver*. By attaching a custom device driver to a program, you can use **Rewrite**, **Reset**, **Write**, **Read**, and other I/O routines to run your device.

Program 13-10 is a unit shell that you can use as a template for your own device driver designs. Line 13 lists the only public procedure in the unit, **AssignDev**, which you'll probably rename for different devices. The procedure is similar to **Assign** or to **AssignCrt** in the **Crt** unit. **AssignDev** prepares a text file (**f**) for an eventual **Reset** or **Rewrite**.

Don't try to use Program 13-10 as listed here. The procedures and functions are unfinished. Notice the {$F+} directive in line 19, which tells Turbo Pascal to compile procedures and functions as *far* routines. A *far* routine can be called from anywhere in memory, not only from the same code segment. A *near* routine must be called only from within its own code segment. Normally, Turbo Pascal compiles procedures and functions as *near* routines. Because system routines located in another segment call the device driver code, the functions must be *far*.

Function **DoNothing** (lines 22–28) simply returns 0, indicating no error. When you have a routine that has no meaning for a specific device, call **DoNothing**. The function also shows the correct form for all device driver routines. Device driver functions receive a single variable parameter **f** of **Dos** unit type **TextRec**, listed in Figure 13-1. You must supply routines for these four basic I/O functions:

1. *Open*—called by **Reset**, **Rewrite**, and **Append**.

2. *Input* and *Output*—called by **Read**, **Readln**, **Write**, **Writeln**, **Eof**, **Eoln**, **SeekEoln**, and **Close**.

3. *Flush*—Called by **Flush** and after **Read**, **Readln**, **Write**, and **Writeln**.

4. *Close*—called by **Close**.

```
TextBuf = array[0..127] of Char;
TextRec = record
            Handle: Word;
            Mode: Word;
            BufSize: Word;
            Private: Word;
            BufPos: Word;
            BufEnd: Word;
            BufPtr: ^TextBuf;
            OpenFunc: Pointer;
            InOutFunc: Pointer;
            FlushFunc: Pointer;
            CloseFunc: Pointer;
            UserData: array[1..16] of Byte;
            Name: array[0..79] of Char;
            Buffer: TextBuf;
          end;
```

Figure 13-1 The **Dos** unit **TextBuf** and **TextRec** data types, which you can use to write custom text file device drivers.

In each of these functions, you can examine the **TextRec.Mode** field to determine the correct action. **Mode** can be any of the values listed in Table 13-3.

Table 13-3 File mode constants

Constant	Value	Action
fmClosed	$D7B0	File is closed
fmInput	$D7B1	Insert input into Buffer
fmOutput	$D7B2	Process characters in Buffer
fmInOut	$D7B3	File is open for read/write

In Program 13-10, the **AssignDev** procedure (lines 81–97) prepares the text file (**f**), first filling it with zero bytes (line 87) and then initializing various fields in the record. The **WITH** statement (lines 89–97) uses a typecast to force Turbo Pascal to consider the **Text** data type as a **TextRec** record. Normally, the insides of **Text** are unavailable to programs. Using a typecast gives you access to the text file's variable normally invisible fields.

Line 95 assigns the address of the **DevOpen** function to field **OpenFunc**. The other **Pointer** fields (see Figure 13-1) may be ignored at this point. The **Handle** $FFFF is the normal value for an unopen file. If you plan to use DOS calls for I/O, you could store the file handle here later when you open the file. Set **Mode** to

fmClosed (line 92), marking the file unopened. Lines 93–94 prepare the address and size of the text file buffer, normally 128 bytes. You could use a longer or shorter buffer if you wish and assign its address to **BufPtr**.

The **fileName** string (see line 13) is ignored in this example. Line 96 sets the first byte of the **Name** character array to zero. If you need to keep track of file names, you can store them here, but you don't have to. In fact, you may as well remove the **fileName** parameter from **AssignDev** if you don't need it.

Program 13-10

```
1:  UNIT UDevice;
2:
3:  (*
4:   *      Device Driver Shell Unit
5:   *      IBM MS/PC-DOS, Turbo Pascal
6:   *)
7:
8:
9:  INTERFACE
10:
11: USES Dos;
12:
13: PROCEDURE AssignDev( VAR f: Text; fileName : String );
14:
15:
16: IMPLEMENTATION
17:
18:
19: {$F+}   { All device functions must be FAR }
20:
21:
22: FUNCTION DoNothing( VAR f : TextRec ) : Integer;
23:
24: { Assign to functions that do nothing }
25:
26: BEGIN
27:    DoNothing := 0   { No error for doing nothing }
28: END; { DoNothing }
29:
30:
31: FUNCTION DevInput( VAR f: TextRec ) : Integer;
32:
33: { Input from device }
34:
35: BEGIN
36: END; { DevInOut }
```

Program 13-10 *cont.*

```
37:
38:
39: FUNCTION DevOutput( VAR f : TextRec ) : Integer;
40:
41: { Output to device }
42:
43: BEGIN
44: END; { DevOutput }
45:
46:
47: FUNCTION DevClose( VAR f : TextRec ) : Integer;
48:
49: { Close file }
50:
51: BEGIN
52: END; { DevClose }
53:
54:
55: FUNCTION DevOpen( VAR f : TextRec ) : Integer;
56:
57: { Called by Reset, Rewrite, Append }
58:
59: BEGIN
60:    WITH f DO
61:    BEGIN
62:       IF Mode = fmInput THEN
63:       BEGIN
64:          InOutFunc := @DevInput;
65:          FlushFunc := @DoNothing
66:       END ELSE
67:       BEGIN
68:          Mode := fmOutput;  { In case mode was fmInOut }
69:          InOutFunc := @DevOutput;
70:          FlushFunc := @DevOutput;
71:       END; { else }
72:       CloseFunc := @DevClose
73:    END; { with }
74:    DevOpen := 0
75: END; { DevOpen }
76:
77:
78: {$F-}  { End of local FAR functions. }
79:
80:
81: PROCEDURE AssignDev;
```

Program 13-10 *cont.*

```
82:
83:    { Initialize file variable }
84:
85:    BEGIN
86:
87:       FillChar( f, SizeOf(f), 0 );   { Zero file variable }
88:
89:       WITH TextRec( f ) DO
90:       BEGIN
91:          Handle    := $FFFF;
92:          Mode      := fmClosed;
93:          BufSize   := SizeOf( Buffer );
94:          BufPtr    := @Buffer;
95:          OpenFunc  := @DevOpen;
96:          Name[0]   := #0   { Ignore filename }
97:       END { with }
98:
99:    END; { AssignDev }
100:
101:
102:   END. { Unit }
```

Using Text Device Drivers

An example device driver will help clarify the preceding discussion. Program 13-11 is a modified copy of the device driver shell in Program 13-10. The purpose of this device driver is to display expanded characters using the same bit patterns for normal-sized letters and symbols. Local procedure **Expander** (lines 19–47) writes a single large character on screen, reading the bit pattern for the character image from ROM (line 36) and displaying large blocks (line 40) or blanks (line 41) for each pattern dot.

The **AssignExp** procedure prepares the device driver. We don't need a file name in this case, and, therefore, the **fileName** field is not included in the procedure declaration (line 13).

DevOpen (lines 78–95) tests the **Mode** field. The driver cannot handle input for **Read** and **Readln** and accordingly sets fields **InOutFunc** and **FlushFunc** (lines 84–85) to the **DoNothing** procedure. Line 88 sets **Mode** to **fmOutput**. (If **Append** opens the file, **Mode** equals **fmInOut** here. If you need to distinguish between **Rewrite** and **Append**, examine **Mode** and take appropriate action. This example treats **Append** and **Rewrite** identically.)

Line 92 assigns the address of the **Close** function to field **CloseFunc**. In this example, closing the file does nothing. In you own drivers, assign the address of a function to deinitialize a device or close a disk file. Line 94 passes an error code back as the function result.

The output routine (lines 53–69) calls procedure **Expander** (line 63) for each character in the text buffer. The **WHILE** loop shows the correct way to process all buffered characters. Again, an error code is passed back as the function result (line 68).

Save Program 13-11 as UEXPAND.PAS and compile to disk, creating the unit file, UEXPAND.TPU. Following the program is an example that shows how to use the custom device driver.

Program 13-11

```
 1:  UNIT UExpand;
 2:
 3:  (*
 4:   *     Expanded Characters Device Driver
 5:   *     IBM MS/PC-DOS, Turbo Pascal
 6:   *)
 7:
 8:
 9:  INTERFACE
10:
11:  USES Crt, Dos;
12:
13:  PROCEDURE AssignExp( VAR f: Text );
14:
15:
16:  IMPLEMENTATION
17:
18:
19:  PROCEDURE Expander( ch : Char );
20:  { Write one expanded-size character }
21:  CONST
22:     Pattern = $FA6E;
23:     Width   = 73;        { 33 for 40-col screens }
24:  VAR
25:     x, y, Segment, Offset, i, j : Word;
26:     EightBits : Byte;
27:  BEGIN
28:     IF WhereX >= Width
29:        THEN FOR i := 1 TO 9 DO Writeln;
30:     x := WhereX; y := WhereY;
31:     Gotoxy( x, y - 8 );
32:     Segment := $F000;
33:     Offset  := Pattern + ( Ord(ch) * 8 );
34:     FOR i := 0 TO 7 DO
35:     BEGIN
36:        EightBits := Mem[ Segment : Offset + i ];
37:        FOR j := 0 TO 7 DO
```

Program 13-11 *cont.*

```
38:       BEGIN
39:          IF EightBits AND $80 <> 0
40:             THEN Write( Chr(177) )
41:             ELSE Write( ' ' ); { 1 blanks }
42:          EightBits := ( EightBits SHL 1 ) MOD 256
43:       END; { for }
44:       Gotoxy( x, WhereY + 1 )  { cr/lf }
45:    END;
46:    Gotoxy( x + 9, y )
47: END; { Expander }
48:
49:
50: {$F+}   { All device functions must be FAR }
51:
52:
53: FUNCTION DevOutput( VAR f: TextRec ) : Integer;
54: { Output expanded text }
55: VAR
56:    k : Word;   { Text buffer index }
57: BEGIN
58:    WITH f DO
59:    BEGIN
60:       k := 0;
61:       WHILE k < BufPos DO
62:       BEGIN
63:          Expander( BufPtr^[k] );
64:          Inc( k )
65:       END; { while }
66:       BufPos := 0
67:    END; { with }
68:    DevOutput := 0
69: END; { DevOutput }
70:
71:
72: FUNCTION DoNothing( VAR f : TextRec ) : Integer;
73: BEGIN
74:    DoNothing := 0
75: END; { DoNothing }
76:
77:
78: FUNCTION DevOpen( VAR f : TextRec ) : Integer;
79: BEGIN
80:    WITH f DO
81:    BEGIN
82:       IF Mode = fmInput THEN
```

Program 13-11 *cont.*

```
 83:        BEGIN
 84:            InOutFunc := @DoNothing;
 85:            FlushFunc := @DoNothing
 86:        END ELSE
 87:        BEGIN
 88:            Mode := fmOutput;
 89:            InOutFunc := @DevOutput;
 90:            FlushFunc := @DevOutput;
 91:        END; { else }
 92:        CloseFunc := @DoNothing
 93:      END; { with }
 94:      DevOpen := 0
 95:  END; { DevOpen }
 96:
 97:
 98:  {$F-}  { End of local FAR functions. }
 99:
100:
101:  PROCEDURE AssignExp;
102:  BEGIN
103:      FillChar( f, SizeOf(f), 0 );   { Zero file variable }
104:      WITH TextRec( f ) DO
105:      BEGIN
106:        Handle    := $FFFF;
107:        Mode      := fmClosed;
108:        BufSize   := SizeOf( Buffer );
109:        BufPtr    := @Buffer;
110:        OpenFunc  := @DevOpen;
111:        Name[0]   := #0
112:      END { with }
113:  END; { AssignExp }
114:
115:
116:  END. { Unit }
```

Using the UExpand Unit

Program 13-12 tests the device driver in Program 13-11. The program uses two units, **Crt** and **UExpand**. (You must have UEXPAND.TPU on disk to compile this example.)

Line 7 passes **Text** file variable **expFile** to **AssignExp**, the public procedure in unit **UExpand**. This initializes the file variable for the **Rewrite** statement in line 9. Then, displaying text with **Write** and **Writeln** statements (line 13) passes characters to the custom device driver, displaying headline-size characters on screen. When you run the program, type a short string and press Enter to see the result.

Program 13-12

```
 1:  PROGRAM TestExpand;
 2:  USES Crt, UExpand;
 3:  VAR
 4:     expFile : Text;
 5:     s : String;
 6:  BEGIN
 7:     AssignExp( expFile );   { Initialize file variable }
 8:     Rewrite( expFile );
 9:     ClrScr;
10:     Write( 'Enter a string: ' );
11:     Readln( s );
12:     GotoXY( 1, 20 );
13:     Write( expFile, s )
14:  END.
```

Increasing Text-File Buffer Size

When reading and writing text files, Turbo Pascal normally uses a 128-byte buffer in memory to hold information on its way to and from disk. This minimum-size buffer saves RAM but can also make disk I/O painfully slow, especially when copying large amounts of text from one file to another. Increasing the buffer size to 256, 512, or even 1024 bytes or larger can add remarkable speed to "I/O-bound" code.

Call the built-in **SetTextBuf** procedure to increase a text file's I/O buffer. The procedure has no effect on files of other data types, in which case buffering is handled by DOS, not by Turbo Pascal. First, you need to declare a new buffer variable and a text file:

```
VAR
    buffer : ARRAY[ 0 .. 511 ] OF Byte;
    t : TEXT;
```

That creates a 512-byte array named **buffer**. The actual format of the variable is unimportant—it doesn't have to be an array of bytes. Anything that's big enough will do. In the code, after assigning a name to text file **t**, attach the buffer to the file variable with:

```
Assign( t, 'FILENAME.TXT' );
SetTextBuf( t, buffer );
Reset( t );
```

Always call **SetTextBuf** after **Assign** and before **Reset**. If the file is already open, **Close** it and then call **SetTextBuf**. Never call **SetTextBuf** to attach a new buffer to an open file. The Turbo Pascal Reference Guide says you may do this if you're careful, but I recommend against it. You could easily destroy information held in the default buffer by attaching a new one at the wrong time.

A second way to call **SetTextBuf** is to add a **Word** parameter equal to the buffer size—useful when the buffer size is variable. (If you don't specify the buffer size, **SetTextBuf** uses the entire buffer space by default.) For example, suppose you have the previous variables (except **buffer**) plus:

```
VAR
    bp : ^Byte;        { Buffer pointer }
    size : Word;       { Size of buffer }
```

Pointer **bp** will address a variable-length buffer on the heap. Variable **size** equals the number of bytes in the buffer. You can then allocate buffer space on the heap and attach that space to a text file with these commands:

```
size := 1024;
GetMem( bp, size );
Assign( t, 'FILENAME.TXT' );
SetTextBuf( t, bp^, size );
Reset( t );
```

When attaching buffer variables to a text file, don't dispose the buffer memory while the file is open. This will almost always lead to a major system crash. To avoid such troubles, follow these guidelines:

- Declare buffer variables global to the entire program. Global variables exist during the program's entire execution lifetime.

- If you must declare buffer variables local to procedures and functions, you *must* **Close** the text file before the routine declaring the buffer variable ends. There are no exceptions to this rule—local variables exist only while their declaring routines are active.

- **Close** files *before* using **Dispose** to recover heap memory attached to a text file. If you do this, don't forget to call **SetTextBuf** again if you later decide to reopen this same text file.

- Don't move buffers around in memory after calling **SetTextBuf**. In other words, if you assign a buffer to another variable, the open text file will still use the original buffer space. You must call **SetTextBuf** again to use a different buffer.

Free Declaration Ordering

In Pascal's original design, **LABEL**, **CONST**, **TYPE**, and **VAR** declarations must appear in that order, with only one of each section within a program, procedure, or function block. Turbo Pascal doesn't care about this rule and allows **TYPE** sections that follow **VAR** declarations, or as many **CONST** sections as you need. You can even declare new types and variables in between procedures and functions.

Up to now, the examples in this book purposely ignored this unique feature. Programs that take advantage of free declaration ordering are not likely to compile with other Pascal compilers. By the way, Turbo Pascal also ignores the **PROGRAM** header, which you see at the top of all examples in this book, except the following. Here, then, is the shortest possible Turbo Pascal program:

```
BEGIN END.
```

Although there is no practical purpose to deleting the **PROGRAM** header, there are times when reversing the normal declaration order has advantages. For a good example, refer to Program 13-13, which has a serious bug.

The program counts down from constant **k** (line 3) to any value you enter (line 19). Procedure **Display** (lines 7–14) recursively calls itself while (**j** < **i**). Unfortunately, this is incorrect—the expression in line 9 should be (**j** < **k**). The programmer goofed.

We've seen this common side-effect bug before. Procedure **Display** has no business referring to global variable **i**, used only in the main program (lines 19–20). To repair the problem, move lines 4–5 to *between* lines 15 and 16 and recompile. Because global variable **i** now comes after the buggy **Display** procedure, the compiler displays:

```
Error 3: Unknown identifier
```

when it gets to line 9. If this were a real program, you'd notice your mistake, change **i** to **k**, and be rid of a nasty bug before it chews up the program's results.

Don't abuse free declaration ordering, scattering your type declarations and variables throughout the source code. But if moving a declaration clarifies your program or helps prevent bugs as in this example, then by all means use this unique Turbo Pascal feature.

Program 13-13 (with errors)

```
 1:   PROGRAM GlobalBug;
 2:   CONST
 3:      k = 100;
 4:   VAR
 5:      i : Integer;
 6:
 7:   PROCEDURE Display( j : Integer );
 8:   BEGIN
 9:      IF j < i THEN    { Incorrect!  Should be j < k! }
10:      BEGIN
11:         Display( j + 1 )
12:      END; { if }
13:      Write( j : 10 )
14:   END; { Display }
```

Program 13-13 (with errors) *cont.*

```
15:
16: BEGIN
17:    Writeln( 'Countdown (with a bug)' );
18:    Write( 'Enter a number from 0 to ', k, ': ' );
19:    Readln( i );
20:    Display( i );
21:    Writeln
22: END.
```

Structured Variable Constants

Chapter 2 introduced simple variable constants—constants that operate as variables with preinitialized values. (Recall that your Turbo Reference Manual calls them "typed constants.") You can also declare structured variable constants, predefining values for arrays, records, sets, or any other Pascal data type. (See Figures 13-2, 13-3, and 13-4.) Although attractive, variable constants have their advantages and disadvantages.

The greatest advantage is that variable constants operate like preinitialized variables. This saves you the step of initializing variables and, therefore, reduces the compiled program size.

variable (typed) constant declaration

Figure 13-2 Railroad diagram for a variable constant declaration. (See also Figures 13-3 and 13-4.)

variable (typed) constant

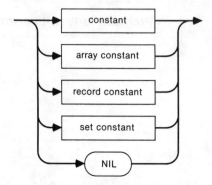

Figure 13-3 Use one of these items after the equal sign in a variable constant declaration (Figure 13-2).

The primary disadvantage is that variable constants are global to the entire program and occupy valuable memory space. A few variable constants probably

array constant

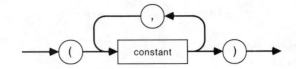

record constant

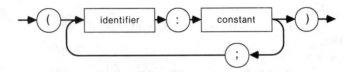

set constant

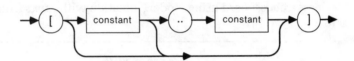

Figure 13-4 Railroad diagrams for array, record, and set variable
constant declarations (Figure 13-2).

won't do much harm, but don't make the mistake of declaring all your variables
this way.

Variable Constant Arrays

A variable constant array is the same as any other array but has preinitialized elements. You can have single-dimension or multiple-dimension constant arrays.

Program 13-14 declares a constant array **MonthNames**, an array of 12 preset
strings. Lines 16–17 print the names of the months. This works because the Turbo
Pascal compiler embeds the predeclared array elements (lines 6–9) directly in the
data segment. Therefore, there is no need to assign strings to the **Months** array—
the month names are already there.

Program 13-14

```
1:   PROGRAM MonthNumbers;
2:   TYPE
3:      Months = ARRAY[ 1 .. 12 ] OF String[3];
4:   CONST
5:      MonthNames :
6:         Months = ( 'Jan', 'Feb', 'Mar',
7:                    'Apr', 'May', 'Jun',
8:                    'Jul', 'Aug', 'Sep',
```

Program 13-14 *cont.*

```
 9:                        'Oct', 'Nov', 'Dec' );
10:    VAR
11:       Month : 1 .. 12;
12:    BEGIN
13:       Writeln;
14:       Writeln( 'Month Numbers' );
15:       Writeln;
16:       FOR Month := 1 TO 12 DO
17:          Writeln( Month:2, ' : ', MonthNames[ Month ] )
18:    END.
```

To declare multiple-dimension constant arrays, use nested parentheses. For a less confusing style, line up opening and closing parentheses as shown in Program 13-15, Chess. The program does not, of course, really play chess. It merely declares a chessboard using modern notation with *ranks* from 1 to 8 and *files* from a to z.

Program 13-15

```
 1:    PROGRAM Chess;
 2:    TYPE
 3:       Piece = ( empty, WPawn, WRook, WKnight, WBishop, WQueen, WKing,
 4:                        BPawn, BRook, BKnight, BBishop, BQueen, BKing );
 5:       Ranks = 1 .. 8;
 6:       Files = ( a, b, c, d, e, f, g, h );
 7:       CheckerBoard = ARRAY[ Ranks, Files ] OF Piece;
 8:
 9:    CONST
10:       Board :
11:        CheckerBoard =
12:        (
13:          ( WRook, WKnight, WBishop, WKing,  WQueen, WBishop, WKnight, WRook ),
14:          ( WPawn, WPawn,   WPawn,   WPawn,  WPawn,  WPawn,   WPawn,   WPawn ),
15:          ( empty, empty,   empty,   empty,  empty,  empty,   empty,   empty ),
16:          ( empty, empty,   empty,   empty,  empty,  empty,   empty,   empty ),
17:          ( empty, empty,   empty,   empty,  empty,  empty,   empty,   empty ),
18:          ( empty, empty,   empty,   empty,  empty,  empty,   empty,   empty ),
19:          ( BPawn, BPawn,   BPawn,   BPawn,  BPawn,  BPawn,   BPawn,   BPawn ),
20:          ( BRook, BKnight, BBishop, BKing,  BQueen, BBishop, BKnight, BRook )
21:        );
22:
23:       PieceNames :
24:         ARRAY[ Piece ] OF String[2] =
25:            ( '..', 'wP', 'wR', 'wN', 'wB', 'wQ', 'wK',
26:                    'bP', 'bR', 'bN', 'bB', 'bQ', 'bK' );
```

Program 13-15 *cont.*

```
27:
28:    PROCEDURE MovePiece( R1 : Ranks; F1 : Files;
29:                         R2 : Ranks; F2 : Files );
30:    BEGIN
31:       Board[ R2, F2 ] := Board[ R1, F1 ];
32:       Board[ R1, F1 ] := empty
33:    END;
34:
35:    PROCEDURE DisplayBoard;
36:    VAR
37:       r : Ranks;
38:       f : Files;
39:    BEGIN
40:       FOR r := 8 DOWNTO 1 DO
41:       BEGIN
42:          Writeln;
43:          Write( r, ': ' );
44:          FOR f := a TO h DO
45:             Write( ' ', PieceNames[ Board[ r, f ] ] )
46:       END;
47:       Writeln;
48:       Writeln;
49:       Writeln( '    a  b  c  d  e  f  g  h' );
50:    END;
51:
52:    BEGIN
53:       Writeln( 'Pawn to Q4 (d2-d4)' );
54:       MovePiece( 2, d, 4, d );
55:       DisplayBoard
56:    END.
```

Board is a variable constant, multidimensional array. That may sound and look complicated. But, as shown here, using a variable constant array efficiently sets up the chessboard, skipping an otherwise messy initialization step. As far as playing ability goes, the program knows one move, Pawn to Q4, or in the modern notation, 2-d to 4-d (see line 54).

You are welcome to finish Program 13-15 with no additional due the author.

Variable Constant Records

Variable constant records are similar to arrays but add field names and colons to predeclared values. Assume you have this record definition:

```
TYPE
   NameRec =
```

```
RECORD
   Name : String[20];
   Age  : Integer
END;
```

You can then declare a variable constant of this structure, with fields set to these values:

```
CONST
   NR : NameRec =
        ( Name : 'GEORGE',
          Age : 25        );
```

Variable Constant Sets

You can also have set constants with predeclared elements. Predefined character sets are especially useful when the set contents won't change during a program run. For example, you can have a set of characters named **Digits** declared this way:

```
TYPE
   CharSet = SET OF Char;
CONST
   Digits : Charset = [ '0' .. '9' ];
```

You don't even need the **TYPE** declaration. The following has the identical effect.

```
CONST
   Digits : SET OF Char = [ '0' .. '9' ];
```

Special Directory Commands

Four directory commands let you work with subdirectories, which are useful for organizing the large amount of space available on a hard disk drive. (You can also use subdirectories with floppy disks, but to a lesser advantage.)

ChDir (Change Directory), **MkDir** (Make Directory), and **RmDir** (Remove Directory) take a single string parameter representing a subdirectory path name such as 'C:\UTIL'or '\TPAS'. The path name can also be a drive letter and colon ('A:'). Suppose you have a subdirectory **LIB** containing a library of procedures and functions. To change the current working directory, you could execute this statement:

```
ChDir( '\PASCAL\LIB' );
```

You can also use **ChDir** to change to a different disk drive. This switches to drive B:

```
ChDir( 'B:' );
```

Procedure **MkDir** creates a new subdirectory if one by that name doesn't already exist. **RmDir** removes a subdirectory, an operation allowed only if the directory is empty.

GetDir has a different format from the previous three commands. The procedure takes two parameters: a drive number equal to 0 for the current drive, 1 for drive A:, 2 for B:, and so on; and a string variable that **GetDir** sets to the current path name. To set a string variable **PathName** to the current directory, use these statements:

```
GetDir( 0, PathName );
Writeln( PathName );
```

Program 13-16 demonstrates the four directory commands. Using the program, you can create a subdirectory, change to a new directory or drive, and remove subdirectories.

Program 13-16

```
 1:   PROGRAM SubDirectories;
 2:   USES Crt;
 3:   TYPE
 4:      MiscString = String[ 64 ];
 5:   VAR
 6:      ch : Char;
 7:      PathName : MiscString;
 8:
 9:   PROCEDURE GetPath;
10:   BEGIN
11:      Write( ' what directory? ' ); Readln( PathName )
12:   END;
13:
14:   {$I-} { i/o check off }
15:   PROCEDURE ChangeDir;
16:   BEGIN
17:      Write( 'Change to' ); GetPath;
18:      ChDir( PathName )
19:   END;
20:
21:   PROCEDURE MakeDir;
22:   BEGIN
23:      Write( 'Make' ); GetPath;
24:      MkDir( PathName )
25:   END;
26:
```

Program 13-16 *cont.*

```
27:   PROCEDURE RemoveDir;
28:   BEGIN
29:      Write( 'Remove' ); GetPath;
30:      RmDir( PathName )
31:   END;
32:   {$I+} { i/o check back on }
33:
34:   BEGIN
35:      ClrScr;
36:      Writeln( 'Sub Directories' );
37:      REPEAT
38:         ClrScr;
39:         GetDir( 0, PathName ); { 0=current drive; 1=A:, 2=B:, etc. }
40:         NormVideo;
41:         Writeln( 'Path is: ', PathName );
42:         Writeln; LowVideo;
43:         Write( 'C.hange, M.ake, R.emove, Q.uit? ' );
44:         REPEAT
45:            ch := Upcase( ReadKey )
46:         UNTIL ch IN [ 'C', 'M', 'R', 'Q' ];
47:         Writeln( ch ); Writeln;
48:         CASE ch OF
49:            'C' : ChangeDir;
50:            'M' : MakeDir;
51:            'R' : RemoveDir
52:         END; { case }
53:         IF IoResult <> 0 THEN
54:         BEGIN
55:            Writeln;
56:            Writeln( 'No directory, bad path, or all files not removed' );
57:            Write( 'Press return...' ); Readln
58:         END
59:      UNTIL ch = 'Q'
60:   END.
```

Custom Exit Procedures

When a Turbo Pascal program ends, several normally invisible events occur. The standard input and output files are closed. A message is displayed if a runtime error caused the program to end prematurely. A return code is passed back to DOS (or to a parent program from a child process). And changed interrupt vectors are restored to their original values, saved earlier by Turbo Pascal runtime routines when the program started.

Linking into the Exit Chain

By following a few simple rules, you can weld your own links to the chain of events after the **END** of a Turbo Pascal program. Your custom exit procedure runs immediately before standard exit events occur, gaining control when:

- The program ends normally.
- A **Halt** statement was executed anywhere in the program.
- An **Exit** statement was executed in the program's outer block.
- A runtime error occurred.

Program 13-17 demonstrates how to write a custom exit procedure. When you run the program, it displays:

```
Welcome to ExitShell
Press <Enter> to end program...
Inside CustomExit procedure
```

The message "Inside CustomExit procedure" appears after you press Enter to end the program, proving that procedure **CustomExit** runs even though the program never calls it directly. To make this happen, ExitShell performs two assignments at the beginning of the program's main body:

```
savedExitProc := exitProc;
exitProc := @CustomExit;
```

The first assignment saves the value of **exitProc**, a **Pointer** variable defined in the **System** unit, which Turbo Pascal automatically links to every compiled program. ExitShell's global variable, **savedExitProc**, holds the original **exitProc** value for the program's duration. In your own programs, always save **exitProc** in a similar global variable. Never assign **exitProc** to a variable declared local to a procedure or function or to a dynamic variable on the heap. The saved **exitProc** must be available after the program ends, and, therefore, only a global variable will do.

The second assignment sets **exitProc** to the address of the custom exit procedure—**CustomExit** in Program 13-17. The @ operator returns the address of **CustomExit**. Because **exitProc** points to the custom exit procedure, Turbo Pascal calls this procedure when the program ends.

Together, these assignments link the custom exit procedure, which has no parameters, into the exit chain. You can name the procedure anything you like.

Inside the exit procedure, assign the saved pointer back to **exitProc**. This preserves the exit chain, letting other processes execute their own exit procedures after yours finishes. Except for this step, there is no limit to what you can do inside a custom exit procedure. You can read and write files, display values, use DOS functions, call other procedures and functions, and perform any other actions as part of your program's shutdown sequence.

A critical step is to declare the exit procedure *far* by surrounding its declaration with the compiler directives {$F + } and {$F – }. (See **CustomExit** in Program 13-17.) Turbo Pascal calls the exit procedure with a *far* Call instruction (technically called an "Inter-Segment Call"). Using the {$F + } directive tells Turbo Pascal to end the procedure with a complementary Inter-Segment *far* Return instruction.

One of the most common mistakes is to forget to declare an exit procedure *far*. Turbo Pascal does not prevent this error, which causes an inevitable disaster from which you'll probably have to reboot to recover. If screwy things happen or if the computer hangs when your program ends, you probably forgot to surround the custom exit procedure declaration with {$F + } and {$F – }.

Program 13-17

```
 1:  PROGRAM ExitShell;
 2:
 3:  { Demonstrate how to write a custom exit procedure }
 4:
 5:  VAR   savedExitProc : Pointer;  { Old ExitProc value }
 6:
 7:
 8:  {$F+} PROCEDURE CustomExit; {$F-}
 9:
10:  { Custom exit procedure }
11:
12:  BEGIN
13:     Writeln( 'Inside CustomExit procedure' );
14:     exitProc := savedExitProc    { Restore saved exitProc pointer }
15:  END; { CustomExit }
16:
17:
18:  BEGIN
19:
20:     savedExitProc := exitProc;   { Save ExitProc pointer }
21:     exitProc := @CustomExit;     { Install custom error procedure }
22:
23:     Writeln;
24:     Writeln( 'Welcome to ExitShell' );
25:     Write( 'Press <Enter> to end program...' );
26:     Readln
27:
28:  END.
```

Customizing a Runtime Handler

Custom exit procedures make it easy to write your own runtime error handler, perhaps displaying a more helpful message than that same ol' line:

```
Runtime error 106 at 0000:001E
```

For an example custom runtime handler, type and compile Program 13-18. As in Program 13-17, two assignments begin **ErrorShell**, saving **exitProc** in **savedExitProc** and assigning to **exitProc** the address of **CustomExit**.

Inside **CustomExit**, an **IF** statement examines two global **System** unit variables, **exitCode** (type **Integer**) and **errorAddr** (type **Pointer**). **ExitCode** holds one of three values: the integer number passed to a **Halt** statement, a runtime error code, or zero if the program ended normally or if an **Exit** statement was executed in the outer program block. **ErrorAddr** addresses the location of a runtime error if one occurred.

To determine the meaning of a nonzero **exitCode** value, check whether **errorAddr** is **NIL**. If so, then no runtime error occurred, and, therefore, **exitCode** holds the value passed to a **Halt** statement. But if **exitCode** is nonzero and if **errorAddr** is not **NIL**, then a runtime error occurred. In this case, **errAddr** specifies the segment and offset address of the runtime error, and **exitCode** equals the error code. (See your Turbo Pascal Manual for a complete list of runtime error codes and their meanings.)

To better understand how to use **exitCode** and **errorAddr**, try the following three experiments.

1. Run Program 13-18. When it asks for an integer value, press 0 and then Enter. The zero value passed to **Halt** is assigned to **exitCode**, which **CustomExit** then examines. Consequently, **CustomExit**'s **IF** statement does not execute, and, therefore, the program silently ends as though it had no custom exit procedure.

2. Run Program 13-18 again, but, this time, type 100. When you press Enter, the program passes 100 to **Halt**, setting **exitCode** to that value. Because no runtime error occurred, **errorAddr** is **NIL** and **CustomExit**'s IF statement executes, displaying the messages:

```
Program halted!
Exit code = 100
```

3. Run Program 13-18 a third time. Type ABC and press Enter. Assigning alphabetic characters to integer variable **num** causes a runtime error during the call to **Readln**, assigning to **errorAddr** the address of the instruction that caused the error and setting **exitCode** to 106, Turbo Pascal's error code for an "Invalid numeric format." Sensing that a runtime error has occurred, **CustomExit**'s **IF** statement does not execute, instead letting Turbo Pascal display its familiar runtime error message.

As you can see from these experiments, **exitCode** and **errorAddr** describe why the program is ending. Table 13-4 lists the possible combinations of the two values. By testing **exitCode** and **errorAddr**, you can write a custom error handler to take different actions before passing control back to DOS or to the parent process that activated the program.

Table 13-4 exitCode and errorAddr combinations

exitCode	errorAddr	Meaning
= 0	= NIL	Normal program end
< > 0	= NIL	Halt(n) executed; exitCode = n
< > 0	< > NIL	Runtime error occurred; exitCode = error code; errorAddr = address

---

Program 13-18

```
1:  PROGRAM ErrorShell;
2:
3:  { Demonstrate how to write a custom halt and
4:    runtime error handler. }
5:
6:  VAR    savedExitProc : Pointer;  { Old ExitProc value }
7:         num : integer;            { Test number }
8:
9:
10: {$F+} PROCEDURE CustomExit; {$F-}
11:
12: { Custom exit and runtime error handler }
13:
14: BEGIN
15:
16:    IF ( exitCode <> 0 ) AND ( errorAddr = NIL ) THEN
17:    BEGIN
18:       Writeln;
19:       Writeln( 'Program halted!' );
20:       Writeln( 'Exit code = ', exitCode )  { Display halt code }
21:    END; { if }
22:
23:    exitProc := savedExitProc    { Restore saved exitProc pointer }
24:
25: END; { CustomExit }
26:
27:
28: BEGIN
29:
30:    savedExitProc := exitProc;  { Save ExitProc pointer }
31:    exitProc := @CustomExit;    { Install custom error procedure }
32:
33:    Writeln;
34:    Writeln( 'Welcome to ErrorShell' );
35:    Writeln;
```

Program 13-18 *cont.*

```
36:     Write( 'Enter an integer value: ' );
37:     Readln( num );
38:     Halt( num )
39:
40:  END.
```

Trapping Runtime Errors

Because **exitCode** and **errorAddr** are variables, you can change their values inside a custom error handler to trap runtime errors and handle them yourself. For example, suppose your custom exit procedure finds that **errorAddr** is not **NIL**, indicating a runtime error has occurred. After taking appropriate action—perhaps displaying the **exitCode** value, deallocating memory, closing files, and so on—set **errorAddr** to NIL and **exitCode** to zero, cancelling the runtime error.

To see how this works, run Program 13-19, a modified version of Program 13-18. Type ABC to force a runtime error as you did in the earlier experiment. You should see a message similar to this:

```
A small problem has developed.
Please jot down the following numbers
and call the programmer at 555-1212.

Address = 0:749
Code    = 106

Thank you for your support!
```

This certainly is more friendly than Turbo Pascal's usual runtime error message. The new exit procedure sets **errorAddr** to **Nil** and **exitCode** to zero, cancelling the runtime error. This way, Turbo Pascal is unaware that an error occurred. If you remove the two assignments in lines 26–27, Turbo Pascal displays its own runtime error message in addition to your custom note.

Program 13-19

```
1:  PROGRAM ErrorShell2;
2:
3:  { Demonstrate how to write a custom halt and
4:    runtime error handler. }
5:
6:  VAR    savedExitProc : Pointer;  { Old ExitProc value }
7:         num : integer;              { Test number }
8:
9:
```

Program 13-19 *cont.*

```
10:  {$F+} PROCEDURE CustomExit; {$F-}
11:  BEGIN
12:     IF errorAddr <> NIL THEN
13:     BEGIN
14:        Writeln( '--------------------------------------' );
15:        Writeln( 'A small problem has developed.'        );
16:        Writeln( 'Please jot down the following numbers' );
17:        Writeln( 'and call the programmer at 555-1212.'  );
18:        Writeln;
19:        Writeln( 'Address = ',
20:           seg(errorAddr^), ':', ofs(errorAddr^) );
21:        Writeln( 'Code    = ', exitCode );
22:        Writeln;
23:        Writeln( 'Thank you for your support!'           );
24:        Writeln( '--------------------------------------' );
25:
26:        errorAddr := NIL;     { Cancel runtime error }
27:        exitCode := 0
28:
29:     END; { if }
30:     exitProc := savedExitProc      { Restore saved exitProc pointer }
31:  END; { CustomExit }
32:
33:
34:  BEGIN
35:
36:     savedExitProc := exitProc;   { Save ExitProc pointer }
37:     exitProc := @CustomExit;     { Install custom error procedure }
38:
39:     Writeln;
40:     Writeln( 'Welcome to ErrorShell' );
41:     Writeln;
42:     Write( 'Enter an integer value: ' );
43:     Readln( num );
44:     Halt( num )
45:
46:  END.
```

Units and Exit Procedures

Another use for custom exit procedures is to add automatic shutdown code to units. Each unit that a program uses can insert its own exit procedure into the chain of events that occurs when the host program ends.

This technique opens countless doors for programmers. A memory management unit might deallocate a list of master pointers stored on the heap. A database unit might close temporary files, dumping buffered data to disk. A telecommunications unit could hang up the phone. These actions are guaranteed to occur even if the program halts prematurely due to a runtime error.

Units install custom exit procedures in the same way as Programs 13-17 and 13-18 demonstrate. In this case, though, because multiple units might install several procedures into the exit chain, it's important to understand the order in which the program and various components in the units run.

As you recall from earlier chapters, a unit may have a main body, called the initialization section. The statements in this section run before the first statement in a program that uses the unit. When a program uses multiple units, the initialization sections in all units run in the same order the unit names appear in the program's **USES** declaration. After all initialization sections finish, the program's statements begin running. Then, when the program ends, any exit procedures installed by the units run in the *opposite* order of the unit declarations in **USES**.

An example helps to clarify these actions. Consider a program that begins like this:

```
PROGRAM DemoExit;
USES UnitA, UnitB, UnitC;
```

The program uses three units, UnitA, UnitB, and UnitC. Figure 13-5 illustrates the order in which the unit initialization sections and exit procedures run. After Turbo Pascal completes its own startup chores, the initialization sections in UnitA, UnitB, and UnitC run (left side of Figure 13-5). Then, when the program ends—either normally, through **Halt** or **Exit**, or due to a runtime error—Turbo Pascal calls the custom exit procedures one by one, this time in the opposite order of the unit declarations (right side of Figure 13-5). In this example, Units A and C attach procedures to the exit chain. Unit B does not have an exit procedure and thus performs no actions when the program ends.

Programs 13-20 through 13-23 correspond with Figure 13-5. To run the complete example, type **UnitA**, **UnitB**, and **UnitC**. Compile each unit to a TPU (Turbo Pascal Unit) disk file. Next, type Program 13-23. Compile and run. You should see these lines on display:

```
Inside Unit A initialization
Inside Unit B initialization
Inside Unit C initialization
Welcome to DemoExit
Inside Unit C exit procedure
Inside Unit A exit procedure
```

Several important details contribute to making this multiple-unit example work correctly. **Unit A** and **Unit C** save **exitProc** in global **Pointer** variables, declared inside each unit's **IMPLEMENTATION** section. You could declare **savedExitProc** in the unit **INTERFACE**s, but because there is no reason for statements outside the unit to use the saved pointers, it's probably best to hide

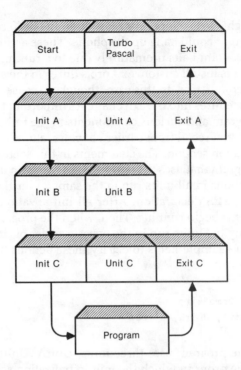

Figure 13-5 Multiple exit procedures in units run in the opposite order
of the unit initialization sections.

savedExitProc variables in the **IMPLEMENTATION**s where items are visible
only to statements inside the units.

The custom exit procedures—**ExitA** and **ExitC** in Programs 13-20 and 13-22
—are declared *far*, but are not listed in the **INTERFACE**. This makes the procedures private to the unit and prevents the host program (or another unit) from calling exit procedures directly, a poor and possibly dangerous practice. As in
Programs 13-17, 13-18, and 13-19, the exit procedures restore the saved **exitProc**
pointers before ending, preserving the exit chain.

Program 13-20

```
 1:   UNIT UnitA;
 2:
 3:   INTERFACE
 4:
 5:   IMPLEMENTATION
 6:
 7:   VAR  savedExitProc : Pointer;  { Old exitProc pointer }
 8:
 9:   {$F+} PROCEDURE ExitA; {$F-}
10:   BEGIN
```

Program 13-20 *cont.*

```
11:     Writeln( 'Inside Unit A exit procedure' );
12:     exitProc := savedExitProc
13: END; { ExitA }
14:
15: BEGIN
16:     savedExitProc := exitProc;
17:     exitProc := @ExitA;
18:     Writeln( 'Inside Unit A initialization' )
19: END.
```

Program 13-21

```
1: UNIT UnitB;
2:
3: INTERFACE
4:
5: IMPLEMENTATION
6:
7: BEGIN
8:     Writeln( 'Inside Unit B initialization' )
9: END.
```

Program 13-22

```
1:  UNIT UnitC;
2:
3:  INTERFACE
4:
5:  IMPLEMENTATION
6:
7:  VAR  savedExitProc : Pointer;  { Old exitProc pointer }
8:
9:  {$F+} PROCEDURE ExitC; {$F-}
10: BEGIN
11:     Writeln( 'Inside Unit C exit procedure' );
12:     exitProc := savedExitProc
13: END; { ExitC }
14:
15: BEGIN
16:     savedExitProc := exitProc;
17:     exitProc := @ExitC;
18:     Writeln( 'Inside Unit C initialization' )
19: END.
```

Program 13-23

```
1:   PROGRAM DemoExit;
2:   USES UnitA, UnitB, UnitC;
3:   BEGIN
4:      Writeln( 'Welcome to DemoExit' )
5:   END.
```

Breaking the Exit Chain

A simple experiment demonstrates what happens if you fail to preserve the exit chain when using multiple exit procedures. Remove line 12 from the **ExitC** procedure in Program 13-22.

When you run the buggy program, **UnitC**'s exit procedure runs but **UnitA**'s does not. This happens because **UnitC** breaks the exit chain by failing to restore the saved **exitProc** pointer; therefore, the pointer to **UnitA**'s exit procedure is lost.

Careful readers may realize that if **exitProc** addresses **ExitC** in **UnitC** and if **ExitC** fails to restore the previous **exitProc** pointer, an infinite loop is the logical result—**ExitC** would end, and Turbo Pascal would repeatedly call **ExitC** as the next exit procedure in the chain.

Turbo Pascal prevents this runaway condition by setting **exitProc** to **Nil** *before* calling each exit procedure in the chain. When a program ends for one of the reasons listed earlier, a portion of the runtime code linked to the program executes the following loop, expressed here in Pascal-like pseudo-code:

```
WHILE exitProc <> NIL DO
BEGIN
    tempProc := exitProc;
    exitProc := NIL;
    Call procedure at tempProc
END; { while }
Perform Turbo Pascal's exit chores
```

Because **exitProc** is **Nil** when **UnitC**'s modified **ExitC** procedure begins running, failing to restore **exitProc** to its saved value ends the runtime loop, causing Turbo Pascal to perform its own exit chores immediately. Knowing this technical detail about how Turbo Pascal works through the exit chain suggests a way to break the chain explicitly—just leave **exitProc** unchanged. (There's no need to set **exitProc** to **Nil**, although doing so is harmless. **ExitProc** is already **Nil** when a custom exit procedure begins.)

Breaking the exit chain is an advanced technique that you should employ only after careful thought. There are times when the method might come in handy, though. Suppose the first of several exit procedures discovers a fatal disk error in a database system of many related units. To prevent subsequent exit procedures from writing to disk and, therefore, displaying multiple disk error messages for the identical condition, the exit procedure could break the exit chain. The program might use an **IF** statement similar to this:

```
{$i-} Close( f ); {$i+}
errnum := IoResult;
IF errnum <> 0
   THEN Writeln( 'Fatal disk error #', errnum )
   ELSE exitProc := savedExitProc;
```

If the **Close** on file **f** fails, the program displays an error message, leaving **exitProc** unchanged (equal to **Nil**) and, therefore, breaking the exit chain. Otherwise, it restores **exitProc** to its saved value, continuing with the next exit procedure in line. This way, disk errors abort the program, preventing other exit procedures from gaining control.

Debugging with Exit Procedures

Program 13-24, **SysDebug**, shows how to use an exit procedure as a debugging device during program development. Adding **SysDebug** to a program's **USES** declaration displays several internal Turbo Pascal variables when the program ends. After debugging, remove **SysDebug** from the **USES** declaration and recompile to create the finished code file.

To use **SysDebug**, type in and compile Program 13-24 to disk. Next, type in Program 13-25, **SDTest**. When you run **SDTest**, type 0, 100, or ABC—just as you did in the earlier experiments. In each case, the program ends by displaying a list of variables similar to the sample in Figure 13-6. (The listed items are discussed at various places in this book.) Notice that, because **CustomExit** does not reset **errorAddr**, Turbo Pascal displays the usual message if a runtime error occurs.

When writing your own units and programs, you can use similar debugging techniques. For example, suppose you have a telecommunications unit named Modem. You could write a separate unit, **ModemDebug**, to dump Modem's global variables after a test program run. Isolating the debugging statements in a separate unit's exit procedure makes it easy to remove the debugging when you're ready to compile the production program. Later, if problems develop, you can quickly add the debugging statements by compiling after reinserting **Modem-Debug** in the program's **USES** declaration.

Custom exit procedures, while not difficult to create, require careful programming. In your own projects, remember to follow these four critical steps:

1. Save **exitProc** in a global **Pointer** variable.

2. Assign to **exitProc** the address of your custom exit procedure.

3. Declare the custom exit procedure *far* by surrounding the declaration with {$F+} and {$F−} compiler directives.

4. Inside the custom exit procedure, restore the saved **exitProc** pointer from the value saved in step 1.

```
System unit and other global variables
--------------------------------------
Memavail    = 463152 bytes
Maxavail    = 463152 bytes
PrefixSeg   = $2973
CSeg        = $298E
DSeg        = $2AC3
SSeg        = $2AED
SPtr        = $3FF4
HeapOrg     = $2EED:0000
HeapPtr     = $2EED:0000
FreePtr     = $9000:0000
FreeMin     = 0
HeapError   = NIL
ExitProc    = NIL
ExitCode    = 106
ErrorAddr   = $0000:009E
RandSeed    = 0
FileMode    = 2
StackLimit  = 0
InOutRec    = 0
Test8087    = 0
Runtime error 106 at 0000:009E.
```

Figure 13-6 Adding **SysDebug** to a **USES** declaration displays several variables when the program ends, as shown in this sample output from Program 13-25 after typing ABC to force a runtime error.

Program 13-24

```
1:  UNIT SysDebug;
2:
3:  { System globals debugging unit }
4:
5:  INTERFACE
6:
7:  IMPLEMENTATION
8:
9:  TYPE  String15 = String[15];    { WPointer string parameter }
10:
11: VAR   savedExitProc : Pointer;  { Old ExitProc value }
12:
13:
14: PROCEDURE WHex( v : word );
15: { Display v as a 4-digit hex string }
```

Program 13-24 *cont.*

```
16:  CONST
17:     digits : ARRAY[ 0 .. 15 ] OF char = '0123456789ABCDEF';
18:  BEGIN
19:     Write( digits[ hi( v ) div 16 ],
20:            digits[ hi( v ) mod 16 ],
21:            digits[ lo( v ) div 16 ],
22:            digits[ lo( v ) mod 16 ]  )
23:  END; { WHex }
24:
25:
26:  PROCEDURE WPointer( description : String15; p : Pointer );
27:  { Display pointer value in 0000:0000 format }
28:  BEGIN
29:     Write( description );
30:     IF p = NIL THEN Write( 'NIL' ) ELSE
31:     BEGIN
32:        Write( '$' );
33:        WHex( Seg(p^) );
34:        Write( ':' );
35:        WHex( Ofs(p^) )
36:     END; { if }
37:     Writeln
38:  END; { WPointer }
39:
40:
41:  PROCEDURE WWord( description : String15; w : Word );
42:  { Display word value in 0000 hex format }
43:  BEGIN
44:     Write( description, '$' );
45:     WHex( w );
46:     Writeln
47:  END; { WWord }
48:
49:
50:  {$F+} PROCEDURE CustomExit; {$F-}
51:
52:  { Display system global variables at exit }
53:
54:  BEGIN
55:     Writeln;
56:     Writeln( 'System unit and other global variables' );
57:     Writeln( '--------------------------------------' );
58:     Writeln( 'Memavail   = ', memavail, ' bytes' );
59:     Writeln( 'Maxavail   = ', maxavail, ' bytes' );
60:     WWord(   'PrefixSeg  = ', prefixSeg );
```

Program 13-24 *cont.*

```
61:      WWord(    'CSeg      = ', cSeg       );
62:      WWord(    'DSeg      = ', dSeg       );
63:      WWord(    'SSeg      = ', sSeg       );
64:      WWord(    'SPtr      = ', sPtr       );
65:      WPointer( 'HeapOrg   = ', heapOrg    );
66:      WPointer( 'HeapPtr   = ', heapPtr    );
67:      WPointer( 'FreePtr   = ', freePtr    );
68:      Writeln(  'FreeMin   = ', freeMin    );
69:      WPointer( 'HeapError = ', heapError  );
70:      WPointer( 'ExitProc  = ', exitProc   );
71:      Writeln(  'ExitCode  = ', exitCode   );
72:      WPointer( 'ErrorAddr = ', errorAddr  );
73:      Writeln(  'RandSeed  = ', randSeed   );
74:      Writeln(  'FileMode  = ', fileMode   );
75:      Writeln(  'StackLimit = ', stackLimit );
76:      Writeln(  'InOutRec  = ', InOutRes   );
77:      Writeln(  'Test8087  = ', Test8087   );
78:
79:      exitProc := savedExitProc     { Restore saved exitProc pointer }
80:
81:  END; { CustomExit }
82:
83:
84:  BEGIN
85:      savedExitProc := exitProc;   { Save ExitProc pointer }
86:      exitProc := @CustomExit       { Install custom exit procedure }
87:  END.
```

Program 13-25

```
 1:  PROGRAM SDTest;
 2:
 3:  { Test SysDebug unit }
 4:
 5:  USES  SysDebug;
 6:
 7:  VAR   num : integer;
 8:
 9:  BEGIN
10:      Writeln( 'Welcome to SysDebug unit test' );
11:      Writeln;
12:      Write( 'Type an exit code : ' );
13:      Readln( num );
14:      Halt( num )
15:  END.
```

Procedure Types

The original Pascal language as designed by Niklaus Wirth (see Bibliography) allowed procedure and function parameters to refer to other procedures and functions. With this ability, programs can pass subroutines to procedures and functions the same way they pass variables of other types. Turbo Pascal 5.0 and later versions now have a similar feature called *procedure types*.

A procedure type defines the format, but not the actual code, of a procedure or function. In the case of a function, a procedure type also defines the type of data that the function returns. Just as with real procedures and functions, procedure types may also declare value and variable parameters. For example, a procedure that takes a string parameter **s** might be defined as a procedure type this way:

```
TYPE
    DisplayProc = PROCEDURE( s : String );
```

DisplayProc defines a procedure type with a single string parameter **s**. Notice that unlike real procedures and functions, a procedure-type declaration does not have a naming identifier. Procedure types might also be parameterless:

```
TYPE
    AnyProc = PROCEDURE;
```

Procedure-type function declarations are similar to those for procedures but use the **FUNCTION** key word and return any of the usual function data types:

```
TYPE
    RealFunc = FUNCTION( n : Real ) : Real;
    StringFunc = FUNCTION : String;
    IntegerFunc = FUNCTION( VAR a, b, c : Integer ) : Integer;
```

The procedure-type functions **RealFunc** and **IntegerFunc** declare value and variable parameters. **StringFunc** is parameterless. As with procedure-type procedures, the function definitions do not have naming identifiers. Procedure-type functions may return the same kinds of values that regular functions return, but with one exception: Function results may not be other procedure data types.

Using Procedure Types

After declaring procedure types, you can declare *procedure variables* of those types:

```
VAR
    displayF : DisplayProc;
    realF    : RealFunc;
    stringF  : StringFunc;
```

The three procedure variables, **displayF**, **realF**, and **stringF**, are actually 32-bit pointers. That doesn't mean you have to manipulate them with pointer routines like **New** and **Dispose**—Turbo Pascal understands that procedure variables address procedures and functions elsewhere in the program. Those procedures and functions must conform to the numbers and types of parameters and function result types defined earlier by the procedure types:

```
{$F+}
PROCEDURE DoubleSpace( s : String );
BEGIN
   Writeln;
   Writeln( s )
END; { DoubleSpace }

FUNCTION Cube( n : Real ) : Real;
BEGIN
   Cube := n * n * n
END; { Cube }

FUNCTION Copyright : String;
BEGIN
   Copyright := '(C) 1989 by Duck Hardware'
END; { Copyright }
```

The procedures and functions must be compiled with the {$F + } far option because, as just explained, procedure variables that will address these routines are actually 32-bit far pointers with segment and offset parts. Like all pointers, procedure-type variables are not initialized when the program runs. You must perform this step by assigning the addresses of actual procedures and functions to the pointer variables:

```
displayF := DoubleSpace;
realF    := Cube;
stringF  := Copyright;
```

That completes the setup phase of writing programs with procedure types and variables. To use the procedures and functions addressed by the procedure variables, **displayF**, **realF**, and **stringF**, insert a variable's identifier at any place where the procedure or function identifier normally could go. For example, the following three statements all display the copyright string assigned to the **Copyright** function:

```
displayF( Copyright );
DoubleSpace( stringF );
displayF( stringF );
```

As usual in this book, variables begin with lowercase letters; procedures and functions, with uppercase letters. The first line calls procedure **DoubleSpace** via the procedure variable **displayF**, passing as a parameter the result of **Copyright**, which returns a **String** data type. The second line does the same, this time calling **DoubleSpace** directly, but passing **stringF** —the procedure-type variable that addresses the **Copyright** function. The third line performs the identical action but uses only procedure-type variables. The three different-looking but similar-acting examples demonstrate that procedure and function identifiers are fully interchangeable with procedure-type variables.

A Procedure-Type Example

Procedure types let you design programs with "hooks," to which you can assign the addresses of custom routines. A good example where this design method is useful is a program that plots the result of a numeric function. The main portion of the program sets up the display, draws x- and y-axis lines, and plots the function as a graph.

Without procedure types, changing the plotted function requires you to rewrite the original source code. Using procedure types to pass the address of a custom function to the plot package simplifies the job—especially if the bulk of the code is precompiled as a separate unit.

Program 13-26 demonstrates how this works. Save the program as PLOTU.PAS and compile to PLOTU.TPU. As the listing shows, the unit has a simple **INTERFACE** section. Line 6 declares the procedure type **PlotFunction**:

```
PlotFunction = FUNCTION( x : Integer ) : Real;
```

Line 8 uses this type in a normal procedure declaration, with a single parameter of type **PlotFunction**:

```
PROCEDURE PlotGraph( pf : PlotFunction );
```

With this design, plotting new functions is a simple matter of writing the function code—which must conform to the **PlotFunction** data type—and passing the function name to **PlotGraph**. Line 70 calls the assigned function to calculate the y coordinate for every possible x value.

An example host program that uses **PlotU** follows the listing for Program 13-26.

Program 13-26

```
1:   UNIT PlotU;
2:
3:   INTERFACE
4:
5:   TYPE
6:       PlotFunction = FUNCTION( x : Integer ) : Real;
```

Program 13-26 *cont.*

```
 7:
 8:   PROCEDURE PlotGraph( pf : PlotFunction );
 9:
10:
11:   IMPLEMENTATION
12:
13:   USES
14:      Crt, Graph;
15:
16:   VAR
17:      graphDriver, graphMode : Integer;        { Graph unit variables }
18:      xMax, yMax, xMin, yMin : Integer;        { x & y coordinate limits }
19:      xCenter, yCenter : Integer;              { Center coordinate }
20:      scale : Integer;                         { Miscellaneous }
21:
22:   PROCEDURE DisplayAxes;
23:   { Draw x and y axes lines with "tick" marks }
24:   VAR x, y, xf, yf, xd, yd : Integer;    { See comments below }
25:   BEGIN
26:      SetColor( LightBlue );
27:      SetLineStyle( DottedLn, 0, NormWidth );
28:      Line( xCenter, yMin, xCenter, yMax );  { Draw x axis }
29:      Line( xMin, yCenter, xMax, yCenter );  { Draw y axis }
30:      SetColor( LightGray );
31:      SetLineStyle( SolidLn, 0, NormWidth );
32:      xf := GetMaxX DIV 20;   { Tick mark at every xf points }
33:      xd := xf DIV 3;         { Length of horizontal tick marks }
34:      yf := GetMaxY DIV 20;   { Tick mark at every yf points }
35:      yd := yf DIV 3;         { Length of vertical tick marks }
36:      FOR x := xMin TO xMax DO
37:        IF ( x MOD xf ) = 0
38:           THEN Line( x, yCenter - yd, x, yCenter + yd );
39:      FOR y := yMin TO yMax DO
40:        IF ( y MOD yf ) = 0
41:           THEN Line( yCenter - xd, y, yCenter + xd, y )
42:   END; { DisplayAxes }
43:
44:   PROCEDURE Initialize;
45:   { Miscellaneous initializations }
46:   BEGIN
47:      xMax := GetMaxX DIV 2;
48:      yMax := GetMaxY DIV 2;
49:      xMin := -xMax;
50:      yMin := -yMax;
51:      xCenter := 0;
```

Program 13-26 *cont.*

```
52:     yCenter := 0;
53:     scale := GetMaxX DIV 8;
54:     SetViewPort( xMax, yMax, GetMaxX, GetMaxY, ClipOff )
55:  END; { Initialize }
56:
57:  PROCEDURE YPlot( x : Integer; y : Real );
58:  { Plot point at x, y }
59:  BEGIN
60:     PutPixel( x, Round( y * scale ), White )
61:  END; { YPlot }
62:
63:  PROCEDURE PlotGraph( pf : PlotFunction );
64:  { Display plot of user's function }
65:  VAR x : Integer;
66:  BEGIN
67:     Initialize;
68:     DisplayAxes;
69:     FOR x := xMin TO xMax DO
70:        YPlot( x, pf( x ) );
71:     REPEAT UNTIL Keypressed;
72:     CloseGraph
73:  END; { PlotGraph }
74:
75:  BEGIN
76:     graphDriver := Detect;
77:     InitGraph( graphDriver, graphMode, '' );
78:     IF GraphResult <> GrOk THEN
79:     BEGIN
80:        Writeln( 'Error initializing graphics' );
81:        Halt( 1 )
82:     END { if }
83:  END.
```

Writing PlotU Host Programs

Program 13-27 demonstrates how to write a host program that calls **PlotGraph** in the **PlotU** unit (Program 13-26). Save as PLOT.PAS and compile. Lines 10–15 contain the function to plot—compiled with {$F + } in effect. Notice that this function has the format required by the **PlotFunction** procedure-type definition (Program 13-26, line 8).

The entire main program reduces to a single statement at line 18, which calls the **PlotGraph**, passing the address of the function to plot. There's no need to modify the **PlotU** package just to plot a different mathematical function. To demonstrate how this works, change **Cos** in line 13 to **Sin**, or invent your own functions. Then, recompile PLOT.PAS and you're done.

Program 13-27

```
1:  PROGRAM Plot;
2:
3:  USES PlotU;
4:
5:  FUNCTION Radians( angle : Integer ) : Real;
6:  BEGIN
7:     Radians := angle * Pi / 180.0
8:  END; { Radians }
9:
10: {$F+}
11: FUNCTION f( x : Integer ) : Real;
12: BEGIN
13:    f := Cos( Radians( x ) )
14: END; { f }
15: {$F-}
16:
17: BEGIN
18:    PlotGraph( f )
19: END.
```

Procedure-Type Complications

Procedure types are useful, especially when designing units such as PLOTU with hooks to which you can attach your own custom routines. But when using procedure types, you should be aware of a few subtle complications the technique introduces.

Procedures and functions addressed by procedure variables must be of your own design—for example, you can't assign the addresses of standard routines such as **Writeln** to procedure variables. The procedures and functions may not nest inside other routines—they must be at the global program level. Procedure variables also may not address interrupt handlers or **InLine** procedures and functions (see Chapter 14).

Another complication involves assignments. As explained earlier, to initialize a procedure variable, you must assign the name of an actual procedure or function to the variable:

```
stringF := Copyright;
```

That assigns the *address* of function **Copyright** to the **StringF** procedure variable. Compare this with the more traditional assignment that involves a function:

```
s := Copyright;
```

In that assignment, function **Copyright** is executed. The function returns a string, which is assigned to string variable **s**. The difference between the two assignments is important. In the first example, **Copyright** does not run. In the second, it does. The dissimilar results are hidden by the similar looking statements.

Usually, Turbo Pascal generates the proper code for such assignments, so there's little need for concern. But, the compiler may not understand your intentions all the time. Suppose the program needs to call a **Reinitialize** procedure if the **stringF** procedure variable is not equal to the address of **Copyright**:

```
IF stringF <> Copyright     {???}
   THEN ReInitialize;
```

That statement may not work correctly. Processing the expression, Turbo Pascal assumes that it should generate function calls to **stringF** and to **Copyright**, and then compare the returned strings. This only makes sense—both identifiers address string functions; therefore, their results are compatible in expressions. But, we want to compare the function *addresses*, not the function *results*. The solution is to use the @ symbol to force Turbo Pascal to compare addresses:

```
IF @stringF <> @Copyright
   THEN ReInitialize;
```

With @ signs, the *address value* of the procedure variable **stringF** is compared with the *address* of the **Copyright** function. Now the expression works correctly.

Be aware of the difference between a procedure variable's address value, and the address of a procedure. As you know, the @ operator returns the address of an identifier. But when applied to a procedure variable, @ returns the variable's *value*, which, as you know, is actually a pointer. If you need to access the address where the procedure variable is stored in memory, you must use a double @@ sign. In other words, to assign the address of the variable **stringF** to a pointer **p**, you have to write:

```
p := @@stringF;     { Assign address of stringF to p }
```

This differs from the usual method for taking the addresses of common variables, such as an integer **i**, which requires only a single @ sign:

```
p := @i;            { Assign address of i to p }
```

Dealing With Heap Errors

When using **New** or **GetMem** to allocate memory for variables on the heap, if enough memory is not available, the program halts with the unfriendly message:

```
Runtime error 203: Heap overflow error
```

To prevent programs from ending when out of memory, you can install your own heap error function, as Program 13-28 demonstrates. Function **HeapError-Trap** (lines 7–12) takes a **Word** parameter **size** and returns type **Integer**. The function must be declared *far* with the compiler directive {$F + } (see line 7) because it will be called from a different code segment.

Line 17 assigns the address of **HeapErrorTrap** to the **System** unit **HeapError** variable. This informs **System** to call the custom function instead of halting if **New** or **GetMem** cannot handle a request to allocate memory. When this happens, parameter **size** equals the number of requested bytes. The custom heap error function can then return one of three values listed in Table 13-5. Remove line 17 and run the program to see the effect of not using a custom heap error handler.

Table 13-5 Heap error function values

Value	Action
0	Halt program with runtime error
1	Have **New** and **GetMem** return **Nil**
2	Retry same **New** or **GetMem**

Usually, return 1 to force **New** and **GetMem** to return a **Nil** pointer instead of halting the program. You can test for this condition, as the **REPEAT** loop demonstrates in Program 13-28, lines 18–20. If the custom heap error handler returns 2, Turbo Pascal retries the **New** or **GetMem** statement that caused the failure. If you write programming to compact the heap after an out-of-memory failure—no small task, which we'll have to leave unimplemented here—then you could return 2 to retry memory allocation requests. Finally, you could return 0, which forces a runtime error to occur, the default condition in the absence of a custom heap error handler.

Program 13-28

```
 1:  PROGRAM HeapOfTrouble;
 2:  TYPE
 3:      Atype = ARRAY[ 1 .. 10000 ] OF Real;
 4:  VAR
 5:      p : ^Atype;
 6:
 7:  {$F+}
 8:  FUNCTION HeapErrorTrap( size : Word ) : Integer;
 9:  BEGIN
10:      HeapErrorTrap := 1    { Forces New, GetMem to return Nil }
11:  END; { HeapErrorTrap }
12:  {$F-}
13:
14:  BEGIN
```

Program 13-28 *cont.*

```
15:      Writeln( 'Memory at start  = ', Memavail );
16:      Writeln( 'Size of variable = ', Sizeof( Atype ) );
17:      HeapError := @HeapErrorTrap;
18:      REPEAT
19:         New( p )
20:      UNTIL p = Nil;
21:      Writeln( 'Memory at end    = ', Memavail );
22:  END.
```

Dealing With the Stack

As you learned in Chapter 7, **New** and **GetMem** allocate memory space for variables on the heap. Local variables in procedures and functions are created on the stack when a statement calls the routines that declare the variables. If there isn't enough memory on the stack to hold the variables, the program halts with:

```
Runtime error 202: Stack overflow error
```

Unlike the heap overflow error discussed in the previous section, there is no way to recover from a stack overflow—it's already too late by the time you discover the problem. The only cure is prevention, using the {$M} compiler directive to change the amount of stack space reserved for your program.

To detect stack overflow errors, Turbo Pascal inserts code to test the stack and heap at the start of each procedure and function. These checks take only a small amount of time—but they do take *some* time. To squeeze every ounce of power out of a program, you can turn off stack error checking by inserting this compiler directive at the start of your program:

```
{$S-}    { Turn off stack error checks }
```

Turning off stack error checking this way is extremely dangerous. If there is not enough stack space to hold local variables when you call procedures and functions, your program will ignore this condition and merrily overwrite whatever other variables or code are in its way. The usual result is a system crash, erased disk files, data destruction, and a loss of hair—yours. Never turn off stack error checking unless you are 100% positive that a stack overflow cannot occur.

Other Memory Concerns

The **System** unit defines three **Pointer** variables, **HeapOrg**, **HeapPtr**, and **FreePtr**, plus one **Word** variable, **FreeMin**, which you can examine and (sometimes) change to manipulate the memory heap. The following paragraphs describe these four variables. For an illustration of these variables and their relation to memory organization, see Appendix B.

HeapOrg points to the low memory start of the heap, which grows toward higher addresses.

HeapPtr points to the current top of the heap, moving to higher addresses as you execute **New** and **GetMem** statements.

FreePtr points to the bottom of the free list, which Turbo Pascal uses to keep track of disposed heap memory variables.

FreeMin equals the minimum space (usually 0) in bytes that Turbo Pascal allows between **HeapPtr** and **FreePtr**.

Passing Command-Line Parameters

When you compile a program to a disk EXE file, you execute the program by typing its name. At the same time, you can type extra commands or other parameters following the program name. For example, if you have the program, SORT, and you want to sort a text file, NAMES.TXT, you might type:

```
A>SORT NAMES.TXT
```

Program 13-29 demonstrates how a program picks up extra parameters like NAMES.TXT from the command line. The program creates one long text file out of a number of other files. You can use it to combine several small programs into a single file, perhaps for uploading to a bulletin board or time-sharing network.

If you type no parameters, the program prints out instructions instead. Line 58 senses how many parameters there are by testing the built-in function, **ParamCount**. If there are no parameters, the **IF** statement calls procedure **Instruct**; otherwise, it calls **Process**. To print instructions, compile the program to an EXE file and run from DOS by typing COMBINE.

To give parameters to the program, enter the name of the output file followed by as many other text files as you want to combine. If you have files named SUB1.PAS and SUB2.PAS, the following combines them into a single file, SUBS.PAS:

```
C>COMBINE SUBS.PAS SUB1.PAS SUB2.PAS
```

The program reads your parameters with procedure **ParamStr**, as shown in lines 31 and 45. **ParamStr** takes an integer value indicating which parameter you want. To display the second parameter, you could use the **Writeln** statement:

```
Writeln( ParamStr( 2 ) );
```

If you're running DOS 3.0 or a later version, you can find out the program's path name by examining **ParamStr(0)**. You can then use **Dos** unit routines to store the path to the program's location, giving you a way to read and write miscellaneous program files there even if people change directories:

```
    pathName := FExpand( paramstr(0) );
    Writeln( 'Program name = ', pathName );
    FSplit( pathName, dir, name, ext );
    Writeln( 'Directory = ', dir );
```

While debugging a program that recognizes parameters, use Turbo Pascal's *Options:Parameters* command to simulate parameter passing. This avoids compiling to an EXE file, exiting Turbo Pascal, and running your program just to test minor corrections.

Program 13-29

```
 1:   PROGRAM Combine;
 2:   USES Crt;
 3:
 4:   PROCEDURE Instruct;
 5:   BEGIN
 6:      Writeln;
 7:      Writeln( 'COMBINE <output> <input1> <input2> ... <inputn>' );
 8:      Writeln; Writeln( '  A>COMBINE New.Txt TextA.Pas TextB.Pas' );
 9:      Writeln;
10:      Writeln( 'The above combines TextA.Pas and TextB.Pas into a new' );
11:      Writeln( 'file, New.Txt. If New.Txt exists, you are asked for' );
12:      Writeln( 'permission to overwrite it.' );
13:      Writeln
14:   END;
15:
16:   FUNCTION FileExists( Var f : Text ) : Boolean;
17:   BEGIN
18:   {$i-} Reset( f ); Close( f ); {$i+}
19:      FileExists := ( IoResult = 0 )
20:   END; { FileExists }
21:
22:   PROCEDURE Process;
23:   VAR
24:      ch        : Char;
25:      Fname     : String[64];
26:      i         : Integer;
27:      Infile,
28:       OutFile  : Text;
29:      s         : String[132];
30:   BEGIN
31:      Fname := ParamStr(1);
32:      IF Length( Fname ) > 0 THEN
33:      BEGIN
34:         Assign( OutFile, Fname );
```

```
35:         IF FileExists( OutFile )
36:            THEN BEGIN
37:                  Write( Fname, ' exists. Overwrite it? ' );
38:                  ch := ReadKey;
39:                  Writeln( ch );
40:                  IF Upcase(ch) <> 'Y' THEN Halt
41:               END;
42:         Rewrite( OutFile );
43:         FOR i := 2 TO ParamCount DO
44:         BEGIN
45:            Fname := ParamStr( i );
46:            Assign( InFile, Fname ); Reset( Infile );
47:            WHILE NOT Eof( InFile ) DO
48:            BEGIN
49:               Readln( Infile, s ); Writeln( OutFile, s )
50:            END;
51:            Close( Infile )
52:         END;
53:         Close( OutFile )
54:      END
55: END; { process }
56:
57: BEGIN
58:    IF ParamCount <= 0 THEN Instruct ELSE Process
59: END.
```

Inside a File Variable

All file variables contain hidden details that Turbo Pascal normally reserves for its own use. With typecasting and the help of the **Dos** unit **FileRec** data type, you can access these details. **FileRec** is defined as:

```
FileRec =
   RECORD
      Handle   : Word;
      Mode     : Word;
      RecSize  : Word;
      Private  : ARRAY[ 1 .. 26 ] OF Byte;
      UserData : ARRAY[ 1 .. 16 ] OF Byte;
      Name     : ARRAY[ 0 .. 79 ] OF Char
   END;
```

To use this record, insert a **USES Dos;** declaration in your program. Then, typecast any file variable to type **FileRec**. For example, Program 13-30 displays the record size for a file of type **Real**.

The statements before the **Writeln** in line 7 assign a name and open the file variable before accessing **FileRec** fields. The variable typecast in line 7 shows how to gain access to the normally hidden fields inside a file variable. Here, the program simply displays the file's record size.

Program 13-30

```
 1:  PROGRAM ShowFileSize;
 2:  USES Dos;
 3:  VAR f : FILE OF Real;
 4:  BEGIN
 5:     Assign( f, 'TEST.$$$' );  { Must open file first }
 6:     Rewrite( f );
 7:     Writeln( 'Record size = ', FileRec(f).RecSize );
 8:     Close( f );
 9:     Erase( f )
10:  END.
```

You can use the same method to access other fields, too. *Handle* is the handle or reference value that DOS returns for file I/O operations. Turbo Pascal calls these DOS routines and stores the DOS handle in the *Handle* field. The *Mode* field can be one of the values from Table 13-3. The *RecSize* field equals the size of file data elements in bytes.

Although Turbo Pascal does not use the *Private* array, don't store any values here. Presumably, future compiler releases will use this field. You may store any data you want in the 16-byte *UserData* array, though. If you need more than 16 bytes, store a pointer in *UserData* to your other variables.

The final field, *Name*, stores the file name originally passed to **Assign**. This field is an ASCIIZ string ending in a null character (ASCII 0), not a Pascal string data type.

Advanced Overlay Management

Turbo Pascal 5.5 adds several advanced features to the **Overlay** unit, first introduced in version 5.0. Most of the time, the information in Chapter 10 is all you need to write overlay programs—overlays are fully compatible in both compiler versions. If you're developing commercial software, though, you'll want to be sure that overlays are working at top efficiency by carefully considering the options discussed here.

Overlay Initializations

As you know, units may have an initialization section, comparable to a program's main block. The initialization code appears between **BEGIN** and **END** at the end of the unit text:

```
UNIT AnyUnit;
INTERFACE
   { Public declarations }
IMPLEMENTATION
   { Private declarations }
BEGIN
   { Perform unit initializations }
END.
```

In a host program that **USES AnyUnit**, unit initialization statements run before the host's first statement executes, which leads to sticky problems when the units are overlays. As explained in Chapter 10, you must call **OverInit** to initialize the **Overlay** unit *before* any overlays can be loaded. But, the overlays must be loaded in order to execute their initialization sections before the program has a chance to call **OverInit**.

One way to resolve this confusion, and ensure that overlay initializations perform in the correct order at the right times, is to call **OverInit** from the initialization section of another unit and then list that unit in a **USES** declaration ahead of all overlays that have their own initialization blocks. Program 13-31 lists a sample unit that you can use for this purpose.

To use the unit, change PROGNAME.OVR in line 10 to the name of your program's overlay file. Compile the unit to OVRSTART.TPU and include a **USES** declaration in your main program similar to this:

```
USES Overlay, Crt, OvrStartup, OvrUnitA, OvrUnitB, OvrUnitC;

{$O OvrUnitA}
{$O OvrUnitB}
{$O OvrUnitC}
```

In this example, overlay units **OvrUnitA**, **OvrUnitB**, and **OvrUnitC** have initialization sections that must run ahead of the main program's first statement. Inserting the **OvrStartup** unit ahead of the overlays calls **OvrInit** (line 10), allowing the overlays to be loaded into memory before executing their initialization code.

Program 13-31

```
1:   UNIT OvrStartup;
2:
3:   INTERFACE
4:
5:   IMPLEMENTATION
6:
7:   USES Overlay;
8:
9:   BEGIN
```

Program 13-31 *cont.*

```
10:      OvrInit( 'PROGNAME.OVR' );
11:      IF OvrResult <> ovrOk THEN
12:      BEGIN
13:         Writeln( 'Overlay error' );
14:         Halt(1)
15:      END; { if }
16:      OvrInitEMS
17:  END. { OvrStartup unit }
```

Overlay Unit Complications

Although the previous section solves the problem of having to call **OvrInit** before executing overlay initialization sections, there are two good reasons to avoid such situations:

- Before running the overlay initialization code, the overlay units must be loaded from disk. With many units, this can slow program startup to a crawl.

- Even though the initialization sections run only once, the initialization code is loaded into memory along with the rest of the unit, wasting RAM and time.

For these reasons, some programmers prefer to stuff initialization statements into yet another overlay unit and eliminate initialization sections from other overlays. When combined with the **OvrStartup** unit (Program 13-31), this reduces startup chores to loading a single overlay and running all initializations.

Optimizing the Overlay Buffer

As Chapter 10 explains, you can call **OvrGetBuf** to find out the size of the overlay buffer, the memory area where overlay units are stored. **OvrSetBuf** can increase the buffer size to allow multiple units to fit together in this memory space, improving performance by reducing disk reads. (Remember, though, if enough EMS RAM is available, there's no advantage to increasing the overlay buffer size.)

Turbo Pascal 5.5 enhances its methods for managing the overlay buffer in an effort to keep the most frequently used code in memory for the longest time. In most programs, the new algorithm—called the *probation-reprieve* method—can reduce the number of times overlays are loaded from disk, often without having to increase the overlay buffer size.

The method works by putting units "on probation" when the unit's code falls within an adjustable *probation area*, usually equal to about a third of the total overlay buffer space. During this time, if any statements call the unit's procedures or functions, when it comes time to load a new overlay into the buffer, the overlay loader "reprieves" the unit that was placed on probation. Instead of moving that unit out to make room in the buffer, the loader releases a less frequently used unit. The reprieved unit then stays in the buffer until the next time more space is needed. As a result, units that work harder tend to stay in RAM longer—and the program runs faster.

Enabling Probation-Reprieve

Switching on the probation-reprieve method is easy—just set the probation area size, normally 0 (off), to any positive value. If you don't do this, the version 5.5 overlay memory manager works as it does in Turbo Pascal 5.0. To enable probation-reprieve buffer management, call **OvrSetRetry**, passing a value somewhere between one half and a third the size of the full overlay buffer:

```
OvrInit( 'PROGNAME.OVR' );
IF OvrResult <> ovrOk THEN Halt(1);
OvrSetBuf( SizeOfBuffer );
OvrSetRetry( SizeOfBuffer DIV 3 );
```

Usually, you'll call **OvrSetBuf** before **OvrSetRetry** to increase the overlay buffer size, in this example, using a previously declared constant **SizeOfBuffer**. To find out the current probation-area size, call **OvrGetRetry**:

```
Writeln( 'Probation area size = ', OvrGetRetry );
```

If you don't like the idea of setting a fixed buffer size, you can increase the default buffer size by adding to **OvrGetBuf**. Then, set the probation area to a third of the adjusted size:

```
OvrSetBuf( OvrGetBuf * 2 );     { Double default buffer size }
OvrSetRetry( OvrGetBuf DIV 3 ); { Set probation area }
```

Calculating the best probation-area size is not always easy. Although Borland recommends a size of a third to one half of the total buffer space, each set of overlays has a unique configuration that results in the most code in memory for the longest times.

To find the best values for your programs, use Turbo Debugger (or the built-in version) to monitor two **Overlay** unit variables, **OvrLoadCount** and **Ovr-TrapCount**. Or, just display the two values in **Writeln** statements. The variables collect statistics that can help you to pick the best probation-area size:

- **OvrLoadCount** measures the number of times units are loaded from disk. Aim for the lowest possible value, indicating that units are staying in memory longer. You can usually reduce a high **OvrLoadCount** by increasing the overlay buffer size with **OvrSetBuf**.

- **OvrTrapCount** counts two items: the number of times units are loaded from disk, and the number of times units are accessed while on probation. Each count represents one interception by the **Overlay** manager of a call to a unit that is either not in memory or is on probation. If **OvrTrapCount** increases at nearly the same rate as **OvrLoadCount**, then the probation-reprieve scheme is not working well—try increasing the probation-area size by calling **OvrSetRetry**. You might also need a larger overlay buffer. If **Ovr-TrapCount** increases at a greater rate than **OvrLoadCount**, then more units are being reprieved—a good sign that you're headed in the right direction. If **OvrTrapCount** increases while **OvrLoadCount** advances slowly or not at all, you've probably hit the ideal configuration. You might even try *reducing* the buffer and probation sizes to minimize memory use.

How the Probation-Reprieve Method Works

Fine-tuning the overlay buffer for peak performance requires a good understanding of how the **Overlay** unit manages memory. For test purposes, assume there are three overlay units of identical size—A, B, and C—plus a main program that loads the overlays in this order:

A B A C A B B C B A B

Figures 13-7 through 13-9 show how the size of the overlay buffer and the amount of probation space affect the performance of this test program. (I prepared the diagrams by hand while examining the overlay buffer contents with a program not listed here. The figures are snapshots of the actual overlay buffer in memory.) The vertical blocks (numbered below and to the left) represent the overlay buffer. The shaded areas represent unused memory. Above the buffers are the values of **OvrTrapCount** listed on top of **OvrLoadCount** for each step. Uppercase letters along the bottom show the progression of calls to overlay routines.

The first test (see Figure 13-7) uses the default buffer size, which is just a little larger than the largest unit. The buffer is always aligned to offsets 0000 at 16-byte "paragraphs" in memory; so there's usually a little waste at the end. The test shows that ten disk reads are required for 11 calls to overlay routines. Obviously, because the buffer can hold only one overlay at a time, the overlay loader has to release the buffer space to load another unit. The only savings in this test comes at step 7, which calls a routine in unit B. Because B is already in the buffer from step 6, no disk read occurs (shown by the dashes above step number 7).

The next test doubles the overlay buffer size, but does not switch on probation-reprieve memory management (see Figure 13-8). Now, two overlays can fit into the buffer together, which should reduce disk reads.

At step 1, unit A is loaded, after which the program calls a routine in B at step 2. Because there's plenty of unused space available, the overlay loader places B after A. As a result, step 3 does not require a disk read—A is already in the buffer. Likewise, step 9 saves another disk read because B is already in the buffer from as far back as step 6.

Only eight disk reads are now required for the 11 steps, a savings of two disk operations from the previous default-buffer test. Increasing the buffer size decreases **OvrLoadCount** (the bottom of the two numbers on top). But, **Ovr-TrapCount** still rises at the same rate as **OvrLoadCount**, indicating that further optimizations are possible.

If you examine Figure 13-8 closely, you'll see another indication that overlay buffer management isn't working as well as it could. Step 4 loads unit C, replacing

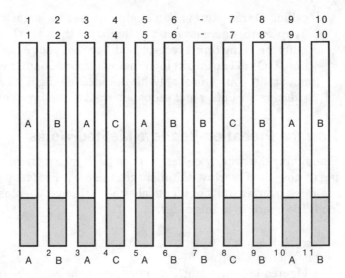

Figure 13-7 Overlay test using the default buffer size.

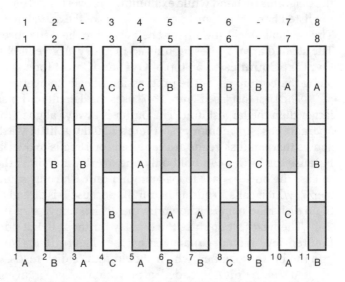

Figure 13-8 Overlay test with double the default buffer size.

unit A in the buffer. Step 5 then calls A, forcing the overlay loader to reload A, thus wasting time. It would have been better to release B at step 4, not A.

Figure 13-9 shows the final test, optimized with probation-reprieve memory management, which can detect these conditions. The buffer size is the same as in the previous test, but the probation area is set to a third of the total buffer. For the purposes of deciding which overlays to place on probation, the overlay loader considers the total buffer to be circular. The probation area includes the free space in the buffer plus extra space extending in the diagrams down and around to the top. For example, at step 1, A is in the probation area. At step 8, overlay B is on probation.

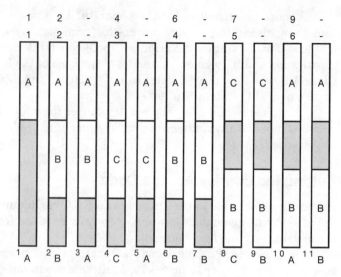

Figure 13-9 Overlay test with probation-reprieve buffer management.

Steps 1–3 are the same as in the previous test. But, at step 3, because A is on probation, the call to one of A's routines causes the overlay loader to give A a reprieve. This means that, when step 4 calls C, the loader throws out the less frequently used unit B; therefore, step 5 does not require another disk read because A is already in memory.

Notice the values on top. Only six disk reads are needed to complete the sequence, a significant savings over the ten disk reads in the first test (Figure 13-7). Also, **OvrTrapCount** reaches a final value of 9 and increases more rapidly than **OvrLoadCount**—a sign of increased reprieval activity.

From examining these tests, you might think that a more simple "least recently used" algorithm (often labeled LRU) would do just as well as the probation-reprieve method. In other words, just count all calls to routines in overlays and, when more space is needed, throw out the units with the lowest LRU counts. That certainly would work, but it requires an increment operation for *each* call to routines in overlays plus space for the LRU values. The probation-reprieve method—which is a little more difficult to use and understand—offers the same benefits in most cases without sacrificing space or performance. The results seem to be especially good in real-life programs with dozens of overlays competing for the same buffer space.

Clearing the Overlay Buffer

Call **OvrClearBuf** to empty the overlay buffer. After this, any calls to overlay unit procedures and functions force the **Overlay** unit to load an overlay from disk or from EMS RAM.

Normally, you don't need to call **OvrClearBuf**. One of the goals of good overlay-buffer management is to keep as much code in memory as possible, not to increase the number of disk reads. You might want to call **OvrClearBuf** during debugging as a worst-case test of program performance, though.

A more practical use for **OvrClearBuf** is to provide some space to store something else in the overlay buffer—for example, saved text behind a pop-up window. Two **System** unit variable (typed) constants locate the overlay buffer's starting and ending segment addresses at the base of the heap. After calling **Ovr-ClearBuf**, you may use the bytes from **OvrHeapOrg:**0000 up to but not including the byte at **OvrHeapEnd:**0000.

Of course, when using the overlay buffer for your own purposes this way, you must not call any routines in overlay units until you're finished with the borrowed space.

Setting the Overlay Access Code

Another new variable in the Turbo Pascal 5.5 **Overlay** unit, **OvrFileMode**, sets the mode value given to DOS when overlays are loaded from disk. Normally, the mode value is 0 (read-only access).

On single-user PCs, the default value rarely if ever needs changing. But on multiple-user systems, such as networks, a different mode value might be needed to allow two or more terminals to open the same overlay .OVR file, perhaps stored on a common file-server disk that all users share. Some networks insist that shared files be opened with read-only status, preventing two or more users from accidentally updating the same data. Even though programs never have any good reason to write data to overlay files, the network software doesn't know that and may prohibit Turbo Pascal overlay code from running on multiple-network terminals.

Table 13-6 lists various bit combinations that make up file-access mode values for DOS 2.0 and 3.0 (plus in-between and later versions). DOS 2.0 recognizes only bits 0–2; other bits are reserved and should be 0. Only three file modes are available: read-only, write-only, and read/write.

Table 13-6 File access modes

DOS 2.0 (and later versions)		
7 6 5 4 3 (reserved)	2 1 0 (access mode)	Hex value
0 0 0 0 0	0 0 0 (Read-only)	$00
	0 0 1 (Write-only)	$01
	0 1 0 (Read/Write)	$02

DOS 3.0 (and later versions)			
7 (inherit)	6 5 4 (denials)	3 (reserved)	Hex value
0 (On)	0 0 0 (Compatibility)	0	$00
1 (Off)			$80
	0 0 1 (Deny read/write)		$10
	0 1 0 (Deny write)		$20
	0 1 1 (Deny read)		$30
	1 0 0 (Deny nothing)		$40

DOS 3.0 uses the full byte except bit 3, which should be 0. Bits 0–2 are the same as in DOS 2.0. Bit 7 determines if child processes (subprograms called by another program) inherit open files from their parents. Bits 4–6 select various "denials." If these three bits are 0, then the value defaults to the compatible bit patterns for DOS 2.0. The other listed settings deny read/write, write, and read-only accesses. When bit 6 is 1 and the other two bits are 0, no denials are recognized.

It's difficult to suggest one correct value for all networks. Some people report that $42 works (deny nothing, enable read/write). Others say $40, $C0, and $A0 are the correct values. You'll just have to experiment. If you think your code will run on a network, you'd be wise to add a global variable that users can change to try out different file-access modes in case problems develop.

Intercepting Overlay Requests

Another new Turbo Pascal 5.5 **Overlay** unit feature lets you intercept calls to the routines that load overlay code from disk. Two declarations in the **Overlay** unit let you hook custom code into the overlay's loader.

```
TYPE
   OvrReadFunc = FUNCTION( ovrSeg : Word ) : Integer;
VAR
   ovrReadBuf : OvrReadFunc;
```

OvrReadFunc is a procedure-type function that takes one **Word** parameter and returns type **Integer**. **OvrReadBuf** is a procedure variable of type **OvrReadFunc**.

When loading overlay units from disk, the overlay loader calls the function addressed by **ovrReadBuf**. A function result of 0 indicates a successful load; a nonzero result indicates an error, causing the overlay manager to generate a runtime error number 209. The **ovrSeg** parameter identifies which of several overlay units to load. Usually, you'll pass this value along to the standard loader after your custom code finishes—the **ovrSeg** value hasn't any other practical use.

Many possible uses come to mind for hooking custom code to the overlay loader. You might use this advanced feature:

- to prevent overlay runtime errors from halting programs, usually caused by a missing overlay file
- to prompt users to insert a diskette containing the overlay file—especially useful on a floppy-disk-only system
- to debug overlays by intercepting calls to the overlay loader

Hooking In an Overlay Function

In addition to performing its own duties, a custom overlay function must call the stock overlay loader. To provide a place to save the address of the loader for later use, create a global variable of type **OvrReadFunc**:

```
VAR
   stockOvrLoader : OvrReadFunc;    { Original loader address }
```

Next, write a custom function with the format of **OvrReadFunc**. As with all procedures and functions addressed by procedure variables, compile the function with the {$F + } *far* option. The function name can be anything you want. Here's a simple example that prompts for a diskette named OVERLAYS:

```
{$F+,I-}    { Compile far code; disable I/O error checks }
FUNCTION OvrPrompter( ovrSeg : Word ) : Integer;
VAR f : FILE;              { For checking if overlay file exists }
    result : Integer;   { Stock loader result code }
BEGIN
   REPEAT
      Assign( f, 'PROGNAME.OVR' );
      REPEAT
        Write( 'Insert diskette OVERLAYS and press Enter...' );
        Readln;
        Reset( f )
      UNTIL IoResult = 0;  { 0 = PROGNAME.OVR found on disk }
      Close( f );
      result := stockOvrLoader( ovrSeg )  { Call stock loader }
   UNTIL result = 0;
   OvrPrompter := result    { Pass 0 result code back to caller }
END; { OvrPrompter }
{$F-,I+}    { Compile near code; enable I/O error checks }
```

The inner **REPEAT** loop cycles until **Reset** successfully opens file PROGNAME.OVR, indicating that the correct diskette is in place. After this, the function calls the stock overlay loader via the **stockOvrLoader** procedure variable, passing the **ovrSeg** parameter, which tells the loader which overlay to retrieve. The outer **REPEAT** loop cycles until the result of this code equals 0, indicating that the overlay has been successfully loaded. Only then is the result (always 0) passed back to the overlay manager through the **OvrPrompter** function identifier.

To enable the custom **OvrPrompter** function, the main program's initialization code must save the stock loader's address and assign the custom function's address to **OvrReadBuf**, the procedure variable declared in the **Overlay** unit:

```
stockOvrLoader := ovrReadBuf;   { Save original loader address }
ovrReadBuf := OvrPrompter;      { Hook in new loader function }
```

Now, every time a call is intercepted to an overlay unit that's not in the overlay buffer, the custom function runs.

Summary

Conditional compilation lets you create programs that compile differently based on the presence or absence of symbols that you define in compiler directives. You can use this technique to customize programs, to write code to run with and without a math coprocessor, and to create programs that compile correctly under different compiler versions.

Variable and value typecasting methods convert data types from one form to another. Variable typecasts must involve variables of equal size. One use for variable typecasts is to access fields in file variables, normally hidden from view.

Mem, **MemW**, **MemL**, **Port**, and **PortW** are special built-in arrays that make it easy to read and write bytes and words in memory or in I/O ports.

Include files help you to write large programs. You can also use the **Dos** unit **Exec** procedure to divide large programs into separate pieces.

Writing your own text file device drivers lets you customize **Read**, **Readln**, **Write**, **Writeln**, **Reset**, and **Rewrite** statements.

Turbo Pascal allows **LABEL**, **TYPE**, **CONST**, and **VAR** declarations to appear in any order, even between procedures and functions. Using this technique can make programs incompatible with other Pascal compilers but is useful in some circumstances and can help prevent side-effect errors.

Variable constants (or typed constants, as the Turbo Pascal Reference Manual calls them) can be structured, letting you define preinitialized arrays, records, and sets.

Turbo Pascal comes with a variety of special commands and variables to use subdirectories, fill and move memory, retrieve command-line parameters, add custom exit procedures to programs, read DOS environment variables, and deal with out-of-memory errors.

Procedure types and procedure-type variables let you pass the addresses of procedures and functions as parameters to other routines. This lets you design code with "hooks" that you can attach to custom code at runtime.

Turbo Pascal 5.5 adds several enhancements to the **Overlay** unit introduced in version 5.0. The enhancements, which include a memory-management technique called probation-reprieve, help to keep frequently used overlays in memory for a longer time, thus improving program speed.

Exercises

13-1. The byte at address $F000:$FFFE indicates the computer model. $FF = IBM PC; $FE = PC/XT; $FD = PCjr; and $FC = PC/AT. Write a program to display your computer type. Use the **Mem** array.

13-2. Take all programs from any chapter (except Chapter 1) and design a menu program that lets you select which program you want. Each program should then return to the menu when it is finished, letting you select another. Use the **Dos** unit **Exec** procedure.

13-3. Rewrite Program 13-15 without using a constant variable array for **Board**. Investigate efficient methods for initializing the array.

13-4. Using a design similar to Program 13-15, write a program, **Checkers**, that sets up a checkerboard and lets two people take turns playing.

13-5. Using conditional compilation, write a program that uses the custom beeper in Program 13-4 or the standard method, using a **Write(Chr(7))** statement. It should be possible to change the program by modifying one symbol definition.

13-6. Write a program to inspect a range of memory bytes in the computer.

13-7. Write a DOS menu program to let people see directories, change to new subdirectories, delete files, and run other programs. It should be possible to select commands with function or single-letter keys. Use the **XtraStuff** unit from Program 10-2 in your answer.

13-8. (Advanced) Design a custom text file device driver to select printer modes. Write an **AssignPrn** procedure to select among various possibilities, perhaps **AssignPrn(f, CompressedText)**, and so on.

13-9. Test the speed advantages of using **FillChar** and **Move** instead of **FOR** loops to fill and move memory.

13-10. (Advanced) Design a custom exit procedure to dump sections of memory to a disk file when a program ends with an error. (In the "old" days of computing, this was called a *core dump*.)

13-11. (Advanced) Modify your answer to exercise 13-10 to write the core dump to the disk file or device specified by a DOS environment variable. For example, you should be able to SET DUMP = PRN to print the core dump or SET DUMP = E:\CORE.DAT to send output to a disk file on a RAM or other disk drive.

Pascal Meets
Assembly Language

- Assembly Versus Machine Language
- Three Machine Language Methods
- Why Use Assembly Language?
- Data Type Formats
- Anatomy of a Pascal Procedure
- Anatomy of a Pascal Function
- Parameters and Variables
- InLine Statements
- InLine Procedures and Functions
- Parameters and InLine Routines
- External Procedures and Functions
- Programming Interrupts
- Adding Assembly Language to Units

14

Adding assembly language to Pascal programs is devil's work. If you're not careful, you can birth an uncontrollable monster that runs wild, destroying every memory byte in its way. Like the Wolf Man, a Pascal program with embedded assembly language can act normally for a while but then become a most unfriendly beast after only innocent provocation from an unwary computer operator.

> Suggestion: If the moon is full, come back to this chapter another day. And don't forget your garlic necklace.

Assembly Versus Machine Language

The term *machine language* refers to the actual bytes that a computer processor interprets as instructions. *Assembly language* is a mnemonic system for writing machine language programs in text form. An *assembler* is a program that converts assembly language text into machine language, or *object code*. A *linker* is a program that combines multiple object-code modules and performs other tasks to create the finished, executable code.

If you have no experience with assembly language, you might have trouble understanding some of the material in this chapter. I assume that you know about bits, bytes, words, addresses, segments, and registers and that you have at least a fundamental knowledge of machine language instructions such as MOV and XOR. I'll explain some of these terms as we go along, but if you're already lost, you might want to read an assembly language tutorial before continuing.

You can use most assemblers to create machine language for eventually attaching to your Pascal programs. Turbo Pascal has its own built-in linker, and you do not need to use DOS LINK.EXE or a similar program. All programming in this chapter is compatible with Borland's Turbo Assembler (TASM) 1.0 and later versions and the Microsoft Macro Assembler (MASM) 4.0 and later versions.

Note: You'll find more information about adding assembly language to Turbo Pascal programs—plus a tutorial on writing stand-alone Turbo Assembler programs in "Ideal mode"—in my book, *Mastering Turbo Assembler*, 1989, Howard W. Sams.

Three Machine Language Methods

Regardless of which assembler you have, Turbo Pascal can attach machine language instructions to programs in three ways:

1. Inline statements.
2. Inline procedures and functions.
3. External routines.

An *inline statement* directly injects machine language into a program's blood stream. You can insert any byte values at any place in a program, code entire procedures and functions in machine language, or insert machine instructions between other Pascal commands with inline statements.

An *inline procedure or function* operates like an assembly language macro, which translates words like PRINT or INKEY into frequently used machine language sequences. Macros are to programmers what shorthand symbols are to a stenographer. Turbo Pascal's inline procedures and functions are similar to an assembler's macros, expanding procedure and function identifiers into machine language instructions instead of making subroutine calls.

An *external routine* is a procedure or function that you write in assembly language, assemble to an object code file with your favorite assembler, and then link into Pascal. This method is particularly useful for replacing tested Pascal routines with optimized assembly language. You might also combine Turbo Pascal with object code files generated by other languages such as C or Prolog.

Why Use Assembly Language?

If adding assembly language to Pascal is so dangerous, why do it? Usually, the answer involves speed. In the hands of an expert willing to use every trick in the microprocessor book, an assembly language program can beat the clock on any compiler's output, even that of top-rated compilers like Turbo Pascal.

Another reason to use assembly language is to manipulate computer hardware, modems, and plotters directly and to do other jobs difficult to accomplish in pure Pascal. Because Turbo Pascal has many hardware-specific facilities—for example, **Mem** and **Port** arrays, logical operators, and explicit addressing techniques—using assembly language for this reason is usually unnecessary.

A third reason for adding assembly language is to save memory. You might be able to save a few bytes by storing variables in processor registers, packing multiple values into bytes and words, and calling subroutines in the ROM BIOS (not a recommended practice). Memory and disk space, though, are inexpensive when compared to the time it takes to save a few bytes. Also, Turbo Pascal's smart linker already keeps program size to a minimum by excluding unneeded runtime routines.

Probably, then, the best reason to mix assembly language and Pascal is to increase program speed. But don't get caught in the speed trap of thinking that the more of your code you convert to assembly language, the faster your program will run. Frederick P. Brooks, Jr. in *The Mythical Man-Month* estimates that all speed problems can be solved by translating from 1 to 5% of a program into machine language. Other studies confirm this assumption, showing that typical programs spend most of their time executing a small percentage of their code. Identifying that critical code and converting it to optimized assembly language often drastically improves a program's operating speed. Converting the other 90 to 95% of a program most often has a negligible effect on speed.

Data Type Formats

Successful assembly language programming requires intimate knowledge of how Turbo Pascal stores variables in memory. You must know how many bytes a **LongInt** variable occupies, how to access fields in records, and how to calculate array indexes. You can no longer rely on the compiler to take care of such details for you and, therefore, this section describes Turbo Pascal's army of data formats, organized into four divisions (Pascal identifiers are capitalized):

1. *Ordinal types*—**Boolean**, **Char**, enumerated, and subranges.
2. *Integer types*—**ShortInt**, **Byte**, **Integer**, **Word**, and **LongInt**.
3. *Real types*—**Single**, **Real**, **Double**, **Extended**, and **Comp**.
4. *Structured types*—pointers, arrays, records, sets, strings, and files.

Figure 14-1 illustrates an imaginary data type to help you better understand

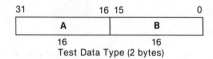

Figure 14-1 Test data type.

the data format diagrams in Figures 14-2 through 14-5. The pretend data type in Figure 14-1 occupies 32 bits with two parts, A and B, each 16 bits long. Bits in part B are numbered from 0 to 15. Bits in part A are numbered from 16 to 31. The most significant bit (MSB) is to the left. The least significant bit is to the right (LSB). In memory, lower addresses are to the right; higher addresses, to the left. In other words, the two bytes are swapped in memory with B physically coming before A.

Ordinal Types

Figure 14-2 diagrams Turbo Pascal's three basic ordinal data types: **Boolean**, **Char**, and enumerated values. Enumerated types with from one to 256 elements occupy one byte. Enumerated types with more than 256 elements occupy two bytes.

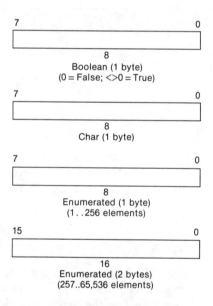

Figure 14-2 Ordinal types.

Integer Types

Figure 14-3 diagrams Turbo Pascal's five integer data types. Subranges (not shown) occupy the smallest possible space. A subrange of −5 . . 120, for example, would be encoded as a **ShortInt** value. The *s* represents the sign bit, which if equal to 1, indicates a negative number in twos-complement form.

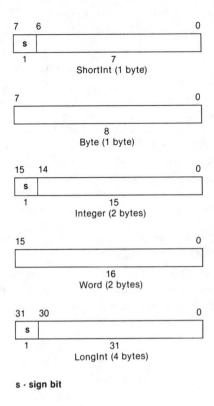

Figure 14-3 Integer types.

Real Types

Figure 14-4 diagrams Turbo Pascal's **Real** data type plus the four math coprocessor types: **Single**, **Double**, **Extended**, and **Comp**. For more information about how to use these types from assembly language, refer to a math coprocessor technical reference.

Structured Types

Figure 14-5 diagrams Turbo Pascal's structured data types: pointers, sets, arrays, records, and strings. Except for pointers, which occupy four bytes, the byte sizes of structured types vary. Use the **Sizeof** function to calculate the size of specific variables.

Arrays are stored with the first element first in memory, followed by the elements with the rightmost array index incrementing first. Record fields are stored in declaration order. Strings begin with a length byte followed by one to 255 character bytes. Strings are not terminated with a null character (ASCII 0) as they are in some languages.

Files are not diagrammed here. Refer to the **Dos** unit types **FileRec** and **TextRec** in the DOS.DOC file on your Turbo Pascal disks for details.

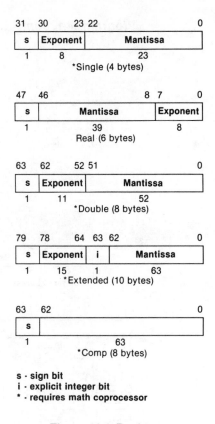

Figure 14-4 Real types.

Anatomy of a Pascal Procedure

When it comes to learning how to add machine language to Pascal programs, there's no better teacher than the compiler itself, which, after all, is an expert machine language encoder! A good way to begin, then, is with a look inside a typical Turbo Pascal procedure.

Program 14-1 is a simple test program with one procedure, **Count**, at lines 3–11. The main body calls **Count**, which counts from 1 to 10 in a **REPEAT** loop. I compiled this program to a disk EXE code file and then disassembled the results to produce the listing in Figure 14-6.

Program 14-1

```
1:  PROGRAM ProcAnatomy;
2:
3:  PROCEDURE Count;
4:  VAR i : Integer;
```

Program 14-1 *cont.*

```
 5:  BEGIN
 6:    i := 0;
 7:    REPEAT
 8:      i := i + 1;
 9:      Writeln( i )
10:    UNTIL i = 10
11:  END; { Count }
12:
13:  BEGIN
14:    Count;
15:  END.
```

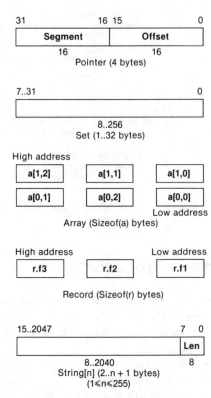

Figure 14-5 Structured types.

Figure 14-6 shows the compiled machine language that Turbo Pascal generates for Program 14-1. For reference, the Pascal statements are repeated in italic with the associated machine language beneath. Read the comments to the right of most lines for a play-by-play description of how the code operates.

If you have the stand-alone Turbo Debugger program, you can view a similar disassembly on your display. (Turbo Pascal's built-in debugger lacks the ability to show you a compiled program's assembled machine code.) After saving Program

14-1 as PROCANAT.PAS, enter these commands to compile and load the result into Turbo Debugger:

```
tpc /v procanat
td procanat
```

You should see the program source code in Turbo Debugger's main window. Press F7 once to execute the program's startup code. Then, press Alt-V C to open the CPU window, and press F5 to expand the window to full screen. This display, which is very useful for learning how the compiler works, shows you the compiled machine language below the associated Pascal statements—nearly identical to Figure 14-6, but with some addresses changed. (The figure shows Turbo Pascal 4.0's output, and you might notice a few minor differences with version 5.5's output.)

Procedure Entry Duties

Several important details are clear from Figure 14-6. At the beginning of **Count**, these two instructions prepare register BP (Base Pointer):

```
PUSH BP
MOV  BP,SP
```

The PUSH instruction saves the current BP value by pushing BP onto the stack. The MOV instruction moves the value of the stack pointer SP register into BP, thus making the two registers address the same location in memory relative to the stack segment register SS.

These two instructions are at the beginning of all procedures. The reason for equating SP and BP is to prepare for addressing variables on the stack. These variables might be parameters, or they might be variables declared local to the procedure. In this example, there is one local variable, integer **i**. The next three instructions prepare space on the stack to hold the variable:

```
MOV  AX,0002
CALL SYSTEM:02AD
SUB  SP,+02
```

The first two instructions call a system routine that checks whether there is enough stack space for the variable—two bytes here. Currently, the routine is located in the SYSTEM segment at offset 02AD. But it is foolhardy to assume that this address will remain unchanged in future compiler versions. Therefore, in your own machine code, it's probably wise never to call routines at explicit addresses.

The second instruction reserves local variable space by subtracting 2 from the current stack pointer SP. As you recall from earlier chapters, local variables are created on the stack when procedures and functions run. The SUB instruction performs this magic, reserving uninitialized stack memory for local variables.

```
 1:  PROGRAM ProcAnatomy;
 2:
 3:  PROCEDURE Count;
 4:  VAR i : Integer;
20A9:0000 55          PUSH   BP              ; push bp register onto stack
20A9:0001 89E5        MOV    BP,SP           ; set bp equal to stack pointer
20A9:0003 B80200      MOV    AX,0002         ; check that stack has 2 bytes,
20A9:0006 9AAD02AF20  CALL   SYSTEM:02AD     ;  enough space for var i
20A9:000B 83EC02      SUB    SP,+02          ; reserve two bytes on stack
                                             ; for integer variable i

 5:  BEGIN
 6:     i := 0;
20A9:000E 31C0        XOR    AX,AX           ; set register ax to 0000
20A9:0010 8946FE      MOV    [BP-02],AX      ; store ax in variable i

 7:     REPEAT
 8:        i := i + 1;
20A9:0013 8B46FE      MOV    AX,[BP-02]      ; load current i value into ax
20A9:0016 40          INC    AX              ; add 1 to ax (i:=i+1)
20A9:0017 8946FE      MOV    [BP-02],AX      ; store new value back in i

 9:        Writeln( i )
20A9:001A BF0001      MOV    DI,0100         ; all this just to write
20A9:001D 1E          PUSH   DS              ;  the value of i plus
20A9:001E 57          PUSH   DI              ;  a carriage return!
20A9:001F 8B46FE      MOV    AX,[BP-02]
20A9:0022 99          CWD
20A9:0023 52          PUSH   DX
20A9:0024 50          PUSH   AX
20A9:0025 31C0        XOR    AX,AX
20A9:0027 50          PUSH   AX
20A9:0028 9A2508AF20  CALL   SYSTEM:0825
20A9:002D 9A8B07AF20  CALL   SYSTEM:078B
20A9:0032 9A7702AF20  CALL   SYSTEM:0277     ; end of Write(i) statement

10:     UNTIL i = 10
20A9:0037 837EFE0A    CMP    Word Ptr [BP-02],+0A  ; compare i with 10
20A9:003B 75D6        JNZ    0013            ; jump to :0013 if i <> 10

11: END; { Count }                          ; prepare to exit Count
20A9:003D 89EC        MOV    SP,BP           ; restore old stack pointer
20A9:003F 5D          POP    BP              ; restore saved bp register
20A9:0040 C3          RET                    ; return to caller

12:
13: BEGIN
20A9:0041 9A0000AF20  CALL   SYSTEM:0       ; call startup routines
20A9:0046 89E5        MOV    BP,SP           ; prepare bp register

14:     Count;
20A9:0048 E8B5FF      CALL   COUNT           ; call Count procedure

15: END.
20A9:004B 89EC        MOV    SP,BP           ; restore stack pointer from bp
20A9:004D 31C0        XOR    AX,AX           ; get ready to end program
20A9:004F 9AF301AF20  CALL   SYSTEM:01F3     ; call shutdown routines
```

Figure 14-6 Program 14-1 disassembled into machine language.

By the way, if you turn off stack error checking with the {$S-} compiler directive, Turbo Pascal generates only the SUB instruction and does not check whether enough stack space is available for local variables.

The rest of the **Count** procedure down to line 11 (END;) executes the statements inside the procedure. You should be able to follow most of this code by reading the comments to the right. (Don't be too concerned with understanding every detail.)

Procedure Exit Duties

The end of a procedure executes three instructions, returning to the machine language instruction following the one that called the procedure:

```
MOV  SP,BP
POP  BP
RET
```

The MOV instruction assigns BP to SP. This restores the stack pointer to its original value before allocating space on the stack for local variables. Recall that BP was equated to SP's value at the start of the procedure. Therefore, as long as no other instructions or subroutines change BP, this is the fastest method to restore the stack pointer before ending the procedure. The second instruction pops BP from the stack restoring BP to the value it had at the procedure start. Finally, a RET instruction continues the program at the instruction following the call to **Count**.

Register Use in Procedures

In your own machine language procedures, you may freely use, and you do not have to preserve, registers AX, BX, CX, DX, DI, and SI. You may change the stack and base pointers SP and BP as described earlier, but you must restore both of these registers before executing RET. You must preserve the data segment register DS, the stack segment register SS, and the code segment register CS. You may use the extra segment register ES for your own purposes. (There's no guarantee that other code will leave ES untouched, though. Always initialize ES before use.)

Anatomy of a Pascal Function

Functions in machine language are similar, but not identical, to procedures. Again, studying a disassembled example is a great way to learn the ropes before writing your own machine language functions. Program 14-2 assigns the squares of values 1 . . 10 to a ten-integer array (lines 11–12), calling function **MySquare** (lines 5–8) for the square of integer parameter **n**.

Program 14-2

```
1:   PROGRAM FuncAnatomy;
2:   VAR i : Integer;
3:       a : ARRAY[ 1 .. 10 ] OF Integer;
4:
5:   FUNCTION MySquare( n : Integer ) : Integer;
6:   BEGIN
7:      MySquare := n * n
8:   END; { MySquare }
9:
10:  BEGIN
11:     FOR i := 1 TO 10 DO
12:         a[i] := MySquare( i )
13:  END.
```

Figure 14-7 lists the machine language that Turbo Pascal generates for Program 14-2. As in the previous example, the Pascal statements are repeated in italic, followed by the associated machine language instructions. Read the comments to the right of most lines for a play-by-play description of how the code operates.

Function Entry Duties

Although the first five machine language instructions in Figure 14-7 are identical to the instructions in Figure 14-6, there is a subtle difference between the startup code for functions and procedures. Procedures reserve stack space for local variables by subtracting a value from the stack pointer register SP. In this example, though, function **MySquare** has no local variables. Yet, the code still subtracts 2 from SP, reserving two bytes on the stack.

The reason for this action is to reserve space for the function result. In this case, the function is type **Integer** and, therefore, two bytes are needed to hold the value. If there were any local variables in the function, additional stack space would be reserved for both the variables and the function result.

The guts of the **MySquare** function first load parameter **n** into register AX, multiply **n** * **n** with an IMUL (Integer Multiply) instruction, and save the result in the space reserved on the stack for the function result.

Function Exit Duties

The **MySquare** function's exit instructions following line 8 (END;) in Figure 14-7 are similar, but not identical, to the instructions that end procedure **Count** in Figure 14-6. The first job is to load register AX with the intermediate function result, currently stored on the stack. This is done by executing:

```
MOV  AX,[BP-02]
```

```
 1:   PROGRAM FuncAnatomy;
 2:   VAR i : Integer;
 3:       a : ARRAY[ 1 .. 10 ] OF Integer;
 4:
 5:   FUNCTION MySquare( n : Integer ) : Integer;
 6:   BEGIN
2E5E:0000 55           PUSH   BP                ; push bp register onto stack
2E5E:0001 89E5         MOV    BP,SP             ; set bp equal to stack pointer
2E5E:0003 B80200       MOV    AX,0002           ; check that stack has 2 bytes,
2E5E:0006 9AAD02642E   CALL   SYSTEM:02AD       ;  enough for function result
2E5E:000B 83EC02       SUB    SP,+02            ; reserve two stack bytes for
                                                ;  intermediate function result
 7:       MySquare := n * n
2E5E:000E 8B4604       MOV    AX,[BP+04]        ; load parameter n into ax
2E5E:0011 F76E04       IMUL   Word Ptr [BP+04]  ; multiply n * n
2E5E:0014 8946FE       MOV    [BP-02],AX        ; store result in stack

2E5E:0017 8B46FE       MOV    AX,[BP-02]        ; load result into ax
2E5E:001A 89EC         MOV    SP,BP             ; restore old stack pointer
2E5E:001C 5D           POP    BP                ; restore saved bp register
2E5E:001D C20200       RET    0002              ; return to caller, releasing
                                                ;  parameter space on stack
 8:   END; { MySquare }
 9:
10:   BEGIN
2E5E:0020 9A0000642E   CALL   SYSTEM:0          ; call startup routines
2E5E:0025 89E5         MOV    BP,SP             ; prepare bp register

11:       FOR i := 1 TO 10 DO
2E5E:0027 C70600000100 MOV    Word Ptr [0000],0001  ; initialize FOR-loop
2E5E:002D EB04         JMP    @+13 (0033)           ; jump to begin FOR-loop
2E5E:002F FF060000     INC    Word Ptr [0000]  ; increment control variable

12:       a[i] := MySquare( i )
2E5E:0033 FF360000     PUSH   [0000]            ; pass i by value to MySquare
2E5E:0037 E8C6FF       CALL   MYSQUARE          ; call MySquare function
2E5E:003A 8B3E0000     MOV    DI,[0000]         ; calculate array index offset
2E5E:003E D1E7         SHL    DI,1              ;  in register di
2E5E:0040 89850000     MOV    [DI+0000],AX      ; store function result in a[i]
2E5E:0044 833E00000A   CMP    Word Ptr [0000],+0A  ; test control variable
2E5E:0049 75E4         JNZ    @+0F (002F)       ; continue or end FOR-loop

13:   END.
2E5E:004B 89EC         MOV    SP,BP             ; restore stack pointer from bp
2E5E:004D 31C0         XOR    AX,AX             ; get ready to end program
2E5E:004F 9AF301642E   CALL   SYSTEM:01F3       ; call shutdown routines
```

Figure 14-7 Program 14-2 disassembled into machine language.

Remember that BP is equated with the stack pointer on entry to the function and, therefore, used here to locate the function space starting two bytes lower than BP. (We'll get to the details of parameter addressing later in this chapter.)

Ordinal and integer functions—those that return data types diagrammed in Figures 14-2 and 14-3—return their results in register AX. Look at the code under the array assignment in line 12. About halfway down, AX is stored in the array following the CALL instruction to **MySquare**.

Ordinal and integer values that occupy single bytes are returned in AL—the least significant half of AX. Refer to Table 14-1 for details on the register assignments for other function result types.

Table 14-1 Function result registers

Function type	Register(s)
Boolean	AL
Char	AL
Enumerated (8-bit)	AL
Enumerated (16-bit)	AX
ShortInt	AL
Byte	AL
Integer	AX
Word	AX
LongInt	DX = high, AX = low words
Single	See note 1
Double	See note 1
Real	DX = high, BX = mid, AX = low words
Extended	See note 1
Comp	See note 1
Pointer	DX = segment, AX = offset
String	See note 2

Note 1. These function types are returned in the math coprocessor top-of-stack register.
Note 2. String functions receive a pointer to a temporary work space created by the caller to the function. The function stores characters at this address, returning the pointer undisturbed on the stack.

Register Use in Functions

The same rules and restrictions for register use in procedures apply to functions. The only exception is that you must return function results in registers as detailed in Table 14-1.

Parameters and Variables

Inside machine language routines, you'll often need to store and retrieve values in Pascal variables. Of course, in Pascal, you simply use the variable's identifier and let the compiler decide where in memory to store values. In machine language, you are responsible for knowing where to find your variables.

As you learned in the previous sections, local variables are stored in temporary stack space created after calling the procedure or function that declared the variables. Callers to procedures and functions push parameters onto the stack. Other variables are stored in the program's data segment.

Figure 14-8 illustrates the stack during a call to a typical procedure. Function calls are similar, but they allocate extra space to hold the function result, as explained earlier. The boxes in the illustration each represent one byte with higher memory addresses at the top. The stack expands toward lower addresses. The organization of variables and other items on the stack during a procedure or function call is known as a *stack frame*.

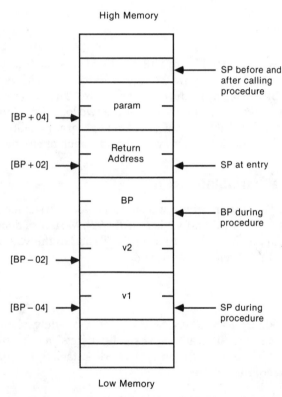

Figure 14-8 Snapshot of a stack frame during a typical procedure.

The notes on the right side of Figure 14-8 show the location of SP and BP at various times during the procedure call. The notes on the left side show the locations of variables relative to register BP. The diagram corresponds with a procedure declared as:

```
PROCEDURE Typical( param : Word );
VAR v1, v2 : Word;
```

This hypothetical procedure has a single **Word** parameter (**param**) and two local **Word** variables (**v1** and **v2**). In machine language, the caller to this procedure executes the instructions:

```
PUSH  AX          ; push one-word parameter
CALL  TYPICAL     ; call procedure
```

This assumes that the parameter to be passed to **Typical** is presently in AX. When **Typical** begins running, SP addresses the *return address*—the location following the CALL instruction. On the stack, the parameter is above the return address. As Figure 14-6 shows, **Typical** first executes these instructions:

```
PUSH BP
MOV  BP,SP
SUB  SP,+04
```

Referring to Figure 14-8, the PUSH instruction stores the current value of BP on the stack, just below the return address. The MOV instruction sets BP equal to SP ("BP during procedure" in the figure). The SUB instruction then subtracts four from SP, reserving four bytes for the two local **Word** variables, **v1** and **v2**. SP now addresses the first byte of **v1**. (A real program would also call Turbo Pascal's stack overflow checker unless you turn off stack checking with {$S – }.)

Local Variables

Use BP minus an offset value to locate local variables on the stack. In Figure 14-8, **v1** is at [BP – 04] and **v2** is at [BP – 02]. Variables declared first in the local **VAR** section are *farthest* away from BP. To assign the value 8 to **v2**, you could use the assembly language instruction:

```
MOV  Word Ptr [BP-02],8
```

Figure 14-8 shows the stack for two-byte variables. To locate a variable of a different size, subtract the variable's byte size plus the total byte sizes of all variables declared *after* the one you need. A stack frame diagram like Figure 14-8 helps avoid confusion.

Value Parameters

Use BP also to locate value parameters passed to a procedure or function. As Figure 14-8 shows, value parameters are stored above the return address. In this sample, the single two-byte **param** is at [BP + 04]—four bytes higher than the location that BP addresses after being initialized at the procedure start. To assign the value 8 to **param**, you could write:

```
MOV  Word Ptr [BP+04],8
```

Figure 14-8 illustrates a common *near* procedure call. Calls to *far* routines—those declared in a unit's interface section, for example—push a four-byte return address. The first parameter above the return address in *far* routines, then, is at [BP + 06].

Parameters are pushed in the order they appear inside the procedure or function parentheses. The first parameter is *farthest* away—at a higher address—from BP. The last declared parameter is just above the return address.

When a procedure or function ends—except for string functions as noted in Table 14-1—the parameter stack space must be removed. To do this, the procedure illustrated in Figure 14-8 ends with these instructions:

```
MOV  SP,BP
POP  BP
RET  0002
```

The MOV instruction deallocates the stack space occupied by local variables **v1** and **v2**, resetting SP to the location in the figure reading "BP during procedure." The POP instruction then restores the original value of BP from the stack, making SP again point to the location "SP at entry."

The RET instruction specifies the optional parameter 0002, telling the processor first to remove the return address from the stack, inserting this address in the instruction pointer register IP, and then adding 2 to SP. Doing this deallocates the two bytes occupied by **param**, returning SP to the value it had before calling the procedure.

Variable Parameters

Variable parameters are passed to procedures and functions as full 32-bit addresses. In Figure 14-8, if **param** was a VAR parameter, then [BP + 04] would locate the four-byte address of **param** on the stack. To use such addresses, programs typically employ the LES instruction and DI register like this:

```
LES  DI,[BP+04]
MOV  Word Ptr ES:[DI],8
```

The LES instruction loads the register combination ES:DI with the data at [BP + 04]. The MOV instruction then uses this address to assign 8 to the variable. This is more complicated (and time-consuming) than referencing value parameters and local variables, which you can directly address on the stack.

Global Variables

Turbo Pascal lumps all global variables, including globals declared in units, in a single data segment. DS:0000 locates the first byte of this data space. Consider a program that declares three global integer variables:

```
PROGRAM Globals;
VAR g1, g2, g3 : Integer;
```

To initialize the three variables to 8, you could write:

```
MOV Word Ptr [0000],8    ; g1 := 8;
MOV Word Ptr [0002],8    ; g2 := 8;
MOV Word Ptr [0004],8    ; g3 := 8;
```

Global variables are stored in declaration order, with the last declared variable at a higher offset relative to DS. Variable (typed) constants are also stored in the data segment but, unlike plain variables, begin with preinitialized values. Plain constants are stored in the code stream as needed. String constants, which are not duplicated even if used multiple times, are also stored in the code segment.

Static Links

Accessing local variables and parameters from within nested procedures and functions is tricky. Consider these procedures:

```
PROCEDURE Outer( a, b : Integer );
VAR i, j : Word;
   PROCEDURE Inner;
   BEGIN
      { inner statements }
   END;
BEGIN
   Inner;
   { outer statements }
END;
```

Procedure **Outer** can access parameters **a** and **b** plus local variables **i** and **j**, as described earlier, relative to BP. However, when **Inner** runs, BP is again initialized for **Inner**'s own stack frame; therefore, the locations of the two parameters and local variables are no longer directly available as offsets from BP.

To solve this dilemma, Turbo Pascal creates a *static link* to variables and parameters from within nested blocks (procedures and functions). The static link tells nested routines how to find an outer routine's variables and parameters. To create the static link in this example, **Outer** pushes the current BP value onto the stack just before calling **Inner**. Suppose **Outer** assigns 5 to local variable **i** and then calls **Inner**. The code would be:

```
MOV  Word Ptr [BP-04],5    ; i := 5
PUSH BP                    ; create static link
CALL INNER                 ; call inner procedure
```

The assignment to **i** uses BP minus an offset value, similar to the arrangement in Figure 14-8. The PUSH instruction passes BP on the stack immediately before calling **Inner**. This is the static link value that **Inner** uses to locate **Outer**'s parameters and local variables. If **Inner** had any parameters, **Outer** would push their values before BP.

When **Inner** begins running, the stack appears similar to Figure 14-8, but with no parameters or local variables. In this case, **param** equals the static link value of BP, located at [BP + 04]. This locates the static link for near procedures and functions. When the outer procedure or function is *far*, the return address of a nested procedure or function's stack is a four-byte value.

With the static link available on the stack, locating the outer routine's parameters and variables is now possible. For example, these instructions inside **Inner** assign 3 to **Outer**'s parameter **a**:

```
MOV  DI,[BP+04]              ; get static link
MOV  Word Ptr SS:[DI+06],3   ; a := 3
```

The first MOV instruction retrieves the static link—the BP value pushed on the stack before calling **Inner**—assigning this value to register DI. The second MOV instruction uses DI as an alternate base pointer with the segment override SS:, telling the processor to locate data in the stack segment. The offset (06) is the same value that **Outer** would use directly with BP to assign 3 to **a**:

```
MOV  Word Ptr [BP+06],3
```

InLine Statements

InLine statements inject bytes directly into Turbo Pascal's code stream. You can insert bytes anywhere inside a procedure or function block or in a main program body. You can also code **InLine** statements in private or public unit routines or in a unit's initialization section. **InLine** statements can go anywhere Turbo Pascal normally allows other kinds of statements.

An **InLine** statement begins with **InLine** followed by a list of byte and word values in parentheses. Separate multiple values with slashes (/). Values that evaluate to eight-bit data types generate one byte of code or data. Values that evaluate to 16-bit data types generate two bytes of code or data. Here's a simple one-byte **InLine** example that disables interrupts:

```
InLine( $FA );   { CLI   ; clear interrupt flag }
```

The $FA byte is the machine language for the CLI instruction, "Clear Interrupt Flag." This enables interrupts:

```
InLine( $FB );   { STI   ; set interrupt flag }
```

The $FB byte represents the STI instruction, "Set Interrupt Flag." You could insert either of these **InLine** statements anywhere in your program to enable and disable interrupts—two jobs that have no direct equivalents in Turbo Pascal. The compiler inserts the $FA and $FB machine language instruction bytes directly into the code file.

Notice the comments to the right of these two **InLine** examples. It's a good idea to document your machine language statements carefully, listing the assembly language text and additional descriptions to explain exactly what each instruction means.

Replacing Pascal with InLine Statements

One use for **InLine** statements is to optimize the code that Turbo Pascal generates. As an example, let's recode function **MySquare** in Program 14-2 using an **InLine** statement.

Examine the machine language for line 7 in Figure 14-7, the disassembly of Program 14-2. Assigning AX to [BP – 02]—the stack space reserved for the intermediate function result—is immediately followed by an assignment to AX of this very same value! Obviously, if AX already equals the function result, there's no need to store AX in the intermediate space. Pascal returns **Integer** function values in AX anyway (see Table 14-1); therefore, the two MOV instructions at 2E5E:0014 and 2E5E:0017 are superfluous. In this example, we can do better than the compiler by recoding the multiplication as an **InLine** statement.

The reason for this apparent inefficiency, by the way, is that Turbo Pascal is a *one-pass compiler*. The compiler evaluates each statement, generating the appropriate machine language before going on to the next statement. When Turbo Pascal compiles the multiplication in line 7 (Figure 14-7), it doesn't know this is the last statement in the function until reaching the **END** key word. By then it's too late to avoid storing AX in the intermediate function result space. If there were other statements after the multiplication, then it would be necessary to store the intermediate function result at [BP – 02], retrieving this value just before ending the function. The compiler simply can't make the appropriate decision in this case, a good example of why high-level language compilers like Turbo Pascal are not as expert as competent assembly language programmers.

Having spotted the inefficiency in Program 14-2, we can recode function **MySquare** with an **InLine** statement. Program 14-3 lists the final result. The **InLine** statement simply copies the bytes from the disassembly in Figure 14-7, skipping the unnecessary assignment to the function value's intermediate stack space.

There are a couple of important details in Program 14-3. First, the original Pascal statement is commented out (line 7) as reference to what the **InLine** statement accomplishes. Besides documenting the code, this also helps programmers transfer the program to different computers—perhaps a Macintosh using a 68000 processor, which can't execute the same **InLine** code. To transfer or *port* the program to the Macintosh, a programmer could remove the **InLine** statements and enable the original Pascal, perhaps later writing 68000 **InLine** statements after debugging the program.

Notice that lines 11–13 in Program 14-3 duplicate the exit code in the original function (Figure 14-7). This is necessary because Turbo Pascal still encodes the startup and exit code for the function as listed at lines 6 and 8 in the figure. To avoid loading AX from the function result's stack space (at address 2E5E:0017 in the figure), the **InLine** statement must end the procedure itself. Unfortunately, there is no way to prevent Turbo Pascal from allocating the unneeded function result space on the stack and, therefore, we still have to recover that space by assigning BP to SP.

I hope you are getting the idea by now that mixing machine language and Pascal is no piece of cake and comes with no guarantee of improved efficiency. In this example, we've managed to cut two MOV instructions—an important improvement that might be critical in a tight situation but, in most cases, probably will have little practical effect. We've saved no space, trading the six bytes saved by discarding two MOVs with a six-byte duplication of the function's exit code. This just proves that adding machine code to Pascal programs is tricky business. Be sure the payoff is worth the effort before going to all this trouble!

Program 14-3

```
 1:  PROGRAM InlineFunction;
 2:  VAR i : Integer;
 3:       a : ARRAY[ 1 .. 10 ] OF Integer;
 4:
 5:  FUNCTION MySquare( n : Integer ) : Integer;
 6:  BEGIN
 7:  (*    MySquare := n * n *)
 8:
 9:      InLine( $8B/ $46/ $04/        { MOV   AX,[BP+04]  ; load n into AX }
10:             $F7/ $6E/ $04/         { IMUL  Word Ptr [BP+04]  ; AX<-n*n }
11:             $89/ $EC/              { MOV   SP,BP        ; restore SP    }
12:             $5D/                   { POP   BP           ; restore BP    }
13:             $C2/ $02/ $00 );       { RET   0002  ; return, deallocate n }
14:
15:  END; { MySquare }
16:
17:  BEGIN
18:     FOR i := 1 TO 10 DO
19:        a[i] := MySquare( i );
20:     FOR i := 1 TO 10 DO
21:        Writeln( 'a[', i:2, '] = ', a[i]:2 )
22:  END.
```

Using Identifiers in InLine Statements

In place of the literal [BP + 04] references in Program 14-3 (lines 9–10), you can use parameter and variable identifiers in **InLine** statements. When you do this, Turbo Pascal replaces the identifiers with the *offset* value representing the location of the variable in the appropriate segment. For example, you can rewrite lines 9–10 like this:

```
InLine( $8B/ $86/ n/  { MOV  AX,n  ; load n into AX }
        $F7/ $AE/ n/  { IMUL n     ; AX<-n*n         }
```

Notice that the original $46 is now $86 and the $6E is $AE, changing the MOV and IMUL instructions to use 16-bit instead of eight-bit offsets. Turbo Pascal replaces parameter **n** with the full 16-bit offset value ($0004), generating this code for these two instructions:

```
8B860400  MOV  AX, Word Ptr [BP+0004]
F7AE0400  IMUL Word Ptr [BP+0004]
```

This illustrates a serious danger when using identifiers in **InLine** statements. You must be absolutely certain that the machine language instructions are able to handle the 16-bit offset values that the compiler inserts in place of identifiers.

Often, however, default 16-bit values are not acceptable. To force Turbo Pascal to insert eight-bit bytes, even though a value or identifier evaluates to a 16-bit word, use the < and > operators. The less-than sign (<) extracts the least significant byte. The greater-than sign (>) extracts the most significant byte. To return to using eight-bit offsets, while specifying parameter identifier **n**, rewrite lines 9–10 this way:

```
InLine( $8B/ $46/ <n/  { MOV  AX,n  ; load n into AX }
        $F7/ $6E/ <n/  { IMUL n     ; AX<-n*n         }
```

Now, we can again use the eight-bit offset forms of MOV and IMUL. The <**n** designation tells the compiler to insert the least significant byte of the 16-bit offset 0004, acceptable in this example because the most significant byte is zero. Of course, if the parameter is more than 255 ($FF) bytes away from BP, then you have to use a 16-bit offset.

You may conclude from these notes that using identifiers in **InLine** statements is too much trouble. But there's a good reason to use <**n** instead of the literal $04 offsets in Program 14-3, lines 9–10. As now written, the program assumes that Turbo Pascal will always organize the stack according to the illustration in Figure 14-8—a potentially dangerous assumption. For instance, if you add an {$F+} directive between lines 4 and 5 in Program 14-3, the compiler generates code for function **MySquare** as a *far* routine. *If you are following along, change the $04 bytes in Program 14-3, lines 9–10, to <n before running the modified program with MySquare declared far!* Calls to **MySquare** then push a four-byte return address on the stack causing parameters to begin at [BP+06] instead of [BP+04]. Obviously, the literal $04 **InLine** offset values will no longer work. (See Figure 14-8.)

By specifying <**n** instead of literal values, the compiler generates the correct offsets for both *far* and *near* routines. Such subtle differences are important to understand, especially when recoding into **InLine** statements unit procedures and functions declared public (in the unit interface), which are *far* by default. You must be certain to use the appropriate data forms for your machine language instructions. The compiler offers no safeguards against errors.

InLine Procedures and Functions

An **InLine** procedure or function is similar to an **InLine** statement. As you have learned, an **InLine** statement is just like any other statement. An **InLine** procedure or function, though, is a kind of shorthand that represents short, machine language sequences. A few examples help explain how this works:

```
PROCEDURE ClrInt; InLine( $FA );
PROCEDURE SetInt; InLine( $FB );
```

An **InLine** procedure starts with the key word **PROCEDURE** followed by the procedure name and a semicolon. After that comes an **InLine** declaration, with exactly the same form as an **InLine** statement. In this case, though, Turbo Pascal does not insert the **InLine** code directly into the code stream. This happens later when you write **ClrInt** or **SetInt**:

```
ClrInt;    { Clear Interrupts }
Writeln( 'Interrupts are off' );
SetInt;    { Enable interrupts }
Writeln( 'Interrupts are on' );
```

In place of **ClrInt**, the compiler inserts the **InLine** byte, $FA, representing the machine language CLI (Clear Interrupt Flag) instruction. In place of **SetInt**, the compiler inserts $FB, the machine language STI (Set Interrupt Flag) instruction. From the Pascal text, it appears that calls are made to the **ClrInt** and **SetInt** procedures, but this is not the case. The procedure identifiers operate similarly to assembly language macros, as mentioned earlier, directly expanding to the **InLine** bytes the identifiers represent.

You can also code **InLine** functions. For example, this function returns the value of the system timer, stored at 0000:046C – 0000:046F:

```
FUNCTION Timer : LongInt;
InLine(
  $31/ $C0/              { XOR AX,AX   ; zero AX }
  $8E/ $C0/              { MOV ES,AX   ; set ES to 0000 }
  $BF/ $6C/ $04/         { MOV DI,046C ; di = offset }
  $26/ $8B/ $05/         { MOV AX,ES:[DI]    ; low word }
  $26/ $8B/ $55/ $02 ); { MOV DX,ES:[DI+02] ; high word }
```

Use this **InLine** function, which returns a **LongInt** value in registers AX:DX (see Table 14-1), as you do any Pascal function. For example, you could display **Timer** values in a **FOR** loop:

```
VAR i : Integer;

FOR i := 1 TO 100 DO
   Writeln( Timer );
```

When Turbo Pascal compiles this loop, it does not call a function subroutine named **Timer**. Instead, it inserts the **InLine** function's code directly into the code stream. As a result, the program saves all the overhead normally associated with calling subroutines—all the stack details described earlier, the CALL and RET instructions, and so on. The **InLine** code works like a function without this overhead and, therefore, improves the speed of the loop.

Another advantage to using **InLine** functions is that the compiler does not reserve space for the function value on the stack as it does for a real function.

Parameters and InLine Routines

You may pass variable and value parameters to **InLine** procedures and functions. The parameters are pushed onto the stack just as they are for normal procedure and function calls. In this case, you are responsible for removing the parameters from the stack in your **InLine** code.

Suppose you need a function to square a 16-bit **Word** value, which you pass to the function by value, returning a **LongInt** result. You could code the function in Pascal:

```
FUNCTION LongSqr( n : Word ) : LongInt;
BEGIN
   LongSqr := LongInt(n) * n
END; { LongSqr }
```

The typecast is necessary to force a long integer result in the multiplication. The equivalent **InLine** function pops the **Word** parameter **n** from the stack into register AX, multiplying AX by AX, leaving the result in DX:AX:

```
FUNCTION LongSqr( n : Word ) : LongInt;

  InLine( $58/          { POP AX  ; pop n into AX    }
          $F7/ $E0 );   { MUL AX  ; DX:AX <- AX x AX }
```

This three-byte function is neat and efficient. Table 14-1 specifies that the DX:AX register pair returns **LongInt** function results. Perhaps by coincidence, or perhaps by design, the MUL instruction leaves the result of the multiplication in the proper registers.

Short **InLine** procedures and functions like **LongSqr** are useful for optimizing code that, if written in Pascal, waste time preparing the stack, referencing variables relative to BP, storing function results in intermediate stack variables, and calling system routines. This observation does not hold true for all procedures and functions, though, and you should use **InLine** routines only for short code that must run as fast as possible.

External Procedures and Functions

The third and final method for mixing assembly language and Pascal requires an assembler—either Turbo Assembler (TASM) 1.0 or the Microsoft Macro Assembler (MASM) 4.0. Later versions of both products and other assemblers may also work.

In this method, you write external assembly language procedures and functions in separate text files, assemble the text to object code files, and link the result into a Pascal program. This approach offers many advantages over **InLine** techniques. For example:

- You can use the many features found in your assembler for declaring data structures.

- You can use assembly language macros (provided you have a macro assembler).

- You can jump to labeled instructions.

- You can work on your assembly language modules apart from the Pascal program.

- You can use your assembler's listing abilities to document your assembly language.

An External Shell

Listing 14-1 is a shell that you can use as a starting place for your own external procedures and functions. Lines and portions of lines beginning with semicolons are comments, which the assembler ignores. The **CODE** key word identifies what follows as a code memory segment. The **WORD** alignment specified in the segment directive could also be **BYTE**, although Turbo Pascal's linker always aligns segments on word boundaries regardless of the setting you specify.

The **ASSUME** directive tells the assembler to assume that register CS is based at this segment. The **PUBLIC** directive exports symbols in the external listing to the Turbo Pascal linker. For every procedure and function in the external listing—and you can have as many as you want—add the routine's name to the **PUBLIC** directive. If you declare a procedure **MyStuff** and a function **AddThings**, you would write:

```
PUBLIC MyStuff, AddThings
```

The dummy procedure in Listing 14-1 starts with a **PROC** directive, identifying **Identifier** as **Near**. If this routine will be linked to a Pascal procedure or function declared *far* (with the {$F + } compiler directive) or to a routine declared in a unit's interface section, then you must change **Near** to **Far**. It's your responsibility to declare *near* and *far* routines—you'll get no help in this regard from the assembler or compiler.

The dummy **Identifier** routine contains the usual entry and exit code plus a few instructions that might be unnecessary in some cases. For example, if you don't change the stack pointer SP, there's no reason to restore SP's value from BP before the procedure ends. The equate (**EQU**) assigns to symbol **params** the addressing details of a parameter located at [BP + 04] on the stack. This step is optional but recommended.

The end of the dummy **Identifier** procedure ends with an **ENDP** directive, matching the previous **PROC**. All **PROC**s must have a corresponding **ENDP**, or you'll receive an error from the assembler.

Finally, the last two lines in Listing 14-1 tell the assembler this is the end of the code segment (**ENDS**) and the end of the entire text file (**END**).

Listing 14-1

```
; Shell for External Procedures and Functions
; For TASM or MASM and Turbo Pascal 4.0, 5.0, and 5.5

CODE            SEGMENT WORD PUBLIC
                ASSUME  CS:CODE
                PUBLIC  Identifier


;--------------------------------------------------------------
; PROCEDURE Identifier( params );
; FUNCTION Identifier( params ) : type;

Identifier      PROC    Near            ; Far if using {$F+} or if
                                        ; routine is declared in a
                                        ; unit interface.

params          EQU     Word Ptr [BP+04]        ; define parameters

                push    bp              ; save bp
                mov     bp,sp           ; address parameters with bp

; insert code here

                mov     sp,bp           ; restore stack pointer
                pop     bp              ; restore bp register
                ret                     ; return to caller

Identifier          ENDP                    ; end of routine


CODE            ENDS                    ; end of CODE segment
                END                     ; end of text
```

Declaring External Data Segments

You can declare a data segment to hold variables for use by external routines. The segment must be named **DATA**. You can assume that register DS addresses this segment, which the linker combines with global variables declared in the Pascal program. There is no way to pass variables by name from an assembly language module to Pascal or vice versa. To declare global data in the assembly language module, use a segment declaration such as this:

```
DATA      SEGMENT WORD PUBLIC
count     dw    5
message   db    "This is a string",0
index     db    ?
DATA      ENDS
```

This segment declares three variables, a 16-bit count, a string message ending in a null character, and an uninitialized byte index. These items are mixed with other Pascal globals in the program's data segment. To find the variables, tell the assembler that DS addresses the data segment. To do this, begin the code segment this way:

```
CODE      SEGMENT WORD PUBLIC
          ASSUME CS:CODE, DS:DATA
```

Inside the code segment, to initialize the index variable to $2000, you could write:

```
MOV  index,2000h
```

Because you told the assembler to assume that DS addresses the data segment and because Turbo Pascal initialized DS for you, there's no need to assign the segment address to DS.

For other variables, you can reserve space on the stack just as Pascal procedures and functions do for local variables. Study Figures 14-6 and 14-7 for hints on how to do this.

An External Example

Listing 14-2 contains two external functions and two external procedures for accessing an asynchronous serial I/O line, perhaps attached to another computer. To save space, the four routines are simplified and do no error checking, but they still are useful for writing programs to transfer information over a serial line. The comments in the listing describe the commands, for which there isn't room to fully explain here. (This is, after all, a Pascal tutorial, not an assembly language primer!)

Use the Turbo Pascal editor—or a programmer's text editor—to enter and save Listing 14-2 as COMM.ASM. Then, if you have TASM, assemble the code with this DOS command:

```
tasm comm
```

To assemble with MASM, use the command:

```
masm comm;
```

The semicolon tells MASM not to prompt for various optional file names. To see the prompts, enter the same command without a semicolon. Turbo Assembler never displays such prompts.

After assembling, you'll have an object code file named COMM.OBJ containing the assembled code in a form ready for linking to a Turbo Pascal program.

Listing 14-2

```
; Communications Externals
; For TASM or MASM and Turbo Pascal 4.0, 5.0, and 5.5

DATA            SEGMENT WORD PUBLIC

thePort         dw      ?                   ; Comm port number

DATA            ENDS                        ; end of DATA segment


CODE            SEGMENT WORD PUBLIC
                ASSUME  CS:CODE, DS:DATA
                PUBLIC  CommInit, CharReady, GetByte, SendByte


;------------------------------------------------------------------
; PROCEDURE CommInit( port : Word; params : Byte );

CommInit        PROC    Near

port            EQU     Word Ptr [BP+06]
params          EQU     Byte Ptr [BP+04]

                push    bp              ; save bp
                mov     bp,sp           ; address parameters with bp

                mov     dx,port         ; move port number into dx
                mov     thePort,dx      ; save port number for later
                mov     al,params       ; get parameters
                mov     ah,0            ; select BIOS init function
                int     14h             ; call BIOS RS232-IO
```

Listing 14-2 *cont.*

```
                pop     bp              ; restore bp register
                ret     10              ; return to caller and
                                        ;  deallocate parameters


CommInit        ENDP                    ; end of CommInit



;----------------------------------------------------------------
; FUNCTION CharReady : Boolean;

CharReady       PROC    Near

                mov     dx,thePort      ; get Comm port number
                mov     ah,3            ; select BIOS status
                int     14h             ; call BIOS RS232-IO

                xchg    ah,al           ; move ah to al
                and     ax,01h          ; return result in bit 0

                ret                     ; return to caller

CharReady       ENDP                    ; end of CharReady



;----------------------------------------------------------------
; FUNCTION GetByte : Char;

GetByte         PROC    Near

                mov     dx,thePort      ; get Comm port number
                mov     ah,2            ; select BIOS receive
                int     14h             ; call BIOS RS232-IO

                ret                     ; return to caller

GetByte         ENDP                    ; end of GetByte



;----------------------------------------------------------------
; PROCEDURE SendByte( theByte : Byte );

SendByte        PROC    Near

theByte         EQU     Byte Ptr [BP+04]
```

Listing 14-2 *cont.*

```
          push    bp                      ; save bp
          mov     bp,sp                   ; address parameters with bp

          mov     al,theByte              ; get the byte to send
          mov     dx,thePort              ; get Comm port number
          mov     ah,1                    ; select BIOS send
          int     14h                     ; call BIOS RS232-IO

          pop     bp                      ; restore bp register
          ret     2                       ; return to caller and
                                          ;   deallocate parameter

SendByte  ENDP                            ; end of SendByte


CODE      ENDS                            ; end of CODE segment
          END                             ; end of text
```

Linking Externals to Pascal

Linking external routines to Pascal programs requires two steps. First, tell the compiler the name and location of the object code file containing the routines. Second, tell the compiler the format of each routine. Lines 5–10 in Program 14-4 demonstrate how to do this.

Line 5 uses the compiler directive {$L COMM}, telling Turbo Pascal to link the routines in the file COMM.OBJ. You do not have to specify the OBJ extension. After this step, tell the compiler about the routines in the object code file, as in lines 7–10.

Notice that lines 7–10 declare Pascal procedures and functions with **EXTERNAL** key words in place of the usual blocks. This tells the compiler that the actual code for these routines is external to the program. Compile the program to disk or memory as you normally do. You don't have to perform any special tasks to link in the assembled object code.

Use these external routines just as you do any other Pascal procedures and functions. For example, line 47 calls the external **CommInit** to initialize serial communications.

While demonstrating how to write external procedures and functions, Program 14-4 is a useful utility for transferring text to other computers and devices such as serial printers that understand a simple I/O protocol called XON-XOFF. Make sure the remote device is ready to receive text and then run the program. Supply the name of a text file to transfer. If you have trouble, press Esc to quit. You might have to adjust the parameters to **CommInit** to match the configuration of the remote device.

Note: When debugging mixed Pascal and assembly language code with
the stand-alone Turbo Debugger, calls to external routines are treated
as indivisible statements. In other words, pressing F7 to step into the
code of an external procedure or function does not show you the individual assembly language instructions as you might expect. One alternative is to switch to the CPU screen by pressing Alt-V C just before
pressing F7 at a call to an external routine. This doesn't show you the
original assembly language source code statements, but it does show
the external routine's disassembled machine code. You can then press
F7 again to execute the individual assembly language instructions.

Program 14-4

```
 1:  PROGRAM SendText;
 2:
 3:  USES Crt;
 4:
 5:  {$L COMM}        { Link the following routines in COMM.OBJ }
 6:
 7:  PROCEDURE CommInit( port : Word; params : Byte ); EXTERNAL;
 8:  FUNCTION CharReady : Boolean; EXTERNAL;
 9:  FUNCTION GetByte : Byte; EXTERNAL;
10:  PROCEDURE SendByte( theByte : Byte ); EXTERNAL;
11:
12:  CONST baud110     = $00;    { Baud rate settings }
13:        baud150     = $20;
14:        baud300     = $40;
15:        baud600     = $60;
16:        baud1200    = $80;
17:        baud2400    = $A0;
18:        baud4800    = $C0;
19:        baud9600    = $E0;
20:
21:        noparity    = $00;    { Parity settings }
22:        oddparity   = $08;
23:        evenparity  = $18;
24:
25:        onestop     = $00;    { Stop bits settings }
26:        twostop     = $04;
27:
28:        len7        = $02;    { Byte length settings }
29:        len8        = $03;
30:
```

Program 14-4 *cont.*

```
31:        XON        = ^Q;   { Flow-control characters }
32:        XOFF       = ^S;
33:
34:
35:   VAR   ch : Char;
36:         f : File OF Char;
37:         fileName : String;
38:         i : Integer;
39:
40:   PROCEDURE CheckKeyboard;
41:   BEGIN
42:     IF Keypressed THEN
43:         IF ReadKey = Chr(27) THEN Halt
44:   END; { CheckKeyboard }
45:
46:   BEGIN
47:     CommInit( 0, baud9600+noparity+onestop+len8 );
48:     Write( 'Send what file? ' );
49:     Readln( fileName );
50:     Assign( f, fileName );
51:     Reset( f );
52:     Writeln( 'Press Esc to stop sending' );
53:     WHILE NOT Eof( f ) DO
54:     BEGIN
55:       IF CharReady THEN
56:       BEGIN
57:         ch := Chr( GetByte );
58:         IF ch = XOFF THEN
59:         REPEAT
60:            CheckKeyboard;
61:            IF CharReady THEN ch := Chr( GetByte )
62:         UNTIL ch = XON
63:       END; { if }
64:       CheckKeyboard;
65:       Read( f, ch );
66:       SendByte( Ord(ch) )
67:     END;
68:     Close( f )
69:   END.
```

Programming Interrupts

As the next example shows, you can also write your own interrupt procedures. Usually, but not always, you'll code the interrupt in assembly language. If you prefer to use Pascal, do so with care. Because interrupts might be activated at any time and from any place, you cannot use Pascal commands that call DOS or BIOS routines, most of which are not reentrant—meaning that, if an interrupted routine is called via mutual recursion by the interrupt handler, problems are almost bound to occur.

To write an interrupt handler, also called an *interrupt service routine*, declare a special Pascal procedure like this:

```
PROCEDURE Service(
   Flags,CS,IP,AX,BX,CX,DX,SI,DI,DS,ES,BP : Word );
   INTERRUPT;
```

The parameters are phony, having the sole purpose of allowing Pascal statements to return values in processor registers. For example, to return a value in register AX, you could write:

```
AX := $1000;      { MOV AX,1000h }
```

If you don't need to reference registers or flags, you may optionally leave them out of the parameter list, cutting from **Flags** to **BP**. In other words, if you need to use CX, then you must declare CX plus all the registers following as in this sample:

```
PROCEDURE Service(
   CX,DX,SI,DI,DS,ES,BP : Word );
   INTERRUPT;
```

The key word **INTERRUPT** identifies the procedure as an interrupt service routine. When the **Service** routine runs, registers AX, BX, CX, DX, SI, DI, DS, ES, and BP are pushed onto the stack. BP and SP are initialized as in a normal procedure for referencing local variables. All registers are pushed onto the stack even if you do not declare the phony register parameters. Also, register DS is initialized to the global data segment, a necessary action because the interrupted process may have changed DS. Therefore, you may reference global variables inside your interrupt service procedure without having to reinitialize DS.

An Example Interrupt Routine

As an example of writing interrupt service routines in Pascal, Program 14-5 displays an independently running timer in the upper-right corner of the display. Before typing and running the program, be aware that installing interrupts in memory can affect the operation of your computer. Line 68 prevents you from breaking out of the program by not allowing you to type the break character, Ctrl-C (or Ctrl-Break). This lets the program remove the interrupt from memory before ending. Not resetting the interrupt would leave the interrupt vector pointing to procedure **ShowTime** (lines 10–39), a dangerous practice that is certain to lead to serious problems.

Because of the sensitive nature of Program 14-5, be sure to save it to disk before running it. If you make any typing errors in the **InLine** statement, you may have to reboot your computer, losing the in-memory program text.

The interrupt service routine, **ShowTime** in lines 10–39, does not have any Pascal statements and, therefore, declares no register parameters. The program prepares interrupt number $1C to display the time of day in the top-right corner of your screen. Use the appropriate value in line 5 for your computer. $B000 is for monochrome displays. $B800 is for color displays and the PCjr (80-column modes only).

The program operates by taking advantage of the IBM PC timer circuits, which execute interrupt number $1C 18.2 times per second. Because the program changes the interrupt $1C vector to the service routine's address, **ShowTime** runs at this same frequency, independently of the other program parts. To demonstrate this independency, an example of *concurrent processing*, procedure **DoWhatever-YouWant** at lines 47–60 lets you enter strings, which the procedure then writes 40 times. This arbitrary action demonstrates that the procedure and the clock interrupt, cycling at 18.2 times per second, run concurrently.

To set up this action, **InitInterrupt** calls **Dos** unit routines **GetIntVec** and **SetIntVec** at lines 43–44 to initialize interrupt $1C to the address of the **Show-Time** interrupt service routine, saving the current interrupt vector in a pointer variable for later restoring. Notice how line 44 uses the @ operator to pass the address of the service routine to **SetIntVec**.

Procedure **DeInitInterrupt** (lines 62–65) reverses this process, restoring interrupt $1C to whatever routine the vector previously addressed. After deinitializing, therefore, the program may safely end with no worry of accidentally leaving the independently executing interrupt routine in memory.

The **InLine** machine language at lines 13–38 decodes the IBM PC timer values located at addresses $0000:046C to $0000:046F. This displays each digit of time in reversed video by simply poking the appropriate characters directly into video display memory (see lines 35, 37, 46, and 48). The comments to the right of the **InLine** code explain how the procedure works.

Program 14-5

```
 1:  PROGRAM Timer;
 2:  USES Crt, Dos;
 3:
 4:  CONST
 5:      DispSeg = $B800;    { Use $B000 for Monochrome display }
 6:
 7:  VAR
 8:      oldVector : Pointer;  { Holds original interrupt $1C vector }
 9:
10:  PROCEDURE ShowTime; INTERRUPT;
11:  { WARNING: Never directly call this procedure! }
12:  BEGIN
13:    InLine(
```

Program 14-5 *cont.*

```
14:    $31/$c0/                        { xor ax,ax         ;ax<-0000              }
15:    $8E/$d8/                        { mov ds,ax                                }
16:    $a1/$6d/$04/                    { mov ax,[046d]     ;get timer div 256     }
17:    $bb/DispSeg/                    { mov bx,DispSeg    ;bx=display addr       }
18:    $8E/$db/                        { mov ds,bx         ;ds=display addr       }
19:    $c7/$06/$9a/$00/$7c/$f0/        { mov word ptr [009a],f07c ;display '|' }
20:    $b7/$70/                        { mov bh,70         ;attribute=reversed    }
21:    $50/                            { push ax           ;save timer value      }
22:    $86/$c4/                        { xchg ah,al        ;ah=timer hi mod 256   }
23:    $d4/$0a/                        { aam               ;make unpacked bcd     }
24:    $0d/$30/$30/                    { or ax,3030        ;convert to ascii      }
25:    $88/$e3/                        { mov bl,ah                                }
26:    $89/$1e/$96/$00/                { mov [0096],bx     ;display 1st hr digit}
27:    $88/$c3/                        { mov bl,al                                }
28:    $89/$1e/$98/$00/                { mov [0098],bx     ;display 2nd hr digit}
29:    $58/                            { pop ax            ;restore timer value }
30:    $b9/$06/$0f/                    { mov cx,0f06       ;calc ax / 4.26        }
31:    $f6/$e5/                        { mul ch            ;  ax<-ax * 15         }
32:    $d3/$e8/                        { shr ax,cl         ;  ax<-ax / 64         }
33:    $d4/$0a/                        { aam                                      }
34:    $0d/$30/$30/                    { or  ax,3030                              }
35:    $88/$e3/                        { mov bl,ah                                }
36:    $89/$1e/$9c/$00/                { mov [009C],bx     ;display 1st min dig.}
37:    $88/$c3/                        { mov bl,al                                }
38:    $89/$1e/$9e/$00 )               { mov [009e],bx     ;display 2nd min dig.}
39: END; { ShowTime }
40:
41: PROCEDURE InitInterrupt;
42: BEGIN
43:    GetIntVec( $1C, oldVector );  { Save old interrupt $1C vector }
44:    SetIntVec( $1C, @ShowTime )   { Set new interrupt $1C vector }
45: END;
46:
47: PROCEDURE DoWhateverYouWant;
48: VAR
49:    i : Integer;
50:    s : String[80];
51: BEGIN
52:    REPEAT
53:       Write( 'Enter a string (RET to quit): ' );
54:       Readln( s );
55:       FOR i := 1 TO 40 DO
56:          Write( s );
57:       Writeln;
58:       Writeln
```

Program 14-5 *cont.*

```
59:      UNTIL Length( s ) = 0
60:   END;
61:
62:   PROCEDURE DeInitInterrupt;
63:   BEGIN
64:      SetIntVec( $1C, oldVector )
65:   END;
66:
67:   BEGIN
68:      CheckBreak := False;    { Must not end program with ^C! }
69:      InitInterrupt;
70:      DoWhateverYouWant;
71:      DeInitInterrupt      { Required before ending program. }
72:   END.
```

Adding Assembly Language to Units

You can use any of the techniques discussed so far to optimize units with assembly language. The following notes will help:

- You may declare **InLine** procedures and functions in a unit's public interface. These routines are then available to host programs, just as though the host declared them directly. Unlike regular procedure and function declarations, **InLine** routines do not require completed bodies in the unit's implementation.

- **InLine** procedures and functions may also be declared in a unit's private implementation. Like other declarations in this section, private **InLine** routines are not available to host programs.

- **InLine** statements must go in the unit's implementation, as do all code-generating statements. You can't insert **InLine** statements in a unit's interface.

- External routines may be public or private. Declare such routines in the unit's interface as though you were going to write their bodies in Pascal. In the unit's interface, declare the same routines with **EXTERNAL** key words in place of their statement bodies.

- In the .ASM file, public external routines must be *far*. Private externals must be *near*. Neglect this rule and your code is certain to crash.

As explained earlier, optimizing critical procedures and functions is one of the best ways to increase runtime performance. Adding assembly language to units makes it easy to keep two versions of your important routines—one version optimized with assembly language and the other written purely in Pascal. If you suspect a bug in your assembly language code, a quick substitution with the original (and, of course, fully tested) Pascal routines will confirm your suspicions.

Because a unit hides the details of its implementation—only the interface's declarations are visible to the outside world—host programs (and host-program programmers) do not have to know whether the actual code is written in Pascal or assembly language. As a real-life example, consider the standard Turbo Pascal **Dos, Crt,** and **Graph** units. Some of these units' routines were written in assembly language; others, in Pascal—facts that you don't need to know when using the units.

To demonstrate how to optimize units with assembly language, Program 14-6 incorporates Listing 4-2's communication routines into a Pascal unit. You'll have to make a few changes to earlier programs before using this unit. Follow these steps:

- Copy Listing 14-2 to a new file named COMMF.ASM. Load this file into your editor and change **Near** to **Far** (four times). In **CommInit** change **port** address [BP + 06] to [BP + 08]. Change **params** address [BP + 04] to [BP + 06]. In **SendByte**, change **theByte** address [BP + 04] to [BP + 06].

- Assemble COMMF.ASM with the command "tasm commf" or "masm commf;" depending on which assembler you have. This creates the file COMMF.OBJ.

- Save Program 14-6 as COMMU.PAS and compile to COMMU.TPU.

- To test the new unit, copy Program 14-4 to a new file named SEND2.PAS. Edit this file and delete lines 5–10. Also, change line 3 to:

```
USES Crt, CommU;
```

After completing these steps, you need only the COMMU.TPU file to compile SEND2.PAS and other host programs that use the assembly language communications routines. You don't need the .ASM or .OBJ files. You also don't need the COMMU.PAS file. (If this were a commercial program, you'd want to supply a .DOC file listing COMMU's interface.)

Notice that Program 14-6's interface and the modified host program show no sign that COMMU's routines are actually written as external assembly language routines. Organizing the unit as illustrated here hides the dirty implementation details from view.

Program 14-6

```
1:   UNIT CommU;        { Communications unit }
2:
3:   INTERFACE
4:
5:   PROCEDURE CommInit( port : Word; params : Byte );
6:   FUNCTION CharReady : Boolean;
7:   FUNCTION GetByte : Byte;
8:   PROCEDURE SendByte( theByte : Byte );
9:
```

Program 14-6 *cont.*

```
10:  IMPLEMENTATION
11:
12:  {$L COMMF}        { Link the following FAR routines in COMMF.OBJ }
13:
14:  PROCEDURE CommInit( port : Word; params : Byte ); EXTERNAL;
15:  FUNCTION CharReady : Boolean; EXTERNAL;
16:  FUNCTION GetByte : Byte; EXTERNAL;
17:  PROCEDURE SendByte( theByte : Byte ); EXTERNAL;
18:
19:  END.
```

Summary

Converting critical routines into machine language can improve the performance of a Pascal program. Turbo Pascal provides three ways to add machine language to programs: **InLine** statements, **InLine** procedures and functions, and external routines.

When adding machine language to Pascal, it's your responsibility to know how to locate variables in memory, prepare a stack frame, and preserve registers. You also must know the storage details of variables—details that the compiler normally handles.

Turbo Pascal lets you write your own interrupt service routines either in Pascal or in machine language.

Exercises

14-1. Take any example Pascal program from earlier examples and use Turbo Debugger to disassemble the compiled machine language.

14-2. Convert Program 14-4 to receive text transmitted from a remote computer.

14-3. (Advanced) Add error checking to the external routines in COMM.ASM (Listing 14-2).

14-4. (Advanced) Code your own interrupt procedure to sound an alarm at a certain time.

14-5. (Advanced) Optimize a Pascal program of your choice by identifying and converting critical routines to assembly language. Use **InLine** statements, **InLine** procedures and functions, or external modules. Run time-trials to prove that your efforts are worth the trouble.

14-6. (Advanced) Convert **MySquare** in Program 14-3 to an **InLine** function. What is the advantage of this method over the one in the listing?

Object-Oriented Programming

- Objectives
- Turbo Pascal's OOP Extensions
- Programming with Turbo Pascal Objects
- Inheritance
- Virtual Methods
- Dynamic Objects
- Streams
- Objects and Variable (Typed) Constants

15

Key Words and Identifiers

CONSTRUCTOR, DESTRUCTOR, Dispose, Fail, HeapFunc, New, OBJECT, Self, TypeOf, VIRTUAL

Objectives

Every once in a while, a new computing concept blows in like a summer breeze on a sultry morning. Structured programming comes to mind. BASIC deserves a place in the sun as do Pascal, the IBM PC, and the Apple II. Now there's something new in the air; something called *object-oriented programming*, which goes by the almost comical acronym, OOP.

This chapter explores Turbo Pascal 5.5's OOP extensions and puts a practical face on what to many programmers is a mysterious stranger with unknown intentions. Who needs OOP and why? What are OOP's advantages and disadvantages? Those are good questions and you *should* be skeptical. OOP is new. OOP is different. And, who knows, after the dust from this new wind settles, all the hOOPla may not have been warranted.

While learning about OOP, keep in mind that everything in this chapter is completely optional. No other chapters require you to know OOP techniques. Most Turbo Pascal programs (and most programmers) do *not* use OOP, although that soon may change. To understand the information in this chapter, you should first read chapters 1 through 7 and be able to do the exercises. A good understanding of pointers and heap memory management is especially helpful. Also, be aware that Turbo Pascal OOP extensions are experimental, and they may be further enhanced in future compiler versions. It's even conceivable that OOP will die out for lack of interest.

But I doubt that will happen. More likely, OOP will be accepted for its real value—a concept that helps programmers solve increasingly complex problems posed by modern personal computers and new advances in operating systems, especially in the area of graphical interfaces. We're fast approaching the time when OOP will be an essential programming tool, and those who learn OOP now will be in a position to control the future of programming.

That is, of course, until the next new breeze drifts ashore.

A Brief History of OOP

OOP's roots began in the late 1960s with a language called Simula 67, which traces its own beginnings to Algol. Simula was designed for writing simulations—still an excellent purpose for OOP techniques. Since then, other OOP languages have appeared with an array of names that reads like the back wall of an ice cream shop: Smalltalk, LOOPS, Flavors, Object Pascal (for the Macintosh), Neon (also for the Mac), Objective C, C++, and Actor (for Microsoft Windows). As you can see, OOP concepts have been around for some time and the OOP field isn't exactly barren.

Why, then, is OOP coming into the forefront now? One reason is the complexity of software that PC programmers are writing. Software source code is becoming longer and more difficult to modify. Time is becoming more expensive, and market competition is ever more fierce. OOP promises to help programmers and software companies become more productive. But whether that promise pans out remains to be seen.

Perhaps programmers have been slow to adopt OOP because none of the current OOP languages implements object-oriented concepts in exactly the same way. Add to this confusion Turbo Pascal's unique OOP extensions—borrowed in part from C++ and Object Pascal—and it's easy to see that there's little consensus among designers about the best way to implement OOP languages. What's more, Microsoft recently released Quick Pascal, compatible in some ways with Turbo Pascal, but different in its OOP extensions.

Don't be dismayed by this apparent jumble. Keep in mind that OOP *concepts* are what matter the most—not the forms. Learn the concepts, and you'll have no trouble with the details. In this department, Turbo Pascal OOP extensions are among the easiest to get to know.

What OOP Can and Can't Do

To understand what OOP can and can't do, you need to learn two new terms: encapsulation and inheritance. (There are many other new terms and phrases that go with OOP, some of which can be confusing at first. I'll introduce the more important terms as the OOP story unfolds. The Glossary of OOP Terms at the end of this chapter explains these terms and more.)

Encapsulation refers to the binding of data and executable code, which are stored separately in procedural languages such as non-OOP Pascal and C. In OOP, an *object* is a data structure, similar to a Pascal **RECORD**, that contains variables and related processes, called *methods*. Instead of writing procedures and functions that act upon data, in OOP you create objects that know how to perform actions on themselves.

Inheritance refers to the ability of new objects to inherit the characteristics—data and methods—of other objects. Similar to the way non-OOP Pascal lets you structure large programs into many small procedures and functions that make up the grand whole, OOP lets you easily create new objects by extending those that already exist. In this way, OOP simplifies building new programs from existing program libraries, usually without having to make extensive modifications to programming that already works.

With OOP, instead of reinventing the wheel every time you start a new program, you simply choose a set of objects that approximate the data and methods you need, and then extend those objects to finish the job. At least, that's the theory. Accomplishing this ideal in practice requires patience and careful programming, especially if you're just learning OOP's ropes.

Turbo Pascal's OOP Extensions

Turbo Pascal's OOP extensions add four new reserved key words, listed in Table 15-1. Three other new identifiers are **Fail** (a new built-in procedure), **Self** (a pointer to an object), and **TypeOf** (a new standard function). You'll meet these new items again later on.

Table 15-1 Turbo Pascal OOP reserved words

Reserved word	Meaning
CONSTRUCTOR	Prefaces an object's constructor methods
DESTRUCTOR	Prefaces an object's destructor methods
OBJECT	Begins object definitions
VIRTUAL	Designates virtual method definitions

Except for these seven new identifiers, everything else about OOP is standard Turbo Pascal. You can use **IF** and **WHILE** statements, assign values to variables, and perform other actions just as before. Everything you already know about procedures, functions, parameters, variables, pointers, and other Pascal elements holds true. You can mix OOP and standard Pascal at will. These facts let you pick up OOP concepts in your own good time without having to learn a new language from scratch. When converting programs to use OOP techniques, you can revise existing code in small chunks, rather than face a complete rewrite—never an enjoyable task.

By the way, Turbo Pascal OOP extensions resemble those in C++ and, to a lesser degree, Object Pascal for the Macintosh. See the Bibliography for references that describe these languages.

Note: Appendix A includes syntax (railroad) diagrams for Turbo Pascal's new object-oriented extensions.

Programming with Turbo Pascal Objects

An *object type*—called a *class* in some other OOP languages—defines an object's contents. Object types are similar to Pascal record definitions such as:

```
DateRec = RECORD
    month : Byte;
    day   : Byte;
    year  : Word;
END; { DateRec }
```

The three data fields **month**, **day**, and **year** are grouped by **DateRec**'s definition, allowing programs to create multipart variables:

```
VAR   today : DateRec;
```

The **today** record is a variable of type **DateRec** with two **Byte** fields and one **Word** field. To assign values to the individual fields in **today**, programs execute statements such as:

```
today.month := 6;
today.day := 6;
today.year := 1989;
```

Or, use a **WITH** statement to simplify the program text:

```
WITH today DO
BEGIN
    month := 6;
    day := 6;
    year := 1989;
END; { with }
```

If this were a real program, at this point, you'd probably begin writing a few procedures to display the date, to let people enter new dates from the keyboard, to advance a **DateRec** variable to the next day, to determine if a year is a leap year, and so on. To perform these operations, you'd then feed **DateRec** variables to your procedures. In essence, that's the standard programming approach in procedural languages like Pascal and C.

Object Data Fields

An OOP solution to the same problem also defines a new data structure, but this time using the **OBJECT** key word in place of **RECORD**:

```
DateObj = OBJECT
```

```
     month : Byte;
     day   : Byte;
     year  : Word;
     PROCEDURE Init( mm, dd, yy : Word );
     FUNCTION StringDate : String;
  END; { DateObj }
```

As before, three data fields **month**, **day**, and **year** store values representing a unique date. Some OOP languages call these fields *instance variables*. Unlike a Pascal record, **PROCEDURE** and **FUNCTION** headers define the format of two routines **Init** and **StringDate** in addition to the object's data fields. These routines are the object's *methods* —the actions that objects know how to perform. Usually, methods do something with an object's data fields, in this example assigning parameters **mm**, **dd**, and **yy** to **month**, **day**, and **year**, and returning the date as a **String**. (The code for these functions comes later.) As explained earlier, merging data and code this way is called encapsulation. The object type **DateObj** encapsulates variables and methods in one handy package.

Remember that the **OBJECT** definition is just that—a definition. An object type is a *design* for an object, not the object itself. An object type occupies no space and contains no code. It merely describes the form of an object—just as a **RECORD** definition describes the form of record variables to be declared later.

An example that fleshes out the **DateObj** object type helps explain more about Turbo Pascal OOP. Compile Program 15-1 as you normally do. You don't need to change any settings or use special option letters to switch on OOP extensions. Turbo Pascal is always OOP ready.

Program 15-1

```
 1:   PROGRAM DateObjects;
 2:
 3:   TYPE
 4:      DateObj = OBJECT
 5:         month : Byte;
 6:         day   : Byte;
 7:         year  : Word;
 8:         PROCEDURE Init( mm, dd, yy : Word );
 9:         FUNCTION StringDate : String;
10:      END; { DateObj }
11:
12:   VAR
13:      today : DateObj;
14:
15:   PROCEDURE DateObj.Init( mm, dd, yy : Word );
16:   BEGIN
17:      month := mm;
18:      day := dd;
```

Program 15-1 *cont.*

```
19:     year := yy
20: END; { Init }
21:
22: FUNCTION DateObj.StringDate : String;
23: VAR
24:     mStr, dStr, yStr : String[10];
25: BEGIN
26:     Str( month, mStr );     { Convert month to string }
27:     Str( day, dStr );       { Convert day to string }
28:     Str( year, yStr );      { Convert year to string }
29:     StringDate := mStr + '/' + dStr + '/' + yStr
30: END; { StringDate }
31:
32: BEGIN
33:     today.Init( 12, 20, 1989 );
34:     Writeln( 'The date is: ', today.StringDate );
35: END.
```

Object Methods

Lines 12–13 in Program 15-1 declare a variable **today** of type **DateObj**. In OOP parlance, a variable of an object data type is called an *object instance*. The object type is *instantiated* in the variable—just a fancy way of saying that memory space is allocated for a variable of the object type. As you know, you can create many variables of any Pascal data types, for instance, a series of **Integers**:

```
VAR  i, j, k : Integer;
```

Similarly, you can declare many instances of object types:

```
VAR  today, yesterday, tomorrow : DateObj;
```

The three object instances **today**, **yesterday**, and **tomorrow** each has its own copies of the data fields defined in **DateObj**. But here comes a big difference between objects and records: Multiple instances of object types *share the same methods*. In Program 15-1, those methods are completed at lines 15–30, appearing much like normal Pascal procedures and functions. Dot notation identifies the routines as object methods. For example, examine line 15:

```
PROCEDURE DateObj.Init( mm, dd, yy : Word );
```

Method **Init** is joined by dot notation to **DateObj**, telling the compiler that **Init** is a method belonging to **DateObj**. This lets you write a non-OOP procedure named **Init** without conflict, although the confusion that introduces is unappealing. Try not to use the same identifiers for methods and other Pascal procedures and functions.

Figure 15-1 illustrates how multiple-object instances (variables) of the same object type have separate copies of the object's data fields but share the same method implementations. This is an important concept to learn.

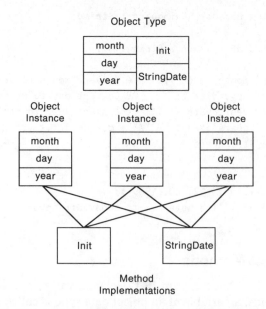

Figure 15-1 Multiple-object instances have separate copies of an object type's data fields but share the same method implementations.

The method implementations (lines 15–30) contain Pascal statements that perform the actions for the **DateObj** object type. **Init** assigns its three parameters to the appropriate object data fields. Most objects contain similar methods to assign new values to an object's instance variables. **DateObj** uses Turbo Pascal's built-in **Str** procedure and three temporary string variables (lines 23–24) to convert the date field values to strings, which are joined together with slashes at line 29 and passed back as the **StringDate** function result.

Lines 33 and 34 call the object methods, assigning date values to **today** and displaying the result. Again, dot notation tells the compiler that this is an object method:

```
today.Init( 12, 20, 1989 );
```

In technical OOP talk, such statements are said to pass the *message* **Init** to the object instance **today**, in effect giving **today** a command to initialize itself. Strictly speaking, the statement does *not* call a procedure named **Init**, although, of course, the compiled machine code performs a subroutine call to **Init**'s address. If this seems arbitrary and confusing, don't dwell on it. The distinction between passing messages to objects and calling procedures and functions is less important in Turbo Pascal OOP than it is in some other OOP languages.

A few more observations about Program 15-1 explain other key OOP concepts:

- An object type such as **DateObj** at lines 4–10 is similar to a unit's interface section, where global functions, procedures, and variables are declared. The method implementations (lines 15–30) are analogous to a unit's implementation section, where the details of the unit's design are hidden from the rest of the program. Like units, objects hide their messy coding details, insulating programmers from becoming mired in too many low-level details.

- Inside a method's implementation, an implied **WITH** statement makes the object's data fields available to statements. Line 17 assigns **mm** to **month**, a field in **DateObj**. An object's data fields are readily available inside the object's method implementations. Because of this, identifiers in method parameter lists—for example, **mm**, **dd**, and **yy** in line 8—must be different from any data fields in the object, such as **month**, **day**, and **year** at lines 5–7. Using the same name for a data field and a method parameter is a common mistake that causes a "Duplicate identifier" compiler error.

- You may access data fields in object instances directly outside of a method's implementation, too. For example, there's nothing to prevent you from writing:

```
today.month := 10;
```

This may seem natural, but there's a good reason for not accessing object data fields directly this way—a reason that will become clear later on. Direct access to object fields is always allowed, but strongly discouraged in Turbo Pascal OOP.

Inheritance

So far, you may be thinking there's not much point to OOP. After all, it would be easy to write a non-OOP version of Program 15-1. OOP's advantages become clearer when you see how new object definitions can inherit the characteristics of other objects. As mentioned earlier, inheritance is one of OOP's major contributions to programming.

Ancestors and Descendants

An object that inherits the characteristics of another object is called a *descendant object*. The object from which the inherited features come is called the *ancestor object*. A most important rule to memorize is that descendant objects can have only one immediate ancestor, as Figure 15-2 illustrates. Conversely, ancestor objects can have an unlimited number of descendants. This relationship is called *single inheritance*. Some OOP languages allow *multiple inheritance*, where a descendant object may have more than one parent. This is not possible in Turbo Pascal—at least not yet. In the figure, the dashed line shows what would be an illegal multiple ancestor relation for the bottom object.

The importance of multiple inheritance is a hotly debated topic in OOP circles—and the outcome of this debate is still uncertain.

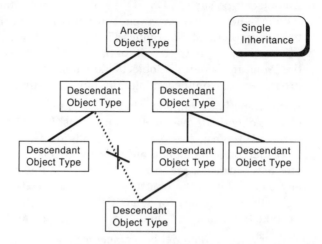

Figure 15-2 Single inheritance allows objects to have many descendants but only one immediate ancestor. Multiple inheritance (represented by the dashed line) is not allowed in Turbo Pascal.

Inherited Data Fields

To create a new object that inherits the characteristics of another object, define a new object type with the ancestor object type name in parentheses. For example, suppose you now need to represent the time *and* the date. If you've done a lot of Pascal programming, you'd probably attempt to define a new date type like this:

```
TimeRec = RECORD
    hour, minute, second : Byte;
    theDate : DateObj;
END; { TimeRec }
```

Turbo Pascal's OOP extensions allow a much better way to accomplish inheritance: Define a new object type that inherits the characteristics of **DateObj**:

```
TimeObj = OBJECT( DateObj )
    hour   : Byte;
    minute : Byte;
    second : Byte;
    PROCEDURE Init( mm, dd, yy, hh, mi, ss : Word );
    FUNCTION StringTime : String;
END; { TimeObj }
```

The new object type, **TimeObj**, defines three data fields **hour**, **minute**, and

second, representing a certain time. Two methods initialize the object (**Init**) and return the time as a string (**StringTime**).

Because **TimeObj** is descended from **DateObj**, the new object contains all features from its ancestor. Every **TimeObj** instance has **hour**, **minute**, and **second** fields *plus* **month**, **day**, and **year** fields from **DateObj**. Descendant objects always inherit all data fields from their ancestors.

Inherited Methods

In addition to inheriting data fields, the new **TimeObj** object type inherits its ancestor's methods, too. Every **TimeObj** instance "knows" how to perform a **StringTime** function—defined by the **TimeObj** object type—and a **StringDate** function—defined by the ancestor **DateObj**.

All **TimeObj** instances also have an **Init** procedure, and this brings up another important OOP concept. Because **TimeObj**'s **Init** function has the same name as its ancestor **Init** from **DateObj**, the descendant's method definition *overrides* the ancestor method. This doesn't mean that the ancestor method disappears. It's still there, beneath the surface of the descendant's replacement method. As you recall, **DateObj**'s **Init** method is defined as:

```
PROCEDURE Init( mm, dd, yy : Word );
```

The new **TimeObj Init** method is defined as:

```
PROCEDURE Init( mm, dd, yy, hh, mi, ss : Word );
```

The overriding **Init** lists all the parameters of the ancestor **Init**, and it adds three new parameters, representing the hour, minute, and seconds for initializing a **TimeObj** object instance. This is a typical OOP setup. The overriding procedures and functions—especially those that initialize object data fields—add new parameters to those in ancestor methods.

> Note: Only methods may be overridden in descendant objects. Data fields may never be overridden; therefore, in a descendant object, new data fields must have identifiers that are unique not only in the object definition, but among all ancestors from which the object descends.

Program 15-2 lists the final result, duplicating all of Program 15-1 and extending **DateObj** with the **TimeObj** object type at lines 12–18. Line 22 declares **appointment** as a **TimeObj** instance.

Study the new method implementations. **TimeObj.Init** at lines 41–47 assigns the three new parameters to the descendant object's data fields, initializing the time. Look closely at line 43. The statement:

```
DateObj.Init( mm, dd, yy );
```

calls the ancestor's **Init** method, passing the other three parameters to initialize the inherited date fields. Prefacing **Init** with the **DateObj** object type identifier and a period tells the compiler which of the identically named **Init**s to use. Although this example has only two object types, another program might have several objects, each descended from another, and each with its own **Init** method. **TimeObj**'s **Init** method implementation could directly assign the date values to the inherited date fields. But, as mentioned before, it's against the spirit of OOP to access data fields in other objects directly.

Lines 49–60 implement a non-OOP procedure to convert values to strings with leading zeros. Lines 62–72 implement the **StringTime** method, similar to the **StringDate** method explained earlier.

Finally, examine lines 77–80. First, a single statement initializes the entire object—assigning date and time values. A **Writeln** statement then displays the date and time. Line 80 proves that **appointment** has a **StringDate** method, inherited from the object's **DateObj** ancestor.

Program 15-2

```
1:   PROGRAM DateObjects2;
2:
3:   TYPE
4:      DateObj = OBJECT
5:         month : Byte;
6:         day   : Byte;
7:         year  : Word;
8:         PROCEDURE Init( mm, dd, yy : Word );
9:         FUNCTION StringDate : String;
10:     END; { DateObj }
11:
12:     TimeObj = OBJECT( DateObj )
13:        hour   : Byte;
14:        minute : Byte;
15:        second : Byte;
16:        PROCEDURE Init( mm, dd, yy, hh, mi, ss : Word );
17:        FUNCTION StringTime : String;
18:     END; { TimeObj }
19:
20:   VAR
21:      today : DateObj;
22:      appointment : TimeObj;
23:
24:   PROCEDURE DateObj.Init( mm, dd, yy : Word );
25:   BEGIN
26:      month := mm;
27:      day := dd;
28:      year := yy
```

Program 15-2 *cont.*

```
29:   END; { Init }
30:
31:   FUNCTION DateObj.StringDate : String;
32:   VAR
33:      mStr, dStr, yStr : String[10];
34:   BEGIN
35:      Str( month, mStr );      { Convert month to string }
36:      Str( day, dStr );        { Convert day to string }
37:      Str( year, yStr );       { Convert year to string }
38:      StringDate := mStr + '/' + dStr + '/' + yStr
39:   END; { ShowDate }
40:
41:   PROCEDURE TimeObj.Init( mm, dd, yy, hh, mi, ss : Word );
42:   BEGIN
43:      DateObj.Init( mm, dd, yy );
44:      hour := hh;
45:      minute := mi;
46:      second := ss
47:   END; { Init }
48:
49:   PROCEDURE Convert( n : Word; VAR s : String; len : Word );
50:   { Convert n to string s of length n, inserting leading 0s }
51:   VAR p : Integer;
52:   BEGIN
53:      Str( n:len, s );        { Do raw number to string conversion }
54:      p := Pos( ' ', s );
55:      WHILE p > 0 DO
56:      BEGIN
57:         s[ p ] := '0';
58:         p := Pos( ' ', s )
59:      END { while }
60:   END; { Convert }
61:
62:   FUNCTION TimeObj.StringTime : String;
63:   VAR
64:      hStr, mStr, sStr : String[10];
65:   BEGIN
66:   {$V-} { Turn off string length checks }
67:      Convert( hour, hStr, 2 );      { Convert hour to string }
68:      Convert( minute, mStr, 2 );    { Convert minute to string }
69:      Convert( second, sStr, 2 );    { Convert second to string }
70:   {$V+} { Turn string length checks on }
71:      StringTime := hStr + ':' + mStr + ':' + sStr
72:   END; { StringTime }
73:
```

Program 15-2 *cont.*

```
74:  BEGIN
75:    today.Init( 12, 20, 1989 );
76:    Writeln( 'The date is: ', today.StringDate );
77:    appointment.Init( 12, 24, 1989, 17, 15, 00 );
78:    Writeln( 'The appointment is at: ',
79:      appointment.StringTime, ' on ',
80:      appointment.StringDate );
81:  END.
```

Turbo Pascal's Smart Linker

One of OOP's possible drawbacks is the fact that new objects inherit everything from their ancestors. But what if you don't need all that the ancestor has to share? You might be tempted in such cases to start over, designing new object types from scratch to avoid wasting memory.

Avoid this temptation. While you can't prevent objects from inheriting ancestor data fields, you can freely extend object methods without worrying about introducing methods that won't ever be used. Turbo Pascal's "smart" linker strips out methods that are never called. If a program never refers to a method, the code for that method is not included in the compiled result. There is no penalty for adding methods that are never used. They take up space only in the program text.

Virtual Methods

The methods in object types such as **DateObj** and **TimeObj** (see Program 15-2, lines 8–9 and 16–17) are *static methods*. A static method header in an object definition is identical in form to a procedure or function header in a unit's interface section.

Virtual methods add the **VIRTUAL** key word to the end of the method definition. For example, to convert **Init** and **StringDate** in Program 15-2 to virtual methods, change lines 8 and 9 to:

```
PROCEDURE Init( mm, dd, yy : Word ); VIRTUAL;
FUNCTION StringDate : String; VIRTUAL;
```

Don't make this change just yet. Virtual methods require special initialization to avoid an almost certain system crash. To understand why this is so, you need to learn the purpose of virtual methods plus another new term, *polymorphism*.

Note: Unlike static methods, unused virtual methods are not stripped by Turbo Pascal's smart linker.

Polymorphism

Virtual methods let you create *polymorphic objects* —literally object instances that can assume different forms when the program runs. A polymorphic object instance might take on the form of itself or any of its descendants.

For example, an object type's root ancestor might be named **Vehicle** with descendants **TwoWheelers** and **FourWheelers** from which **Cart**, **Bicycle**, and **Automobile** are descended. All such objects share some of the same characteristics—the ability to go, to stop, to accelerate, and so on. Suppose you create an object instance of type **Automobile**:

```
VAR  MyWheels : Automobile;
```

You then want to tell the object to stop. Because there's a world of difference in the way you stop a cart, a bicycle, and an automobile, each object type defines its own **Stop** method, overriding its ancestor's method. To stop any object takes only a simple statement:

```
MyWheels.Stop;
```

But now a complication sets in. Suppose also that the root ancestor object **Vehicle** defines a data field **Velocity** and another method called **SlowDown**. The implementation for **SlowDown** might be something like this:

```
PROCEDURE Vehicle.SlowDown;
BEGIN
   IF Velocity > 0
      THEN Velocity := Velocity - 1;
   IF Velocity = 0
      THEN Stop
END; { SlowDown }
```

All objects descending from **Vehicle** slow down in exactly the same way. (At least they do for our purposes.) Because descendant objects inherit the methods of their ancestors, it's perfectly legal to write:

```
MyWheels.SlowDown
```

If this causes **Velocity** to reach 0, the **IF** statement in **SlowDown** calls the **Stop** method.

But which **Stop** method?

Obviously, we want **SlowDown** to use the **Stop** method that applies to an **Automobile**. Unfortunately, this is not what happens. Because **SlowDown** is implemented as a method in the root ancestor **Vehicle**, the compiler generates code to call **Vehicle.Stop**, not **Automobile.Stop**.

Fixing this problem is easy—just make **Stop** virtual. By doing this, you are telling the compiler that the actual **Stop** method to use isn't known until the **Slow-Down** method executes. At that time, you want the code to examine the type of object that's slowing down and, if the velocity reaches 0, to call the appropriate **Stop** method that applies to this type of **Vehicle**.

A more general explanation illustrates this problem, which virtual methods neatly solve. Program 15-3 defines two objects, **Object1** and **Object2** at lines 4–11. **Object1** defines two methods, **MethodA** and **MethodB**. A descendant object inherits these methods but replaces **MethodA** with its own version.

Examine the method implementations. Each **MethodA** simply displays a message so we know which method is running. **Object1**'s **MethodB** does the same, but also calls **MethodA**.

Two object instances, **Item1** of type **Object1** and **Item2** of type **Object2**, are declared at lines 13–15. The main body of the program (lines 34–35) calls **MethodB**, displaying:

```
Inside Object1's MethodA
Inside MethodB
Inside Object1's MethodA
Inside MethodB
```

But this is not correct. When **Item2** activates **MethodB** inherited from **Object1**, we want the statement at line 24 to call the new **MethodA** that **Object2** defines as a replacement for the ancestor's method. Figure 15-3 illustrates the problem. **MethodB**'s implementation is hard wired during compilation to **MethodA** in **Object1**, a process called *early binding*. **Object2**'s replacement **MethodA** can never be called by **MethodB**. The solution, as you'll see in the next program, is to convert **MethodA** to a virtual method.

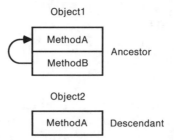

Figure 15-3 **MethodB** is tightly bound to **Object1**'s **MethodA**, preventing it from calling **Object2**'s replacement **MethodA**.

Program 15-3

```
1:   PROGRAM StaticTrouble;
2:
3:   Type
4:      Object1 = OBJECT
5:         PROCEDURE MethodA;
6:         PROCEDURE MethodB;
7:      END;
```

Program 15-3 *cont.*

```
 8:
 9:    Object2 = OBJECT( Object1 )
10:       PROCEDURE MethodA;
11:    END;
12:
13: VAR
14:    Item1 : Object1;
15:    Item2 : Object2;
16:
17: PROCEDURE Object1.MethodA;
18: BEGIN
19:    Writeln( 'Inside Object1''s MethodA' )
20: END;
21:
22: PROCEDURE Object1.MethodB;
23: BEGIN
24:    MethodA;
25:    Writeln( 'Inside MethodB' )
26: END;
27:
28: PROCEDURE Object2.MethodA;
29: BEGIN
30:    Writeln( 'Inside Object2''s MethodA' )
31: END;
32:
33: BEGIN
34:    Item1.MethodB;
35:    Item2.MethodB
36: END.
```

Constructors

Object types that define virtual methods require a special method called a *constructor*. The purpose of a constructor is similar to that of the **Init** method in Program 15-1. Object constructors are syntactically identical to procedure methods but use the key word **CONSTRUCTOR** in place of **PROCEDURE**. A constructor may have parameters, but it doesn't have to. Constructors can be inherited just like other methods and can be replaced by new methods defined in descendants.

Every object that defines one or more virtual methods *must* have a constructor. If you don't define a constructor method in an object with virtual procedures and functions, the program will fail to operate. There are no exceptions to this rule.

A constructor performs two services. It can initialize data fields in the object instance—just as **Init** does in Program 15-1. And it always initializes an object's

Virtual Method Table (VMT), which is stored in the program's global data segment (see Appendix B's memory map).

A VMT stores two kinds of information—the size of the object and a set of pointers to the object type's methods. The method pointers in the VMT allow an object instance to use inherited methods in ancestor objects that in turn use replacement methods in the descendant. The constructor links the object instance to its VMT, allowing the object to locate its methods. This linkage occurs at run time, a process called *late binding*.

> Note: Turbo Pascal creates a VMT for object *types* defined in a program. Multiple object *instances* (variables) of the same type share a single VMT. The VMT is stored in the program's data segment along with other global variables. VMT's are not stored in object instances.

Figure 15-4 shows the new arrangement after making **MethodA** virtual. **MethodB** in **Object1** now locates **MethodA** by consulting the VMT rather than calling the method directly, as it did in Figure 15-3. There still is only one copy of **MethodB**'s code in memory. But, because **Object2** inherits **MethodB** from **Object1**, and because **MethodB** now consults the object's VMT for virtual method calls, **MethodB** now calls the replacement **MethodA** in **Object2** while still calling the original **MethodA** in **Object1** as before.

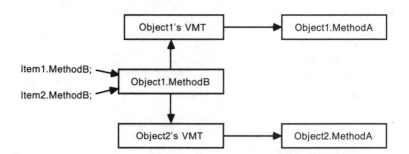

Figure 15-4 Objects consult the VMT for the addresses of virtual methods.

Program 15-4 puts these observations to the test. The program is nearly identical to Program 15-3, but adds a constructor **Init** definition to **Object1** at line 7. Also, the key word **VIRTUAL** is added to the two **MethodA** definitions at lines 8 and 13. This tells the compiler to generate code that consults the VMT for every call to **MethodA**. The actual **MethodA** that runs depends on the type of the object instance.

Another change is at lines 20–23, listing the **Init** constructor's implementation. In this example, the constructor is empty. In practice, a constructor usually performs various initialization duties, assigns values to variables, prepares pointers, and so forth. But, despite appearances, the seemingly empty constructor is not a do-nothing shell. It still performs the vital (if invisible) service of initializing an object instance to address the correct VMT for this object type.

The final change is at lines 42–43, which activate the **Init** constructor for each object instance (variable). **Object2** inherits the constructor from **Object1**, just as it inherits the other methods. **Init** must be called for each object instance. If you have 100 object instances of the same object type, this rule means that you have to call the **Init** constructor 100 times—once per object instance.

Because of these changes, running the program now correctly displays:

```
Inside Object1's MethodA
Inside MethodB
Inside Object2's MethodA
Inside MethodB
```

> Note: Run Program 15-4 under control of the built-in or stand-alone Turbo Debugger. Press F7 repeatedly to execute statements one at a time. Notice that when **MethodB** first calls **MethodA**, it uses the version for **Object1** (line 25 in the listing). The second time, it calls **MethodA** for **Object2** (line 36). You are seeing virtual methods in action.

Program 15-4

```
 1:  {$R+}     { Check for uninitialized objects }
 2:
 3:  PROGRAM VirtualPleasure;
 4:
 5:  Type
 6:     Object1 = OBJECT
 7:        CONSTRUCTOR Init;
 8:        PROCEDURE MethodA; VIRTUAL;
 9:        PROCEDURE MethodB;
10:     END;
11:
12:     Object2 = OBJECT( Object1 )
13:        PROCEDURE MethodA; VIRTUAL;
14:     END;
15:
16:  VAR
17:     Item1 : Object1;
18:     Item2 : Object2;
19:
```

Program 15-4 *cont.*

```
20:   CONSTRUCTOR Object1.Init;
21:   BEGIN
22:      { Initializes object's VMT }
23:   END;
24:
25:   PROCEDURE Object1.MethodA;
26:   BEGIN
27:      Writeln( 'Inside Object1''s MethodA' )
28:   END;
29:
30:   PROCEDURE Object1.MethodB;
31:   BEGIN
32:      MethodA;
33:      Writeln( 'Inside MethodB' )
34:   END;
35:
36:   PROCEDURE Object2.MethodA;
37:   BEGIN
38:      Writeln( 'Inside Object2''s MethodA' )
39:   END;
40:
41:   BEGIN
42:      Item1.Init;
43:      Item2.Init;
44:      Item1.MethodB;
45:      Item2.MethodB
46:   END.
```

Catching Constructor Errors

The two most important rules about constructors to remember are:

- Every object with one or more virtual methods must define (or inherit) a constructor method, even if that constructor has no direct duties to perform.

- The program must call the constructor for each object instance (variable) of that object type.

Failing to obey either rule is catastrophic. You have to remember the first rule yourself. Switching on the {$R + } switch (normally used to check array index and integer subranges) lets Turbo Pascal help you to remember the second.

Line 1 of Program 15-4 demonstrates how the {$R + } switch works. To see what happens if you forget to call an object instance's constructor, change line 43 to:

```
(* Item2.Init; *)
```

In other words, turn the statement into a comment. Recompile and run. You should receive error 210, "Object not initialized." If you also delete line 1, the program will crash when it tries to call the object's methods without first linking the object to its VMT. (You don't have to try this. If you do, be prepared to reboot.)

Checking for object VMT errors takes time and space. The compiler must generate subroutine calls around *every* use of all virtual methods. For this reason, after testing your program, be sure to reset the R switch to its normal state {$R – }, or to remove the switch altogether.

Assigning Objects

You can of course assign one object instance to another of a compatible type. But in objects with virtual methods, the results may be unexpected. For example, if you have the object type:

```
ObjectType = OBJECT
   x, y : Word;
   CONSTRUCTOR init( xx, yy : Word );
   { ... virtual methods }
END;
```

And if you define two variables of type **ObjectType**:

```
VAR  obj1, obj2 : ObjectType;
```

You might be tempted to initialize **obj1** and assign it to **obj2** like this:

```
obj1.init( 4, 3 );
obj2 := obj1;           { ??? }
```

Such assignments are dangerous. Because **ObjectType** declares virtual methods, its constructor must be called for every object in order to link the object instance with the appropriate VMT, locating the addresses of the object's methods. To satisfy this requirement, the previous assignment must be followed by:

```
obj2.init( 4, 3 );
```

Even though you already initialized **obj1** and assigned it to **obj2**, you still *must* call **obj2**'s **init** constructor. If you don't do this, **obj2**'s pointer to its VMT will not be set up, and calls to **obj2** methods will fail. Remember always to call each object instance's constructor, even after copying one object to another.

You may wonder why assignment statements don't copy VMT pointers along with everything else in objects. The reason is that ancestor object instances may be assigned to instances of their descendants, which begin with a copy of the ancestor's fields. Descendant objects have their own VMTs unique from ancestor VMTs, and copying the ancestor's VMT pointer to a descendant's VMT pointer would be a serious error.

Virtual Methods and Constructors

As you've seen, virtual methods allow precompiled code (procedures and functions inherited from ancestor objects) to call new methods in descendant objects. Imagine the possibilities this opens. If you purchase a toolkit from a software supplier, even if you don't have the original source code, you can write new methods and have the existing routines in the toolkit call your custom code! For this reason, it's wise to make most methods virtual. If you make them static, you may prevent people (and yourself) from extending existing code later.

A few other notes will help you to use virtual methods and constructors effectively:

- Make methods virtual by adding the **VIRTUAL** key word to the end of the method definition in the object type. This is the only place the **VIRTUAL** key word may appear.

- Methods that override ancestor virtual methods must be virtual, and they must have identical names and parameter lists. Overriden static methods and constructors may have different parameter lists.

- Make sure that each object type that uses virtual methods defines or inherits at least one constructor method.

- Never forget to call a constructor for each object instance of any object type that defines virtual methods.

- Constructors can *never* be virtual. This only makes sense. If a constructor initializes the VMT, which holds the addresses of an object type's virtual methods, you'd be unable to use a virtual constructor because the VMT wouldn't be initialized before the constructor ran at least one time!

- Objects may have multiple constructors, a useful technique when objects must be initialized in different ways depending on other circumstances. In such cases, you must call only one of an object's many constructors to ensure that the VMT link is initialized. You don't have to call every constructor defined in the object type.

- Calling a constructor more than once is perfectly okay. The VMT is initialized only on the first such use. But, be aware that constructors often allocate memory on the heap for other variables. Unless you do something to recover that memory, calling constructors in succession could cause the heap to become permanently fragmented.

Dynamic Objects

Until now, example object instances have been plain Pascal variables, declared in the program's **VAR** section. A more popular OOP strategy is to declare pointers to object types and allocate space for object instances at runtime. A few observations explain why this OOP technique is vital:

- A single pointer may address object instances of its own object base type or of object instances of *any descendant type*.

- The reverse is not true: A pointer to an object instance may not address an instance of an ancestor object type.

- The object's constructor simplifies memory management by cooperating with an extended form of **New** to allocate space for object instances on the heap.

- The object can also define a *destructor*. Along with constructors, destructors simplify memory management by cooperating with an extended form of **Dispose** to delete object instances from the heap.

The first two of these points may seem odd at first. A pointer to an object type may address object instances of that type or any of its descendants. For example, using the earlier analogy, a pointer to type **Vehicle** might address a **Cart**, a **Bicycle**, or an **Automobile**, all of which descend from objects **FourWheelers** and **TwoWheelers**. Figure 15-5 illustrates this concept, which bends Pascal's normally strict type-checking rules. Shaded boxes represent inherited characteristics in descendant objects. Each descendant adds its own features (data fields and methods), shown as the unshaded box at the bottom of each new object type. Descendant objects inherit the data fields of their ancestors; therefore, a pointer to **Vehicle** can safely manipulate the inherited **Vehicle** and **FourWheelers** data at the top of a **Cart** object instance. But the reverse is not true. A pointer to a **Bicycle** object must not attempt to treat that object as though it were a **Cart**—there are no **Bicycle** and **TwoWheeler** fields in a **Cart** object instance, and writing to those nonexistent fields could overwrite other data in memory, causing a serious bug.

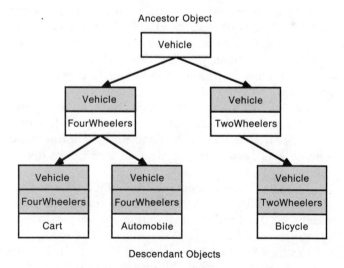

Figure 15-5 Pointers to objects are fully compatible with descendants of those objects.

Can you see the importance of this idea and how it relates to virtual methods? If you write code with pointers to objects that metamorphize (change form) at runtime, then the object instances themselves *must* be able to decide which methods are the correct ones to use. There's no way you can possibly know in advance which polymorphic object a pointer will actually address at runtime. As explained before, virtual methods allow this freedom by looking up method addresses in the object's VMT. Pointers to such objects take full advantage of OOP polymorphism—the ability of objects to assume different forms when the program runs.

An excellent example of dynamic objects and polymorphism is a simple linked list. Your Turbo Pascal OOP Guide contains a similar example, defining a **Node** object that contains two pointers: one to the next node and one to the variable-length data stored in memory. (If you have that book handy, a diagram of this structure appears on page 55.)

This is a typical setup. A different—and, perhaps, more purely polymorphic—approach lets the nodes metamorphize, taking whatever form is needed to store integers, real numbers, and strings on the same list. The objects themselves take care of what is usually a messy job of managing memory and pointers—without the need for nonpolymorphic **Node** objects linked together. The next sections put this idea to work.

Constructors and Destructors

Program 15-5 implements two simple objects that can manage linked lists containing any data types. Line 11 introduces a new key word, **DESTRUCTOR**. Destructors typically perform cleanup chores for objects created in heap memory. Often, such objects themselves contain pointers to other data, and the destructor disposes this memory in preparation for releasing the memory occupied by the object instance.

Like a constructor, a destructor is identical to a procedure method except that **DESTRUCTOR** replaces **PROCEDURE**. Destructors are almost always virtual, allowing future code to inherit an ancestor object's definitions and redefine the destructor's duties, perhaps disposing new data fields and performing other jobs. Destructors may be static, however, in cases where such enhancements are unnecessary.

Destructors are usually named **Done**, although you can choose a different name if you want. Unlike constructors, objects that define virtual methods do not require destructors. Also, an object may define multiple destructors, useful when objects need different disposal techniques depending on other circumstances.

Lines 34–36 implement the **Item** object's **Done** destructor. In this example, there are no statements in the destructor implementation. Even so, the destructor contains machine code that simplifies memory management, as explained after the listing.

Compile Program 15-5 to create LISTU.TPU. The program is in the form of a unit, with the object type definitions in the interface section and the methods hidden neatly away in the implementation.

Note: Some people recommend defining only one destructor per object type, as this more closely mirrors the way languages such as C++ operate. Future Turbo Pascal versions may take advantage of this arrangement, automatically calling an object's designated destructor when the program disposes object instances or when those instances are no longer within the scope of currently active procedures and functions. That's pure guesswork, however, and you are certainly free to define multiple destructors in object types. But if you want to gamble on my crystal ball, limit your objects to one destructor with *no* parameters.

Program 15-5

```
1:   UNIT ListU;
2:
3:   INTERFACE
4:
5:   TYPE
6:
7:      ItemPtr = ^Item;
8:      Item = OBJECT
9:         next : ItemPtr;
10:        CONSTRUCTOR Init;
11:        DESTRUCTOR Done; VIRTUAL;
12:        PROCEDURE Print; VIRTUAL;
13:     END;
14:
15:     List = OBJECT
16:        root : ItemPtr;
17:        CONSTRUCTOR Init;
18:        PROCEDURE InsertItem( n : ItemPtr );
19:        PROCEDURE DisposeList;
20:        PROCEDURE PrintList;
21:     END; { List }
22:
23:
24:   IMPLEMENTATION
25:
26:
27:   { Item }
28:
29:   CONSTRUCTOR Item.Init;
30:   BEGIN
```

Program 15-5 *cont.*

```
31:      next := Nil
32:  END;
33:
34:  DESTRUCTOR Item.Done;
35:  BEGIN
36:  END;
37:
38:  PROCEDURE Item.Print;
39:  BEGIN
40:     Writeln;    { Start new display line }
41:  END;
42:
43:
44:  { List }
45:
46:  CONSTRUCTOR List.Init;
47:  BEGIN
48:     root := Nil;
49:  END;
50:
51:  PROCEDURE List.InsertItem( n : ItemPtr );
52:  BEGIN
53:    n^.next := root;
54:     root := n
55:  END;
56:
57:  PROCEDURE List.PrintList;
58:  VAR   ip : ItemPtr;
59:  BEGIN
60:     ip := root;
61:     WHILE ( ip <> Nil ) DO
62:     BEGIN
63:       ip^.Print;
64:       ip := ip^.next
65:     END; { while }
66:  END;
67:
68:  PROCEDURE List.DisposeList;
69:  VAR   ip : ItemPtr;
70:  BEGIN
71:     WHILE root <> Nil DO
72:     BEGIN
73:       ip := root;
74:       root := ip^.next;
75:       Dispose( ip, Done )
```

Program 15-5 *cont.*

```
76:     END { while }
77: END;
78:
79:
80: END. { ListU }
```

Extended New( ) and Dispose( )

As you recall from Chapter 7, the standard procedure **New** allocates space on the heap for a variable addressed by a pointer. You can use the standard **New** to create object instances on the heap. For example, if **op** is a pointer to a **Cart** object type, you could write:

```
New( op );
```

But you now are faced with finishing the initialization of your object instance, calling the constructor to set up the link to the object's VMT:

```
op^.Init;
```

There's an easier way to perform both of these steps with one statement. **New** now allows you to pass the name of the object's constructor as a second parameter:

```
New( op, Init );
```

This allocates space on the heap for the object instance, calls the constructor, and initializes the VMT (if necessary). You'll almost always create new dynamic objects this way.

You can also use **New** as a function that returns a pointer to an instance of the object data type. (This form of **New** also works with other Pascal data types, too.) If **OpTypePtr** is a pointer type to an object type named **OpType** with a constructor named **Init**, and **op** is of type **OpTypePtr**, this statement allocates heap space for the object instance and assigns the pointer to **op**:

```
op := New( OpTypePtr, Init );
```

The effect is no different from the earlier example, so you'll rarely use **New** this way. **New**'s real value as a function comes when passing the address of newly allocated objects to other methods, leading to statements such as:

```
Variable.Insert( New( OpTypePtr, Init( 'String', 14, 3.14159 ) ) );
```

Get used to this sort of code, which is commonplace in OOP. In this hypothetical example, **New** allocates space for an object instance of type **OpType**, calling the object's constructor **Init** with three parameters and passing the result (an **OpTypePtr** pointer) to **Variable.Insert** (not shown), a method that requires a pointer to an instance of type **OpTypePtr** as a parameter.

The familiar **Dispose** procedure is also extended, taking a pointer to an object instance as its first parameter and the name of a destructor as the second:

```
Dispose( op, Done );
```

Using **Dispose** this way calls the **Done** destructor (presumably defined in **OpType**) and disposes the memory occupied by the object instance addressed by **op**. Unlike **New, Dispose** can't be used as a function.

Dispose truly comes into its own when polymorphic objects are involved. Most often, descendant objects redefine what a virtual destructor **Done** accomplishes. Depending on what type of object a pointer addresses, **Dispose** must be able to call the appropriate destructor—a fact that can't be known until runtime.

Program 15-5 demonstrates this use of **Dispose** at line 75 inside the **List** object's **DisposeList** method. This code releases the memory occupied by listed items—which might contain any kind of data. Because the code is written before the list items are defined, it's impossible for **DisposeList** to know ahead of time what kind of data will be stored in the list.

> Note: I hope that last sentence makes a little light go on in your head. Think about this. How is it possible to program a method that disposes a list of items when we haven't even decided what or even how big those items will be? But that's exactly what OOP is all about—the ability to write code for the unforeseen future. **DisposeList** is a *finished* method. It is not a shell. It will not require modification to handle new kinds of data later. This is polymorphism at work—providing future programs with the ability to create objects of new forms, which existing code such as **DisposeList** will be able to handle with ease.

Now, let's throw some data into a list and see what happens. Program 15-6 uses **ListU** and creates three new object types at lines 7–27. **IntObj** stores integers. **RealObj** stores real numbers. **StrObj** stores strings. Each of these objects is a direct descendant of **Item** (see Program 15-5, lines 8–13). Consequently, each of the new object types inherits a **next** field of type **ItemPtr** plus three methods.

IntObj and **RealObj** update two of those methods, **Init** and **Print**. Because these object types require no special handling for disposal, they simply inherit **Item**'s destructor. The new object types add a single field each—an integer (line 9) and a real number (line 16). Thanks to polymorphism, a pointer to **Item** can address **IntObj** and **RealObj** object instances.

Line 23 in **StrObj** defines a pointer to a **String**. The new object could define a string variable directly, but the pointer allows variable-length strings to occupy only as much heap space as needed. Because this requires custom code to allocate space for strings on the heap, **StrObj** replaces the **Done** destructor with a new version that cleans up this additional memory.

Compile and run Program 15-6. (You must first compile Program 15-5 and name the result LISTU.TPU.)

Program 15-6

```
1:  PROGRAM ListDemo;
2:
3:  USES ListU;
4:
5:  TYPE
6:
7:     IntObjPtr = ^IntObj;
8:     IntObj = OBJECT( Item )
9:        i : Integer;
10:        CONSTRUCTOR Init( ii : Integer );
11:        PROCEDURE Print; VIRTUAL;
12:     END; { IntObj }
13:
14:     RealObjPtr = ^RealObj;
15:     RealObj = OBJECT( Item )
16:        r : Real;
17:        CONSTRUCTOR Init( rr : Real );
18:        PROCEDURE Print; VIRTUAL;
19:     END; { RealObj }
20:
21:     StrObjPtr = ^StrObj;
22:     StrObj = OBJECT( Item )
23:        s : ^String;
24:        CONSTRUCTOR Init( ss : String );
25:        DESTRUCTOR Done; VIRTUAL;
26:        PROCEDURE Print; VIRTUAL;
27:     END; { StrObj }
28:
29:
30:  VAR
31:
32:     itemList : List;
33:
34:
35:  { IntObj }
36:
37:  CONSTRUCTOR IntObj.Init( ii : Integer );
38:  BEGIN
39:     Item.Init;
```

Program 15-6 *cont.*

```
40:     i := ii;
41: END;
42:
43: PROCEDURE IntObj.Print;
44: BEGIN
45:     Item.Print;
46:     Write( 'Integer = ', i );
47: END;
48:
49:
50: { RealObj }
51:
52: CONSTRUCTOR RealObj.Init( rr : Real );
53: BEGIN
54:     Item.Init;
55:     r := rr;
56: END;
57:
58: PROCEDURE RealObj.Print;
59: BEGIN
60:     Item.Print;
61:     Write( 'Real = ', r );
62: END;
63:
64:
65: { StrObj }
66:
67: CONSTRUCTOR StrObj.Init( ss : String );
68: BEGIN
69:     Item.Init;
70:     GetMem( s, Length( ss ) + 1 );
71:     s^ := ss
72: END;
73:
74: DESTRUCTOR StrObj.Done;
75: BEGIN
76:     FreeMem( s, Length( s^ ) + 1 );
77:     Item.Done
78: END;
79:
80: PROCEDURE StrObj.Print;
81: BEGIN
82:     Item.Print;
83:     Write( 'String = ', s^ );
84: END;
```

Program 15-6 *cont.*

```
 85:
 86:
 87:   BEGIN
 88:     itemList.Init;
 89:     Writeln( 'Memory before insertions = ', MemAvail );
 90:     itemList.InsertItem( New( RealObjPtr, Init( 123.456 ) ) );
 91:     itemList.InsertItem( New( IntObjPtr, Init( 451 ) ) );
 92:     itemList.InsertItem( New( StrObjPtr, Init( 'Fahrenheit' ) ) );
 93:     Writeln( 'Memory after insertions  = ', MemAvail );
 94:     itemList.PrintList;
 95:     itemList.DisposeList;
 96:     Writeln;
 97:     Writeln;
 98:     Writeln( 'Memory after disposal    = ', MemAvail );
 99:     Writeln
100:   END.
```

How the ListDemo Works

The best way to understand how the previous two programs work, and how polymorphism allows the appropriate methods to recognize objects of different forms, is to run the code under control of Turbo Debugger. If you're using the integrated version, just press F7 to step through the program one statement at a time. If you're using the stand-alone debugger, execute the DOS commands:

```
tpc /b /v listdemo
td listdemo
```

This assumes you've named the text file LISTDEMO.PAS. The /b switch rebuilds the program (compiling LISTU.PAS to LISTU.TPU). The /v switch adds debugging information to the result.

Figure 15-6 illustrates the structure that Programs 15-5 and 15-6 create in memory. A list head named **itemList** begins the list, with a field **root** addressing the first listed object. Each of the three objects on the list—of types **RealObj**, **IntObj**, and **StrObj**—inherits **Item**'s properties, including a **next** pointer to the next listed item. Each object defines its own data field, **r**, **i**, and **s**. Notice that **s** is a pointer to a string for which space is allocated separately. The other two objects store their data directly.

After compiling Program 15-6 (and loading into Turbo Debugger if you're using the stand-alone model), press F7 to single step through the code. As the program progresses, **InsertItem** adds new object instances to the list, adjusting the **root** and **next** pointers. Parameter **n** (see line 51 in Program 15-5) addresses an **ItemPtr**. Remember, because of polymorphism, **n** might actually address any **Item** descendant.

After creating the list, you'll enter **PrintList** (lines 57–66 in Program 15-5).

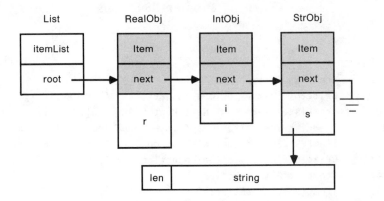

Figure 15-6 A list of polymorphic objects that take on new forms
at runtime.

There, a **WHILE** loop cycles, starting by setting a local **ItemPtr** variable **ip** to **root** and progressing from **next** pointer to **next** pointer. Line 63 activates the **Print** method. (OOP purists would say such statements "pass a **Print** message to the object instance at **ip.**") Exactly which **Print** method runs depends on the object type addressed by **ip**. As you'll see when you step through this code, the program magically runs the **IntObj, RealObj**, and **StrObj** print methods to display the correct data for each listed object. In effect, *the objects themselves do the printing*.

Similarly, **DisposeList** at lines 68–77 in Program 15-5 removes individual objects from the heap, calling the extended **Dispose** at line 75 and passing the virtual destructor named **Done. RealObj** and **IntObj** objects inherit **Item**'s stock **Done**, which doesn't execute any statements. **StrObj** objects call the replacement **Done** in program 15-6 lines 74–78, where **FreeMem** disposes the separately stored string space (see Figure 15-6) before passing control to **Item.Done**, completing the disposal.

As you can see from these experiments, Programs 15-5 and 15-6 make good use of polymorphism, allowing lower-level programming in **PrintList** and **DisposeList** to acquire new abilities—merely by defining new objects, not by revising the code. Master this concept, and you'll move to the front of the OOP pack in no time.

The Self Pseudo-Variable

You might wonder how object methods are able to refer to data fields inside object instances. For example, line 61 in Program 15-6 displays the value of real number **r**, a field in the **RealObj** object type. But the actual object instance is stored in heap memory, and the exact location of this variable may change each time the program runs. How does the **Write** statement know where **r** is?

Object methods know the location of the associated object instances through a normally invisible pointer named **Self**—a pseudo-variable that you can't change.

Self acts as a **VAR** parameter of the object type. Knowing this, you can rewrite line 61 this way:

```
Write( 'Real = ', Self.r );
```

Most of the time you won't need to do this. But, if there was another variable named **r** within the scope of that statement, you could use **Self** to specify which **r** to use—the variable or the field in the object instance.

Self is passed as a 32-bit pointer on the stack to every object method, whether or not the method declares other parameters. A neat trick is to add **Self** to Turbo Debugger's Watch window (press Ctrl-F7 and type "SELF"), letting you inspect the address and data to which **Self** points. The stand-alone debugger shows the object data type that **Self** addresses as the code executes various methods. The built-in debugger shows only the object instance's address.

Dealing With Memory Errors

Lines 67–72 in Program 15-6 neglect the always present possibility that enough memory won't be available to hold a new string. Simple programs such as this one can get away with ignoring this error—a memory shortage will halt the program when **GetMem** at line 70 executes.

Such Stone-Age error handling won't do for a finished product, though. As explained in Chapter 16, you can install a custom **HeapFunc** function to trap out-of-memory conditions. Instead of halting the program, **GetMem** and **New** return **Nil** pointers if the amount of memory you request isn't available. Other statements can then take whatever action is necessary.

When using a custom **HeapFunc** function in conjunction with OOP constructors, a subtle problem sneaks in through the back door. Because programs usually call constructors via the extended form of **New** as lines 90–93 in Program 15-6 demonstrate, Turbo Pascal must reserve heap memory for the object instance that's being constructed *before* the constructor code runs. Inside the object constructor, if a call to **GetMem** or **New** fails, the program has to be careful to dispose the space that's been allocated to the object instance.

To make this happen, use the standard procedure **Fail**, which has no parameters. **Fail** immediately exits the constructor, disposing all memory allocated to the object instance. You can't use **Fail** anywhere else—only inside a constructor's implementation.

Program 15-7 demonstrates the correct way to use **Fail**. The program uses LISTU.TPU (Program 15-5) and is similar to Program 15-6. To save space, only **StrObj** is defined at lines 8–13.

The custom **HeapFunc** function appears at lines 22–28. The function must be compiled with the {$F+} switch in effect, allowing the function to be called from other code segments. Also, **HeapFunc** may not be nested inside any other procedure or function. Returning a function result of 1 causes **New** and **GetMem** to return **Nil** pointers instead of halting the program when out of memory. Line 60 installs the new heap error function by assigning **HeapFunc**'s address to the special **System** variable **HeapError**.

Closely examine **StrObj**'s **Init** constructor and **Done** destructor at lines 33–50, comparing these with the previous versions in Program 15-6, lines 67–78. The new code tests whether **GetMem** sets pointer **s** to **Nil** (Program 15-7, line 37). If so, the program is out of memory, and the **IF** statement calls **Fail** at line 40 to deallocate the object instance that the constructor is constructing.

Notice that line 39 calls the **Done** destructor for the object that's under construction. This ensures that all deallocation steps are performed in case of errors during an object's construction, and it's usually wise to call the object's destructor this way before executing **Fail**. As a consequence, lines 47–48 must test whether **s** is **Nil** before calling **FreeMem**. Careful memory management requires that **Done** (and other destructors) be prepared to clean up partially constructed object instances.

Because of these changes, the main program must now initialize and insert new object instances differently than before (see lines 63–68). First, **New** attempts to create and initialize a new object, assigning the object instance's address to pointer **sp**. If this fails, because of the custom **HeapFunc**, **sp** will be **Nil**; otherwise, **itemList.Insert** inserts the new object onto the list.

Program 15-7

```
 1:  PROGRAM ListFailDemo;
 2:
 3:  USES ListU;
 4:
 5:  TYPE
 6:
 7:     StrObjPtr = ^StrObj;
 8:     StrObj = OBJECT( Item )
 9:        s : ^String;
10:        CONSTRUCTOR Init( ss : String );
11:        DESTRUCTOR Done; VIRTUAL;
12:        PROCEDURE Print; VIRTUAL;
13:     END; { StrObj }
14:
15:
16:  VAR
17:
18:     itemList : List;
19:     sp : StrObjPtr;
20:
21:
22:  {F+}      { Switch on "far" code generation }
23:  FUNCTION HeapFunc( size : Word ) : Integer;
24:  { Allow New and GetMem to return Nil when out of memory }
25:  BEGIN
26:     HeapFunc := 1;
```

Program 15-7 *cont.*

```
27:  END; { HeapFunc }
28:  {$F-}     { Switch off "far" code generation }
29:
30:
31:  { StrObj }
32:
33:  CONSTRUCTOR StrObj.Init( ss : String );
34:  BEGIN
35:     Item.Init;
36:     GetMem( s, Length( ss ) + 1 );
37:     IF s = Nil THEN
38:     BEGIN          { Out of memory! }
39:        Done;          { Deallocate string object s pointer }
40:        Fail           { Exit and dispose object instance }
41:     END ELSE
42:        s^ := ss;   { Assign string to heap space }
43:  END;
44:
45:  DESTRUCTOR StrObj.Done;
46:  BEGIN
47:     IF s <> Nil
48:        THEN FreeMem( s, Length( s^ ) + 1 );
49:     Item.Done
50:  END;
51:
52:  PROCEDURE StrObj.Print;
53:  BEGIN
54:     Item.Print;
55:     Write( 'String = ', s^ );
56:  END;
57:
58:
59:  BEGIN
60:     HeapError := @HeapFunc;     { Install custom heap function }
61:     itemList.Init;
62:     Writeln( 'Memory before insertions = ', MemAvail );
63:     New( sp, Init( 'This is the first string' ) );
64:     IF sp <> Nil THEN itemList.InsertItem( sp );
65:     New( sp, Init( 'This is the second string' ) );
66:     IF sp <> Nil THEN itemList.InsertItem( sp );
67:     New( sp, Init( 'This is the last string' ) );
68:     IF sp <> Nil THEN itemList.InsertItem( sp );
69:     Writeln( 'Memory after insertions  = ', MemAvail );
70:     itemList.PrintList;
71:     itemList.DisposeList;
```

Program 15-7 *cont.*

```
72:     Writeln;
73:     Writeln;
74:     Writeln( 'Memory after disposal    = ', MemAvail );
75:     Writeln
76:  END.
```

Boolean-Function Constructors

It is unfortunate that, while fixing one problem, Program 15-7 has introduced another that may not be obvious. To understand the danger, consider what happens if you create a static object of type **StrObj**. (The phrase *static object* refers to an object instance declared in a Pascal **VAR** section. A *dynamic object* is one that is addressed by a pointer.)

For an experiment, add a new variable at line 20 in Program 15-7:

```
stringObject : StrObj;
```

Variable **stringObject** is a static object—an object instance declared as a plain Pascal variable. Next, delete lines 61–75, replacing the main program body with:

```
stringObject.Init( 'This is a test string' );
stringObject.Print;
stringObject.Done;
```

When you compile and run the modified program, the first statement initializes the static **stringObject** instance, assigning to it the string "This is a test string." The **Print** method then displays the string, and **Done** cleans up the object before the program ends, disposing the memory space occupied by the string characters.

Figure 15-7 illustrates how the static object appears in memory. Field **s** addresses a dynamic string variable on the heap. When the **Done** method executes, this memory is disposed by **FreeMem** at line 48. Because the object is a static variable in the data segment, it is *not* disposed. Like all global variables, **stringObject** remains in the data segment at all times. And, as for other common variables, **New** and **Dispose** can't manage static objects. **New** and **Dispose** operate only with pointers to dynamic variables.

And that's the problem. After creating a static object, if the program attempts to link that object onto a **List** object, the static variable will become part of that list. This is easy to do with OOP! A list of polymorphic instances can contain dynamic objects in heap memory, global static objects in the program's data segment, and local variables on the stack. Figure 15-8 illustrates how such a setup might appear, threading together many objects stored in various memory segments. Obviously, managing this structure takes careful programming.

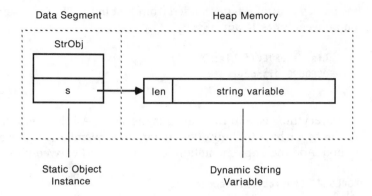

Figure 15-7 A static object in the data segment addressing a dynamic
string variable on the heap.

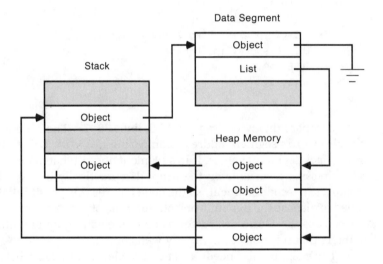

Figure 15-8 Polymorphic objects in various memory locations, all linked
to a common list.

Consider what happens when the list is disposed by the **List** object's **Dispose-List** method (Program 15-5, lines 68–77). Line 75 calls **Dispose**, activating the object instance's **Done** destructor. But **Dispose** can operate only on pointers to dynamic variables on the heap. At line 75, **ItemPtr ip** might address a static object in the data segment, causing **Dispose** to fail when it attempts to release this memory.

Obviously, **DisposeList** must be revised to deal with objects that weren't created by **New**. Or does it? Remember that new objects inherit everything from their ancestors. A better plan is to create a new list object type and *replace the DisposeList method with fresh code that handles static object instances.* To make this change, copy Program 15-7 to a new file named STATIC.PAS. Define a new object type named **StaticList**, descended from **List** in LISTU.TPU. Add this new definition between lines 14 and 15:

```
StaticList = OBJECT( List )
    PROCEDURE DisposeList;
END;
```

Everything else in **List** remains the same. All the methods work as before. We don't even have to think about them. All we want is to replace the **DisposeList** method. Add the implementation for that method between lines 57 and 58:

```
PROCEDURE StaticList.DisposeList;
VAR   ip : ItemPtr;
BEGIN
   WHILE root <> Nil DO
   BEGIN
     ip := root;
     root := ip^.next;
     IF ( Seg( ip^ ) <> DSeg ) AND ( Seg( ip^ ) <> SSeg )
        THEN Dispose( ip, Done )
        ELSE ip^.Done
   END { while }
END;
```

Compare this with Program 15-5, lines 68–77. The code is nearly the same, but checks **ip**'s segment address, comparing this with **DSeg** (data segment) and **SSeg** (stack segment) values. If **ip**'s segment doesn't match either of these, it must be addressing a variable on the heap. (It's practically impossible to store object instances in a code segment, so the code ignores this possibility.) **Dispose** is then called to dispose the dynamic object. But if the object is not on the heap, the **ELSE** clause runs the **Done** destructor as before, cleaning up any other variables and pointers that this object might very well contain.

The program also needs a static variable. Add this line between lines 19 and 20:

```
myString : StrObj;    { A "static" object instance }
```

Also change **itemList**'s type at line 18 to:

```
itemList : StaticList;
```

Finally, add a statement between lines 68 and 69 to initialize the static **my-String** object and insert it onto the list:

```
IF myString.Init( 'Initializing a static object instance!' )
   THEN itemList.InsertItem( @myString );
```

Notice that the constructor **Init** is used here as a **Boolean** function, a special allowance that Turbo Pascal makes specifically to handle the situation where static objects contain pointers to dynamic variables (which could be other objects, of course). If the constructor returns via **Fail**, then **Init** returns **False**; otherwise, it returns **True**. Notice that **itemList**'s method **InsertItem** is used as before, but this time, because **myString** is a static object, the @ operator is used to pass the address of **myString** to the method, which expects to receive a pointer to an **Item** or to any of its descendants.

When you run the modified program, you'll see that the static object's string displays along with the others, proving that the new list now includes objects in the heap and in the global data segment.

There's an even more important observation to make. You've made a major change to the LISTU.TPU unit, replacing the **DisposeList** method with a new implementation. And you did this without modifying the original unit. If LISTU.TPU were a commercial toolkit for which the source code was not available, you still could have made this change. Everything else in the program operates as it did before—but the original **List** object is extended to handle static as well as dynamic object instances. This is one of the great benefits of OOP—the ability to add new methods and information to existing code without revising statements that already work.

Streams

The usual Pascal methods for reading and writing disk files don't work so well with polymorphic objects, which can assume different forms and sizes at runtime. A file of an object base type might contain "records" of that object type and any of its descendants. To handle this, Borland includes with Turbo Pascal the file OBJECTS.PAS, which contains a set of object types to implement *streams*, offering one answer to the problem.

A few example programs demonstrate how you can use streams to read and write files of polymorphic objects. Also, OBJECTS.PAS contains its own methods for creating linked lists—similar to the earlier example programs in this chapter. For reference, you may want to print a copy of the OODEMOS.DOC file (also on your Turbo Pascal master disks) and OBJECTS.PAS.

> The programs in this section require the four files OBJECTS.PAS, STREAM.OBJ, DOSSTM.OBJ, and BUFSTM.OBJ from your Turbo Pascal master disks. Make sure these files are in the current directory and then compile OBJECTS.PAS to disk, creating OBJECTS.TPU.

An OOP Database

If you've ever used a commercial database system, you probably know one of the major problems with software that stores fixed-size records in files. Such an arrangement ignores the fact that information in the real world rarely fits so neatly into a one-size-takes-all cubbyhole. For example, in a name-and-address database, you'd want to store different information about your personal entries than you would for your business contacts. Few database systems allow this level of flexibility.

In OOP, it's easy. To demonstrate, the next three programs implement a polymorphic database—admittedly lacking many features that a fully fledged program would need, but capable enough to demonstrate the highlights of using streams to read and write polymorphic objects in disk files.

The first step is to create an object that defines the fixed information—fields that all database entries share. Because other programs need this information, Program 15-8 is in the form of a unit. Save the program as ADDRU.PAS and compile to disk, creating ADDRU.TPU.

Program 15-8

```
 1:   UNIT AddrU;
 2:
 3:   INTERFACE
 4:
 5:   USES Objects;
 6:
 7:   TYPE
 8:
 9:       NameStr = String[ 30 ];
10:       AddressStr = String[ 30 ];
11:       CityStZipStr = String[ 30 ];
12:       PhoneStr = String[ 12 ];
13:
14:       AddrObjPtr = ^AddrObj;
15:       AddrObj = OBJECT( Node )
16:          name : NameStr;
17:          address : AddressStr;
18:          cityStZip : CityStZipStr;
19:          phone : PhoneStr;
20:          CONSTRUCTOR Init( na : NameStr; ad : AddressStr;
21:             csz : CityStZipStr; ph : PhoneStr );
22:          CONSTRUCTOR Load( VAR s : Stream );
23:          PROCEDURE Store( VAR s : Stream );
24:          PROCEDURE Display; VIRTUAL;
25:       END; { AddrObj }
26:
27:       AddressList = OBJECT( List )
28:          PROCEDURE DisplayList;
29:       END; { AddressList }
30:
```

Program 15-8 *cont.*

```
31:
32:    IMPLEMENTATION
33:
34:
35:    { AddrObj }
36:
37:    CONSTRUCTOR AddrObj.Init( na : NameStr; ad : AddressStr;
38:            csz : CityStZipStr; ph : PhoneStr );
39:    BEGIN
40:      name := na;
41:      address := ad;
42:      cityStZip := csz;
43:      phone := ph;
44:    END;
45:
46:    CONSTRUCTOR AddrObj.Load( VAR s : Stream );
47:    BEGIN
48:      s.Read( name, SizeOf( NameStr ) );
49:      s.Read( address, SizeOf( AddressStr ) );
50:      s.Read( cityStZip, SizeOf( CityStZipStr ) );
51:      s.Read( phone, SizeOf( PhoneStr ) );
52:      IF s.Status <> 0 THEN Fail
53:    END;
54:
55:    PROCEDURE AddrObj.Store( VAR s : Stream );
56:    BEGIN
57:      s.Write( name, SizeOf( NameStr ) );
58:      s.Write( address, SizeOf( AddressStr ) );
59:      s.Write( cityStZip, SizeOf( CityStZipStr ) );
60:      s.Write( phone, SizeOf( PhoneStr ) );
61:    END;
62:
63:    PROCEDURE AddrObj.Display;
64:    BEGIN
65:      Writeln;
66:      Writeln( ';;;;;;;;;;;;;' );
67:      Writeln( name );
68:      Writeln( address );
69:      Writeln( cityStZip );
70:      Writeln( phone );
71:    END;
72:
73:
74:    { AddressList }
75:
```

Program 15-8 *cont.*

```
76:  PROCEDURE AddressList.DisplayList;
77:  VAR
78:     temp : AddrObjPtr;
79:  BEGIN
80:     temp := AddrObjPtr( First );
81:     WHILE ( temp <> Nil ) DO
82:     BEGIN
83:       temp^.Display;
84:       temp := AddrObjPtr( Next( temp ) )
85:     END { while }
86:  END;
87:
88:  END. { AddrU }
```

Lines 9–12 in ADDRU.PAS define four string types. If you want, you can change the lengths of these strings.

Lines 14–25 define the **AddrObj** object type and a pointer to that type, **AddrObjPtr**. In this object are four data fields of the string types defined earlier. Every database object has **name, address, cityStZip**, and **phone** fields.

There are four methods in **AddrObj**. The first two of these are constructors, **Init** and **Load**. There are two ways that programs will create **AddrObj** instances; therefore, the object definition needs two constructors—one to create new object instances in memory, and one to load objects saved in disk files.

Constructor **Init**'s parameters are assigned directly to the four data fields, thus initializing the record with four new strings (see lines 37–44).

Constructor **Load**'s parameter is a single variable of type **Stream**. All objects that use streams must have a similar constructor named **Load**. Examine lines 46–53. The four statements read the object's four fields—presumably from the disk file currently managed by the stream identified by **Load**'s parameter. The **Steam.Read** method has the form:

```
Stream.Read( VAR buf; size : Word ); VIRTUAL;
```

The first parameter is the identifier of the variable stored on disk, usually a field in the object type. The second parameter represents the size of this data in bytes. The method is virtual and can be replaced, although you probably won't need to do that.

Line 52 examines **Stream**'s **Status** value—an **Integer** field in the **Stream** object. This breaks the rules of OOP that discourage direct access to object data fields. But, in this case, simply examining **Status** is harmless. It would be wasteful to call a function just to return this same value. If **Status** is not 0, a disk error has occurred; otherwise, the **Read**s were successful.

Lines 55–61 perform the reverse operation, writing the object's four data fields to disk with **Stream**'s **Write** method, which has the identical parameters as

Read. Store is a static method in **AddrObj** (see line 23). All objects that use streams must define a **Load** constructor and a **Store** method this way.

The final method in **AddrObj** is **Display** (see line 24). This method simply displays the contents of the object for test purposes and is not required for using streams.

In addition to this fundamental object, we also need a way to store names and addresses in memory. To do this and to demonstrate OBJECTS.PAS's list objects, lines 27–29 define a new object **AddressList** descended from **List**. All the internal details for creating linked lists are completely handled by this object—all we need here is a new method to display a list's contents. This is easily done by adding a new **DisplayList** method.

DisplayList's implementation (lines 76–86) resembles the **PrintList** method in Program 15-5, lines 57–66. A temporary pointer runs through the polymorphic objects on the list, activating the **Display** method for each (line 83). Different here are the **First** and **Next** methods in lines 80 and 84. **First** returns a pointer to the first item in the linked list. **Next** advances a pointer to the next item, returning **Nil** when reaching the end of the list. (Actually, OBJECTS.PAS lists are circular and, therefore, have no beginning or end. Even so, the **List** object is designed to allow code such as the **WHILE** loop here to function correctly.)

Methods **First** and **Next** are defined in the **List** object type in file OBJECTS.PAS. These methods each return a pointer of type **NodePtr**, which addresses another object named **Node** defined as:

```
NodePtr = ^Node;
Node = OBJECT( Base )
   next : NodePtr;
   FUNCTION Prev : NodePtr;
END;
```

If variable **temp** (line 78) were of type **NodePtr**, there would be no way to activate the **Display** method—which is not defined in **Node** but, rather, in **Node**'s descendant, **AddrObj**. For this reason, the results of **First** and **Next** must be recast to pointers of type **AddrObjPtr** to allow the statement in line 83 to call **Display**.

Using type casting this way is controversial. Some say type casts should not be necessary in OOP; others insist they are. In general, a type cast appears to be needed when, as in this example, a descendant adds a new method to an object type, while *another* descendant (for example, **List**) contains methods that declare parameters and function results addressing the original ancestor. To make such references recognize a descendant's new features, a type cast to the descendant type is needed.

Another important fact to know about **Node** objects is that they are descended from an abstract object type called **Base**, which is never instantiated (declared as variables). The design for **Base** seems almost too simple to be of any use:

```
BasePtr = ^Base;
Base = OBJECT
```

```
    DESTRUCTOR Done; VIRTUAL;
END;
```

Every object descended from **Base** inherits a virtual **Done** destructor. Because of this, descendant objects are guaranteed to have a pointer to the object type's VMT—a requirement of streams.

So what does all this have to do with linked lists and streams? Interestingly, the **Stream** object is also descended from **Base**:

```
Stream = OBJECT( Base )
   { ... contents of Stream (see OBJECTS.PAS) }
END;
```

Consequently, our **AddrObj** in Program 15-8 and the **Stream** object type are cousins! (Or, maybe they're siblings. Anyway, they're descended from the same ancestral stock.)

Before proceeding, make sure you understand Program 15-8. You don't have to study everything in OBJECTS.PAS. In fact, that's one of the advantages of OOP—the ability to use existing tools without having to become an expert in every low-level detail.

The next step in creating an OOP database is to define a few more objects that add items unique to the information to be stored on disk. Program 15-9 is another unit with two such object types, **Personal** and **Business**. Save the text as PERSONU.PAS and compile to the disk file, PERSONU.TPU.

Program 15-9

```
 1:  UNIT PersonU;
 2:
 3:  INTERFACE
 4:
 5:  USES Objects, AddrU;
 6:
 7:  TYPE
 8:
 9:     PersonalPtr = ^Personal;
10:     Personal = OBJECT( AddrObj )
11:        age : Integer;
12:        homePhone : PhoneStr;
13:        CONSTRUCTOR Init( na : NameStr; ad : AddressStr;
14:           csz : CityStZipStr; ph : PhoneStr;
15:           ag : Integer; hp : PhoneStr );
16:        CONSTRUCTOR Load( VAR s : Stream );
17:        PROCEDURE Store( VAR s : Stream );
18:        PROCEDURE Display; VIRTUAL;
19:     END; { Personal }
```

Program 15-9 *cont.*

```
20:
21:      BusinessPtr = ^Business;
22:      Business = OBJECT( AddrObj )
23:         balance : Real;
24:         contact : NameStr;
25:         CONSTRUCTOR Init( na : NameStr; ad : AddressStr;
26:            csz : CityStZipStr; ph : PhoneStr;
27:            ba : Real; co : NameStr );
28:         CONSTRUCTOR Load( VAR s : Stream );
29:         PROCEDURE Store( VAR s : Stream );
30:         PROCEDURE Display; VIRTUAL;
31:      END; { Business }
32:
33:      AddressFile = OBJECT( BufStream )
34:         PROCEDURE RegisterTypes; VIRTUAL;
35:      END; { AddressFile }
36:
37:
38:   IMPLEMENTATION
39:
40:
41:   { Personal }
42:
43:   CONSTRUCTOR Personal.Init( na : NameStr; ad : AddressStr;
44:      csz : CityStZipStr; ph : PhoneStr;
45:      ag : Integer; hp : PhoneStr );
46:   BEGIN
47:      AddrObj.Init( na, ad, csz, ph );
48:      age := ag;
49:      homePhone := hp;
50:   END;
51:
52:   CONSTRUCTOR Personal.Load( VAR s : Stream );
53:   BEGIN
54:      AddrObj.Load( s );
55:      s.Read( age, SizeOf( Integer ) );
56:      s.Read( homePhone, SizeOf( PhoneStr ) );
57:      IF s.Status <> 0 THEN Fail
58:   END;
59:
60:   PROCEDURE Personal.Store( VAR s : Stream );
61:   BEGIN
62:      AddrObj.Store( s );
63:      s.Write( age, SizeOf( Integer ) );
64:      s.Write( homePhone, SizeOf( PhoneStr ) );
```

Program 15-9 *cont.*

```
65:   END;
66:
67:   PROCEDURE Personal.Display;
68:   BEGIN
69:      AddrObj.Display;
70:      Writeln( 'Age = ', age );
71:      Writeln( 'Home phone = ', homePhone );
72:   END;
73:
74:
75:   { Business }
76:
77:   CONSTRUCTOR Business.Init( na : NameStr; ad : AddressStr;
78:      csz : CityStZipStr; ph : PhoneStr;
79:      ba : Real; co : NameStr );
80:   BEGIN
81:      AddrObj.Init( na, ad, csz, ph );
82:      balance := ba;
83:      contact := co;
84:   END;
85:
86:   CONSTRUCTOR Business.Load( VAR s : Stream );
87:   BEGIN
88:      AddrObj.Load( s );
89:      s.Read( balance, SizeOf( Real ) );
90:      s.Read( contact, SizeOf( NameStr ) );
91:      IF s.Status <> 0 THEN Fail
92:   END;
93:
94:   PROCEDURE Business.Store( VAR s : Stream );
95:   BEGIN
96:      AddrObj.Store( s );
97:      s.Write( balance, SizeOf( Real ) );
98:      s.Write( contact, SizeOf( NameStr ) );
99:   END;
100:
101:   PROCEDURE Business.Display;
102:   BEGIN
103:      AddrObj.Display;
104:      Writeln( 'Balance = $', balance:0:2 );
105:      Writeln( 'Contact = ', contact );
106:   END;
107:
108:
109:   { AddressFile }
```

Program 15-9 *cont.*

```
110:
111:   PROCEDURE AddressFile.RegisterTypes;
112:   BEGIN
113:     BufStream.RegisterTypes;
114:     Register( TypeOf( AddrObj  ), @AddrObj.Store,  @AddrObj.Load  );
115:     Register( TypeOf( Personal ), @Personal.Store, @Personal.Load );
116:     Register( TypeOf( Business ), @Business.Store, @Business.Load );
117:   END;
118:
119:
120:   END. { PersonU }
```

Although PERSONU.PAS is longer than ADDRU.PAS, if you examine the code closely, you'll see that the two programs are very much alike. The **Personal** and **Business** object types (lines 10–19 and 22–31) are descended from **AddrObj**. Consequently, every instance of these new types has **name, address**, and other data fields defined in **AddrObj**. All the new objects need to do is define unique fields: **age** and **homePhone** in **Personal**; and **balance** and **contact** in **Business**.

In addition, the **Init** constructors add new parameters to initialize the inherited fields and the new additions. This is a typical OOP design. Pay special attention to the constructor implementations at lines 43–50 and 77–84. In each case, the ancestor **AddrObj.Init** constructor initializes the inherited fields. The new **Init** parameters are assigned to the object's unique fields. In this way, the extended constructors completely initialize instances of the new object types.

The other constructor and two methods—**Load, Store**, and **Display** —are similar to those described before. The method implementations use **AddrObj.Load** and **AddrObj.Store** to read and write the **AddrObj** inherited fields. They also add new statements to read and write fields unique to the new object types. The new **Display** methods do the same—first calling **AddrObj.Display** to display the inherited fields and then adding new statements to display the unique data.

In addition to the new **AddrObj** descendants, another object **AddressFile** is defined at lines 33–35. This object is descended from **BufStream**—itself a descendant of **Stream** in OBJECTS.PAS. A **BufStream** object adds memory buffering to the fundamental disk file routines in OBJECTS.PAS. Storing data in buffers speeds disk I/O by transferring data in larger chunks to and from disk. You can use the other file object types in OBJECTS.PAS if you want, but in most cases, **BufStream** is faster and easier.

AddressFile defines only one replacement method, **RegisterTypes**, which prepares a stream to read and write various objects. Those objects *must* be descended from **Base**. The implementation for **AddressFile** (lines 111–117) shows how to prepare a stream. First, the ancestor **RegisterTypes** method is called (line 113). Then, each type to be stored in disk files is passed to method **Register**, which has the form:

```
Stream.Register( typePtr, storePtr, loadPtr : Pointer );
```

Stream defines the **Register** method, which **BufStream** and **AddressFile** inherit. The first parameter addresses the VMT of the object type to be stored in disk files. The other two parameters address the **Load** and **Store** methods in the object type definitions.

Making the first parameter, **typePtr**, address the object's VMT poses a special problem. At this point, the program hasn't yet declared any instances of the object type to store in disk files; therefore, Turbo Pascal defines a new function **TypeOf** specifically to return the VMT address of an object type. As lines 115–116 show, use statements such as **TypeOf(Personal)** and **TypeOf(Business)** to register the VMT addresses.

The **storePtr** and **loadPtr** parameters address the **Load** and **Store** implementations for this object type's methods of those names. Use the @ sign as shown at lines 115–116 to pass the method addresses to **Register**.

Registering the object types gives the stream the necessary information it needs to read and write objects of those types. Object instances can be mixed in any order in disk files. The stream stores information in the file to distinguish one object instance from another.

The final step is to write the database program. Program 15-10 lists one example, using the units in the previous two listings. Save the text as ADDRESS.PAS, compile, and run. Press enter and read the on screen messages to create a sample database, clear memory, and read the data back from disk.

Program 15-10

```
 1:   PROGRAM Address;
 2:
 3:   USES Objects, AddrU, PersonU;
 4:
 5:   VAR
 6:
 7:      namesList : AddressList;      { List of objects }
 8:      namesFile : AddressFile;      { File of objects }
 9:
10:
11:   { non-OOP procedure }
12:
13:   PROCEDURE Message( s : String );
14:   BEGIN
15:      Writeln;
16:      Write( '---- (', MemAvail, ') Press <Enter> to ', s );
17:      Readln;
18:   END; { Message }
19:
20:
21:   BEGIN
22:
```

Program 15-10 *cont.*

```
23:    message( 'create list in memory' );
24:
25:    namesList.Clear;      { Initialize empty list }
26:
27:    namesList.Append
28:    ( New
29:       ( PersonalPtr, Init    { create new personal object }
30:          (
31:                'A. Friend',            { name }
32:                '47 Western Way',       { address }
33:                'Our Town, PA 19876',   { city state zip }
34:                '212-555-1212',         { daytime phone }
35:                35,                     { age in years }
36:                '000-1212'              { home phone }
37:          )
38:       )
39:    );
40:
41:    namesList.Append
42:    ( New
43:       ( BusinessPtr, Init    { create new business object }
44:          (
45:                'Cookies Incorporated', { name }
46:                '100 Park Place',       { address }
47:                'New York, NY 10010',   { city state zip }
48:                '717-555-1212',         { company phone }
49:                3549.79,                { balance }
50:                'Mr. T. F. Cookie'      { contact }
51:          )
52:       )
53:    );
54:
55:    namesList.Append
56:    ( New
57:       ( PersonalPtr, Init    { create new personal object }
58:          (
59:                'E. Z. Pickins',        { name }
60:                '23 Easy Street',       { address }
61:                'Anyplace, TX 77665',   { city state zip }
62:                '800-555-1212',         { daytime phone }
63:                62,                     { age in years }
64:                '(unlisted)'            { home phone }
65:          )
66:       )
67:    );
```

Program 15-10 *cont.*

```
68:
69:     Message( 'display list in memory' );
70:     namesList.DisplayList;
71:
72:     Message( 'write list to disk' );
73:     namesFile.Init( 'NAMES.XXX', SCreate, 1024 );
74:     namesList.Store( namesFile );
75:     namesFile.Done;
76:
77:     Message( 'delete list from memory' );
78:     namesList.Delete;
79:
80:     Message( 'display empty list' );
81:     namesList.DisplayList;
82:
83:     Message( 'read list from disk' );
84:     namesFile.Init( 'NAMES.XXX', SOpen, 1024 );
85:     namesList.Load( namesFile );
86:     namesFile.Done;
87:
88:     Message( 'display list in memory' );
89:     namesList.DisplayList;
90:
91:     Message( 'delete list from memory' );
92:     namesList.Delete;
93:     Message( 'end program' );
94:
95: END.
```

The main body in ADDRESS.PAS starts a new list by activating the **Clear** method in **namesList**, an object instance of type **AddressList**, descended from **List** in OBJECTS.PAS. Always begin new lists this way.

Lines 27–67 create new database entries with the extended form of **New** and the **Init** constructor in the **Personal** and **Business** objects. The indented style should help you to pick through this code. Of course, a full database system would need ways to let people enter new information from the keyboard. The basic idea remains the same, however.

Notice that the parameters to **Init** change depending on the type of object created. (Compare lines 31–36, 45–50, and 59–64.) In each case, the **namesList.Append** method (lines 27, 41, and 55) links the polymorphic object instances onto a list in memory. Line 70 displays the listed objects, just to prove they are there.

The three statements at lines 73–75 demonstrate how to open a file and store a series of object instances on disk. The first statement uses the **BufStream.Init** constructor:

```
BufStream.Init( fileName : FNameStr; mode, size : Word );
```

The first **BufStream.Init** parameter is the file name to create, in this example, NAMES.XXX. (I used XXX as the extension because it's unlikely you'll have another file by that name in your directory. You can use any name you want.) The **mode** parameter should be one of the stream access values (defined in OBJECTS.PAS):

```
SCreate     = $3C00;    { Create new file }
SOpenRead   = $3D00;    { Read-only access }
SOpenWrite  = $3D01;    { Write-only access }
SOpen       = $3D02;    { Read and write access }
```

Use these values to open files with different access parameters. The final **BufStream.Init** parameter represents the buffer size in bytes. 1024 is a good choice, but you can use larger or smaller values if you prefer. For best results, buffers should be able to hold the data from several objects at once, but they do not have to be exact multiples of any specific object instance size.

After using **Init** to create the new file, call **Store** in the **List** object to write the data to disk, passing the **BufStream** object instance as the lone parameter. This method (defined and implemented in OBJECTS.PAS) calls the **Store** method for each object on the linked list, writing all data to disk.

Finally, call the **Done** destructor to close the file (see line 75).

To demonstrate that the operation worked, lines 78 and 81 delete the list from memory and display the empty list, proving the objects are gone. After this, the statements at lines 84–86 read the data from disk, creating a new list in memory. These statements are similar to those used to write the data earlier. In this case, the second **Init** parameter is set to **SOpen** to open the file. And, the **Load** method is used at line 85 to read the data from disk. This uses the **Load** constructors in the **Personal** and **Business** objects to read information from disk and create the new object instances in memory.

Line 89 then displays the list, which now has the data that was deleted earlier, proving that the information was stored and retrieved. Finally, just to show that the heap is properly cleaned of all object instances, line 92 again deletes the list before the program ends.

Note: Because individual objects stored in disk files vary in size, OBJECTS.PAS does not define a random-access method corresponding to a non-OOP **Seek**. Consequently, all disk reads and writes must be sequential—you can't jump to the middle of a disk file and read or write an individual object at that location. One way to eliminate this disadvantage is to create a separate index that points to the beginning of each stored object—an advanced technique that requires careful programming.

Objects and Variable (Typed) Constants

When you need a preinitialized object instance, you can declare a variable constant (also known as a typed constant) of any object type. For example, using **DateObj** from Program 15-1, the following declares a variable constant initialized to July 4, 1976:

```
CONST
   CelebrationDate : DateObj =
      ( month : 7; day : 4; year : 1976 );
```

CelebrationDate is the variable constant's identifier, which you can use just like any other object variable. The colon (:) tells Turbo Pascal that a data type follows (**DateObj** here). After the equal sign comes a series of expressions inside parentheses. Each expression begins with a field name (**month, day, year**) followed by a colon and the initial value. Semicolons separate multiple fields. This is the same format used to declare variable constant records. (See Chapter 13.)

You may assign initial values only to object data fields. You can't refer to an object's methods in the constant declaration—only in program statements. For example, this displays **CelebrationDate**:

```
Writeln( 'Party day = ', CelebrationDate.StringDate );
```

The next program explains a few other details about variable constant objects. Program 15-11 is similar to Program 15-1, but Program 15-11 adds a variable constant at lines 14–16 and uses the **Dos** unit's **GetDate** routine (see line 41) to determine today's date. This information is passed to the **Today** object's **Init** constructor (line 42). Lines 43–44 then display **Today** and the preinitialized variable constant **VersionDate**.

Lines 10–11 declare **Init** as a constructor and **StringDate** as a virtual function. As you recall, objects with virtual methods must have at least one constructor, which the program must call in order to initialize the object's pointer to its VMT. If you forget this step, the object won't be able to find its methods, and the program is almost certain to crash.

That rule is a little different for preinitialized variable constant objects. As line 42 shows, **Init** must be called for **Today**, a simple object variable. But the constructor does not have to be called for **VersionDate**. In fact, doing so would overwrite the data field values in the object, negating the purpose of declaring preinitialized variable constants. For this reason, Turbo Pascal automatically initializes the object's VMT pointer—you do not have to call a variable constant's constructor method, even if the object declares virtual methods.

Program 15-11

```
1:  PROGRAM OOPConstants;
2:
```

Program 15-11 *cont.*

```
3:  USES Crt, Dos;
4:
5:  TYPE
6:     DateObj = OBJECT
7:        month : Byte;
8:        day   : Byte;
9:        year  : Word;
10:       CONSTRUCTOR Init( mm, dd, yy : Word );
11:       FUNCTION StringDate : String; VIRTUAL;
12:    END; { DateObj }
13:
14: CONST
15:    VersionDate : DateObj =
16:       ( month : 4; day : 3; year : 1988 );
17:
18: VAR
19:    Today : DateObj;
20:    year, month, day, dayOfWeek : Word;
21:
22: CONSTRUCTOR DateObj.Init( mm, dd, yy : Word );
23: BEGIN
24:    month := mm;
25:    day := dd;
26:    year := yy;
27: END; { DateObj.Init }
28:
29: FUNCTION DateObj.StringDate : String;
30: VAR
31:    mStr, dStr, yStr : String[10];
32: BEGIN
33:    Str( month, mStr );
34:    Str( day, dStr );
35:    Str( year, yStr );
36:    StringDate := mStr + '/' + dStr + '/' + yStr;
37: END; { DateObj.StringDate }
38:
39:
40: BEGIN
41:    GetDate( year, month, day, dayOfWeek );
42:    Today.Init( month, day, year );
43:    Writeln( 'Today   = ', Today.StringDate );
44:    Writeln( 'Version = ', VersionDate.StringDate );
45: END.
```

Summary

Object-Oriented Programming, or OOP, is Turbo Pascal's newest addition. OOP concepts, which have been in existence for years, promise to help programmers deal with increasingly complex requirements in writing programs for more sophisticated hardware and operating systems. Whether OOP catches on or passes as just another fad remains to be seen. The subject is enjoying heightened attention, and most signs suggest that OOP is here to stay.

In Turbo Pascal OOP, an object is similar to a record but uses the **OBJECT** key word in place of **RECORD**. Object type definitions contain both data fields and methods—definitions for procedures and functions that the object knows how to perform. This combination of data and process is known as encapsulation, one of OOP's most important contributions.

Objects may inherit the characteristics of other objects, another important OOP concept. In Turbo Pascal, as in most OOP languages, descendant objects may have many descendants, but only a single ancestor (which might be descended from a more distant ancestor object). This is called single inheritance. A few OOP languages, but not Turbo Pascal, implement multiple inheritance, where one object may be descended from more than one parent. The importance of multiple inheritance to OOP is unclear.

Polymorphism refers to the ability of object instances to assume new forms at runtime. With OOP, it's possible to write code that uses object methods without knowing ahead of time the exact type of the object instance defining those methods. Polymorphism allows existing programs to be extended, often without requiring modifications to source code that already works.

Turbo Pascal OOP extensions include seven new identifiers: **CONSTRUCTOR, DESTRUCTOR, OBJECT, VIRTUAL, Fail, Self**, and **TypeOf**. Except for these uniquely OOP items, everything else about Turbo Pascal programming remains the same.

The addresses of static methods (those defined without the **VIRTUAL** key word) are known at compile time—a concept called early binding. Because static method addresses are hard wired into the code, calls to static methods are slightly faster than calls to virtual methods, which require the program to consult the object's VMT for method addresses, a process called late binding, which occurs at runtime.

Virtual methods are advantageous because they can be replaced by new objects and used by code that was compiled before the new object is defined. Static methods cannot be replaced this way.

Extended forms of **New** and **Dispose** simplify memory management of dynamic objects created in heap memory. Object constructors and destructors cooperate with **New** and **Dispose** to allocate space for object instances and to dispose of that memory after the objects are no longer needed.

Streams (defined in OBJECTS.PAS on the Turbo Pascal master disks) implement one way to store polymorphic objects in disk files.

Exercises

15-1. Create an object that represents a computer's diskette drive. What data fields might such an object need? What methods does it need to know how to perform?

15-2. What does a constructor do?

15-3. What does a destructor do?

15-4. How may constructors and destructors may an object type define?

15-5. What are the main differences between static and virtual methods?

15-6. Suppose you need to store names and addresses for the members of a club, listing their interests, the dates they joined, and whether they've paid their dues. Add this new object to Program 15-9's database.

15-7. Write an OOP simulation of a lunar lander, a computer game that's available on most bulletin boards and time-sharing systems. Use objects to simulate the lander's engine, fuel supply, and guidance systems.

Glossary of OOP Terms

Dozens of new terms and phrases, many of which are more confusing than helpful, have stalled the acceptance of OOP. The following glossary describes object-oriented terms that have appeared in many different sources. Turbo Pascal doesn't use or even require you to understand all these terms. In fact, the Turbo Pascal Object-Oriented Programming Guide specifically avoids many of the more confusing entries. But, because some of you will want to examine other OOP languages (particularly C++), I've included terms that apply to those languages, too. All the following terms and phrases have appeared somewhere in print.

Abstract class An object definition that is never instantiated—in other words, an object type used only as the basis for defining other objects, never to declare object instance variables. A good example of an abstract class is a location on a computer screen. Probably, you'd never need an actual variable of type **Location**. But, you might need a variable of an object descended from the abstract **Location** class, perhaps a character at a certain spot on the display.

Ancestor An object from which another object is descended. Ancestor objects may have any number of descendants, but a descendant object may have only one immediate ancestor, a concept known as *single inheritance*. Some OOP languages, but not Turbo Pascal, allow *multiple inheritance*, where descendant objects may have more than one immediate ancestor.

Class A synonym for an "object type" in Turbo Pascal. A class defines the data fields and method headers of a single object, which might be descended from another object class.

Constructor A special method, prefaced in Turbo Pascal with the key word **CONSTRUCTOR**, and usually called as the second parameter in the extended **New** standard procedure. All objects that define one or more virtual methods must have at least one constructor, which initializes the object's VMT, containing the addresses of those virtual methods. Programs must call at least one of those constructor methods for each object instance of such types. Failure to follow this rule will almost certainly cause the program to crash. When called via **New**, constructors automatically allocate memory for an instance of the object type; otherwise, they operate as common procedure methods. Usually, constructors also allocate memory space for variables addressed by pointer fields in objects. If such allocations fail, use **Fail** to exit the constructor and dispose of the object's allocated space. Objects may define multiple constructors. Constructor methods are always static, never virtual.

Descendant Inherits all the data fields and methods from its immediate ancestor, which may have inherited properties from its own ancestor. An object may have any number of descendants, but in Turbo Pascal (as in most OOP languages), only one immediate ancestor.

Destructor A special method, prefaced in Turbo Pascal with the key word **DESTRUCTOR**, and usually called as the second parameter in the extended **Dispose** standard procedure. When called via **Dispose**, destructors dispose of the memory occupied by dynamic object instances; otherwise, destructors operate as common procedure methods. Usually, a destructor's duties include disposing of memory allocated to pointer fields defined in the object. Because descendant objects may add additional such fields, destructors should be virtual, allowing the new objects to add statements to dispose of the additional variables. Destructors may be static in rare circumstances, though. An object may define more than one destructor.

Dynamic object An object instance for which space is allocated in heap memory, addressed by a pointer to the object type. See also *Static object*. The word "dynamic" refers to the fact that such object instances are created and destroyed by **New** and **Dispose** statements in the program at runtime.

Early binding The addresses of static methods (those without a **VIRTUAL** key word) are hard wired (bound) into the program during compilation, in other words, early in the game. The phrase "early binding" describes this process. Because of early binding, calls to static methods run a tiny bit faster than calls to virtual methods.

Encapsulation Object types combine (encapsulate) definitions for data fields (as in Pascal records) and also definitions for methods—procedures and functions that describe operations an object can perform.

Fail A new Pascal standard procedure for use only inside an object's constructor method. Executing **Fail** causes the constructor to end (similar to the way **Exit** works). When the constructor was called by the extended **New** procedure, **Fail** executes code that removes the heap memory allocated to the object, presumably because of another memory allocation problem, usually when attempting to reserve heap space for a pointer field. When the constructor was called directly (most often for a static object declared as a variable), **Fail** causes the constructor identifier to return **False**. (Constructors can be used as procedures or as **Boolean** functions.)

Inheritance Objects can inherit the properties (data fields and methods) of other objects. Inheritance is one of OOP's prime features. See also *Ancestor*.

Instance A variable of an object type, similar to the way an integer variable is an "instance" of type **Integer**. An object instance may be a plain variable declared in a Pascal **VAR** section, or it may be addressed by a pointer to the object type. Also called an object instance.

Late binding The addresses of virtual methods are stored in the object type's VMT. An object instance's constructor method links the object instance with the proper VMT in the data segment, allowing the object to locate its method code in memory. This linkage is performed when the object is initialized by a constructor at runtime, a process known as late binding. Because virtual method addresses are stored in the VMT, an additional lookup operation is needed for each virtual method activation. For this reason, virtual method calls run more slowly than calls to static methods. See also *Early binding*.

Message OOP purists never say that a program "calls" an object's methods. Instead, they say that statements "pass messages" (method names) to objects, telling objects to perform operations on themselves. In pure OOP, one doesn't initialize objects; one passes an object a message to initialize itself. One doesn't print an object's data. One gives an object a message to print what it contains.

In practice (and especially in Turbo Pascal), such semantic jargon is best learned and forgotten. True, in some OOP languages, the notion of passing messages is important—but mostly because those languages were designed to emphasize this importance in the first place. The concept of message passing isn't as vital to OOP as some would have you believe. Procedures and functions still run just as they do in non-OOP Pascal—whether you "call" them or pass them as "messages" to objects.

Method A procedure or function definition in an object type (a class in standard OOP lingo). Methods describe the operations that objects know how to perform.

Method Implementation Contains the actual statements that flesh out an object type's definition. The implementation of a method is shared by all object instances of the object type. Statements in object methods are the same as in non-OOP procedures and functions.

Multiple inheritance See *Ancestor*

Object instance See *Instance*

Object type An object type (also called a class) defines an object's data fields and methods. An object type is a definition for an object, not the object itself. Programs can declare object instances (variables) of object types, and they can declare pointers to objects, just as they can declare pointers to other data types.

Overloading Turbo Pascal ignores this important OOP concept, which refers to the ability for object methods to have the same names but different parameter lists. An example of overloading is the familiar Pascal **WriteLn** procedure, which can have no parameters or many of different kinds. Even with OOP, however, it's not possible to write similar Pascal procedures of your own.

OOP languages such as C++ allow "operator overloading," actually just an extension of the idea that methods can have identical names but different forms in the same object definition. Operator overloading allows you to define new data types and write numerical expressions such as X = X * Y. With operator overloading, X might be an array object, and the expression might be performing a complex array multiplication. Accomplishing this requires overloading the = and * operators, allowing the compiler to generate code that implements the expression.

Turbo Pascal does not (yet?) allow operator and method overloading. The term is so frequently used in OOP circles, though, that you should be aware of what it means.

Override Methods in descendant objects can override methods of the same names in their ancestors. In Turbo Pascal, overriding is automatic—just give the new method the same name as the old. In some other OOP languages, overriding methods might need a special key word.

Overridden static objects and constructors may have different parameter lists in the descendant object definitions. Overridden virtual methods must have the same names and parameter lists.

Paradigm ("Para-dime") This word actually refers to a Marx Brothers joke where Chico says, "I sell you a paradigm for a quarter" and Harpo buys several. Honk. Honk.

Okay, there is a serious meaning. In general, a paradigm is a conceptual model. In programming, a paradigm is a conceptual model for building computer programs. An important paradigm in computer science history is the concept of structured programming. OOP is a relatively new paradigm—a new conceptual model for programmers to use for writing code.

Polymorphism One of OOP's most important concepts, polymorphism refers to the ability of objects to assume different forms but still be type-compatible with existing code. A good example of a polymorphic object is a graphics shape. A location on a graphics screen might be the ancestor of a visible pixel, which might be the ancestor of a square, from which a three-dimensional box is descended, and so on. The objects are polymorphic in the sense that a pointer to a location might actually address a pixel, a square, or a box. Program statements can perform operations (pass messages to) polymorphic objects without knowing in advance the actual form of the object. In OOP, you can tell a polymorphic graphics object to move to a new location without having to hard wire statements that know how to process specific object types. At runtime, the object instance itself decides how to handle the message, moving its shape by whatever means are necessary.

Self Every object method implementation receives a normally invisible 32-bit pointer that addresses the object instance (variable) in memory. This pointer is named **Self**, which acts like a **VAR** parameter of the object's type. You can't assign new values to **Self**. **Self** assumes the data type of the object that defined the method; therefore, you don't have to use a caret (^) to dereference the pointer as you do with common Pascal pointers. If the object contains a data field named **count**, **Self.Count** refers to the object instance's data field.

Normally, there's no need to use **Self** this way—you can simply use **Count** as though you had declared it as a variable in the method implementation. Use **Self** only to resolve identifier conflicts—for example, with a global variable that's also named **Count**.

Single inheritance See *Ancestor*

Static method All methods in Turbo Pascal object type definitions are static by default. Virtual methods require the **VIRTUAL** key word. Other methods are static. Constructors are always static.

Static method addresses are calculated at runtime; therefore, calls to such methods are faster than calls to virtual methods. Also, the smart linker can remove unused static methods from compiled code. See *Early binding* and *Late binding*

Static object An object instance declared as a Pascal variable in a **VAR** section is a static object. The term is slightly misleading because object instances declared local to procedures and functions are temporarily allocated space on the stack, just as for other local variables. (Usually the word "static" refers only to global variables.) See *Dynamic object*

Virtual method Use the key word **VIRTUAL** to define a virtual method inside an object type definition. A virtual method may be a procedure or function, and it may or may not have parameters. Constructors may not be virtual methods. Destructors may be virtual. They probably should be virtual in most cases.

The addresses for virtual methods are stored in the object type's VMT; therefore, calls to virtual methods require an additional lookup operation to load this address. The addresses of static methods are known at compile time, and, for this reason, static method calls operate a little faster than virtual method calls.

Virtual methods are usually preferred in OOP because existing code can use overridden virtual methods in object descendants. Static methods can't be used this way. If an ancestor object method A calls another method B in that object, and if a descendant object replaces B with a new method, method A will still call the original B unless B is virtual.

Virtual method table (VMT) There is one VMT per object type definition in the program. No matter how many object instances (variables) of that type, there is still only one VMT. All VMTs are stored in the program's global data segment in the program's .EXE disk file.

Only objects that define one or more virtual methods and constructors have VMTs. The constructors in such objects link object instances to the correct VMTs, allowing the object instances to locate their methods. Failing to initialize objects with virtual methods by calling at least one constructor almost always leads to a system crash. Use the {$R+} switch to detect this condition. VMTs also store the size of the object instance, a value that **New** and **Dispose** use to allocate and dispose memory space for objects.

Turbo Pascal Encyclopedia

16

The alphabetical reference in this chapter describes all Turbo Pascal procedures and functions. Each section has four parts, listing a routine's syntax, location, description, and an example. The following explains these sections.

1. *Syntax.* Using a form similar to a typical Pascal declaration, this section lists the procedure or function name, the function data type, and any parameters. For example, the syntax for function **Chr** is:

```
FUNCTION Chr( n : Byte ) : Char;
```

This tells you that **Chr** takes a single **Byte** parameter (**n**) and returns the **Char** data type. If you were to write your own **Chr** function, you'd declare it as listed here.

Occasionally, the syntax breaks with standard Pascal style. For example, **Writeln**, which takes a variable number of parameters or none at all, cannot be written in Pascal. Function **Abs**, which returns a data type equal to the type of its argument, is another example. For these and other nonstandard declarations, refer to Table 16-1 for a description of various symbols and notations you'll encounter from time to time.

2. *Location.* Most Turbo Pascal procedures and functions are stored in units. Native routines plus those in the **System** unit, which automatically envelopes every program, are listed as belonging to **System**. Other routines are located in other units. To use a procedure or function, insert the unit name in a **USES** declaration. You may omit or include the **System** unit as you wish. See Chapters 9 and 10 for more information about using units.

3. *Description.* This section describes how to use the procedure or function. After reading the brief overview here, if you need more help, check the index

for pages with additional details. Also check the table of contents and key word lists at chapter beginnings.

4. *Example*. The programming example shows how to use the procedure or function in a real program. Each example is a complete program, ready to type and run. I tried to choose examples that demonstrate key features and problems, although, in order to keep this chapter within a reasonable size, programs are often simplistic. Even so, running the examples on your computer should answer many of your questions. Unlike other programs in this book, the examples here have no line numbers.

Graph unit examples require driver and, in some cases, character font files on disk as Chapter 11 explains. These programs also require you to have appropriate graphics hardware.

Table 16-1 Encyclopedia symbols and notations

Symbol	Description
|	or—as in Byte | Integer (Byte or Integer)
[<item>]	the <item> is optional
. . .	a continuing sequence of one or more items
<ident>	identifier
<type>	any type except <file>
<ordinal>	<integer>|Char|Boolean |<enumerated type>
<enumerated type>	(<ident>, <ident>, . . . , <ident>)
<number>	<integer>|<real>
<integer>	<signed integer>|<unsigned integer>
<signed integer>	ShortInt|Integer|LongInt
<unsigned integer>	Byte|Word
<real>	Real|<IEEE real>
<IEEE real>	Single|Double|Extended|Comp
<pointer>	Pointer|<typed pointer>
<typed pointer>	^<type>|<file>
<file>	<text file>|<untyped file>|<typed file>
<untyped file>	FILE
<typed file>	FILE OF <type>
<text file>	TEXT|FILE OF CHAR
<string>	<string variable>|<string constant>
<string variable>	<typed string>|String
<typed string>	String[n] where $0 < n \le 255$
<proc>	Procedure or Function
<constructor>	Object constructor method
<destructor>	Object destructor method
<pointer type>	Pointer data type

Using the Encyclopedia

If you purchased the listings on disk (see the last page inside the back cover for an order form), programs are stored in files named X<id>.PAS where <id> is the procedure or function name. For example, the listing for the **Pred** function is stored in XPRED.PAS. See the README file on your disk for a few oddball cases where names are changed or abbreviated.

If you did not purchase the disks, you might want to follow a similar file-naming convention when typing the examples. By saving the listings on disk, you'll build a library of tests for every Turbo Pascal procedure and function. When upgrading your compiler to new versions, these programs give you a useful way to test changes and improvements.

A few parameter names differ in spelling and capitalization from the names used in the Turbo Pascal manuals and in the unit interface .DOC text files on your master disks. In all cases, these changes are for clarity and have no effect on the operation and use of the procedures and functions. Where the Turbo Pascal manuals and the .DOC text files disagree, I relied on the .DOC file as the authority.

Abs

Syntax

```
FUNCTION Abs( n : <number> ) : <number>;
```

Location

System

Description

Abs returns the absolute (unsigned) value of **n**. The function result is of the same type as its parameter, which may be of any numerical type. For example, **Abs**(– 5) returns 5, **Abs**(– 100.25) returns 100.25, and **Abs**(3.141) returns 3.141.

Example

```
PROGRAM xAbs;
VAR i:integer; r:real; l:longint;
BEGIN
   FOR i := -10 to 10 DO Writeln( 'i=', i, ' abs(i)=', abs(i) );
   r := -2567; Writeln( 'r=', r, ' abs(r)=', abs(r) );
   l := -maxlongint; Writeln( 'l=', l, ' abs(l)=', abs(l) )
END.
```

Addr

Syntax

```
FUNCTION Addr( VAR id : <ident> ) : Pointer;
```

Location

System

Description

Addr returns the memory address of **id**, which may be any variable, procedure, or function identifier. The function result is a 32-bit pointer containing two 16-bit values representing the segment and offset where **id** exists in memory.

You may use the result of **Addr** anywhere you could use a pointer variable of any type with one exception: You cannot directly dereference **Addr** with a following caret (^). As the example shows, to dereference the pointer, you must first assign the result of **Addr** to a pointer variable and then dereference the variable.

If **id** is an array, it may have an index as in **id[5]** to find the address of a specific array element. You may also specify fields in records to find their addresses. If **id** is a record, then **Addr(id.name)** locates the address of the **name** field in **id**.

The @ operator is a convenient shorthand for **Addr**. When using @, you do not have to surround **id** with parentheses. The shorthand character produces the same result as the function.

Example

```
PROGRAM xAddr;
VAR
   p, q : Pointer;
   r : RECORD a, b : integer END;

PROCEDURE p1;
BEGIN
   Writeln('Inside p1')
END; {p1}

BEGIN
   p := Addr(p1);   { Assign address of procedure p1 to p }
   q := @p1;        { Same as above statement }
   IF p <> q
      THEN Writeln( 'p<>q!' )  { This will never appear }
      ELSE Writeln( 'p1 is at ', Seg(p^), ':', Ofs(p^) );

   r.a := 10; r.b := 20;  { Assign values to a record }
```

```
    p := Addr(r.a);          { p points to r.a in memory }
    q := @r.b;               { q points to r.b in memory }

    Writeln( 'a=', Integer(p^) );   { Display r.a value }
    Writeln( 'b=', Integer(q^) )    { Display r.b value }
END.
```

Append

Syntax

```
PROCEDURE Append( VAR f : TEXT );
```

Location

System

Description

Append opens text file **f** ready to accept new lines at the current end of the file. The only legal operations on a file opened with **Append** are **Write(f)** and **Writeln(f)**. Before using **Append**, **Assign** a file name to file variable **f**.

Example

```
PROGRAM xAppend;
VAR tf : TEXT;
BEGIN
   Assign( tf, 'TEST.TXT' );
   Rewrite( tf );
   Writeln( tf, 'This is line #1' );
   Close( tf );

   Append( tf );
   Writeln( tf, 'This is line #2' );
   Close( tf )
END.
```

Arc

Syntax

```
PROCEDURE Arc( x, y : Integer; stAngle, endAngle, radius: Word );
```

Location

Graph

Description

Arc draws a semicircle anchored at coordinate (x,y) in the color passed to **SetColor**. Words **stAngle** and **endAngle** are the end points of the arc. You can imagine these points as being on the tips of lines equal in length to **radius** extending from the center of a circle on which the arc lies.

The example draws a pseudo-three-dimensional tube out of arcs by varying the position of the arc while increasing its size and length.

Example

```
PROGRAM xArc;
USES Crt, Graph;
VAR graphDriver, graphMode, x, y : integer;
    MaxX : word;
BEGIN
   DetectGraph( graphDriver, graphMode );
   InitGraph( graphDriver, graphMode, '' );
   MaxX := GetMaxX;
   y := 10;
   FOR x := 25 TO MaxX - 75 DO
   BEGIN
      SetColor( x MOD 16 );
      Arc( x, y, y MOD 360, x MOD 360, x DIV 10 );
      y := y + ( x MOD 2 )
   END;
   REPEAT UNTIL Keypressed;
   CloseGraph
END.
```

Arctan

Syntax

```
FUNCTION Arctan( r : <real> ) : <real>;
```

Location

System

Description

Arctan returns the arctangent in radians of angle **r**, also expressed in radians. To convert angles to radians, use the **Radians** function listed in the example.

Example

```
PROGRAM xArctan;
VAR angle : Integer;

FUNCTION Radians( angle : Integer ) : Real;
BEGIN
   Radians := Abs( angle Mod 360 ) * Pi / 180.0
END; { Radians }

BEGIN
   angle := 0;
   WHILE ( angle < 360 ) DO
   BEGIN
      Writeln( 'Angle=', angle:3, ' Arctan in radians=',
         ArcTan( Radians(angle) ):8:3 );
      angle := angle + 15
   END { while }
END.
```

Assign

Syntax

```
PROCEDURE Assign( VAR f : <file>; filename : <string> );
```

Location

System

Description

Before using **Reset** or **Rewrite** on file variable **f**, assign a file name with this procedure. The **filename** string, which can be from zero to 79 characters long, may refer to a disk file with or without a path as in C:\UTIL\TEST.TXT, or it may refer to a device such as CON (console) or PRN (printer).

If **filename** is null (the string length equals zero) and if file **f** is a text file, then resetting **f** directs input through the standard input file. Rewriting **f** with a null **filename** directs output through the standard output file.

The example shows how to use **Assign** in two ways. File **tf** is a text file, directed to standard output. File **temp** is a plain file, used here to determine whether file TURBO.EXE is on disk. Because **tf** is directed through standard output, you can redirect the result of the program to another file instead of the console. Compile the program to XASSIGN.EXE and type these commands. The result of running the program goes into file TEST.TXT, which the second command then displays:

```
XASSIGN>TEST.TXT
TYPE TEST.TXT
```

Example

```
PROGRAM xAssign;
VAR temp:FILE; tf:TEXT;
BEGIN
    Assign( tf, '' );                  { Assign null string to tf }
    Rewrite( tf );                     { Direct tf to standard output }
    Write( tf, 'TURBO.EXE is ' );      { Write to standard output }
    Assign( temp, 'TURBO.EXE' );       { Assign file name to temp }
    {$i-} Reset( temp ); {$i+}         { Test if file exists }
    IF IoResult <> 0                   {   it does only if ioresult = 0 }
       THEN Write( tf, 'not ' )
       ELSE Close( temp );
    Writeln( tf, 'here!' );
    Close( tf )
END.
```

AssignCrt

Syntax

```
PROCEDURE AssignCrt( VAR f : TEXT );
```

Location

Crt

Description

AssignCrt associates any text file variable with the **Crt** unit's direct-video output routines. After rewriting the file assigned to the **Crt**, **Write** and **Writeln** statements that use the file display text on screen as fast as possible.

This can be useful in programs that write to the standard output file. To display a message on screen, perhaps an error message or prompt and *not* redirect that message to the current output file, use **AssignCrt** to assign a file to the CRT. Using this file ensures that output displays via fast direct-video routines, even if standard output is redirected elsewhere.

The example demonstrates how to do this. File **crtf** is assigned to the CRT. File **outf** is assigned to standard output (by using a null file name in the **Assign** statement). Compile the program to XASSIGNC.EXE and type XASSIGNC> TEST.TXT, redirecting output to a disk text file. The first string is displayed on the screen; the second is redirected to TEST.TXT.

Example

```
PROGRAM xAssignCrt;
USES Crt;
VAR crtf, outf : TEXT;
BEGIN
   ClrScr;
   AssignCrt( crtf );     { Assign crtf to CRT output }
   Rewrite( crtf );
   Assign( outf, '' );   { Assign outf to standard output }
   Rewrite( outf );
   Writeln( crtf, 'This line goes directly to the CRT' );
   Writeln( outf );
   Writeln( outf, 'This line goes to standard output' );
   Close( crtf ); Close( outf )
END.
```

Bar

Syntax

```
PROCEDURE Bar( x1, y1, x2, y2 : Integer );
```

Location

Graph

Description

Bar draws a filled rectangle with corners at (x1,y1) and (x2,y2). Use **SetFillStyle**

to prepare the color and pattern used to fill the bar. The example displays a vertical blue bar near the center of the screen.

Example

```
PROGRAM xBar;
USES Crt, Graph;
VAR graphDriver, graphMode : Integer;
    x1, y1, x2, y2 : Integer;
BEGIN
   graphDriver := Detect;
   InitGraph( graphDriver, graphMode, '' );
   x1 := GetMaxX DIV 2;    { Center screen }
   y1 := GetMaxY DIV 4;    { Lower mid screen }
   x2 := x1 + 25;          { Width of bar }
   y2 := y1 * 2;           { Height of bar }
   SetFillStyle( 1, 3 );   { Pattern, Color }
   Bar( x1, y1, x2, y2 );  { Draw filled bar }
   REPEAT UNTIL Keypressed;
   CloseGraph
END.
```

Bar3d

Syntax

```
PROCEDURE Bar3D( x1, y1, x2, y2 : Integer; depth : Word; top : Boolean );
```

Location

Graph

Description

Bar3D draws a filled pseudo-three-dimensional rectangle. The example is similar to the program for **Bar**. The new program also displays a blue bar in the center of the screen, but this time, the bar has an outlined top and side, giving the illusion of depth.

Parameters (x1,y1) and (x2,y2) define the upper-left and lower-right corners of the face of the bar. Set **depth** to higher values to increase the illusion of depth. Set **top** true to draw the top of the bar. Set **top** false to not draw the top, perhaps to stack another bar on top of this one.

Example

```
PROGRAM xBar3D;
USES Crt, Graph;
```

```
VAR graphDriver, graphMode : Integer;
    x1, y1, x2, y2, depth : Integer;
    top : Boolean;
BEGIN
    graphDriver := Detect;
    InitGraph( graphDriver, graphMode, '' );
    x1 := GetMaxX DIV 2;      { Center screen }
    y1 := GetMaxY DIV 4;      { Lower mid screen }
    x2 := x1 + 25;            { Width of bar }
    y2 := y1 * 2;             { Height of bar }
    depth := 10;             { Depth of illusion }
    top := true;             { Draw top on bar }
    SetFillStyle( 1, 3 );    { Pattern, Color }
    Bar3D( x1, y1, x2, y2, depth, top );   { Draw filled 3D bar }
    REPEAT UNTIL Keypressed;
    CloseGraph
END.
```

BlockRead

Syntax

```
PROCEDURE BlockRead( VAR f : FILE; VAR v : <type>; n : Word [;result : Word ] );
```

Location

System

Description

BlockRead reads **n** 128-byte blocks of untyped file **f** directly into variable **v**, usually an array. (Use **Reset** with an optional parameter to change from 128 to a different block byte size.) Whatever **v**'s type, it's your responsibility to ensure that **v** can hold as many bytes as **BlockRead** requests from the file.

   The optional **result** parameter equals the number of blocks actually read from file **f**. Use this value to determine whether the **BlockRead** was successful. You can also use **result** to know how many blocks were actually read from a file of unknown size. For example, this reads from zero to 10 blocks of a test file:

```
VAR a:ARRAY[1..10] OF ARRAY[0..127] OF Byte
    result:integer;

Assign( f, 'TEST.DAT' );
Reset( f );
```

```
BlockRead( f, a, 10, result );
Writeln( result, ' blocks loaded' );
```

The example shows how to load the first 128 bytes of a file TEST.DAT into a 256-byte array. When you run the program, you'll see that this fills only half of the array. Change the **Reset** statement to **Reset(f,256)** to fill the array completely.

Example

```
PROGRAM xBlockRead;
VAR f : FILE;
    a : ARRAY[0..255] OF Byte;
    i, result : integer;
BEGIN
   FillChar( a, sizeof(a), 0 );   { Fill array with zeros }
   Assign( f, 'TEST.DAT' );       { Assign file name to f }
   Reset( f );                    { Open for 128-byte block reads }
   BlockRead( f, a, 1, result );  { Read 128 bytes into array }
   IF result = 1                  { Check if result=num blocks }
      THEN Writeln( 'Successful read' )  { If so, read successful }
      ELSE Writeln( 'Disk read error' ); { Else read unsuccessful }
   FOR i := 0 TO 255 DO Write( a[i]:4 ); { Display array contents }
   Writeln;
   Close( f )
END.
```

BlockWrite

Syntax

```
PROCEDURE BlockWrite( VAR f : FILE; VAR v : <type>; n : Word [;result : Word ] );
```

Location

System

Description

BlockWrite writes **n** 128-byte blocks to untyped file **f**, starting from the first byte of variable **v**. (Use **Rewrite** with an optional parameter to change from 128 to a different block byte size.) It's your responsibility to ensure that the number of blocks **BlockWrite** writes corresponds with the size of **v**.

The optional **result** parameter equals the number of blocks actually written to file **f**. You can use this value as a verification of **BlockWrite**'s success.

The example creates a file, TEST.DAT, containing 256 bytes with successive values from zero to 255. After running the program, use the **BlockRead** example to read the contents of TEST.DAT.

Example

```
PROGRAM xBlockWrite;
VAR f : FILE;
    a : ARRAY[0..255] OF Byte;
    i, result : integer;
BEGIN
   FOR i := 0 TO 255 DO   { Fill array with values from 0 to 255 }
      a[i] := i;
   Assign( f, 'TEST.DAT' );        { Assign file name to f }
   Rewrite( f, 256 );              { Open for 256-byte block writes }
   BlockWrite( f, a, 1, result ); { Write 256 bytes from array }
   IF result = 1                   { Check if result=num blocks }
      THEN Writeln( 'Successful write' )  { If so, write successful }
      ELSE Writeln( 'Disk write error' ); { Else write unsuccessful }
   Close( f )
END.
```

ChDir

Syntax

```
PROCEDURE ChDir( path : <string> );
```

Location

System

Description

ChDir changes the current subdirectory or drive letter to the **path** string. Check **IoResult** after **ChDir** to determine if the change was successful. The example prompts for a new path name, changing the current directory if the path exists or displaying an error message if not. This is similar to the way the DOS CHDIR and CD commands work.

Example

```
PROGRAM xChDir;
VAR path : String[64];
BEGIN
   Write( 'New path? ' );
   Readln( path );
```

```
      {$i-} ChDir( path ); {$i+}
      IF IoResult <> 0
        THEN Writeln( path, ' does not exist' )
    END.
```

Chr

Syntax

```
FUNCTION Chr( n : Byte ) : Char;
```

Location

System

Description

Chr returns the character with ASCII value **n**. If a variable is not in the range 0 . . 255, then the character returned equals **n** modulo 256. In other words, if **i** is an Integer equal to 256, **Chr(i)** produces the same result as **Chr(0)**. The example displays the alphabet by cycling **i** through the ASCII values for the letters A through Z.

Example

```
PROGRAM xChr;
VAR i : Byte;
BEGIN
   Writeln( 'A programmer''s ABCs:' );
   FOR i := 65 TO 90 DO
      Write( Chr( i ) );
   Writeln
END.
```

Circle

Syntax

```
PROCEDURE Circle( x, y : Integer; radius : Word );
```

Location

Graph

Description

Circle draws an unfilled circle with its center at coordinate (x,y). The **radius** equals the radius of the circle in pixels adjusted for the display's aspect ratio. Use **SetColor** to change the color of the circle.

The example draws a bull's eye by increasing the radius until the circle fills about half the display.

Example

```
PROGRAM xCircle;
USES Crt, Graph;
VAR graphDriver, graphMode : integer;
    radius, xMax, yMax, color : Integer;
BEGIN
   graphDriver := Detect;
   InitGraph( graphDriver, graphMode, '' );
   xMax := GetMaxX; yMax := GetMaxY;
   radius := 10; color := 0;
   WHILE radius < (xMax DIV 4) DO
   BEGIN
      SetColor( color MOD 16 );   { Set drawing color }
      Circle( xMax DIV 2, yMax DIV 2, radius );  { x, y, radius }
      radius := radius + 5;        { Increase circle size }
      color := color + 1          { Change colors }
   END; { while }
   REPEAT UNTIL Keypressed;
   CloseGraph
END.
```

ClearDevice

Syntax

```
PROCEDURE ClearDevice;
```

Location

Graph

Description

Call **ClearDevice** to erase the graphics screen (or to reset another graphics device). When erasing the display, **ClearDevice** resets CP to (0,0) in the upper-left corner.

Run the example and press Enter to clear the screen with **ClearDevice**. Notice that this changes CP to (0,0), the starting point for the first random line drawn in the **REPEAT** loop. Press Esc to quit.

Example

```
PROGRAM xClearDevice;
USES Crt, Graph;
VAR graphDriver, graphMode : integer;
    cMax, xMax, yMax : Integer;
    done : Boolean; ch : Char;
BEGIN
    Writeln( 'Press <Esc> to halt; <Enter> to clear device' );
    Write( 'Press <Enter> now to begin...' );
    Readln;
    graphDriver := Detect;
    InitGraph( graphDriver, graphMode, '' );
    xMax := GetMaxX; yMax := GetMaxY;
    cMax := GetMaxColor;
    done := False;
    REPEAT
        SetColor( Random(cMax) );
        LineTo( Random(xMax), Random(yMax) );
        IF Keypressed THEN
        BEGIN
            ch := ReadKey;
            IF ch = CHR(13) THEN ClearDevice
                ELSE done := ( ch = CHR(27) )
        END { if }
    UNTIL done;
    CloseGraph
END.
```

ClearViewPort

Syntax

```
PROCEDURE ClearViewPort;
```

Location

Graph

Description

ClearViewPort erases the viewport to the current background color, set by **SetBkColor**, and resets CP to (0,0) in the upper-left corner of the viewport window.

In general, when clearing the entire screen, use the faster **ClearDevice** instead of **ClearViewPort**. Use **ClearViewPort** only to clear windows not open to the entire display.

Example

```
PROGRAM xClearViewPort;
USES Crt, Graph;
CONST Message = 'Press Enter to ClearViewPort...';
VAR graphDriver, graphMode : integer;
    xMax, yMax : Integer;
BEGIN
   graphDriver := Detect;
   InitGraph( graphDriver, graphMode, '' );
   xMax := GetMaxX; yMax := GetMaxY;
   SetColor( Yellow );
   Line( 0, 0, xMax DIV 2, yMax DIV 2 );
   OutTextXY( 0, yMax - TextHeight(Message), Message );
   REPEAT UNTIL ReadKey = CHR(13);
   ClearViewPort;
   OutText( '<-- CP is here' );
   OutTextXY( 0, yMax - TextHeight('M'), 'Press Enter to quit' );
   REPEAT UNTIL ReadKey = CHR(13);
   CloseGraph
END.
```

Close

Syntax

```
PROCEDURE Close( VAR f : <file> );
```

Location

System

Description

Close cancels all input or output to file **f** and writes to disk any modified data held in memory. To avoid losing data, after writing to a file, always **Close** the file variable before ending your program.

The example opens text file **tf** to XCLOSE.PAS. After reading and displaying the lines from the file, the program closes **tf**. Because it is an error to close an already closed file, or a file that never was opened, the second **Close** produces:

```
Runtime error 103: File not open
```

This differs from earlier versions of Turbo Pascal, which allowed closing a closed file.

Example

```
PROGRAM xClose;
VAR tf:TEXT; s:String;
BEGIN
   Assign( tf, 'XCLOSE.PAS' );  { Open this text file }
   Reset( tf );
   WHILE NOT Eof(tf) DO
   BEGIN
      Readln( tf, s ); Writeln( s )   { Display text from file }
   END; { while }
   Close( tf );  { Close tf when done using the file }
   Writeln;
   Writeln( 'File is closed' );
   Close( tf )   { Incorrect!  This produces runtime error 103 }
END.
```

CloseGraph

Syntax

```
PROCEDURE CloseGraph;
```

Location

Graph

Description

CloseGraph reverses what **InitGraph** does, removing the graphics driver from memory and returning the display to a text mode. Use **CloseGraph** when your program is completely finished displaying graphics.

The example displays a red circle and waits for you to press Enter. It then calls **CloseGraph** to remove the graphics driver from memory before displaying the message, "End of program."

Example

```
PROGRAM xCloseGraph;
USES Graph;
VAR graphDriver, graphMode : integer;
BEGIN
   graphDriver := Detect;
```

```
    InitGraph( graphDriver, graphMode, '' );
    SetColor( 4 );                { Set drawing color }
    Circle( 175, 85, 100 );  { x, y, radius }
    Readln;                       { Pause }
    CloseGraph;                   { End graphics display }
    Writeln( 'End of program' )
END.
```

ClrEol

Syntax

```
PROCEDURE ClrEol;
```

Location

Crt

Description

ClrEol clears the display from the cursor position to the end of the line or to the rightmost border of the current window. After clearing, the cursor returns to its original position.

The example fills the screen with x characters and then uses **ClrEol** to clear a space for you to enter your name. This is a typical use for the procedure—clearing areas on screen to let people type something there.

Example

```
PROGRAM xClrEol;
USES Crt;
VAR i, j : integer; s : String;
BEGIN
    FOR i := 1 TO 24 DO
        FOR j := 1 TO 80 DO
            Write( 'x' );
    Gotoxy( 10, 10 );
    Write( 'Enter your name: ' );
    ClrEol;
    Readln( s )
END.
```

ClrScr

Syntax

```
PROCEDURE ClrScr;
```

Location

Crt

Description

ClrScr erases the entire display or current window and places the cursor at the home position in the top-left corner.

The example first calls **ClrScr** to erase the display and "home" the cursor. It then fills the screen with x characters and asks you to press Enter to end the program. The last two statements show a typical way to end programs, calling **ClrScr** and repositioning the cursor so the DOS prompt appears on the bottom line of a blank screen.

Example

```
PROGRAM xClrScr;
USES Crt;
VAR i, j : integer;
BEGIN
   ClrScr;              { Erase display and "home" the cursor }
   FOR i := 1 TO 24 DO    { Fill screen with x characters }
      FOR j := 1 TO 80 DO
         Write( 'x' ); Writeln;
   Write( 'Press <Enter> to end program...' );
   Readln;
   ClrScr;              { Erase display }
   GotoXY( 1, 25 )   { Position cursor on bottom line }
END.
```

Concat

Syntax

```
FUNCTION Concat( s1, s2, ... , sn : <string> ) : String;
```

Location

System

Description

Concat concatenates, or joins, strings $s_1, s_2, \ldots, s_n$—which may be string variables, literal strings, or single characters—into a single string. Programs may assign the resulting string to a string variable or pass the result (by value only) as a parameter to another function or procedure.

Assigning the result of **Concat** to a string variable does not produce an error if the result is longer than the declared variable length. **Concat** automatically cuts the result to fit in the variable.

Instead of using **Concat**, you can also join strings with plus signs. There are two good reasons for using **Concat**, though. First, many other Pascal compilers have a **Concat** function but few allow the plus sign alternative. Second, **Concat** makes it obvious that you are adding strings together. A string expression such as $A+B+C$ might appear to be adding values when it is actually concatenating strings, leading to confusion when you or someone else reads the program.

Example

```
PROGRAM xConcat;
VAR s,s1,s2,s3,s4:String;
BEGIN
   s1:='what goes ';
   s2:='up ';
   s3:='must come ';
   s4:='down ';
   Writeln( Concat( s1, s2, s3, s4 ) );
   s := Concat( s1, s4, s3, s2 );
   Writeln( s );
   s := s4 + s3 + s1 + s2;
   Writeln( s )
END.
```

Copy

Syntax

```
FUNCTION Copy( s : <string>; index, len : Integer ) : String;
```

Location

System

Description

Copy returns a string containing **len** characters from string **s**, beginning at character **s[index]**. If there are fewer than **len** characters from **s[index]** to the end of the string, then **Copy** returns only as many characters as it can.

Example

```
PROGRAM xCopy;
VAR s:String;
BEGIN
   s := 'Mastering Turbo Pascal';
   Writeln( Copy( s, 6, 4 ) );     { writes ring }
   s := Copy( s, 17, 6 );
   Writeln( s )                    { writes Pascal }
END.
```

Cos

Syntax

```
FUNCTION Cos( r : <real> ) : <real>;
```

Location

System

Description

Cos returns the cosine of **r** in radians. Use the function in the example to convert angles to radians.

Example

```
PROGRAM xCos;
VAR angle : Integer;

FUNCTION Radians( angle : Integer ) : Real;
BEGIN
   Radians := Abs( angle Mod 360 ) * Pi / 180.0
END; { Radians }

BEGIN
   angle := 0;
   WHILE ( angle < 360 ) DO
   BEGIN
      Writeln( 'Angle=', angle:3, ' Cos in radians=',
         Cos( Radians(angle) ):8:3 );
      angle := angle + 15
   END { while }
END.
```

CSeg

Syntax

```
FUNCTION CSeg : Word;
```

Location

System

Description

CSeg returns the value of the code segment register CS equal to the segment address of the currently executing code. Remember that programs and units have their own code segments, and, therefore, **CSeg** can be different depending on which section of the program is running.

The example displays the first 16 bytes from the program's own code segment. It does this by assigning to byte pointer **p** the value of **CSeg** as the segment address plus integer **i** as the offset. The **Write** statement then displays the byte values in decimal from addresses CS:0000 to CS:000F.

Because the actual address of the code segment is not known until the program runs, **CSeg** may not be used in **Absolute** declarations.

Example

```
PROGRAM xCSeg;
VAR p : ^Byte; i : Integer;
BEGIN
   FOR i := 0 TO 15 DO
   BEGIN
      p := Ptr( CSeg, i );
      Write( p^:4 )
   END; { for }
   Writeln
END.
```

Dec

Syntax

```
PROCEDURE Dec( VAR n : <ordinal> [; count : LongInt] );
```

Location

System

Description

Dec subtracts one, or an optional **count**, from an integer, character, Boolean, or enumerated variable. Given an integer variable **n**, the following statements are logically identical:

```
n := n - 1;    { Subtract 1 from n }
Dec( n );      { Subtract 1 from n }
```

Using **Dec** is faster than the equivalent expression because of the way Turbo Pascal compiles the two statements. The expression, $n := n - 1$, compiles to the assembly language commands:

```
MOV AX,[0000]        ;n := n - 1
DEC AX
MOV [0000],AX
```

In other words, the variable at address 0000 is first moved into a register (AX), the register is decremented by one, and the result is stored back in the variable in memory. With **Dec**, Turbo Pascal reduces these three commands to the single and faster instruction:

```
DEC Word Ptr[0000]        ; n := n - 1
```

Example

```
PROGRAM xDec;
VAR i:integer;
BEGIN
   i:=10;
   WHILE i > 0 DO
   BEGIN
      Writeln( i );
      Dec( i )
   END { while }
END.
```

Delay

Syntax

```
PROCEDURE Delay( ms : Word );
```

Location

Crt

Description

Delay pauses the program for approximately **ms** milliseconds (0.001 second). **Delay(1000)** pauses for about 1 second. The value of **ms** may range from 0 (no delay) to 65535 (about 65.5 seconds).

The accuracy of the delay depends on the accuracy of the computer's internal clock, which on most systems is no better than about +/− 0.12 second. Because of this, delays of less than ¼ second (**Delay(250)**) are probably unreliable.

The example uses **Delay** to count off 10 seconds. Because **Delay** is initialized by a software timing loop, delays are independent of computer processor speed.

Example

```
PROGRAM xDelay;
USES Crt;
VAR i : Integer;
BEGIN
   Write( 'Press return to begin...' );
   Readln;
   FOR i := 1 TO 10 DO
   BEGIN
     Delay( 1000 );
     Write( i:4 )
   END; { for }
   Writeln
END.
```

Delete

Syntax

```
PROCEDURE Delete( VAR s : <string variable>; index, len : Integer );
```

Location

System

Description

Delete removes **len** characters from string **s** starting at **index**. If there are fewer than **len** characters from **index** to the end of the string, **Delete** chops off the string end.

Example

```
PROGRAM xDelete;
VAR s : String;
```

```
BEGIN
  s := 'Mastering Turbo Pascal';
  Delete( s, 1, 16 );              { s='Pascal' }
  Writeln( s );
  Delete( s, Pos('s',s), 3 );  { s='Pal' }
  Writeln( s );
  Delete( s, 2, 128 );              { s='P' }
  Writeln( s )
END.
```

DelLine

Syntax

```
PROCEDURE DelLine;
```

Location

Crt

Description

Call **DelLine** to delete one text line at the cursor location in the current window, moving up any lines below and blanking the bottom line of the display. After deleting a line, the cursor position does not change.

The example displays 24 numbered lines and then positions the cursor on line 10. Press the Enter key to delete ten lines and notice how the lines below move up.

Example

```
PROGRAM xDelLine;
USES Crt;
VAR i : integer; ch : char;
BEGIN
  ClrScr;
  FOR i := 1 TO 24 DO
    Writeln( 'This is line number ', i );
  GotoXY( 1, 10 );
  FOR i := 1 TO 10 DO
  BEGIN
    ch := Readkey;    { Pause for any keypress }
    DelLine          { Delete line at cursor }
  END { for }
END.
```

DetectGraph

Syntax

```
PROCEDURE DetectGraph( VAR graphDriver, graphMode : Integer );
```

Location

Graph

Description

Call **DetectGraph** to determine whether the computer supports graphics and, if so, which **graphDriver** is appropriate to use. As the example demonstrates, pass the results returned by **DetectGraph** to **InitGraph**, selecting a graphics display appropriate for this system and optionally changing **graphMode** to select a different mode for this driver.

If function **GraphResult** does not equal **GrOK** after calling **InitGraph**, then it is either not possible to display graphics on this system or one or more of Turbo Pascal's graphics driver files are missing (see Chapter 11).

The example shows how to write graphics programs that work on most systems, selecting a graphics mode and drawing a circle, or writing the message "No graphics available" if the computer cannot display graphics.

Example

```
PROGRAM xDetectGraph;
USES Crt, Graph;
VAR graphDriver, graphMode : integer;
    xMax, yMax : word;
BEGIN
   DetectGraph( graphDriver, graphMode );
   InitGraph( graphDriver, graphMode, '' );
   IF GraphResult <> GrOK
    THEN
      Writeln( 'No graphics available' )
    ELSE
      BEGIN   { Draw a circle }
         xMax := GetMaxX;
         yMax := GetMaxY;
         SetColor( 3 );
         Circle( xMax DIV 2, yMax DIV 2, xMax DIV 4 );
         REPEAT UNTIL Keypressed;
         CloseGraph
      END { else }
END.
```

DiskFree

Syntax

```
FUNCTION DiskFree( drive : Byte ) : LongInt;
```

Location

Dos

Description

DiskFree tells you how many bytes are available on a disk in a drive. The disk may be a floppy, a hard drive, a RAM disk, or any other type of drive.

The **drive** parameter selects a disk drive according to this scheme: 0 equals the current drive, 1 equals drive A:, 2 equals B:, and so on. If **DiskFree** does not recognize a **drive** value, it returns − 1.

Use **DiskFree** to determine if files will fit on disk. For example, a copy program might call **DiskFree** and, if enough room is not available to transfer a file from another drive, ask for a blank disk.

Compile the example to FREE.EXE and type FREE at the DOS prompt to find out how much space remains on the current disk. Type FREE d where d is a drive letter (A, B, C, etc.) to find out how much space remains on a different drive.

Example

```
PROGRAM xDiskFree;
USES Dos;
VAR drive : Byte; s : String;
BEGIN
   IF ParamCount = 0
   THEN
     drive := 0   { Use current drive if none other specified }
   ELSE
     BEGIN
        s := ParamStr(1);
        drive := 1 + Ord( UpCase(s[1]) ) − Ord('A')
     END; { else }
   Writeln( DiskFree( drive ), ' bytes free' )
END.
```

DiskSize

Syntax

```
FUNCTION DiskSize( drive : Byte ) : LongInt;
```

Location

Dos

Description

DiskSize returns the total number of bytes on a disk drive, including both occupied and free space. Set parameter **drive** to 0 for the current drive; 1 for drive A:, 2 for B:, and so on. **DiskSize** returns − 1 if it does not recognize the **drive** parameter you specify.

The example shows how to use **DiskSize** along with **DiskFree** to report the total size of a disk, the number of available bytes, and the number of bytes occupied by files. Compile the program to DISKSIZE.EXE and type DISKSIZE for a report of the current drive. Type DISKSIZE d where d is a drive letter (A, B, C, etc.) for a report of a different drive.

Example

```
PROGRAM xDiskSize;
USES Dos;
VAR drive : Byte; s : String; totalSize, freeBytes : LongInt;
BEGIN
   IF ParamCount = 0
    THEN drive := 0   { Use current drive if none other specified }
    ELSE BEGIN
         s := ParamStr(1);
         drive := 1 + Ord( UpCase(s[1]) ) - Ord('A')
      END; { else }
   totalSize := DiskSize( drive );
   freeBytes := DiskFree( drive );
   Writeln( 'Bytes on disk  = ', totalSize:8 );
   Writeln( 'Bytes free     = ', freeBytes:8 );
   Writeln( 'Bytes occupied = ', totalSize - freeBytes:8 )
END.
```

Dispose

Syntax

```
PROCEDURE Dispose( p : <pointer> );
PROCEDURE Dispose( p : <pointer>, d : <destructor> );
```

Location

System

Description

Dispose deallocates memory occupied by the variable addressed by **p**. Other dynamic variables on the heap are undisturbed, and the deallocated space will be used, if possible, for future variables created by **New**.

Turbo Pascal links disposed memory spaces in a chain of pointers and other information called the *free list*, stored as high as possible on the heap. As you dispose variables, the free list grows toward lower addresses, itself occupying more and more space. It's possible for the free list to grow so large it can hold no more free memory pointers. This usually happens only if you dispose many small (one- or two-byte) variables. Avoid the condition by allocating larger areas with **New**— create an array of 20 single bytes, for example, instead of creating 20 separate byte variables with **New**.

Turbo Pascal attempts to keep the free list short by combining adjacent memory areas. If you dispose two variables physically next to each other, Turbo Pascal combines the memory the two variables occupy into a single block.

Starting with Turbo Pascal 5.5, **Dispose** is extended to handle cleanup chores for dynamic objects addressed by pointers (see the second syntax definition). Such objects most often have *destructor* methods that perform various duties just before disposing the space occupied by objects. For example, a destructor might unlink an object from a list of other objects, or it might transfer the information in an object to another variable.

You can always perform these and other cleanup chores with common methods and then call **Dispose** to deallocate the object's memory. But, when objects inherit the properties of other objects, it's frequently impossible to know which of many such polymorphic objects is the right one to dispose. This information— and, specifically, the size of the object—is available only at runtime.

The primary purpose of the new **Dispose** is to call an object's *destructor* method and, after the code finishes, to dispose the correct amount of memory occupied by the object. This is possible because an object's size is found in the object's VMT (Virtual Method Table) at runtime. For example, if an object named **OType** is addressed by a pointer **oPtr** and if that object has a *destructor* named **AllDone,** then a single statement calls **AllDone** and disposes the object's memory:

```
Dispose( oPtr, AllDone );
```

When designing dynamic objects to be addressed by pointers, it's a good idea to include an empty *destructor* method even if there are no other cleanup chores to perform. This lets you use the new form of **Dispose** to deallocate the correct number of bytes with a simple procedure call. Also, it's wise to make all *destructor* methods virtual, so that inheriting objects may add their own cleanup chores to their ancestors' *destructor* methods.

See Chapter 15 for more information on object-oriented programming concepts. The example shows the more traditional way to call **Dispose**, creating a string variable on the heap and displaying the amount of memory available at the start of the program, after creating the heap variable and after disposing the memory the variable occupies.

Example

```
PROGRAM xDispose;
VAR p : ^String;
BEGIN
   Writeln( 'Memory at start of program = ', memavail );
   New( p );          { Create a string variable on the heap }
   p^ := 'This string is on the heap.';  { Assign string }
   Writeln( p^ );   { Display string }
   Writeln( 'Memory before dispose = ', memavail );
   Dispose( p );     { Reclaim used heap space }
   Writeln( 'Memory after dispose  = ', memavail )
END.
```

DosExitCode

Syntax

```
FUNCTION DosExitCode : Word;
```

Location

Dos

Description

DosExitCode retrieves the value passed to a parent program from a child process, started by **Exec**. If you end a child process with **Halt(n)**, you can retrieve **n** with **DosExitCode**.

The example demonstrates how this works. Compile the first program to a disk file, TEST.EXE. Compile the second program to DOSEXIT.EXE. Run DOSEXIT from DOS and type a halt value.

The Turbo Pascal Reference Guide incorrectly claims that **DosExitCode** returns 0 in the high byte if no errors occurred plus a halt value in the low byte of the function: 1 if ^C ended the child process, 2 for device errors, and 3 if the child ends via **Keep**. These standard DOS values are not returned by Turbo Pascal's critical runtime code responsible for trapping DOS errors.

At this time, the only reliable use for **DosExitCode** is to check if the result equals 0. If not, the value is either a **Halt** code or an indication that an error has occurred. Perhaps a later version will repair this bug. You can use the example program to test how **DosExitCode** works with your current and future compiler versions.

Example

```
{$M 1024, 0, 0}
PROGRAM Test;
VAR n : Word;
BEGIN
   Write( 'Halt with what value? ' );
   Readln( n );
   Halt( n )
END.

{$M 1024, 0, 0 }
PROGRAM xDosExitCode;
USES Dos;
VAR code : Word;
BEGIN
   Exec( 'TEST.EXE', '' );
   Writeln;
   Writeln( 'Back in xDosExitCode' );
   code := DosExitCode;
   Writeln( 'DosExitCode = ', code );
   Writeln( 'High byte   = ', Hi(code) );
   Writeln( 'Low byte    = ', Lo(code) )
END.
```

DosVersion

Syntax

```
FUNCTION DosVersion : Word;
```

Location

Dos

Description

Call **DosVersion** for the current DOS version number. The function returns the result as a 16-bit word with the major version number in the low byte and the minor revision number in the high byte. The second **Writeln** statement in the example displays the current DOS version with the help of the **Lo** and **Hi** functions, which extract the individual bytes from the full word value.

Example

```
PROGRAM xDosVersion;
USES Crt, Dos;
VAR version : Word;
BEGIN
   version := DosVersion;
   Writeln( 'DosVersion value = ', version );
   Writeln( 'DOS version is ',
      Lo( version ), '.', Hi( version ) )
END.
```

DrawPoly

Syntax

```
PROCEDURE DrawPoly( numPoints : Word; VAR polyPoints );
```

Location

Graph

Description

Use **DrawPoly** to connect a series of coordinates stored in an array of **PointType** records. This is faster and easier than using separate **Line** or **LineTo** commands to do the same thing.

Parameter **numPoints** should equal the number of **PointType** records stored in **polyPoints**. Because **polyPoints** is not typed, the array can be as large as you need.

The example shows how to use **DrawPoly**. Array **polyPoints** holds the coordinates of three points on a triangle in the center of the display. We need four array records to close the triangle, drawing each of the three sides and returning to the starting place. After preparing the array, **DrawPoly** connects the dots. Change the 4 to 3 in **DrawPoly** to see why you need four and not three array records to draw a triangle.

Example

```
PROGRAM xDrawPoly;
USES Crt, Graph;
VAR graphDriver, graphMode : integer;
    xMax, yMax, xMaxD4, yMaxD4 : word;
     polyPoints : ARRAY[ 1 .. 4 ] OF PointType;
BEGIN
   DetectGraph( graphDriver, graphMode );
   InitGraph( graphDriver, graphMode, '' );
   xMax := GetMaxX; yMax := GetMaxY;
   xMaxD4 := xMax DIV 4;   yMaxD4 := yMax DIV 4;
   polyPoints[1].x := xMaxD4;
   polyPoints[1].y := yMaxD4;
   polyPoints[2].x := xMax-xMaxD4;
   polyPoints[2].y := yMaxD4;
   polyPoints[3].x := xMax DIV 2;
   polyPoints[3].y := yMax-yMaxD4;
   polyPoints[4]    := polyPoints[1];
   SetColor( 12 );
   DrawPoly( 4, polyPoints );    { Connect coordinates }
   REPEAT UNTIL Keypressed;
   CloseGraph
END.
```

DSeg

Syntax

FUNCTION DSeg : Word;

Location

System

Description

DSeg returns the value of the data segment register DS. This equals the segment address where program and unit global variables are stored in memory. Programs can have only one data segment totaling a maximum of 65,520 bytes.

The example uses **DSeg** to assign addresses to pointer **p**, displaying the first 16 bytes of the program's data segment.

Because the actual address of the data segment is not known until the program runs, **DSeg** may not be used in **Absolute** declarations.

Example

```
PROGRAM xDSeg;
VAR p : ^Byte; i : Integer;
BEGIN
   FOR i := 0 TO 15 DO
   BEGIN
      p := Ptr( DSeg, i );
      Write( p^:4 )
   END; { for }
   Writeln
END.
```

Ellipse

Syntax

```
PROCEDURE Ellipse( x, y : Integer; stAngle, endAngle : Word; xRadius, yRadius : Word );
```

Location

Graph

Description

Ellipse draws a full or partial oval or circular outline. Set **stAngle** to 0 and **end-Angle** to 360 to display a closed outline. Set the two variables to other values in the range of 0 to 360 to draw arcs. Parameters **x** and **y** anchor the center of the oval to this coordinate on the display. Words **xRadius** and **yRadius** specify the width and height of the oval. Unless your display's aspect ratio is 1.0, meaning pixels are perfectly square (unusual in PC graphics), if **xRadius** equals **yRadius**, then **Ellipse** does *not* draw a circle as you might expect. (See **GetAspectRatio**.)

The example draws successive and overlapping ovals in various colors. The first **Ellipse** varies the **xRadius** parameter. The second varies **yRadius**.

Example

```
PROGRAM xEllipse;
USES Crt, Graph;
VAR graphDriver, graphMode : integer;
    xMax, yMax, radius : integer;
BEGIN
   graphDriver := Detect;
   InitGraph( graphDriver, graphMode, '' );
   xMax := GetMaxX; yMax := GetMaxY;
   radius := 10;
```

```
          WHILE radius < yMax DIV 2 DO
          BEGIN
             SetColor( 1 + ABS( Random(MaxColors) ) );
             Ellipse( xMax DIV 2, yMax DIV 2,
                     0, 360, radius, 50 );
             Ellipse( xMax DIV 2, yMax DIV 2,
                     0, 360, 50, radius );
             radius := radius + 10
          END;
          REPEAT UNTIL Keypressed;
          CloseGraph
       END.
```

EnvCount

Syntax

```
FUNCTION EnvCount : Integer;
```

Location

Dos

Description

Call **EnvCount** for the number of strings in the DOS environment, which stores RAM variables such as PATH and PROMPT. To set an environment variable, use the SET command. For example, typing SET TMP = \e: sets the TMP environment variable equal to the string '\e:'. Most people place such commands in their AUTOEXEC.BAT file to enable various settings at boot time. (See the **EnvStr** function for more information about reading environment variables.)

The sample displays current environment variables and calculates the total amount of space occupied, adding to this the number of strings to account for the null (ASCII 0) separators between variables plus 1 for the extra null at the end of the DOS environment block.

Example

```
PROGRAM xEnvCount;
USES Crt, Dos;
VAR
   i, numStrings : Integer;
   totalSize : LongInt;
BEGIN
   numStrings := EnvCount;
   totalSize := 0;
```

```
      FOR i := 1 to numStrings DO
      BEGIN
         Writeln( EnvStr( i ) );
         totalSize := totalSize + Length( EnvStr( i ) )
      END; { for }
      Writeln;
      totalSize := 1 + totalSize + numStrings;
      Writeln( totalsize, ' byte(s) in ', numStrings, ' variables' )
   END.
```

EnvStr

Syntax

```
FUNCTION EnvStr( index : Integer ) : String;
```

Location

Dos

Description

Call **EnvStr** with **index** equal to an environment variable's position in the DOS environment block. If the value of **index** is not within the range of 1 .. **EnvCount**, **EnvStr** returns a null (zero-length) string.

Programs can use **EnvStr** along with **EnvCount** to search for a particular environment variable, initialized by the DOS SET command. The example program demonstrates this by searching for and displaying the setting of the PATH variable (if found).

Example

```
PROGRAM xEnvStr;
USES Crt, Dos;
VAR
   i : Integer;
   found : Boolean;
BEGIN
   found := False;
   WHILE ( i <= EnvCount ) AND ( NOT Found ) DO
   BEGIN
      IF Pos( 'PATH', EnvStr( i ) ) = 1
         THEN found := True
         ELSE Inc( i )
   END; { while }
   IF NOT found THEN Writeln( 'No PATH variable found' ) ELSE
```

```
        BEGIN
            Writeln( 'Value of PATH is:' );
            Writeln( Copy( EnvStr( i ), 6, 255 ) )
        END
    END.
```

Eof

Syntax

FUNCTION Eof(VAR f : <file>) : Boolean;

Location

System

Description

Eof returns true after a **Read** or **Readln** statement reads the last element of data in a file. In the special case of a disk text file, **Eof** is true when reaching a Ctrl-Z (ASCII 26) character. This fact is important only when processing text files as the example demonstrates.

Example

```
PROGRAM xEof;
VAR tf : TEXT; ch : Char;
BEGIN
    Assign( tf, 'XEOF.PAS' );
    Reset( tf );
    WHILE NOT Eof( tf ) DO
    BEGIN
        Read( tf, ch );
        Write( ch )
    END; { while }
    Close( tf )
END.
```

Eoln

Syntax

```
FUNCTION Eoln( VAR f : TEXT ) : Boolean;
```

Location

System

Description

Eoln returns true when reaching the end of a line in a text file (**f**). Use **Eoln** when processing text one character at a time in programs that need to know where the ends of lines are.

The example is the same as the example for **Eof**. This time, the program uses **Eoln** to add an extra blank line, double-spacing the text.

Example

```
PROGRAM xEoln;
VAR tf : TEXT; ch : Char;
BEGIN
   Assign( tf, 'XEOLN.PAS' );
   Reset( tf );
   WHILE NOT Eof( tf ) DO
   BEGIN
      IF Eoln( tf )
         THEN Writeln;  { Add extra blank line }
      Read( tf, ch );
      Write( ch )
   END; { while }
   Close( tf )
END.
```

Erase

Syntax

```
PROCEDURE Erase( VAR f : <file> );
```

Location

System

Description

Erase permanently erases file **f** from the disk directory. Before erasing, **Assign** a name to **f**. If the file is open, close it before erasing. Erasing an open file is a poor programming practice and can cause bugs. File **f** may be any type of file but is usually untyped.

The example erases its own backup file, XERASE.BAK, or displays an error message if the file does not exist. Notice how {$i–} and {$i+} surround **Erase** to allow the program to check **IoResult** after erasing. If the result is zero, then the file was successfully erased. Otherwise, an error occurred—probably because the file does not exist.

Example

```
PROGRAM xErase;
CONST FileName = 'XERASE.BAK';
VAR f : FILE;
BEGIN
   Write( FileName );
   Assign( f, 'XERASE.BAK' );
   {$i-} Erase( f ); {$i+}
   IF IoResult = 0
      THEN Writeln( ' erased' )
      ELSE Writeln( ' does not exist' )
END.
```

Exec

Syntax

```
PROCEDURE Exec( path, cmdline : String );
```

Location

Dos

Description

A program calls **Exec** to load and run another program, called a *child process*. The original program—the parent—is suspended while the child runs.

The first string parameter, **path**, specifies the path and file name of the child process to run. The second string parameter, **cmdline**, contains a command to pass to the child program, similar to an argument you type on the DOS command line.

Before using **Exec**, you must allow enough memory for the child process. The best way to do this is to use the {$M} directive at the start of the program. The example sets three memory parameters—the stack, minimum heap value, and maximum heap value—to 1024 bytes. This limits the amount of space reserved for the parent program, leaving room for the child process.

One of the most common uses for **Exec** is to perform DOS commands from inside a Turbo Pascal program. As the example shows, **Exec** makes it easy to display directories by starting COMMAND.COM as a child process and passing it a command, DIR *.* here. The /C in the **cmdline** string tells DOS that this is a second copy of COMMAND.COM.

Another use for **Exec** is to divide a large program into pieces and then call each piece as a child process under control of a parent. This gives the illusion that a single monster program is running when, in fact, the beast is composed of many smaller demons.

Example

```
{$M 1024, 0, 0}
PROGRAM xExec;
USES Dos;
BEGIN
   Writeln( 'Press return for directory...' );
   Readln;
   Exec( GetEnv( 'COMSPEC' ), '/C DIR *.*' );
   Writeln;
   Writeln( 'Back from exec...' );
END.
```

Exit

Syntax

```
PROCEDURE Exit;
```

Location

System

Description

Exit leaves the current block. If the block is nested inside other blocks, the next outer block begins running at the statement following the one that activated the block containing **Exit**. If a procedure or function exits, the next statement to run is the one following the statement that called the procedure or function. If the main program exits, the program immediately ends.

The example uses two **Exit** statements. The first **Exit** ends the program after displaying a message if you do not type a file name as in XEXIT XEXIT.PAS. The second **Exit** ends the program if the file you name isn't on disk.

When exiting a program, it's possible to have Turbo Pascal automatically call a custom routine as part of the sequence of events that occur before returning to DOS. See Chapter 13 for details.

Example

```
PROGRAM xExit;
VAR tf:TEXT; s:String;
BEGIN
   IF ParamCount = 0 THEN
   BEGIN
      Writeln( 'Type XEXIT <file> to list a text file' );
      Exit
   END; { if }
   Assign( tf, ParamStr(1) );
   {$i-} Reset( tf ); {$i+}
   IF IoResult <> 0 THEN
   BEGIN
      Writeln( 'Cannot find ', ParamStr(1) );
      Exit
   END; { if }
   WHILE NOT Eof( tf ) DO
   BEGIN
      Readln( tf, s );
      Writeln( s )
   END; { while }
   Close( tf )
END.
```

Exp

Syntax

```
FUNCTION Exp( r : <real> ) : <real>;
```

Location

System

Description

Exp returns the exponential of **r**, equal to **e** raised to the power of **r**. The value of **e** is 2.7182818285, the base of the natural logarithms.

The example demonstrates how to use **Exp** to calculate the return on an investment compounded "continuously" as some banks advertise. The program works because when **r** is the interest rate, e^r equals the yearly amount of the investment per dollar, compounded continuously. (Knuth, D. E., *Fundamental Algorithms, The Art of Computer Programming*, Volume 1, Second Edition. Reading, Mass.: Addison-Wesley, 1968, p. 23.)

Example

```
PROGRAM xExp;
VAR amount, investment, rate: real; years : integer;
BEGIN
   Write( 'Amount invested yearly?' );
   Readln( amount );
   Write( 'Interest rate? (e.g. 0.09 = 9%) ' );
   Readln( rate );
   Write( 'How many years? ');
   Readln( years );
   investment := 0;
   WHILE years > 0 DO
   BEGIN
      investment := ( investment + amount ) * exp(rate);
      years := years - 1
   END; { while }
   Writeln( 'Investment at end of period = $', investment:0:2 )
END.
```

Fail

Syntax

```
PROCEDURE Fail;
```

Location

System

Description

Use **Fail** to exit an object's constructor method, usually when **GetMem** or **New** return **Nil**, indicating an out-of-memory error. For this to work, you must install a **HeapFunc** function. (See **HeapFunc** in this chapter.)

If **New** created the object instance on the heap, then **Fail** deallocates the object's memory space. If the object instance is a plain Pascal variable, **Fail** does not have this effect. In most cases, just before calling **Fail**, you should call the object's destructor (if it has one) to clean up any partially allocated variables addressed by pointer data fields in the object. This is a typical OOP strategy, but it isn't strictly required.

When constructors are used as **Boolean** functions, **Fail** causes the function to return **False**. If the constructor ends normally (without calling **Fail**), the constructor returns **True**.

Example

(For a complete object-oriented example, see Program 15-7, **ListFailDemo**. The constructor implementation **Init** from that program is repeated here, showing how to use **Fail**.)

```
CONSTRUCTOR StrObj.Init ( ss : String);
BEGIN
   Item.Init;
   GetMem( s, Length( ss ) + 1 );
   IF s = Nil THEN
   BEGIN                { Out of memory! }
      Done;                { Deallocate string object s pointer }
      Fail                 { Exit and dispose object instance }
   END ELSE
      s^ := ss; { Assign string to heap space }
END;
```

FExpand

Syntax

```
FUNCTION FExpand( path : PathStr ) : PathStr;
```

Location

Dos

Description

Function **FExpand** returns a **PathStr** string expanded to include the drive letter and any subdirectories for another **PathStr**, usually a file name. The **Dos** unit defines **PathStr** as **String[79]**.

The function is particularly useful in programs that let people change directories (perhaps by executing **ChDir**). Because the current directory may change, the program needs to know the complete path name to various files.

The example program displays the current directory, expanding all file names to include disk drive letters and subdirectory names.

Example

```
PROGRAM xFExpand;
USES Dos;
```

```
VAR sr : SearchRec;
BEGIN
   Writeln;
   FindFirst( '*.*', 0, sr );
   WHILE DosError = 0 DO
   BEGIN
      Writeln( FExpand( sr.name ) );
      FindNext( sr )
   END; { While }
   Writeln
END.
```

FilePos

Syntax

```
FUNCTION FilePos( VAR f : <untyped file>|<typed file> ) : LongInt;
```

Location

System

Description

FilePos returns the current file pointer position, or record number, of open file **f**. The file may not be type **TEXT**. It may be a file of **Char**.

FilePos equals the **LongInt** number of the record that will be affected by the next read or write. On an untyped file, **FilePos** returns the number of the next 128-byte or other size disk block to be processed. On a typed file, **FilePos** returns the number of the next file element to be processed. After resetting a file, **FilePos** always returns 0, the record number of the first element in all files.

One use for **FilePos** is to back up one or more records from the current position. For example, suppose a program reads ten records out of a file. To back up to record number 9, use the statement:

```
Seek( f, FilePos(f)-2 );
```

To read the same record again, **Seek** to **FilePos(f) – 1**. To advance to a certain record beyond the current one, add a positive integer to **FilePos** in a similar **Seek** statement. The example demonstrates this idea by creating a file of 100 integers, seeking to 50, and then backing up to 40.

Example

```
PROGRAM xFilePos;
VAR f : FILE Of Integer; i : Integer;
```

```
BEGIN
   Assign( f, 'TEST.DAT' );
   Rewrite( f );
   FOR i := 1 TO 100 DO
      Write( f, i );
   Seek( f, 49 );
   Read( f, i );
   Writeln( 'Should equal 50 -- ', i );
   Seek( f, FilePos(f)-11 );
   Read( f, i );
   Writeln( 'Should equal 40 -- ', i );
   Close( f )
END.
```

FileSize

Syntax

```
FUNCTION FileSize( VAR f : <untyped file>|<typed file> ) : LongInt;
```

Location

System

Description

Use **FileSize** to determine how many records there are in file **f**. The file may not be type **TEXT**. On an untyped file, **FileSize** returns the number of 128-byte or other size disk blocks in the file. On a typed file, **FileSize** returns the number of records the file contains.

   The example shows how to use **FileSize** to prepare for appending new records to the end of an existing file. The program writes 100 integers to disk, closes and reopens the file, appends another 100 integers, and displays the results. This works because the first component of all files is numbered zero. Seeking **FileSize**(f), therefore, positions the file pointer just after the last record or to an empty file's beginning.

Example

```
PROGRAM xFileSize;
VAR f : FILE Of Integer; i : Integer;
BEGIN
   Assign( f, 'TEST.DAT' );
   Rewrite( f );
```

```
     FOR i := 1 TO 100 DO          { Create 100-integer file }
        Write( f, i );
     Close(f);                     { Close file }
     Reset( f );                   { Reopen file }

     Seek( f, FileSize(f) );       { Prepare to append records }
     FOR i := 1 TO 100 DO          { Append another 100 integers }
        Write( f, i );

     Reset( f );                   { Display file contents }
     WHILE NOT Eof(f) DO
     BEGIN
        Read( f, i ); Write( i:4 )
     END; { while }
     Close( f )
  END.
```

FillChar

Syntax

```
PROCEDURE FillChar( VAR v; n : Word; c : <ordinal> );
```

Location

System

Description

FillChar fills **n** bytes of variable **v** of any type with bytes or characters **c**. If **v** is an array, it may be indexed to indicate where to begin filling; otherwise, the starting point is the first byte of **v**. Technically, **v** may be a file variable, although filling files with values is a poor if not a dangerous practice.

Turbo Pascal does not check whether you fill too many bytes. Filling beyond the size of your variable overwrites portions of memory, probably destroying data, your program or both. Use the **Sizeof** function as shown in the example to avoid this problem.

One use for **FillChar** is to zero an array—in other words, to fill an array with zero bytes. The example shows how to do this to an array of 100 integers. The second **FillChar** fills the same array with the value 2, setting all of the two-byte integer array values to 514. This seemingly odd result occurs because **FillChar** operates on bytes, not on integers or any other data type. Assigning 2 to each of the two bytes that make up an integer gives the integer the value 514. Therefore, filling an integer array with 2s effectively assigns 514 to every integer in the array.

Example

```
PROGRAM xFillChar;
VAR a : ARRAY[1..100] OF Integer;
    i : Integer;
BEGIN
   FillChar( a, Sizeof(a), 0 );

   Writeln( 'After filling with 0:' );
   Writeln;
   FOR i := 1 TO 100 DO
      Write( a[i]:4 );
   Writeln;

   FillChar( a, Sizeof(a), 2 );

   Writeln;
   Writeln( 'After filling with 2:' );
   Writeln;
   FOR i := 1 TO 100 DO
      Write( a[i]:4 );
   Writeln
END.
```

FillEllipse

Syntax

```
PROCEDURE FillEllipse( x, y : Integer; xRadius, yRadius : Word );
```

Location

Graph

Description

Similar to **Ellipse**, **FillEllipse** draws a filled ellipse with the center at (x, y), the width equal to (**xRadius** * 2), and the height equal to (**yRadius** * 2). Unlike **Ellipse**, **FillEllipse** can't draw partial ovals (arcs).

Call **SetColor** to change the outline color of a filled ellipse. Call **SetFillPattern** or **SetFillStyle** to change fill patterns and colors as the example demonstrates.

Example

```
PROGRAM xFillEllipse;
USES Crt, Graph;
VAR graphDriver, graphMode : Integer;
    x, direction, count, xMax, yMax : Integer;
```

```
BEGIN
   graphDriver := Detect;
   InitGraph( graphDriver, graphMode, '' );
   xMax := GetMaxX; yMax := GetMaxY;
   x := 20; direction := 1; count := 5;
   Randomize;
   SetColor( White );
   REPEAT
      IF ( x > xMax - 50 ) OR ( x <= 0 ) THEN
      BEGIN
         direction := direction * -1;
         count := count + 5
      END; { if }
      SetFillStyle( Random( 12 ), 1 + ABS( Random(MaxColors) ) );
      FillEllipse( x, yMax DIV 2,
         count + Random( xMax DIV 6 ),
         count + Random( yMax DIV 4 ) );
      x := x + ( 50 * direction )
   UNTIL Keypressed;
   CloseGraph
END.
```

FillPoly

Syntax

```
PROCEDURE FillPoly( numPoints : Word; VAR polyPoints );
```

Location

Graph

Description

After creating a polygon—an array of coordinate points —call **FillPoly** to fill the enclosed shape with a certain pattern and color. Parameter **numPoints** specifies how many (x,y) coordinates are in array **polyPoints**.

The example creates polygons of 13 points selected at random. It draws the polygon outline with **DrawPoly** and then fills the shape with **FillPoly**. The result resembles Japanese origami, the art of folding paper into birds and other animals and figures. Press any key to stop the demonstration.

Example

```
PROGRAM xFillPoly;
USES Crt, Graph;
```

```
CONST NumPoints = 13;
     pat : FillPatternType =
     ( $11, $22, $44, $88, $11, $22, $44, $88 );
VAR graphDriver, graphMode : integer;
   xMax, yMax, i : integer;
   polyPoints : ARRAY[ 1 .. NumPoints ] OF PointType;
BEGIN
   graphDriver := Detect;
   InitGraph( graphDriver, graphMode, '' );
   xMax := GetMaxX; yMax := GetMaxY;
   Randomize;
   REPEAT
     ClearViewPort;
     FOR i := 1 TO NumPoints DO   { Create random polygon }
     BEGIN
        polyPoints[i].x := ABS( Random(xMax) );
        polyPoints[i].y := ABS( Random(yMax) )
     END; { for }
     polyPoints[NumPoints] := polyPoints[1];  { Complete shape }
     SetColor( 1 + Random(MaxColors) );
     DrawPoly( NumPoints, polyPoints );   { Connect the dots }
     SetFillPattern( pat, 1 + Random(MaxColors) );
     FillPoly( NumPoints, polyPoints );   { Fill polygon }
     Delay(1500)   { Pause between screens }
   UNTIL Keypressed;
   CloseGraph
END.
```

FindFirst

Syntax

```
PROCEDURE FindFirst( path : String; attr : Word; VAR sr : SearchRec );
```

Location

Dos

Description

FindFirst locates the first file name entry in a disk directory matching various attributes. See **FindNext** for details on how to use this procedure.

Example

See the example for **FindNext**.

FindNext

Syntax

```
PROCEDURE FindNext( VAR sr : SearchRec );
```

Location

Dos

Description

FindNext and **FindFirst** locate file name entries in disk directories. The example explains the proper way to use the two procedures to display a listing of the files on disk.

The first step is to call **FindFirst**, passing a string, an attribute value, and the identifier of a **SearchRec** (**sr** here). The string can be anything you normally would type after a DOS DIR command. For example, the string 'C:\TPAS*.PAS' locates all the files ending in PAS in the TPAS subdirectory on drive C:. The integer attribute can be zero or any of the following:

```
ReadOnly   =    $01
Hidden     =    $02
SysFile    =    $04
VolumeID   =    $08
Directory =     $10
Archive    =    $20
AnyFile    =    $3F
```

A zero attribute locates all normal files on disk—the same files that a DOS DIR command displays. A nonzero attribute locates only files with matching attributes. The special value $3F finds all files regardless of their attributes.

You can combine attributes for special purposes. For example, **Archive + ReadOnly** locates only files with both the archive and read-only bits turned on in their attribute values.

Both **FindFirst** and **FindNext** fill a **SearchRec** record with the result of searching the disk directory. This record has the structure:

```
SearchRec=
   RECORD
      Fill : ARRAY[ 1 .. 21 ] OF Byte;
      Attr : Byte;
      Time : LongInt;
      Size : LongInt;
      Name : String[12]
   END;
```

DOS initializes the **Fill** array when you call **FindFirst** and then uses the array contents for each subsequent call to **FindNext**. Field **Attr** is the attribute byte for this file entry. The **Time** represents the date and time the file was most recently changed. The **Size** equals the size of the file in bytes. Finally, the **Name** string is the name of the file, with an extension if there is one.

Notice how the example examines **DosError**, an integer variable in the **Dos** unit. If **DosError** is not zero after either **FindFirst** or **FindNext** then all entries have been located, and the directory search can end.

Example

```
PROGRAM xFind;
USES Dos;
CONST Blank = ' ';   { One blank character }
VAR sr : SearchRec;
BEGIN
  Writeln;
  FindFirst( '*.*', 0, sr );
  WHILE DosError = 0 DO
  BEGIN
    WITH sr DO
        Write( name, Blank:16-Length(name) );
    FindNext( sr )
  END; { While }
  Writeln
END.
```

FloodFill

Syntax

```
PROCEDURE FloodFill( x, y : Integer; border : Word );
```

Location

Graph

Description

FloodFill paints an enclosed shape with the color and pattern set by **SetFillStyle** or **SetFillPattern**. Assign to parameters **x** and **y** the coordinate values of any pixel inside the shape. This location is called the *seed*—the place where filling begins. Assign to **border** the color value (0 to 15) of the shape's outline.

If the shape's outline is broken, the paint will leak into the areas around the shape. If the outline is a different color than **border** specifies, then **FloodFill** will ignore the shape's outline.

The example draws an oval inside a box. Press Enter to fill the space around the ellipse with light cyan. Press Enter again to fill the oval with red. Notice how **SetFillPattern** tells the graphics kernel to use constant **pat**, making a kind of herringbone brush for painting rather than a solid color, the normal fill pattern.

Example

```
PROGRAM xFloodFill;
USES Crt, Graph;
CONST pat : FillPatternType =
      ( $11, $22, $44, $88, $88, $44, $22, $11 );
      OutlineColor = Yellow;
VAR graphDriver, graphMode : integer;
    cx, cy, xMaxD4, yMaxD4, xMax, yMax : integer;

PROCEDURE Box( x1, y1, x2, y2 : Integer );
BEGIN
   MoveTo( x1, y1 );
   LineTo( x2, y1 );  LineTo( x2, y2 );
   LineTo( x1, y2 );  LineTo( x1, y1 )
END; { Box }

BEGIN
   graphDriver := Detect;
   InitGraph( graphDriver, graphMode, '' );
   xMax := GetMaxX; yMax := GetMaxY;
   xMaxD4 := xMax DIV 4; yMaxD4 := yMax DIV 4;
   cx := xMax DIV 2; cy := yMax DIV 2;
   SetColor( OutlineColor );
   Box( xMaxD4, yMaxD4, xMax-xMaxD4, yMax-yMaxD4 );
   Ellipse( cx, cy, 0, 360, xMaxD4 DIV 2, yMaxD4 DIV 2 );

{ Fill space around the ellipse }
   Readln;
   SetFillPattern( pat, LightCyan );
   FloodFill( xMaxD4 + 1, yMaxD4 + 1, OutlineColor );

{ Fill space inside the ellipse }
   Readln;
   SetFillPattern( pat, Red );
   FloodFill( cx, cy, OutlineColor );

   REPEAT UNTIL Keypressed;
   CloseGraph
END.
```

Flush

Syntax

```
PROCEDURE Flush( VAR f : TEXT );
```

Location

System

Description

Flush writes buffered sectors from open text file **f** to disk. When you write information to disk files, Turbo Pascal and DOS save the information in memory buffers. Only when these buffers become full does DOS send the information on its way to disk. Flushing the file writes to disk all characters temporarily held in memory.

Example

```
PROGRAM xFlush;
VAR f : TEXT; ch : CHAR;
BEGIN
   Assign( f, 'TEST.TXT' );
   Rewrite( f );
   FOR ch := 'A' TO 'Z' DO  { Data saved in disk buffer }
      Write( f, ch );
   Flush( f );    { Data safe if power should fail }
END.
```

Frac

Syntax

```
FUNCTION Frac( r : <real> ) : <real>;
```

Location

System

Description

Frac returns the value of real number **r** minus its whole number part. For example, **Frac(pi)** equals 0.14159.

Example

```
PROGRAM xFrac;
VAR r : Real; i : Integer;
BEGIN
   FOR i := 1 TO 20 DO
   BEGIN
      r := Random + Random * 100;
      Writeln( 'r=', r:8:4, '  frac(r)=', frac(r):7:4 )
   END { for }
END.
```

FreeMem

Syntax

```
PROCEDURE FreeMem( VAR p : <pointer>; len : Word );
```

Location

System

Description

FreeMem deallocates **len** heap bytes addressed by **p**. It assumes that **p** addresses a variable containing at least **len** bytes. Deallocating more than that number could cause serious bugs.

Usually, employ **FreeMem** after reserving memory on the heap with **GetMem**. After using the reserved memory, call **FreeMem** to make the bytes available for other uses. This is similar to the way **Dispose** deallocates variables created on the heap, although with **FreeMem**, it's up to you to specify the number of bytes to free.

Example

```
PROGRAM xFreeMem;
VAR p : ^Real;
BEGIN
   Writeln( 'MemAvail before GetMem  : ', MemAvail );
   GetMem( p, 10 );  { more than enough room }
   Writeln( 'MemAvail after GetMem   : ', MemAvail );
   p^ := pi;
   Writeln( 'Value on heap=', p^ );
   Writeln( 'MemAvail before FreeMem : ', MemAvail );
   FreeMem( p, 10 ); { deallocate p^ }
   Writeln( 'MemAvail after FreeMem  : ', MemAvail )
END.
```

FSearch

Syntax

```
FUNCTION FSearch( path : PathStr; DirList : String ) : PathStr;
```

Location

Dos

Description

FSearch searches a list of directories specified by **DirList** for a file name in **path**. The most common use of **FSearch** is to search multiple directories for a specific file. For example, if the current PATH environment variable is C:\-TP;C:\TD;C:\DOS, then passing that string to **FSearch** with **path** equal to TPC.CFG locates that file if it exists in any of the listed directories.

The example uses **GetEnv** to retrieve the current value of the PATH environment variable, passing this value to **FSearch** to look for TPC.CFG among all PATH directories.

Be aware that the result of **FSearch** locates only the first occurrence of a file. It does not locate multiple copies of files with the same names.

Example

```
PROGRAM xFSearch;
USES Crt, Dos;
CONST
   CONFIG = 'TPC.CFG';
VAR
   fileName : PathStr;
BEGIN
   fileName := FSearch( CONFIG, GetEnv( 'PATH' ) );
   IF Length( fileName ) > 0
      THEN Writeln( FExpand( fileName ) )
      ELSE Writeln( CONFIG, ' not found' )
END.
```

FSplit

Syntax

```
PROCEDURE FSplit( path : PathStr; VAR dir : DirStr;
    VAR name : NameStr; VAR ext : ExtStr );
```

Location

Dos

Description

In programs that keep track of file names, it's often necessary to separate a path specification like C:\TP\MYPROG.PAS into its various parts. **FSplit** makes this easy to do. Pass the original path name in the first parameter, **path.** The results are returned in the other parameters—the directory name in **dir**, the file name in **name,** and the file extension in **ext.** The **Dos** unit defines the data types for these parameters.

Run the example program and enter the name of any file in the current directory. (XFSPLIT.PAS is a good choice if you saved the program by that name.) The program calls **FExpand** to expand the plain file name before calling **FSplit** to extract the various parts for display.

Notice that the example carefully checks whether the file exists before calling **FExpand.** This is necessary because **FExpand** merely assumes that the specified file exists in the current directory.

Example

```
PROGRAM xFSplit;
USES Crt, Dos;
VAR
    path : PathStr;
    dir : DirStr;
    name : NameStr;
    ext : ExtStr;
    f : FILE;
BEGIN
    Write( 'Enter a file name: ' );
    Readln( path );
    Assign( f, path );
    {$i-} Reset( f ); {$i+}
    IF IoResult <> 0
      THEN
        Writeln( 'File not found' )
      ELSE
        BEGIN
```

```
            path := FExpand( path );
            FSplit( path, dir, name, ext );
            Writeln( 'Path : ', path );
            Writeln( 'Dir  : ', dir );
            Writeln( 'Name : ', name );
            Writeln( 'Ext  : ', ext )
         END { else }
      END.
```

GetArcCoords

Syntax

```
PROCEDURE GetArcCoords( VAR arcCoords : ArcCoordsType );
```

Location

Graph

Description

Immediately after drawing a semicircle with **Arc**, call **GetArcCoords** for the (x,y) coordinates of the arc's center and two end points. The procedure takes a variable of type **ArcCoordsType** defined in Graph as:

```
TYPE
   ArcCoordsType =
      RECORD
         x, y              : Integer;
         xStart, yStart    : Integer;
         xEnd, yEnd        : Integer
      END;
```

Coordinate (x,y) is the center of the circle of which the arc is a part. (xStart,yStart) equals the starting point, and (xEnd,yEnd) equals the ending point of the arc.

The example marks the three coordinates with Xs of different colors: red for the center, blue for the start, and green for the end points.

Example

```
PROGRAM xGetArcCoords;
USES Crt, Graph;
VAR graphDriver, graphMode : integer;
    xMax, yMax : Integer;
    arcCoords : ArcCoordsType;
```

```
PROCEDURE DrawX( x, y : Integer );
BEGIN
   Line( x-5, y, x+5, y );
   Line( x, y-5, x, y+5 )
END; { DrawX }

BEGIN
   graphDriver := Detect;
   InitGraph( graphDriver, graphMode, '' );
   xMax := GetMaxX; yMax := GetMaxY;
   SetColor( Yellow );
   Arc( xMax DIV 2, yMax DIV 2, 45, 135, yMax DIV 4 );
   GetArcCoords( arcCoords );
   WITH arcCoords DO
   BEGIN
      SetColor( Red   ); DrawX( x, y );
      SetColor( Blue  ); DrawX( xStart, yStart );
      SetColor( Green ); DrawX( xEnd, yEnd )
   END;
   REPEAT UNTIL Keypressed;
   CloseGraph
END.
```

GetAspectRatio

Syntax

```
PROCEDURE GetAspectRatio( VAR xAsp, yAsp : Word );
```

Location

Graph

Description

Because individual display dots, or pixels, are not perfectly square, horizontal and vertical lines of the same number of pixels may appear to be different lengths. The aspect ratio of a graphics device, usually the display, accounts for this difference allowing you to draw perfectly square boxes and round circles.

The example shows how to use **GetAspectRatio**. The procedure returns two **Word** values, **xAsp** and **yAsp**. Dividing floating point equivalents of **xAsp** by **yAsp** calculates the real number **ratio**. This result tells how many pixels to draw horizontally to equal the visual length of a vertical line so many pixels long.

After these calculations, the example sets **yLen** to 100, the length of the vertical lines the program will eventually draw. This value divided by the aspect ratio equals **xLen**, the number of pixels to draw horizontal lines. Finally, the program uses **xLen** and **yLen** to display a yellow box. Because the program accounts for the display's aspect ratio, the box is perfectly square—or as nearly perfect as possible.

For an experiment, set **ratio** to 1.0 instead of to the result of the floating point division. When you run the modified program, the box probably is not square.

Example

```pascal
PROGRAM xGetAspectRatio;
USES Crt, Graph;
VAR graphDriver, graphMode : integer;
    xLen, yLen, xMax, yMax : integer;
    xAsp, yAsp : word;
    ratio : real;

FUNCTION Float( n : LongInt ) : Real;
BEGIN
   Float := n
END; { Float }

BEGIN
   graphDriver := Detect;
   InitGraph( graphDriver, graphMode, '' );
   xMax := GetMaxX; yMax := GetMaxY;
   GetAspectRatio( xAsp, yAsp );
   ratio := Float( xAsp ) / Float( yAsp );
   SetColor( Yellow );
   xlen := Trunc( 100.0 / ratio );    { Adjust xlen }
   ylen := 100;
   Line( 0, 0, xlen, 0 );             { Draw box }
   Line( xlen, 0, xlen, ylen );
   Line( xlen, ylen, 0, ylen );
   Line( 0, ylen, 0, 0 );
   REPEAT UNTIL Keypressed;
   CloseGraph
END.
```

GetBkColor

Syntax

```
FUNCTION GetBkColor : Word;
```

Location

Graph

Description

GetBkColor returns the color value of the graphics background. When a graphics program starts, the background color normally is black. Use **SetBkColor** to change the background color.

The example shows one way to use **GetBkColor**. Drawing a filled bar in a color equal to **GetBkColor** plus one guarantees that the pattern is never the same color as the background. Drawing in the background color is invisible. In your own programs, whenever the color of the background might change, use a similar technique to make sure that objects you draw over various background colors are visible.

Example

```
PROGRAM xGetBkColor;
USES Crt, Graph;
VAR graphDriver, graphMode : integer;
    xMax, yMax, xMaxD4, yMaxD4 : integer;
BEGIN
   graphDriver := Detect;
   InitGraph( graphDriver, graphMode, '' );
   xMax := GetMaxX; yMax := GetMaxY;
   xMaxD4 := xMax DIV 4; yMaxD4 := yMax DIV 4;
   WHILE NOT Keypressed DO
   BEGIN
      SetBkColor( Random(MaxColors) );
      SetFillStyle( XHatchFill, GetBkColor+1 );
      Bar( xMaxD4, yMaxD4, xMax-xMaxD4, yMax-yMaxD4 );
      Delay( 1000 )
   END; { while }
   CloseGraph
END.
```

GetCBreak

Syntax

```
PROCEDURE GetCBreak( VAR break : Boolean );
```

Location

Dos

Description

Execute **GetCBreak** to determine the current state of the DOS Ctrl-Break switch. Pass a **Boolean** variable (**ctrlBreak** in the example program) to **GetCBreak.** You can then examine the switch by inspecting the variable or toggle the setting on and off (see the **SetCBreak** procedure).

When Ctrl-Break checking is on, pressing the Ctrl-Break keys immediately ends a program at the next DOS system call. When Ctrl-Break checking is off, pressing these keys ends the program only during console and auxiliary (serial communications) I/O and printer output. (Normally, Ctrl-Break checking should be off. Turn it on only for debugging purposes.)

Example

```
PROGRAM xGetCBreak;
USES Crt, Dos;
VAR ctrlBreak : Boolean;
BEGIN
   GetCBreak( ctrlBreak );
   Writeln( 'Control-Break checking is: ', ctrlBreak );
END.
```

GetColor

Syntax

```
FUNCTION GetColor : Word;
```

Location

Graph

Description

Use **GetColor** to discover the current drawing color. Normally, the drawing color is white (15), unless you changed colors by calling procedure **SetColor**.

The example is similar to the program for **GetBkColor**. This time, the drawing color varies at random, creating rectangle outlines of various hues. To ensure visible outlines, the program changes the background color to **GetColor** + 1.

Example

```
PROGRAM xGetColor;
USES Crt, Graph;
VAR graphDriver, graphMode : integer;
    xMax, yMax, xMaxD4, yMaxD4 : integer;
BEGIN
   graphDriver := Detect;
   InitGraph( graphDriver, graphMode, '' );
   xMax := GetMaxX; yMax := GetMaxY;
   xMaxD4 := xMax DIV 4; yMaxD4 := yMax DIV 4;
   WHILE NOT Keypressed DO
   BEGIN
      SetLineStyle( SolidLn, SolidFill, ThickWidth );
      SetColor( 1 + Random(MaxColors) );
      Rectangle( xMaxD4, yMaxD4, xMax-xMaxD4, yMax-yMaxD4 );
      SetBkColor( GetColor+1 );
      Delay( 1000 )
   END; { while }
   CloseGraph
END.
```

GetDate

Syntax

```
PROCEDURE GetDate( VAR year, month, day, dayOfWeek : Word );
```

Location

Dos

Description

GetDate reads the current system date, which is correct only if your computer has a hardware clock or if you set the date beforehand.

After calling **GetDate**, **Year** equals the current year, for example 1989 or 2001, requiring no correction. The **month** is a value from 1 (January) to 12 (December). The **day** equals the day of the month. And **dayOfWeek** equals 0 for Sunday, 1 for Monday, and so on, up to 6 for Saturday.

By using **GetDate**'s values as indexes to variable string array constants, the example displays the date in the form: Tue 20-Oct-1987.

Example

```
PROGRAM xGetDate;
USES Dos;
CONST Days : ARRAY[ 0 .. 6 ] OF String[3] =
        ( 'Sun', 'Mon', 'Tue', 'Wed', 'Thu', 'Fri', 'Sat' );
      Months : ARRAY[ 1 .. 12 ] OF String[3] =
        ( 'Jan', 'Feb', 'Mar', 'Apr', 'May', 'Jun', 'Jul',
          'Aug', 'Sep', 'Oct', 'Nov', 'Dec' );
VAR year, month, day, dayofweek : Word;
BEGIN
   GetDate( year, month, day, dayofweek );
   Writeln( Days[dayofweek], ' ', day,
            '-', Months[month], '-', year )
END.
```

GetDefaultPalette

Syntax

```
PROCEDURE GetDefaultPalette( VAR palette : PaletteType );
```

Location

Graph

Description

After calling **InitGraph,** the **Graph** unit initializes a default palette record of type **PaletteType.** This record has two fields, **size** of type **byte,** equal to the number of palette entries, and **colors,** an array of **ShortInt.** The value at **colors[0]** represents the background color. The values at **colors[1 .. size – 1]** represent all available pixel colors.

Use **GetDefaultPalette** to make a copy of the default palette saved by the **Graph** unit. After doing this, you can modify the palette values, perhaps calling **SetAllPalette** to change colors instantly on screen. Then, you can restore the saved palette later. The example shows how to do this, displaying an animated globe that reminds me of those crepe paper hangups you see at parties.

Example

```
PROGRAM xGetDefaultPalette;
USES Crt, Graph;
VAR graphDriver, graphMode : Integer;
    i, j, xMax, yMax : Integer;
    newPalette, savedPalette : PaletteType;
```

```
BEGIN
   graphDriver := Detect;
   InitGraph( graphDriver, graphMode, '' );
   xMax := GetMaxX; yMax := GetMaxY;
   i := 1; j := 1;
   GetDefaultPalette( savedPalette );
   newPalette := savedPalette;
   WHILE i < yMax DIV 2 DO
   BEGIN
      Delay( 100 );
      SetColor( 1 + ( j MOD ( newPalette.size - 1 ) ) );
      Ellipse( xMax DIV 2, yMax DIV 2, 0, 360, i, yMax DIV 3 );
      Inc( i, 4 );
      Inc( j )
   END; { while }
   WHILE NOT Keypressed DO WITH newPalette DO
   BEGIN
      Delay( 100 );
      j := colors[ size - 1 ];
      FOR i := size - 1 DOWNTO 1 DO
         colors[ i ] := colors[ i - 1 ];
      colors[ 1 ] := j;
      SetAllPalette( newPalette )
   END; { while }
   SetAllPalette( savedPalette );
   CloseGraph
END.
```

GetDir

Syntax

```
PROCEDURE GetDir( drive : Byte; VAR path : String );
```

Location

System

Description

GetDir returns **path** equal to the current directory in **drive**. **Drive** 0 represents the current disk drive and directory—the one that typing the DOS DIR command would list. **Drive** 1 stands for drive A:, 2 for B:, 3 for C:, and so on.

The example displays the current path on the current drive and on drive A:. Insert a formatted diskette into drive A: before running this program.

Example

```
PROGRAM xGetDir;
VAR s : String;
BEGIN
   GetDir( 0, s );
   Writeln( 'Current path ........... ', s );
   GetDir( 1, s );
   Writeln( 'Path on drive A: ....... ', s )
END.
```

GetDriverName

Syntax

```
FUNCTION GetDriverName : String;
```

Location

Graph

Description

To display the name of the current graphics driver, first call **InitGraph** as you normally do to initialize graphics, then call the **String** function **GetDriverName**. The example program demonstrates how the function works, assigning its result to a string variable **s**, displayed before the program ends.

Example

```
PROGRAM xGetDriverName;
USES Crt, Graph;
VAR graphDriver, graphMode : integer;
    s : String;
BEGIN
   graphDriver := Detect;
   InitGraph( graphDriver, graphMode, '' );
   IF GraphResult <> grOk
    THEN
      Writeln( 'No graphics' )
    ELSE
      BEGIN
        s := GetDriverName;
        CloseGraph;
        Writeln( 'Graphics driver is: ', s )
      END { else }
END.
```

GetEnv

Syntax

```
FUNCTION GetEnv( envVar : String ) : String;
```

Location

Dos

Description

Function **GetEnv** returns a string equal to the value of the environment variable **envVar.** To use the function, pass **envVar** equal to the name of the environment variable you want to inspect—for example, PATH or TMP—as in the example, which sets string **path** to the value of the COMSPEC environment variable. The example then uses this information to change to the directory that contains COMMAND.COM, probably C:\ or A:\.

Example

```
PROGRAM xGetEnv;
USES Crt, Dos;
VAR path : PathStr; dir : DirStr;
    name : NameStr; ext : extStr;
BEGIN
    Writeln( 'Changing to COMMAND.COM directory...' );
    path := GetEnv( 'COMSPEC' );
    FSplit( path, dir, name, ext );
    ChDir( dir );
    GetDir( 0, dir );
    Writeln( 'Directory is ', dir )
END.
```

GetFAttr

Syntax

```
PROCEDURE GetFAttr( VAR f; VAR attr : Word );
```

Location

Dos

Description

GetFAttr returns the attribute value stored along with file names in disk directories. By examining the attribute, you can find out if a file name is a subdirectory, if it was recently backed up, if it is a system or hidden file, or combinations of these and other attributes.

Before using **GetFAttr**, assign a file name to any file variable. Then pass the file variable (**f**) and a **Word** variable (**attr**) to **GetFAttr**. The file does not have to be open. When **GetFAttr** ends, **attr** equals the attribute of the file.

The example shows how to use **GetFAttr** along with one of several constants defined in the **Dos** unit. ANDing **attr** with one or more constants makes it easy to tell if this file has specific attributes. In addition to **Archive**, you may use the attributes: **ReadOnly**, **Hidden**, **SysFile**, **VolumeID**, and **Directory**. For example, use an **IF** statement like this to identify a read-only, hidden file:

```
IF attr AND ( ReadOnly+Hidden )
    THEN { file has read-only, hidden attributes }
```

Example

```
PROGRAM xGetFAttr;
USES Dos;
VAR f : File; attr : Word; name : String;
BEGIN
   Write( 'File name? ' );
   Readln( name );
   IF Length( name ) > 0 THEN
   BEGIN
      Assign( f, name );
      GetFAttr( f, attr );
      IF DosError <> 0
       THEN
         Writeln( 'Error reading file' )
       ELSE
         BEGIN
            Writeln( 'Attribute = ', attr );
            IF attr AND Archive = 0
               THEN Writeln( 'File is backed up' )
               ELSE Writeln( 'File is not backed up' )
         END { else }
   END { if }
END.
```

GetFillPattern

Syntax

```
PROCEDURE GetFillPattern( VAR fillPattern : FillPatternType );
```

Location

Graph

Description

After changing fill patterns with **SetFillPattern**, call **GetFillPattern** to preserve the fill pattern array. The procedure takes a variable defined in **Graph** as:

```
TYPE
   FillPatternType =
       ARRAY[ 1 .. 8 ] OF Byte;
```

Use **GetFillPattern** to preserve the current fill pattern when changing to a new setting. Then pass the saved array to **SetFillPattern** to restore the original pattern. The example displays the default pattern contents, an array of eight bytes equal to 255 or $FF in hexadecimal.

Example

```
PROGRAM xGetFillPattern;
USES Crt, Graph;
VAR graphDriver, graphMode : integer;
    pattern : FillPatternType;
    i : Byte;
BEGIN
   graphDriver := Detect;
   InitGraph( graphDriver, graphMode, '' );
   GetFillPattern( pattern );
   CloseGraph;
   Writeln( 'Fill pattern:' );
   FOR i := 1 TO 8 DO
      Writeln( 'Pattern[', i, '] = ', pattern[i] )
END.
```

GetFillSettings

Syntax

```
PROCEDURE GetFillSettings( VAR fillInfo : FillSettingsType );
```

Location

Graph

Description

Call **GetFillSettings** to find out the current line drawing pattern and color. Pass a **FillSettingsType** record to **GetFillSettings**. This record has the structure:

```
FillSettingsType =
   RECORD
      pattern : Word;
      color   : Word
   END;
```

Example

```
PROGRAM xGetFillSettings;
USES Crt, Graph;
VAR graphDriver, graphMode : integer;
    fst : FillSettingsType;
BEGIN
   graphDriver := Detect;
   InitGraph( graphDriver, graphMode, '' );
   GetFillSettings( fst );
   CloseGraph;
   WITH fst DO
   BEGIN
      Writeln( 'Pattern = ', pattern );
      Writeln( 'Color   = ', color )
   END { with }
END.
```

GetFTime

Syntax

```
PROCEDURE GetFTime( VAR f; VAR time : LongInt );
```

Location

Dos

Description

Call **GetFTime** for any open file (**f**) to set **time** to the encoded date and time the file was created or most recently closed. Unlike **GetFAttr**, **GetFTime** requires the file to be open.

Example

```
PROGRAM xGetFTime;
USES Dos;
TYPE Str2=String[2];
VAR f : FILE; name : String;
    time : LongInt; datentime : DateTime;

FUNCTION D2( n : Integer ):Str2;
VAR s:Str2;
BEGIN
   Str( n:2, s );
   IF n < 10 THEN s[1] := '0';
   D2 := s
END; { D2 }

BEGIN
   Write( 'File name? ' );
   Readln( name );
   IF Length( name ) > 0 THEN
   BEGIN
      Assign( f, name );
      Reset( f );
      GetFTime( f, time );
      IF DosError <> 0
        THEN
          Writeln( 'Error reading file' )
```

```
            ELSE
              BEGIN
                Writeln( 'Time value = ', time );
                UnpackTime( time, datentime );
                WITH datentime DO
                  Writeln(
                    'Date = ', d2(month), '/', d2(day), '/', year,
                    ' Time = ', d2(hour), ':', d2(min), '.', d2(sec) )
              END; { else }
            Close( f )
        END { if }
    END.
```

GetGraphMode

Syntax

```
FUNCTION GetGraphMode : Integer;
```

Location

Graph

Description

GetGraphMode returns a value representing the computer's video graphics mode. You can use this value to switch back to graphics after switching to a text display.

The example first initializes graphics in the usual way, draws a box, displays a message, and waits for you to press Enter. It then switches to a text display by calling **RestoreCrtMode**. Just before the switch, the program calls **Get-GraphMode**, saving the current graphics mode in **oldmode**. After you again press Enter, the program restores the original graphics display by passing **oldmode** to **SetGraphMode**.

When you run the program the first time, the box color is light magenta. When the program returns to the original graphics display, though, the box is white. This demonstrates that switching to a previous graphics mode reinitializes drawing colors and does not preserve any objects on display.

Example

```
PROGRAM xGetGraphMode;
USES Graph;
VAR graphDriver, graphMode : integer;
    oldmode : Integer;
BEGIN
```

```
    graphDriver := Detect;
    InitGraph( graphDriver, graphMode, '' );
    SetColor( LightMagenta );
    Rectangle( 100, 100, 150, 150 );
    Writeln( 'This is the graphics page' );
    Write( 'Press <Enter>...' );
    Readln;
    oldmode := GetGraphMode;
    RestoreCrtMode;
    Writeln( 'This is on the text page' );
    Write( 'Press <Enter>...' );
    Readln;
    SetGraphMode( oldmode );
    Rectangle( 100, 100, 150, 150 );
    Writeln( 'Back on the graphics page' );
    Write( 'Press <Enter>...' );
    Readln;
    CloseGraph
END.
```

GetImage

Syntax

```
PROCEDURE GetImage( x1, y1, x2, y2 : Integer; VAR bitMap );
```

Location

Graph

Description

GetImage copies a portion of the graphics screen into a variable, usually an array of bytes. The captured image has its upper-left corner at coordinate (x1,y1) and its lower-right corner at coordinate (x2,y2). The pixels from this image are copied into the **bitmap** variable along with width and height information.

It is important to understand that pixels and not bits are copied by **GetImage**. Because the number of memory bits that a pixel occupies depends on the graphics mode, you cannot precalculate image sizes in bits unless you are writing a program for a fixed video mode.

Most of the time, call **ImageSize** to reserve enough memory for an image, storing the pixels on the heap as the example shows. Pointer **image** addresses an array of an unknown number of bytes. The program calls **GetMem** to reserve **ImageSize** bytes on the heap. If this works (**image** is not **NIL**), then the program saves a portion of the display in the reserved heap space. Finally, the program replicates the saved image by calling **PutImage**, filling the screen with an interesting plaid pattern.

Example

```pascal
PROGRAM xGetImage;
USES Crt, Graph;
CONST x1=100; y1=100; x2=227; y2=163;
TYPE ByteArray = ARRAY[0..0] OF Byte;
     ByteArrayPtr = ^ByteArray;
VAR graphDriver, graphMode : integer;
    xMax, yMax : integer;
    x, y, xSize, ySize, i : integer;
    image : ByteArrayPtr;
BEGIN
   graphDriver := Detect;
   InitGraph( graphDriver, graphMode, '' );
   xMax := GetMaxX; yMax := GetMaxY;
   Randomize;
   FOR i := 1 TO 100 DO
   BEGIN  { Draw a few lines at random }
      SetColor( 1+Random(MaxColors) );
      LineTo( Random(xMax), Random(yMax) )
   END; { for }
   GetMem( image, ImageSize( x1, y1, x2, y2 ) );  { Reserve memory }
   IF image <> NIL THEN BEGIN
      GetImage( x1, y1, x2, y2, image^ );  { Copy display image }
      ClearViewPort;
      xSize := Succ(x2-x1); ySize := Succ(y2-y1); x := 0;
      WHILE x < xMax DO BEGIN
         y := 0;
         WHILE y < yMax DO BEGIN
            PutImage( x, y, image^, NormalPut );  { Replicate image }
            y := y + ySize
         END; { while }
         x := x + xSize
      END { while }
   END; { if }
   REPEAT UNTIL Keypressed;
   CloseGraph
END.
```

GetIntVec

Syntax

```
PROCEDURE GetIntVec( intNo : Byte; VAR vector : Pointer );
```

Location

Dos

Description

GetIntVec assigns to a pointer variable the address of a hardware or software interrupt, called a *vector*. The example sets **charPtr** to the address of interrupt $1F. It then displays the first 130 bytes stored at that location. In this case, the data is not an interrupt routine but the bit patterns that make up part of the graphics character set stored in ROM.

Example

```
PROGRAM xGetIntVec;
USES Dos;
TYPE ByteArray=ARRAY[0..0] OF Byte;
VAR charPtr : Pointer;
    i : Integer;
BEGIN
   GetIntVec( $1F, charPtr );  { Get address of interrupt $1F }
   FOR i := 1 TO 130 DO
      Write( ByteArray(charPtr^)[i]:8 );
   Writeln
END.
```

GetLineSettings

Syntax

```
PROCEDURE GetLineSettings( VAR lineInfo : LineSettingsType );
```

Location

Graph

Description

Call **GetLineSettings** to assign to fields in a **LineSettingsType** record the current line drawing style, pattern, and thickness. These are either the default values or the values most recently passed to **SetLineStyle**.

The example displays the line settings for the computer's default graphics display.

Example

```
PROGRAM xGetLineSettings;
USES Graph;
VAR graphDriver, graphMode : integer;
    lineInfo : LineSettingsType;
BEGIN
   graphDriver := Detect;
   InitGraph( graphDriver, graphMode, '' );
   GetLineSettings( lineInfo );
   WITH lineInfo DO
   BEGIN
     Writeln( 'Default line settings' );
     Writeln( 'Line Style = ', lineStyle );
     Writeln( 'Pattern    = ', pattern );
     Writeln( 'Thickness  = ', thickness );
     Writeln;
     Write( 'Press Enter...' );
     Readln
   END; { with }
   CloseGraph
END.
```

GetMaxColor

Syntax

```
FUNCTION GetMaxColor : Word;
```

Location

Graph

Description

The range 0 . . **GetMaxColor** includes all the color values you may pass to **SetColor** in the current graphics mode. **GetMaxColor** + 1 equals the total number of colors available, including the background color number, 0.

The example fills the screen with horizontal and vertical lines in all possible colors (except the background). The more colors your system has, the better this program looks.

Example

```
PROGRAM xGetMaxColor;
USES Crt, Graph;
VAR graphDriver, graphMode : integer;
    x, y, xMax, yMax, color : integer;
BEGIN
   graphDriver := Detect;
   InitGraph( graphDriver, graphMode, '' );
   xMax := GetMaxX; yMax := GetMaxY;
   x := 0; y := 0;
   Rectangle( 0, 0, xMax, yMax );
   FOR color := 1 TO GetMaxColor DO
   BEGIN
      SetColor( color );
      Line( x, 0, x, yMax );
      Line( 0, y, xMax, y );
      x := x + ( xMax DIV GetMaxColor );
      y := y + ( yMax DIV GetMaxColor )
   END; { color }
   REPEAT UNTIL Keypressed;
   CloseGraph
END.
```

GetMaxMode

Syntax

```
FUNCTION GetMaxMode : Integer;
```

Location

Graph

Description

Similar to **GetModeRange**, **GetMaxMode** returns the maximum number you can pass to **SetGraphMode**, selecting different display options for a certain adapter card and graphics driver. **GetModeRange** works only for standard BGI drivers. **GetMaxMode** works for all drivers, even those from other vendors. Because **GetMaxMode** interrogates the driver itself for its maximum mode number, it's probably best to call this function instead of **GetModeRange.** The example displays a brief list of statistics including the maximum mode number for the default graphics driver.

Example

```
PROGRAM xGetMaxMode;
USES Graph;
VAR graphDriver, graphMode : integer;
    xMax, yMax, maxMode : Integer;
    driver : String;
BEGIN
    graphDriver := Detect;
    InitGraph( graphDriver, graphMode, '' );
    IF GraphResult <> grOk
     THEN
       Writeln( 'No graphics' )
     ELSE
       BEGIN
          xMax := GetMaxX; yMax := GetMaxY;
          maxMode := GetMaxMode;
          driver := GetDriverName;
          CloseGraph;
          Writeln( 'Default driver is ', driver );
          Writeln( 'x Max = ', xMax );
          Writeln( 'y Max = ', yMax );
          Writeln( 'Maximum mode = ', maxMode )
       END { else }
END.
```

GetMaxX

Syntax

```
FUNCTION GetMaxX : Integer;
```

Location

Graph

Description

After calling **InitGraph** to initialize a graphics display, **GetMaxX** returns the maximum horizontal screen coordinate value. For example, in a display of 640 horizontal by 350 vertical pixels, **GetMaxX** returns 639. This is one less than the number of horizontal pixels because the minimum coordinate value is always 0.

Example

See **GetMaxY**.

GetMaxY

Syntax

```
FUNCTION GetMaxY : Integer;
```

Location

Graph

Description

After calling **InitGraph** to initialize a graphics display, **GetMaxY** returns the maximum vertical screen coordinate value. For example, in a display of 640 horizontal by 350 vertical pixels, **GetMaxY** returns 349. This is one less than the number of vertical pixels because the minimum coordinate value is always 0.

Most often you will use **GetMaxX** and **GetMaxY** together as in the example. Instead of using constants for display coordinate limits, call these functions to discover the maximum x and y coordinate values your program can use. This way, you can write programs that work correctly regardless of the display's resolution.

Example

```
PROGRAM xGetMaxXY;
USES Crt, Graph;
VAR graphDriver, graphMode : Integer;
    xMax, yMax, xMin, yMin : Integer;
BEGIN
   graphDriver := Detect;
   InitGraph( graphDriver, graphMode, '' );
   xMax := GetMaxX; yMax := GetMaxY;
   xMin := 0;       yMin := 0;
   WHILE ( xMax > 0 ) AND ( yMax > 0 ) DO
   BEGIN
     SetColor( 1 + Random(MaxColors) );
     Line( xMin, yMin, xMax, yMin );
     Line( xMax, yMin, xMax, yMax );
     Line( xMax, yMax, xMin, yMax );
     Line( xMin, yMax, xMin, yMin );
     xMax := xMax - 1; yMax := yMax - 1;
     xMin := xMin + 1; yMin := yMin + 1
   END; { while }
   REPEAT UNTIL Keypressed;
   CloseGraph
END.
```

GetMem

Syntax

```
PROCEDURE GetMem( VAR p : <pointer>; n : Word );
```

Location

System

Description

GetMem reserves **n** bytes of memory on the heap and assigns the address of the first byte of that memory to **p**. **GetMem** is similar to **New**, except it lets you specify the number of bytes to reserve, up to 65,521 bytes for each call to **GetMem**.

As the example shows, **GetMem** can allocate space for record variants, which **New** does not allow in Turbo Pascal. Reserving space for only the integer field of a free union record takes two bytes. Reserving space for this same record by using **New** would take six bytes, the size of the record's real number field. This is equivalent to the statement, **New(p,b)**, which most Pascal compilers, but not Turbo, recognize as a command to reserve memory only for field **b**.

Example

```
PROGRAM xGetMem;
TYPE rec =
        RECORD
            CASE Integer OF
                1 : ( a : Real );
                2 : ( b : Integer )
            END;
VAR p : ^rec;
BEGIN
   Writeln( 'Memory before GetMem=', Memavail );
   GetMem( p, 2 );
   Writeln( 'Memory after GetMem =', Memavail );
   p^.b := MaxInt;
   Writeln( p^.b, ' takes ', Sizeof(p^.b), ' bytes of storage.' );
   Freemem( p, 2 );
   Writeln( 'Memory after FreeMem=', Memavail )
END.
```

GetModeName

Syntax

```
FUNCTION GetModeName( graphMode : Integer ) : String;
```

Location

Graph

Description

Most graphics drivers support two or more display modes, referenced by number (e.g., see **GetMaxMode** and **SetGraphMode**). These modes also have names, returned by the **String** function **GetModeName.** The function supports standard BGI drivers as well as those from other vendors.

Instead of hardwiring graphics mode names into your programs, always use **GetModeName**, perhaps in a menu that lets people select among available modes. This way, your program will be compatible with future modifications and drivers. The example displays the current graphics driver name and all possible modes.

Example

```
PROGRAM xGetModeName;
USES Graph;
VAR graphDriver, graphMode, i : Integer;
BEGIN
    graphDriver := Detect;
    InitGraph( graphDriver, graphMode, '' );
    IF GraphResult <> grOk
      THEN
        Writeln( 'No graphics' )
      ELSE
        BEGIN
          Writeln( 'Graphics driver is: ', GetDriverName );
          FOR i := 0 TO GetMaxMode DO
             Writeln( 'Mode ', i, ' : ', GetModeName(i) );
          Writeln;
          Write( 'Press Enter...' );
          Readln;
          CloseGraph
        END { else }
END.
```

GetModeRange

Syntax

```
PROCEDURE GetModeRange( graphDriver : Integer; VAR loMode, hiMode : Integer );
```

Location

Graph

Description

Pass any graphics driver to **GetModeRange** to set two variables, **loMode** and **hiMode** to the minimum graphics mode values you can then pass to **InitGraph**. **GetModeRange** tells you how many different display modes are available for a particular driver. The example displays a table of mode ranges for all Turbo Pascal graphics drivers.

Example

```
PROGRAM xGetModeRange;
USES Graph;
CONST ModeNames : ARRAY[ 1 .. 10 ] OF String[8] =
      ( 'CGA     ', 'MCGA    ', 'EGA     ', 'EGA64   ',
        'EGAMono ', 'RESERVED', 'HercMono', 'Att400  ',
        'VGA     ', 'PC3270  ' );
VAR graphDriver, loMode, hiMode : integer;
BEGIN
   Writeln( 'Graphics Driver Mode Ranges' );
   Writeln;
   FOR graphDriver := 1 TO 10 DO
   BEGIN
      GetModeRange( graphDriver, loMode, hiMode );
      Writeln( ModeNames[graphDriver], ' = ',
               loMode:2, ' ..', hiMode:2 )
   END { for }
END.
```

GetPalette

Syntax

```
PROCEDURE GetPalette( VAR palette : PaletteType );
```

Location

Graph

Description

To read the current color palette, call **GetPalette** with a variable of type **Palette-Type** defined as:

```
TYPE
   PaletteType =
      RECORD
         size : Byte;
         colors : ARRAY[ 0 .. MaxColors ] OF ShortInt
      END;
```

Field **size** equals the number of entries in the **colors** array. The example displays the current palette settings for the default graphics mode, listing the color number (equal to the **palette.colors** array index), the value stored in the array, and drawing a bar in that color. Notice that, to change bar colors, the program passes the **colors** array *index*—not the arrayed value—to **SetFillStyle**.

Example

```
PROGRAM xGetPalette;
USES Crt, Graph;
VAR graphDriver, graphMode : integer;
    h, i, xMax : Integer;
    palette : PaletteType;
    s : String;
BEGIN
   graphDriver := Detect;
   InitGraph( graphDriver, graphMode, '' );
   xMax := GetMaxX;
   GetPalette( palette );
   h := TextHeight( 'M' ) + 8;
   FOR i := 0 TO palette.size-1 DO
   BEGIN
      Str( i:2, s );
      MoveTo( 0, i * h );
      OutText( 'Color #' + s + ' = ' );
      Str( palette.colors[i]:3, s );
      OutText( s + ' :: ' );
      SetFillStyle( SolidFill, i );
      Bar( GetX, GetY, xMax, GetY+4 )
   END; { for }
   REPEAT UNTIL Keypressed;
   CloseGraph
END.
```

GetPaletteSize

Syntax

```
FUNCTION GetPaletteSize : Integer;
```

Location

Graph

Description

GetPaletteSize returns the size of the **colors** field in a palette record, equal to the **size** field. Calling this function is easier than (and has the same effect as) reading the current palette with **GetPalette** or **GetDefaultPalette** and inspecting the **size** field. The example demonstrates how to use **GetPaletteSize** along with **GetMaxColor** to randomize palette colors, producing a "shimmering pick-up sticks " effect—at least that's what it looks like to me.

Example

```
PROGRAM xGetPaletteSize;
USES Crt, Graph;
VAR graphDriver, graphMode : integer;
    i, xMax, yMax : Integer;
BEGIN
   graphDriver := Detect;
   InitGraph( graphDriver, graphMode, '' );
   xMax := GetMaxX; yMax := GetMaxY;
   FOR i := 1 TO 100 DO
   BEGIN
      SetColor( 1 + Random( GetMaxColor - 1 ) );
      Line( ABS( Random( xMax ) ),
            ABS( Random( yMax ) ),
            ABS( Random( xMax ) ),
            ABS( Random( yMax ) ) )
   END; { for }
   WHILE NOT Keypressed DO
   BEGIN
      IF i >= GetPaletteSize THEN i := 1 ELSE Inc( i );
      Delay( 10 );
      SetPalette( i, 1 + Random( GetMaxColor - 1 ) )
   END; { while }
   CloseGraph
END.
```

GetPixel

Syntax

```
FUNCTION GetPixel( x, y : Integer ) : Word;
```

Location

Graph

Description

GetPixel returns the color value of the pixel at coordinate (x,y). Use the procedure as a kind of sensor to check for borders or objects on display.

The example displays a series of boxes and then cycles variables **x** and **y** through every possible coordinate value. Before displaying randomly colored dots, **GetPixel** checks for the color of the boxes. Whenever the program locates a box edge, it toggles variable **penDown**—a simple algorithm for filling about half of the box areas on screen. The result is a confetti-colored set of outlined boxes.

Example

```
PROGRAM xGetPixel;
USES Crt, Graph;
CONST BorderColor=Red;
VAR graphDriver, graphMode : integer;
    i, xMax, yMax, x, y : integer;
    penDown : Boolean;

PROCEDURE Box( x1, y1, x2, y2 : Word );
BEGIN
   SetColor( BorderColor );
   Line( x1, y1, x2, y1 );
   Line( x2, y1, x2, y2 );
   Line( x2, y2, x1, y2 );
   Line( x1, y2, x1, y1 )
END; { Box }

BEGIN
   graphDriver := Detect;
   InitGraph( graphDriver, graphMode, '' );
   xMax := GetMaxX; yMax := GetMaxY;
   Randomize;
   FOR i := 1 TO 15 DO
     Box( Random( xMax ), Random( yMax ),
          Random( xMax ), Random( yMax ) );
   FOR x := 0 TO xMax DO
```

```
        BEGIN
           penDown := FALSE;
           FOR y := 0 TO yMax DO
              IF ( GetPixel( x,   y ) = BorderColor ) AND
                 ( GetPixel( x+1, y ) = BorderColor )
                 THEN penDown := NOT penDown
                 ELSE IF penDown
                         THEN PutPixel( x, y, Random(MaxColors) )
           END; { for }
           REPEAT UNTIL Keypressed;
           CloseGraph
        END.
```

GetTextSettings

Syntax

```
PROCEDURE GetTextSettings( VAR textInfo : TextSettingsType );
```

Location

Graph

Description

GetTextSettings returns a record containing five fields that describe the current graphics text settings. These settings affect the appearance of text displayed by **OutText** and **OutTextXY**. The **TextSettingsType** record has the following structure:

```
TextSettingsType =
   RECORD
      font      : Word;  { Font number }
      direction : Word;  { Horizontal or vertical direction }
      charSize  : Word;  { Relative size}
      horiz     : Word;  { Horizontal justification }
      vert      : Word   { Vertical justification }
   END;
```

Example

```
PROGRAM xGetTextSettings;
USES Graph;
VAR graphDriver, graphMode : integer;
    tsRec : TextSettingsType;
BEGIN
```

```
   graphDriver := Detect;
   InitGraph( graphDriver, graphMode, '' );
   GetTextSettings( tsRec );
   WITH tsRec DO
   BEGIN
      Writeln( 'Font ......... ', font );
      Writeln( 'Direction .... ', direction );
      Writeln( 'CharSize ..... ', charSize );
      Writeln( 'Horiz ........ ', horiz );
      Writeln( 'Vert ......... ', vert )
   END; { with }
   Readln;
   CloseGraph
END.
```

GetTime

Syntax

```
PROCEDURE GetTime( VAR hour, minute, second, sec100 : Word );
```

Location

Dos

Description

Call **GetTime** to read the current time of day. The procedure returns four **Word**
variables equal to the hour, minute, second, and hundredths of seconds. Because most PC clocks are interrupt driven, the hundredths value is not very accurate. Don't trust it for less than about ¼ second. The hour is a 24-hour value.
As the example shows, to display 12-hour time, subtract 12 from the hour if
greater than 12.

Example

```
PROGRAM xGetTime;
USES Dos;
VAR hour, minute, second, sec100 : Word;

FUNCTION D2( n : Word ) : Word;
BEGIN
   IF n < 10 THEN Write('0');
   D2 := n
END; { D2 }
```

```
BEGIN
   GetTime( hour, minute, second, sec100 );
   IF hour > 12
      THEN hour := hour - 12;
   Writeln( 'The time is ',
      D2(hour), ':', D2(minute), ':', D2(second) )
END.
```

GetVerify

Syntax

```
PROCEDURE GetVerify( VAR verify : Boolean );
```

Location

Dos

Description

When the DOS *verify* switch is True, disk writes are followed by automatic disk reads to verify that data written to disk probably was stored correctly. When the *verify* switch is False, disk writes are not followed by disk reads. Because write-verification slows disk I/O considerably, most people leave this switch off.

Call function **GetVerify** to inspect the state of the DOS *verify* switch. You can change the switch setting from DOS by typing "verify ON" or "verify OFF". Or, from inside a program, use the **SetVerify** procedure.

Example

```
PROGRAM xGetVerify;
USES Dos;
VAR verify : Boolean;
BEGIN
   GetVerify( verify );
   Writeln( 'Verify switch is: ', verify )
END.
```

GetViewSettings

Syntax

```
PROCEDURE GetViewSettings( VAR viewPort : ViewPortType );
```

Location

Graph

Description

To read the current viewport settings, call **GetViewSettings** with a variable of type **ViewPortType** defined as:

```
TYPE
   ViewPortType =
      RECORD
         x1, y1, x2, y2 : Integer;
         clip : Boolean
      END;
```

      GetViewSettings fills in the record fields with the minimum (x1,y1) and maximum (x2,y2) display coordinates. It also sets **clip** true if clipping is on or false if clipping is off. The example uses this information to outline the display and show the current clipping value.

Example

```
PROGRAM xGetViewSettings;
USES Crt, Graph;
VAR graphDriver, graphMode : integer;
    viewport : ViewPortType;
BEGIN
   graphDriver := Detect;
   InitGraph( graphDriver, graphMode, '' );
   GetViewSettings( viewport );
   WITH viewport DO
   BEGIN
      Rectangle( x1, y1, x2, y2 );
      MoveTo( 10, y2 DIV 2 );
      OutText( 'Clipping = ' );
      IF clip
         THEN OutText( 'TRUE' )
         ELSE OutText( 'FALSE' )
   END; { with }
   REPEAT UNTIL Keypressed;
   CloseGraph
END.
```

GetX

Syntax

```
FUNCTION GetX : Integer;
```

Location

Graph

Description

GetX returns the internal x (horizontal) coordinate value affected by **MoveTo**, **LineTo**, **LineRel**, **MoveRel**, and **OutText** statements. See **GetY** for additional details.

Example

See example for **GetY**.

GetY

Syntax

```
FUNCTION GetY : Integer;
```

Location

Graph

Description

GetY returns the internal y (vertical) coordinate value affected by **MoveTo**, **LineTo**, **LineRel**, **MoveRel**, and **OutText** statements. Along with **GetX**, the function lets you pinpoint where drawing next appears—except in graphics routines such as **Circle** that let you specify other (x,y) coordinates.

The example demonstrates several subtleties of coordinate positioning in the Turbo Pascal graphics kernel. First, the program displays a blue dot at screen center. It then shows the current **GetX** and **GetY** values, which both remain equal to their initialized zero values. This proves that **PutPixel** does not affect the internally saved (x,y) coordinate. In the next step, the program calls **MoveTo** to position the graphics coordinate to mid screen. As you can see when you run the program, this and the **OutText** statement change the internally saved (x,y) graphics coordinate.

Example

```
PROGRAM xGetXY;
USES Graph;
VAR graphDriver, graphMode : integer;
BEGIN
   graphDriver := Detect;
   InitGraph( graphDriver, graphMode, '' );
   PutPixel( GetMaxX DIV 2, GetMaxY DIV 2, Blue );
   Writeln( 'GetX=', GetX, ' GetY=', GetY );
   MoveTo( GetMaxX DIV 2, GetMaxY DIV 2 );
   OutText( 'Testing GetX and GetY' );
   Writeln( 'GetX=', GetX, ' GetY=', GetY );
   ReadLn;
   CloseGraph
END.
```

GotoXY

Syntax

```
PROCEDURE GotoXY( x, y : Byte );
```

Location

Crt

Description

GotoXY positions the cursor at display coordinate (x,y). The upper-left corner of the display, or "home" position, has the coordinate (1,1). In an 80-column by 25 line display, the bottom-right corner has the coordinate (80,25).

The example shows how to use **GotoXY** to center a message on display. Extract function **Center** for your own programs. (I borrowed the message from signs along the Pennsylvania Turnpike in case you're interested.)

By the way, some people say "Go-toxy" while others pronounce it "Goto-X-Y." It's your choice.

Example

```
PROGRAM xGotoXY;
USES Crt;
CONST Wait = 3000;

PROCEDURE Center( message : String );
BEGIN
   GotoXY( 1, 12 );
```

```
   ClrEol;
   GotoXY( 40-( Length(message) DIV 2 ), 12 );
   Write( message )
END; { Center }

BEGIN
   ClrScr; Delay( Wait );
   Center( 'You can drive'   ); Delay( Wait );
   Center( 'a mile a minute' ); Delay( Wait );
   Center( 'but there''s no' ); Delay( Wait );
   Center( 'future in it.'   ); Delay( Wait )
END.
```

GraphDefaults

Syntax

```
PROCEDURE GraphDefaults;
```

Location

Graph

Description

Call **GraphDefaults** to restore all graphics settings, CP, the viewport, and other parameters, to the values these items have immediately following **InitGraph**. **GraphDefaults** does not clear the screen, however. To do that, follow **GraphDefaults** with **ClearDevice**. (You could also use the slower **ClearViewPort** but, because **GraphDefaults** opens the viewport to full screen, **ClearDevice** is faster.)

Run the example to see a restricted view of random circles in the upper-left corner of your screen. Press the space bar to call **GraphDefaults**, opening the window to full screen but not clearing the display. Press Esc to end the demonstration.

Example

```
PROGRAM xGraphDefaults;
USES Crt, Graph;
VAR graphDriver, graphMode : integer;
    done : Boolean; ch : Char;
BEGIN
   graphDriver := Detect;
   InitGraph( graphDriver, graphMode, '' );
   SetViewPort( 10, 10, 110, 110, True );
```

```
        done := False;
        REPEAT
            SetColor( 1+Random(GetMaxColor) );
            Circle( Random(GetMaxX), Random(GetMaxY), Random(25) );
            IF Keypressed THEN
            BEGIN
                ch := ReadKey;
                IF ch = Chr(32)
                    THEN BEGIN Write( Chr(7) ); GraphDefaults END
                    ELSE done := ( ch = Chr(27) )
            END { if }
        UNTIL done;
        CloseGraph
END.
```

GraphErrorMsg

Syntax

```
FUNCTION GraphErrorMsg( errorCode : Integer ) : String;
```

Location

Graph

Description

GraphErrorMsg returns a string that describes a graphics error. You can pass error code values to **GraphErrorMsg** or pass the result of function **GraphResult**.

The example displays error messages for values − 15 to 0, which indicates no error.

Example

```
PROGRAM xGraphErrorMsg;
USES Graph;
VAR graphDriver, graphMode, i : integer;
BEGIN
    graphDriver := Detect;
    InitGraph( graphDriver, graphMode, '' );
    Writeln( 'Graphics Error Messages' );
    Writeln;
    FOR i := 0 DOWNTO -15 DO
        Writeln( i:3, ' : ', GraphErrorMsg(i) );
    Readln;
    CloseGraph
END.
```

GraphResult

Syntax

```
FUNCTION GraphResult : Integer;
```

Location

Graph

Description

Certain graphics operations return error codes through the **GraphResult** function. See Table 11-3 for a list of error codes and their meanings.

The example calls **SetTextStyle** with a font number that you can enter when the program begins. Try numbers 1 and 2. Then enter a bad number such as 4000, for which there is no corresponding character font file on disk. Checking **GraphResult** in this situation prevents **OutText** from displaying a message when the font selection fails.

Example

```
PROGRAM xGraphResult;
USES Graph;
VAR graphDriver, graphMode : Integer;
  fontNumber : Integer;
BEGIN
   Write( 'Font number? ' );
   Readln( fontNumber );
   graphDriver := Detect;
   InitGraph( graphDriver, graphMode, '' );
   SetColor( LightBlue );
   SetTextStyle( FontNumber, 0, 4 );
   IF GraphResult = GrOK
      THEN OutText( 'Font selected' )
      ELSE Writeln( 'Error in SetTextStyle' );
   Readln;
   CloseGraph
END.
```

Halt

Syntax

```
PROCEDURE Halt[( n : Word )];
```

Location

System

Description

Halt immediately ends the program, returning to the Turbo Pascal integrated editor or to DOS if the program was compiled to disk and run from the command line. You may halt a program at any place in its execution.

There are two ways to call **Halt**. The first passes no parameter. The second passes an integer value representing an error code. Zero means no error. Any other value indicates a problem. Batch files can check the **Halt** code through the ERRORLEVEL command. A program can check the **Halt** code of a subprogram (called a child process) through the **DosExitCode Dos** unit variable.

The example demonstrates this second use of **Halt**. First type and compile to disk XHALTB.PAS, creating XHALTB.EXE. Next, type and run XHALT.PAS, either in memory or from disk. XHALT calls XHALTB with an **Exec** statement, running XHALTB as a child process, which ends with a **Halt(3)** statement. The parent program (XHALT) then continues where it stopped, displaying the **Halt** error code held by **DosExitCode**.

Example

XHALTB.PAS

```
{$M 2000,1000,1000}
PROGRAM xHaltB;
BEGIN
   Write( 'Inside HALTB. Press <Enter>...' );
   Readln;
   Halt( 3 );
   Writeln( 'This line is not displayed' )
END.
```


XHALT.PAS

```
{$M 2000,1000,1000}
PROGRAM xHalt;
USES Dos;
BEGIN
```

```
      Writeln( 'Running HALTA' );
      Exec( 'XHALTB.EXE', '' );
      Writeln( 'Back from HALTB' );
      Writeln( 'DOSExitCode=', DOSExitCode )
END.
```

HeapFunc

Syntax

```
{$F+}
FUNCTION HeapFunc( size : Word ) : Integer;
{$F-}
```

Location

Description

HeapFunc is not a function that you can call. It's a design for a function that you create and then tell Turbo Pascal to call when a heap error occurs.

The example explains how **HeapFunc** works. Most important are the {$F + } and {$F – } compiler directives, which tell the compiler this is a *far* routine. If you forget this step, the program is sure to crash and all the king's programmers won't be able to repair the damage to memory.

Inside the custom **HeapFunc**, a simple assignment returns 1 as the function result. Doing this changes the way **New** and **GetMem** operate. Normally, these two procedures cause a runtime error to occur when you try to allocate variables too large to fit in the available memory on the heap. By assigning the address of **HeapFunc** to the **System** unit **HeapError** pointer, though, instead of a runtime error, **New** and **GetMem** now return **NIL** if there isn't enough memory.

Run the example, which creates large arrays on the heap until running out of space. You should see the message, "Out of Memory," proving that **New** returned **NIL**. Now, remove the assignment to **HeapError** and run the program again. This time, you receive a runtime error, halting the program at **New**.

Example

```
PROGRAM xHeapFunc;
USES Crt;
TYPE BigArray = ARRAY[ 1 .. 10000 ] OF Integer;
VAR p : ^BigArray;

{$F+} FUNCTION HeapFunc( size : Word ) : Integer; {$F-}
BEGIN
```

```
      HeapFunc := 1
END; { HeapFunc }

BEGIN
   HeapError := @HeapFunc;
   REPEAT
      IF Keypressed THEN Halt;  { For safety }
      Writeln( 'Memory = ', Memavail );
      New( p );
      IF p = NIL THEN
      BEGIN
         Writeln( 'Out of memory' );
         Halt
      END
   UNTIL False
END.
```

Hi

Syntax

```
FUNCTION Hi( n : <integer> ) : Byte;
```

Location

System

Description

Hi returns the high, or most significant, byte of the **Word** or **Integer** value **n**. The result is always in the range 0 to 255.

Example

```
PROGRAM xHi;
VAR i : Word;
BEGIN
   i := 0;
   WHILE i < MaxInt DO
   BEGIN
      Writeln( 'i=', i:5, '  High byte=', Hi(i):3 );
      i := i + ( MaxInt DIV 10 )
   END { while }
END.
```

HighVideo

Syntax

```
PROCEDURE HighVideo;
```

Location

Crt

Description

HighVideo sets the high intensity bit of a display character. After calling **HighVideo**, characters displayed through **Write** and **Writeln** statements will appear brighter or in different colors than normal. Depending on the display mode in effect, though, **HighVideo** may not change text the way you always expect. For that reason, it's a good idea to test what **HighVideo** does before assuming anything about the results.

The example displays a reference of text in 16 colors before and after calling **HighVideo**. On monochrome monitors, you see different text attributes instead of colors.

Example

```
PROGRAM xHighVideo;
USES Crt;
VAR color : Integer;
BEGIN
   ClrScr;
   Writeln( 'HighVideo Color Text Demonstration' );
   Writeln( '-----------------------------------' );
   FOR color := 0 TO 15 DO
   BEGIN
     NormVideo;
     Write( 'Color=', color:2 );
     TextColor( color );
     Write( '   Normal video    ' );
     HighVideo;
     Writeln( 'High video' )
   END { for }
END.
```

ImageSize

Syntax

```
FUNCTION ImageSize( x1, y1, x2, y2 : Integer ) : Word;
```

Location

Graph

Description

Use **ImageSize** to determine the number of bytes a bit-map image occupies. The image is a rectangle with its upper-left corner at (x1,y1) and its lower-right corner at (x2,y2). **ImageSize** accurately tells you how many bytes it takes for a variable to hold the video buffer bytes that make up the image plus width and height information, regardless of the display mode you are using.

The example shows how to create an array of bytes and reserve **ImageSize** bytes on the heap, assigning a pointer (**image**) to this memory. Before doing this, the program fills the screen with 30,000 randomly colored pixels. **GetImage** then captures the image, which a **FOR** loop displays using the **Sin** function for a three-dimensional effect.

Example

```
PROGRAM xImageSize;
USES Crt, Graph;
CONST x1=100; y1=100; x2=227; y2=163;
TYPE ByteArray = ARRAY[0..0] OF Byte;
     ByteArrayPtr = ^ByteArray;
VAR graphDriver, graphMode : integer;
    xMax, yMax, x, y, i : integer;
    image : ByteArrayPtr;

FUNCTION Radians( angle : Word ) : Real;
BEGIN
   Radians := Abs( angle Mod 360 ) * Pi / 180.0
END; { Radians }

BEGIN
   graphDriver := Detect;
   InitGraph( graphDriver, graphMode, '' );
   xMax := GetMaxX; yMax := GetMaxY;
   Randomize;
   FOR i := 1 TO 30000 DO
      PutPixel( Random(xMax), Random(yMax), Random(MaxColors) );
   GetMem( image, ImageSize( x1, y1, x2, y2 ) );  { Reserve memory }
```

```
       IF image <> NIL THEN
       BEGIN
          GetImage( x1, y1, x2, y2, image^ );  { Copy display image }
          ClearViewPort;
          y := 0;
          FOR x := 0 TO xMax-(x2-x1) DO
          BEGIN
             PutImage( x, 100+Trunc( Sin(Radians(y))*50.0 ),
                       image^, NormalPut );
             y := y + 1
          END { for }
       END; { if }
       REPEAT UNTIL Keypressed;
       CloseGraph
    END.
```

Inc

Syntax

```
PROCEDURE Inc( VAR n : <ordinal> [; count : LongInt ] );
```

Location

System

Description

Inc increments an ordinal variable **n** either by 1 or by an optional **count**. The variable may be any integer, character, Boolean, or enumerated data type. The procedure is equivalent to the expression:

```
n := Succ( n );
```

This expression is inferior because Turbo Pascal generates machine language instructions to directly increment variables passed to **Inc**. The example shows how to use **Inc** to count from one to ten and to display the alphabet.

Example

```
PROGRAM xInc;
VAR n : Integer; ch : Char;
BEGIN
   n := 0;
   WHILE n < 20 DO        { Count to 20 by 2s }
   BEGIN
```

```
    Inc( n, 2 );
    Writeln( n )
  END; { while }
  Writeln;

  ch := 'A';
  WHILE ch <= 'Z' DO     { Display the alphabet }
  BEGIN
    Write( ch );
    Inc( ch )
  END; { while }
  Writeln
END.
```

InitGraph

Syntax

```
PROCEDURE InitGraph( VAR graphDriver : Integer; VAR graphMode : Integer;
  pathToDriver : String );
```

Location

Graph

Description

Call **InitGraph** to initialize the display to any graphics mode. Before calling **Init-Graph**, set **graphDriver** and **graphMode** to the graphics hardware and mode you want to use. See Table 11-2 for a list of possible values. Initializing nonexistent graphics modes can lock the computer, forcing you to reboot. String **pathTo-Driver** is the path name where the Turbo Pascal graphics driver files (those ending in .BGI) are located.

To have the graphics kernel automatically select the best possible graphics mode, set **graphDriver** to the constant, **Detect**.

After calling **InitGraph**, use the **GraphResult** function to check for errors. If **GraphResult** equals **GrOk**, then you can assume the graphics display is initialized and ready for drawing.

The example shows the correct way to use **InitGraph** to initialize a graphics display. If no errors occur, the program displays a few details about the display and draws some colored circles to prove that you can mix graphics and text on the same screen.

Example

```
PROGRAM xInitGraph;
USES Graph;
```

```
VAR graphDriver, graphMode : integer;
    i, xMax, yMax : integer;
BEGIN
   Write( 'Default display.  Press <Enter>...' );
   Readln;
   graphDriver := Detect;
   InitGraph( graphDriver, graphMode, '' );
   IF GraphResult = GrOk THEN
   BEGIN
     xMax := GetMaxX; yMax := GetMaxY;
     Writeln( 'Graphics display' );
     Writeln( '----------------' );
     Writeln( 'Graph driver = ', graphDriver );
     Writeln( 'Graph mode   = ', graphMode );
     Writeln( 'Maximum x coordinate = ', xMax );
     Writeln( 'Maximum y coordinate = ', yMax );
     FOR i := 1 TO 50 DO
     BEGIN
        SetColor( Random(MaxColors) );
        Circle( Random(xMax), Random(yMax), Random(50) )
     END; { for }
     Readln;
     CloseGraph
   END { if }
END.
```

InLine

Syntax

```
InLine( c1/ c2/ c3/ .../ cn : Byte|Word );
```

Location

System

Description

InLine statements inject machine language instructions and data directly into a Pascal program. Because **InLine** is not itself a procedure or function, but rather a special technique for adding machine code to Pascal programs, its syntax is different from most other routines in this chapter.

There are two ways to write an **InLine** statement. The first looks like any other Pascal statement. The second resembles an assembly language macro. The example demonstrates both forms. Procedure **WriteAChar** contains an **InLine** statement with machine language instructions to send a single character to the standard DOS output file, usually the display. In this case, the values inside the **InLine** statement run every time the program calls **WriteAChar**.

Procedure **DirectWrite** shows how to use the second **InLine** form. In this case, the **InLine** statement follows the procedure declaration. In the program's main body, Turbo Pascal inserts the **InLine** bytes in place of **DirectWrite**.

There are several rules to follow when designing machine language code in **InLine** statements. These are:

- Values in the range 0 to 255 cause one byte to be inserted. Values greater than 255 cause two bytes to be inserted.

- Identifiers generate offset values, which are up to you to use properly. In the example, **ch** is replaced by its offset on the stack (because the variable is a parameter and all parameters are stored on the stack). If **ch** were a global variable, then the offset generated would be relative to the data segment in which **ch** is stored.

- To force Turbo Pascal to generate the least significant byte of a two-byte value, preface the value or constant identifier with <. To generate the most significant byte, preface the value with >.

- Remember that variable identifiers are replaced by the offset address of the variable—not their values. In other words, referencing an integer **Num** does not insert the value of **Num** into the program code. It inserts **Num**'s address.

- Because **InLine** routines like **DirectWrite** in the example are macros and not real Pascal procedures or functions, you cannot take their addresses with @ or pass their identifiers to **Addr**, **Ofs**, and **Seg**.

- Notice in the example that the first **InLine** statement references **ch** as a variable on the stack at location **[BP + ch]**. In the second case, the **InLine** statement pops this same variable from the stack. The first case doesn't do this because procedure **WriteAChar** is responsible for removing its local variables from the stack. The second case is not a procedure call, but a macro expansion, and, therefore, **DirectWrite** must itself remove any parameters from the stack.

- Use **InLine** statements only where they make a real difference or where they perform operations impossible or awkward to do in Pascal. It's a good idea to program entirely in Pascal and, after testing the program, convert key routines to assembly language. It's generally not a good idea to program with **InLine** statements from the start. If you are doing that, then why bother using a Pascal compiler?

Example

```
PROGRAM xInLine;
USES Crt;
CONST CR = #13; LF = #10;   { Carriage return & line feed characters }
```

```
    VAR ch : Char;

    PROCEDURE WriteAChar( ch : Char );
    BEGIN
        InLine( $B4/ $02/       { MOV AH, 02    ; DOS output function }
                $8A/ $56/ <ch/   { MOV DL, [BP+ch] ; DL = char   }
                $CD/ $21         { INT 21h        ; Call DOS   }
              )
    END; { WriteAChar }

    PROCEDURE DirectWrite( ch : Char );

        InLine( $B4/ $02/       { MOV AH, 02    ; DOS output function }
                $5A/            { POP DX        ; Pop ch into DL }
                $CD/ $21 );     { INT 21h       ; Call DOS }

BEGIN
    ClrScr;
    WriteAChar( CR ); WriteAChar( LF );
    FOR ch := 'A' TO 'Z' DO
        WriteAChar( ch );

    DirectWrite( CR ); DirectWrite( LF );
    FOR ch := 'A' TO 'Z' DO
        DirectWrite( ch )
END.
```

Insert

Syntax

```
PROCEDURE Insert( source : String; VAR destination : String; index : Byte );
```

Location

System

Description

Insert inserts the **source** string, which may be literal or a variable, into the **destination** string starting at **destination**'s **index** character. If the insertion causes the string to become longer than its maximum declared length, no error results, but characters pushed beyond the end of the string are irretrievably lost.

The procedure is good for adding all sorts of items to strings. For instance, the example contains a function, **Dollars**, which accepts a **Word** value **n** and returns a string formatted with a dollar sign and decimal place.

Example

```
PROGRAM xInsert;
VAR n : Integer;

FUNCTION Dollars( n : Word ) : String;
VAR s : String;
BEGIN
   Str( n:5, s );
   WHILE Length(s) < 3 DO
      Insert( '0', s, 1 );
   Insert( '.', s, Length(s)-1 );
   Dollars := '$' + s
END; { Dollars }

BEGIN
   Randomize;
   FOR n := 1 TO 25 DO
      Writeln( Dollars( Random(MaxInt) ) )
END.
```

InsLine

Syntax

```
PROCEDURE InsLine;
```

Location

Crt

Description

InsLine inserts a blank line at the cursor's position in the current text display window, causing any lines below to move down one line and pushing the bottom line irretrievably off the display. After a line is inserted, the cursor position does not change. The example uses **InsLine** to simulate someone inserting text with a word processor.

Example

```
PROGRAM xInsLine;
USES Crt;
```

```
         VAR i : Integer;
         BEGIN
            ClrScr;
            GotoXY( 1, 1 );
            Writeln( 'Blasting Turbo Rascal' );
            Writeln( 'by Tom Duck' );

            GotoXY( 1, 2 );
            FOR i := 1 TO 8 DO BEGIN
               Delay(500);
               InsLine
            END; { for }

            GotoXY( 1, 2 );
            Writeln( 'Second edition' );
            Writeln( 'for version 4.0' );

            GotoXY( 1, 4 );
            FOR i := 1 TO 6 DO BEGIN
               Delay(500);
               DelLine
            END
         END.
```

InstallUserDriver

Syntax

```
FUNCTION InstallUserDriver( name : String;
   autoDetectPtr : Pointer ) : Integer;
```

Location

Graph

Description

Call **InstallUserDriver** to load a custom graphics driver, which you may have
received from the manufacturer of a graphics card that supports special modes,
possibly in addition to the usual CGA, EGA, and VGA displays. Suppose this
driver is named 3DG.BGI. To force the **Graph** unit to use the driver, execute the
commands:

```
graphDriver := InstallUserDriver( '3DG.BGI', Nil );
IF graphDriver = GrError THEN Halt;
```

```
InitGraph( graphDriver, graphMode, '' );
IF GraphResult = GrOk THEN
BEGIN
   { insert graphics commands here }
   CloseGraph
END; { if }
```

When used this way, **InstallUserDriver** takes two parameters: the name of the driver and a **Nil** pointer, which defeats an optional auto-detection scheme. **InstallUserDriver** returns an **Integer** value. If this value equals **GrError,** then the BGI device table is full and the program should halt. Unless you are loading several custom drivers simultaneously, you'll rarely see this error. If the program doesn't detect an error, it can then pass the **InstallUserDriver** result to **Init-Graph,** which calls low-level routines in the new driver to initialize graphics. If **GraphResult** equals **GrOk** after this step, all **Graph** unit commands use the new driver's low-level graphics routines.

More advanced graphics drivers and video hardware allow **InitGraph** to detect their presence automatically. To enable this feature, you need to write a detection function, similar to **Detect3DG** in the example. The function must be *far* — compiled with {$F + } in effect—and it should return **GrError** if it fails to detect the custom driver or hardware; otherwise, the function should return a mode number representing the default graphics configuration. (The example function is a dummy that always returns an error.)

Next, call **InstallUserDriver** as the example demonstrates, passing the address of the custom detection function as the second parameter (@**Detect3DG**). This causes the **Graph** unit to link **Detect3DG** into the built-in detection logic for common modes such as CGA, EGA, and VGA displays. If **InstallUserDriver** does not return **GrError,** then pass the constant **Detect** to **InitGraph** as most graphics programs normally do. **InitGraph** then calls **Detect3DG.** If the custom function returns a positive value or 0, **InitGraph** loads and initializes the custom driver. If the custom function returns **GrError** (as it always does in the example), then **InitGraph** proceeds with its normal auto-detection duties. This process lets you write graphics programs that work with custom hardware or software drivers, but still work correctly on more common systems.

Note that **InitGraph** calls the auto-detection **Detect3DG** function, even though you pass the function address to **InstallUserDriver.**

Example

```
PROGRAM xInstallUserDriver;
USES Graph;
VAR userDriver, graphDriver, graphMode : Integer;
    xMax, yMax : Integer;

{$F+}
FUNCTION Detect3DG : Integer;
CONST
```

```
      DriverFound = False; { Dummy value }
      DefaultMode = 3;     { Default }
   BEGIN
      IF DriverFound
         THEN Detect3DG := DefaultMode
         ELSE Detect3DG := GrError
   END; { Detect3DG }
   {$F-}


   BEGIN
      userDriver := InstallUserDriver( '3DG.BGI', @Detect3DG );
      IF userDriver = GrError THEN
      BEGIN
         Writeln( 'Graphics-driver table is full' );
         Halt( 1 )
      END; { if }

   {----- Method #1 disabled, (pass userDriver to InitGraph): }
   (* graphDriver := userDriver; *)

   {----- Method #2 enabled, (let InitGraph auto-detect driver): }
      graphDriver := Detect;

      InitGraph( graphDriver, graphMode, '' );  { Calls Detect3DG! }
      IF GraphResult <> grOk
       THEN
         Writeln( 'Error initializing graphics' )
       ELSE
         BEGIN
            xMax := GetMaxX; yMax := GetMaxY;
            Ellipse( xMax DIV 2, yMax DIV 2, 0, 360, xMax DIV 6, 50 );
            Readln;
            CloseGraph
         END { else }
   END.
```

InstallUserFont

Syntax

```
FUNCTION InstallUserFont( fontFileName : String ) : Integer;
```

Location

Graph

Description

The BGI **Graph** unit comes with several standard fonts. **InstallUserFont** loads other font files, perhaps purchased from a software company or supplied with a special video card. The example shows the correct way to use the function. Pass the name of the font disk file to **InstallUserFont**, which returns a number that you can later pass to **SetTextStyle**. Calling **GraphResult** after **InstallUserFont** does not detect font-loading errors. Instead, examine **GraphResult** after calling **SetTextStyle** with the font number returned by **InstallUserFont**. If an error occurs at this time, you can select a different font as the example demonstrates.

Example

```
PROGRAM xInstallUserFont;
USES Crt, Graph;
VAR userFont, graphDriver, graphMode : Integer;
    x, y, size : Integer;
    sizeStr : String[2];
BEGIN
    userFont := InstallUserFont( '3DG.CHR' );
    graphDriver := Detect;
    InitGraph( graphDriver, graphMode, '' );
    IF GraphResult <> grOk
      THEN
        Writeln( 'Error initializing graphics' )
      ELSE
        BEGIN
          SetTextStyle( userFont, HorizDir, 2 );
          IF GraphResult <> GrOk
            THEN userFont := SansSerifFont;
          x := 0; y := 0;
          FOR size := 1 TO 7 DO
          BEGIN
            SetTextStyle( userFont, HorizDir, size );
            y := 4 + y + TextHeight( 'M' );
            Str( size, sizeStr );
            OutTextXY( x, y, 'Testing font size=' + sizeStr )
          END; { for }
          REPEAT UNTIL Keypressed;
          CloseGraph
        END { else }
END.
```

Int

Syntax

```
FUNCTION Int( r : <real> ) : <real>;
```

Location

System

Description

Int returns the integer part of real number **r**, equal to the value of **r** minus its fractional part. For example, **Int**(3.141) = 3.0 and **Int**(65538.2) = 65538.0.

Despite its name, the function returns a real number, not an integer. The example shows this clearly, displaying:

```
Pi= 3.1415926536E+00    Int(pi)= 3.0000000000E+00
```

Example

```
PROGRAM xInt;
BEGIN
   Writeln( 'Pi=', pi, '    Int(pi)=', int(pi) )
END.
```

Intr

Syntax

```
PROCEDURE Intr( intNo : Byte; VAR regs : Registers );
```

Location

Dos

Description

Intr calls the software interrupt specified by **intNo**, passing the register values in record **regs**.

The example shows how to use **Intr** to change the cursor from its usual underline shape to a fat block. Consult a DOS or PC technical reference for a list of interrupt numbers and their meanings.

Example

```
PROGRAM xIntr;
USES Dos;
VAR reg : Registers;
BEGIN
   WITH reg DO
   BEGIN
      ah := 1;      { Set cursor type }
      ch := 0;
      cl := 7
   END; { with }
   Intr( $10, reg )
END.
```

IoResult

Syntax

```
FUNCTION IoResult : Word;
```

Location

System

Description

IoResult returns the input/output (I/O) error code result if I/O error checking is turned off with the compiler option {$I – }. **IoResult** has the intended side effect of resetting Turbo Pascal's internal error code and is valid only on its first use following the I/O operation.

Error codes match those returned by DOS. See a DOS technical reference or your Turbo Pascal Manual for a list of error codes and their meanings.

The example lists a handy function, **FileExists**, that uses **IoResult** to test whether a certain file exists on disk. Press Enter to end the program.

Example

```
PROGRAM xIoResult;
VAR fileName : String;

FUNCTION FileExists( fname : String ) : Boolean;
VAR f : FILE;
BEGIN
   Assign( f, fname );
   {$I-} Reset( f ); {$I+}
   FileExists := ( Ioresult = 0 )
```

```
    END; { FileExists }

BEGIN
   Writeln( 'File check' );
   REPEAT
      Write( 'Name? ' );
      Readln( fileName );
      IF Length( fileName ) > 0 THEN
      IF FileExists( fileName )
         THEN Writeln( 'file exists' )
         ELSE Writeln( 'file does not exist' )
   UNTIL Length( fileName ) = 0
END.
```

Keep

Syntax

```
PROCEDURE Keep( exitCode : Word );
```

Location

Dos

Description

Keep causes a program or child process to terminate and stay resident (TSR) in memory. The *entire* program stays, including all memory allocated to it; therefore, be sure to use the {$M} directive to reduce reserved memory to the absolute minimum before **Keep**.

The example shows how to use **Keep** to install an interrupt in memory. Procedure **Crawl** is a simple routine that counts up to 30,000 before ending. By attaching this routine to interrupt vector $1C, the PC ROM BIOS timer calls the new routine once for every hardware timer tick—about 18.2 times per second. This slows the computer to a crawl!

Compile the example to a disk code file KEEP.EXE. *Do not run this program from inside the integrated Turbo Pascal editor!* Quit Turbo Pascal and type KEEP to install the program in memory. Try executing commands such as DIR and TYPE, which now run as fast as ants stuck in honey.

You might use the example to debug programs that run too fast, slowing actions to a crawl. Reboot to restore your computer to full speed.

Example

```
{ !!!!!!!!!!!!!!!!!!!!!!!!!!!!!!!!!!!!!!!!!!!!!!!!!!!!!!!!!!!!!!!!!!!!
  WARNING: This program stays resident until you reboot. Do not
```

```
run more than once without rebooting. DO NOT RUN FROM INSIDE
INTEGRATED TURBO PASCAL EDITOR.
!!!!!!!!!!!!!!!!!!!!!!!!!!!!!!!!!!!!!!!!!!!!!!!!!!!!!!!!!!!!!!! }
```

```
{$M 1024, 0, 0}    { Use minimum amount of memory }
{$N-,S-}           { No coprocessor, no stack overflow checking }
PROGRAM xKeep;
USES Dos;

PROCEDURE Crawl( Flags,CS,IP,AX,BX,CX,DX,SI,DI,DS,ES,BP : Word );
INTERRUPT;
VAR k : Word;
BEGIN
   FOR k := 1 TO 30000 DO {wait}
END; { Crawl }

BEGIN
   SetIntVec( $1C, @Crawl );  { Install timer interrupt }
   Keep( 0 )  { Terminate, stay resident }
END.
```

Keypressed

Syntax

```
FUNCTION Keypressed : Boolean;
```

Location

Crt

Description

Keypressed returns true if a character is waiting to be read from the keyboard.

The most common use for **Keypressed** is to read a character only *after* someone types something. This allows the program to continue if no characters are waiting. One example where this technique might be useful is in a game where certain keys move figures on screen. With **Keypressed**, the game action continues until a key is pressed. You might find the following statements inside the program:

```
IF Keypressed THEN
   CASE ReadKey OF
      'U' : Up;
      'D' : Down
   END { case }
```

Another use for **Keypressed** is to clear the keyboard input buffer. This buffer fills with characters that you type while other program events are occurring. The example shows how to empty the buffer by calling **Readkey** while **Keypressed** returns true. By doing this, you can force people to give programs instructions at critical points, preventing them from answering Yes to questions they haven't yet seen.

Example

```
PROGRAM xKeypressed;
USES Crt;
VAR i : Integer;

PROCEDURE Pause;
VAR ch : Char;
BEGIN
   Write( 'Press Space to continue...' );
   WHILE Keypressed DO      { Throw away buffered typing }
      ch := ReadKey;
   REPEAT
      IF Keypressed THEN
         IF ReadKey = CHR(32)  { Wait for Space character }
            THEN Exit
   UNTIL false
END; { Pause }

BEGIN
   FOR i := 1 TO 50 DO
   BEGIN
      Delay(50);
      Writeln( 'Start typing now' );
   END; { for }
   Writeln;
   Pause;
   Writeln( 'Ending program' )
END.
```

Length

Syntax

```
FUNCTION Length( s : <string> ) : Integer;
```

Location

System

Description

Length returns the length of string **s**, which may be variable, literal, or constant. The length of the string is equal to the number of characters it contains, not the declared string length. A zero-length string is called a *null string*.

The example shows how to use **Length** to center text on display. You can use **Center** in your own programs to center messages, program titles, and so on.

Example

```
PROGRAM xLength;
USES Crt;

PROCEDURE Center( s : String );
BEGIN
   Writeln( s : 40 + (Length(s) DIV 2) )
END; { Center }

BEGIN
   ClrScr;  Center( 'Welcome to' );
   Writeln; Center( '** Monster Spreadsheet **' );
   Writeln; Center( '"The program that ate Wallstreet"' );
   Writeln; Center( 'written by ByteMan' );
   GotoXY( 1, 25 );
   Readln
END.
```

Line

Syntax

```
PROCEDURE Line( x1, y1, x2, y2 : Integer );
```

Location

Graph

Description

Use **Line** to draw lines of various styles and colors, connecting the two coordinates (x1,y1) and (x2,y2). Call **SetColor** before **Line** to change the line's color. Use **SetLineStyle** to change the thickness and style of the line.

Example

```
PROGRAM xLine;
USES Crt, Graph;
```

```
        VAR graphDriver, graphMode : Integer;
            xMin, yMin, xMax, yMax : Integer;
        BEGIN
            graphDriver := Detect;
            InitGraph( graphDriver, graphMode, '' );
            xMax := GetMaxX;
            yMax := GetMaxY;
            xMin := 0;
            yMin := 0;
            WHILE ( xMin < xMax ) OR ( yMin < yMax ) DO
            BEGIN
                Delay(50);
                SetColor( Random(MaxColors) );
                Line( xMin, yMin, xMax, yMin );
                Line( xMin, yMax, xMax, yMax );
                Inc( xMin ); Inc( yMin );
                Dec( xMax ); Dec( yMax )
            END; { while }
            REPEAT UNTIL Keypressed;
            CloseGraph
        END.
```

LineRel

Syntax

```
PROCEDURE LineRel( dx, dy : Integer );
```

Location

Graph

Description

Call **LineRel** (Line Relative) to draw a line from the current coordinate (x,y) to (x + dx, y + dy). Because **LineRel** takes only two parameters, it is faster than **Line**, which takes four. Use **LineRel** to write programs that draw figures the same way at any starting location.

The example displays a series of boxes in various colors for an animated display. The four calls to **LineRel** draw boxes with only two variables, **xMax** and **xMin**.

Example

```
PROGRAM xLineRel;
USES Crt, Graph;
```

```
VAR graphDriver, graphMode : Integer;
    xMax, yMax : Integer; color : Word;
BEGIN
   graphDriver := Detect;
   InitGraph( graphDriver, graphMode, '' );
   Randomize;
   WHILE NOT Keypressed DO
   BEGIN
      xMax := GetMaxX; yMax := GetMaxY;
      MoveTo( 0, 0 );
      color := 1 + Random( MaxColors );
      WHILE xMax > 1 DO
      BEGIN
         SetColor( Random( color ) );
         LineRel( xMax, 0 );
         LineRel( 0, yMax );
         LineRel( -xMax, 0 );
         LineRel( 0, -yMax );
         Dec( xMax, 2 ); Dec( yMax, 2 );
         MoveTo( Succ( GetX ), Succ( GetY ) )
      END { while }
   END; { while }
   CloseGraph
END.
```

LineTo

Syntax

```
PROCEDURE LineTo( x, y : Integer );
```

Location

Graph

Description

Use **LineTo** to draw lines starting from the current coordinate to (x,y). After **LineTo**, the current coordinate changes to (x,y); therefore, you can use this procedure to draw continuing lines where each starting point is the end point of the last. Use **MoveTo** to preset the current coordinate before drawing with **LineTo**.

The example draws lines at random in a recursive procedure **Lines** that also erases each line it draws in a pulsating pattern. Reduce **TimeDelay** to speed up the action and change **MaxLines** to draw different numbers of lines.

Example

```
PROGRAM xLineTo;
USES Crt, Graph;
CONST MaxLines = 125;  TimeDelay = 50;
VAR graphDriver, graphMode : Integer;
    xMax, yMax : Integer;

PROCEDURE Lines( n : Integer );
VAR x1, y1, x2, y2 : Integer;
BEGIN
   Delay( TimeDelay );
   IF n < MaxLines THEN
   BEGIN
      x1 := GetX; y1 := GetY;
      SetColor( 1 + Random( MaxColors ) );
      x2 := Random( xMax ); y2 := Random( yMax );
      LineTo( x2, y2 );
      Lines( n + 1 )
   END; { if }
   Delay( TimeDelay );
   SetColor( Black );
   Line( x1, y1, x2, y2 )    { Erase }
END; { Lines }

BEGIN
   graphDriver := Detect;
   InitGraph( graphDriver, graphMode, '' );
   xMax := GetMaxX; yMax := GetMaxY;
   WHILE NOT Keypressed DO
      Lines( 1 );
   CloseGraph
END.
```

Ln

Syntax

```
FUNCTION Ln( r : <real> ) : <real>;
```

Location

System

Description

Ln returns the natural logarithm of real number **r**. $Ln(r) = \log_e r$ where base $e = 2.7182818285$. If **r** is zero or negative, a runtime error 207 (Invalid floating point operation) is generated, halting the program.

Example

```
PROGRAM xLn;
VAR r : Real;
BEGIN
   Writeln( 'Ln demonstration' );
   Writeln( 'Type 0 to quit' );
   Writeln;
   REPEAT
     Write( 'Value? ' );
     Readln( r );
     IF r > 0.0
        THEN Writeln( 'Ln = ', ln(r) )
   UNTIL r <= 0.0
END.
```

Lo

Syntax

```
FUNCTION Lo( i : <integer> ) : Byte;
```

Location

System

Description

Lo returns the low, or least significant, byte of the **Word** or **Integer** value **i**. The result is always in the range 0 to 255.

Example

```
PROGRAM xLo;
VAR n : Integer;
BEGIN
   n := 1;
   WHILE n > 0 DO
   BEGIN
     n := n SHL 1;
     Writeln( 'n=', n:6,
```

```
                    '  high byte=', hi(n):6,
                    '  low byte=', lo(n):6 );
          END
     END.
```

LowVideo

Syntax

```
PROCEDURE LowVideo
```

Location

Crt

Description

LowVideo clears the high-intensity bit of a display character. After calling **LowVideo**, characters displayed through **Write** and **Writeln** statements appear dimmer or in different colors than after calling **HighVideo**. **LowVideo** clears the high-intensity bit of character bytes stored in the video display buffer.

Depending on the display mode in effect, though, **LowVideo** may not change text the way you always expect. For that reason, it's a good idea to test what **LowVideo** does before assuming anything about the results.

The example displays a reference of text in 16 colors before and after calling **LowVideo**. On monochrome monitors, you see different text attributes instead of colors.

Example

```
PROGRAM xLowVideo;
USES Crt;
VAR color : Integer;
BEGIN
   ClrScr;
   Writeln( 'LowVideo Color Text Demonstration' );
   Writeln( '----------------------------------' );
   FOR color := 0 TO 15 DO
   BEGIN
      HighVideo;
      Write( 'Color=', color:2 );
      TextColor( color );
      Write( '   High video   ' );
      LowVideo;
      Writeln( 'Low video' )
   END { for }
END.
```

Mark

Syntax

```
PROCEDURE Mark( VAR p : Pointer );
```

Location

System

Description

Mark records the current address of the Pascal heap top, setting **p** equal to that value. After calling **Mark**, you can restore the heap to its original size by passing **p** to **Release**. Although **p** may be any pointer variable, it is usually an untyped **Pointer** variable.

The example displays the amount of available memory before calling **New** to allocate space for an array of real numbers on the heap. After filling and displaying the array's contents, the program calls **Release** with the pointer (**heap**) initialized by **Mark**. As you can see when you run the program, this reclaims the memory the array previously occupied.

Example

```
PROGRAM xMark;
TYPE Items = ARRAY[1..100] OF Real;
VAR heap : Pointer; i : Integer;
    a : ^Items;
BEGIN

   Mark( heap );

   Writeln( 'Memory before new    = ', Memavail );
   New( a );
   Writeln( 'Memory after new     = ', Memavail );
   FOR i := 1 TO 100 DO
      a^[i] := Random;
   FOR i := 1 TO 100 DO
      Write( a^[i]:10 );

   Writeln;
   Release( heap );
   Writeln( 'Memory after release = ', Memavail )

END.
```

MaxAvail

Syntax

```
FUNCTION MaxAvail : LongInt:
```

Location

System

Description

MaxAvail returns the maximum undivided amount of memory available on the heap. This is equal to either the total amount of heap space available or the size of the largest disposed dynamic variable, whichever is greater.

If **MaxAvail** is less than the size of the variable you want to place on the heap, there is little to do but end the program with an out-of-memory error.

The example reserves 65,535-byte blocks on the heap while **MaxAvail** reports at least that much memory available. The program reports the size of the largest available memory space before and after reserving blocks, and after releasing one block by calling **FreeMem**.

Example

```
PROGRAM xMaxAvail;
VAR p : Pointer;
BEGIN
   Writeln( 'Before GetMem, MaxAvail=', MaxAvail );
   WHILE MaxAvail > 65535 DO
      GetMem( p, 65535 );
   Writeln( 'After GetMem,  MaxAvail=', MaxAvail );
   FreeMem( p, 65535 );
   Writeln( 'After FreeMem, MaxAvail=', MaxAvail )
END.
```

MemAvail

Syntax

```
FUNCTION MemAvail : LongInt;
```

Location

System

Description

MemAvail returns the number of free bytes available on the heap. Because of fragmented free spaces between objects on the heap, this may be greater than the amount of free space available for individual variables. (See also **MaxAvail**.)

Example

```
PROGRAM xMemAvail;
BEGIN
   Write( 'There are ', MemAvail );
   Writeln( ' bytes available on the heap' );
END.
```

MkDir

Syntax

```
PROCEDURE MkDir( path : <string> );
```

Location

System

Description

MkDir creates a new subdirectory of the name specified by the **path** string. This is similar to the DOS MKDIR (MD) command. If I/O error checking is off with the {$i–} compiler directive, you can check **IoResult** after **MkDir** to determine the success or failure of creating the subdirectory.

Example

```
PROGRAM xMkDir;
VAR path : String;
BEGIN
   Write( 'Create what directory? ' );
   Readln( path );
   IF Length( path ) > 0 THEN
   BEGIN
      {$i-} MkDir( path ); {$i+}
      IF IoResult = 0
         THEN Writeln( path, ' created' )
         ELSE Writeln( 'Error creating directory' )
   END { if }
END.
```

Move

Syntax

```
PROCEDURE Move( VAR source, destination : <type>|<file>; n : Word );
```

Location

System

Description

Move transfers **n** bytes of **source** to **destination** using fast memory move instructions. The source and destination variables may be different or the same types. They may also be the same variable—a large array, for example, in which you want to shift data from one part of the array to another.

Index the source or destination arrays to indicate a starting position. If the source and destination are the same variable, then **Move** controls the direction of byte transfers to prevent overlapping bytes.

The example fills an array with characters starting with A, displays the array contents, and then moves the first 50 characters to the last 50. This is similar to the way some word processors might move characters during an insertion.

Example

```
PROGRAM xMove;
VAR ChArray : ARRAY[ 1 .. 100 ] OF Char;
    i : Integer;
BEGIN
   FOR i := 1 TO 100 DO
      ChArray[i] := Chr( Ord('a') + i );
   Writeln( 'Before:' );
   FOR i := 1 TO 100 DO
      Write( ChArray[i] );
   Writeln;

   Move( ChArray[1], ChArray[50], 50 );

   Writeln( 'After:' );
   FOR i := 1 TO 100 DO
      Write( ChArray[i] );
   Writeln;
END.
```

MoveRel

Syntax

```
PROCEDURE MoveRel( dx, dy : Integer );
```

Location

Graph

Description

Calling **MoveRel** changes the current coordinate by a relative amount equal to x + dx and y + dy. The *d* in dx and dy stands for *delta*, a term that typically represents a relative change in something.

As the example shows, **MoveRel** operates invisibly. For an experiment, try replacing **MoveRel** with **LineRel**, which works identically to **MoveRel** but leaves a trail behind while moving.

Example

```
PROGRAM xMoveRel;
USES Crt, Graph;
VAR i, graphDriver, graphMode : Integer;
BEGIN
   graphDriver := Detect;
   InitGraph( graphDriver, graphMode, '' );
   MoveTo( 10, GetMaxY DIV 2 );
   FOR i := 1 TO 36 DO
   BEGIN
      SetColor( 1 + Random( MaxColors ) );
      Circle( GetX, GetY, GetX );
      MoveRel( i, 0 )
   END; { for }
   REPEAT UNTIL Keypressed;
   CloseGraph
END.
```

MoveTo

Syntax

```
PROCEDURE MoveTo( x, y : Integer );
```

Location

Graph

Description

Use **MoveTo** to change the current coordinate to a specific display location, without drawing a line or making any other changes to the display.

MoveTo comes in handy for restoring the current coordinate to a previous setting. The example uses this idea in procedure **Outline**, which draws a white border around the display. By saving the current coordinate in two local variables, **oldx** and **oldy**, the procedure can restore this coordinate after outlining the screen.

Example

```
PROGRAM xMoveTo;
USES Crt, Graph;
VAR graphDriver, graphMode : Integer;
    y, xMax, yMax : Word;

PROCEDURE Outline;
VAR oldx, oldy : Word;
BEGIN
   oldx := GetX; oldy := GetY;
   MoveTo( 0, 0 );
   LineTo( xMax, 0 );
   LineTo( xMax, yMax );
   LineTo( 0, yMax );
   LineTo( 0, 0 );
   MoveTo( oldx, oldy )
END; { Outline }

BEGIN
   graphDriver := Detect;
   InitGraph( graphDriver, graphMode, '' );
   xMax := GetMaxX; yMax := GetMaxY;
   MoveTo( xMax DIV 2, yMax DIV 2 );
   y := yMax DIV 2;
   Outline;
   WHILE NOT Keypressed DO
   BEGIN
      Delay(50);
      SetColor( 1 + Random(MaxColors) );
      LineTo( 1+Random(xMax-2), y (*1+Random(yMax-2)*) );
      y := y + Random(15);
      IF y >= yMax THEN
      BEGIN
         y := 1; MoveTo( GetX, y )
      END
   END; { while }
   CloseGraph
END.
```

MsDos

Syntax

```
PROCEDURE MsDos( VAR regs : Registers );
```

Location

Dos

Description

MsDos calls a standard DOS operating system routine. Variable **regs** is a record
defined in the **Dos** unit (see Chapter 9).

To call a DOS routine, place the routine's number in **regs.ah**, set other fields
for this operation and pass the **regs** record to **MsDos**. When the routine ends, **regs**
fields contain any results returned by DOS.

The example shows how to turn on disk-write verification, causing DOS to
read and check every disk sector after writing to disk. You might want to use this
idea for extra safety in programs that write to disk files. Change al: = 1 to al: = 0 to
turn off verification or use the DOS command, *verify* OFF.

Note: The **Dos** unit in Turbo Pascal 5.0 and later versions contains a
procedure **SetVerify** that can turn disk-write verification on and off.

Example

```
PROGRAM xMsDos;
USES Dos;
VAR regs : Registers;
BEGIN
   Writeln( 'Turn on disk-write verification' );
   WITH regs DO
   BEGIN
     ah := $2E;    { Set Verify Flag }
     al := 1;      { 1=on, 0=off }
     dl := 0       { Required by DOS 1.0, 2.0 only }
   END; { with }

   MsDos( regs )   { Call DOS }

END.
```

New

Syntax

```
PROCEDURE New( VAR p : <typed pointer> );
FUNCTION New( <pointer type> [, c : <constructor>] ) : Pointer;
```

Location

System

Description

New creates a dynamic variable of **p**'s base type and assigns the address of the first byte in the variable to **p**. After **New(p)**, the contents of the variable, represented by **p^**, are uninitialized.

The maximum variable size that each call to **New** can create is 65,521 bytes, even though the heap might contain much more free space. You can use this space by calling **New** more than once.

Unlike some other compilers, Turbo Pascal does not allow allocation of variant record parts by specific tag field values.

Starting with Turbo Pascal 5.5, **New** is extended in two ways (see the second syntax definition). The first extension, which applies to all uses of **New**, allows you to write statements such as:

```
p := New( PType );
```

where **PType** is a pointer type, and **p** is a pointer variable, usually but not necessarily of type **PType**. Using **New** as a function leads to certain dangers. For example, *don't* write expressions such as:

```
IF New( PType ) THEN ...
```

That simply throws away heap space by allocating a variable of type **PType** and then discarding the pointer to that space.

The all new **New** also plays a role in object-oriented programming. Objects are often allocated space in heap memory and usually have constructor procedures to initialize themselves. Because the constructors must be called for every new instance of the object, **New** handles both the allocation and initialization steps in one easy motion.

If **oPtr** is a pointer to an object named **OType**, which has a constructor named **OInit** that takes two integer parameters, you can initialize and allocate space for the object with:

```
oPtr := New( OType, OInit( 123, 456 ) );
```

See Chapter 15 for more information on object-oriented programming concepts. The example shows the more traditional way to call **New**.

Example

```
PROGRAM xNew;
TYPE realArray = ARRAY[1..100] OF Real;
VAR p : ^realArray; i : Integer;
BEGIN
   Writeln( 'Creating array of real numbers on the heap' );

   New( p );  { Reserve space for the array, assigning the
                array's address to p. }

   FOR i := 1 TO 100 DO    { Assign random values to array }
      p^[i] := Random;

   FOR i := 1 TO 100 DO    { Display values }
      Write( p^[i]:10 );


   Writeln

END.
```

NormVideo

Syntax

```
PROCEDURE NormVideo;
```

Location

Crt

Description

NormVideo restores text displays to the background and foreground colors originally set when the program started running. Use **NormVideo**, **HighVideo**, and **LowVideo** along with **TextColor** and **TextBackground** to display characters in various colors and attributes. Be aware that different monitors and video cards respond differently to the same settings.

The example displays a table of all possible color combinations, in **LowVideo** and **HighVideo**. Notice how **NormVideo** makes it easy to insert blanks between each combination in the displayed table. You can use the table to select character attributes when designing screens.

Example

```
PROGRAM xNormVideo;
USES Crt;
CONST Blank=' ';  { Single blank space }
VAR i, bColor, fColor : Integer;
BEGIN
   ClrScr;
   Writeln(
      'Text Attributes  Columns=TextColor, Rows=TextBackground' );
   Writeln(
      'First character=LowVideo, second character=HighVideo' );
   Writeln(
      '--------------------------------------------------------' );
   Writeln; Writeln; Write( Blank );
   FOR i := 0 TO 15 DO Write( i:4 );

   FOR bColor := 0 TO 15 DO
   BEGIN
      Writeln;
      Write( bColor:2 );
      FOR fColor := 0 TO 15 DO
      BEGIN
         NormVideo;
         Write( Blank );
         TextColor( fColor );
         TextBackground( bColor );
         LowVideo;
         Write( Blank, 'A' );
         HighVideo;
         Write( 'A' )
      END; { for }
      NormVideo
   END; { for }
END.
```

NoSound

Syntax

```
PROCEDURE NoSound;
```

Location

Crt

Description

NoSound stops the tone started by procedure **Sound**. Because sound continues after calling **Sound**, you must call **NoSound** or the tone will continue—even after the program ends!

The example shows how to design your own bell procedure, which many programmers prefer over using the standard **Write(Chr(7))** beep. The delays determine the length and separation of each tone. Try removing **NoSound** and running the program. Then run the original program to turn off the noise.

Example

```
PROGRAM xNoSound;
USES Crt;
VAR i : Integer;
BEGIN
   ClrScr;
   FOR i := 1 TO 10 DO
   BEGIN
      Delay(150);
      Write( #14:4 );
      Sound(2000);
      Delay(150);
      NoSound
   END
END.
```

Odd

Syntax

```
FUNCTION Odd( n : <integer> ) : Boolean;
```

Location

System

Description

Odd returns true if integer **n** is an odd number. You can also use **Odd** to test the least significant bit (lsb) of **n** in binary. If **Odd(n)** is true, then lsb = 1, else lsb = 0.

The example shows another way to put this useful function to work. The expression:

```
IF Odd( Random( MaxInt ) )
   THEN A
   ELSE B;
```

executes both A and B about 50% of the time. You might use this idea in a game or a simulation to make 50/50 decisions, as in the example, which flips an imaginary coin, counting the number of heads and tails.

Example

```
PROGRAM xOdd;
USES Crt;
VAR done : Boolean; heads, tails : LongInt;
BEGIN
   Writeln( 'Heads I Win, Tails You Lose' );
   Writeln;
   Writeln( 'Flipping a coin.' );
   Write(' Press <Enter> to stop...' );
   heads := 0; tails := 0; done := FALSE;
   REPEAT
      IF Odd( Random(MaxInt) )
         THEN heads := heads + 1
         ELSE tails := tails + 1;
      IF Keypressed THEN
         done := ( Readkey = Chr(13) )
   UNTIL done;
   Writeln;
   Writeln( 'Heads = ', heads );
   Writeln( 'Tails = ', tails )
END.
```

Ofs

Syntax

```
FUNCTION Ofs( v : <ident> ) : Word;
```

Location

System

Description

Ofs returns the 16-bit offset address where **v** is located. Usually, **v** is a variable, but it can also be a procedure or function identifier.

Finding the offset address of pointer variables requires care. **Ofs(p)** returns the address of the pointer variable itself—in other words, the address where the pointer is stored in memory. **Ofs(p^)** returns the address of the variable addressed by the pointer. Using the wrong form can produce very hard-to-find bugs.

The example displays the offset address of both a pointer variable (**p2**) and the number the pointer addresses. The other pointers are not used.

Example

```
PROGRAM xOfs;
VAR p1, p2, p3 : ^Real;
BEGIN
   New( p1 ); New( p2 ); New( p3 );
   p2^ := Pi;
   Writeln( 'Offset address of p2  = ', ofs(p2) );
   Writeln( 'Offset address of p2^ = ', ofs(p2^) );
END.
```

Ord

Syntax

```
FUNCTION Ord( v : <ordinal> ) : LongInt;
```

Location

System

Description

Ord returns the ordinal number representing the order of **v** in a set of scalar values. With an enumerated data type, **Ord** returns the order of elements as originally declared. If Color = (Red,White,Blue), then Ord(Red) = 0, Ord(White) = 1, and Ord(Blue) = 2.

The ordinal number of a character **c** equals the ASCII value of that character. For example, **Ord('A') = 65** and **Ord('B') = 66**.

The example shows how to use **Ord** to convert character digits '0' to '9' to equivalent decimal values. Type any character to see the ASCII value. Type a digit key to see the ASCII and decimal values, returned by function **ValCh**, which uses **Ord** to convert ASCII digit characters to decimal equivalents. The **REPEAT** loop also uses **Ord** to end when character **ch** equals 27, the ASCII value for the Esc key.

Example

```
PROGRAM xOrd;
USES Crt;
CONST ASCIIEsc = 27;  { ASCII value for Esc key }
VAR ch : Char;
```

```
FUNCTION ValCh( ch : Char ) : Byte;
BEGIN
   ValCh := Ord( ch ) - Ord( '0' )
END; { ValCh }

BEGIN
   REPEAT
     Writeln;
     Write( 'Type 0..9 or Esc to quit: ' ); ch := ReadKey;
     Writeln;
     Writeln( 'The character you typed is : ', ch );
     Writeln( 'Its ASCII value is        : ', Ord(ch) );
     IF ch in [ '0' .. '9' ] THEN
     Writeln( 'Its value in decimal is    : ', ValCh(ch) );
   UNTIL Ord(ch) = ASCIIEsc
END.
```

OutText

Syntax

```
PROCEDURE OutText( textString : String );
```

Location

Graph

Description

Use **OutText** to display text on graphics displays in the current font, direction, and size set by **SetTextStyle** and in the justification set by **SetTextJustify**.

You can pass literal or variable strings to **OutText**. On screen, the text appears at the current coordinate, which you can change by calling **MoveTo**.

Example

```
PROGRAM xOutText;
USES Crt, Graph;
VAR graphDriver, graphMode : integer;
    charSize, y : Word;
BEGIN
   graphDriver := Detect;
   InitGraph( graphDriver, graphMode, '' );
   y := 0; Randomize;
   FOR charSize := 1 TO 8 DO
   BEGIN
     SetColor( 1+Random(MaxColors) );
```

```
      MoveTo( 0, y );
      SetTextStyle( 1, 0, charSize );
      OutText( 'This is a test. ABCDEFG 1234567890' );
      y := y + TextHeight('M') + 1
   END; { while }
   REPEAT UNTIL Keypressed;
   CloseGraph
END.
```

OutTextXY

Syntax

```
PROCEDURE OutTextXY( x, y : Integer; textString : String );
```

Location

Graph

Description

OutTextXY is nearly identical to **OutText** except for the addition of two parameters, **x** and **y**, representing the coordinate where the first character of string **textString** appears. The two statements:

```
MoveTo( x, y );
OutText( s );
```

are equivalent to:

```
OutTextXY( x, y, s );
```

One difference, however, is that after **OutText**, CP (current point) changes to the end of the string. After **OutTextXY**, CP remains unchanged.

Example

```
PROGRAM xOutTextXY;
USES Crt, Graph;
VAR graphDriver, graphMode : integer;
    charSize, y : Word;
BEGIN
   graphDriver := Detect;
   InitGraph( graphDriver, graphMode, '' );
   y := 0; Randomize;
   FOR charSize := 3 TO 9 DO
```

```
   BEGIN
      SetColor( 1+Random(MaxColors) );
      SetTextStyle( 2, 0, charSize );
      OutTextXY( 0, y, 'This is a test. ABCDEFG 1234567890' );
      y := y + TextHeight('M') + 1
   END; { while }
   REPEAT UNTIL Keypressed;
   CloseGraph
END.
```

OvrClearBuf

Syntax

```
PROCEDURE OvrClearBuf;
```

Location

Overlay

Description

After calling **OvrClearBuf** to clear all overlays from the overlay buffer, the next call to a procedure or function in an overlay unit will load the unit from disk or from EMS RAM.

In most programs, there's rarely any good reason to call **OvrClearBuf**. For debugging custom overlay-loader routines (see **OvrReadFunc**), you can call **Ovr-ClearBuf** to force disk reads (or EMS RAM transfers) on the next call to an overlay routine.

If you need extra memory (especially if the overlay buffer is large), you can call **OvrClearBuf** and then use the buffer memory for other purposes—that is, between calls to routines in overlay units. The overlay buffer is located at **OvrHeapOrg:0000** up to but not including the byte at **OvrHeapEnd:0000**, which is also the base of the heap.

The example configures the **Dos** unit as an overlay (the only standard Turbo Pascal unit for which this is possible) and then calls two routines in the unit, **GetDate** before clearing the buffer and **DosVersion** after. Because this example is so small, you might not see any disk activity.

Example

```
{$O+,F+}    { Use overlays, Generate FAR code }
PROGRAM xOvrClearBuf;
USES Overlay, Crt, Dos;
{$O Dos}
VAR version, year, month, day, weekday : Word;
```

```
BEGIN
   OvrInit( 'XOVRCLEA.OVR' );
   IF OvrResult <> OvrOk THEN Halt;
   GetDate( year, month, day, weekday );
   Writeln( 'Today''s date is: ', day, '-', month, '-', year );
   Write( 'Press Enter to load Dos overlay...' );
   Readln;
   OvrClearBuf;              { Empty overlay buffer }
   version := DosVersion;    { Reloads Dos unit overlay into buffer }
   Writeln( 'Dos version is: ', Lo( version ), '.', Hi( version ) );
END.
```

OvrGetBuf

Syntax

```
FUNCTION OvrGetBuf : LongInt;
```

Location

Overlay

Description

OvrGetBuf returns the size in bytes of the current overlay buffer. Call **OvrSetBuf** to increase the buffer size. The default buffer size equals the number of bytes in the largest overlay unit.

The example is in three files: OVERU1.PAS, OVERU2.PAS, and XOVRGETB.PAS. The first two overlay unit files are used by other overlay examples in this chapter. The third file demonstrates how to call **OvrGetBuf** to display the overlay buffer size.

Example

```
(* OVERU1.PAS *)

{$O+,F+}     { Use overlays, Generate FAR code }
UNIT OverU1;
{ Test overlay unit }
INTERFACE
PROCEDURE WriteHi( n : Word );
IMPLEMENTATION
PROCEDURE WriteHi( n : Word );
BEGIN
   Write( Hi( n ) )
END; { WriteHi }
END.
```

```
(* OVERU2.PAS *)

{$O+,F+}     { Use overlays, Generate FAR code }
UNIT OverU2;
{ Test overlay unit }
INTERFACE
PROCEDURE WriteLo( n : Word );
IMPLEMENTATION
PROCEDURE WriteLo( n : Word );
BEGIN
   Write( Lo( n ) )
END; { WriteLo }
END.



(* XOVRGETB.PAS *)

{$O+,F+}     { Use overlays, Generate FAR code }
PROGRAM xOvrGetBuf;
USES Overlay, Dos, OverU1, OverU2;
{$O Dos}
{$O OverU1}
{$O OverU2}
VAR version : Word;
BEGIN
   OvrInit( 'XOVRGETB.OVR' );
   IF OvrResult <> OvrOk THEN Halt;
   { For test purposes only, the next several statements load
     overlay units (4 times) from disk or from EMS RAM. }
   Write( 'DOS version = ' );
   WriteLo( DosVersion );
   Write( '.' );
   WriteHi( DosVersion );
   Writeln;
   Writeln( 'Size of overlay buffer = ', OvrGetBuf, ' bytes' );
END.
```

OvrGetRetry

Syntax

```
FUNCTION OvrGetRetry : LongInt;
```

Location

Overlay

Description

OvrGetRetry returns the size of the probation area, which usually occupies from one third to half of the total overlay buffer size. Units that fall within this area are put "on probation," during which time if any statements call procedures and functions in the unit, the unit is given a "reprieve." When buffer space is needed for another overlay, the overlay loader tries to keep reprieved units in memory. This helps to keep frequently used overlays in the buffer for longer times, thus improving program performance by limiting disk reads.

The example displays the size of the probation area before and after calling **OvrSetRetry**, which changes the probation size. Units **OverU1** and **OverU2** are from **OvrGetBuf**'s example.

Example

```
{$O+,F+}    { Use overlays, Generate FAR code }
PROGRAM xOvrGetRetry;
USES Overlay, Dos, OverU1, OverU2;
{$O Dos}
{$O OverU1}
{$O OverU2}
VAR version : Word;
BEGIN
    OvrInit( 'XOVRGETR.OVR' );
    IF OvrResult <> OvrOk THEN Halt;
    { For test purposes only, the next several statements load
      overlay units (4 times) from disk or from EMS RAM. }
    Writeln( 'Size of overlay buffer = ', OvrGetBuf, ' bytes' );
    Writeln( 'Size of probation area before = ', OvrGetRetry, ' bytes' );
    OvrSetRetry( OvrGetBuf DIV 3 );      { 1/3 total buffer space }
    Write( 'DOS version = ' );
    WriteLo( DosVersion );
    Write( '.' );
    WriteHi( DosVersion );
    Writeln;
    Writeln( 'Size of probation area after  = ', OvrGetRetry, ' bytes' );
END.
```

OvrInit

Syntax

```
PROCEDURE OvrInit( fileName : String );
```

Location

Overlay

Description

All programs that enable overlays must call **OvrInit** before other statements call procedures and functions in overlay units. The **fileName** string should be set to the program's .OVR file name. For example, if the main program text is STARS.PAS, Turbo Pascal saves the main code in STARS.EXE and the overlays in STARS.OVR. To initialize overlays for this program, use the statements:

```
OvrInit( 'STARS.OVR' );
IF OvrResult <> OvrOk THEN
BEGIN
   Writeln( 'Error loading overlays' );
   Halt
END; { if }
```

Usually, it's wise to follow **OvrInit** with a check of the **OvrResult** variable (typed) constant. If this value does not equal **OvrOk**, then the overlay file is missing or damaged and the program must not continue.

Turbo Pascal 5.5 allows you to attach an overlay file to the end of the .EXE file. You can then delete the .OVR file. To do this, compile all units and the main program *without* Turbo Debugger information. Then execute the DOS commands:

```
COPY /B STARS.EXE + STARS.OVR
DEL STARS.OVR
```

Also change the **OvrInit** parameter to load the .EXE instead of the .OVR file:

```
OvrInit( 'STARS.EXE' );
```

The example demonstrates how to call **OvrInit** and check for errors. Compile to XOVRINIT.EXE and run. Then delete the XOVRINIT.OVR file and run a second time to see the error message. Units **OverU1** and **OverU2** are from **OvrGetBuf**'s example.

Example

```
{$O+,F+}    { Use overlays, Generate FAR code }
PROGRAM xOvrInit;
```

```
USES Overlay, Dos, OverU1, OverU2;
{$O Dos}
{$O OverU1}
{$O OverU2}
VAR version : Word;
BEGIN
   OvrInit( 'XOVRINIT.OVR' );
   IF OvrResult <> OvrOk THEN
   BEGIN
      Writeln( 'Overlay error, code ', OvrResult );
      Halt( OvrResult )
   END; { if }
   { For test purposes only, the next several statements load
     overlay units (4 times) from disk or from EMS RAM. }
   Write( 'DOS version = ' );
   WriteLo( DosVersion );
   Write( '.' );
   WriteHi( DosVersion );
   Writeln;
END.
```

OvrInitEMS

Syntax

```
PROCEDURE OvrInitEMS;
```

Location

Overlay

Description

OvrInitEMS detects whether the system has EMS (Expanded Memory System) RAM. If enough EMS RAM is available, **OvrInitEMS** loads the program's .OVR overlay file into that memory. Then, instead of reading overlay units from disk, the overlay loader transfers overlays from EMS RAM to the overlay buffer for execution. Because the entire program remains in RAM, performance increases dramatically.

   OvrInitEMS does not eliminate the need for a main-memory overlay buffer. But, if EMS RAM is available, you may want to use the smallest buffer possible—there's not much of an advantage to increasing the overlay buffer size with **Ovr-SetBuf** if all overlays are stored in EMS RAM. (Transferring overlay units from EMS RAM to the overlay buffer does take *some* time, so for the very best results, you can use both EMS RAM and a large overlay buffer. In most cases, the benefits from such an arrangement will be small.)

Checking for errors after calling **OvrInitEMS** as in the example is optional. If enough EMS RAM is not available to hold overlays, the program uses main memory just as it does if no EMS RAM exists. Units **OverU1** and **OverU2** are from **OvrGetBuf**'s example.

Example

```
{$O+,F+}     { Use overlays, Generate FAR code }
PROGRAM xOvrInitEMS;
USES Overlay, Dos, OverU1, OverU2;
{$O Dos}
{$O OverU1}
{$O OverU2}
VAR version : Word;
BEGIN
   OvrInit( 'XOVREMS.OVR' );
   IF OvrResult <> OvrOk THEN Halt;
   OvrInitEMS;     { Detect and use EMS RAM if available }
   IF OvrResult <> OvrOk THEN
      Writeln( 'EMS error detected, code ', OvrResult );
   { For test purposes only, the next several statements load
     overlay units (4 times) from disk or from EMS RAM. }
   Write( 'DOS version = ' );
   WriteLo( DosVersion );
   Write( '.' );
   WriteHi( DosVersion );
   Writeln;
END.
```

OvrReadFunc

Syntax

```
OvrReadFunc = FUNCTION( ovrSeg : Word ) : Integer;
```

Location

Overlay

Description

OvrReadFunc is a procedure-type function, in other words, a design for a function that you can write, not a real function in the **Overlay** unit. Attaching a custom **OvrReadFunc** function to the **Overlay** unit traps calls to the overlay loader, letting you add new operations just before overlays are loaded from disk or from EMS RAM. The function must be compiled with the {$F + } *far* option.

There are three main reasons for installing an **OverReadFunc** function:

- To prompt for people to insert a diskette containing the overlay file.
- To prevent programs from halting due to disk errors while reading overlays.
- To debug overlays by intercepting overlay-loader calls.

To attach a custom overlay-loader function, create a variable of type **Ovr-ReadFunc** for saving the original overlay-loader address (**stockOvrLoader** in the example). Then, write a custom function with the same format as **Ovr-ReadFunc** (see **OvrDebugger** in the example). Switch on {$F + } to compile this function as a *far* subroutine. The function parameter **ovrSeg** identifies the overlay to be loaded. Pass this value to the original overlay loader with a statement such as:

```
OvrDebugger := stockOvrLoader( ovrSeg );  { Call overlay loader }
```

This calls the stock overlay loader and returns the result code as **OvrDebugger**'s function value. To check for errors during loading, thus preventing a program from halting if the .OVR file can't be found, save the stock overlay loader's result code in a temporary variable and loop until the result is 0:

```
REPEAT
    tempInteger := stockOvrLoader( ovrSeg );
    IF tempInteger <> 0 THEN
    { ... Insert message to check disks, etc. }
UNTIL tempInteger = 0;
```

Only if the **OvrReadFunc** function returns a nonzero value will a runtime error halt the program; therefore, this code prevents accidental interruptions due to overlay problems. (A better example would give people a way to end the program if they can't correct the overlay problem.)

The example is similar to **OvrInit**'s, but displays several overlay values during each call to the overlay loader. This proves that the overlay loader is intercepting the calls to **DosVersion** and to **WriteLo** and **WriteHi** routines in units **OverU1** and **OverU2** from **OvrGetBuf**'s example.

Example

```
{$O+,F+}    { Use overlays, Generate FAR code }
PROGRAM xOvrReadFunc;
USES Overlay, Dos, OverU1, OverU2;
{$O Dos}
{$O OverU1}
{$O OverU2}
```

```
        VAR version : Word;
            stockOvrLoader : OvrReadFunc;

        {$F+}
        FUNCTION OvrDebugger( ovrSeg : Word ) : Integer;
        BEGIN
           Writeln;
           Writeln( '----- OvrDebugger start' );
           Writeln( ' OvrTrapCount = ', OvrTrapCount );
           Writeln( ' OvrLoadCount = ', OvrLoadCount );
           Writeln( ' OvrFileMode  = ', OvrFileMode  );
           Writeln( ' OvrHeapOrg   = ', OvrHeapOrg, ':0000' );
           Writeln( ' OvrHeapPtr   = ', OvrHeapPtr, ':0000' );
           Writeln( ' OvrHeapEnd   = ', OvrHeapEnd, ':0000' );
           Writeln( ' OvrHeapSize  = ', OvrHeapSize, ' paragraphs' );
           Writeln;
           Write( 'Press Enter to load overlay...' );
           Readln;
           OvrDebugger := stockOvrLoader( ovrSeg )   { Call overlay loader }
        END; { OvrDebugger }
        {$F-}

        BEGIN
           OvrInit( 'XOVRREAD.OVR' );
           IF OvrResult <> OvrOk THEN Halt;
           stockOvrLoader := ovrReadBuf;        { Save overlay-loader address }
           ovrReadBuf := OvrDebugger;           { Attach custom function }
           { For test purposes only, the next several statements load
             overlay units (4 times) from disk or from EMS RAM. }
           Write( 'DOS version = ' );
           WriteLo( DosVersion );
           Write( '.' );
           WriteHi( DosVersion );
           Writeln;
        END.
```

OvrSetBuf

Syntax

```
PROCEDURE OvrSetBuf( size : LongInt );
```

Location

Overlay

Description

Call **OvrSetBuf** to increase the size of the overlay buffer. A larger overlay buffer allows the **Overlay** unit to store multiple overlays in memory, thus increasing performance by reducing disk reads. Call **OverSetBuf** as soon as possible after calling **OvrInit** to initialize overlays. When also enabling EMS RAM with **OvrInitEMS**, it's probably not necessary to call **OvrSetBuf**. If overlays are already in memory, there's little advantage to increasing the overlay buffer size.

OvrSetBuf has no effect in two situations: when the **size** value is smaller than the largest overlay unit and after you've executed **New** to create pointer-addressable variables on the heap, from which the overlay unit takes space for the overlay buffer.

The example doubles the default buffer size by passing to **OvrSetBuf** a value equal to twice **OvrGetBuf**, which returns the size of the current buffer. An **IF** statement avoids increasing the buffer size if EMS RAM is available. Units **OverU1** and **OverU2** are from **OvrGetBuf**'s example.

Example

```
{$O+,F+}    { Use overlays, Generate FAR code }
PROGRAM xOvrSetBuf;
USES Overlay, Dos, OverU1, OverU2;
{$O Dos}
{$O OverU1}
{$O OverU2}
VAR version : Word;
BEGIN
   OvrInit( 'XOVRSETB.OVR' );
   IF OvrResult <> OvrOk THEN Halt;
   Writeln( 'Default overlay buffer size = ', OvrGetBuf, ' bytes' );
   OvrInitEMS;    { Detect and use EMS RAM if available }
   IF OvrResult <> OvrOk THEN
   BEGIN
      Writeln( 'EMS RAM not available' );
      OvrSetBuf( OvrGetBuf * 2 );    { Double the buffer size }
      Writeln( 'Overlay buffer size increased to ', OvrGetBuf, ' bytes' )
   END ELSE
      Writeln( 'Overlays loaded into EMS RAM' );
   { For test purposes only, the next several statements load
     overlay units (4 times) from disk or from EMS RAM. }
   Write( 'DOS version = ' );
   WriteLo( DosVersion );
   Write( '.' );
   WriteHi( DosVersion );
   Writeln;
END.
```

OvrSetRetry

Syntax

```
PROCEDURE OvrSetRetry( size : LongInt );
```

Location

Overlay

Description

Use **OvrSetRetry** to designate a portion of the overlay buffer as the "probation" area. Normally, the size of this area is 0, making the **Overlay** unit function as in Turbo Pascal 5.0. Setting the probation area to a positive value enables the "probation-reprieve" overlay memory-management method, introduced in Turbo Pascal 5.5.

This new buffer-management method helps keep frequently used overlay units in memory for longer periods of time. When a unit's code falls within the designated probation area, any calls to routines in the unit cause the entire unit to be given a reprieve the next time more space is needed for another overlay. (See Chapter 13 for a detailed description of how this method works.)

Borland recommends assigning from one third to half of the total buffer size to the probation area. For best results, examine the values of **OvrTrapCount** (the number of intercepted calls to overlays on probation or not in memory) and **Ovr-LoadCount** (the number of times overlays are loaded into memory) while experimenting with different probation sizes. Strive for a setting that causes **OvrTrapCount** to advance more rapidly than **OvrLoadCount**.

Example

See example for **OvrGetRetry**.

PackTime

Syntax

```
PROCEDURE PackTime( VAR t : dateTime; VAR p : LongInt );
```

Location

Dos

Description

Use **PackTime** to convert date and time values in a **DateTime** record into a single

LongInt value **p** in the packed format stored with file entries in disk directories. Use **UnPackTime** to go the other direction, unpacking a **LongInt** value into a **DateTime** record.

The example uses **PackTime** to stuff the current date and time into **LongInt** variable **p**, passed to **SetFTime** to let you update any file to today's date.

Example

```
PROGRAM xPackTime;
USES Dos;
VAR f : File; fname : String; junk : Word;
    theDate : DateTime; p : LongInt;
BEGIN
   Writeln( 'Change a file''s date and time' );
   Write( 'File name? ' );
   Readln( fname );
   Assign( f, fname );
   Reset( f );
   WITH theDate DO
   BEGIN
      GetDate( year, month, day, junk );
      GetTime( hour, min, sec, junk )
   END; { with }

   PackTime( theDate, p );

   SetFTime( f, p );
   Close( f )
END.
```

ParamCount

Syntax

```
FUNCTION ParamCount : Word;
```

Location

System

Description

ParamCount returns the number of arguments entered after the program name on the DOS command line. Suppose you have the program TEST.EXE on disk. If you run the program from DOS with the following command, **ParamCount** will equal two:

```
A>TEST INPUT.TXT OUTPUT.TXT
```

Use the Options:Parameters command to perform the equivalent of this command when using Turbo Pascal's integrated compiler. This simulates passing parameters to programs rather than forcing you to return to DOS just to test programs such as these.

One typical use for **ParamCount** is to know when to display program instructions. If **ParamCount** is zero and the program requires one or more parameters, then the person who started the program probably needs help. Compile the example to a disk file TEST.EXE and type TEST with and without parameters to see the difference.

Example

```
PROGRAM xParamCount;
VAR i : Integer;
BEGIN
   IF ParamCount = 0 THEN
   BEGIN { Display instructions }
      Writeln;
      Writeln( 'Run the program this way:' );
      Writeln;
      Writeln( '  TEST <p1> <p2> <p3> ... <pn>' );
      Writeln;
      Writeln( 'where <p1>..<pn> are parameters you want' );
      Writeln( 'to pass to TEST. For example, you could type:' );
      Writeln;
      Writeln( '  TEST INTEXT.TXT OUTTEXT.TXT' )
   END ELSE
   BEGIN { Display parameters }
      Writeln( 'You typed ', ParamCount, ' parameters:' );
      FOR i := 1 TO ParamCount DO
         Writeln( i:2, ' : ', ParamStr(i) )
   END { else }
END.
```

ParamStr

Syntax

```
FUNCTION ParamStr( n : Word ) : String;
```

Location

System

Description

When you are executing a program from DOS, or in memory with optional command line parameters, **ParamStr** returns parameter string **n**, if it exists. Use **ParamCount** to determine the number of parameters waiting to be read.

The example shows how to use **ParamStr** to pick up a parameter file name passed to a program from the DOS command line. Compile the program to TEST.EXE and type TEST <file name> to type a text file to the display, similar to the way the DOS TYPE command works. Type TEST alone to see an error message reminding you to type a file name.

Under DOS 3.0 and later versions, **ParamStr(0)** returns the name of the current program. To assign the program name to a string variable **progName**, write:

```
IF Lo( DosVersion ) < 3
   THEN progName := ''
   ELSE progName := ParamStr( 0 );
```

Example

```
PROGRAM xParamStr;
VAR tf : Text; s : String;
BEGIN
   IF ParamCount = 0
    THEN Writeln( 'Error: no file name specified' )
    ELSE BEGIN
      Assign( tf, ParamStr(1) );
      Reset( tf );
      WHILE NOT EOF(tf) DO
      BEGIN
         Readln( tf, s );
         Writeln( s )
      END; { while }
      Close( tf )
   END { else }
END.
```

Pi

Syntax

```
FUNCTION Pi : <real>;
```

Location

System

Description

Pi returns the value of π, previously a constant in earlier Turbo Pascal versions. Because **Pi** is now a function, its precision changes when you compile a program with the {$N+} directive, enabling math coprocessor data types.

The example displays the extended value of **Pi**, enabling a math coprocessor or emulation with the directives {$N+,E+}. Remove the directives and run the example to see **Pi**'s default value. For reference, both values are listed below.

```
Pi = 3.14159265358979E+0000    (Coprocessor or emulation)
Pi = 3.1415926536E+00          (No coprocessor)
```

Example

```
{$N+,E+}    { Enable coprocessor or emulation }
PROGRAM xPi;
BEGIN
   Writeln( 'Pi = ', pi )
END.
```

PieSlice

Syntax

```
PROCEDURE PieSlice( x, y : Integer; stAngle, endAngle, radius : Word );
```

Location

Graph

Description

PieSlice draws a filled wedge with the sharp point at coordinate (x,y). The starting angle (**stAngle**) and ending angle (**endAngle**) represent the width of the wedge, with greater angles running counterclockwise. The **radius** changes the wedge length.

Use **SetColor** to change the wedge outline. Use **SetFillStyle** to change the wedge fill color and pattern. The example uses **PieSlice** to display a chart of the 16 colors available in EGA and VGA displays.

Example

```
PROGRAM xPieSlice;
USES Crt, Graph;
VAR graphDriver, graphMode : integer;
    color, stAngle, radius, xCenter, yCenter : word;
BEGIN
```

```
      graphDriver := Detect;
      InitGraph( graphDriver, graphMode, '' );
      xCenter := GetMaxX DIV 2;
      yCenter := GetMaxY DIV 2;
      radius := GetMaxX DIV 4;
      stAngle := 0;
      FOR color := 0 TO 14 DO
      BEGIN
         stAngle := stAngle + 24;
         SetFillStyle( SolidFill, color );
         PieSlice( xCenter, yCenter, stAngle, stAngle+24, radius )
      END; { for }
      REPEAT UNTIL Keypressed;
      CloseGraph
   END.
```

Pos

Syntax

```
FUNCTION Pos( pattern, search : <string> ) : Byte;
```

Location

System

Description

Pos returns the index position where the **pattern** exists in the **search** string. If **Pos** doesn't find **pattern** anywhere in **search**, the function returns zero.

The example shows a common use for **Pos**, prompting for file names with a default extension, in this case, .PAS. Run the program and type the name of a Pascal source code file to display. For example, if you type TEST, the program tries to list TEST.PAS. But if you type TEST.TXT, **Pos** finds the period in the file name and does not add the default extension.

Example

```
PROGRAM xPos;
VAR tf : Text; s, filename : String;
BEGIN
   Write( 'List what file? [.PAS] ' );
   Readln( fileName );
   IF Pos( '.', fileName ) = 0
      THEN fileName := fileName + '.PAS';
   Writeln( 'Listing ', fileName );
```

```
      Assign( tf, fileName );
      Reset( tf );
      WHILE NOT EOF(tf) DO
      BEGIN
         Readln( tf, s );
         Writeln( s )
      END; { while }
      Close( tf )
   END.
```

Pred

Syntax

```
FUNCTION Pred( v : <ordinal> ) : <ordinal>;
```

Location

System

Description

Pred returns the scalar predecessor of **v**, which can be any ordinal type such as **Integer**, **Char**, or an enumerated type of your own making. For example, if type Color = (Red,White,Blue), then Pred(Blue) = White, and Pred(White) = Red. Pred(Red) is undefined. Also, Pred(True) = False, Pred(1) = 0, Pred(2) = 1, and so on.

Example

```
PROGRAM xPred;
VAR i : Integer;
BEGIN
   Writeln( 'Countdown courtesy of Pred(v)' );
   Writeln;
   i := 100;
   WHILE i > 0 DO
   BEGIN
      Write( i:4 );
      i := Pred( i )
   END { while }
END.
```

Ptr

Syntax

```
FUNCTION Ptr( segment, offset : Word ) : Pointer;
```

Location

System

Description

Ptr returns a **Pointer** equal to the 32-bit memory address specified by **segment** and **offset**. You can assign the function result to any pointer variable.

Use **Ptr** to create pointers to known locations in memory, as in the example, which points variable **lowTime** to the low word value of the PC interrupt timer. When you run the program, you'll see the value at the address in **lowTime** constantly changing.

Example

```
PROGRAM xPtr;
USES Crt;
VAR lowTime : ^Word;
BEGIN
   lowTime := Ptr( 0000, $046C );
   WHILE NOT KeyPressed DO
   BEGIN
      GotoXY( 1, WhereY );
      Write( lowTime^ )
   END { while }
END.
```

PutImage

Syntax

```
PROCEDURE PutImage( x, y : Integer; VAR bitMap; mode : Word );
```

Location

Graph

Description

PutImage copies a saved graphics image from a variable **bitMap**, usually an array of bytes, to the display. The upper-left corner of the image is at coordinate (x,y). Parameter **mode** specifies the logical operation used to combine image bits with pixels already on display. (The **Graph** unit calls this **BitBlt**, an apparent, and somewhat misleading, reference to a hardware *blitter*, a device used for high-speed graphics on computers such as the Amiga. PCs do not have blitter devices.) Set this value to one of the five constants: **NormalPut**, **XORPut**, **OrPut**, **AndPut**, **NotPut**. **NormalPut** mode copies the image over anything on display. The other modes use exclusive-OR, OR, AND, or NOT logic to combine bits with display pixels. The image width and height were previously saved by **GetImage** in **bitMap**.

Normally, you'll save images with **GetImage** and then redisplay them elsewhere with **PutImage**. The example shows how to use this technique to bounce a red rubber ball around on screen. After drawing the ball, **GetImage** saves the pixels in a byte array addressed by pointer **image**. Then, a **WHILE** loop cycles, displaying the ball with calls to **PutImage** until you press any key to end the program.

Example

```
PROGRAM xPutImage;
USES Crt, Graph;
CONST radius = 10;
TYPE ByteArray = ARRAY[0..0]] OF Byte;
     ByteArrayPtr = ^ByteArray;
VAR graphDriver, graphMode : integer;
    xc, yc, x1, y1, x2, y2, xMax, yMax : integer;
    diameter, dx, dy, x, y : integer;
    image : ByteArrayPtr;
BEGIN
   graphDriver := Detect;
   InitGraph( graphDriver, graphMode, '' );
   xMax := GetMaxX; yMax := GetMaxY;
   xc := XMax DIV 2; yc := YMax DIV 2;
   x1 := (xc-radius)-1; y1 := (yc-radius)-4;
   x2 := (xc+radius)+1; y2 := (yc+radius)+4;
   diameter := radius+radius;
   SetColor( White );                 { Draw red rubber ball }
   Circle( xc, yc, radius );
   SetFillStyle( SolidFill, Red );
   FloodFill( xc, yc, White );
   GetMem( image, ImageSize( x1, y1, x2, y2 ) );  { Reserve memory }
   IF image <> NIL THEN
   BEGIN
      GetImage( x1, y1, x2, y2, image^ );  { Copy display image }
      ClearViewPort;
      dx := 1; dy := 1; y := yc; x := xc;
      WHILE NOT Keypressed DO
```

```
    BEGIN
        PutImage( x, y, image^, NormalPut );  { Display ball }
        x := x + dx;
        y := y + dy;
        IF ( y >= YMax-diameter ) OR ( y <= 0 ) THEN dy := -dy;
        IF ( x >= XMax-diameter ) OR ( x <= 0 ) THEN dx := -dx
    END { while }
  END; { if }
  CloseGraph
END.
```

PutPixel

Syntax

```
PROCEDURE PutPixel( x, y : Integer; pixel : Word );
```

Location

Graph

Description

PutPixel displays a single pixel on the graphics display. The exact format of parameter **pixel** depends on the display mode, but you generally can set **pixel** to a color constant (0 to 15 for EGA graphics) to display dots of those colors.

The example is similar to the program for **Plot**. The display fills with a starry-sky pattern, which seems to reach equilibrium after running for a minute or so. The program also gives you a visual way to check Turbo Pascal's random number generator. If the display fills evenly, the generator is working.

Example

```
PROGRAM xPutPixel;
USES Crt, Graph;
VAR graphDriver, graphMode : integer;
    xMax, yMax : integer; color : word;
BEGIN
    graphDriver := Detect;
    InitGraph( graphDriver, graphMode, '' );
    xMax := GetMaxX; yMax := GetMaxY;
    WHILE NOT KeyPressed DO
    BEGIN
        IF Random(400) > 2
            THEN color := 0
            ELSE color := 1+Random(MaxColors);
```

```
         PutPixel( Random( XMax ),    { x }
                   Random( YMax ),    { y }
                   color            )
      END; { while }
      CloseGraph
   END.
```

Random

Syntax

```
FUNCTION Random : Real;
FUNCTION Random( modulus : Word ) : Word;
```

Location

System

Description

Random returns the next value in a random sequence, optionally seeded (initial-ized) by **Randomize**. The first form returns a real number **r** in the range:

$$0.0 < = r < 1.0$$

The second form returns an integer or word value **n** in the range:

$$0 < = n < modulus$$

The modulus may be any positive whole number from 0 to 65,535. You may assign the result to any **Byte**, **ShortInt**, **Integer**, **Word**, or **LongInt** variable. As-signing **Random(n)** to a signed integer variable produces positive values if **n** is less or equal to **MaxInt**. If **n** is greater than **MaxInt**, both negative and positive integers are produced. This trick does not always have the expected results, though. For example, consider this expression:

```
i := Random( 65535 );
```

If **i** is integer, then the expression assigns the equivalent of the range 0 to 65,534. Because the modulus (65,535) is never generated, and because 65,535 in binary equals -1 as a signed integer, this expression skips -1 in the random se-quence! To get negative values correctly, use an expression such as:

```
i := Random(100)-50;
```

This sets **i** to a value from −50 to +49, exactly 100 possible values (including −1) evenly distributed over the range.

One common use for **Random** is to let programs make decisions in simulations. To do this, you might decide that certain operations should occur about 25% of the time; others at 75%; and so on. The example shows how to program such events. It assumes that the expression:

```
IF Random(100) < 25
   THEN DoEvent;
```

will call **DoEvent** about 25% of the time because **Random(100)** is about three times more likely to produce values in the range 25 to 99 than it is in the range 0 to 24.

When you run the example, press Enter to see a report of the counts and frequencies of values produced in the range 0 to 24, 0 to 49, 0 to 74, and 0 to 99.

Example

```
PROGRAM xRandom;
USES Crt;
VAR counts : ARRAY[ 1 .. 4 ] OF LongInt;
    i, n : Integer;
    ch : Char;
BEGIN
   FOR i := 1 TO 4 DO
      counts[i] := 0;
   Writeln( 'Counting...' );
   WHILE NOT Keypressed DO
   BEGIN
      n := Random(100);
      IF n < 25 THEN Inc( counts[1] );
      IF n < 50 THEN Inc( counts[2] );
      IF n < 75 THEN Inc( counts[3] );
      Inc( counts[4] )
   END; { while }
   ch := Readkey;  { throw out keypress }
   FOR i := 1 TO 4 DO
      Writeln( i, ' :', counts[i]:8,
         100.0*((1.0*counts[i]) / (1.0*counts[4])):10:3, ' %' )
END.
```

Randomize

Syntax

```
PROCEDURE Randomize;
```

Location

System

Description

Call **Randomize** to seed the random number generator, beginning a new random sequence each time the program runs. If you do not call **Randomize**, then programs will repeat the same random sequence.

Run the example several times to produce different sets of 10 random numbers. Then, remove **Randomize** and run the program several more times. Without **Randomize**, all random number sets are now identical.

Example

```
PROGRAM xRandomize;
VAR i : Integer;
BEGIN
   Randomize;
   FOR i := 1 TO 10 DO
      Write( Random(MaxInt):8 );
   Writeln
END.
```

Read

Syntax

```
PROCEDURE Read( [f : <file>;] v1, v2, ..., vn );
```

Location

System

Description

Use **Read** to input one or more variables from a file, which might be a disk file or a device such as a modem or keyboard. If < file > is not specified, **Read** loads variables from the standard input text file, normally the keyboard.

Read also can read several variables at the same time. The variables do not have to be of the same type. Separate the variable identifiers with commas as in this statement, which reads a character (**ch**), an integer (**i**), and a real number (**r**):

```
Read( ch, i, r );
```

When this statement executes, the program pauses for you to type the three items. You can press Enter after typing each item, or you can press Space after the character and integer and press Enter after the real number. The same rule does not hold for string variables, which must be terminated with Enter. For example, the statement:

```
Read( s, i );
```

reads a string (**s**) and an integer (**i**). You must press Enter after typing the string (or there must be a carriage return after the string if you are reading from a disk text file). Then you can type, or read from disk, the integer value.

The example shows how to read a text file one character at a time with **Read**.

Example

```
PROGRAM xRead;
VAR tf:Text; ch:Char;
BEGIN
   Write( 'Press <Enter> to read file...' );
   Read( ch );
   Assign( tf, 'XREAD.PAS' );
   Reset( tf );
   WHILE NOT EOF(tf) DO
   BEGIN
      Read( tf, ch );
      Write( ch )
   END { while }
END.
```

ReadKey

Syntax

```
FUNCTION ReadKey : Char;
```

Location

Crt

Description

ReadKey returns one character from the keyboard. The function is particularly convenient for reading control keys, arrow keys, and function keys, when you want complete control over the display. Unlike **Read** and **Readln**, **ReadKey** never displays anything.

To read keyboard commands, you can use **ReadKey** along with **Upcase** and **Keypressed**. If **Keypressed** is true, then call **ReadKey** to find out which key was typed. For example, you can write:

```
IF Keypressed THEN
CASE Upcase( ReadKey ) OF
   'A' : ChoiceA;
   'B' : ChoiceB;
   'C' : ChoiceC
END; { case }
```

This does not recognize function, arrow, and other special keys, which return two values, a null (ASCII 0) plus a second character representing the key. To do this, first, check for a null. Then, use **ReadKey** a second time to find out which special key was typed. Here's the program:

```
IF ReadKey = CHR(0) THEN
IF ReadKey = 'P'
   THEN DoDownArrow;
```

The statements call **DoDownArrow** only if you press the down arrow key, which generates the two ASCII characters, null and P. See Table 9-3 for a list of all two-character sequences you can use this way.

The example uses **ReadKey** in a handy program for checking ASCII values. Use it to discover what characters certain keys produce. Type Esc to quit.

Example

```
PROGRAM xReadKey;
USES Crt;
VAR ch : Char;
BEGIN
   Writeln( 'Display ASCII character values' );
   Writeln( 'Type ESC to quit' );
   Writeln;
   REPEAT
      Write( 'Char? ' );
      ch := ReadKey;
      Writeln( ch, ' : ASCII value = ', Ord(ch) );
   UNTIL ch = CHR(27)
END.
```

ReadLn

Syntax

```
PROCEDURE Readln( [f : TEXT;] v1, v2, ..., vn );
```

Location

System

Description

Readln (read line) operates identically to **Read**, but with one major difference: It can read only from text files. **Read** can read variables from any kind of file. **Readln** can read variables only from text files.

Most often you will use **Readln** to read strings when you want someone to type a response to a prompt and press Enter when they're done. For example, this asks you to type a file name:

```
VAR fname : String;

Write( 'File? ' );
Readln( fname );
```

Even though **Readln** reads from text files, you may read variables other than strings. For example, this pauses and waits for you to type a real number:

```
VAR r : Real;

Write( 'Value? ' );
Readln( r );
```

You can also use **Readln** to read disk text files. Unlike the **Read** example, though, because **Readln** reads an entire line at a time into a string variable, no line can exceed the maximum string length of 255 characters.

Example

```
PROGRAM xReadln;
VAR tf:Text; s:String;
BEGIN
   Write( 'Press <Enter> to read file...' );
   Readln;
   Assign( tf, 'XREADLN.PAS' );
   Reset( tf );
   WHILE NOT EOF(tf) DO
   BEGIN
```

```
            Readln( tf, s );
            Writeln( s )
        END { while }
    END.
```

Rectangle

Syntax

```
PROCEDURE Rectangle( x1, y1, x2, y2 : Integer );
```

Location

Graph

Description

Rectangle displays a rectangle with its upper-left corner at coordinate (x1,y1) and its lower coordinate at (x2,y2). Change the rectangle's color with **SetColor**.

The example draws randomly colored and sized rectangles until you press any key to stop the program. Lower the **Delay** value to increase program speed.

Example

```
PROGRAM xRectangle;
USES Crt, Graph;
VAR graphDriver, graphMode : integer;
    xMax, yMax : integer;
BEGIN
   graphDriver := Detect;
   InitGraph( graphDriver, graphMode, '' );
   xMax := GetMaxX; yMax := GetMaxY;
   WHILE NOT Keypressed DO
   BEGIN
      Delay(50);
      SetColor( 1+Random(MaxColors) );
      Rectangle( Random(XMax), Random(YMax),
                 Random(XMax), Random(YMax) )
   END; { while }
   REPEAT UNTIL Keypressed;
   CloseGraph
END.
```

RegisterBGIdriver

Syntax

```
FUNCTION RegisterBGIdriver( driver : Pointer ) : Integer;
```

Location

Graph

Description

Call **RegisterBGIdriver** to register a graphics driver previously loaded into memory. Pass the driver's address in pointer **driver**, telling the graphics kernel where to find this driver. If **RegisterBGIdriver** returns a negative value, then an error occurred and you must not use the loaded driver. Otherwise, when you later initialize the driver with **InitGraph**, the graphics kernel will use the in-memory copy instead of loading the BGI driver file from disk.

The technique is useful to rapidly switch between two or more graphics drivers and modes. Preloading the drivers onto the heap avoids time-wasting disk reads for every switch.

The example demonstrates how to load two driver files, CGA.BGI and EGAVGA.BGI. Procedure **LoadOneDriver** reads the file after allocating exactly as much memory as needed to hold the entire file. (The program halts with a run-time error if enough memory is not available.)

The main body of the example calls **InitGraph** three times, switching between CGA and EGA modes. Press the Space bar to switch. Notice that when you do this, the disk drive light does not come on. To write this same program without preloading and registering the different drivers, you would have to insert **CloseGraph** commands between the calls to **InitGraph**.

Example

```
{ NOTE: This program requires both EGA and CGA video hardware }

PROGRAM xRegisterBGIdriver;
USES Crt, Graph;
VAR graphDriver, graphMode : Integer;

PROCEDURE LoadOneDriver( fileName : String );
VAR
   f : FILE;
   fp : Pointer;
   bytes : LongInt;
BEGIN
   Assign( f, fileName );
   Reset( f, 1 );
```

```
        bytes := FileSize( f );
        GetMem( fp, bytes );
        BlockRead( f, fp^, bytes );
        Close( f );
        IF RegisterBGIdriver( fp ) < O THEN
        BEGIN
            Writeln( 'Error registering ', filename );
            Writeln( 'Graphics error : ', GraphErrorMsg( GraphResult ) );
            Halt
        END { if }
    END; { LoadOneDriver }


    PROCEDURE DrawLines;
    BEGIN
        REPEAT
            SetColor( 1 + Random(GetMaxColor) );
            LineTo( Random(GetMaxX), Random(GetMaxY) )
        UNTIL Keypressed;
        CloseGraph;
        IF ReadKey = Chr(27) THEN Halt
    END; { DrawLines }

    BEGIN
        LoadOneDriver( 'CGA.BGI' );
        LoadOneDriver( 'EGAVGA.BGI' );

        graphDriver := CGA; graphMode := CGACO;
        InitGraph( graphDriver, graphMode, '' );
        DrawLines;

        graphDriver := EGA; graphMode := EGAHi;
        InitGraph( graphDriver, graphMode, '' );
        DrawLines;

        graphDriver := CGA; graphMode := CGAC1;
        InitGraph( graphDriver, graphMode, '' );
        DrawLines
    END.
```

RegisterBGIfont

Syntax

```
FUNCTION RegisterBGIfont( font : Pointer ) : Integer;
```

Location

Graph

Description

Call **RegisterBGIfont** to register a graphics font previously loaded into memory. Pass the font's address in pointer **font**, telling the graphics kernel where to find this font. If **RegisterBGIfont** returns a negative value, then an error occurred and you must not use the loaded font. Otherwise, when you later select the font with **SetTextStyle**, the graphics kernel will use the in-memory copy instead of loading the CHR font file from disk.

The technique is useful when you want to switch between two or more fonts. Preloading the font patterns onto the heap avoids repeated disk reads for every new character style.

The example demonstrates how to load four font files—TRIP.CHR, LITT.CHR, SANS.CHR, and GOTH.CHR. Procedure **LoadOneFont** reads the file after allocating exactly as much memory as needed to hold the entire file. (The program halts with a runtime error if enough memory is not available.)

The main body of the program calls **SetTextStyle** to switch to a new character style for each string passed to **OutText**. If the font patterns were not preloaded into memory, each such call would cause the graphics kernel to reload the font file from disk, a time-wasting action the example avoids.

Example

```
PROGRAM xRegisterBGIfont;
USES Crt, Graph;
VAR graphDriver, graphMode : Integer;

PROCEDURE LoadOneFont( fileName : String );
VAR
    f : FILE;
    fp : Pointer;
    bytes : LongInt;
BEGIN
    Assign( f, fileName );
    Reset( f, 1 );
    bytes := FileSize( f );
    GetMem( fp, bytes );
    BlockRead( f, fp^, bytes );
```

```
        Close( f );
        IF RegisterBGIfont( fp ) < 0 THEN
        BEGIN
            Writeln( 'Error registering ', filename );
            Writeln( 'Graphics error : ', GraphErrorMsg( GraphResult ) );
            Halt
        END { if }
    END; { LoadOneFont }

    BEGIN
        LoadOneFont( 'TRIP.CHR' );
        LoadOneFont( 'LITT.CHR' );
        LoadOneFont( 'SANS.CHR' );
        LoadOneFont( 'GOTH.CHR' );

        graphDriver := Detect;
        InitGraph( graphDriver, graphMode, '' );
        SetColor( LightBlue );
        MoveTo( 10, 50 );
        SetBkColor( White );

        OutText( 'This ' );
        SetTextStyle( TriplexFont, HorizDir, 4 );
        OutText( 'program ' );
        SetTextStyle( SmallFont, HorizDir, 8 );
        OutText( 'uses ' );
        SetTextStyle( SansSerifFont, HorizDir, 3 );
        OutText( 'multiple ' );
        SetTextStyle( GothicFont, HorizDir, 5 );
        OutText( 'fonts.' );

        REPEAT UNTIL Keypressed;
        CloseGraph
    END.
```

Release

Syntax

```
PROCEDURE Release( VAR p : Pointer );
```

Location

System

Description

Release resets the heap top to the address of **p**, previously set by **Mark**. Any **New** variables created before **Release** are invalid. Parameter **p** may be any pointer type, although it usually is a generic **Pointer**. Calling **Release** also erases any disposed areas on the heap, which Turbo Pascal tracks in a list, also stored on the heap.

Example

```
PROGRAM xRelease;
TYPE a = ARRAY[1..1000] OF Real;
     aptr = ^a;
VAR heap : Pointer;
    v : aptr;
BEGIN
   Mark( heap );
   Writeln( 'Memory before new    =', Memavail:8 );
   New( v );
   Writeln( 'Memory after new     =', Memavail:8 );

   Release( heap );

   Writeln( 'Memory after release =', Memavail:8 )
END.
```

Rename

Syntax

```
PROCEDURE Rename( VAR f : <file>; filename : <string> );
```

Location

System

Description

Rename changes the directory name of file **f** to **filename**, which may be a literal or variable string. Before renaming, **Assign** the file's current name to file variable **f**. The file should not be open. Also, to avoid duplicate file names in the same directory, **filename** should not already exist. You can check this, as in the example, by resetting the file before renaming. Usually, the file to be renamed is an untyped **FILE**, but it can be any other file type, too.

Example

```
PROGRAM xRename;
VAR f : FILE; s : String;
BEGIN
   Write( 'Rename what file? ' );
   Readln( s );
   IF Length( s ) > 0 THEN
   BEGIN
      Assign( f, s );
      {$i-} Reset( f ); {$i+}
      IF IoResult <> 0
       THEN
         Writeln( 'Can''t find ', s )
       ELSE
         BEGIN
            Write( 'New name? ' );
            Readln( s );
            IF Length( s ) > 0
               THEN Rename( f, s )
         END { else }
   END { if }
END.
```

Reset

Syntax

```
PROCEDURE Reset( VAR f : <file> [; n : Word] );
```

Location

System

Description

Reset opens or resets to the beginning an already open file. Resetting a text file prepares the file for reading only. Resetting other file types prepares for reading and writing. Before resetting, **Assign** a file path name to **f**. A null string resets a text file to the standard input (DOS handle 0).

When **f** is an untyped **FILE**, you may use an optional value **n** to specify the number of bytes that **BlockRead** and **BlockWrite** transfer at one time. If you do not specify a value, **n** defaults to 128. Usually, for best results, set **n** to 512, the size of one disk sector.

Surround a **Reset** statement with the compiler directives, {$i –} and {$i +}, turning off automatic I/O error detection. Then, check **IoResult**. If zero, the file is open and ready to use. If not zero, an error occurred and you must not use the file. The example shows how to use this technique to check whether a file exists on disk.

Example

```
PROGRAM xReset;
VAR f : File; fileName : String;
BEGIN
   Write( 'File? ' );
   Readln( fileName );
   IF Length( fileName ) > 0 THEN
   BEGIN
      Assign( f, fileName );
      {$i-} Reset( f ); {$i+}
      IF IoResult = 0 THEN
      BEGIN
         Writeln( 'File exists!' );
         Close( f )
      END ELSE
         Writeln( 'File does not exist' )
   END { if }
END.
```

RestoreCrtMode

Syntax

`PROCEDURE RestoreCrtMode;`

Location

Graph

Description

Call **RestoreCrtMode** to return to the original display screen before calling **Init-Graph**. After that, call **SetGraphMode** to go back to the graphics screen.

   RestoreCrtMode erases the display and homes the cursor. As the example shows, you can use this procedure to switch back and forth between graphics and text screens. Press Enter to switch and Esc to quit. Unfortunately, switching modes does not preserve any graphics or text previously on display.

Example

```
PROGRAM xRestoreCrtMode;
USES Crt, Graph;
```

```
CONST Esc = #27;
VAR graphDriver, graphMode : integer;
    i, xMax, yMax : word;

PROCEDURE Bubbles;
VAR i : Integer;
BEGIN
   FOR i := 1 TO 100 DO
   BEGIN
      SetColor( Random(1+GetMaxColor) );
      Circle( Random(xMax), Random(yMax), Random(75) )
   END { for }
END; { Bubbles }

BEGIN
   graphDriver := Detect;
   InitGraph( graphDriver, graphMode, '' );
   xMax := GetMaxX; yMax := GetMaxY;
   REPEAT
      SetGraphMode( graphMode );
      Bubbles;
      IF ReadKey <> Esc THEN
      BEGIN
         RestoreCrtMode;
         Writeln( 'Press Enter for graphics; Esc to quit...' )
      END { if }
   UNTIL ReadKey = Esc;
   CloseGraph
END.
```

Rewrite

Syntax

```
PROCEDURE Rewrite( VAR f : <file> [; n : Word] );
```

Location

System

Description

Rewrite creates a new disk file for output or readies a text device such as a printer or modem. Before rewriting, **Assign** a file name to file variable **f**. Rewriting a text file prepares it for writing only. Rewriting other kinds of files prepares for reading and writing.

Rewriting an existing disk file erases the file's contents and creates a new file of the same name, now empty. To prevent accidents, be sure to rewrite existing files only if you want to erase them.

The optional parameter **n** specifies the number of bytes read by **BlockRead** or written by **BlockWrite** when **f** is an untyped **FILE**. If **n** is not specified, the number defaults to 128. For best results, set **n** to 512, the size of one disk sector.

Surround a **Rewrite** statement with the compiler directives, {$i−} and {$i+}, turning off automatic I/O error detection. Then, check **IoResult**. If zero, then the file is open and ready to use. If not zero, an error occurred, and you must not use the file.

The example shows how to use **Rewrite** to copy a text file, in this case, creating XREWRITE.BAK from XREWRITE.PAS. Type the program and save as XREWRITE.PAS, then run to create the backup.

Example

```
PROGRAM xRewrite;
VAR inFile, outFile : Text; s : String;
BEGIN
   Writeln( 'Backing up XREWRITE.PAS...' );
   Assign( outFile, 'XREWRITE.BAK' );   { Erase old backup }
   {$i-} Erase( outFile ); {$i+}        { Ignore any error }
   IF IoResult <> 0 THEN {do nothing};
   Assign( inFile, 'XREWRITE.PAS' );    { Open input file  }
   Reset( inFile );
   Rewrite( outFile );                  { Create output file }
   WHILE NOT Eof( inFile ) DO
   BEGIN
      Readln( inFile, s );
      Writeln( outFile, s )
   END; { while }
   Writeln( 'done' );
   Close( inFile );
   Close( outFile )
END.
```

RmDir

Syntax

```
PROCEDURE RmDir( path : <string> );
```

Location

System

Description

RmDir removes the subdirectory that **path** specifies. If there are any files in the directory, DOS generates an error and does not remove the directory. Use **IoResult** to detect this error.

RmDir operates identically to the DOS RMDIR and RD commands.

The example uses **RmDir** along with **MkDir** to create a temporary subdirectory, \TEMP. A program might do this to make certain it has enough space for temporary data files, removing both the files and directory before ending. Before using **RmDir**, it's important to remove any files in the directory, or you'll receive an error.

Example

```
PROGRAM xRmDir;
VAR err : Integer;
BEGIN
   Writeln( 'Creating \TEMP...' );
   {$i-} MkDir( '\TEMP' ); {$i+}
   err := IoResult;
   IF ( err = 0 ) OR ( err = 5 {already exists} ) THEN
   BEGIN

      { Store data in \TEMP subdirectory }

      { Delete files before continuing }

      Writeln( 'Deleting \TEMP...' );
      {$i-} RmDir( '\TEMP' ); {$i+}
      IF IoResult <> 0
         THEN Writeln( 'Error removing \TEMP' )

   END { if }
END.
```

Round

Syntax

```
FUNCTION Round( r : <real> ) : LongInt;
```

Location

System

Description

Round returns the long integer value of **r** rounded to the nearest whole number. **Round**(1.4999) = 1,   **Round**(1.5000) = 2,   **Round**   (−1.4999) = −1,   **Round** (−1.5000) = −2, and so on.

You can assign **Round**'s result to any **ShortInt**, **Byte**, **Integer**, or **LongInt** variable, but you risk receiving a range error for types other than **LongInt**. The example shows how to avoid this error by checking the real number before rounding. (Although the program checks for negative values, too, the **Random** statement produces only positive numbers.)

Example

```
PROGRAM xRound;
VAR r : Real; i : Integer;
BEGIN
   Randomize;
   r := Random * 50000.0;
   Writeln( 'r = ', r:0:5 );
   IF ( -32767.0 <= r ) AND ( r <= 32768 ) THEN
   BEGIN
      i := Round( r );
      Writeln( 'i = ', i )
   END ELSE
      Writeln( 'Result is outside Integer range' )
END.
```

RunError

Syntax

```
PROCEDURE RunError;
PROCEDURE RunError( errorCode : Word );
```

Location

System

Description

RunError comes in two flavors: one with no parameters and one with a single **Word** parameter **errorCode**. Similar to **Halt**, **RunError** stops a running program in its tracks. Unlike **Halt**, **RunError** simulates a runtime error, just as though the program stopped due to a real critical problem.

Pass the value of any Turbo Pascal runtime error number to **RunError** to simulate how the program will respond if that error actually occurs. Use the parameterless form of **RunError** to halt the program with no specific runtime error number. (In that case, a runtime error "0" is reported, even though 0 is not a valid runtime error value.)

One use for **RunError** is to debug a critical error handler (see Chapter 13, *Customizing a Runtime Handler*). Executing **RunError** halts the program and runs the error-handler code.

The example demonstrates another use for **RunError** —forcing a runtime error to occur after you've replaced Turbo Pascal's normal error-handling logic. Although not shown in the example, you might do this after changing how **New** and **GetMem** detect out-of-memory errors (see **HeapFunc** in this chapter for details). As the example shows, if **MaxAvail** reports too little memory available, **RunError** can generate an out-of-memory error (code 1). (Of course, a real program would do this only as a last resort after closing files and performing other duties before shutting down.) To see **RunError** 's result, remove the $ from the top line and insert a $ between { and M in the second.

Example

```
{$M 1024, 65535, 65535}    { 64K heap }
{ M 1024,     0,     0}    { Minimum heap }
PROGRAM xRunError;
CONST size = 2048;
VAR p : Pointer;
BEGIN
   Writeln( 'Before: MemAvail=', MemAvail,
      ' MaxAvail=', MaxAvail );
   IF MaxAvail < size
      THEN RunError( 1 )         { Out of memory }
      ELSE GetMem( p, size ); { Allocate heap space }
   Writeln( size, ' bytes allocated' );
   Writeln( 'After: MemAvail=', MemAvail,
      ' MaxAvail=', MaxAvail );
END.
```

Sector

Syntax

```
PROCEDURE Sector( x, y : Integer;
    stAngle, endAngle, xRadius, yRadius : Word );
```

Location

Graph

Description

The strangely named **Sector** operates the same as **Ellipse**, but it fills an ellipse with the current fill pattern and color (see **SetFillStyle** and **SetFillPattern**). Use **SetColor** to change the ellipse's outline color. The parameters are identical to and have the same effects as the parameters for **Ellipse**.

The example fills the display with a variety of filled ellipses. Several variables ensure that the program operates correctly with all display types.

Example

```
PROGRAM xSector;
USES Crt, Graph;
VAR graphDriver, graphMode : Integer;
    x, y, xMax, yMax, xSize, ySize : Integer;
    xSizeD2, ySizeD2, xSizeT2, ySizeT2 : Integer;
BEGIN
   Randomize;
   graphDriver := Detect;
   InitGraph( graphDriver, graphMode, '' );
   xMax := GetMaxX; yMax := GetMaxY;
   xSize := xMax DIV 8; ySize := yMax DIV 4;
   xSizeD2 := xSize DIV 2; ySizeD2 := ySize DIV 2;
   xSizeT2 := xSize * 2; ySizeT2 := ySize * 2;
   y := ySizeD2;
   WHILE y < ( yMax - ySizeD2 ) DO
   BEGIN
      x := xSizeD2;
      WHILE x < ( xMax - xSizeD2 ) DO
      BEGIN
        SetColor( 1 + Random( MaxColors ) );
        SetFillStyle( 1 + Random( 11 ), 1 + Random( MaxColors ) );
        Sector( x, y, Random( 360 ), Random( 45 ),
           xSizeD2 - 6, ySizeD2 - 6 );
        x := x + xSize
      END; { while }
      y := y + ySize
   END; { while }
   REPEAT UNTIL Keypressed;
   CloseGraph
END.
```

Seek

Syntax

```
PROCEDURE Seek( VAR f : <untyped file>|<typed file>; rn : LongInt );
```

Location

System

Description

Seek positions the internal file pointer to record **rn** in file **f** so that the next read or write to the file occurs at position **rn**. The file must be open before seeking. You can use any file type except **TEXT**. To **Seek** in text files, declare the file variable as a **FILE OF Char**.

The first record in all files is number 0; therefore, seeking to record 0 is similar to resetting the file to its beginning. Seeking to one record beyond the last record in a file prepares for expanding existing files. Use this method when you want to append nontext files.

The example shows how to seek characters in a text file, reading the program's own text (XSEEK.PAS) and displaying the thirteenth character, k. Because the first record—or character in this case—is number 0, seeking to 12 locates the thirteenth, not the twelfth, record.

Example

```
PROGRAM xSeek;
VAR tf : FILE OF Char; ch : Char;
BEGIN
    Assign( tf, 'XSEEK.PAS' );
    Reset( tf );
    Seek( tf, 12 );
    Read( tf, ch );
    Writeln( 'ch=', ch );
    Close( tf )
END.
```

SeekEof

Syntax

```
FUNCTION SeekEof( VAR f : TEXT ) : Boolean;
```

Location

System

Description

This function is similar to **Eof** except that **SeekEof** looks ahead for the end of file marker ^Z (ASCII 26), skipping tabs, blanks, and end-of-line carriage return and line feed characters. File **f** must be **TEXT**. It cannot be **FILE OF CHAR**.

      The function is true when it finds a ^Z (ASCII 26) ahead of the current character or at the physical end of the file, whichever comes first.

      When reading text files, **SeekEof** helps you to avoid reading extra blank lines after the last line of text. The example shows how to do this. Run the program and then type the name of any text file for a report on the total number of lines plus the total number of nonblank lines.

Example

```
PROGRAM xSeekEof;
VAR tf : TEXT; c1, c2 : LongInt; s : String;
BEGIN
   Write( 'File name? ' );
   Readln( s );
   Assign( tf, s );
   Reset( tf );
   c1 := 0; c2 := 0;

   WHILE NOT Eof(tf) DO          { Read all lines }
   BEGIN
      Readln( tf, s );
      Inc( c1 )
   END; { while }

   Reset( tf );

   WHILE NOT SeekEof(tf) DO     { Read only nonblank lines }
   BEGIN
      Readln( tf, s );
      Inc( c2 )
   END; { while }

   Writeln; Writeln;
   Writeln( 'Total number of lines    = ', c1 );
   Writeln( 'Number of nonblank lines = ', c2 )
END.
```

SeekEoln

Syntax

```
FUNCTION SeekEoln( VAR f : TEXT ) : Boolean;
```

Location

System

Description

This function is similar to **Eoln** except that **SeekEoln** looks ahead for the end-of-line carriage return and line feed markers, skipping tabs and blanks. When reading text files, **SeekEoln** avoids reading extra blank characters after the last significant character on each line. File **f** must be **TEXT**. It cannot be **FILE OF CHAR**.

The function is true when it finds a carriage return (ASCII 13) and line feed (ASCII 10) ahead of the current character. It is also true at the physical end of the file.

The example reads any text file, ignoring blanks and control characters. Change **SeekEoln** to **Eoln** to see the differences between these similar functions.

Example

```
PROGRAM xSeekEoln;
VAR tf : TEXT; ch : Char; filename : String;
BEGIN
   Write( 'File name? ' );
   Readln( filename );
   Assign( tf, filename );
   Reset( tf );
   WHILE NOT Eof( tf ) DO
   BEGIN
     WHILE NOT SeekEoln( tf ) DO
     BEGIN
        Read( tf, ch );
        Write( ch )
     END; { while }
     Readln( tf );
     Writeln
   END; { while }
   Close( tf )
END.
```

Seg

Syntax

```
FUNCTION Seg( v : <ident> ) : Word;
```

Location

System

Description

Seg returns the segment address of a variable, procedure, or function, **v**. Finding the address of pointer variables requires care. **Seg**(p) returns the segment of the pointer variable itself. **Seg**(p^) returns the segment address of the variable addressed by the pointer. See also **Ofs**.

The example displays the segment address of a variable and a procedure. When you run the program, you'll see these values are different, proving that Turbo Pascal stores its global variables and procedure code in different memory segments.

Example

```
PROGRAM xSeg;
VAR i : Integer;

PROCEDURE x;
BEGIN
   Writeln( 'x' )
END;

BEGIN
   Writeln( 'Seg(i)    = ', seg(i) );
   Writeln( 'Seg(x)    = ', seg(x) )
END.
```

SetActivePage

Syntax

```
PROCEDURE SetActivePage( page : Word );
```

Location

Graph

Description

SetActivePage tells the Turbo Pascal graphics kernel on which memory page to draw. The procedure works only on systems with multiple graphics pages, such as EGA, VGA, and Hercules. It does not work with CGA graphics.

Together, **SetActivePage** and **SetVisualPage** make it easy to design smooth animation sequences with a technique known as page swapping or ping ponging. The idea is to draw new graphics on an invisible page while viewing the most recent frame. Then, switch frames bringing the new graphics into view and preparing to draw on the other page.

The example demonstrates the difference page swapping makes, expanding a circle, with each new outline a different frame in the animation. To see how page swapping smooths the action, initialize variable **visual** to 0, drawing and displaying on the same graphics page. Without page swapping, you can see each circle being formed. With page swapping, all drawing occurs backstage—you see only the results.

Example

```
PROGRAM xSetActivePage;
USES Crt, Graph;
VAR graphDriver, graphMode : integer;
    radius, xc, yc : word;
    active, visual, temp : word;
BEGIN
{ Note: Requires multipage EGA or VGA display }
    graphDriver := EGA;  { or VGA }
    graphMode := EGAHi;  { and VGAMed }
    InitGraph( graphDriver, graphMode, '' );
    xc := GetMaxX DIV 2; yc := GetMaxY DIV 2; radius := 10;
    active := 0; visual := 1;
    WHILE NOT Keypressed DO
    BEGIN
        SetActivePage( active );
        SetVisualPage( visual );
        ClearViewPort;
        SetColor( 1+Random(GetMaxColor) );
        Circle( xc, yc, radius );
        SetVisualPage( active );
        temp := active;
        active := visual;
        visual := temp;
        radius := radius + 10;
        IF radius > yc THEN
            radius := 10
    END; { while }
    CloseGraph
END.
```

SetAllPalette

Syntax

```
PROCEDURE SetAllPalette( VAR palette );
```

Location

Graph

Description

Use **SetAllPalette** to change the actual colors you see for the color values you pass to **SetColor**. A palette is merely a translation between these color values and the values passed to the graphics hardware.

The **palette** parameter is untyped to allow it to grow or shrink to the exact size you need for different video graphics modes. Usually, though, **palette** is of type **PaletteType**, defined in the **Graph** unit as:

```
PaletteType =
   RECORD
      size : Byte;
      colors : ARRAY[ 0 .. MaxColors ] OF ShortInt
   END;
```

The **size** byte tells how many values follow in the **colors** array. Each array index is a different color, from 0 to **MaxColors**, a constant also defined in **Graph**. (Use **GetMaxColor** to discover the maximum color value for different modes.) By inserting a new color value into the **colors** array, you tell Turbo Pascal to convert one color to another. Passing the whole record to **SetAllPalette** instantly changes any graphics now on display to the new colors.

The example shows how to use **SetAllPalette** to achieve an animation effect simply by scrambling palette colors until you press a key to stop the program.

Setting any palette color to −1 tells Turbo Pascal to not change that setting. The example uses this technique to preserve the background color (colors[0]) without having to know what that color value is.

Example

```
PROGRAM xSetAllPallette;
USES Crt, Graph;
VAR graphDriver, graphMode : integer;
    i, cMax, xMax, yMax : integer;
    palette : PaletteType;
BEGIN
   graphDriver := Detect;
   InitGraph( graphDriver, graphMode, '' );
```

```
       xMax := GetMaxX; yMax := GetMaxY; cMax := GetMaxColor;
       Randomize;
       FOR i := 1 TO 75 DO
       BEGIN
          SetColor( 1+Random(cMax) );
          Circle( Random(xMax), Random(yMax), Random(100) )
       END; { for }
       palette.size := cMax+1;      { Number of colors in palette }
       palette.colors[0] := -1;     { No change to background color }
       WHILE NOT KeyPressed DO
       BEGIN
          Delay(150);
          FOR i := 1 TO cMax DO
             palette.colors[ i ] := Random(cMax+1);
          SetAllPalette( palette )
       END; { while }
       CloseGraph
    END.
```

SetAspectRatio

Syntax

```
PROCEDURE SetAspectRatio( xAsp, yAsp : Word );
```

Location

Graph

Description

The **Graph** unit keeps an internal value called the *aspect ratio*, which compensates for the fact that pixels on most PC graphics displays are not perfectly square. If a display's aspect ratio were not taken into account, circles would not be round because horizontal and vertical radii of the same numbers of pixels would have different visible lengths.

In some custom and VGA display modes, pixels are square (a ratio of 1/1). No compensation is required on such displays to draw round circles. On other displays, the ratio is anything but square. Among other defaults, **Graph** unit uses values of 4167/10,000 for CGA and 7750/10,000 for EGA displays.

Most of the time, these defaults work well. But monitors are often misaligned, and in such cases, **SetAspectRatio** can make helpful adjustments. A graphics program might provide aspect-ratio variables as an optional service to let users fine-tune their displays.

The example program draws circles with several different aspect ratios in effect. See Chapter 11 and **GetAspectRatio** for more information about this subject.

Example

```
PROGRAM xSetAspectRatio;
USES Graph;
VAR graphDriver, graphMode : integer;

PROCEDURE RoundAbout;
VAR ch : Char;  { Throw-away character }
   xAsp, yAsp : Word;
BEGIN
   GetAspectRatio( xAsp, yAsp );
   Writeln( 'X=', xAsp, ' Y=', yAsp,
      ' Ratio=', (1.0 * xAsp) / yAsp );
   Circle( GetMaxX - ( GetMaxX DIV 3 ),
      GetMaxY DIV 2, GetMaxY DIV 4 );
   Readln;
END; { RoundAbout }


BEGIN
   graphDriver := Detect;
   InitGraph( graphDriver, graphMode, '' );
   RoundAbout;
   SetAspectRatio( 1, 1 );
   RoundAbout;
   SetAspectRatio( 1, 2 );
   RoundAbout;
   SetAspectRatio( 2, 1 );
   RoundAbout;
   SetAspectRatio( 3, 2 );
   RoundAbout;
   CloseGraph
END.
```

SetBkCol

Syntax

```
PROCEDURE SetBkColor( color : Word );
```

Location

Graph

Description

Call **SetBkColor** to change the background color. Parameter **color** selects a color value from the current palette (see **SetAllPalette**). Set **color** to zero to change the background to black, the default color for all graphics modes.

The example cycles the graphics display through all possible background colors for the default palette. Press any key to end the program.

Example

```
PROGRAM xSetBkColor;
USES Crt, Graph;
VAR graphDriver, graphMode : integer;
    color : Word;
BEGIN
   graphDriver := Detect;
   InitGraph( graphDriver, graphMode, '' );
   WHILE NOT Keypressed DO
   BEGIN
     color := 0;
     WHILE color <= GetMaxColor DO
     BEGIN
        SetBkColor( color );
        Delay( 500 );
        IF Keypressed
           THEN color := GetMaxColor;
        Inc( color )
     END { for }
   END; { while }
   CloseGraph
END.
```

SetCBreak

Syntax

```
PROCEDURE SetCBreak( break : Boolean );
```

Location

Dos

Description

Call **SetCBreak** to turn on DOS's Ctrl-Break switch (**break = True**) or to turn it off (**break = False**). Normally, you should leave the switch off. But, if you want to be able to interrupt programs at any time a DOS function is called—useful during debugging, especially in programs that tend to get "locked up"—turn on Ctrl-Break by passing **True** to **SetCBreak**. With Ctrl-Break off, pressing Ctrl-C or Ctrl-Break keys interrupts a program only during console I/O, printing, or communications. (Most communications programs do not call DOS for serial I/O, thus bypassing the Ctrl-Break switch.)

The example demonstrates how to use **SetCBreak** along with its sister procedure **GetCBreak**, which returns the current Ctrl-Break switch setting.

Example

```
PROGRAM xSetCBreak;
USES Crt, Dos;
VAR break : Boolean;
BEGIN
   GetCBreak( break );
   Writeln( 'Control-Break checking is: ', break );
   SetCBreak( NOT break );
   GetCBreak( break );
   Writeln( 'Control-Break checking is: ', break );
   SetCBreak( False );
   GetCBreak( break );
   Writeln( 'Control-Break checking is: ', break );
END.
```

SetColor

Syntax

```
PROCEDURE SetColor( color : Word );
```

Location

Graph

Description

Pass a color number to **SetColor** to change the color used by **LineTo**, **LineRel**, **Line**, **Rectangle**, **DrawPoly**, **Arc**, **Circle**, **Ellipse**, **PieSlice** (outline only), **OutText**, and **OutTextXY**.

Parameter **color** is an index into the current color palette, not a color value as stored in video display memory. Because of this, the actual color you see might not match one of the color constants listed in the **Graph** unit. For example, if you write **SetColor(Red)**, you could see a different color if you had previously changed the palette or if the hardware doesn't display red for this color number.

The example displays a series of bars in all possible colors for the graphics mode on your computer. The first bar is the same as the background and is, therefore, invisible.

Example

```
PROGRAM xSetColor;
USES Crt, Graph;
VAR graphDriver, graphMode : integer;
    x, xMax, yMax, color, width, height : word;
BEGIN
   graphDriver := Detect;
   InitGraph( graphDriver, graphMode, '' );
   xMax := GetMaxX; yMax := GetMaxY;
   width := ( Succ(xMax) DIV Succ(GetMaxColor) ) DIV 2;
   height := ( Succ(yMax) DIV 4 );
   x := 0;
   FOR color := 0 TO GetMaxColor DO
   BEGIN
      SetColor( color );
      Rectangle( x, yMax, x + width, height );
      SetFillStyle( LtSlashFill, color );
      FloodFill( x+1, yMax-1, color );
      x := x + width + width
   END; { for }
   REPEAT UNTIL KeyPressed;
   CloseGraph
END.
```

SetDate

Syntax

```
PROCEDURE SetDate( year, month, day : Word );
```

Location

Dos

Description

Call **SetDate** to change the computer's system date. Parameter **year** must be the full year—1987 or 1999 for example. Parameter **month** should be in the range 1 to 12, and **day** should be the month's day number.

The example finds the day of the week for any date by setting the system date and then calling the **Dos** unit routine **GetDate**. Before the program ends, it calls **SetDate** a second time to reset today's date. (Don't trust the results of this example too far. The program's accuracy is only as good as DOS's date routines, which may have bugs on some early systems and which may not be able to handle dates before January 1, 1980.)

Example

```
PROGRAM xSetDate;
USES Dos;
CONST DayNames : ARRAY[0..6] OF String[3] =
    ( 'Sun', 'Mon', 'Tue', 'Wed', 'Thu', 'Fri', 'Sat' );
VAR oldyear, oldmonth, oldday, olddayofweek : Word;
    newyear, newmonth, newday, newdayofweek : Word;
    year, month, day : Word;
BEGIN
    GetDate( oldyear, oldmonth, oldday, olddayofweek );
    Write( 'Year? (ex. 1987) : ' ); Readln( year );
    Write( 'Month? (ex. 11)  : ' ); Readln( month );
    Write( 'Day? (ex. 25)    : ' ); Readln( day );
    SetDate( year, month, day );
    GetDate( newyear, newmonth, newday, newdayofweek );
    Writeln( 'Day of week : ', DayNames[newdayofweek] );
    SetDate( oldyear, oldmonth, oldday )
END.
```

SetFAttr

Syntax

```
PROCEDURE SetFAttr( VAR f; attr : Word );
```

Location

Dos

Description

SetFAttr stores the attribute value **attr** along with a file name in a disk directory. It changes nothing in the file itself; only the file's directory entry. By changing the attribute, you can hide files, modify the archive bit—which tells if the file was recently backed up—or mark the file read-only, preventing it from being deleted or changed.

Before using **SetFAttr**, assign a file name to any file variable. Then pass the file variable (**f**) and a **Word** variable (**attr**) to **GetFAttr**. The file must not be open.

To preserve other attribute settings, use **GetFAttr** before calling **SetFAttr**. Add or subtract combinations of the constant values:

```
ReadOnly   = $01    Hidden   = $02
SysFile    = $04    VolumeID = $08
Directory  = $10    Archive  = $20
```

To test whether a file has a certain attribute combination, AND the attribute with the sum of one or more constants. If the result is zero, then the file does not have the attributes. If not zero, then the file has at least one of the settings.

To change an attribute, OR the sum of one or more constant values to turn on attributes, or NOT-AND the sum to turn off attributes.

The example shows how to use these techniques to first check whether a file TEST.TXT has ReadOnly or Hidden attributes. If not, the program turns on these settings by ORing them into the file's current attribute bits; otherwise, it turns the settings off by NOT-ANDing the settings. Run the program once to hide TEST.TXT in the directory and to mark it read-only, preventing you from deleting it. Run the program again to reset the file's attributes to normal. You need a test file named TEST.TXT for the example to work.

Example

```
PROGRAM xSetFAttr;
USES DOS;
VAR f : FILE; attr, settings : Word;
BEGIN
   Assign( f, 'TEST.TXT' );
   GetFAttr( f, attr );
   settings := ReadOnly + Hidden;
   IF (attr AND settings) = 0
     THEN SetFAttr( f, (attr OR settings) )      { Turn on }
     ELSE SetFAttr( f, (attr AND NOT settings) ) { Turn off }
END.
```

SetFillPattern

Syntax

```
PROCEDURE SetFillPattern( pattern : FillPatternType; color : Word );
```

Location

Graph

Description

SetFillPattern changes the bit pattern and color used by **Bar, Bar3D, FillEllipse, FillPoly, FloodFill, PieSlice**, and **Sector**. The **pattern** is a variable of this type:

```
TYPE
   FillPatternType =
      ARRAY[ 1 .. 8 ] OF Byte;
```

Insert bit pattern bytes into the pattern array and call **SetFillPattern** with a color value. In the example, a **REPEAT** loop cycles until you press any key to quit. Each time through the loop, an inner **FOR** loop rotates to the left the bits in the pattern array. Filling a bar with this pattern causes an undulating animation that would be difficult to achieve with other methods.

Example

```
PROGRAM xSetFillPattern;
USES Crt, Graph;
VAR graphDriver, graphMode : integer;
    xc, yc, x1, y1, x2, y2 : Integer;
    pattern : FillPatternType;
    i : Byte;
BEGIN
   graphDriver := Detect;
   InitGraph( graphDriver, graphMode, '' );
   xc := GetMaxX DIV 2; yc := GetMaxY DIV 2;
   FOR i := 1 TO 8 DO
      pattern[i] := i;
   x1 := xc - 50; y1 := yc - 50;
   x2 := xc + 50; y2 := yc + 50;
   REPEAT
      SetFillPattern( pattern, red );
      Bar( x1, y1, x2, y2 );
      FOR i := 1 TO 8 DO
         pattern[i] := ( pattern[i] SHL 1 ) OR pattern[i] SHR 7
   UNTIL Keypressed;
   CloseGraph
END.
```

SetFillStyle

Syntax

```
PROCEDURE SetFillStyle( pattern : Word; color : Word );
```

Location

Graph

Description

Call **SetFillStyle** to select one of several predefined fill patterns for **Bar, Bar3D, FillEllipse, FillPoly, FloodFill, PieSlice**, and **Sector**. Pass a **color** number plus one of these **pattern** constants, as defined in the **Graph** unit's interface:

```
EmptyFill       = 0;   { fills area in background color }
SolidFill       = 1;   { fills area in solid fill color }
LineFill        = 2;   { --- fill }
LtSlashFill     = 3;   { /// fill }
SlashFill       = 4;   { /// fill with thick lines }
BkSlashFill     = 5;   { \\\ fill with thick lines }
LtBkSlashFill   = 6;   { \\\ fill }
HatchFill       = 7;   { light hatch fill }
XHatchFill      = 8;   { heavy cross hatch fill }
InterleaveFill  = 9;   { interleaving line fill }
WideDotFill     = 10;  { widely spaced dot fill }
CloseDotFill    = 11;  { closely spaced dot fill }
UserFill        = 12;  { user defined fill }
```

The example displays randomly colored and sized bars using all possible fill patterns except zero, which fills in the background color. Press any key to end the demonstration.

Example

```
PROGRAM xSetFillStyle;
USES Crt, Graph;
VAR graphDriver, graphMode : integer;
    xMax, yMax : Integer;
BEGIN
   graphDriver := Detect;
   InitGraph( graphDriver, graphMode, '' );
   xMax := GetMaxX; yMax := GetMaxY;
   WHILE NOT Keypressed DO
   BEGIN
     SetFillStyle( 1+Random(11), 1+Random(GetMaxColor) );
     Bar( Random(xMax), Random(yMax),
          Random(xMax), Random(yMax) )
   END; { while }
   CloseGraph
END.
```

SetFTime

Syntax

```
PROCEDURE SetFTime( VAR f; time : LongInt );
```

Location

Dos

Description

Call **SetFTime** to change the date and time for a file's directory entry. The procedure never changes the file itself, only the date and time you see when listing the file name with the DOS DIR command.

File **f** must be open. Parameter **time** must be in the packed format required by DOS. To set a specific time, assign fields in a **DateTime** record and call **Pack-Time** to convert the record to the packed long integer value. Then call **SetFTime** to change the file date and time.

If you write to a file and then call **SetFTime**, when you close the file, DOS will update the date and time, erasing your change. To avoid this problem, **Reset** the file you want to change. As long as you do not write to the file, **Close** will not update the date and time.

The example changes TEST.TXT's date to last year by reading the file's date and time with **GetFTime**, unpacking the long integer value into a **DateTime** record, subtracting one from the year field, repacking, and then calling **SetFTime**.

Example

```
PROGRAM xSetFTime;
USES Dos;
VAR f : FILE; time : LongInt;
    daterec : DateTime;
BEGIN
   Assign( f, 'TEST.TXT' );
   Reset( f );
   GetFTime( f, time );
   UnPackTime( time, daterec );
   WITH daterec DO
      year := year - 1;
   PackTime( daterec, time );
   SetFTime( f, time );
   Close( f )
END.
```

SetGraphBufSize

Syntax

```
PROCEDURE SetGraphBufSize( bufSize : Word );
```

Location

Graph

Description

Before calling **InitGraph**, if you plan to fill complex polygons or other shapes with patterns, you might have to expand a special memory buffer set aside by the graphics kernel. Pass to **SetGraphBufSize** the number of bytes in **bufSize** that you want to reserve for the kernel's fill work space.

Normally, you will rarely need to increase the default setting of 4K, large enough to fill polygons with over 600 points. You might call **SetGraphBufSize** as in the example, though, to reduce the buffer size and gain a little extra memory for other purposes when filling relatively uncomplicated shapes.

Example

```
PROGRAM xSetGraphBufSize;
USES Crt, Graph;
CONST NumPoints = 75;
VAR graphDriver, graphMode : integer;
    i, xMax, yMax : integer;
    polyPoints : ARRAY[ 1 .. NumPoints ] OF PointType;
BEGIN
   Randomize;
   SetGraphBufSize( 1024 );  { 1/4 the normal 4K allotment }
   graphDriver := Detect;
   InitGraph( graphDriver, graphMode, '' );
   xMax := GetMaxX; yMax := GetMaxY;
   FOR i := 1 TO NumPoints DO
   BEGIN
      polyPoints[i].x := Random(xMax);
      polyPoints[i].y := Random(yMax)
   END; { for }
   SetFillStyle( XHatchFill, LightMagenta );
   FillPoly( NumPoints, polyPoints );
   REPEAT UNTIL Keypressed;
   CloseGraph
END.
```

SetGraphMode

Syntax

```
PROCEDURE SetGraphMode( mode : Integer );
```

Location

Graph

Description

Call **SetGraphMode** to restore a previous graphics mode after switching to a text screen. Parameter **mode** should be the value returned by **GetGraphMode**, although it can also be a different value if you want to switch between various graphics modes in the same program.

The example shows one way to use **SetGraphMode**. The program begins normally, automatically detecting and initializing a graphics display. It then saves the current graphics mode in **oldmode** and calls **RestoreCrtMode** to return to the text screen. After displaying a message, **SetGraphMode** returns to the graphics display until you press a key to end the example.

Example

```
PROGRAM xSetGraphMode;
USES Crt,Graph;
VAR graphDriver, graphMode : integer;
    i, oldmode, xMax, yMax : Integer;
BEGIN
   graphDriver := Detect;
   InitGraph( graphDriver, graphMode, '' );
   IF GraphResult = GrOk THEN
   BEGIN
      xMax := GetMaxX; yMax := GetMaxY;
      oldmode := GetGraphMode;
      RestoreCrtMode;
      Writeln( 'Ready for graphics!' );
      Writeln;
      Write( 'Press <Enter> to continue...' );
      Readln;

      SetGraphMode( oldmode );

      REPEAT
         SetColor( Random(1+GetMaxColor) );
         Rectangle( Random(xMax), Random(yMax),
                    Random(xMax), Random(yMax) );
```

```
        UNTIL Keypressed;
        CloseGraph
    END { if }
END.
```

SetIntVec

Syntax

```
PROCEDURE SetIntVec( intNo : Byte; vector : Pointer );
```

Location

Dos

Description

Interrupt vectors are the addresses of routines you want to run when a specific interrupt occurs. The interrupt itself is identified by a number ranging from 0 to hex $FF. Programs can interrupt themselves via software interrupts—a call to a DOS function for example. Or, programs can be interrupted by hardware-generated interrupts—perhaps from a keypress or an incoming character from a modem.

Call **SetIntVec** to change the vector address of any PC interrupt. Because many computer operations depend on the correct vectors, changing vectors indiscriminately can cause serious problems. For instance, if you fiddle with the absolute disk read and write vectors, hex $25 and $26, you could temporarily lose the ability to use your disk drives.

The example shows how to set a pointer variable, **address**, to a specific location. In your own programs, replace the first 0000 with the segment and the second 0000 with the offset addresses of your interrupt routine. Then pass the interrupt number (here $60) plus the address to **SetIntVec**. After that, when this interrupt occurs, your interrupt routine will begin running.

Example

```
PROGRAM xSetIntVec;
USES Dos;
VAR address : Pointer;
BEGIN
    address := Ptr( 0000, 0000 );
    SetIntVec( $60, address )
END.
```

SetLineStyle

Syntax

```
PROCEDURE SetLineStyle( lineStyle : Word; pattern : Word; thickness : Word );
```

Location

Graph

Description

Call **SetLineStyle** to change the thickness and bit pattern used by **LineTo**, **LineRel**, **Line**, **Rectangle**, and **DrawPoly**. **Arc**, **Circle**, **Ellipse**, and **PieSlice** outlines are always solid—you cannot change their line styles with **SetLineStyle**.
   Parameter **lineStyle** may be one of the following constant values:

```
SolidLn   = 0;
DottedLn  = 1;
CenterLn  = 2;
DashedLn  = 3;
UserBitLn = 4;
```

   Parameter **thickness** may be **NormWidth** (1) or **ThickWidth** (3). As the example proves, a thickness of 2 does not draw a double-width line as you might expect. Only thicknesses of 1 and 3 have any effect.
   If you set parameter **lineStyle** to the constant **UserBitLn**, lines are drawn with the bits in parameter **pattern**. **SetLineStyle** ignores **pattern** for any other **lineStyle** value. For example, to draw a finely dotted horizontal line with the repeating binary pattern 01010101 . . . , you could write:

```
pattern := $5555;
SetLineStyle( UserBitLn, pattern, NormWidth );
SetColor( Red );
Line( 0, 10, GetMaxX, 10 );
```

   The example displays test lines in all possible standard settings. Notice that line thicknesses 1 and 2 draw identical lines.

Example

```
PROGRAM xSetLineStyle;
USES Crt, Graph;
VAR graphDriver, graphMode : integer;
    y, xMax, yMax : word;
    lineStyle, pattern, thickness : word;
    lsStr, pStr, tStr : String[8];
```

```
BEGIN
    graphDriver := Detect;
    InitGraph( graphDriver, graphMode, '' );
    xMax := GetMaxX; yMax := GetMaxY;
    y := 4;
    pattern := 0;  { Ignored unless lineStyle = UserBitLn }
    FOR thickness := 1 TO 3 DO
    FOR lineStyle := 0 TO 3 DO
    BEGIN
        SetColor( Red );
        SetLineStyle( lineStyle, pattern, thickness );
        Line( 0, y, xMax, y );
        Str( lineStyle, lsStr );
        Str( pattern, pStr );
        Str( thickness, tStr );
        SetColor( White );
        OutTextXY( 0, y+8,
            'Style='+lsStr+'  Pattern='+pStr+'  Thickness='+tStr );
        y := y + 28
    END;
    REPEAT UNTIL Keypressed;
    CloseGraph
END.
```

SetPalette

Syntax

PROCEDURE SetPalette(colorNum : Word; color : ShortInt);

Location

Graph

Description

As described in the description to **SetAllPalette**, color numbers are translated to the actual color values stored in the video display memory to produce certain hues on screen. The translations between color numbers and the hues they produce are stored in a palette. Use **SetPalette** to change one palette entry, affecting the color you see (**color**) for one color number (**colorNum**).

The example demonstrates how to use this procedure to produce an interesting illusion. By rotating all but palette entry zero, the background color, lines take on the colors of their neighbors. Because changing palette entries has an immediate visual effect, the lines appear to move.

Example

```
PROGRAM xSetPalette;
USES Crt,Graph;
VAR graphDriver, graphMode : integer;
    maxcolor, temp, c, y, xMax, yMax : word;
    colors : ARRAY[ 0 .. 15 ] OF Word;
BEGIN
   graphDriver := Detect;
   InitGraph( graphDriver, graphMode, '' );
   xMax := GetMaxX; yMax := GetMaxY; y := 0;
   maxColor := GetMaxColor;
   SetLineStyle( SolidLn, 0, ThickWidth );
   FOR c := 0 TO maxColor DO
   BEGIN
      colors[c] := c;              { Save colors in array }
      SetColor( c );
      y := y + 20;
      Line( 0, y, xMax, y )        { Fill screen with lines }
   END; { for }
   WHILE NOT Keypressed DO          { "Rotate" colors }
   BEGIN
      Delay(300);                   { Adjust to change speed }
      temp := colors[1];
      FOR c := 1 TO maxColor DO
      BEGIN
         IF c = maxColor
            THEN colors[c] := temp
            ELSE colors[c] := colors[c+1];
         SetPalette( c, colors[c] )
      END { for }
   END; { while }
   CloseGraph
END.
```

SetRGBPalette

Syntax

```
PROCEDURE SetRGBPalette( colorNum, redValue, greenValue,
   blueValue : Integer );
```

Location

Graph

Description

Use this special **Graph** procedure to set the red, green, and blue (RGB) color values for IBM-8514 256-color displays. Set **colorNum** to the palette index value you want to change, in the range 0 to 255. For compatibility with other display formats, the first 16 (index values 0 to 15) IBM-8514 palette entries match EGA and VGA display colors. Use **SetRGBPalette** to modify these colors.

Only the least-significant 6 bits of the low bytes in each of the three **Integer** parameters, **redValue**, **greenValue**, and **blueValue**, are used, limiting color values to the range 0 to 64.

It's possible to use **SetRGBPalette** to modify some VGA display colors, but in this case, Borland specifies that **colorNum** should be limited to the values 0 to 15, even for 256-color displays. At this time, better control of 256-color VGA displays is available only with a special version of the BGI **Graph** unit, which Borland plans to distribute free of charge on bulletin boards and time-share services such as Compuserve.

The example examines the automatically selected graphics driver (**graphDriver**) and calls either **SetRGBPalette** or **SetPalette** to modify the displayed colors of vertical lines drawn in all available colors. Because palette entries control the colors of pixels already on display, the effects of modifying the palette values like this are instantaneous.

Example

```
PROGRAM xSetRGBPalette;
USES Crt, Graph;
VAR graphDriver, graphMode : Integer;
    x, xMax, yMax, color, width, height : Word;
BEGIN
   graphDriver := Detect;
   InitGraph( graphDriver, graphMode, '' );
   xMax := GetMaxX; yMax := GetMaxY;
   width := ( Succ(xMax) DIV Succ(GetMaxColor) ) DIV 2;
   height := ( Succ(yMax) DIV 4 ); x := 0;
   FOR color := 0 TO GetMaxColor DO
   BEGIN
     SetColor( color );
     Line( x, yMax, x, height );
     Line( x + 1, yMax, x + 1, height );
     x := x + ( width * 2 )
   END; { for }
   WHILE NOT Keypressed DO
   FOR color := 1 TO GetMaxColor DO
     IF graphDriver = IBM8514
        THEN SetRGBPalette( color, Random(65), Random(65), Random(65) )
        ELSE SetPalette( color, Random( GetMaxColor + 1 ) );
   CloseGraph
END.
```

SetTextBuf

Syntax

```
PROCEDURE SetTextBuf( VAR f : TEXT; VAR buf [; size : Word] );
```

Location

System

Description

When reading and writing large text files, you might be able to improve I/O speed by increasing the size of the buffer Turbo Pascal fills with characters on their way to and from disk.

Normally, text files have a 128-byte buffer, large enough for most purposes. To increase buffer size, declare a variable, usually an array of **Byte** or **Char**, and pass the variable along with the file to **SetTextBuf**. Do this either before or immediately after resetting or rewriting the file. Changing the text buffer after reading or writing text might accidentally discard information stored in the default buffer.

Unless you add a **size** parameter, Turbo Pascal uses the entire buffer. In other words, the default condition is:

```
SetTextBuf( f, buffer, sizeof(buffer) );
```

Usually, this is best. To use only part of a buffer, pass the number of bytes as the third parameter. For example, to use 512 bytes of a buffer, you could write:

```
SetTextBuf( f, buffer, 512 );
```

Use the example to experiment reading large text files. Change the buffer size (or remove the **SetTextBuf** statement) and note how long it takes to read through a file. Also, watch your disk drive light. With larger buffer sizes, you should see less disk activity, which usually means better program speed.

Example

```
PROGRAM xSetTextBuf;
VAR tf : TEXT;
    buf : ARRAY[0..1023] OF Char;
    fileName, s : String;
BEGIN
   Write( 'Display what text file? ' );
   Readln( fileName );
   Assign( tf, fileName );
   SetTextBuf( tf, buf );   { Use entire buffer }
   Reset( tf );
```

```
      WHILE NOT Eof(tf) DO
      BEGIN
         Readln( tf, s );
         Writeln( s )
      END; { while }
      Close( tf )
   END.
```

SetTextJustify

Syntax

```
PROCEDURE SetTextJustify( horiz, vert : Word );
```

Location

Graph

Description

Call **SetTextJustify** to change where **OutText** displays text in relation to the current point (CP) or to the coordinate passed to **OutTextXY**. For the **horiz** parameter, use one of these constants:

```
LeftText   = 0;
CenterText = 1;
RightText  = 2;
```

For the **vert** parameter, use one of these constants:

```
BottomText = 0;
CenterText = 1;
TopText    = 2;
```

The example helps explain how **SetTextJustify** affects the appearance of text on screen. Run the program and press Enter several times to display a message. A white dot shows the current point in relation to where text appears for various justification settings.

Example

```
PROGRAM xSetTextJustify;
USES Crt, Graph;
VAR graphDriver, graphMode : Integer;
    xCenter, yCenter : Word;
    horiz, vert : Integer;
```

```
BEGIN
    graphDriver := Detect;
    InitGraph( graphDriver, graphMode, '' );
    xCenter := GetMaxX DIV 2; yCenter := GetMaxY DIV 2;
    FOR vert := 0 TO 2 DO
        FOR horiz := 0 TO 2 DO
        BEGIN
            SetTextJustify( horiz, vert );
            ClearViewPort;
            SetColor( Magenta );
            OutTextXY( xCenter, yCenter, 'Happy New Year!' );
            SetColor( White );
            Rectangle( xCenter, yCenter, xCenter+1, yCenter+1 );
            IF ReadKey = CHR(27) THEN
            BEGIN
                CloseGraph;
                Halt
            END { if }
        END; { for / for }
    CloseGraph
END.
```

SetTextStyle

Syntax

```
PROCEDURE SetTextStyle( font, direction : Word; charSize : Word );
```

Location

Graph

Description

SetTextStyle changes three text characteristics: the font, the direction, and the size. To select a different font, use one of these constants:

```
DefaultFont    = 0;
TriplexFont    = 1;
SmallFont      = 2;
SansSerifFont  = 3;
GothicFont     = 4;
```

The default font is an 8 × 8 bit-mapped image. The other fonts are stroked (vectored). If the font is not in memory, **SetTextStyle** attempts to load the associated

CHR file from disk, in the path specified for **InitGraph**. If the font file is not on disk, **SetTextStyle** returns an error through **GraphResult**.

The direction and size parameters let you display text horizontally or vertically and scale characters to different sizes. Set the direction to either of the constants **HorizDir** or **VertDir**. Set the size to any positive value greater than zero. The actual size you see on screen has no relation to the point sizes (typically in $1/72$-inch increments) used in typesetting. Using the same size values for different fonts does not draw characters in the same relative sizes on screen.

The example displays two messages in vertical and horizontal directions. Notice how **TextWidth** and **TextHeight** position the text.

Example

```
PROGRAM xSetTextStyle;
USES  Crt, Graph;
CONST Size = 4;
VAR   graphDriver, graphMode : Integer;
      x, y : Word;
BEGIN
   graphDriver := Detect;
   InitGraph( graphDriver, graphMode, '' );
   x := TextWidth( 'M' ) * 4;
   y := TextHeight( 'M' ) * 2;
   SetTextStyle( SansSerifFont, VertDir, Size );
   OutTextXY( x, y, 'Going up' );
   SetTextStyle( SansSerifFont, HorizDir, Size );
   OutTextXY( x, y, '    Stepping out' );
   REPEAT UNTIL Keypressed;
   CloseGraph
END.
```

SetTime

Syntax

```
PROCEDURE SetTime( hour, minute, second, sec100 : Word );
```

Location

Dos

Description

Call **SetTime** to change the computer's system time to the **hour**, **minute**, **second**, and **sec100** (hundredths of seconds) specified by these parameters.

As the example demonstrates, programs can set the time to zero, perform an operation to be timed (a nested **FOR** loop here) and then call **GetTime** to read the result. The program displays how long it takes to cycle one million times—an important benchmark of the computer processor's speed and Turbo Pascal's **FOR** loop overhead. After running this program, you might want to reset your computer's clock to the current time. To do this, either reboot or use the DOS TIME command.

Example

```
PROGRAM xSetTime;
USES DOS;
VAR i, j : Integer;
    hour, minute, sec, sec100 : Word;
BEGIN
   SetTime( 0, 0, 0, 0 );
   FOR i := 1 TO 100 DO
      FOR j := 1 TO 10000 DO { nothing };
   GetTime( hour, minute, sec, sec100 );
   Writeln( 'Hours     = ', hour );
   Writeln( 'Minutes   = ', minute );
   Writeln( 'Seconds   = ', sec );
   Writeln( 'Hundredths = ', sec100 )
END.
```

SetUserCharSize

Syntax

```
PROCEDURE SetUserCharSize( multX, divX, multY, divY : Word );
```

Location

Graph

Description

Most of the time, you can select character font sizes by passing a size number to **SetTextStyle**. For better control, use **SetUserCharSize**, which lets you adjust the horizontal and vertical ratio used to draw characters.

Parameters **multX** and **divX** control the horizontal size. Parameters **multY** and **divY** control the vertical. Use a ratio less than 1 to shrink characters to less than their usual dimensions. For example, if **multX/divX** equals 0.25, then characters display one-fourth their normal width. Likewise, if **multY/divY** equals 3.5, then characters display about 3½ times their normal height.

After calling **SetUserCharSize**, you must call **SetTextStyle** to select a character font and direction. Pass the constant **UserCharSize** as the third **SetText-**

Style parameter, telling the graphics kernel to use your ratio instead of the default. Because **SetTextStyle** loads a font CHR file from disk, you might want to preload and register the font ahead of time (see **RegisterBGIfont**), especially if you switch ratios frequently.

The example displays two messages, the first 3.5 times as tall as usual (7/2), and the second about 2.7 (8/3) times as wide on EGA or better systems and about 1.4 (4/3) times as wide on CGA displays. Try experimenting with different ratios in the three calls to **SetUserCharSize**.

Example

```
PROGRAM xSetUserCharSize;
USES Crt, Graph;
VAR graphDriver, graphMode : integer;
BEGIN
   graphDriver := Detect;
   InitGraph( graphDriver, graphMode, '' );
   SetUserCharSize( 1, 1, 7, 2 );
   SetTextStyle( SansSerifFont, HorizDir, UserCharSize );
   OutTextXY( 0, 50, 'Tall in the saddle' );
   IF graphDriver = CGA
      THEN SetUserCharSize( 4, 3, 1, 1 )
      ELSE SetUserCharSize( 8, 3, 1, 1 );
   SetTextStyle( SansSerifFont, HorizDir, UserCharSize );
   OutTextXY( 0, 150, 'Wide in the ride' );
   REPEAT Until Keypressed;
   CloseGraph
END.
```

SetVerify

Syntax

```
PROCEDURE SetVerify( verify : Boolean );
```

Location

Dos

Description

When the DOS *verify* switch is **True**, disk writes are followed by automatic disk reads to verify that data written to disk probably was stored correctly. When the *verify* switch is **False**, disk writes are not followed by disk reads. Because write-verification slows disk I/O considerably, most people leave this switch off.

Call function **SetVerify** to change the switch setting (similar to the way the DOS VERIFY command works). Call the related **GetVerify** procedure to inspect the state of the DOS *verify* switch. The example toggles the switch on and off.

Example

```
PROGRAM xSetVerify;
USES Dos;
VAR verify : Boolean;
BEGIN
   GetVerify( verify );
   verify := NOT verify;
   SetVerify( verify );
   Writeln( 'Verify switch is: ', verify )
END.
```

SetViewPort

Syntax

```
PROCEDURE SetViewPort( x1, y1, x2, y2 : Integer; clip : Boolean );
```

Location

Graph

Description

Changing the graphics viewport with **SetViewPort** defines the boundaries of the visible portion of the display. Coordinate (x1,y1) represents the top-left corner of the new display window while (x2,y2) represents the bottom-right corner. If **clip** is **True**, then lines drawn outside of the new boundaries are invisible. If it's **False**, then lines are not restricted to the window boundaries. In place of **True** and **False**, you can use the **Graph** constants, **ClipOn** and **ClipOff**.

After calling **SetViewPort**, the top-left corner of the new window has the coordinate (0,0), not (x1,y1). You can use this fact to shift the origin—the anchor point or home position of the logical coordinate grid. Negative coordinate values lie to the left and above the origin. Positive coordinate values lie to the right and below. Shifting the viewport to center (0,0) sometimes makes graphics programs easier to write. To do this, execute the instructions:

```
xCenter := GetMaxX DIV 2; yCenter := GetMaxY DIV 2;
SetViewPort( xCenter, yCenter, GetMaxX, GetMaxY, ClipOff );
```

Example

```
PROGRAM xSetViewPort;
USES Crt, Graph;
VAR graphDriver, graphMode : integer;
    xCenter, yCenter, xcd2, ycd2 : integer;
BEGIN
   graphDriver := Detect;
   InitGraph( graphDriver, graphMode, '' );
   xCenter := GetMaxX DIV 2; yCenter := GetMaxY DIV 2;
   xcd2 := xCenter DIV 2; ycd2 := yCenter DIV 2;
   Randomize;
   SetViewPort( xCenter-xcd2, yCenter-ycd2,
                xCenter+xcd2, yCenter+ycd2, ClipOn );
   WHILE NOT Keypressed DO
   BEGIN
      SetColor( 1+Random(GetMaxColor) );
      LineTo( Random(GetMaxX)-xcd2, Random(GetMaxY)-ycd2 )
   END; { while }
   CloseGraph
END.
```

SetVisualPage

Syntax

```
PROCEDURE SetVisualPage( page : Word );
```

Location

Graph

Description

In graphics modes that support multiple pages, **SetVisualPage** brings the display number **page** into view. When combined with **SetActivePage**, this procedure lets you view one graphics display while drawing on another. Rapidly flopping the two pages—viewing the previously hidden page and drawing on the one now invisible—can produce smooth animations, similar to the effect of flipping the pages in an animated cartoon book.

For an example of how to use **SetVisualPage** and for more information, see **SetActivePage**.

Example

See **SetActivePage**.

SetWriteMode

Syntax

```
PROCEDURE SetWriteMode( writeMode : Integer );
```

Location

Graph

Description

To change the logic by which **Graph** combines pixels in lines and other shapes with existing pixels, pass one of the following values to **SetWriteMode**:

```
CopyPut  = 0;
XORPut   = 1;
ORPut    = 2;
ANDPut   = 3;
NOTPut   = 4;
```

The **Graph** unit defines these constants to add readability to programs. For example, to change the write mode to **ANDPut**, execute the statement:

```
SetWriteMode( ANDPut );
```

Each write-mode method has a different effect. The default value **CopyPut** causes new pixels to overwrite existing shapes. The other values combine new pixels according to the rules of Boolean logic operators XOR, OR, AND, and NOT (see Chapter 2).

One of the more useful of these values is **XORPut**, which has the property of being able to toggle bits on and off without prior knowledge of the original bit value. When applied to graphics, this property lets programs draw shapes on top of other shapes and then remove the topmost shape simply by redrawing that shape! As if by magic, the shape below remains untouched by the operation.

The example demonstrates the effect of drawing lines with the write mode set to **XORPut**. First, the program fills the screen with a complex background pattern, drawn by the **Bar** procedure. Then, an array of color and coordinate values is filled with random values. A **FOR** loop uses these values to draw ten lines over the complex background. Another **FOR** loop then redraws the same lines in reverse. Press < Enter > repeatedly to see how **XORPut** allows these lines to remove themselves from the display, completely restoring other lines and the background pattern below.

Example

```
PROGRAM xSetWrite;
USES Crt, Graph;
TYPE rec = RECORD color : Word;
             x1, y1, x2, y2 : Integer
           END;
VAR graphDriver, graphMode : Integer;
    i : Integer;
    v : ARRAY[ 1 .. 10 ] OF rec;


PROCEDURE SetValues( i, c : Word;
   x, y, xx, yy : Integer );
BEGIN
   WITH v[ i ] DO
   BEGIN
     color := c;
     x1 := x; y1 := y;
     x2 := xx; y2 := yy
   END { with }
END; { SetValues }


BEGIN
   graphDriver := Detect;
   InitGraph( graphDriver, graphMode, '' );
   SetFillStyle( XHatchFill, Red );
   Bar( 0, 0, GetMaxX, GetMaxY );
   FOR i := 1 TO 10 DO
     SetValues( i, 1 + Random( GetMaxColor ),
        Random( GetMaxX ), Random( GetMaxY ),
        Random( GetMaxX ), Random( GetMaxY ) );
   SetWriteMode( XORPut );
   SetLineStyle( SolidLn, 0, ThickWidth );
   FOR i := 1 TO 10 DO WITH v[i] DO
   BEGIN
     SetColor( color );
     Line( x1, y1, x2, y2 )
   END; { for }
   FOR i := 10 DOWNTO 1 DO WITH v[i] DO
   BEGIN
     Readln;
     SetColor( color );
     Line( x1, y1, x2, y2 )
   END; { for }
   REPEAT UNTIL Keypressed;
   CloseGraph
END.
```

Sin

Syntax

```
FUNCTION Sin( r : <real> ) : <real>;
```

Location

System

Description

Sin returns the sine of r, which must be expressed in radians. The example requires a graphics display.

Example

```
PROGRAM xSin;
USES Crt,Graph;
VAR graphDriver, graphMode : integer;
    x, y, yc : integer;

FUNCTION Radians( angle : Integer ) : Real;
BEGIN
   Radians := Abs( angle Mod 360 ) * Pi / 180.0
END; { Radians }

BEGIN
   graphDriver := Detect;
   InitGraph( graphDriver, graphMode, '' );
   yc := GetMaxY DIV 2;
   FOR x := 0 TO GetMaxX DO
      PutPixel( x, yc+Round(yc * Sin(Radians(x))), Green );
   REPEAT UNTIL Keypressed;
   CloseGraph
END.
```

SizeOf

Syntax

```
FUNCTION SizeOf( v : <type> | <file> ) : Word;
```

Location

System

Description

SizeOf returns the number of bytes occupied by a variable **v** or by any data type. Use this function with **Move** and **FillChar** to prevent accidental overwriting of memory beyond addresses occupied by variables.

The example displays a chart of Turbo Pascal's common data types along with the number of bytes variables of those types occupy in memory.

Example

```
PROGRAM xSizeOf;
BEGIN
   Writeln( 'Types          Bytes' );
   Writeln( '==================' );
   Writeln( 'Byte ........ ', Sizeof( Byte ) );
   Writeln( 'ShortInt .... ', Sizeof( ShortInt ) );
   Writeln( 'Integer ..... ', Sizeof( Integer ) );
   Writeln( 'Word ........ ', Sizeof( Word ) );
   Writeln( 'LongInt ..... ', Sizeof( LongInt ) );
   Writeln( 'Real ........ ', Sizeof( Real ) );
   Writeln( 'Char ........ ', Sizeof( Char ) );
   Writeln( 'Boolean ..... ', Sizeof( Boolean ) )
END.
```

Sound

Syntax

```
PROCEDURE Sound( hz : Word );
```

Location

Crt

Description

Sound turns on a **hz** (hertz or cycles per second) tone. The frequency is approximate. The tone stays on while other statements execute until you call **NoSound**.

Example

```
PROGRAM xSound;
USES Crt;
VAR frequency : Integer;
```

```
BEGIN
   WHILE NOT Keypressed DO
   BEGIN
      Write( 'Whoop...' );
      FOR frequency := 500 TO 900 DO
      BEGIN
         Delay(1);
         Sound( frequency )
      END; { for }
      NoSound;
      Delay(75)
   END { while }
END.
```

SPtr

Syntax

FUNCTION SPtr : Word;

Location

System

Description

SPtr returns the 16-bit value of the processor stack pointer, which decreases toward zero as the program uses stack space for local variables and also for procedure and function calls. You might examine the stack pointer in a program that turns off stack checking with the compiler directive {$S–} to see if your memory fuel tank is getting low.

The example calls a recursive bean counter, counting up to ten and displaying the stack pointer at each level in the recursion. Function **SSeg** returns the stack segment value, which never changes. When you run the program, you see a display similar to this:

```
Beans =  0  SPtr = 5643 :3FBA
Beans =  1  SPtr = 5643 :3FC0
Beans =  2  SPtr = 5643 :3FC6
Beans =  3  SPtr = 5643 :3FCC
Beans =  5  SPtr = 5643 :3FD8
Beans =  7  SPtr = 5643 :3FE4
Beans =  9  SPtr = 5643 :3FF0
Beans = 10  SPtr = 5643 :3FF6
```

Example

```
PROGRAM xSPtr;

FUNCTION WHex( v : word ) : Char;
CONST
   digits : ARRAY[ 0 .. 15 ] OF char = '0123456789ABCDEF';
BEGIN
   Write( digits[ hi( v ) div 16 ],
          digits[ hi( v ) mod 16 ],
          digits[ lo( v ) div 16 ],
          digits[ lo( v ) mod 16 ]  );
   WHex := Chr(0) { Null, so WHex can go in Write statements }
END; { WHex }

PROCEDURE BeanCounter( beans : Integer );
BEGIN
   IF beans > 0
      THEN BeanCounter( beans - 1 );
   Writeln( 'Beans =', beans:3,
      ' SPtr = ', WHex(SSeg), ':', WHex(SPtr) )
END; { BeanCounter }

BEGIN
   BeanCounter( 10 )
END.
```

Sqr

Syntax

```
FUNCTION Sqr( n : <number> ) : <number>;
```

Location

System

Description

Sqr returns the square of an integer or real number. The result, which is of the same type as its parameter, is equivalent to **n∗n**.

The square of even small integers may produce unexpected results. For example, **Sqr**(250) is −3036, not 62,500, which is greater than the largest possible positive integer value. Because any value squared is a positive number, you can usually avoid this problem by assigning **Sqr** to a **Word** or **LongInt** variable instead of to an **Integer** or **ShortInt**.

Example

```
PROGRAM xSqr;
CONST number = 212;
VAR int : Integer; long : LongInt;
BEGIN
   int := number;
   int := Sqr(int);
   long := Sqr(number);
   Writeln( 'Sqr(number):' );
   Writeln( '-----------------------' );
   Writeln( 'Integer result = ', int  );
   Writeln( 'LongInt result = ', long )
END.
```

Sqrt

Syntax

```
FUNCTION Sqrt( ( n : <real> ) : <real>;
```

Location

System

Description

Sqrt returns the square root of a real number. Unlike some functions that return the type of their arguments, **Sqrt** always returns a real-number result.

Example

```
PROGRAM xSqrt;
VAR r : Real;
BEGIN
   Write( 'Square root of ? ' );
   Readln( r );
   Writeln( '  _____' );      { 2 blanks + 8 underlines }
   Writeln( '\/', r:0:3, '=':8, Sqrt(r):10:3 )
END.
```

SSeg

Syntax

```
FUNCTION SSeg : Word;
```

Location

System

Description

SSeg returns the value of the stack segment register, SS. This equals the base address where local variables (those declared inside procedures and functions) are stored along with return addresses. See **SPtr** for an example of **SSeg** in action.

Example

See **SPtr**.

Str

Syntax

```
PROCEDURE Str( i[:n] : <integer>; VAR s : <string var> );
PROCEDURE Str( r[:n[:d]] : <real>; VAR s : <string var> );
```

Location

System

Description

Str converts real number values **r** or integer values **i** to string variables **s**. Optional formatting expressions right-justify values in **n** columns and **d** decimal places within the string.

You can specify the maximum number of decimals only for real numbers. For example, **Str**(r:8:2,s) converts real number **r** to string **s** in eight columns with two decimal places. This is identical to the numeric formatting rules for numbers in **Write** and **Writeln** statements.

The example displays several numbers as strings, using a variety of formatting options. The first two **Writeln** statements display a column reference line.

Example

```
PROGRAM xStr;
```

```
VAR s : String;
BEGIN
   Writeln( '0         1         2         3'              );
   Writeln( '012345678901234567890123456789012345678901234567890123456789' );
   Str( Pi, s     ); Writeln( s );
   Str( Pi:8:2, s ); Writeln( s );
   Str( Maxint, s ); Writeln( s );
   Str( 255:6, s  ); Writeln( s );
END.
```

Succ

Syntax

```
FUNCTION Succ( v : <ordinal> ) : <ordinal>;
```

Location

System

Description

Succ returns the scalar successor of **v**. For example, if type Color = (Red,White, Blue), then Succ(White) = Blue, and Succ(Red) = White. Succ(Blue) is undefined. Also, Succ(False) = True, and Succ(0) = 1, Succ(1) = 2, etc.

Example

```
PROGRAM xSucc;
VAR i : Integer;
BEGIN
   Writeln( 'Counting via Succ()' );
   Writeln;
   i := 0;
   WHILE i < 100 DO
   BEGIN
      i := Succ( i );
      Write( i:8 )
   END; { while }
   Writeln
END.
```

Swap

Syntax

```
FUNCTION Swap( i : <integer> ) : <integer>;
```

Location

System

Description

Swap exchanges the high (most significant) and low (least significant) bytes of a 16-bit integer or word variable. You can also swap other integer types such as **ShortInt** and **Byte**, but the results are not particularly useful for these single-byte quantities.

Example

```
PROGRAM XSwap;
USES Crt;
VAR
   s : shortint;
   i : integer;
   l : longint;
   b : byte;
   w : word;
BEGIN
   s := 15;      s := Swap(s); writeln( 's=', s );
   b := 255;     b := Swap(b); writeln( 'b=', b );
   i := 240;     i := Swap(i); writeln( 'i=', i );
   w := 240;     w := Swap(w); writeln( 'w=', w );
   l := 900000;  l := Swap(l); writeln( 'l=', l )
END.
```

SwapVectors

Syntax

```
PROCEDURE SwapVectors;
```

Location

Dos

Description

When a program begins, Turbo Pascal's **System** unit copies a series of low-memory interrupt vectors, which address critical ROM and DOS routines such as the keyboard interrupt handlers. Some of these vectors are then replaced with the addresses of Turbo Pascal's own critical code. Later, just before the program hands control back to DOS, the **System** unit restores the original vectors. If you need to do this at other times, call **SwapVectors**.

The example uses **SwapVectors** to restore interrupt vectors before calling **Exec** to execute a DOS command. This lets DOS use its own critical routines. A second call to **SwapVectors** restores the Turbo Pascal vectors before the program continues.

Example

```
{$M 1024, 0, 0}
PROGRAM xSwapVectors;
USES Dos;
BEGIN
   Writeln( 'Press Enter for wide directory...' );
   Readln;
   SwapVectors;
   Exec( GetEnv( 'COMSPEC' ), '/C DIR *.* /W' );
   SwapVectors;
   Writeln;
   Writeln( 'Press Enter to continue...' );
   Readln;
   { ... continue program }
END.
```

TextBackground

Syntax

```
PROCEDURE TextBackground( color : Byte );
```

Location

Crt

Description

TextBackground selects the background color of the entire text display, regardless of the current window boundaries. After **TextBackground**, **ClrScr** clears the screen to the new color. Characters with the same **TextColor** as the background are invisible.

Example

```
PROGRAM xTextBackground;
USES Crt;
VAR ch : Char; color : Byte;
BEGIN
   ClrScr;
   FOR color := 0 TO 15 DO
   BEGIN
     TextBackGround( color );
     Writeln;
     IF color < 8
        THEN LowVideo
        ELSE HighVideo;
     FOR ch := 'A' TO 'Z' DO
     Write( ch:2 )
   END; { for }
   Writeln
END.
```

TextColor

Syntax

```
PROCEDURE TextColor( color : Byte );
```

Location

Crt

Description

TextColor selects the foreground color for displaying characters. Characters with the same color as the background are invisible.

Example

```
PROGRAM xTextColor;
USES Crt;
VAR ch : Char; color : Byte;
BEGIN
   ClrScr;
   FOR color := 0 TO 15 DO
   BEGIN
     TextBackground( color );
     Writeln;
```

```
        FOR ch := 'A' TO 'Z' DO
        BEGIN
           TextColor( Ord(ch) MOD 16 );
           Write( ch:2 )
        END { for }
     END; { for }
     Writeln
  END.
```

TextHeight

Syntax

```
FUNCTION TextHeight( textString : <string> ) : Word;
```

Location

Graph

Description

TextHeight returns the height in pixels of a literal or variable string. Use this value to space text vertically, or, as in the example, to draw boxes around text in different fonts and sizes.

Example

```
PROGRAM xTextHeight;
USES Crt,Graph;
CONST message = 'Happy Holidays';
VAR graphDriver, graphMode : integer;
    xCenter, yCenter, x1, x2, y1, y2, h, w : integer;
BEGIN
   graphDriver := Detect;
   InitGraph( graphDriver, graphMode, '' );
   xCenter := GetMaxX DIV 2; yCenter := GetMaxY DIV 2;

   SetTextJustify( CenterText, CenterText );
   SetTextStyle( TriplexFont, HorizDir, 4 );

   h := TextHeight( message ) + 4;
   w := TextWidth( message ) + 4;

   x1 := xCenter - ( w DIV 2 );
   x2 := xCenter + ( w DIV 2 );
   y1 := yCenter - ( h DIV 2 );
```

```
        y2 := yCenter + ( h DIV 2 );

        SetColor( Red );
        Rectangle( x1, y1, x2, y2 );
        SetColor( Green );
        OutTextXY( xCenter, yCenter, message );

        REPEAT UNTIL Keypressed;
        CloseGraph

    END.
```

TextMode

Syntax

```
PROCEDURE TextMode( mode : Word );
```

Location

Crt

Description

TextMode selects a text display mode. Pass one of the following constants to **TextMode** in parentheses:

```
BW40      --    40 columns, monochrome
C040      --    40 columns, color
BW80      --    80 columns, monochrome
C080      --    80 columns, color
Mono      --    MDA or Hercules only
Font8x8   --    EGA 43-line or VGA 50-line modes
```

You can also use **C40** in place of **CO40** and **C80** in place of **CO80**, provided for compatibility with version 3.0 programs.

When programs begin and every time you call **TextMode**, the display mode is stored in the **Crt Word** variable, **lastMode**. Passing **lastMode** to **TextMode**, then, does *not* return to the previous text display as you might expect.

As the example demonstrates, add the special constant **Font8x8** to **CO80** to turn on 43-line EGA or 50-line VGA displays. Don't run this program unless you have EGA or VGA video. Then, to return to the previous display, use the statement:

```
TextMode( Lo( lastMode ) );
```

Example

```
PROGRAM xTextMode;

{ Note: Requires EGA or VGA video card }

USES Crt;
VAR color : Integer;
BEGIN
   TextMode( Co80 + Font8x8  );   { EGA=43 lines, VGA=50 lines }
   ClrScr;
   Writeln( '    Tiny Text Color Demonstration' );
   Writeln( '------------------------------------' );
   FOR color := 0 TO 15 DO
   BEGIN
      NormVideo;
      Write( 'Color=', color:2 );
      TextColor( color );
      Write( '   Normal video   ' );
      HighVideo;
      Writeln( 'High video' )
   END; { for }
   REPEAT UNTIL Keypressed;
   TextMode( Lo( lastMode ) )   { Restore original display }
END.
```

TextWidth

Syntax

```
FUNCTION TextWidth( textString : <string> ) : Word;
```

Location

Graph

Description

TextWidth returns the width of **textString** in pixels. Use this function along with **TextHeight** to design graphics text displays in different fonts and sizes. The example is a primitive text editor—actually just a typing demonstration—that shows one way to simulate carriage returns and line feeds on graphics displays.

Example

```
PROGRAM xTextWidth;
USES Crt,Graph;
```

```
        VAR graphDriver, graphMode : Integer;
            xMax, yMax : Integer; ch : Char;
        BEGIN
           graphDriver := Detect;
           InitGraph( graphDriver, graphMode, '' );
           xMax := GetMaxX; yMax := GetMaxY;
           SetTextStyle( SansSerifFont, HorizDir, 4 );
           OutTextXY( 0, 0, 'Type Esc to quit...' );
           MoveTo( 0, TextHeight('M') + 6 );
           REPEAT
              ch := ReadKey;
              OutText( ch );
              IF (ch = CHR(13) ) OR (GetX + TextWidth('M') > xMax) THEN
              BEGIN { carriage return, line feed }
                 MoveTo( 0, GetY + TextHeight('M') + 6 );
                 IF GetY + TextHeight('M') >= yMax
                    THEN ClearViewPort { new page }
              END { if }
           UNTIL ch = Chr(27);
           CloseGraph
        END.
```

Trunc

Syntax

FUNCTION Trunc(r : <real>) : LongInt;

Location

System

Description

Trunc returns the **LongInt** equivalent value of a real number **r** minus **r** 's fractional part. The function operates similarly to **Int**, but returns a **LongInt** instead of a real-number result.

   If you attempt to assign **Trunc** to an **Integer** variable, and if range checking is turned on with the compiler directive {$R +}, a runtime error 201 halts the program. With range checking off ({$R −}), this error is not detected and the program does not halt, although the assigned value is meaningless. To avoid this problem, test **r** before passing to **Trunc**. For example:

```
IF (-32768.0 <= r ) AND ( r <= 32767.0 )
   THEN n := Trunc(r)
   ELSE Writeln( 'Real number out of range' )
```

Example

```
PROGRAM xTrunc;
VAR i : Integer; r : Real;
BEGIN
   Randomize;
   FOR i := 1 TO 20 DO
   BEGIN
     r := Random * 20000;
     Writeln( 'r=', r:11:4, '  trunc(r)=', trunc(r):6 )
   END
END.
```

Truncate

Syntax

```
PROCEDURE Truncate( VAR f : <file> );
```

Location

System

Description

Use **Truncate** to delete from the current file marker to the end of the file. The present file marker then becomes the new end of file, and all information beyond that point is permanently lost. File **f** may be any type except **TEXT**. To truncate text files, use **FILE OF CHAR**.

The example creates a file of 100 numbers and then truncates from record number 50 to the end of the file. Remember that the first record is number 0. Seeking to record 50, then, locates the fifty-first record—the first to be truncated in this test.

Example

```
PROGRAM xTruncate;
VAR f : FILE OF Integer; i : Integer;

PROCEDURE DisplayFile;
VAR n : Integer;
BEGIN
   Reset( f );
   WHILE NOT EOF( f ) DO
   BEGIN
     Read( f, n );
```

```
                Write( n : 8 )
         END; { while }
         Writeln; Writeln
      END; { DisplayFile }

      BEGIN
         Assign( f, 'TEST.DAT' );    { Create file of 100 numbers }
         Rewrite( f );
         FOR i := 1 TO 100 DO
            Write( f, i );

         Writeln( 'Before truncating:' );
         DisplayFile;

         Seek( f, 50 );     { Delete all records from #50 to end of file }
         Truncate( f );

         Writeln( 'After truncating:' );
         DisplayFile;

         Close( f )
      END.
```

TypeOf

Syntax

```
FUNCTION TypeOf( <type identifier> ) : Pointer;
```

Location

System

Description

TypeOf returns the address of an object type's VMT (Virtual Method Table). Be sure to set *type identifier* to the name of an object type definition—not to the name of a variable (instance) of that type.

The VMT stores the addresses of virtual methods defined in the object. It also stores the size of an instance of this object type. Only objects with one or more virtual methods or a constructor have VMTs.

TypeOf is required by streams—a way to read and write other objects in disk files. Streams are included in OBJECTS.PAS and documented in OODEMOS.PAS, two files distributed on the Turbo Pascal 5.5 master disks.

Example

(For a complete object-oriented example, see Programs 15-8, 15-9, and 15-10. Procedure method **AddressFile.RegisterTypes** from Program 15-9 is repeated here, showing one way to use **TypeOf.**)

```
PROCEDURE AddressFile.RegisterTypes;
BEGIN
  BufStream.RegisterTypes;
  Register( TypeOf( AddrObj  ), @AddrObj.Store,  @AddrObj.Load  );
  Register( TypeOf( Personal ), @Personal.Store, @Personal.Load );
  Register( TypeOf( Business ), @Business.Store, @Business.Load );
END;
```

UnpackTime

Syntax

```
PROCEDURE UnpackTime( p : LongInt; VAR t : DateTime );
```

Location

Dos

Description

Call **UnpackTime** with a long integer **p** equal to the packed date and time format, as returned by **GetFTime**. Also pass a **DateTime** record **t**. The procedure unpacks the encoded date and time into the record fields, **year**, **month**, **day**, **hour**, **min**, and **sec**.

For an example of **UnpackTime** in action, turn to the notes for **GetFTime**.

Example

See **GetFTime**.

Upcase

Syntax

```
FUNCTION Upcase( ch : Char ) : Char;
```

Location

System

Description

Upcase converts character **ch** from lower- to uppercase. The function affects only characters in the range a to z. Punctuation, digits, and uppercase characters return unchanged.

The equivalent **Dncase** (upper- to lowercase) function, not in Turbo Pascal, is shown in the example.

Example

```
PROGRAM xUpcase;
CONST Blank=' ';
VAR ch : CHAR;

FUNCTION Dncase( ch : Char ) : Char;
BEGIN
   IF ( 'A' <= ch ) AND ( ch <= 'Z' )
      THEN Dncase := Chr( Ord(ch) + 32 )
END; { Dncase }

BEGIN
   Writeln( 'ch:Upcase' );
   FOR ch := 'a' TO 'z' DO
      Write( ch, Upcase(ch), Blank );
   Writeln; Writeln;
   Writeln( 'ch:Dncase' );
   FOR ch := 'A' TO 'Z' DO
      Write( ch, Dncase(ch), Blank );
   Writeln
END.
```

Val

Syntax

```
PROCEDURE Val( s : <string>; VAR n : <number>; VAR e : Integer );
```

Location

System

Description

Val converts string **s** to a real or integer number **n**. If **n** is a real number, then the string may be in scientific notation and may or may not have a decimal part. If **n** is an integer, the string must be a whole number. **Val** returns an error code in integer variable **e** equal to the index position in string **s** where **Val** finds a bad character. If **e** is zero, then the conversion was successful.

When you run the example, type a number like 3.14159 to convert from a string to a **Real** variable. Type errors like 3.14QB6 to see how the **ELSE** clause handles bad characters.

Example

```
PROGRAM xVal;
VAR r : Real; s : String; e : Integer;
BEGIN
    Write( 'Enter a number: ' )
    Readln( s );
    Val( s, r, e );
    IF e = 0
        THEN Writeln( 'No errors. Value = ', r )
        ELSE Writeln( '^':16+e, '--- Error!' )
END.
```

WhereX

Syntax

```
FUNCTION WhereX : Byte;
```

Location

Crt

Description

WhereX returns the horizontal cursor coordinate. As the example shows, this function and its brother **WhereY** are useful for writing procedures to move the cursor around the screen.

Another use for **WhereX** is to move the cursor up or down a few lines without changing its column position. For example, this statement moves the cursor up four lines:

```
GotoXY( WhereX, WhereY-4 );
```

Example

```
PROGRAM xWhereXY;
USES Crt;
VAR x, i : Integer;
```

```
    PROCEDURE GoUp;
    BEGIN
        Gotoxy( WhereX, WhereY-1 );
    END;

    PROCEDURE GoLeft;
    BEGIN
        Gotoxy( WhereX-1, WhereY )
    END;

    BEGIN
        ClrScr;
        GotoXY( 40, 12 );
        Write( ' <-- Center of screen' );
        FOR i := 1 TO 4 DO GoUp;
        For i := 1 TO 15 DO GoLeft;
        x := WhereX;
        Write( ' <-- Up 4, left 15' );
        GotoXY( x, WhereY );
        REPEAT UNTIL Keypressed
    END.
```

WhereY

Syntax

```
FUNCTION WhereY : Byte;
```

Location

Crt

Description

WhereY returns the vertical cursor coordinate. Along with **WhereX**, this function is useful for writing procedures to move the cursor around the screen.

Example

See **WhereX**.

Window

Syntax

```
PROCEDURE Window( x1, y1, x2, y2 : Byte );
```

Location

Crt

Description

Window sets the text display window to the upper-left corner (x1,y1) and lower-right corner (x2,y2). **Window(1,1,80,25)** resets the display to its maximum opening.

After changing the window, output to the display is restricted to the new borders. Scrolling occurs inside the window and does not disturb text elsewhere on the screen. Screen operations like **ClrScr**, **ClrEol**, and **GotoXY** operate within the current window. In other words, **GotoXY(1,1)** locates the upper-left corner of the new window, not necessarily the upper-left corner of the display.

Window does not save text *behind* the window. After you write to a new window, anything on the screen at the same position is lost.

The example displays randomly selected and colored text in three windows that scroll separately. Notice that the program must keep track of the cursor location in each window and that it must execute **GotoXY** after **Window** to place the cursor inside the window before displaying text there.

Example

```
PROGRAM xWindow;
USES Crt;
VAR y1, y2, y3 : Integer;

PROCEDURE RandText;
VAR i : Integer;
BEGIN
   Delay(75);
   FOR i := 1 TO 25 DO
   BEGIN
      TextColor( 1+Random(15) );
      Write( Chr( 32+Random(144) ) )
   END; { for }
   Writeln
END; { RandText }

BEGIN
   ClrScr;
   y1 := 11; y2 := 11; y3 := 13;
```

```
        WHILE NOT Keypressed DO
        BEGIN
           Window( 1, 1, 26, 11 );
           GotoXY( 1, y1 );
           RandText;
           y1 := WhereY;
           Window( 20, 13, 45, 23 );
           GotoXY( 1, y2 );
           RandText;
           y2 := WhereY;
           Window( 50, 5, 75, 17 );
           GotoXY( 1, y3 );
           RandText;
           y3 := WhereY
        END
     END.
```

Write

Syntax

```
PROCEDURE Write( [f : <file>;] v1, v2, ..., vn );
```

Location

System

Description

Use **Write** to send values to an output file, which might be the display, the printer, a modem, or a disk file. If <file> is not specified, **Write** and **Writeln** default to the standard output, normally the console. For text, the output file may be redirected from the DOS command line if you do not use the **Crt** unit. In programs that use **Crt**, **Write** (and **Writeln**) display text much faster but cannot be redirected.

Separate multiple items with commas inside **Write**'s parentheses. The items may be of different types. When writing to text files, the items may be literal constants or variables. When writing to data files, items must be variables.

When writing to text files or to the default output, Boolean variables automatically convert to the strings True and False.

Optional formatting commands write integer, real, and string variables in fixed column widths. The command **i:n** right-justifies integer **i** or string **s** in **n** columns, while **r:n:d** right-justifies real number **r** with **d** decimal places in **n** columns.

When writing data files, **Write** transfers one or more records to the current file position.

Example

```
PROGRAM xWrite;
CONST
   n = 1234;
   s = 'The Write Stuff';
BEGIN
   Write( 'pi=', pi:1:8, ' n=', n, ' s=', s )
END.
```

Writeln

Syntax

```
PROCEDURE Writeln( [f : <file>;] v1, v2, ..., vn );
```

Location

System

Description

Writeln operates identically to **Write** except for two differences: You can use this procedure only with text files (including text devices like the display console and a printer), and after the last item written, **Writeln** appends carriage return and line feed control characters.

Normally, use **Writeln** when you want to display text and send the cursor to the start of a new line. Use **Write** when you want to display text and leave the cursor positioned after the last character written. Use **Writeln** with no parameters to start a new line without displaying any text.

Like **Write**, **Writeln** can handle any number of parameters, which can be strings, characters, or simple types that Turbo Pascal can convert to text. When writing items such as real numbers or integers, remember that these are converted to a character format.

In programs that don't use the Crt unit, **Writeln**'s output can be redirected from the DOS command line. To test this, compile the example to a disk file, XWRITELN.EXE. Typing XWRITELN alone sends text to the default output, the display. Typing XWRITELN > PRN sends the output to the printer. Typing XWRITELN > TEST.TXT sends the output to a disk text file, TEST.TXT.

Example

```
PROGRAM xWriteln;
BEGIN
   Writeln( 'You can redirect this text to a file.' );
   Writeln( 'Follow the instructions in the description.' );
   Writeln( 'That''s all folks!' )
END.
```

Appendixes

A

Turbo Pascal Railroad Diagrams

The following railroad diagrams describe the syntax of Turbo Pascal. Portions of the same diagrams appear throughout the book, sometimes in slightly altered form. See Chapter 1 for a description on how to read and use railroad diagrams.

letter

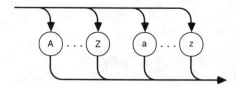

digit

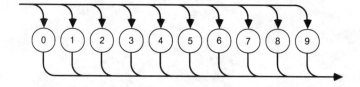

hex digit

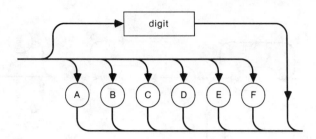

identifier

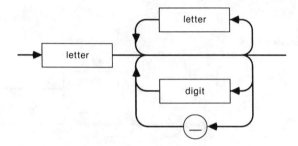

unsigned integer

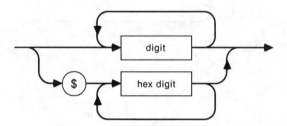

unsigned number

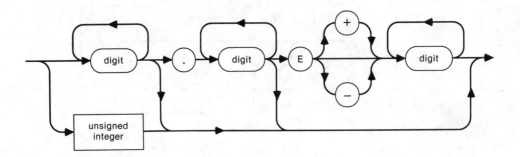

string constant

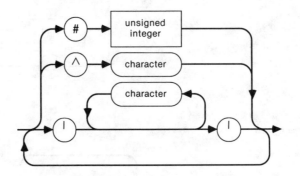

unsigned constant

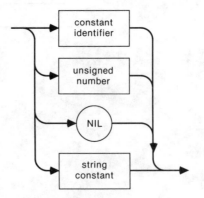

constant

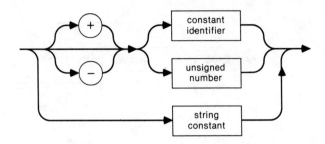

simple type

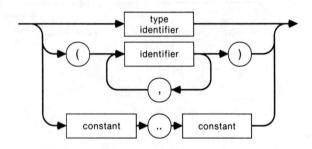

field list

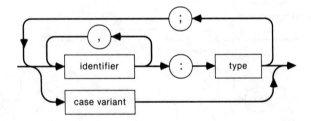

case variant

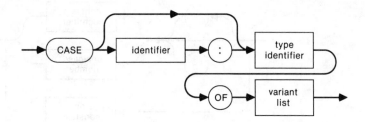

variant list

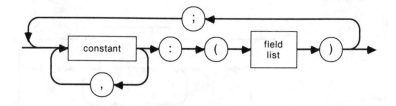

data type

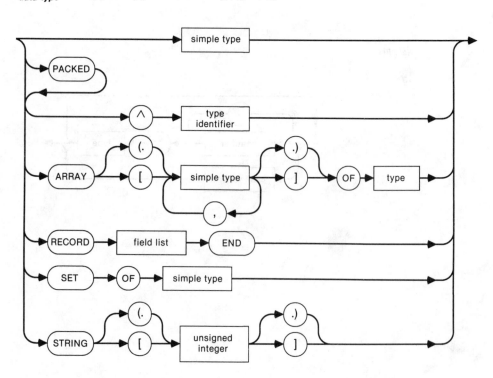

file type

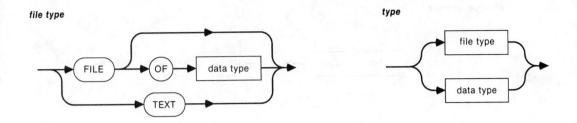

type

factor

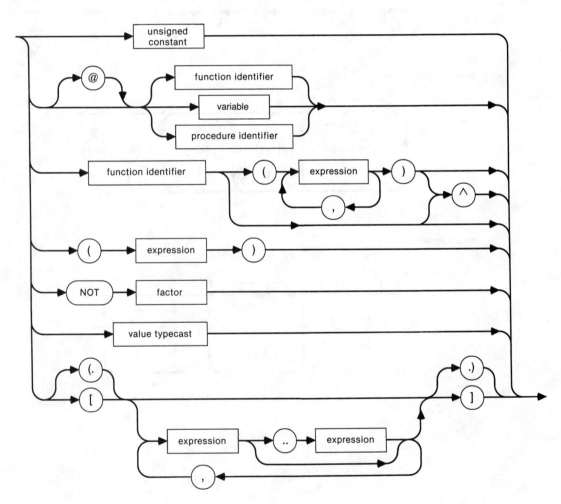

value typecast

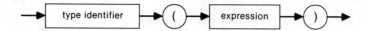

variable typecast

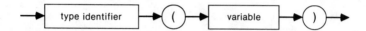

term

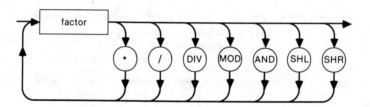

simple expression

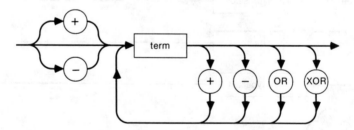

expression

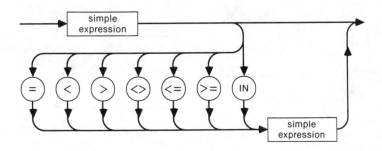

variable

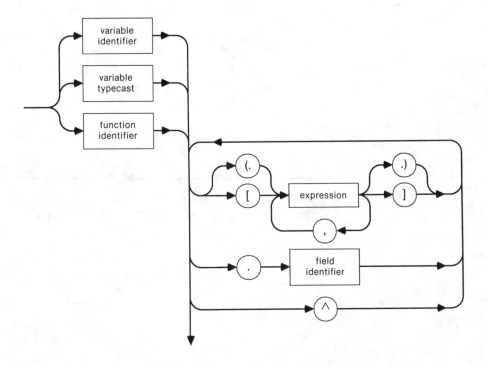

inline element

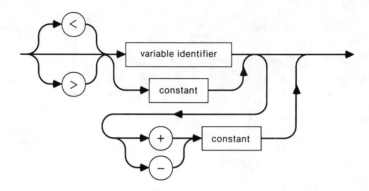

inline directive

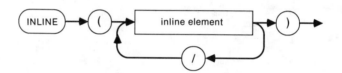

procedure body

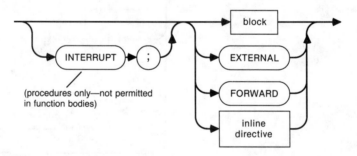

(procedures only—not permitted
in function bodies)

parameter list

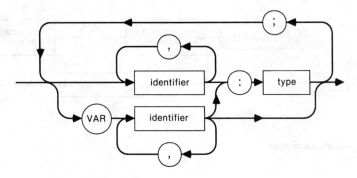

parameters

function declaration

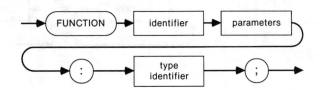

procedure declaration

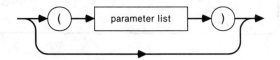

absolute address

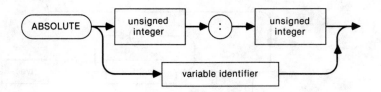

variable declaration

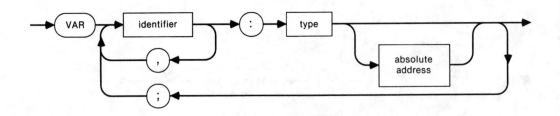

type declaration

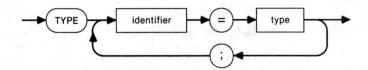

set constant

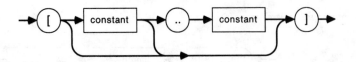

record constant

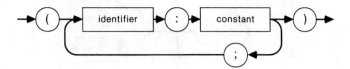

array constant

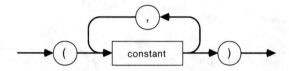

variable (typed) constant

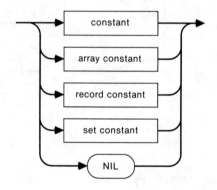

constant declaration

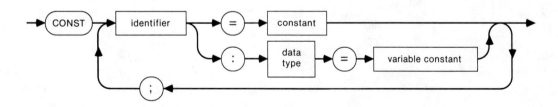

label declaration

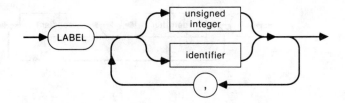

for statement

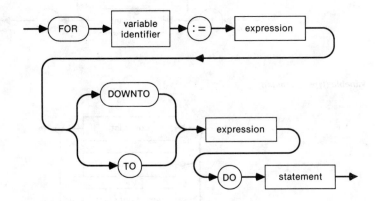

repeat statement

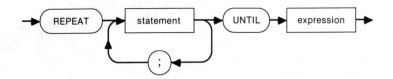

while statement

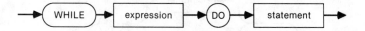

case statement

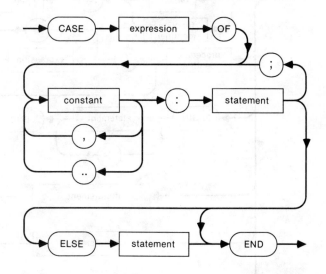

if statement

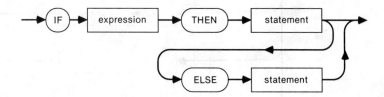

statement

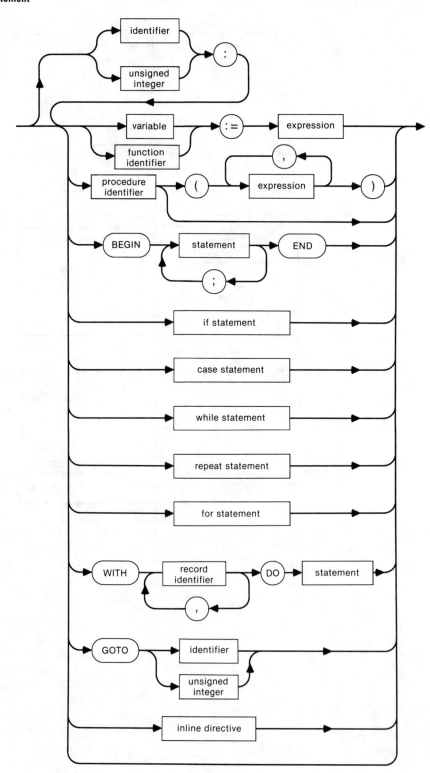

block

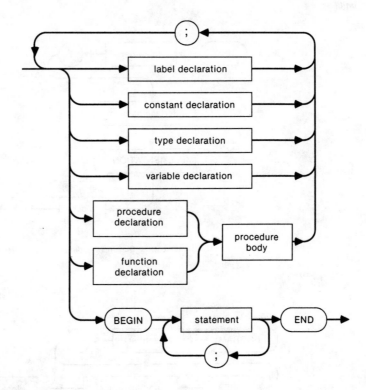

interface part

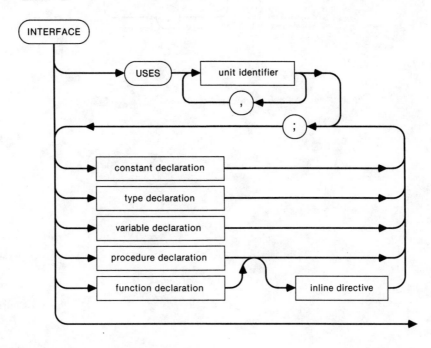

unit

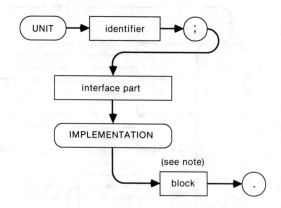

Note: BEGIN Statement; ...; Statement optional

program

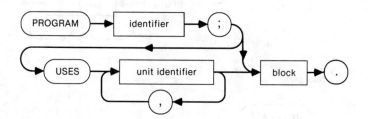

Object-Oriented Diagrams

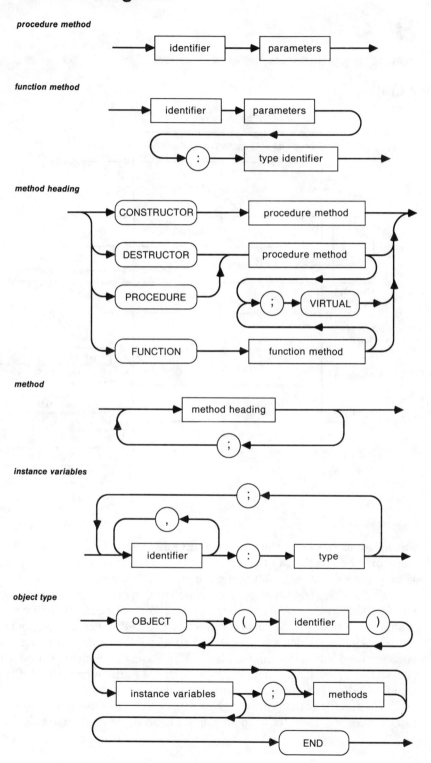

procedure method

function method

method heading

method

instance variables

object type

B

Memory Map

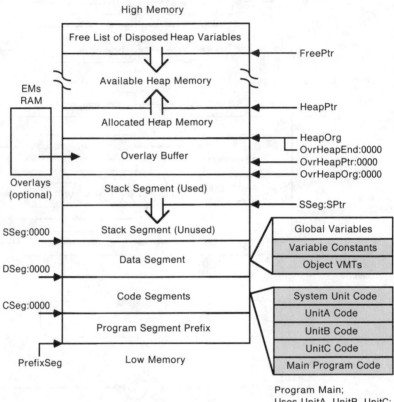

High Memory

Free List of Disposed Heap Variables — FreePtr

Available Heap Memory

EMs RAM

Allocated Heap Memory — HeapPtr

HeapOrg
OvrHeapEnd:0000
Overlay Buffer — OvrHeapPtr:0000
OvrHeapOrg:0000

Overlays (optional)

Stack Segment (Used)

SSeg:0000 — SSeg:SPtr

Stack Segment (Unused)

Global Variables
Variable Constants
Object VMTs

Data Segment

DSeg:0000

Code Segments

System Unit Code
UnitA Code

CSeg:0000

UnitB Code
UnitC Code

Program Segment Prefix

Main Program Code

PrefixSeg   Low Memory

Program Main;
Uses UnitA, UnitB, UnitC;

Shaded areas represent the compiled .EXE file image as stored on disk. (Overlay units may be attached to this image.) Other areas are allocated at runtime. The main program and each unit occupy distinct code segments up to 64K; therefore, the value of **CSeg** (register CS) changes depending on which module's code is executing. **DSeg** (register DS) and **SSeg** (register SS) do not change during normal program runs. The top of the stack is located at **SSeg:SPtr.** The data segment contains global variables, which are allocated at runtime. It also contains variable (typed) constants and Virtual Method Tables (VMTs), both of which are stored in the .EXE file. DOS creates the 256-byte Program Segment Prefix when it loads the program into RAM. **PrefixSeg** addresses this memory.

The freelist of dynamic variables released by **Dispose** grows down from the top of memory (**FreePtr**). The occupied heap of dynamic variables created by

New grows up from the start of the heap (**HeapOrg**). Space between **FreePtr** and **HeapPtr** has never been used.

The overlay buffer begins at **OvrHeapOrg** and extends to the start of the heap. **OvrHeapEnd** marks the top of the overlay buffer. **OvrHeapPtr** floats between these areas as new overlays are loaded into the buffer. These three word-values address paragraph boundaries at offset addresses of 0000. See Chapter 10 for more information on the layout of the overlay buffer.

C

Compiler Directives

Table C-1 Compiler directives

Directive	Default	Version 4	5	5.5	Description
A +/−	+		x	x	Word-align 16-bit and larger data
B +/−	+	x	x	x	Short-circuit Boolean expressions
D +/−	+	x	x	x	Generate debug information
E +/−	+		x	x	Numeric coprocessor emulation
F +/−	−	x	x	x	Compile far procedure or function
I +/−	+	x	x	x	Check for I/O errors
I filename		x	x	x	Include text from file
L +/−	+	x			Link buffer in memory
L +/−	+		x	x	Include local symbols for debugging
L filename		x	x	x	Link external routines in file
M i,j,k		x	x	x	Set memory (i = stack, j = heap min, k = heap max)
N +/−	−	x	x	x	Allow math coprocessor numeric types
O +/−	−		x	x	Enable overlay code generation
O unitname			x	x	Convert unit to overlay module
R +/−	−	x	x	x	Check for range errors
R +/−	−			x	Verify object instance VMT link
S +/−	+	x	x	x	Check for stack overflow
T +/−	−	x			Generate TPM map file
U filename		x			Open alternate unit file filename.TPU
V +/−	+	x	x	x	Check string VAR parameter lengths

Notes: Enter switch (+/−) directives in the form {$c + }, {$c − }, (* $c + *), or
(* $c − *), where c is an option directive letter. Enable options with
+; disable with −. Enter parameter options such as *I filename* in the
form {$c filename} or (* $c filename *). In the M option, i, j, and k
are unsigned long integers.

Table C-2 Conditional compilation directives

Directive	Description
DEFINE symbol	Define symbol for future use
UNDEF symbol	Undefine symbol
IFDEF symbol	Compile next statements if symbol defined
IFNDEF symbol	Compile next statements if symbol not defined
IFOPT directive	Compile next statements if directive set
ELSE	Compile next statements if IF . . . failed
ENDIF	End of IF . . . ELSE conditional section

Note: A *symbol* is equivalent to an identifier.

D

ASCII Character Codes

Dec	Hex	Char		Dec	Hex	Char	Dec	Hex	Char	Dec	Hex	Char
0	00	NUL	(^@)	33	21	!	66	42	B	99	63	c
1	01	SOH	(^A)	34	22	"	67	43	C	100	64	d
2	02	STX	(^B)	35	23	#	68	44	D	101	65	e
3	03	ETX	(^C)	36	24	$	69	45	E	102	66	f
4	04	EOT	(^D)	37	25	%	70	46	F	103	67	g
5	05	ENQ	(^E)	38	26	&	71	47	G	104	68	h
6	06	ACK	(^F)	39	27	'	72	48	H	105	69	i
7	07	BEL	(^G)	40	28	(	73	49	I	106	6A	j
8	08	BS	(^H)	41	29	)	74	4A	J	107	6B	k
9	09	HT	(^I)	42	2A	*	75	4B	K	108	6C	l
10	0A	LF	(^J)	43	2B	+	76	4C	L	109	6D	m
11	0B	VT	(^K)	44	2C	,	77	4D	M	110	6E	n
12	0C	FF	(^L)	45	2D	-	78	4E	N	111	6F	o
13	0D	CR	(^M)	46	2E	.	79	4F	O	112	70	p
14	0E	SO	(^N)	47	2F	/	80	50	P	113	71	q
15	0F	SI	(^O)	48	30	0	81	51	Q	114	72	r
16	10	DLE	(^P)	49	31	1	82	52	R	115	73	s
17	11	DC1	(^Q)	50	32	2	83	53	S	116	74	t
18	12	DC2	(^R)	51	33	3	84	54	T	117	75	u
19	13	DC3	(^S)	52	34	4	85	55	U	118	76	v
20	14	DC4	(^T)	53	35	5	86	56	V	119	77	w
21	15	NAK	(^U)	54	36	6	87	57	W	120	78	x
22	16	SYN	(^V)	55	37	7	88	58	X	121	79	y
23	17	ETB	(^W)	56	38	8	89	59	Y	122	7A	z
24	18	CAN	(^X)	57	39	9	90	5A	Z	123	7B	{
25	19	EM	(^Y)	58	3A	:	91	5B	[	124	7C	|
26	1A	SUB	(^Z)	59	3B	;	92	5C	\	125	7D	}
27	1B	ESC		60	3C	<	93	5D	]	126	7E	~
28	1C	FS		61	3D	=	94	5E	^	127	7F	DEL
29	1D	GS		62	3E	>	95	5F	_			
30	1E	RS		63	3F	?	96	60	`			
31	1F	US		64	40	@	97	61	a			
32	20	SP		65	41	A	98	62	b			

E

Operator Precedence

Level	Operator	Description	Allowed operand types
1:	@	Address of	Procedure, Function, Variable
	–	Unary minus	Integer, Real
	NOT	Negate	Boolean, Integer
2:	*	Times	Integer, Real, Set
	/	Divide	Real, Set
	DIV	Integer divide	Integer
	MOD	Modulus	Integer
	AND	Logical AND	Boolean, Integer
	SHL	Shift left	Integer
	SHR	Shift right	Integer
3:	+	Plus	Integer, Real, String, Set
	–	Minus	Integer, Real, Set
	OR	Logical OR	Boolean, Integer
	XOR	Exclusive OR	Boolean, Integer
4:	=	Equal	All
	< >	Not equal	All
	<	Less than	All
	>	Greater than	All
	< =	Less or equal	All
	> =	Greater or equal	All
	IN	Set membership	Set

Notes: Operators at level 1 have higher precedences than operators at level 2, operators at level 2 have higher precedences than operators at level 3, and so on. Integer types include Byte, ShortInt, Word, Integer, and LongInt. Real types include Single, Double, Extended, and Comp—which require a math coprocessor—and Real which is always available.

Bibliography

Brooks, Frederick P. *The Mythical Man-Month*. Addison-Wesley, 1975. Amusing collection of essays on managing large software projects.

Duncan, Ray. *Advanced MS-DOS*. Microsoft Press, 1986. You won't find a better DOS reference. Also discusses routines in the PC ROM BIOS. Requires knowledge of assembly language and some C.

Grogono, Peter. *Programming in Pascal. Rev ed*. Addison-Wesley, 1980. Introduction to programming in standard Pascal. Many good examples.

Jensen, Kathleen, and Wirth, Niklaus. *Pascal User Manual and Report, 2nd ed*. Springer-Verlag, 1974. The classic Pascal reference. Part one, The User Manual, written by Jensen, is a concentrated overview of programming in Pascal and contains many short examples. The Report, written by Pascal inventor, Niklaus Wirth, describes the syntax of standard Pascal. Pretty much out of date by now, but worth a look.

Kernighan, Brian W., and Plauger, P.J. *Software Tools in Pascal*. Addison-Wesley, 1981. Practical guide to software development with emphasis on writing useful programs in Pascal.

Knuth, Donald E. *The Art of Computer Programming, Vols. 1,2,3, 2nd ed*. Addison-Wesley, 1973. Penultimate reference for professional programmers and students working in any computer language.

Ledgard, Henry F., et al. *Pascal With Style; Programming Proverbs*. Hayden Book Company, 1979. Thoughtful hints and suggestions for developing a good programming style.

Liffick, W. Blaise. *The BYTE Book of Pascal*. BYTE Publications, 1979. Looks at Pascal compiler design. Contains many programs, from text formatters to chess, written for a variety of Pascal compilers.

Schmucker, Kurt J., *Object-Oriented Programming for the Macintosh*. Object Pascal for the Mac and Turbo Pascal OOP extensions share some of the same concepts and forms, although the two languages are not source-code compatible. Still, this is a good book if you want to learn more about OOP.

Wiener, Richard S., and Pinson, Lewis J. *An Introduction to Object-Oriented Programming and C++*. Addison-Wesley, 1988. Although this book contains no Pascal programs, it describes OOP concepts in C++, upon which Turbo Pascal's OOP extensions are based. Requires a strong knowledge of C.

Wirth, Niklaus. *Algorithms + Data Structures = Programs*. Prentice-Hall, 1976. Still one of the best books on advanced Pascal programming.

Answers to Selected Exercises

The exercises at the ends of chapters were chosen to illustrate various Pascal features discussed in the chapters. The answers in this section will help you to fine-tune your understanding of details that may give you trouble on a first reading. Of course, no book has all the answers and this book is no exception. You will, therefore, find a few missing numbers and several missing chapters in the material that follows.

Chapter 1

1-1.
```
PROGRAM Alphabet;
BEGIN
    Writeln( 'Pack my box with five dozen liquor jugs.' )
END.
```

1-2.
```
PROGRAM Announcement;
BEGIN
    Writeln( '"It''s eleven o''clock," she said,' );
    Writeln( '"Why aren''t you in bed?"' )
END.
```

1-5.
```
PROGRAM Triplicate;
VAR
    s : string[20];
BEGIN
    Write( 'Enter any string: ' );
    Readln( s );
    Writeln( s, s, s )
END.
```

Chapter 2

2-1.
```
PROGRAM WaterWeight;
CONST
   LbsPerGallon = 8.33;
VAR
   Gallons : Real;
BEGIN
   Writeln( 'Weight of water' );
   Writeln;
   Write( 'Number of gallons? ' );
   Readln( Gallons );
   Writeln( 'Weight = ', Gallons * LbsPerGallon:8:2,
            ' pounds.' )
END.
```

2-2.
```
PROGRAM Fahrenheit;
VAR
   Fdegrees, Cdegrees : Real;
BEGIN
   Writeln( 'Celsius to Fahrenheit conversion' );
   Writeln;
   Write( 'Degrees Celsius? ' );
   Readln( Cdegrees );
   Fdegrees := ( ( Cdegrees * 9.0 ) / 5.0 ) + 32.0;
   Writeln( 'Degrees Fahrenheit = ', Fdegrees:8:2 )
END.
```

2-3.
```
PROGRAM Water;
{ Boiling point of water at various altitudes }
{ Author: Tom Swan }
CONST
   Factor = 550;   { One degree less per Factor feet }
   BoilingPoint = 212;    { Degrees Fahrenheit }
VAR
   Altitude, Temperature : Real;
BEGIN
   Writeln( 'Boiling point of water' );
   Writeln;
   Write( 'Altitude? ' );
   Readln( Altitude );
   Temperature := BoilingPoint - ( Altitude / Factor );
   Writeln( 'Temperature = ', Temperature:8:2,
            ' degrees Fahrenheit' )
END.
```

2-4. The number of decimal places is declared as a variable constant. This makes
it easy to specify a default value of two. Another possibility would be to de-

clare **Decimals** as an integer variable, initializing somewhere with the assignment statement **Decimals: = 2**.

```pascal
PROGRAM WaterWeight;
{ Modified for variable number of decimal places }
CONST
   LbsPerGallon = 8.33;
   Places = 8;               { Fixed number columns }
   Decimals : integer = 2;   { Variable decimal places }
VAR
   Gallons : Real;
BEGIN
   Writeln( 'Weight of water' );
   Writeln;
   Write( 'Number of gallons? ' );
   Readln( Gallons );
   Write( 'Number of decimal places? ' );
   Readln( Decimals );
   Writeln( 'Weight = ',
       Gallons * LbsPerGallon:Places:Decimals, ' pounds.' )
END.
```

Chapter 3

```pascal
3-1. PROGRAM WhileCountDown;
     VAR
        i : Integer;
     BEGIN
        Writeln( 'While countdown' );
        i := 10;
        WHILE i > 0 DO
        BEGIN
           Writeln( i );
           i := i - 1
        END
     END.
```

```pascal
3-2. PROGRAM Celsius2;
     VAR
        Fdegrees, Cdegrees : Real;
        Answer : Char;
     BEGIN
        Writeln( 'Fahrenheit to Celsius conversion' );
        Writeln;
        REPEAT
           Write( 'Degrees Fahrenheit ? ' );
```

```
        Readln( Fdegrees );
        Cdegrees := ( ( Fdegrees - 32.0 ) * 5.0 ) / 9.0;
        Writeln( 'Degrees Celsius = ', Cdegrees:8:2 );
        Writeln;
        Write( 'Another (y/n)? ' );
        Readln( Answer )
    UNTIL ( Answer <> 'Y' ) AND ( Answer <> 'y' )
END.
```

3-3.
```
PROGRAM Color3;
VAR
    Choice : Integer;
    UserQuits : Boolean;
BEGIN
    Writeln( 'Complementary Colors #3' );
    UserQuits := False;
    REPEAT
      Writeln;
      Writeln(' 1=Blue          2=Green        3=Orange        4=Purple' );
      Writeln(' 5=Red           6=Yellow       7=Yellow-green  8=Red-purple' );
      Writeln(' 9=Blue-green 10=Red-orange 11=Blue-purple   12=Yellow-orange' );
      Writeln;
      Write( 'Color? (0 to quit) ' );
      Readln( Choice );
      Write( 'Complement is: ' );
      CASE Choice OF
          0 : UserQuits := True;
          1 : Writeln( 'Orange' );
          2 : Writeln( 'Red' );
          3 : Writeln( 'Blue' );
          4 : Writeln( 'Yellow' );
          5 : Writeln( 'Green' );
          6 : Writeln( 'Purple' );
          7 : Writeln( 'Red-purple' );
          8 : Writeln( 'Yellow-green' );
          9 : Writeln( 'Red-orange' );
         10 : Writeln( 'Blue-green' );
         11 : Writeln( 'Yellow-orange' );
         12 : Writeln( 'Blue-purple' )
         ELSE Writeln( 'Error: try again.' )
      END
    UNTIL UserQuits
END.
```

3-4. There are many correct answers to writing a factorial program. The answer below is easy to understand, but it may not be the most efficient solution.

```
PROGRAM Fact;
VAR
```

```
            Value : Integer;
            Result : Real;
        BEGIN
            REPEAT
                Write( 'Value? (-1 to end) ' );
                Readln( Value );
                IF Value >= 0 THEN
                BEGIN
                    Result := 1;
                    WHILE Value > 0 DO
                    BEGIN
                        Result := Result * Value;
                        Value := Value - 1
                    END;
                    Writeln( 'Factorial + ', Result:1:0 )
                END
            UNTIL Value = -1
        END.
```

3-5. If you had trouble with this one, enter and run the answer here, then "play computer," writing down the variables on paper while executing the program statements by hand. This should help explain how the program works. The method is called a "binary search" because of the way the high and low guesses are divided by two in line 10 to form new guesses. This narrowing down of possibilities is guaranteed to compute the correct result in seven attempts or less. Any more than that and the program knows you're cheating.

```
PROGRAM NumberGame;
VAR
    Answer, High, Low, Guess : Integer;
BEGIN
    Writeln( 'Think of a number from 1 to 100,' );
    Write( 'then press return...' );
    Readln;
    High := 100; Low := 1;
    REPEAT
        Guess := ( Low + High ) DIV 2;
        Write( 'I guess ', Guess,
            '. 1=Correct, 2=Low, 3=High ? ' );
        Readln( Answer );
        IF Answer = 2
            THEN Low := Guess = 1
            ELSE IF Answer = 3
                    THEN High := Guess - 1
    UNTIL ( High < Low ) OR ( Answer = 1 );
    IF Answer = 1
        THEN Writeln( 'I win!' )
```

```
            ELSE Writeln( 'You cheated!!!' )
      END.
```

Chapter 4

```
4-1. PROGRAM Area;
     VAR
         Selection : Integer;

     PROCEDURE Square;
     VAR a, b : Real;
     BEGIN
        Writeln( 'Square' );
        Write( 'Length side a? ' ); Readln( a );
        Write( 'Length side b? ' ); Readln( b );
        Writeln( 'Area=', a*b:1:2 )
     END; { Square }

     PROCEDURE Pyramid;
     VAR n, b, h : Real;
     BEGIN
        Writeln( 'Pyramid' );
        Write( 'Number of faces? ' ); Readln( n );
        Write( 'Length of base? ' ); Readln( b );
        Write( 'Height? ' ); Readln( h );
        Writeln( 'Area=', (n*b*h)/2:1:2 )
     END; { Pyramid }

     PROCEDURE Cube;
     VAR a : Real;
     BEGIN
        Writeln( 'Cube' );
        Write( 'Length of one side? ' ); Readln( a );
        Writeln( 'Area=', 6*Sqr(a):1:2 )
          {Note: Sqr(n) is a predeclared function.}
     END; { Cube }

     PROCEDURE Cylinder;
     VAR r, h : Real;
     BEGIN
        Writeln( 'Cylinder' );
        Write( 'Radius? ' ); Readln( r );
        Write( 'Height? ' ); Readln( h );
        Writeln( 'Area=', (2*Pi*r)*h:1:2 )
     END; { Cylinder }
```

```
        BEGIN
          Writeln( 'Compute the area' );
          Writeln;
          Write( '1=square, 2=pyramid, 3=cube, 4=cylinder? ' );
          Selection := 0; { end on pressing Enter }
          Readln( Selection );
          CASE Selection OF
            1 : Square;
            2 : Pyramid;
            3 : Cube;
            4 : Cylinder
          END
        END.
```

4-2.
```
    PROGRAM Current;
    VAR
        Voltage, Resistance : Real;

    FUNCTION Amperes : Real;
    BEGIN
        Amperes := Voltage / Resistance
    END; { Amperes }

    BEGIN
        Writeln( 'Calculate current in Amperes' );
        Write( 'Voltage? ' ); Readln( Voltage );
        Write( 'Resistance (ohms)? ' ); Readln( Resistance );
        Writeln( 'Current = ', Amperes:1:2, ' amperes' )
    END.
```

4-3. Six functions are used in this version of the program. The first three functions calculate E, I, and R. The next three prompt for volts, amperes, and ohms.

```
    PROGRAM OhmsLaw;
    VAR
        Choice : Char;

    FUNCTION E( Amps, Ohms : Real ) : Real;
    { Solve for E=voltage }
    BEGIN
        E := Amps * Ohms
    END;

    FUNCTION I( Volts, Ohms : Real ) : Real;
    { Solve for I=current }
    BEGIN
        I := Volts / Ohms
```

```
END;

FUNCTION R( Volts, Amps : Real ) : Real;
{ Solve for R=resistance }
BEGIN
   R := Volts / Amps
END;

FUNCTION Voltage : Real;
{ Prompt for voltage }
VAR n : Real;
BEGIN
   Write( 'Volts? ' );
   Readln( n );
   Voltage := n
END;

FUNCTION Current : Real;
{ Prompt for current }
VAR n : Real;
BEGIN
   Write( 'Current (amps)? ' );
   Readln( n );
   Current := n
END;

FUNCTION Resistance : Real;
{ Prompt for resistance }
VAR n : Real;
BEGIN
   Write( 'Resistance (ohms)? ' );
   Readln( n );
   Resistance := n
END;

BEGIN
   Writeln( 'Welcome to Ohm''s Law' );
   REPEAT
     Writeln;
     Write( 'E=voltage, I=current, R=resistance or Q=quit? ' );
     Readln( Choice );
     CASE Upcase( Choice ) OF
       'E' : Writeln( E( Current, Resistance ):1:2, ' volts' );
       'I' : Writeln( I( Voltage, Resistance ):1:2, ' amperes' );
       'R' : Writeln( R( Voltage, Current   ):1:2, ' ohms' )
     END { case }
```

```
                UNTIL Upcase( Choice ) = 'Q'
        END.
```

4-6. Make the following changes to Program 4-7 to print the alphabet in normal order.

```
 7:  IF ch > 'A' THEN B( ch );
13:  A( pred( ch ) )
17:  A('Z')
```

4-7.
```
PROGRAM TestPETC;

PROCEDURE PETC;
{ Press Enter To Continue }
VAR
    Ch : Char;
BEGIN
    Writeln;
    Write( 'Press Enter to continue...' );
    Readln        { Wait for Enter key }
END; { PETC }


BEGIN
    Writeln( 'Test PETC procedure' );
    PETC;
    Writeln( 'Program continues' )
END.
```

Chapter 5

5-1.
```
PROGRAM DateCheck;
TYPE
    DateRec =
        RECORD
            Year : Integer;
            Month : 1 .. 12;
            Day : 0 .. 31
        END;
VAR
    TestDate : DateRec;

FUNCTION LeapYear( VAR Date : DateRec ) : Boolean;
{ True if date is a leap year }
{ From Program 3-12 }
BEGIN
    WITH Date DO
        IF Year MOD 100 = 0
```

```
            THEN LeapYear := ( Year MOD 400 ) = 0
            ELSE LeapYear := ( Year MOD   4 ) = 0
END; { LeapYear }


FUNCTION GoodDate( VAR Date : DateRec ) : Boolean;
{ True if Date is legal }
CONST
   Days : ARRAY[ 1 .. 12 ] OF byte =
            (31,28,31,30,31,30,31,31,31,31,30,31);
VAR
   LastDay : Integer;
BEGIN
   WITH Date DO
   BEGIN
      IF LeapYear( Date )
         THEN Days[2] := 29
         ELSE Days[2] := 28;
      GoodDate := ( Year  >=  0 ) AND
                  ( Month >=  1 ) AND
                  ( Month <= 12 ) AND
                  ( Day   >=  1 ) AND
                  ( Day   <= Days[Month] )
   END
END; { GoodDate }


BEGIN
   WITH TestDate DO
   BEGIN
      Write( 'Year? ' ); Readln( Year );
      Write( 'Month? ' ); Readln( Month );
      Write( 'Day? ' ); Readln( Day )
   END; { with }
   IF GoodDate( TestDate )
      THEN Writeln( 'Date may be okay' )
      ELSE Writeln( 'Date is not okay' )
END.
```

5-2. ```
PROGRAM TFOrdinals;

PROCEDURE BooleanOrd(b : Boolean);
BEGIN
   Writeln('Ordinal value of ', b, ' = ', ord(b))
END;

BEGIN
   BooleanOrd(True);
   BooleanOrd(False);
```
```

```
        BooleanOrd( NOT True );
        BooleanOrd( NOT(NOT True AND NOT False) )
END.
```

5-3.
```
PROGRAM VertAndDiag;
VAR
    i : Integer;
    s : String[80];
BEGIN
    Write( 'String? ' ); Readln( s );
    Writeln;
    Writeln( 'Vertical:' );
    FOR i := 1 TO Length( s ) DO
        Writeln( s[i] );
    Writeln;
    Writeln( 'Press Enter...' );
    Readln;
    Writeln( 'Diagonal' );
    FOR i := 1 TO Length( s ) DO
        Writeln( s[i]:i )
END.
```

5-5. To solve this problem, you first need to decide on the kind of index to use. You might start with an enumerated data type:

```
TYPE
    City = ( Atlanta, Baltimore, Boston, Chicago,
             Dallas, LosAngeles, NewYork );
```

Next, declare the mileage array indexed by the new type.

```
VAR
    Miles : ARRAY[ City, City ] OF Real;
```

Defining the data structures often simplifies writing the program. To assign mileages, you could use assignments like these:

```
Miles[ Atlanta, Dallas ] := 822;
Miles[ Chicago, Boston ] := 1004;
```

With these suggestions as starting points, you should be able to finish the program.

5-8. Depending on how you enter names, sorting by last name can be tricky. Everything proceeds smoothly as long as all entries are in last-name-first order. Because assumptions such as these are prime sources of program bugs, a better solution is to use separate fields in the **Member** record for last names, first names, and middle initials. Because you can then directly compare two last names, this makes sorting easier. Another problem arises if names are in upper- and lowercase. To deal with this problem, you may have to convert to all uppercase before sorting. (Converting fields to uppercase before comparing in the sort procedure causes operating times to suffer. Why?)

5-10. This is easily done with a set of **DaysOfWeek**.

```
TYPE
   DaySet = SET OF DaysOfWeek;
   Employee = RECORD
                 Name : String[40];
                 Days : DaySet
              END;
```

Then, to record the days an employee works is a simple assignment. Assume **A** is an array of **Employee** records indexed by **Number**.

```
A[ Number ].Days := [ Mon .. Wed, Fri, Sat ];
```

It's now easy to print the chart. A nested **FOR** loop seems best.

```
Writeln( '  #  Sun  Mon  Tue  Wed  Thu  Fri  Sat' );
   FOR Number := 1 TO LastEmployee DO
BEGIN
   Writeln;
   Write( Number:3 );
   FOR Day := Sun TO Sat DO
      IF Day IN A[ Number ].Days
         THEN Write( '*':5 )
         ELSE Write( ' ':5 )
END; { for }
```

Chapter 6

6-1.
```
PROGRAM SdrawKcab;
VAR
   InFile : Text;
   FileName : String[64];
   OneLine : String[132];
   i : integer;
BEGIN
   Write( 'File name? ' ); Readln( FileName );
   Assign( InFile, FileName );
   Reset( InFile );
   WHILE NOT eof( InFile ) DO
   BEGIN
      Readln( InFile, OneLine );
      FOR i := Length( OneLine ) DOWNTO 1 DO
         Write( OneLine[ i ] );
      Writeln
   END
END.
```

6-3. The simplest approach is to use a constant maximum number of lines for each new output file. For example:

```
WHILE NOT Eof( InFile ) DO
BEGIN
   StartOutput;
   FOR i := 1 TO MaxLines DO
     IF NOT Eof( InFile ) THEN
         BEGIN
             Readln( InFile, OneLine );
             Writeln( OutFile, OneLIne )
         END;
   Close( OutFile )
END;
```

The procedure **StartOutput** has to create the new output file. Most important is to give each file a new name. **FileNumber** is a global integer variable.

```
PROCEDURE StartOutput;
BEGIN
   FileNumber := FileNumber + 1;
   str( FileNumber, s );
   Assign( OutFile, FileName + '.' + s );
   Rewrite( OutFile )
END;
```

6-4. You can improve program speed by not resetting the input file if requested line numbers are greater than the last line read. This is a trick employed by word-processing programs. When you advance, say, from page 10 to page 11, there is no reason to reread the previous pages again. For clarity, the changes to Program 6-12 are in uppercase.

```
PROGRAM SeekStrings;
VAR
   {...}
   OLDLINE : Integer;
BEGIN
   {...}
   OLDLINE := 0;
   REPEAT
      {...}
      IF LineNumber > 0 THEN
      BEGIN
         IF OLDLINE > LINENUMBER THEN
         BEGIN
            Reset( TextFile );
            OLDLINE := 0
         END;
         FOR i := OLDLINE=1 TO LineNumber DO
            Readln( TextFile, OneLine );
```

```
          Writeln( LineNumber, ': ', OneLine );
          OLDLINE := LINENUMBER
       END { if }
    UNTIL LineNumber = 0;
    Close( TextFile )
 END.
```

6-5. There is no single correct answer here, although some encryption methods are better than others. Basically, you need to read blocks of data, change each byte according to a formula, and write the blocks back to disk. After reading a block, a simple **FOR** loop converts the bytes.

```
FOR i := 0 TO 511 DO
  Encrypt( Block[i] );
```

Of course, that doesn't say anything about the encryption method. You could add a constant value to each byte; use a translation table that says A is T, B is C, C is Q, and so on; or mathematically change each byte some other way. Chapter 12, for example, discusses logical operations on integers. One of those operations is called the *exclusive or*, written XOR. You could use XOR to write the simple encryption loop like this:

```
FOR i := 0 TO 511 DO
   Block[i] := Block[i] XOR
      Key[ 1 + i MOD Length( Key ) ];
```

Chapter 7

7-1. You can store any kind of data in a linked list. The link fields are the same; just change the other fields in the record. This declaration links 80-character strings.

```
ItemPointer = ^Item;
Item = RECORD
          NextItem : ItemPointer;
          OneString : String[80]
       END;
```

You can then treat **OneString** fields as you do any other string variables. **ItemRec** is a variable of type **Item**.

```
New( ItemRec );
Readln( InFile, ItemRec^.OneString );
```

Notice how the caret tells Pascal you want to access the data stored at the address of **ItemRec**. That data is a record; therefore, you can use a period as shown to access individual fields.

7-3. Exchanging two 40-character strings causes the computer to access memory hundreds of times. It has to copy each character of string A to a temporary holding area (C), then copy B to A, and finally copy C to B. Exchanging a set of pointers—as long as the pointers are shorter than the data to which they point—is faster because it reduces this memory shuffling. Using the **Item** declaration from Program 7-5, the following procedure exchanges two sets of **Left** and **Right** pointers.

```
PROCEDURE Exchange( A, B : ItemPointer );
{ Exchange data addressed by A and B by adjusting link fields }
VAR
   TempLeft, TempRight : ItemPointer;
BEGIN
   WITH A^ DO
   BEGIN
     TempLeft := Left; TempRight := Right;
     Left := B^.Left; Right := B^.Right
   END;
   WITH B^ DO
   BEGIN
     Left := TempLeft; Right := TempRight
   END
END; { Exchange }
```

Chapter 12

```
12-1. PROGRAM Hypotenuse;
      VAR
         A, B : real;

      PROCEDURE GetNum( VAR R : Real );
      VAR
         s : string[20]; e : integer;
      BEGIN
         REPEAT
            Readln( s );
            Val( s, r, e );
            IF e <> 0
               THEN writeln( 'Error in number, try again...' )
         UNTIL e = 0
      END; { GetNum }


      BEGIN
         Writeln( 'Find the Hypotenuse of a right triangle' );
         Writeln;
         Writeln( 'Enter length of side A' );
         GetNum( A );
         Writeln( 'Enter length of side B' );
         GetNum( B );
```

```
      Writeln( 'Hypotenuse = ', Sqrt( A*A + B*B ):8:2 )
   END.
```

12-5. Octal (base 8) digits range from 0 to 7. Because this takes three bits (in binary 000 to 111), you must imagine an eight-bit byte to have a zero bit to its left, making a total of nine bits. The value 255 decimal ($FF hexadecimal or 1111 1111 in binary) is, therefore, 377 in octal or, with its imaginary bit, 011 111 111 in binary. The answer uses divisions to isolate groups of three bits in bytes. This works because divisors that are powers of two (64 and 8 in the answer) have the effect of shifting left all the bits in a byte. Thus, 64 or 2^6 shifts bits six places left; 8 or 2^3 shifts three places, and so on.

```
PROGRAM OctalTest;
VAR
   Value : integer;

FUNCTION OctalDigit( n : Byte ) : Byte;
BEGIN
   OctalDigit := n MOD 8
END;


PROCEDURE OctalByte( n : Byte );
BEGIN
   Write( ' ', OctalDigit( n DIV 64 ),
              OctalDigit( n DIV 8  ),
              OctalDigit( n ) )
END; { OctalByte }


BEGIN
   Writeln( 'Octal notation' );
   Writeln;
   Write( 'Value? ' ); Readln( Value );
   OctalByte( Hi( Value ) );
   OctalByte( Lo( Value ) )
END.
```

Chapter 15

15.1
```
DiskDrive = OBJECT
   speed : Integer;
   open : Boolean;
   diskInserted : Boolean;
   CONSTRUCTOR Init;
   DESTRUCTOR Done;
   PROCEDURE InsertDisk;
   PROCEDURE EjectDisk;
```

```
      FUNCTION IsOpen : Boolean;
      PROCEDURE SetSpeed( s : Integer )
   END;
```

There are other possibilities. This exercise is designed to have you think about the properties of a diskette drive and how to represent those properties with an OOP object. Simulating real-world objects like disk drives and motors is one of OOP's primary uses.

15-2. A constructor initializes a link between an object and its VMT in objects that define one or more virtual methods. Constructors also allocate space via **New** for dynamic objects in heap memory. In addition to these standard effects, constructors may also perform other object initializations.

15-3. When called via **Dispose**, a destructor disposes the memory occupied by a dynamic object instance on the heap. In addition, destructors may perform other clean up chores.

15-4. Object types may define an unlimited number of constructors and destructors.

15-5. A static method's address is known at compile time. A virtual method's address must be looked up at runtime from the object's VMT. Replaced static methods in descendant objects can't be called by method implementations in the object's ancestors. Replaced virtual methods can be called by an ancestor's precompiled code.

Program Index

Index

Mastering Turbo Pascal Files
Tom Swan

This book demonstrates how to produce full-scale, integrated, power-user-type programs that use graphics, database access, cursor control, editing, menus, and windows.

This is an advanced guidebook and reference for professional and semi-professional programmers working with Borland International's Turbo Pascal for the IBM® PC. It explains how to use Turbo Pascal to create command and menu-driven applications for dealing with file management, data compatibility, text processing, games, graphics, and communications.

Mastering Turbo Pascal Files details how to write programs to read and write disk files of all kinds and explains the recent advances in disk storage devices, including 3.5-inch microfloppies, WORM drives, and others. Dozens of complete, tested, and practical programs are provided, as is Swan's personal collection of file programming "packages."

Topics covered include:

- File Fundamentals
- In Sequence and At Random
- Text and the Single Character
- Files in the Raw
- Directing the Directory
- Problems of a Sort
- Searches for Tomorrow
- Multi-User Mysteries

320 Pages, 7½ x 9¾, Softbound
ISBN: 0-672-22592-1
No. 22592, $18.95

Pascal Programs for Games & Graphics
Tom Swan

This outstanding collection of 22 unusually sophisticated games and graphics helps users realize Apple Pascal's full potential.

The powerful graphics editor enables users to custom-design character sets, change pictures up to full screen, and print a hard copy of the finished pictures as easily as working with text. Learn to design new alphabets, too.

Topics covered include:

- Moire Art
- Lasergraph
- Light Bikes
- Character Designer
- Touchup
- Printfoto
- Pascal Library - Procedures and Functions
- Xtrastuff

224 Pages, 7 x 9¼, Softbound
ISBN: 0-8104-6271-0
No. 46271, $17.95

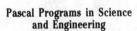

Pascal Programs in Science and Engineering
Gilder and Barrus

This text contains 112 Apple Pascal programs to tackle problems that confront students. Programs are organized into three sets: general math such as derivatives, integrals, curve fitting; basic electricity and electronics; computer-aided design of amplifiers, power supplies, and active and passive filters. All programs are ready to run, easy to modify.

350 Pages, 6¾ x 9¾, Softbound
ISBN: 0-8104-6265-6
No. 46265, $21.95

Pascal with Excellence
Ledgard with Tauer

Improve your software programs with this easy-to-read book of ke concepts in structured programming.

The book is comprised of progra ming proverbs—short, specific kernels of wisdom designed to make the process of programmin more creative and more rewardin They cover such concerns as con ceptualizing, coding, documenting testing, debugging, and maintainin and modifying programs. Each pr verb is followed by examples of good and bad program segments and is then put to the test in a scenario of top-down programmin

Topics covered include:

- A Good Start is Half the Race— Question and Define the Problem; Think First, Code Later
- Structure is Logic— Black-Box Your Subroutines
- Coding the Problem— Spaces Have Meaning, Get the Syntax Correct Now, Your Output is Not Only for You
- And of Course. . .— Don't Be Afraid to Start Over
- Program Standards— General Requirements Control Structures
- Potpourri— Global Variables Recursion
- Top-Down Programming
- Appendices: Summary of Program Standards, Final Program for Kriegspiel Checkers, Bibliography

256 Pages, 7 x 9¼, Softbound
ISBN: 0-8104-6490-X
No. 46490, $16.95

Visit your local book retailer or call
800-257-5755